The Collins World Atlas

Wm. Collins Sons
& Co. Ltd.
P.O. Box.
Glasgow. G4 0NB

The Collins World Atlas

First Published 1970
Revised 1972, 1973
Reprinted 1974
Revised 1975, 1977
Printed & Bound in Scotland by Wm. Collins Sons & Co. Ltd.

Contents

SYMBOLS 4

CLIMATE OF THE CONTINENTS

EUROPE Climatic Graphs & Regions 5
ASIA Climatic Graphs & Regions 6
AFRICA Climatic Graphs & Regions 7
AUSTRALASIA Climatic Graphs & Regions 8
NORTH AMERICA Climatic Graphs & Regions 9
SOUTH AMERICA Climatic Graphs & Regions 10

EUROPE

Physiography & Geology *1 : 20 000 000* 11
Land Cover *1 : 16 000 000* 12–13
Climate *1 : 32 000 000* 14–15
Mineral Resources & Population *1 : 32 000 000* 16
Industry, G. N. P. & Economic Groups *1 : 32 000 000* 17
Political *1 : 20 000 000* 18

BRITISH ISLES

Physiography & Geology *1 : 5 000 000* 19
Land Cover *1 : 3 500 000* 20–21
Climate (Seasonal Precipitation & Temperature) 22
Agriculture (Distribution of Oats; Hay & Silage; Wheat; Roots, Fruit & Market Gardening; Dominant Crops; Beef Cattle; Dairy Cattle; Sheep) 23
Population & Communications *1 : 5 000 000* 24
Political *1 : 5 000 000* 25
Power, Mineral Resources & Industry *1 : 7 000 000* 26
LONDON REGION *1 : 400 000* 27
SOUTHERN ENGLAND *1 : 1 000 000* 28–29
WALES & SOUTHWEST ENGLAND *1 : 1 000 000* 30–31
NORTHERN ENGLAND *1 : 1 000 000* 32–33
SOUTHERN SCOTLAND & NORTHEAST ENGLAND *1 : 1 000 000* 34–35
NORTHERN SCOTLAND *1 : 1 000 000* 36–37
IRELAND *1 : 1 400 000* 38–39

REGIONS OF EUROPE

FRANCE *1 : 5 000 000* 40
SPAIN & PORTUGAL *1 : 5 000 000* 41
ITALY & THE BALKANS *1 : 5 250 000* 42–43
GERMANY & THE ALPS *1 : 4 000 000* 44
THE LOW COUNTRIES *1 : 2 000 000* 45
SCANDINAVIA & ICELAND *1 : 7 500 000* 46
EASTERN EUROPE *1 : 9 500 000* 47
UNION OF SOVIET SOCIALIST REPUBLICS *1 : 20 000 000* 48–49

ASIA

Physiography & Geology *1 : 40 000 000* 50–51
Land Cover *1 : 40 000 000* 52–53
Climate (Seasonal Precipitation & Temperature) 51 & 53
Mineral Resources 55
Population 55
Political *1 : 40 000 000* 54–55
SOUTHWEST ASIA *1 : 9 000 000* 56–57
SOUTH ASIA *1 : 14 000 000* 58–59
SOUTHEAST ASIA *1 : 15 000 000* 60–61
CHINA & JAPAN *1 : 16 000 000* 62–63

AFRICA

Physiography & Geology *1 : 37 000 000* 64
Land Cover *1 : 37 000 000* 65
Climate (Seasonal Precipitation & Temperature) 66
Mineral Resources 65
Population 67
Political *1 : 37 000 000* 67
NORTHERN AFRICA *1 . 20 000 000* 68–69
WEST AFRICA *1 : 10 000 000* 70–71
CENTRAL & EAST AFRICA *1 : 10 750 000* 72–73
SOUTHERN AFRICA *1 : 10 600 000* 74

AUSTRALASIA

Physiography & Geology *1 : 27 000 000* 75
AUSTRALIA
Land Cover *1 : 20 000 000* 76
Climate (Seasonal Precipitation & Temperature; Variability of Rainfall; Water Supply) 77
Mineral Resources 78
Population 78
AUSTRALIA *1 : 20 000 000* 79
SOUTHEAST AUSTRALIA *1 : 7 500 000* 80

NEW ZEALAND
Land Cover *1 : 6 000 000* 81
Climatic Types *1 : 12 000 000* 81
Agriculture *1 : 12 000 000* 82
Mineral Resources *1 : 12 000 000* 81
Population *1 : 12 000 000* 82
General *1 : 6 000 000* 82

NORTH AMERICA

Physiography & Geology *1 : 35 000 000* 83
Land Cover *1 : 25 000 000* 84–85
Climate (Seasonal Precipitation & Temperature) 86
Mineral Resources *1 : 35 000 000* 87
Population *1 : 35 000 000* 88
Political *1 : 35 000 000* 89
UNITED STATES OF AMERICA *1 : 12 000 000* 90–91
CANADA *1 : 17 000 000* 92–93
NORTHEAST U.S.A. & SOUTH CENTRAL CANADA *1 : 5 000 000* 94–95
CENTRAL AMERICA & THE CARIBBEAN *1 : 12 500 000* 96–97

SOUTH AMERICA

Physiography & Geology 99
Land Cover *1 : 25 000 000* 98–99
Climate (Seasonal Precipitation & Temperature) 100
Mineral Resources *1 : 50 000 000* 101
Population *1 : 50 000 000* 101
Political *1 : 35 000 000* 102
SOUTHEAST BRAZIL & NORTH ARGENTINA *1 : 12 000 000* 103
POLAR REGIONS *1 : 50 000 000* 104

WORLD

Physiography & Structure 105
Physical *1 : 85 000 000* 106–107
Climate (Seasonal Temperature and Precipitation; Annual Precipitation) 108–109
Agriculture *1 : 72 500 000* 110–111
Political *1 : 72 500 000* 112–113
Population & Communications *1 : 72 500 000* 114–115
Airways 116

COMPREHENSIVE INDEX 117–172

GENERAL MAPS

The symbols used on general maps in this atlas are explained below. Thematic map symbols are explained in keys alongside each map.

Relief

- Land contour
- ▲ 29028 Spot height (feet)
- Pass
- Permanent ice cap

Relief

Feet	Metres
16404	5000
9843	3000
6562	2000
3281	1000
1640	500
656	200
0	Sea Level
656	200
13123	4000
22966	7000

Hydrography

- Submarine contour
- • 36200 Ocean depth (feet)
- Reef
- River
- Intermittent river
- Falls/Dam
- Gorge
- Canal
- Lake/Reservoir
- Intermittent lake
- Marsh/Swamp

Communications

- Tunnel — Railway
- Tunnel — Road
- Desert track

Administration

- International boundary
- Undefined boundary
- Internal boundary
- National capitals

Settlement

Calcutta	Over 1,000,000 inhabitants
Dortmund	500,000–1,000,000 inhabitants
Veracruz	100,000–500,000 inhabitants
Timbuktu	Under 100,000 inhabitants

Lettering

Various styles of lettering are used in this atlas, each style for a different type of feature.

Physical features	*ALPS*	*Congo Basin*	*Nicobar Islands*	*Mt Cook*
Hydrographic features	*PACIFIC OCEAN*	*Red Sea*	*Lake Erie*	*Amazon*

Country name CHILE Internal division IOWA Territorial admin. *(Fr.)*

BRITISH ISLES GENERAL MAPS

Additional or variant symbols used on these maps.

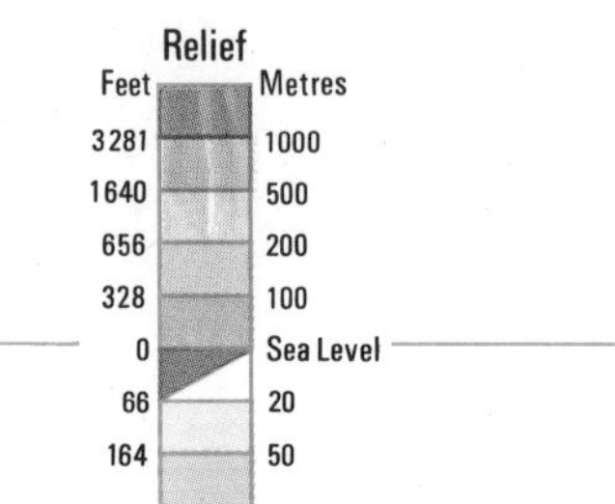

Relief

Feet	Metres
3281	1000
1640	500
656	200
328	100
0	Sea Level
66	20
164	50

- Access Point — Motorway
- Main road
- International airport
- Other airport

- National boundary
- County or Region boundary

- Built-up area
- Over 1 000 000 inhabitants
- 500 000–1 000 000 inhabitants
- 100 000–500 000 inhabitants
- 25 000–100 000 inhabitants
- 10 000–25 000 inhabitants
- Under 10 000 inhabitants

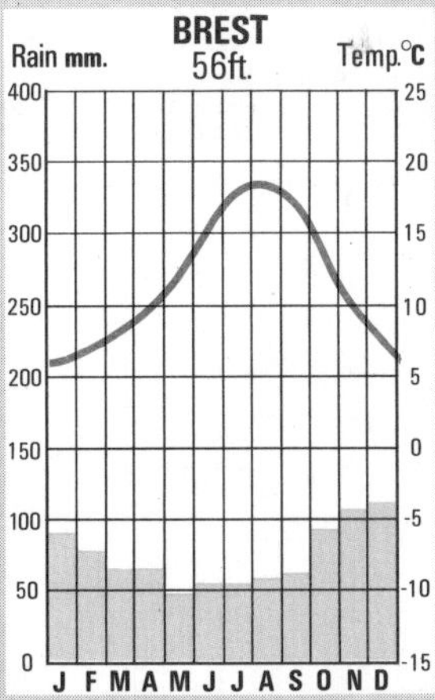

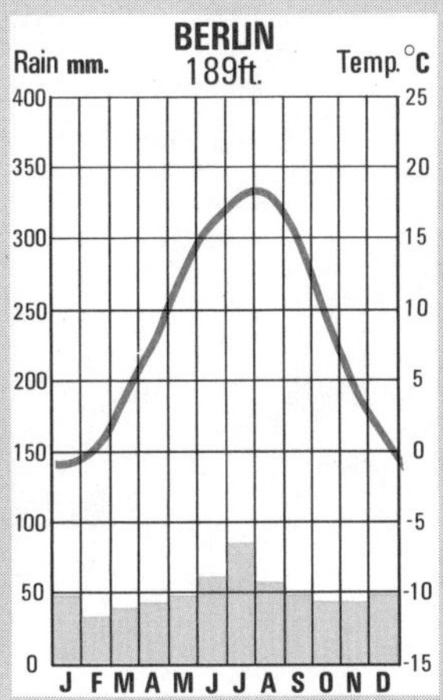

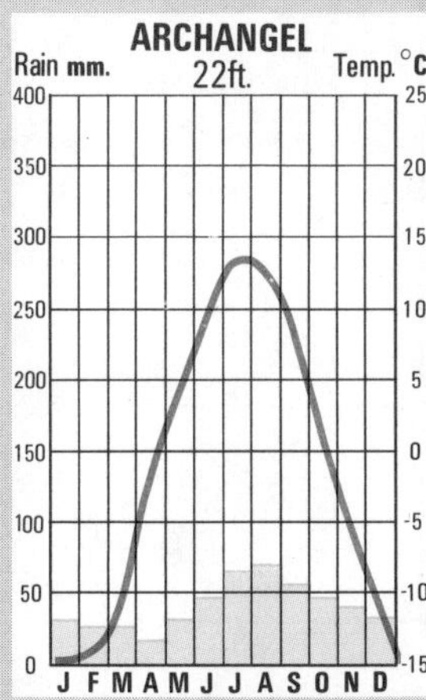

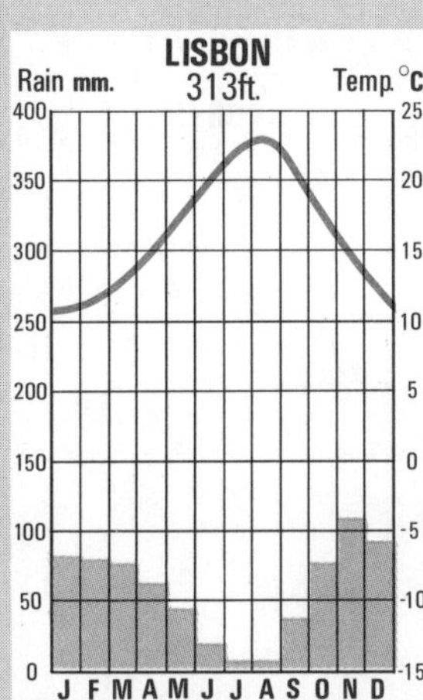

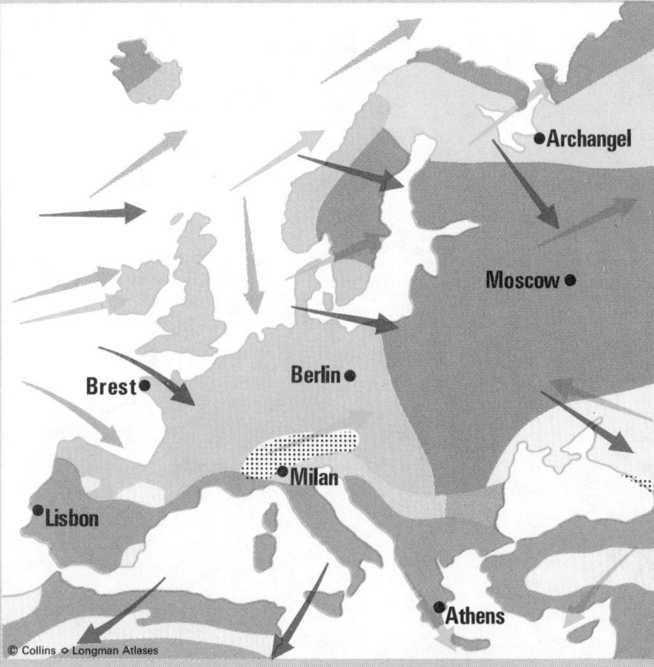

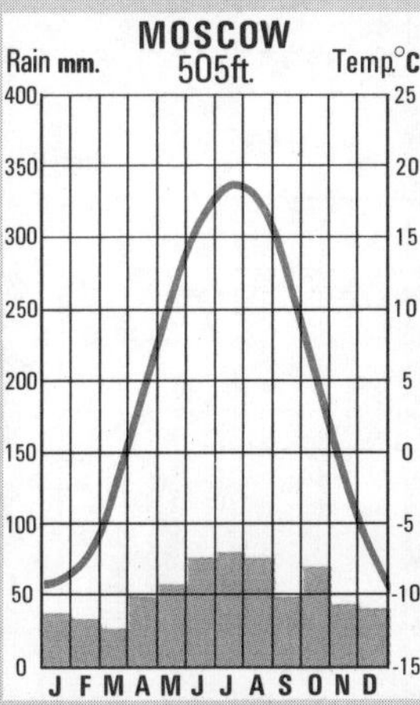

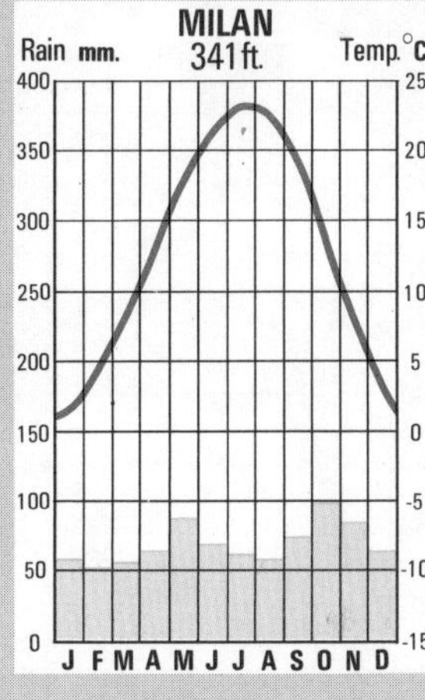

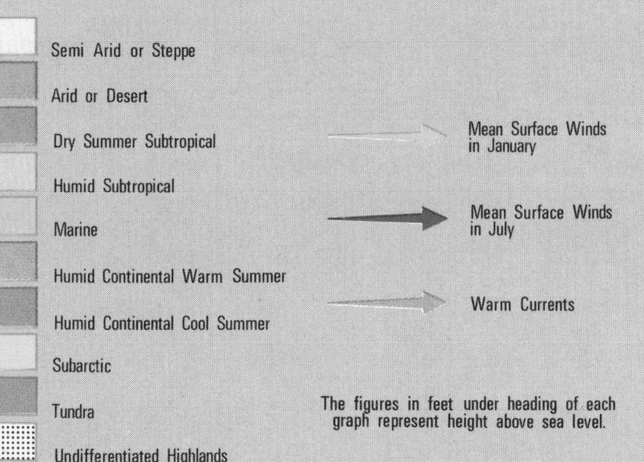

The figures in feet under heading of each graph represent height above sea level.

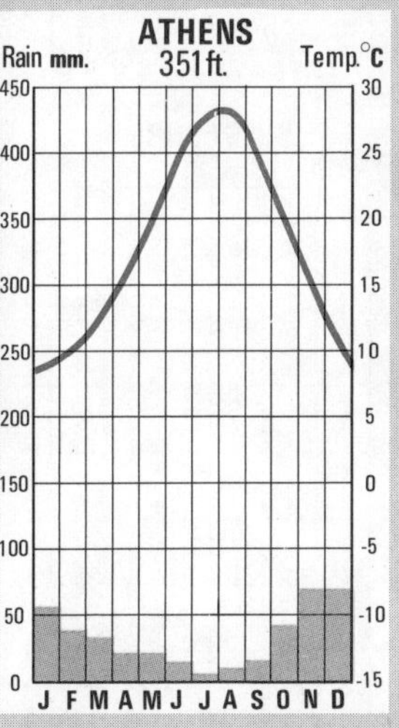

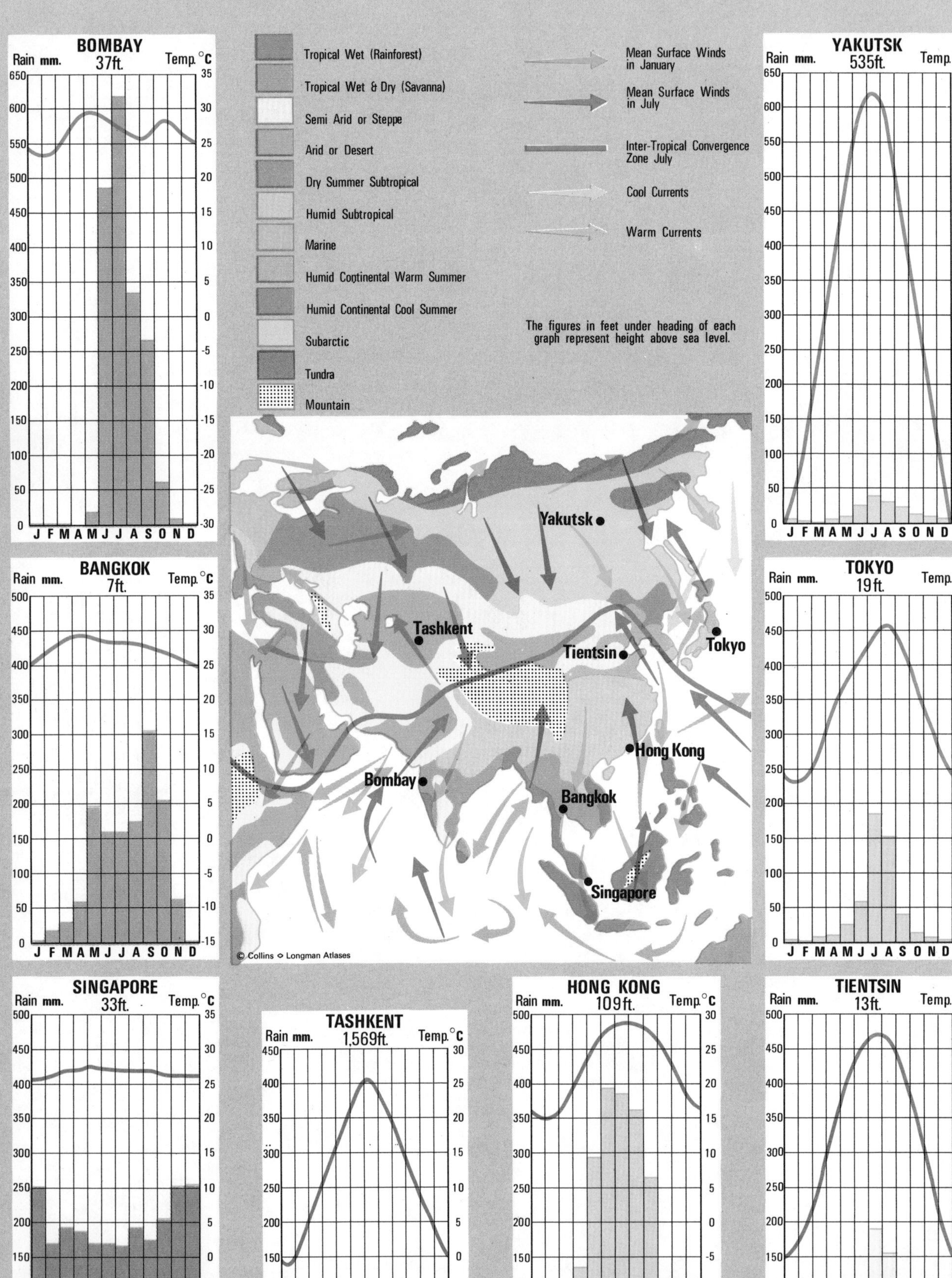
BOMBAY
37ft.
Rain mm.
Temp. °C
BANGKOK
7ft.
SINGAPORE
33ft.
TASHKENT
1,569ft.
HONG KONG
109ft.
TIENTSIN
13ft.
YAKUTSK
535ft.
TOKYO
19ft.
J F M A M J J A S O N D
Tropical Wet (Rainforest)
Tropical Wet & Dry (Savanna)
Semi Arid or Steppe
Arid or Desert
Dry Summer Subtropical
Humid Subtropical
Marine
Humid Continental Warm Summer
Humid Continental Cool Summer
Subarctic
Tundra
Mountain
Mean Surface Winds in January
Mean Surface Winds in July
Inter-Tropical Convergence Zone July
Cool Currents
Warm Currents
The figures in feet under heading of each graph represent height above sea level.
Yakutsk
Tashkent
Tientsin
Tokyo
Hong Kong
Bombay
Bangkok
Singapore
© Collins ◇ Longman Atlases

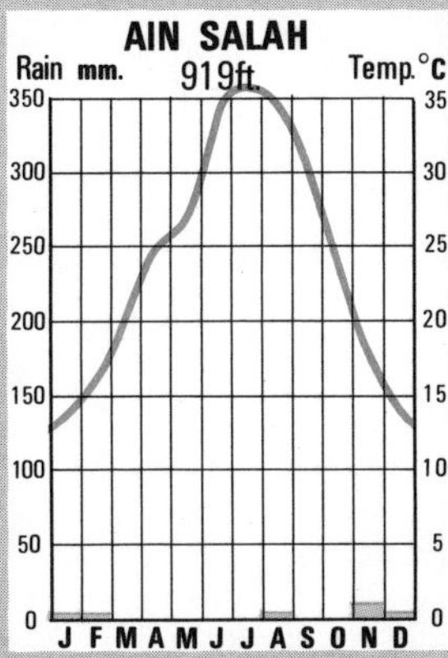

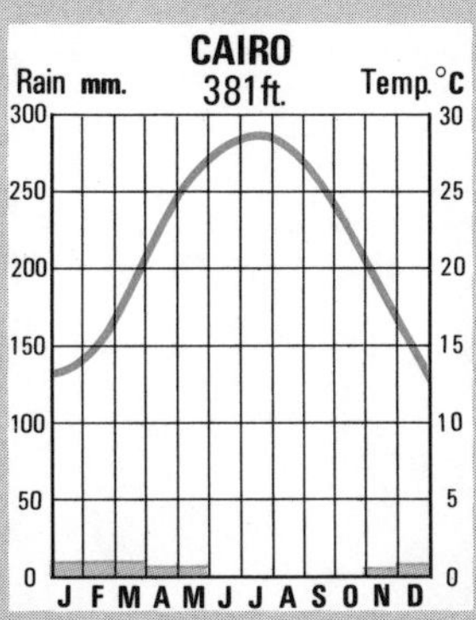

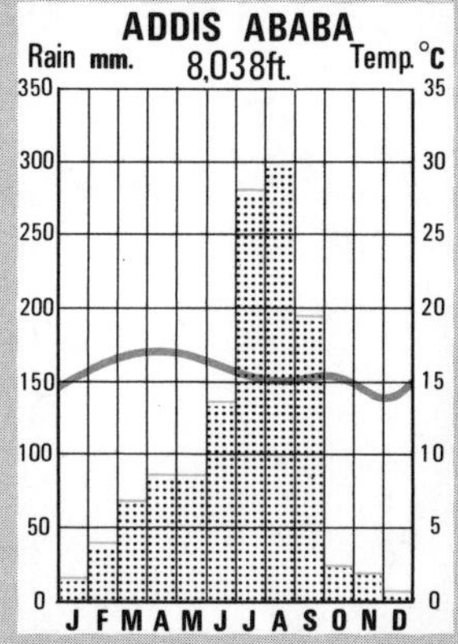

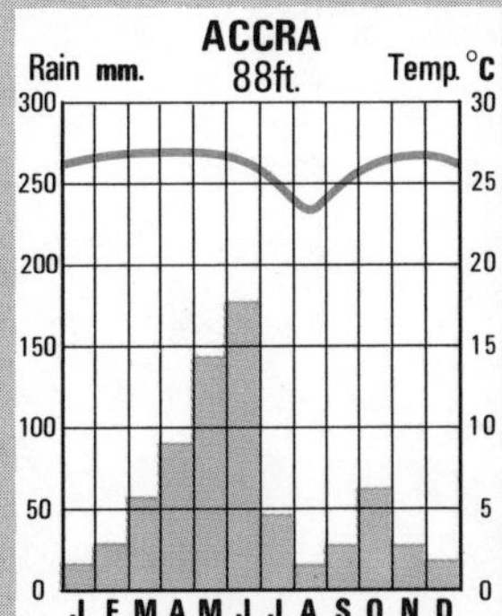

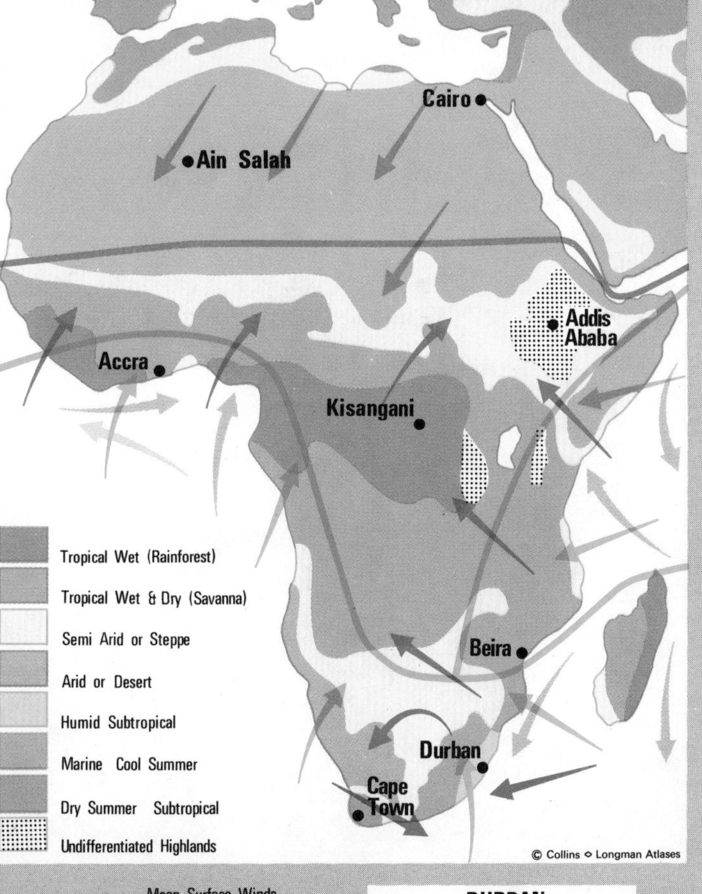

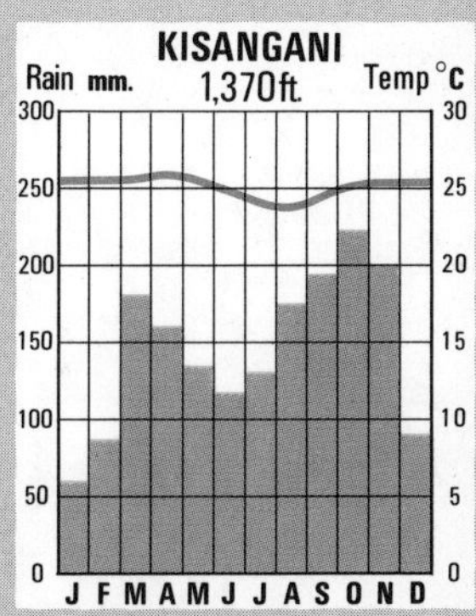

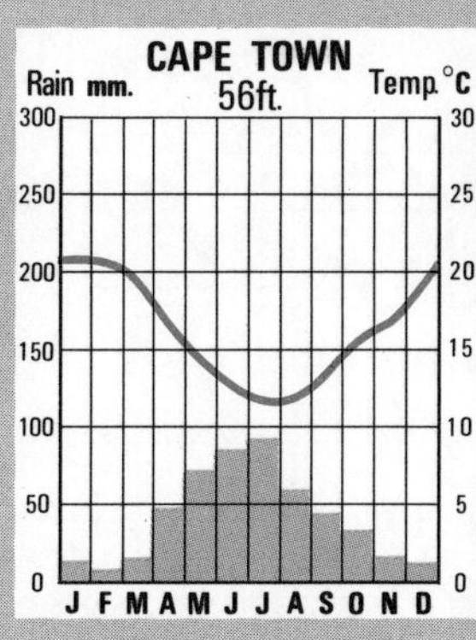

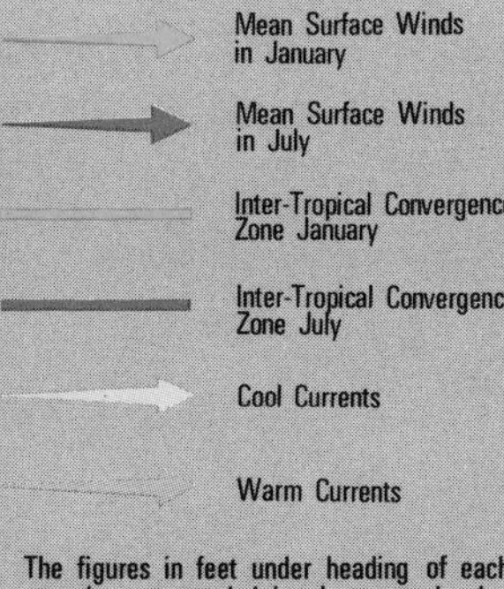

The figures in feet under heading of each graph represent height above sea level.

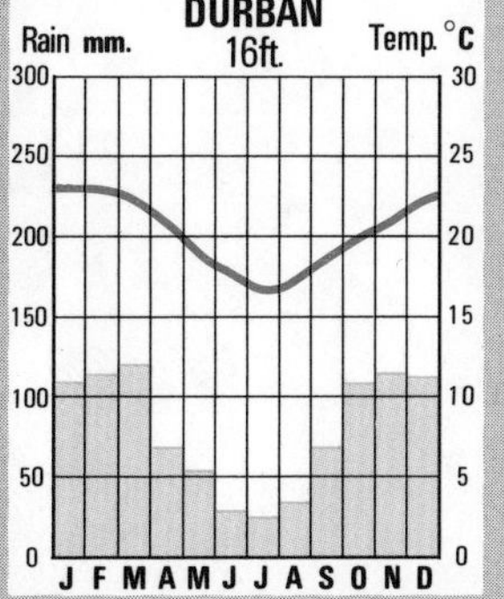

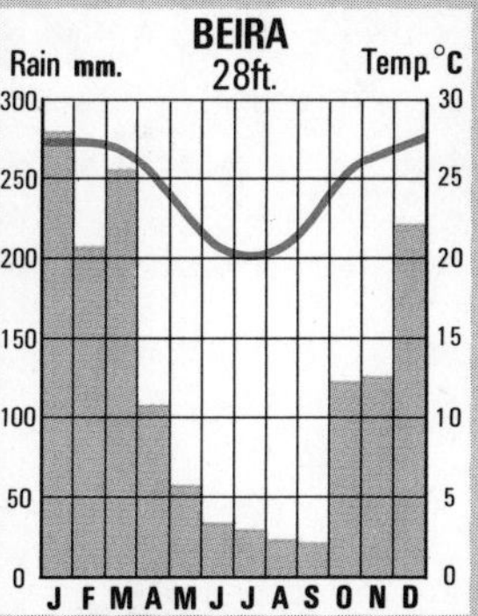

AUSTRALASIA Climatic Graphs & Regions

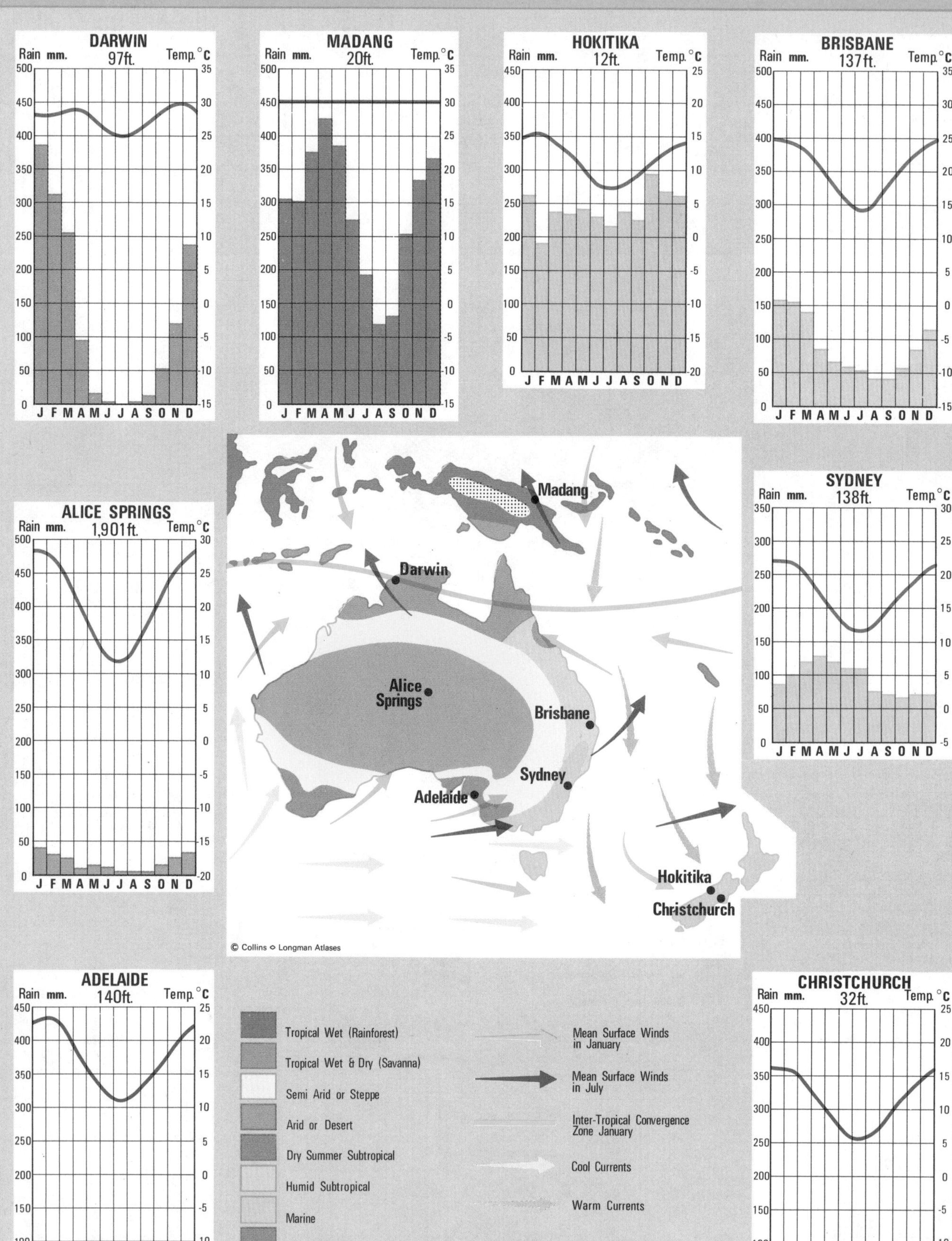

Tropical Wet (Rainforest)

Tropical Wet & Dry (Savanna)

Semi Arid or Steppe

Arid or Desert

Dry Summer Subtropical

Humid Subtropical

Marine

Humid Cool Summer

Undifferentiated Highlands

Mean Surface Winds in January

Mean Surface Winds in July

Inter-Tropical Convergence Zone January

Cool Currents

Warm Currents

The figures in feet under heading of each graph represent height above sea level.

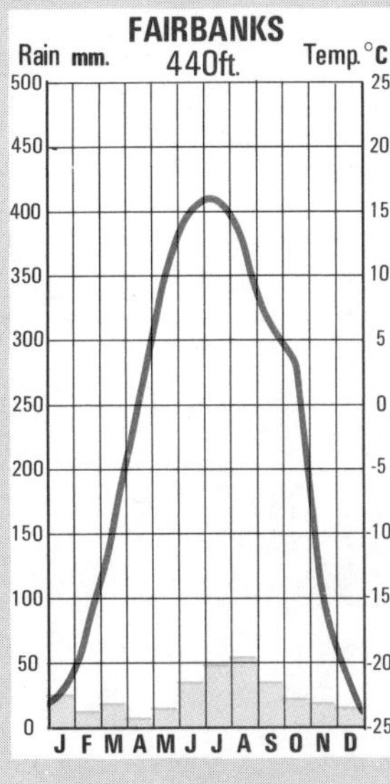

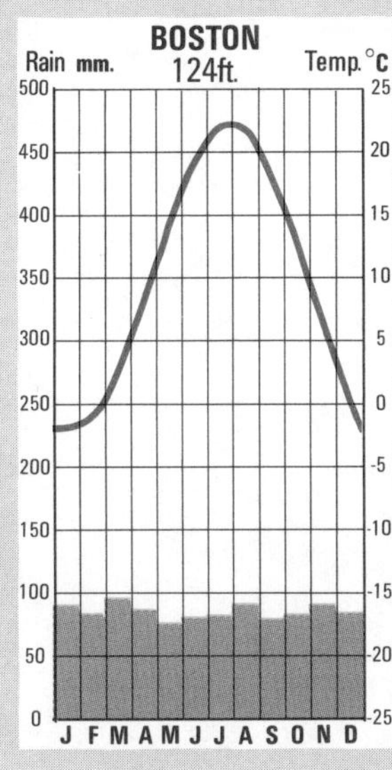

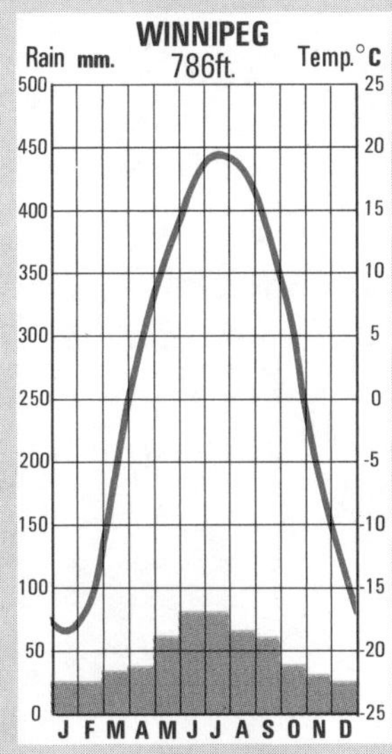

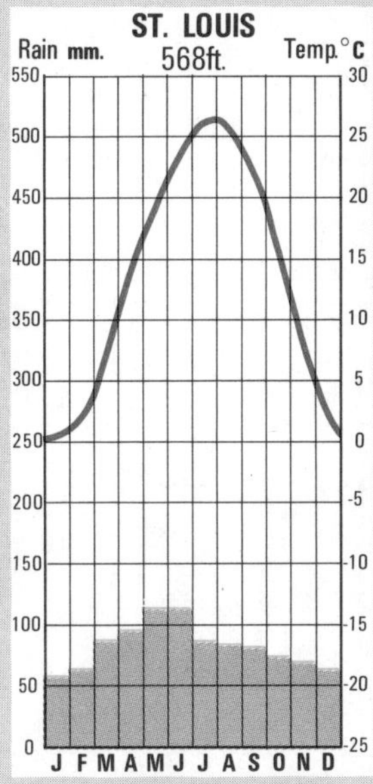

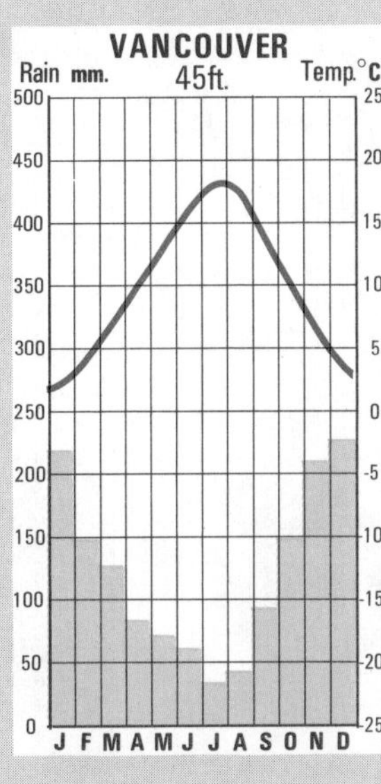

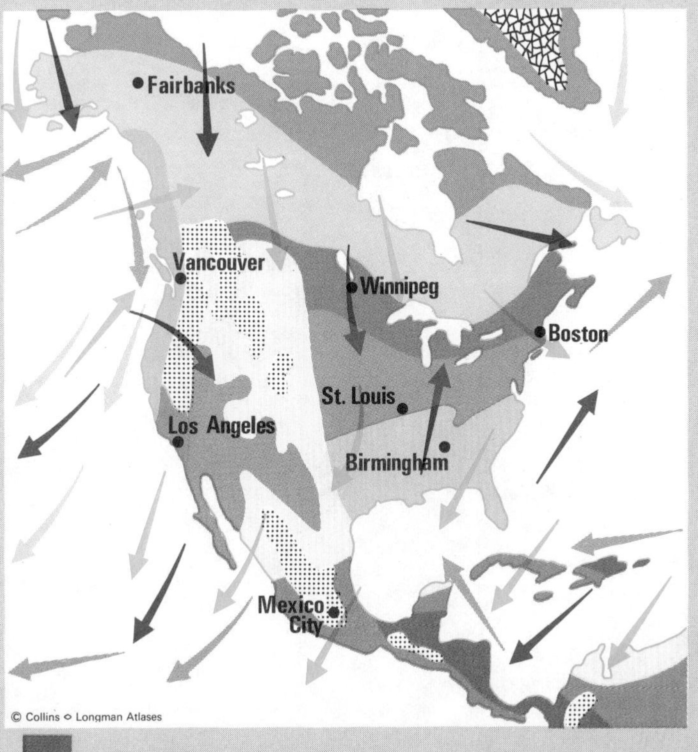

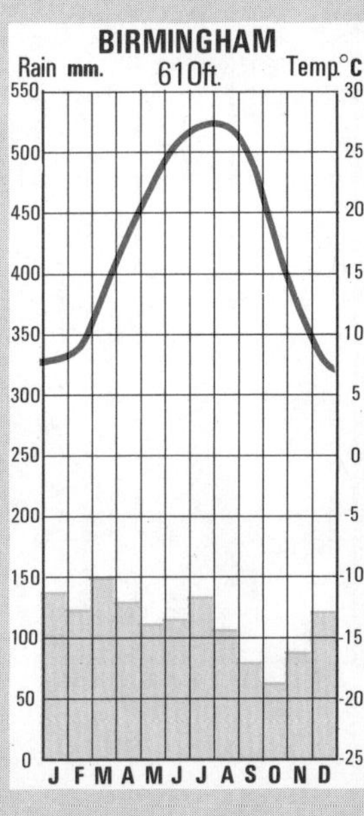

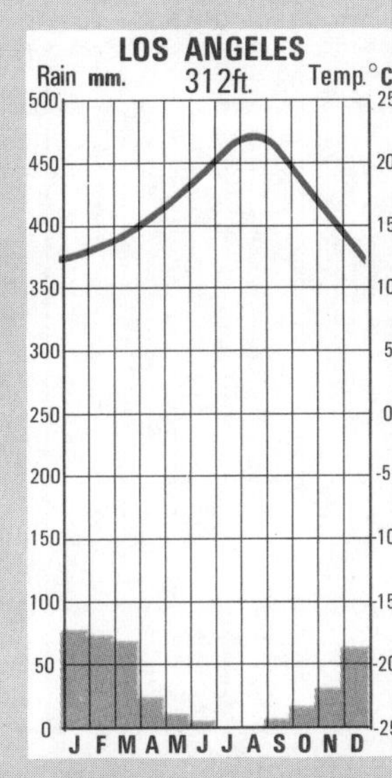

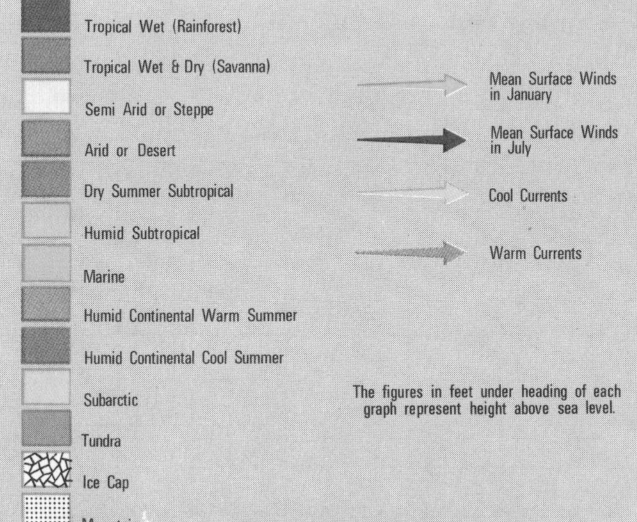

The figures in feet under heading of each graph represent height above sea level.

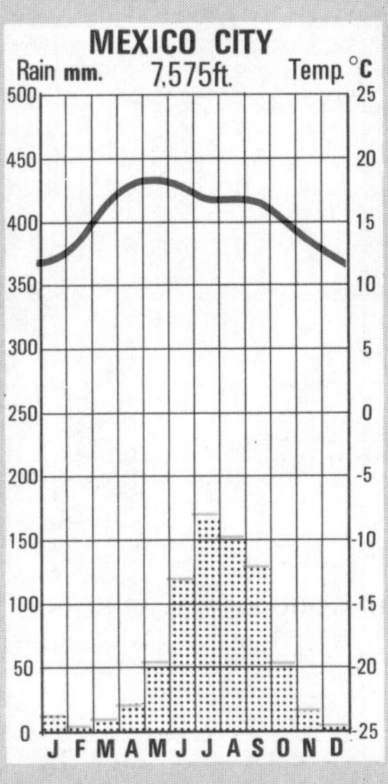

SOUTH AMERICA Climatic Graphs & Regions

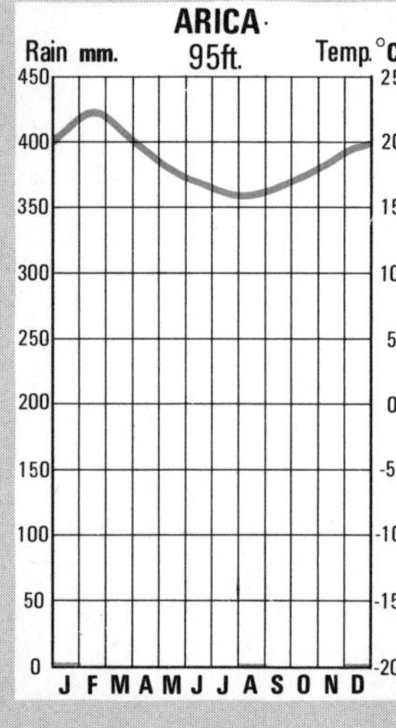

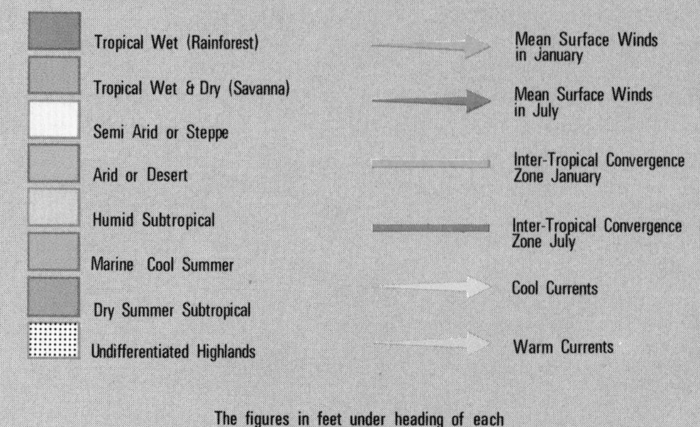

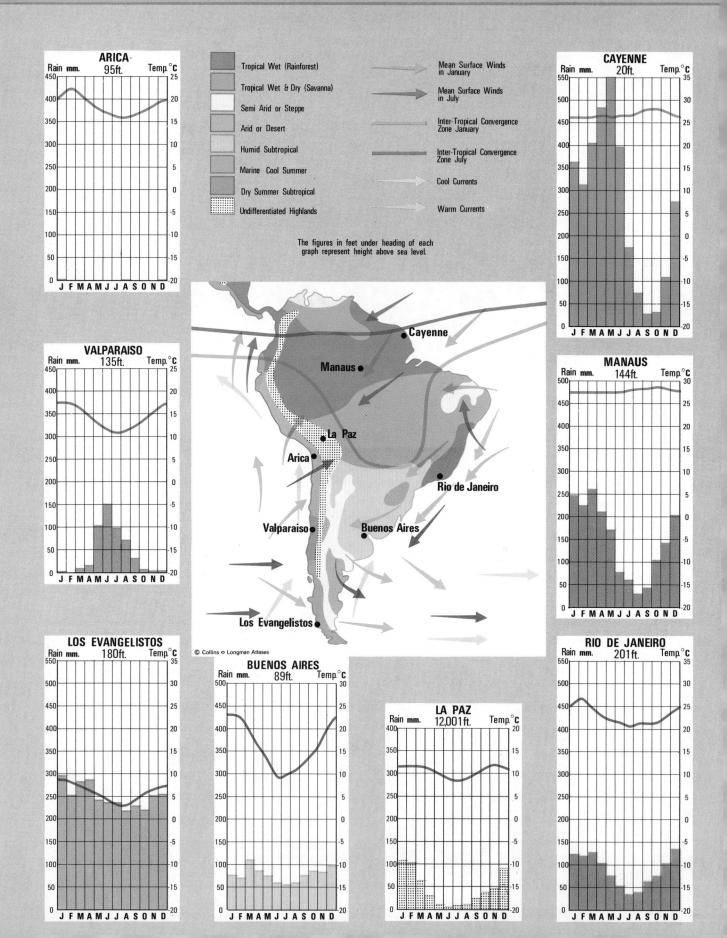

The figures in feet under heading of each graph represent height above sea level.

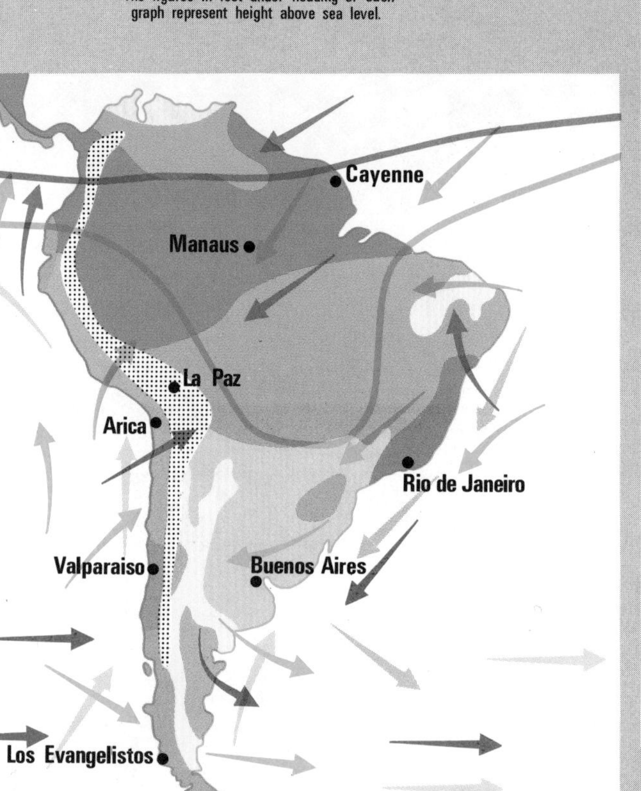

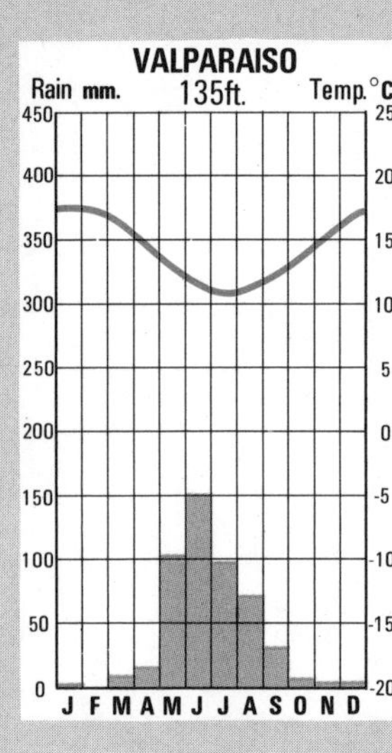

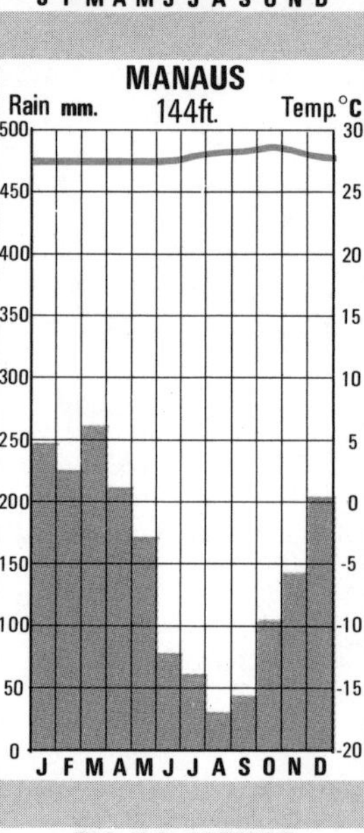

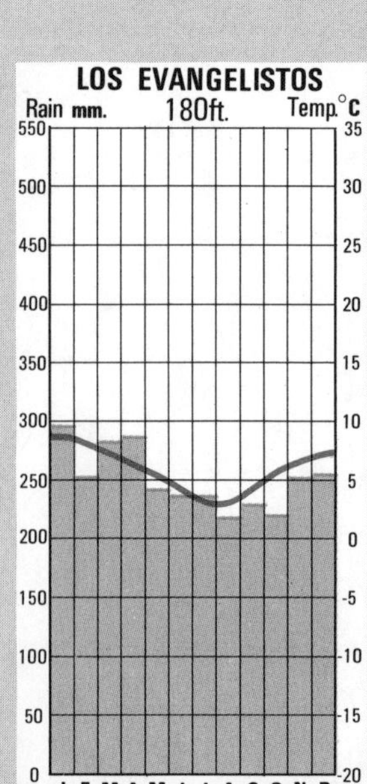

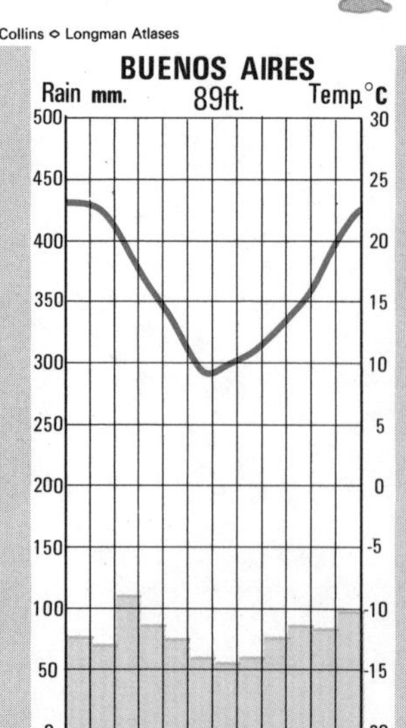

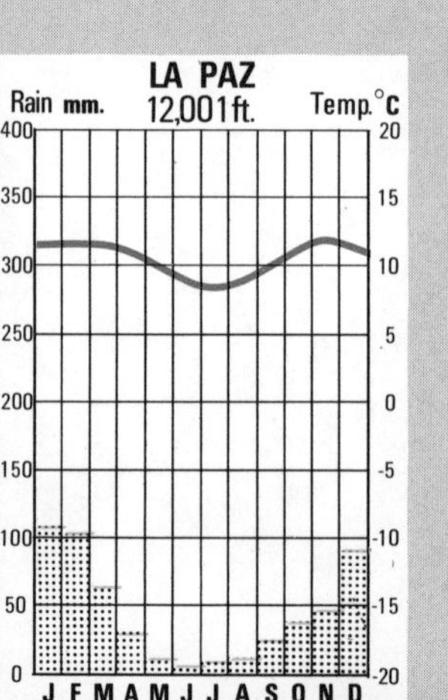

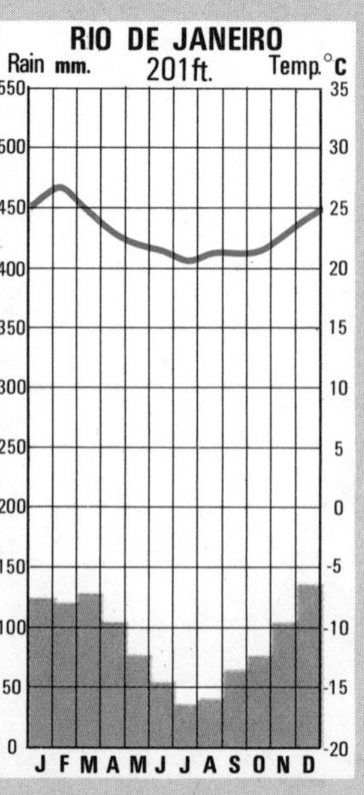

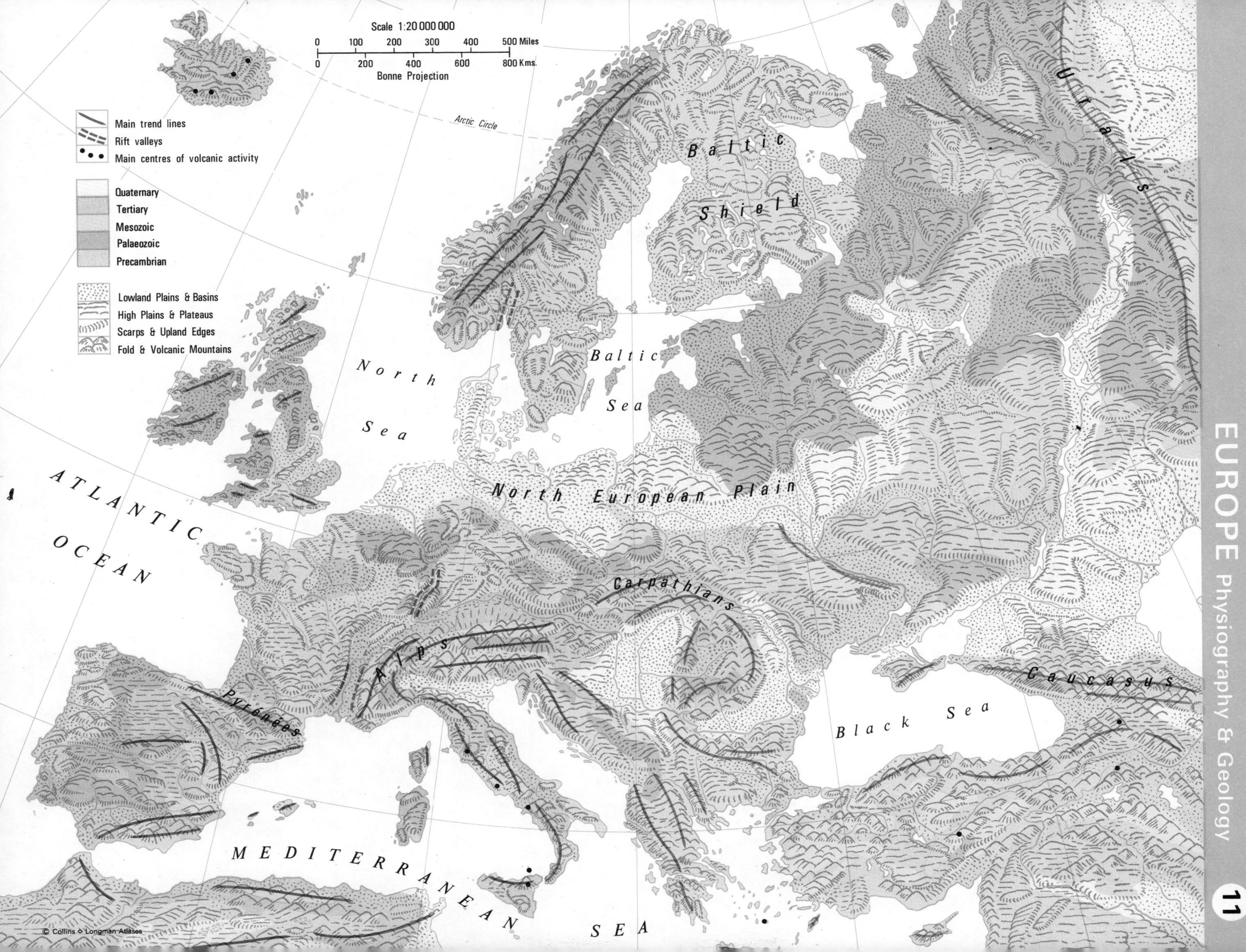
Scale 1:20 000 000
0 100 200 300 400 500 Miles
0 200 400 600 800 Kms.
Bonne Projection
Arctic Circle
Main trend lines
Rift valleys
Main centres of volcanic activity
Quaternary
Tertiary
Mesozoic
Palaeozoic
Precambrian
Lowland Plains & Basins
High Plains & Plateaus
Scarps & Upland Edges
Fold & Volcanic Mountains
Baltic Shield
Urals
North Sea
Baltic Sea
North European Plain
ATLANTIC OCEAN
Carpathians
Alps
Pyrénées
Caucasus
Black Sea
MEDITERRANEAN SEA

Permanent ice and snow
Tundra and alpine
Desert
Semi-desert
Grassland, heath, marsh and steppe
Forest and woodland
Cultivated land
Scale 1:16 000 000
0 100 200 300 400 500 Miles
0 200 400 600 800 Kms.
Conic Projection
ARCTIC
NORWEGIAN SEA
ATLANTIC OCEAN
NORTH SEA
ICELAND
Hekla 4892
Arctic Circle
Faroe Is.
Shetland Is.
Orkney Is.
Hebrides
Ben Nevis 4406
Ireland
Great Britain
Thames
Land's End
English Channel
SCANDINAVIA
Lofoten Is.
North Cape
Tornio
Gulf of Bothnia
Gulf of Finland
L. Peipus
8103
Mälaren
Åland Is.
Vänern
Vättern
Skagerrak
Gotland
Jutland
Baltic Sea
Bornholm
North European
Weser
Elbe
Rhine
Vistula
Bug
Meuse
Ardennes
Oder
Sudeten Mts.
Ore Mts.
Bohemian Forest
Seine
Loire
Vosges
Black Forest
Danube
Moravian Heights
Carpathians
Bay of Biscay
C. Finisterre
Massif Central
Jura Mts
Inn
Mt. Blanc 15781
The Alps
Hungarian Plain
Cantabrian Mts.
Garonne
Cevennes
Rhone
Po
Drava
Mures
Sava
Transylvanian Alps
Douro
Meseta
Pyrénées
Pico de Aneto 11168
Ebro
Gulf of Lions
Ligurian Sea
Apennines
Adriatic Sea
Dinaric Alps
Balkans
Tagus
Corsica
Tiber
Guadiana
C. St. Vincent
Sierra Morena
Guadalquivir
Sardinia
Tyrrhenian Sea
Balearic Is.
Pindus Mts
Olympus 9550
Str. of Gibraltar
Sierra Nevada
MEDITERRANEAN
Ionian Sea
Tell Atlas
High Atlas
Saharan Atlas
Sicily
Mt Etna 10958
Malta

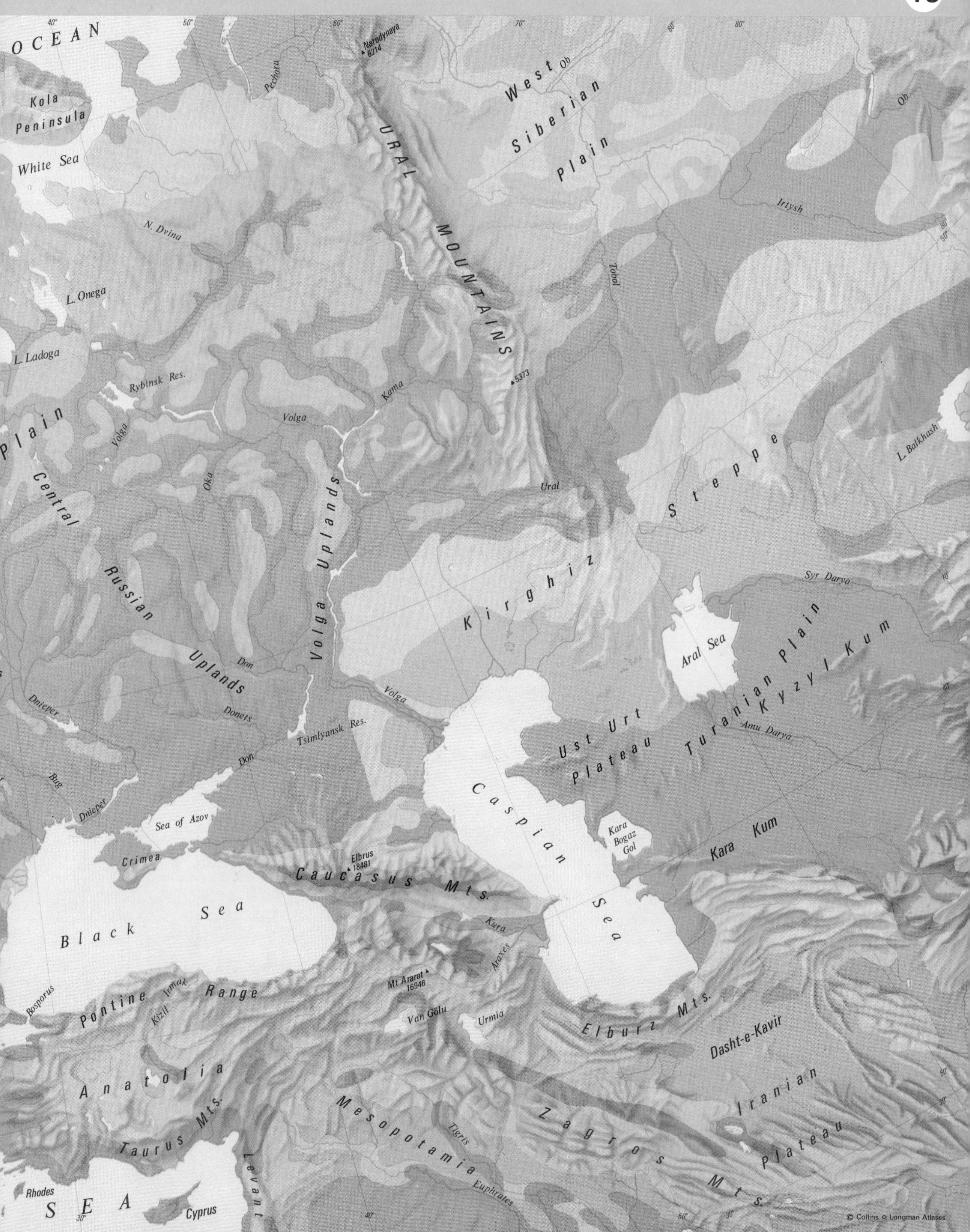
OCEAN
Kola Peninsula
White Sea
Narodynaya 6214
Pechora
West Siberian Plain
Ob
URAL MOUNTAINS
N. Dvina
L. Onega
L. Ladoga
Rybinsk Res.
Irtysh
Tobol
Kama
5373
Volga
Plain
Central Russian Uplands
Oka
Volga Uplands
Ural
Steppe
L. Balkhash
Kirghiz
Syr Darya
Aral Sea
Turanian Plain
Kyzyl Kum
Don
Dnieper
Doners
Tsimlyansk Res.
Ust Urt Plateau
Amu Darya
Bug
Sea of Azov
Caspian Sea
Kara Bogaz Gol
Kara Kum
Crimea
Elbrus 18481
Caucasus Mts.
Black Sea
Kura
Araxes
Bosporus
Pontine Range
Irmak
Kizil
Mt. Ararat 16946
Van Gölu
Urmia
Elburz Mts.
Dasht-e-Kavir
Anatolia
Taurus Mts.
Mesopotamia
Tigris
Euphrates
Zagros Mts.
Iranian Plateau
Levant
Rhodes
SEA
Cyprus
© Collins ○ Longman Atlases

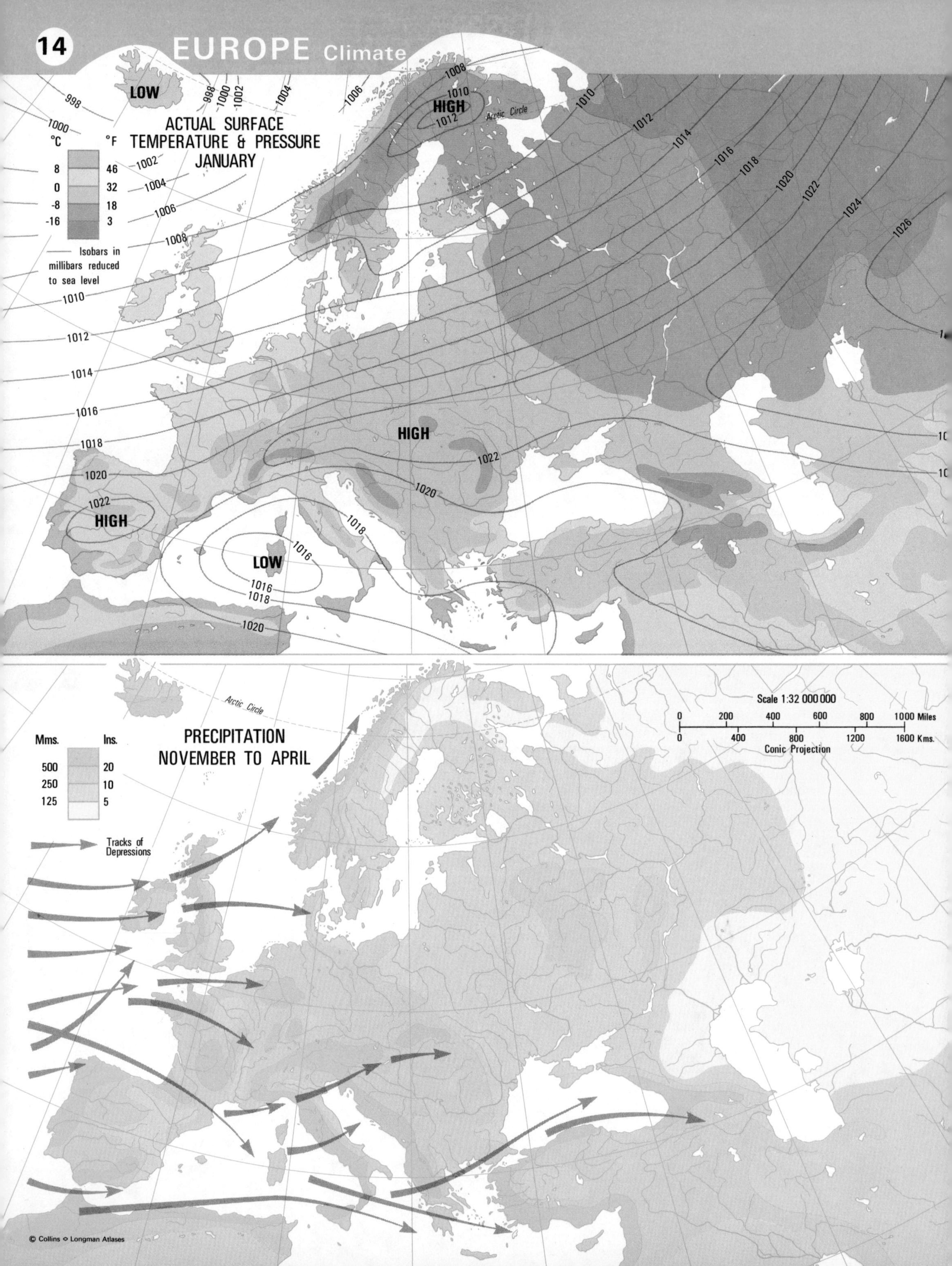

ACTUAL SURFACE TEMPERATURE & PRESSURE JANUARY
°C °F
8 46
0 32
-8 18
-16 3
Isobars in millibars reduced to sea level
LOW
HIGH
HIGH
HIGH
LOW
Arctic Circle
998
1000
1002
1004
1006
1008
1010
1012
1014
1016
1018
1020
1022
1024
1026
PRECIPITATION NOVEMBER TO APRIL
Mms. Ins.
500 20
250 10
125 5
Tracks of Depressions
Scale 1:32 000 000
0 200 400 600 800 1000 Miles
0 400 800 1200 1600 Kms.
Conic Projection

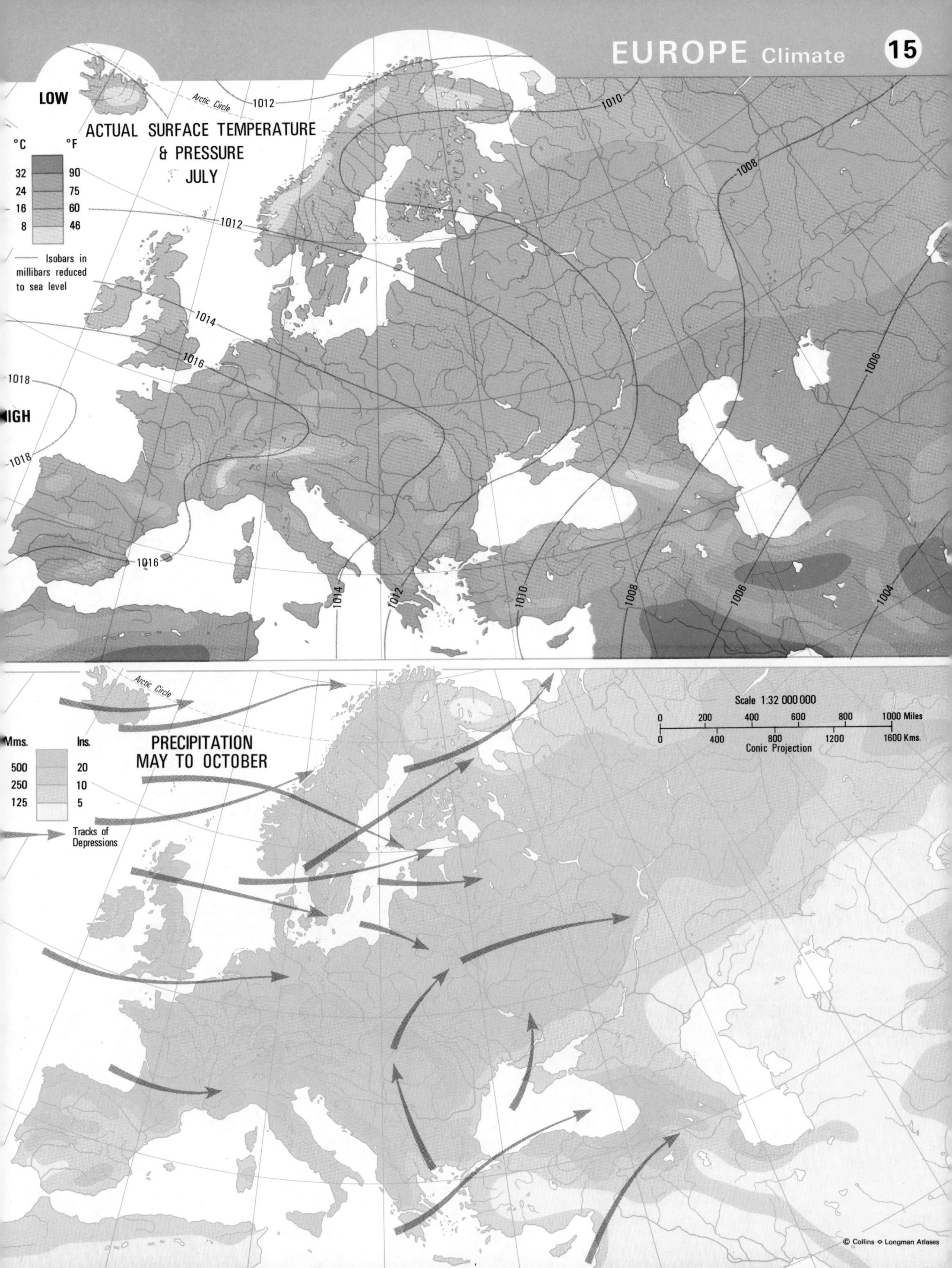
LOW
ACTUAL SURFACE TEMPERATURE
& PRESSURE
JULY
°C
°F
32
90
24
75
16
60
8
46
Isobars in millibars reduced to sea level
Arctic Circle
1012
1010
1008
1014
1016
1018
HIGH
1006
1004
PRECIPITATION
MAY TO OCTOBER
Mms.
Ins.
500
20
250
10
125
5
Tracks of Depressions
Scale 1:32 000 000
0 200 400 600 800 1000 Miles
0 400 800 1200 1600 Kms.
Conic Projection

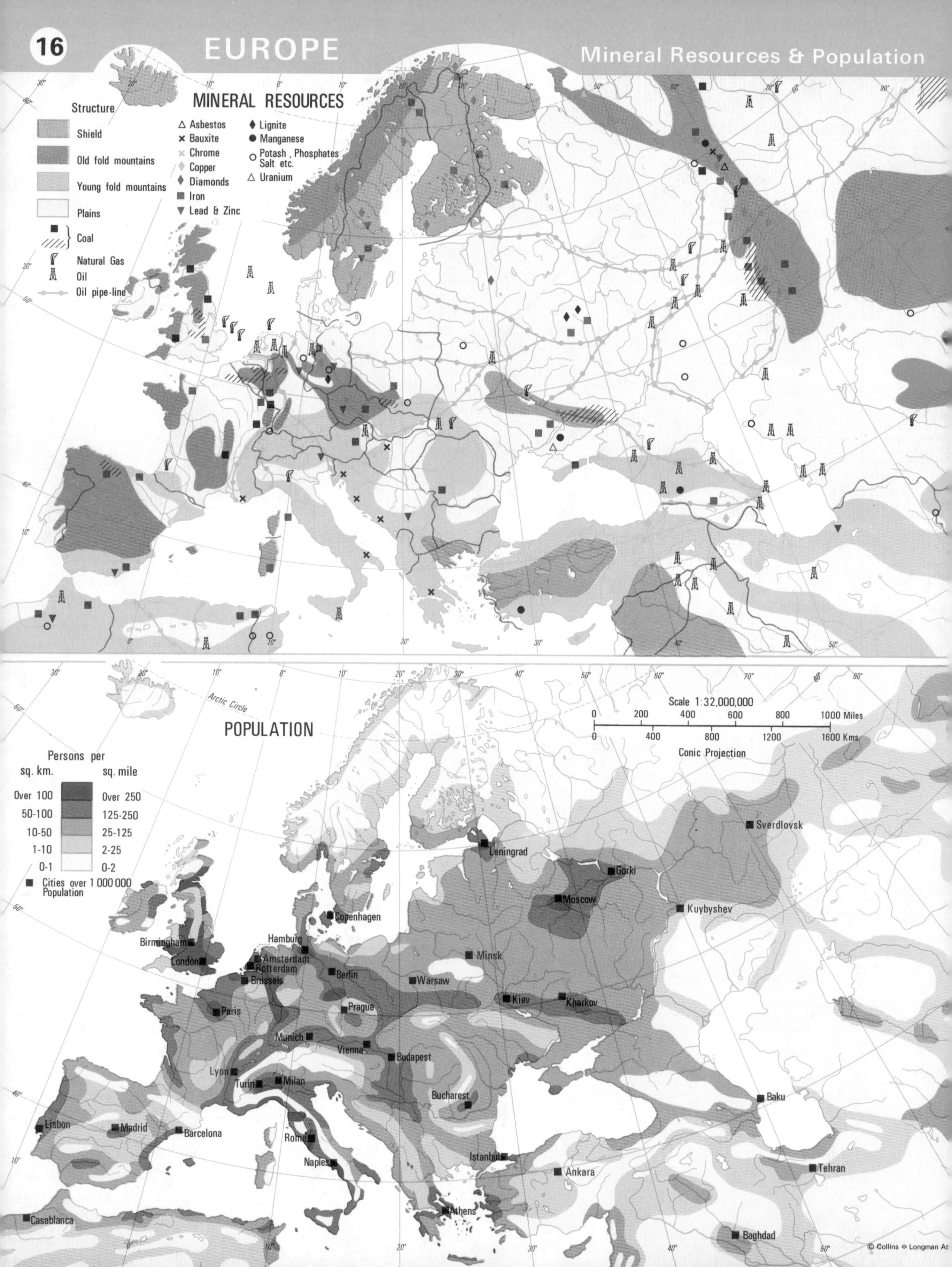
MINERAL RESOURCES
Structure
Shield
Old fold mountains
Young fold mountains
Plains
Coal
Natural Gas
Oil
Oil pipe-line
Asbestos
Bauxite
Chrome
Copper
Diamonds
Iron
Lead & Zinc
Lignite
Manganese
Potash, Phosphates Salt etc.
Uranium
POPULATION
Arctic Circle
Persons per
sq. km.
sq. mile
Over 100
50-100
10-50
1-10
0-1
Over 250
125-250
25-125
2-25
0-2
Cities over 1 000 000 Population
Scale 1:32,000,000
0 200 400 600 800 1000 Miles
0 400 800 1200 1600 Kms
Conic Projection
Sverdlovsk
Leningrad
Gorki
Moscow
Kuybyshev
Copenhagen
Birmingham
London
Hamburg
Amsterdam
Rotterdam
Brussels
Berlin
Minsk
Warsaw
Kiev
Kharkov
Paris
Prague
Munich
Vienna
Budapest
Lyon
Turin
Milan
Bucharest
Baku
Lisbon
Madrid
Barcelona
Rome
Naples
Istanbul
Ankara
Tehran
Athens
Casablanca
Baghdad

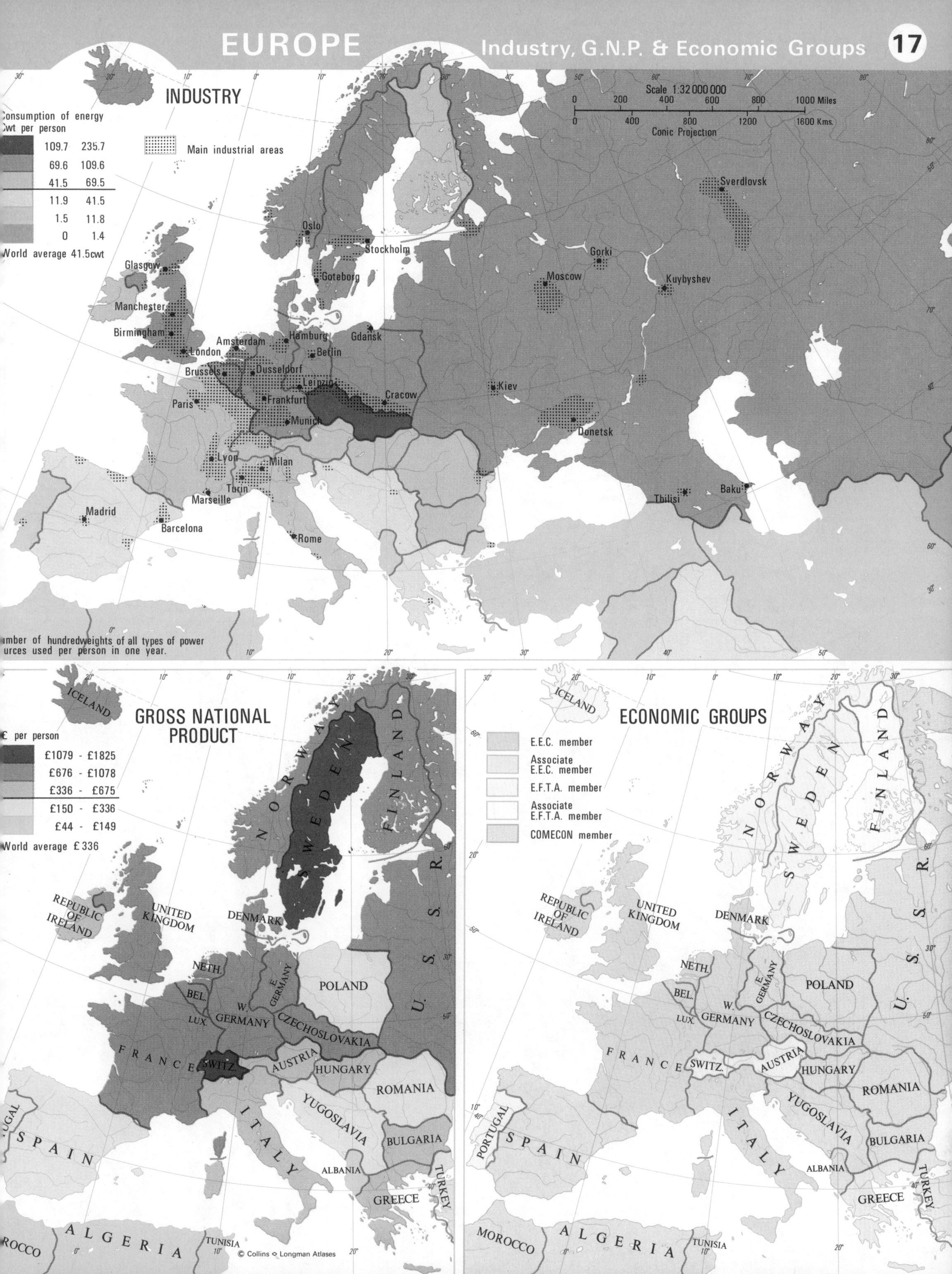
INDUSTRY
Consumption of energy
Cwt per person
109.7 235.7
69.6 109.6
41.5 69.5
11.9 41.5
1.5 11.8
0 1.4
World average 41.5cwt
Main industrial areas
Scale 1:32 000 000
0 200 400 600 800 1000 Miles
0 400 800 1200 1600 Kms.
Conic Projection
Sverdlovsk
Oslo
Stockholm
Gorki
Glasgow
Goteborg
Moscow
Kuybyshev
Manchester
Birmingham
Amsterdam
Hamburg
Gdansk
London
Berlin
Brussels
Dusseldorf
Leipzig
Kiev
Paris
Frankfurt
Cracow
Munich
Donetsk
Lyon
Milan
Turin
Marseille
Tbilisi
Baku
Madrid
Barcelona
Rome
Number of hundredweights of all types of power sources used per person in one year.
GROSS NATIONAL PRODUCT
£ per person
£1079 - £1825
£676 - £1078
£336 - £675
£150 - £336
£44 - £149
World average £336
ICELAND
NORWAY
SWEDEN
FINLAND
U. S. S. R.
REPUBLIC OF IRELAND
UNITED KINGDOM
DENMARK
NETH.
E. GERMANY
POLAND
BEL.
W. GERMANY
LUX.
CZECHOSLOVAKIA
FRANCE
SWITZ.
AUSTRIA
HUNGARY
ROMANIA
YUGOSLAVIA
BULGARIA
SPAIN
ITALY
ALBANIA
TURKEY
GREECE
ALGERIA
TUNISIA
MOROCCO
ECONOMIC GROUPS
E.E.C. member
Associate E.E.C. member
E.F.T.A. member
Associate E.F.T.A. member
COMECON member
PORTUGAL

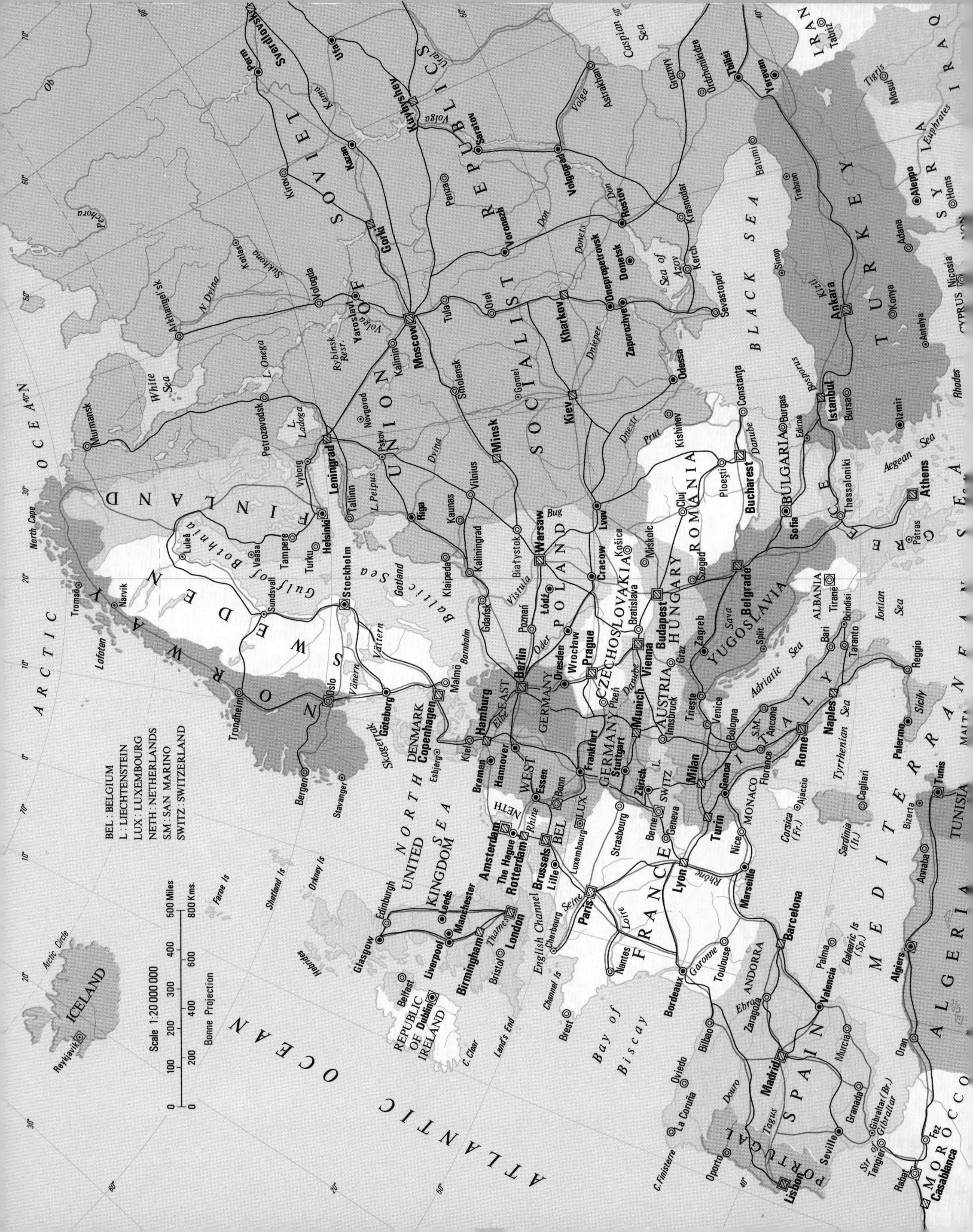
ARCTIC OCEAN
ATLANTIC OCEAN
NORTH SEA
BLACK SEA
MEDITERRANEAN SEA
Baltic Sea
Bay of Biscay
Caspian Sea
Aegean Sea
Ionian Sea
Adriatic Sea
Tyrrhenian Sea
White Sea
Sea of Azov
Gulf of Bothnia
English Channel
ICELAND
Reykjavik
REPUBLIC OF IRELAND
Dublin
UNITED KINGDOM
London
NORWAY
Oslo
SWEDEN
Stockholm
FINLAND
Helsinki
DENMARK
Copenhagen
UNION OF SOVIET SOCIALIST REPUBLICS
Moscow
Leningrad
POLAND
Warsaw
EAST GERMANY
Berlin
WEST GERMANY
Bonn
CZECHOSLOVAKIA
Prague
AUSTRIA
Vienna
HUNGARY
Budapest
ROMANIA
Bucharest
BULGARIA
Sofia
YUGOSLAVIA
Belgrade
ALBANIA
Tiranë
GREECE
Athens
TURKEY
Ankara
ITALY
Rome
FRANCE
Paris
SPAIN
Madrid
PORTUGAL
Lisbon
MOROCCO
Rabat
ALGERIA
Algiers
TUNISIA
Tunis
SYRIA
IRAQ
IRAN
CYPRUS
Nicosia
MONACO
ANDORRA
NETH
BEL
LUX
SWITZ
Amsterdam
Brussels
Luxembourg
Berne
BEL : BELGIUM
L : LIECHTENSTEIN
LUX : LUXEMBOURG
NETH : NETHERLANDS
S.M : SAN MARINO
SWITZ : SWITZERLAND
Scale 1:20 000 000
0 100 200 300 400 500 Miles
0 200 400 600 800 Kms.
Bonne Projection

Tertiary
Mesozoic
Palaeozoic
Precambrian
Igneous rocks of various ages
Lowland Plains & Basins
High Plains & Plateaus
Scarps & Upland Edges
Fold & Volcanic Mountains
Main fault line
MOINE THRUST
Northwest Highlands
GREAT GLEN FAULT
Grampian Mountains
HIGHLAND BOUNDARY FAULT
Ochil Hills
SOUTHERN UPLANDS FAULT
Southern Uplands
Cheviot Hills
CRAVEN FAULT
Pennines
Lake District
Antrim Mts.
Wicklow Mts.
Macgillycuddy's Reeks
Cambrian Mountains
Cotswolds
Chiltern Hills
North Downs
South Downs
Exmoor
Dartmoor
Scale 1:5 000 000
0 50 100 150 Miles
0 50 100 150 200 Kms.
Conic Projection

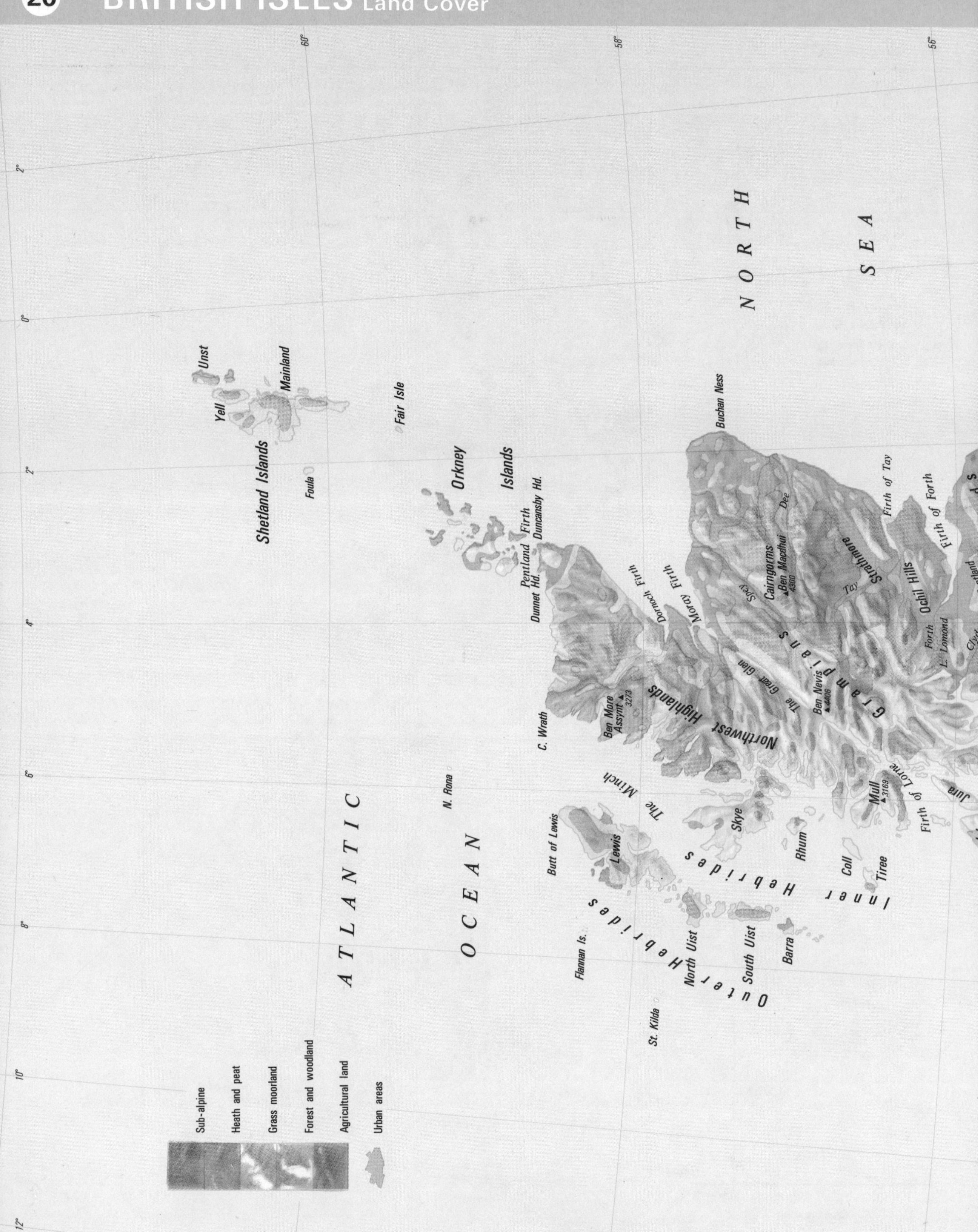

Sub-alpine
Heath and peat
Grass moorland
Forest and woodland
Agricultural land
Urban areas
ATLANTIC
OCEAN
NORTH
SEA
Shetland Islands
Unst
Yell
Mainland
Fair Isle
Foula
Orkney
Islands
Pentland Firth
Duncansby Hd.
Dunnet Hd.
Buchan Ness
Firth of Tay
Firth of Forth
Dee
Cairngorms
Ben Macdhui
4300
Strathmore
Tay
Ochil Hills
Pentland
Spey
Moray Firth
Dornoch Firth
Forth
L. Lomond
Clyde
Grampians
The Great Glen
Ben Nevis
4406
Northwest Highlands
Ben More Assynt
3273
C. Wrath
N. Rona
The Minch
Butt of Lewis
Lewis
Skye
Rhum
Mull
3169
Firth of Lorne
Jura
Islay
Coll
Tiree
Inner Hebrides
Outer Hebrides
Flannan Is.
North Uist
South Uist
Barra
St. Kilda
60°
58°
56°
2°
0°
4°
6°
8°
10°
12°

Channel
Firth of
South
Cheviot
L. Foyle
Antrim Plateau
Galloway
Tyne
Sperrin Mts.
Belfast L.
Solway Firth
Pennines
Lough Neagh
Lagan
Donegal Bay
L. Erne
Mull of Galloway
St. Bee's Hd.
Lake
Scafell Pike
3210
District
Tees
Yorkshire Moors
Vale of York
York Wolds
Mourne Mts.
2796
Isle of Man
Flamborough Hd.
54°
Achill I.
Morecambe Bay
Ribble
IRISH SEA
Spurn Hd.
Humber
Vale of Trent
Lincoln Wolds
Connemara
L. Corrib
Boyne
Mersey
The Peak
Liffey
Shannon
Anglesey
Sl. Bloom
Wicklow Mts.
3039
Snowdon
3560
L. Derg
Dee
Trent
The Wash
Cambrian Mts.
Severn
Barrow
The Fens
Golden Vale
Cardigan Bay
East Anglia
Galty Mts.
Nene
Gt. Ouse
Blackwater
52°
Carrauntoohill
3414
Carnsore Pt.
Wye
Vale of Evesham
St. George's Channel
St. David's Hd.
Tywi
Cotswold Hills
Chilterns
The Naze
Cape Clear
Thames
Sheppey
North Foreland
North Downs
Bristol Channel
Mendip Hills
Salisbury Plain
South Foreland
Lundy
The Weald
Exmoor
South Downs
Dungeness
Strait of Dover
Scale 1:3 500 000
0 25 50 75 100 Miles
0 25 50 75 100 125 150 Kms.
Conic Projection
Beachy Head
High Willhays
2038
Isle of Wight
Dartmoor
Portland Bill
50°
Start Point
ENGLISH CHANNEL
Land's End
Isles of Scilly
Lizard Point
Guernsey
Channel Islands
Jersey
Normandy
10°
8°
6°
4°
2°
0°

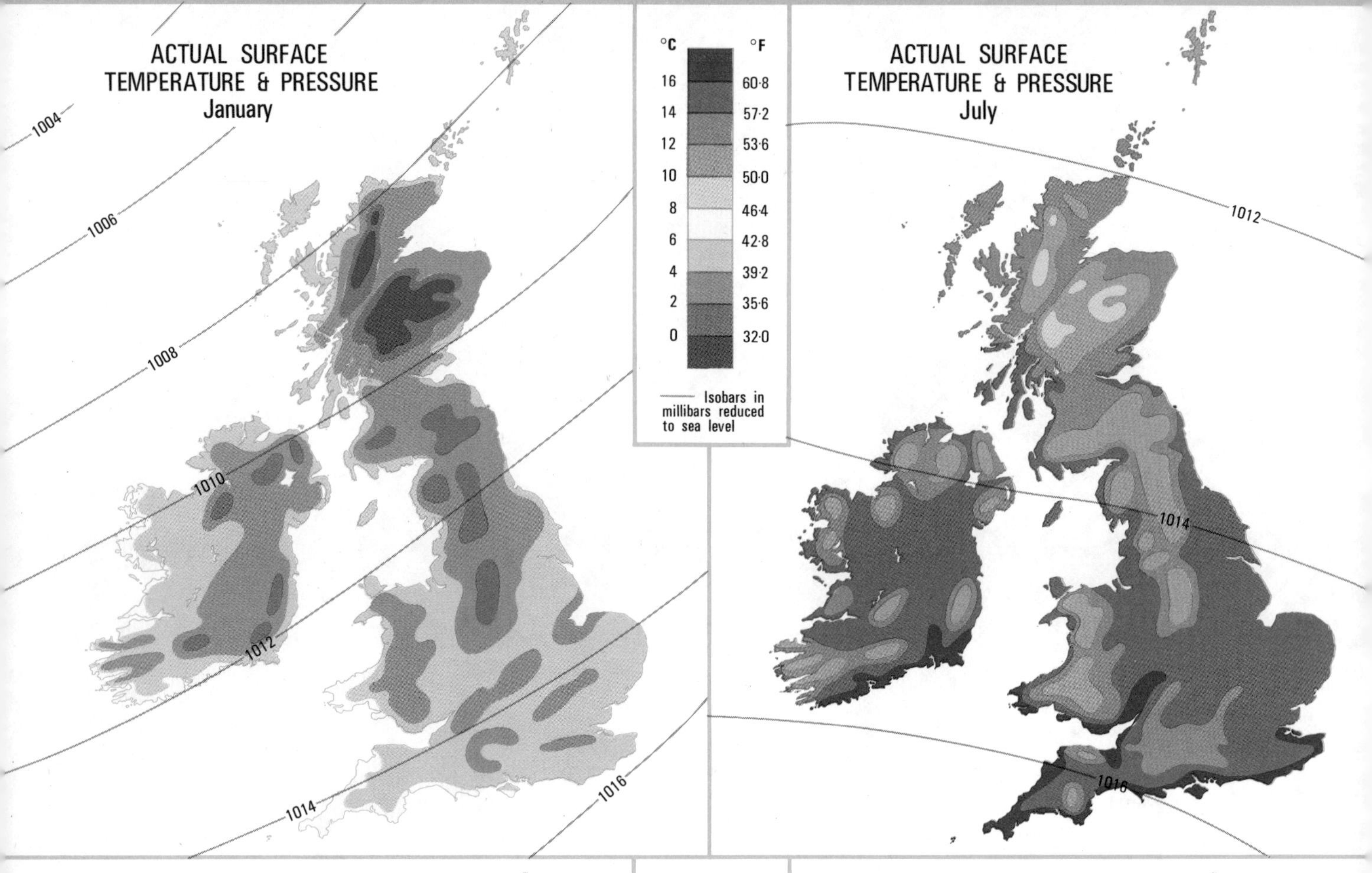
ACTUAL SURFACE
TEMPERATURE & PRESSURE
January
1004
1006
1008
1010
1012
1014
1016
°C
°F
16
60·8
14
57·2
12
53·6
10
50·0
8
46·4
6
42·8
4
39·2
2
35·6
0
32·0
Isobars in millibars reduced to sea level
ACTUAL SURFACE
TEMPERATURE & PRESSURE
July
1012
1014
1016

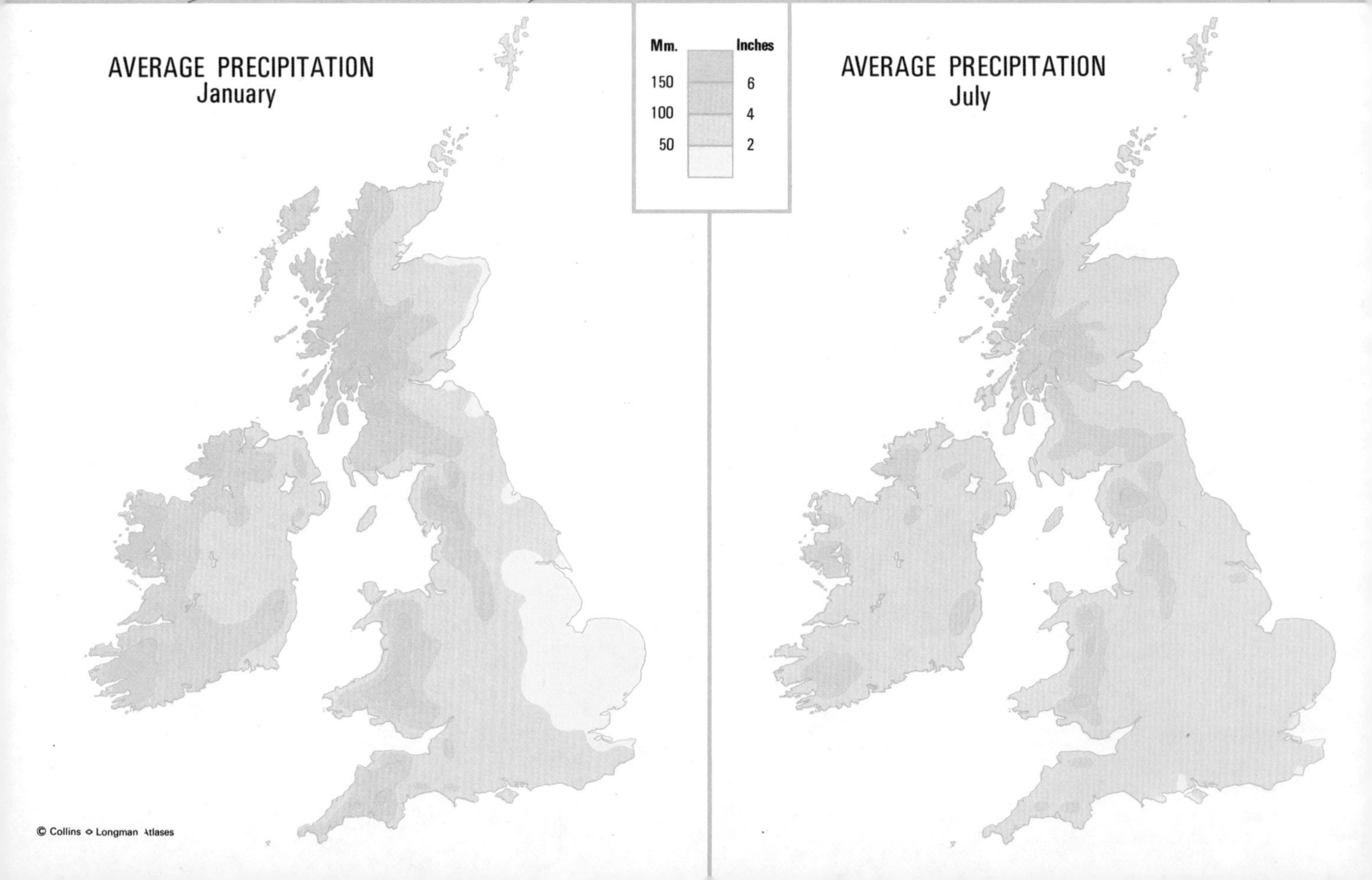
AVERAGE PRECIPITATION
January
Mm.
Inches
150
6
100
4
50
2
AVERAGE PRECIPITATION
July

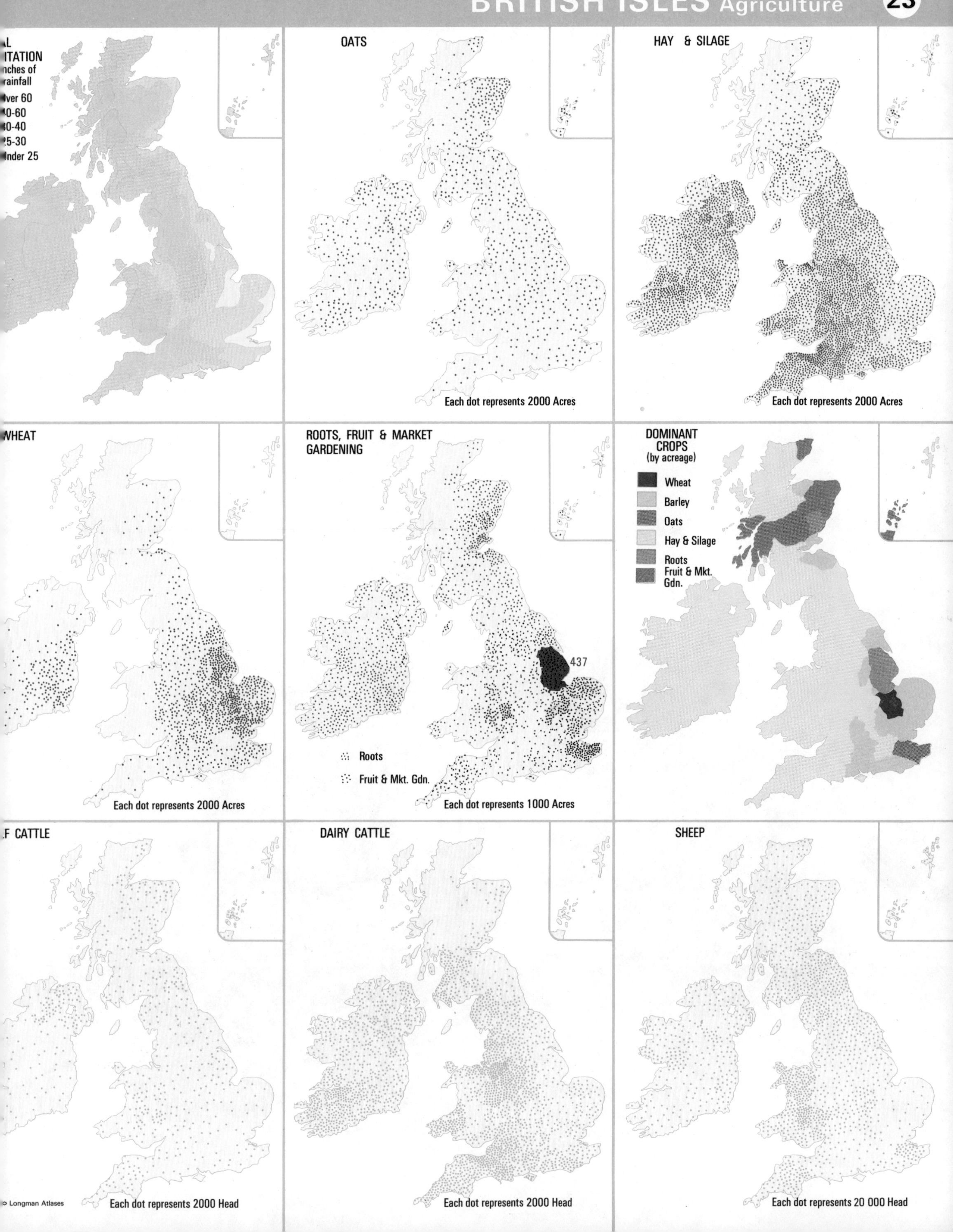
L
ITATION
nches of
rainfall
ver 60
0-60
0-40
5-30
nder 25
OATS
Each dot represents 2000 Acres
HAY & SILAGE
Each dot represents 2000 Acres
WHEAT
Each dot represents 2000 Acres
ROOTS, FRUIT & MARKET GARDENING
437
Roots
Fruit & Mkt. Gdn.
Each dot represents 1000 Acres
DOMINANT CROPS
(by acreage)
Wheat
Barley
Oats
Hay & Silage
Roots
Fruit & Mkt. Gdn.
F CATTLE
Each dot represents 2000 Head
DAIRY CATTLE
Each dot represents 2000 Head
SHEEP
Each dot represents 20 000 Head

POPULATION
Persons per sq. km.
Persons per sq. ml.
over 150
over 400
20-150
50-400
0.4-20
1-50
under 0.4
under 1
Cities over 250,000 population
Main Road
Main Railway
Scale 1:5 000 000
0 25 50 75 100 Miles
0 50 100 150 Kms.
Conic Projection
Glasgow
Edinburgh
Newcastle upon Tyne
Belfast
Dublin
Kingston upon Hull
Leeds
Bradford
Liverpool
Manchester
Sheffield
Stoke-on-Trent
Nottingham
Wolverhampton
Leicester
Birmingham
Coventry
London
Cardiff
Bristol
Plymouth

International boundary
National boundary
County or region boundary
Historic counties in Northern Ireland
Metropolitan county
Greater London
Administrative headquarters (those underlined contain the offices of more than one county)
The local government boundaries for England & Wales shown on this map were officially approved by an Act of Parliament in October 1972, and those for Scotland and Northern Ireland in October 1973. The sub-division of Counties and Regions is not shown.
SCOTLAND
9 Regions
3 Island Authorities
53 Districts
NORTHERN IRELAND
1 Region
26 Districts
ENGLAND
39 Counties
6 Metropolitan Counties
Greater London
36 Metropolitan Districts
296 Non-Metropolitan Districts
WALES
8 Counties
37 Districts
REPUBLIC OF IRELAND
26 Counties
ORKNEY
Kirkwall
SHETLAND
Lerwick
WESTERN ISLES
Stornoway
HIGHLAND
Inverness
GRAMPIAN
Aberdeen
TAYSIDE
Dundee
FIFE
Cupar
CENTRAL
Stirling
LOTHIAN
Edinburgh
STRATHCLYDE
Glasgow
BORDERS
Newtown St Boswells
DUMFRIES & GALLOWAY
Dumfries
DONEGAL
Lifford
Londonderry
Antrim
Tyrone
Belfast
Fermanagh
Armagh
Down
Monaghan
ISLE OF MAN
Douglas
Sligo
SLIGO
LEITRIM
Carrick-on-Shannon
CAVAN
Cavan
MONAGHAN
LOUTH
Dundalk
MAYO
Castlebar
ROSCOMMON
Roscommon
LONGFORD
Longford
Navan
MEATH
Mullingar
WEST MEATH
GALWAY
Galway
DUBLIN
Dublin
Tullamore
OFFALY
KILDARE
Naas
Port Laoise
LAOIS
WICKLOW
Wicklow
CLARE
Ennis
Carlow
CARLOW
Kilkenny
KILKENNY
TIPPERARY
Limerick
LIMERICK
Clonmel
WEXFORD
Wexford
Tralee
KERRY
WATERFORD
Waterford
CORK
Cork
NORTHUMBERLAND
Newcastle upon Tyne
TYNE & WEAR
Carlisle
Durham
DURHAM
CLEVELAND
Middlesbrough
CUMBRIA
Northallerton
NORTH YORKSHIRE
HUMBERSIDE
Kingston upon Hull
LANCASHIRE
Preston
WEST YORKSHIRE
Wakefield
Barnsley
SOUTH YORKSHIRE
Manchester
G.M.
MERSEYSIDE
Liverpool
Lincoln
LINCOLNSHIRE
Mold
CLWYD
CHESHIRE
Chester
DERBYSHIRE
Matlock
NOTTINGHAMSHIRE
Nottingham
Caernarvon
GWYNEDD
Stafford
STAFFORDSHIRE
Shrewsbury
SALOP
LEICESTERSHIRE
Leicester
Norwich
NORFOLK
Birmingham
W.M.
CAMBRIDGESHIRE
Cambridge
Warwick
WARWICKSHIRE
NORTHAMPTONSHIRE
Northampton
SUFFOLK
Ipswich
Bedford
BEDFORDSHIRE
POWYS
Llandrindod Wells
Worcester
HEREFORD & WORCESTER
DYFED
Carmarthen
Gloucester
GLOUCESTERSHIRE
Oxford
OXFORDSHIRE
BUCKINGHAMSHIRE
Aylesbury
HERTFORDSHIRE
Hertford
Chelmsford
ESSEX
WEST GLAMORGAN
Swansea
MID GLAMORGAN
GWENT
Cwmbran
Bristol
AVON
S.G.
Cardiff
Trowbridge
WILTSHIRE
Reading
BERKSHIRE
Kingston upon Thames
GREATER LONDON
SURREY
Maidstone
KENT
SOMERSET
Taunton
HAMPSHIRE
Winchester
WEST SUSSEX
Chichester
EAST SUSSEX
Lewes
DEVON
Exeter
DORSET
Dorchester
Newport
ISLE OF WIGHT
CORNWALL
Truro
G.M. GREATER MANCHESTER
S.G. SOUTH GLAMORGAN
W.M. WEST MIDLANDS
Scale 1:4 000 000
0 20 40 60 80 100 Miles
0 40 80 120 160 km
Conic Projection

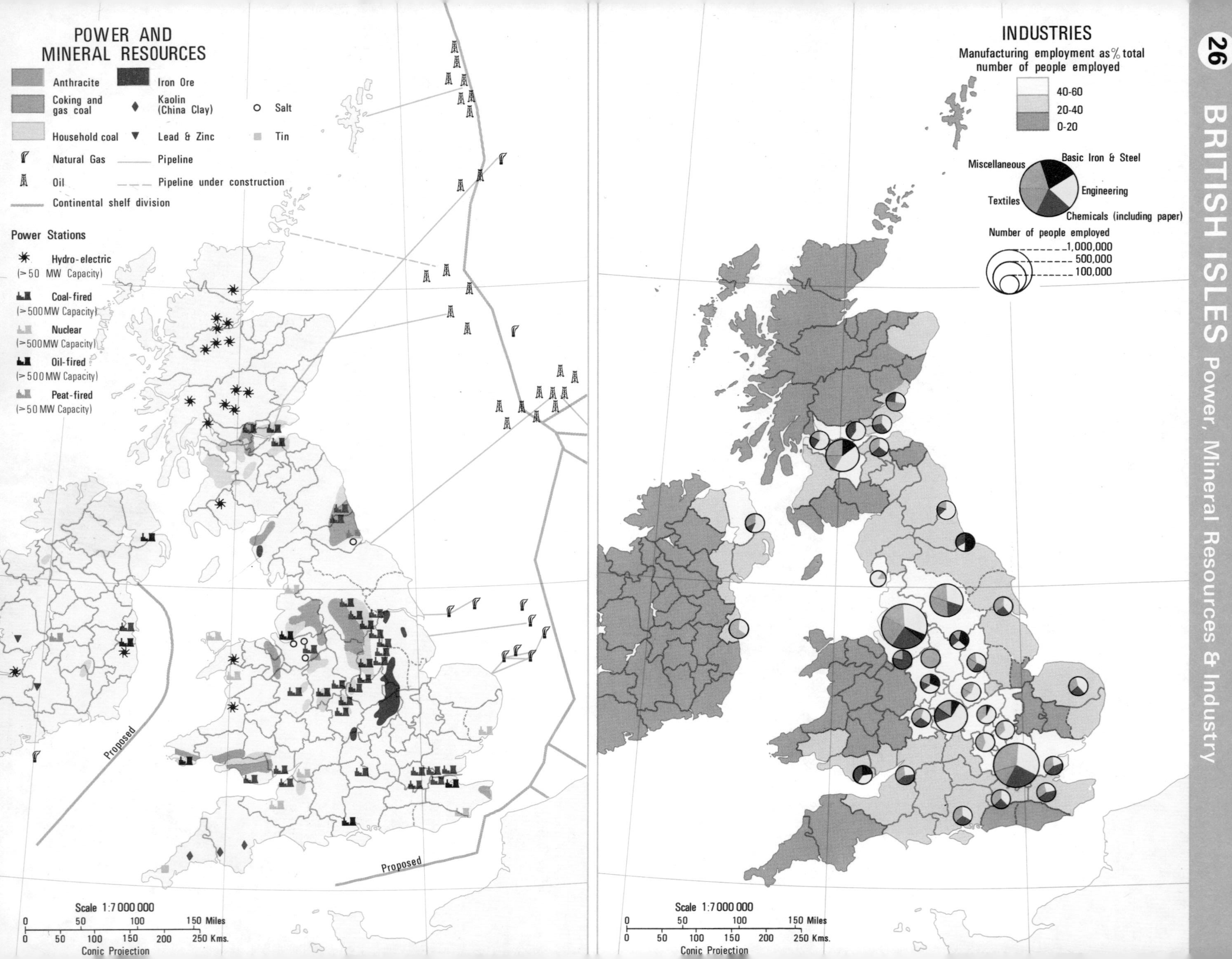

POWER AND MINERAL RESOURCES
Anthracite
Iron Ore
Coking and gas coal
Kaolin (China Clay)
Salt
Household coal
Lead & Zinc
Tin
Natural Gas
Pipeline
Oil
Pipeline under construction
Continental shelf division
Power Stations
Hydro-electric (> 50 MW Capacity)
Coal-fired (> 500 MW Capacity)
Nuclear (> 500 MW Capacity)
Oil-fired (> 500 MW Capacity)
Peat-fired (> 50 MW Capacity)
Proposed
Proposed
Scale 1:7 000 000
0 50 100 150 Miles
0 50 100 150 200 250 Kms.
Conic Projection
INDUSTRIES
Manufacturing employment as % total number of people employed
40-60
20-40
0-20
Miscellaneous
Basic Iron & Steel
Engineering
Textiles
Chemicals (including paper)
Number of people employed
1,000,000
500,000
100,000
Scale 1:7 000 000
0 50 100 150 Miles
0 50 100 150 200 250 Kms.
Conic Projection

Motorway
'A' Road
'B' Road
Woodland
Relief
Feet Metres
656 200
328 100
0 Sea Level
Scale 1:400 000
0 5 10 Miles
0 5 10 15 Kms
Lambert Conformal Conic Projection
HERTFORDSHIRE
BUCKINGHAMSHIRE
ESSEX
BERKSHIRE
SURREY
KENT
GREATER LONDON
Chelmsford
Harlow
Welwyn Garden City
St Albans
Hemel Hempstead
Watford
High Wycombe
Rickmansworth
Cheshunt
Brentwood
Basildon
Chigwell
Maidenhead
Slough
Staines
Egham
Sunbury
Walton -on- Thames
Chertsey
Esher
Ewell
Epsom
Banstead
Woking
Leatherhead
Guildford
Farnborough
Aldershot
Reigate
Dartford
Gravesend
Grays
Rochester
Gillingham
Chatham
Maidstone
Thames
Medway
© Collins – Longman Atlases

LEICESTERSHIRE
STAFFORDSHIRE
SALOP
POWYS
WEST MIDLANDS
WARWICKSHIRE
NORTHAMPTONSHIRE
HEREFORD AND WORCESTER
GLOUCESTERSHIRE
OXFORDSHIRE
BUCKINGHAMSHIRE
GWENT
MID GLAMORGAN
SOUTH GLAMORGAN
AVON
WILTSHIRE
BERKSHIRE
SOMERSET
HAMPSHIRE
DORSET
DEVON
ISLE OF WIGHT
BRISTOL CHANNEL
Bridgwater Bay
Lyme Bay
Poole Bay
The Solent
Spithead
Shrewsbury
Telford
Wolverhampton
Walsall
West Bromwich
Dudley
Birmingham
Solihull
Coventry
Nuneaton
Leicester
Rugby
Northampton
Kidderminster
Bromsgrove
Redditch
Worcester
Hereford
Great Malvern
Stratford-upon-Avon
Banbury
Cheltenham
Gloucester
Oxford
Swindon
Reading
Newport
Cardiff
Bristol
Bath
Weston-super-Mare
Bridgwater
Taunton
Yeovil
Salisbury
Winchester
Southampton
Portsmouth
Bournemouth
Poole
Weymouth
Basingstoke
Newbury
Chippenham
Trowbridge
Andover
Eastleigh
Havant
Chichester
Aylesbury
Bletchley
Wellingborough
Maidenhead
Farnborough
Aldershot
Exmouth
Dorchester
Christchurch
Lymington
Newport
Ryde
Sandown
Shanklin
Ventnor
Cowes
Fareham
Gosport
Isle of Portland
Chesil Beach
The Needles
St Catherine's Pt
Selsey Bill
St Alban's or St Aldhelm's Hd
Durlston Hd
Vale of White Horse
Vale of Evesham
Vale of Berkeley
Forest of Dean
Salisbury Plain
Mendip Hills
Quantock Hills
Brendon Hills
Black Down Hills
North Dorset Downs
South Dorset Downs
New Forest
Marlborough Downs
Hampshire Downs
Berkshire Downs
Brecon Beacons
Black Mountains
Clun Forest
Wenlock Edge
The Long Mynd
Malvern Hills
Severn
Thames
Avon
Wye
Kennet
M4
M5
M6
M1
M40
M3
M27
M45
M50
52°
51°
3°
2°
1°

Relief

Feet	Metres
3281	1000
1640	500
656	200
328	100
0	Sea Level
66	20
164	50

Spot Heights in Feet ▲4406

Scale 1:1 000 000

0 10 20 30 40 Miles

0 10 20 30 40 50 60 Kms.

Lambert Conformal Conic Projection

West from Greenwich 0° East from Greenwich

1° 2° 52° 51°

LINCOLNSHIRE
NORFOLK
CAMBRIDGESHIRE
SUFFOLK
HERTFORDSHIRE
ESSEX
GREATER LONDON
KENT
EAST SUSSEX
FRANCE
PAS DE CALAIS
NORD
STRAIT OF DOVER

Saxthorpe
Bacton
North Walsham
Aylsham
Waxham
Stalham
Coltishall
Norfolk Broads
Hoveton
Winterton-on-Sea
King's Lynn
Glen
Deeping Fen
Market Deeping
Welland
Crowland
The Fens
Nene
Wisbech
Marshland Fen
Great Ouse
Nar
East Dereham
Wensum
Bure
Caister-on-Sea
Yarmouth Roads
Great Yarmouth
Swaffham
Norwich
Thorney
Guyhirn
Outwell
Downham Market
▲267
Watton
Wymondham
▲244
Yare
Reedham
Peterborough
March
Bedford Levels
Wissey
Old Fletton
Whittlesey
Farcet Fen
Methwold
Attleborough
Stilton
Littleport
Breckland
Lowestoft
Ramsey
Chatteris
Little Ouse
Bungay
Beccles
Kessingland
Wangford Fen
Brandon
Thetford
Harleston
Isle of Ely
Ely
Diss
Mildenhall
Waveney
Halesworth
Blyth
Southwold
Huntingdon
St Ives
Soham
Eye
Godmanchester
Lark
Ixworth
Kimbolton
Cottenham
Little Fen
Kentford
Yoxford
Burwell
Histon
Newmarket
Bury St. Edmunds
Debenham
Framlingham
St Neots
Saxmundham
Cambridge
Leiston
Stowmarket
Deben
Great Shelford
▲420
Wickham Market
Alde
Aldeburgh
Needham Market
Sawston
Sandy
Linton
Biggleswade
Haverhill
Orford
Woodbridge
Orford Ness
Melbourn
Great Chesterford
▲413
Stour
Sudbury
Hadleigh
Ipswich
Hollesley Bay
Shefford
Royston
Saffron Walden
Bawdsey
Stotfold
▲410
East Anglian Heights
Baldock
Newport
Bures
Nayland
Letchworth
Thaxted
Stour
Felixstowe
Buntingford
Halstead
Manningtree
Harwich
Hitchin
Stevenage
Great Bardfield
Colne
Stansted Mountfitchet
Colchester
Luton
Braintree
Coggeshall
Thorpe-le-Soken
The Naze
Standon
Great Dunmow
Wivenhoe
Walton on the Naze
Bishop's Stortford
Kelvedon
Brightlingsea
Frinton
Harpenden
Welwyn Garden City
Sawbridgeworth
Tiptree
Ware
Chelmer
Witham
Mersea I.
Hatfield
Hertford
Harlow
West Mersea
Clacton on Sea
Hoddesdon
M11
St Albans
M10
Chelmsford
Maldon
Blackwater
Cheshunt
Waltham Abbey
Bradwell-on-Sea
Potters Bar
Epping
Chipping Ongar
Ingatestone
South Woodham Ferrers
Southminster
Epping Forest
Enfield
Roding
Chigwell
Billericay
Wickford
Burnham-on-Crouch
Barnet
Crouch
Foulness Pt
Harrow
Redbridge
Brentwood
Rayleigh
Foulness I.
Havering
Basildon
S. Benfleet
Stanford le Hope
Canvey
Shoeburyness
London
Grays
Southend-on-Sea
Thames Haven
Hounslow
Tilbury
Grain
Richmond-upon-Thames
Swanscombe
Sheerness
Bexley
Dartford
Medway
Minster
Kingston-upon-Thames
Gravesend
Queenborough
Leysdown-on-Sea
Margate
Esher
Bromley
Rochester
Isle of Sheppey
Whitstable
Herne Bay
North Foreland
Sutton
Gillingham
Isle of Thanet
Broadstairs
Epsom
Croydon
Kingsdown
Chatham
Sittingbourne
The Swale
Ramsgate
Faversham
M2
Pegwell Bay
Banstead
▲771
Borough Green
Stour
Canterbury
Sandwich
Goodwin Sands
Caterham
North Downs
Maidstone
▲645
M20
Sevenoaks
Westerham
▲756
Reigate
Oxted
Charing
Gt. Stour
Aylesham
Deal
Dorking
Walmer
Leith Hill
▲965
Tonbridge
Paddock Wood
Medway
Beult
Wye
▲583
Horley
Headcorn
Kennington
St Margaret's at Cliffe
Capel
Lingfield
Marden
Vale of Kent
Ashford
South Foreland
M23
Southborough
Royal Tunbridge Wells
Temple Ewell
Lyminge
Dover
Crawley
East Grinstead
Bethersden
Forest Row
Cranbrook
Hamstreet
Folkestone
Dunkirk
The Weald
Crowborough
Tenterden
Hythe
Sandgate
Horsham
Ashdown Forest
Wadhurst
Hawkhurst
Romney Marsh
Grand Fort Philippe
Billingshurst
▲646
Ticehurst
Dymchurch
Cuckfield
Mayfield
Isle of Oxney
Gravelines
Haywards Heath
Northiam
New Romney
Calais
Burgess Hill
Uckfield
Rother
Heathfield
Lydd
Aa
Audruicq
Ouse
Rye
Adur
Battle
Brede
Henfield
Ditchling Beacon
▲813
Rye Bay
Dungeness
Guînes
Cap Gris-Nez
▲522
Ardres
Steyning
Lewes
Hailsham
Shoreham-by-Sea
Hove
Hastings
Southwick
Polegate
Marquise
Worthing
Brighton
▲713
Bexhill
▲554
Newhaven
St Omer
Cuckmere
Seaford
Eastbourne
Boulogne
Beachy Hd
Liane
Desvres
▲656
Samer
Fauquembergues
Hucqueliers

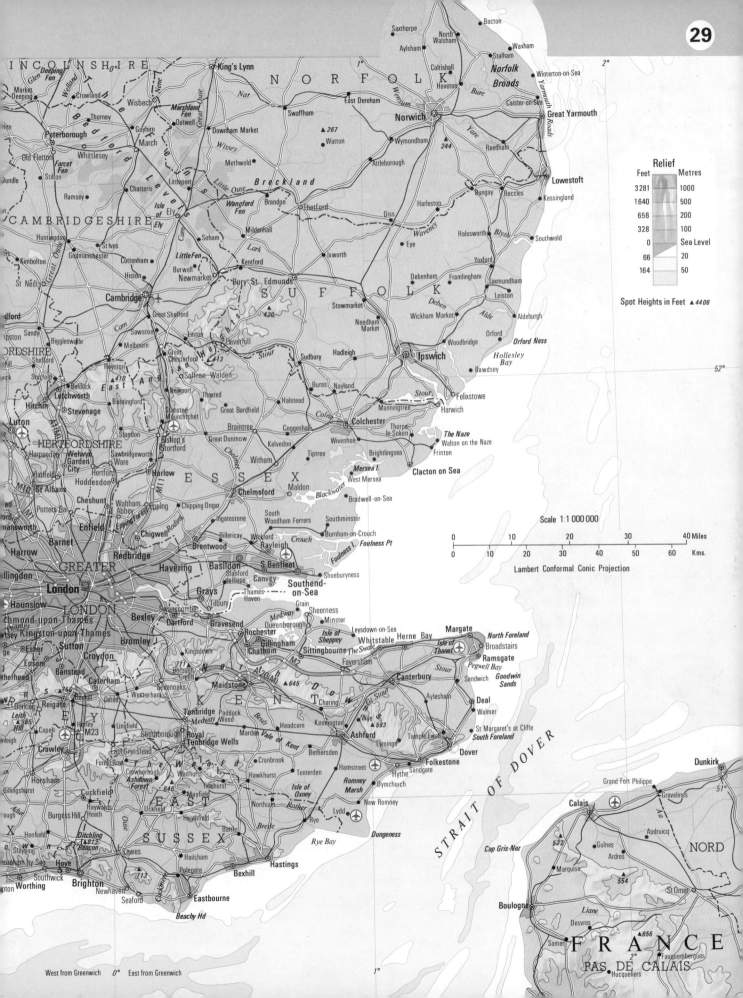

IRISH SEA
ST GEORGE'S CHANNEL
CARDIGAN BAY
MERSEYSIDE
CHESHIRE
LANCASHIRE
STAFFORDSHIRE
SALOP
CLWYD
GWYNEDD
POWYS
DYFED
HEREFORD AND WORCESTER
CAMBRIAN MOUNTAINS
Snowdon
Anglesey
Liverpool
Manchester
Chester
Wrexham
Shrewsbury
Hereford
Aberystwyth
Cardigan
Caernarvon
Holyhead
Bangor
Llandudno
Colwyn Bay
Prestatyn
Barmouth
Aberdovey
Towyn
New Quay
Aberayron
Fishguard Bay
St David's Hd
Bardsey
Tremadog Bay
Menai Str
Clwydian Range
Clun Forest
Black Mountains
Scale 1:1 000 000
0 10 20 30 40 Miles
0 10 20 30 40 50 60 Kms.
Lambert Conformal Conic Projection

Relief
Feet Metres
3281 1000
1640 500
656 200
328 100
0 Sea Level
66 20
164 50
328 100
Spot Heights in Feet ▲4406
BRISTOL CHANNEL
ENGLISH CHANNEL
Carmarthen Bay
Bridgwater Bay
Lyme Bay
Lundy
SOUTH GLAMORGAN
MID GLAMORGAN
GWENT
AVON
SOMERSET
DEVON
DORSET
CORNWALL
Dartmoor Forest
Exmoor Forest
Bodmin Moor
Mendip Hills
Brendon Hills
Quantock Hills
Blackdown Hills
Swansea
Neath
Port Talbot
Llanelli
Cardiff
Newport
Barry
Bristol
Bath
Weston-super-Mare
Bridgwater
Taunton
Yeovil
Exeter
Torbay
Plymouth
Barnstaple
Bideford
Tiverton
Okehampton
Launceston
Bodmin
Truro
St Austell
Falmouth
Penzance
Newquay
Camborne
Redruth
Helston
Dorchester
Weymouth
Isles of Scilly
St Mary's
St Martin's
St Agnes
Bryher
Hugh Town
Seven Stones
Wolf Rock
Land's End
Lizard Pt
Hartland Pt
Start Pt
Bolt Hd
Eddystone
CHANNEL ISLANDS
Alderney
Guernsey
Sark
Jersey
St Helier
St Peter Port
FRANCE
Same Scale
5° West from Greenwich
51°
50°
4°
3°
6°W
2°W
2°30′W
49°30′
© Collins ◇ Longman Atlases

DUMFRIES AND GALLOWAY
The Machers
Wigtown Bay
Garlieston
Port William
Whithorn
Isle of Whithorn
Burrow Hd
Kirkcudbright
Kirkcudbright Bay
SOLWAY FIRTH
Silloth
Abbey Town
Wigton
Thursby
Carlisle
Eden
Wetheral
NORTHUMBERLAND
Newcastle upon Tyne
Tyne
Ryton
Blaydon
Whickham
Consett
Derwent
Alston
Kirkoswald
Aspatria
Caldbeck
Caldew
M6
Maryport
Flimby
Ellen
Seaton
Workington
Cockermouth
Derwent
3053 Skiddaw
Mts
Penrith
Collier Law 1692
Stanhope
Tow Law
Wear
Weardale
Wolsingham
Crook
DURHAM
Cross Fell
Middleton in Teesdale
Bishop Auckland
Keswick
Pooley Bridge
Derwent Wr
Crummock Wr
Whitehaven
Cleator Moor
Lake District
Ullswater
3118 Helvellyn
Hawes Water
Shap
Appleby
2591
Teesdale
Tees
Barnard Castle
St Bees Hd
St Bees
Ennerdale Wr
Egremont
CUMBRIA
3210 Scafell Pike
Wast Water
Ambleside
Brough
Bowes
Kirkby Stephen
Rogan's Seat 2203
Richmond
Seascale
Esk
Coniston
Windermere
Gt Shunner Fell 2340
Swale
Leyburn
Black Combe 1969
Bootle
Broughton in Furness
Coniston Wr
Kendal
Sedbergh
Hawes
Wensleydale
Aysgarth
Millom
Ulverston
Grange-over-Sands
Milnthorpe
Arnside
Kirkby Lonsdale
Whernside 2419
Langstrothdale Chase
Cover
Lune
Greta
Ingleborough 2373
Ingleton
Pen-y-ghent 2231
Gt Whernside 2310
Nidderdale
YORK
PENNINES
Dalton-in-Furness
Barrow-in-Furness
Isle of Walney
Morecambe Bay
Carnforth
Morecambe
High Bentham
Ribble
Wharfe
Settle
Hilpsford Pt
Heysham
Lancaster
Ward's Stone 1836
Glasson
Ribblesdale
Hellifield
Wharfedale
Forest of Bowland
Slaidburn
Hodder
Skipton
Ilkley
1340
Fleetwood
Rossall Pt
Preesall
Garstang
LANCASHIRE
Barnoldswick
Earby
Silsden
Cleveleys
Thornton
Wyre
Pendle Hill 1831
Clitheroe
Colne
Keighley
Guiseley
Bingley
Great Eccleston
Nelson
Blackpool
M55
Longridge
Whalley
Brierfield
Shipley
Bradford
Kirkham
Gt Harwood
Burnley
Lytham St Anne's
Preston
Accrington
Hebden Bridge
Halifax
Blackburn
Forest of Rossendale
Tarleton
Leyland
Darwen
Haslingden
Rawtenstall
Bacup
Todmorden
Brighouse
Elland
Southport
Chorley
1534
Ramsbottom
Adlington
Rufford
Rochdale
Huddersfield
Burscough
Horwich
Bury
GREATER
Marsden
Formby
Formby Pt
Ormskirk
Skelmersdale
Wigan
M61
Bolton
M62
Heywood
Oldham
Meltham
Holmfirth
Farnworth
Radcliffe
Saddleworth Moor
Liverpool Bay
Maghull
Rainford
Ashton in Makerfield
Atherton
Middleton
Crosby
Kirkby
Leigh
Manchester
Ashton-under-Lyne
MERSEYSIDE
Bootle
M57
Eccles
Wallasey
St Helens
Prescot
Newton le Willows
Urmston
Salford
Hyde
Hadfield
Bleaklow Hill
Birkenhead
Liverpool
Warrington
Sale
Stockport
Glossop
Hoylake
M53
M62
MANCHESTER
Marple
Kinder Scout 2088
High Peak
West Kirby
Wirral
Widnes
Altrincham
Cheadle
New Mills
Heswall
Bebington
Mersey
Runcorn
M56
Wilmslow
Hathersage
Neston
Dee
Ellesmere Port
Frodsham
Weaver
Knutsford
Whaley Bridge
Chapel en le Frith
The Skerries
Cemaes Bay
Carmel Hd
Amlwch
Holyhead Bay
Red Wharf Bay
Puffin I.
Gt Ormes Hd
Llandudno
Prestatyn
Holyhead
Llanerchymedd
Benllech
Conwy Bay
Conwy
Tywyn
Colwyn Bay
Rhyl
Anglesey
Beaumaris
Holy I.
Llangefni
Penmaenmawr
Abergele
Holywell
Flint
Rhosneigr
Menai Bridge
Llanfairfechan
Elwy
Clwyd
Macclesfield
Bangor
Denbigh
Northwich
CHESHIRE
Buxton
Aberffraw
Port Dinorwic
Bethesda
Connah's Quay
Caernarvon
Mold
Buckley
Chester
Kelsall
Winsford
Holmes Chapel
Middlewich
Llanberis
Llanrwst
Clwydian Range
Tarporley
Congleton
Menai Str
1102
1603
Harrington
Caernarvon Bay
3560 Snowdon
Ruthin
Sandbach
Biddulph
Leek
Dove
Penygroes
Betws-y-Coed
Alsager
Kidsgrove
Farndon
Crewe
53°
GWYNEDD
CLWYD
Nantwich
Wrexham
Blaenau Ffestiniog
2194 Carnedd y Filiast
Rhosllanerchrugog
Ruabon
Newcastle-under-Lyme
Stoke-on-Trent
Audlem
1860
Nefyn
Llangollen
Overton
Corwen
Dee
Tudweiliog
Lleyn Peninsula
Criccieth
Penrhyndeudraeth
Ffestiniog
Porthmadog
Whitchurch
Trentham
Upper Tean
Bala
2800
Llandrillo
Berwyn
2713
Ceiriog
Ellesmere
Market Drayton
Pwllheli
Tremadog Bay
Harlech
Whittington
Stone
Uttoxeter
Abersoch
Y Llethr 2475
Llanbedr
Llanuwchllyn
Aran Fawddwy 2970
Llangynog
Oswestry
Wem
Hodnet
Eccleshall
Roden
Trent
West Felton
Tanat
Stafford
Lake Vyrnwy
Llanfyllin
Harmer Hill
Burton upon Trent
Barmouth
Dolgellau
2927 Cader Idris
Dinas Mawddwy
Vyrnwy
SALOP
Newport
Rugeley
Fairbourne
POWYS
Severn
Shrewsbury
Wellington
STAFFORDSHIRE
Cannock
Llangadfan
54°
4°
2°
3°
IRISH SEA
Pt of Ayre
Andreas
Bride
Jurby Hd
Ramsey Bay
Ramsey
Kirk Michael
Snaefell 2034
Maughold Hd
Peel
Laxey
ISLE OF MAN
Crosby
Clay Hd
1585 South Barrule
Douglas
Port Erin
Castletown
Langness

West from Greenwich
East from Greenwich
Scale 1:1 000 000
0 10 20 30 40 Miles
0 10 20 30 40 50 60 Kms.
Lambert Conformal Conic Projection
Relief
Feet Metres
3281 1000
1640 500
656 200
328 100
0 Sea Level
66 20
164 50
328 100
Spot Heights in Feet ▲4406
NORTH SEA
CLEVELAND
HUMBERSIDE
LINCOLNSHIRE
NORFOLK
LEICESTERSHIRE
NOTTINGHAMSHIRE
North York Moors
Cleveland Hills
Yorkshire Wolds
Lincoln Wolds
Vale of Pickering
Vale of York
Holderness
THE WASH
Flamborough Head
Bridlington Bay
Spurn Hd
Gibraltar Pt
Holkham Bay
Blakeney Pt
Tees Bay
Sherwood Forest
Isle of Axholme
Holland Fen
Deeping Fen
The Marsh
South Shields
Sunderland
Hartlepool
Redcar
Middlesbrough
Stockton-on-Tees
Whitby
Scarborough
Filey
Bridlington
York
Kingston upon Hull
Grimsby
Cleethorpes
Scunthorpe
Doncaster
Lincoln
Skegness
Boston
Grantham
Nottingham
King's Lynn
Hunstanton
Cromer
Sheringham
Loughborough
Mansfield
Worksop
Rotherham
Barnsley
Wakefield
Pontefract
Castleford
Selby
Goole
Beverley
Hornsea
Withernsea
Louth
Mablethorpe
Spalding
Newark-on-Trent
Gainsborough
Market Rasen
Horncastle
Sleaford
Fakenham
East Dereham

ATLANTIC
OCEAN
NORTH CHANNEL
HIGHLAND
ARGYLL
NORTHERN IRELAND
LONDONDERRY
ANTRIM
TYRONE
DOWN
FIRTH OF LORNE
FIRTH OF CLYDE
SOUND OF JURA
Sound of Mull
Sound of Islay
Sound of Gigha
Kilbrannan Sound
Sound of Bute
Kyles of Bute
Rathlin Sound
Gulf of Corryvreckan
Belfast Lough
LOUGH NEAGH
Lough Foyle
Luce Bay
Wigtown Bay
Irvine Bay
Culzean Bay
Sorisdale
Coll
Arinagour
Caoles
Tiree
Scarinish
Hynish Bay
Hynish
Skerryvore
Ardmore Pt
Tobermory
Dervaig
L. Frisa
Treshnish Pt
Treshnish Is
L. Tuath
Ulva
L. na Keal
Staffa
Ben More
3169
Mull
Glen More
Iona
Fionnphort
Bunessan
L. Scridain
Ross of Mull
Sd of Iona
Torran Rocks
L. Buie
Lochbuie
Salen
Drimnin
Morvern
Lochaline
Duart Pt
Lochdonhead
Lismore
Loch Linnhe
Loch Sunart
Strontian
Ben Hiant
1729
Corran
North Ballachulish
Kinlochleven
Ballachulish
Glen Coe
3766
Bidean nam Bian
Blackwater Res.
L. Laidon
Rannoch Moor
Kinloch Rannoch
L. Rannoch
Glen Lyon
Breadalbane
Portnacroish
2657
Creach Bheinn
Glen Kinglass
Ben Cruachan
3689
Taynuilt
Connel
Oban
Kerrera
Dalmally
Glen Orchy
Tyndrum
Killin
Glen Dochart
3708
Ben Lui
Crianlarich
3843
Ben More
Lochearnhead
L. Voil
Kilninver
Kilchrenan
Loch Awe
1932
Seil
Luing
Garvellachs
Scarba
Inveraray
Ardlui
3092
L. Katrine
The Trossachs
L. Venachar
Aberfoyle
Arrochar
3192
Ben Lomond
Loch Lomond
Luss
Drymen
Balfron
Dubh Artach
Colonsay
Scalasaig
Oronsay
Ford
L. Craignish
Kilmartin
Crinan
Strachur
Lochgoilhead
L. Long
Loch Fyne
Loch Eck
Garelochhead
Ardentinny
Helensburgh
Balloch
Alexandria
Dumbarton
Kilcreggan
Gourock
Greenock
Port Glasgow
Clydebank
Erskine
Bearsden
Milngavie
Kilmacolm
Renfrew
Johnstone
Paisley
Rutherglen
Barrhead
M8
Jura
1564
Killchianaig
L. Tarbert
Lagg
2571
Paps of Jura
Rubha A'Mhail
Nave
Ardnave Pt
Port Askaig
Islay
L. Gorm
Coul Pt
Port Charlotte
L. Indaal
Bowmore
1609
Beinn Bheigeir
Portnahaven
Rhinns Pt
Laggan Bay
Ardmore Pt
Port Ellen
Mull of Oa
Ardrishaig
Lochgilphead
Achahoish
1840
Sliabh Gaoil
Tarbert
Knapdale
L. Caolisport
Pt of Knap
Kilberry Hd
Kilfinan
Tighnabruaich
Kames
Ardlamont Pt
1658
Colintraive
Dunoon
Sandbank
L. Striven
Innellan
Port Bannatyne
Rothesay
Bute
Kingarth
Millport
Cumbraes
Wemyss Bay
Skelmorlie
Largs
Lochwinnoch
Kilbirnie
Beith
Dalry
West Kilbride
Seamill
Kilwinning
Ardrossan
Saltcoats
Stevenston
Irvine
Kilmarnock
Stewarton
Newton Mearns
Galston
Newmilns
Darvel
Cunninghame
1383
Skipness
Gigha
Cara
Kintyre
Beinnan Tuirc
1491
Carradale
Lochranza
2866
Goat Fell
Arran
Brodick
Lamlash
Holy I.
Dippin Hd
Garroch Hd
Machrihanish
Campbeltown
Johnston's Pt
Southend
Sanda
Mull of Kintyre
Troon
Prestwick
Ayr
Heads of Ayr
Tarbolton
Mauchline
Kyle
Auchinleck
Cumnock
New Cumnock
Maidens
Maybole
Patna
Dalmellington
Girvan
Ailsa Craig
Carrick
Carrick Forest
Merrick
2765
2669
Rhinns of Kells
Bennane Hd
Ballantrae
Benerairld
1436
Milleur Pt
Kirkcolm
L. Ryan
Stranraer
The Rhinns
Glenluce
Water of Luce
Newton Stewart
Kirkcowan
Creetown
Wigtown
The Machars
Garlieston
Whithorn
Port William
Isle of Whithorn
Burrow Hd
Portpatrick
Port Logan
Drummore
Mull of Galloway
Rathlin I.
Fair Head
Giant's Causeway
Benbane Hd
Inishowen Hd
Inishowen Peninsula
Malin
Culdaff
Carndonagh
2019
Moville
Greencastle
Portrush
Portstewart
Bushmills
Ballycastle
1695
Knocklayd
Castlerock
Coleraine
Armoy
Runabay Hd
Cushendun
Red Bay
Cushendall
Trostan
1817
Antrim Mountains
Garron Pt
Carrowkeel
Muff
Limavady
Ballykelly
Eglinton
Ballymoney
Bush
Bann
Londonderry
Garvagh
Kilrea
Cloughmills
Collin Top
1426
Glenarm
Claudy
Dungiven
Portglenone
Ballymena
Agnew's Hill
1563
Larne
Island Magee
Mullaghmore
1825
2240
Sperrin Mountains
Glenelly
Owenkillew
Maghera
Draperstown
Castledawson
L. Beg
Randalstown
Magherafelt
The Six Towns
Ballyclare
Black Hd
Whitehead
Carrickfergus
1735
Moneymore
Antrim
M2
1778
Creggan
Cookstown
Ballinderry
Glengormley
Newtownabbey
Whiteabbey
Bangor
Groomsport
Copeland I.
Donaghadee
Holywood
Crumlin
Belfast
Lagan
Newtownards
Comber
Greyabbey
Ballywalter
Beragh
Sixmilecross
Stewartstown
Dungannon
56°
55°
7°
6°
5°
© Collins • Longman Atlases
West From Greenwich

Scale 1:1 000 000
0 10 20 30 40 Miles
0 10 20 30 40 50 60 Kms.
Lambert Conformal Conic Projection
Relief
Feet Metres
3281 1000
1640 500
656 200
328 100
0 Sea Level
66 20
164 50
328 100
656 200
Spot Heights in Feet ▲4406
NORTH SEA
Montrose
Lunan Bay
Brechin
Pitlochry
Kirkmichael
Kirriemuir
Forfar
Bridge of Cally
Alyth
Glamis
Carmyllie
Arbroath
Blairgowrie
Dunkeld
Coupar Angus
Strathmore
Sidlaw Hills
Carnoustie
Dundee
Monifieth
Buddon Ness
Inchcape or Bell Rock
Tayport
Newport-on-Tay
Wormit
Bankfoot
Stanley
Guildtown
New Scone
Methven
Perth
Carse of Gowrie
Firth of Tay
St Andrews Bay
St Andrews
Crieff
Bridge of Earn
Newburgh
Abernethy
Strathearn
Cupar
Eden
Auchterarder
Blackford
Auchtermuchty
Ochil Hills
Fife Ness
Crail
Largo Ward
Falkland
Milnathort
Leslie
Kinross
Markinch
Anstruther
Pittenweem
Glenrothes
Leven
Elie & Earlsferry
I. of May
Buckhaven & Methil
Dollar
Tillicoultry
Alva
Dunblane
Alloa
Clackmannan
Cowdenbeath
Lochgelly
Kirkcaldy
FIRTH OF FORTH
Dunfermline
M90
Kincardine
Kinghorn
Burntisland
North Berwick
Bass Rock
Culross
Rosyth
Gullane
Grangemouth
Larbert
Falkirk
Bo'ness
M9
Inverkeithing
Inchkeith
Queensferry
Tyne
Dunbar
Leith
Longniddry
Prestonpans
Tranent
Haddington
East Linton
Linlithgow
Cumbernauld
Edinburgh
Musselburgh
Cockburnspath
Bathgate
Dalkeith
Ormiston
Gifford
St Abb's Hd
Coldingham
Eyemouth
Armadale
Loanhead
Bonnyrigg
Balerno
Livingston
Lammermuir Hills
Airdrie
M8
Whitburn
Gorebridge
Shotts
West Calder
Fauldhouse
Penicuik
Lammermuir
Chirnside
Motherwell
Wishaw
Forth
Leadburn
Pentland Hills
Moorfoot Hills
Duns
Whiteadder Wr.
Berwick-upon-Tweed
Carluke
West Linton
Carstairs
Carnwath
Eddleston
Lauder
Greenlaw
Merse
Ancroft
Norham
Holy I.
Lanark
Blyth Bridge
Peebles
Stow
Gordon
Coldstream
Lowick
Farne Is
Bamburgh
Seahouses
Biggar
Innerleithen
Galashiels
Belford
Kelso
Broughton
Tweed
Melrose
Roxburgh
Wooler
Douglas
Tinto Hills
Selkirk
St Boswells
Snook Pt
Dun Rig
2433
Yarrow
Ettrick Forest
Culter Fell
The Cheviot
2676
1036
Embleton
Abington
Crawford
Broad Law
2723
St Mary's Loch
Teviot
Jedburgh
Teviotdale
Longhoughton
Leadhills
White Coomb
2696
Hawick
Cheviot Hills
Glanton
Aln
Alnwick
Green Lowther
2404
Sanquhar
Coquet I.
Shilbottle
Amble
Daer Resr.
Moffat
2270
Ettrick Pen
Teviothead
Rothbury
Coquet
Cauldcleuch Head
1996
1975
Peel Fell
Rochester
Tosson Hill
1447
Rothbury Forest
Felton
Lowther Hills
2286
Queensberry
Rede
Otterburn
Longhorsley
Kielder Forest
Ashington
Thornhill
Eskdale
Newcastleton
NORTHUMBERLAND
Morpeth
Newbiggin-by-the-Sea
Langholm
Sighty Crag
1702
Wansbeck
Bedlington
Blyth
Lochmaben
Dunscore
1416
Cockerbie
Bewcastle Fells
Bellingham
Cramlington
Seaton Delaval
DUMFRIES AND GALLOWAY
Dumfries
Ecclefechan
Canonbie
Bewcastle
Wark Forest
N Tyne
Ponteland
Killingworth
Whitley Bay
Longbenton
Gosforth
Tynemouth
Annan
Gretna
Longtown
Gilsland
Irthing
Haltwhistle
Haydon Bridge
Corbridge
Hexham
Newcastle upon Tyne
Ryton
Blaydon
Wallsend
South Shields
Jarrow
TYNE AND WEAR
Prudhoe
Whickham
Gateshead
A194(M)
Sunderland
Criffel
1866
Dalbeattie
Bowness-on-Solway
Esk
Eden
M6
Brampton
Cold Fell
2041
Allen
S Tyne
Washington
Kirkbean
Kirkbride
Carlisle
Wetheral
Consett
Stanley
Houghton-le-Spring
Silloth
SOLWAY FIRTH
Thursby
Wigton
Derwent
Annfield Plain
Chester-le-Street
Seaham
Abbey Town
Alston
Hetton-le-Hole
Easington
Durham
Collier Law
1692
Aspatria
Caldbeck
Caldew
Kirkoswald
Stanhope
Tow Law
Brandon
Peterlee
Wear
Weardale
Wolsingham
Crook
Willington
Wingate
Maryport
Flimby
Ellen
CUMBRIA
Cross Fell
2930
DURHAM
Spennymoor
Hartlepool
Penrith
Sedgefield
Tees Bay
Workington
Seaton
Cockermouth
Middleton in Teesdale
Bishop Auckland
CLEVELAND
Redcar
Marske-by-the-Sea
3053
Skiddaw
Shildon
Aycliffe
Billingham
2591
Teesdale
Tees
Pooley Bridge
Keswick
Appleby
Barnard Castle
Gainford
Stockton-on-Tees
Middlesbrough
Guisborough
Eston
Whitehaven
Derwent Wr
Crummock Wr
Ullswater
Shap
Darlington
Thornaby-on-Tees
56°
55°
2°
1°
3°

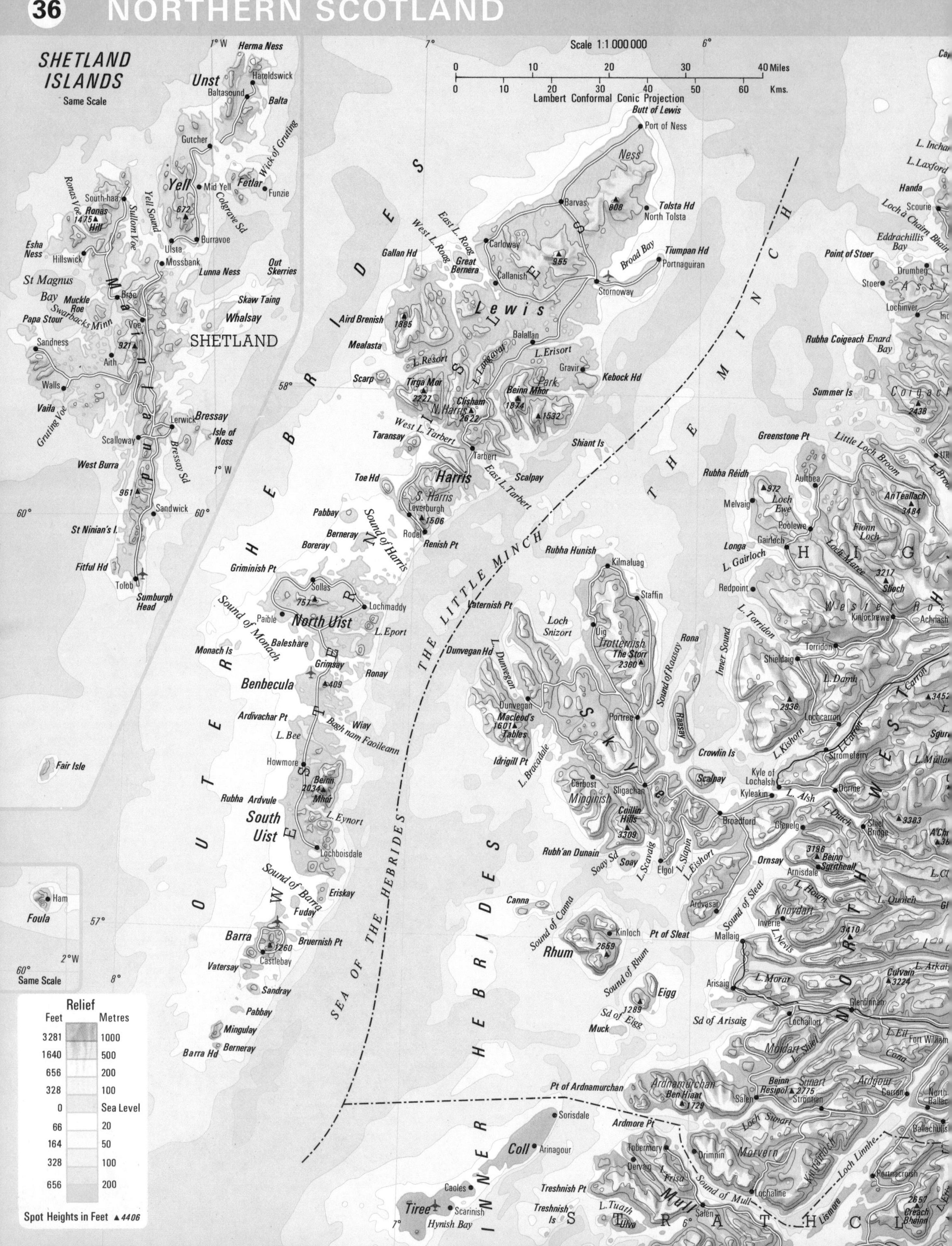

SHETLAND ISLANDS
Same Scale
Herma Ness
Unst
Haroldswick
Baltasound
Balta
Gutcher
Yell
Mid Yell
Fetlar
Funzie
Wick of Gruting
Colgrave Sd
Yell Sound
Ronas Voe
South-haa
Ronas Hill
1475
672
Sullom Voe
Ulsta
Burravoe
Esha Ness
Hillswick
Mossbank
Lunna Ness
Out Skerries
St Magnus Bay
Muckle Roe
Swarbacks Minn
Brae
Skaw Taing
Whalsay
Papa Stour
Voe
Mainland
Sandness
921
Aith
SHETLAND
Walls
Vaila
Gruting Voe
Lerwick
Bressay
Isle of Noss
Scalloway
Bressay Sd
West Burra
961
Sandwick
St Ninian's I.
Fitful Hd
Tolob
Sumburgh Head
Fair Isle
Ham
Foula
60°
1° W
2° W
57°
60° Same Scale
Scale 1:1 000 000
0 10 20 30 40 Miles
0 10 20 30 40 50 60 Kms.
Lambert Conformal Conic Projection
7°
6°
58°
8°
Butt of Lewis
Port of Ness
Ness
Barvas
808
Tolsta Hd
North Tolsta
Carloway
East L. Roag
West L. Roag
Gallan Hd
Great Bernera
Callanish
955
Broad Bay
Tiumpan Hd
Portnaguiran
Stornoway
Lewis
Aird Brenish
1885
Mealasta
Balallan
L. Erisort
L. Resort
L. Langavat
Gravir
Kebock Hd
Park
Scarp
Tirga Mor
2227
Clisham
N. Harris
2622
Beinn Mhor
1874
1532
Taransay
West L. Tarbert
Tarbert
East L. Tarbert
Harris
S. Harris
Toe Hd
Scalpay
Shiant Is
Leverburgh
1506
Rodel
Renish Pt
Pabbay
Berneray
Boreray
Sound of Harris
Griminish Pt
Sollas
757
Lochmaddy
Paible
North Uist
L. Eport
Sound of Monach
Monach Is
Baleshare
Grimsay
Ronay
Benbecula
409
Ardivachar Pt
Wiay
L. Bee
Bagh nam Faoileann
Howmore
Beinn Mhor
2034
Rubha Ardvule
South Uist
L. Eynort
Lochboisdale
Sound of Barra
Eriskay
Fuday
Barra
1260
Bruernish Pt
Castlebay
Vatersay
Sandray
Pabbay
Mingulay
Berneray
Barra Hd
OUTER HEBRIDES
WESTERN ISLES
SEA OF THE HEBRIDES
THE LITTLE MINCH
THE MINCH
Rubha Hunish
Kilmaluag
Staffin
Vaternish Pt
Loch Snizort
Uig
Trotternish
The Storr
2360
Rona
Dunvegan Hd
L. Dunvegan
Dunvegan
Macleod's Tables
1601
Sound of Raasay
Raasay
Inner Sound
Portree
SKYE
Idrigill Pt
L. Bracadale
Crowlin Is
Carbost
Minginish
Sligachan
Scalpay
Cuillin Hills
3309
Broadford
Rubh'an Dunain
Soay Sd
Soay
L. Scavaig
L. Slapin
L. Eishort
Elgol
Canna
Sound of Canna
Kinloch
Pt of Sleat
Rhum
2659
Sound of Rhum
Eigg
1289
Sd of Eigg
Muck
INNER HEBRIDES
Pt of Ardnamurchan
Sorisdale
Ardmore Pt
Coll
Arinagour
Caoles
Tiree
Scarinish
Hynish Bay
Treshnish Pt
Treshnish Is
L. Tuath
Ulva
Tobermory
Dervaig
L. Frisa
Mull
Salen
Sound of Mull
Drimnin
Morvern
Lochaline
Kingairloch
Loch Linnhe
Lismore
STRATHCLYDE
Ardnamurchan
Ben Hiant
1729
Salen
Beinn Resipol
2775
Sunart
Strontian
Loch Sunart
Ardgour
Corran
Moidart
L. Shiel
Lochailort
Glenfinnan
L. Eil
Fort William
Sd of Arisaig
Arisaig
L. Morar
Mallaig
Culvain
3224
L. Arkaig
Inverie
Knoydart
3410
L. Nevis
Sound of Sleat
Ardvasar
L. Hourn
L. Quoich
Ornsay
Arnisdale
3196
Beinn Sgritheall
Glenelg
Kyleakin
L. Alsh
L. Duich
Shiel Bridge
3383
Kyle of Lochalsh
Dornie
Stromeferry
L. Kishorn
Lochcarron
L. Carron
2936
Shieldaig
L. Damh
Torridon
L. Torridon
Kinlochewe
Achnash
Redpoint
L. Gairloch
Gairloch
Longa
Melvaig
Rubha Réidh
972
Loch Ewe
Aultbea
Poolewe
Fionn Loch
Loch Maree
3217
Slioch
An Teallach
3484
Little Loch Broom
Greenstone Pt
Summer Is
2438
Rubha Coigeach
Enard Bay
Lochinver
Stoer
Drumbeg
Point of Stoer
Eddrachillis Bay
Loch a Chairn Bhain
Scourie
Handa
L. Laxford
L. Inchard
HIGHLAND
WESTER ROSS
SOUTH WEST
MORAR
Relief
Feet Metres
3281 1000
1640 500
656 200
328 100
0 Sea Level
66 20
164 50
328 100
656 200
Spot Heights in Feet ▲4406

PENTLAND FIRTH
Brough Ness
Stroma
Muckle Skerry
Dunnet Hd
John O' Groats
Duncansby Hd
Dunnet Bay
Dunnet
Whiten Hd
Strathy Pt
Durness
L. Eriboll
Ben Hutig
Kyle of Tongue
Portskerra
Dounreay
Thurso
Halkirk
Sinclair's Bay
Noss Hd
Reiss
L.Watten
Wick
Bettyhill
Tongue
L. Hope
Ben Hope 3042
Ben Loyal 2504
L. Loyal
Strath More
Naver
Strathnaver
Halladale
Strath Halladale
Beinn nam Bad Mor 952
Ben Griam More 1936
942
Lybster
Ben Hee 2864
Altnaharra
L. Naver
Ben Klibreck 3154
Kinbrace
Morven 2313
Dunbeath
Berriedale
Strath of Kildonan
Beinn Dhorain 2060
Helmsdale
L. Shin
Cassley
Brora
Ben Horn 1706
Lairg
Oykel Bridge
Oykel
Fleet
Golspie
Carron
Bonar Bridge
Dornoch
Dornoch Firth
Tarbat Ness
Portmahomack
2302
Beinn Tharsuinn 2270
Tain
Hill of Fearn
Easter Ross
L. Morie
L. Glass
Alness
Invergordon
3429 Ben Wyvis
Cromarty Firth
Cromarty
MORAY FIRTH
Evanton
Garve
Dingwall
Black Isle
Fortrose
Strathpeffer
Conon
Muir of Ord
Moray Firth
Beauly F.
Beauly
Inverness
The Aird
Strathglass
Dores
Strathnairn
Enrick
Drumnadrochit
Loch Ness
Invermoriston
Glen Mor
Fort Augustus
L. Oich
2658
Monadhliath Mountains
3087
Kingussie
Newtonmore
Spey
Creag Meagaidh 3700
Laggan
Dalwhinnie
Glen Spean
Loch Ericht
Ben Alder 3765
Forest of Atholl
Glen Garry
Blair Atholl
Kinloch Rannoch
L. Rannoch
3546 Schiehallion
L. Tummel
Tummel
Pitlochry
L. Laidon
Rannoch Moor
Glen Lyon
Ben Lawers 3984
Lawers
Kenmore
Aberfeldy
Tay
Breadalbane
Killin
Loch Tay
Dunkeld
Braan
Bankfoot
Strath Tay
Nairn
Ferness
Findhorn
Tomatin
2162
Strathdearn
Carrbridge
Aviemore
Burghead
Findhorn
Lossiemouth
Elgin
Forres
Lossie
Spey Bay
Garmouth
Fochabers
Buckie
Portknockie
Cullen
Portsoy
Banff
Macduff
Troup Hd
Rosehearty
Kinnairds Hd
Fraserburgh
Rattray Hd
Knock Hill 1409
Rothes
Keith
Deveron
Turriff
New Pitsligo
Strichen
Buchan
Cuminestown
Mintlaw
Peterhead
Ugie
Boddam
Buchan Ness
Cruden Bay
New Deer
Fyvie
Ythan
571
Ellon
Newburgh
Carn na Loine 1799
Strathspey
Charlestown of Aberlour
2755 Ben Rinnes
Dufftown
Huntly
Strathbogie
GRAMPIAN
Formartine
Oldmeldrum
Insch
Garioch
Inverurie
Kintore
Dyce
Don
Aberdeen
Grantown-on-Spey
Strath Avon
2563 Corryhabbie Hill
The Buck 2368
Lumsden
Tomintoul
Carn Mor 2636
Alford
Avon
Geal Charn 2692
Cairn Gorm 4084
3843 Ben Avon
4300 Ben Macdhui
Cairngorms
HIGHLANDS
Mar
Tarland
Hill of Fare 1545
Aboyne
Dee
Banchory
Ballater
Braemar
Badenoch
3786 Lochnagar
3077 Mt Keen
2555 Mt Battock
Glen Dye
1747 Kerloch
Stonehaven
3502 Glas Maol
Glen Esk
Fettercairn
Laurencekirk
Inverbervie
Glen Tilt
3671 Beinn a'Ghlo
Glenshee
Glen Clova
Glen Prosen
West Water
Edzell
Brechin
Montrose
TAYSIDE
Kirkmichael
Strathardle
Isla
S. Esk
Kirriemuir
Forfar
Strathmore
Bridge of Cally
Alyth
Blairgowrie
Glamis
Carmyllie
Arbroath
Lunan Bay
Coupar Angus
Sidlaw Hills
Carnoustie
Dundee
Monifieth
Buddon Ness
GRAMPIAN
NORTH SEA
ORKNEY ISLANDS
Same Scale
Mull Hd
Noup Hd
Papa Westray
North Ronaldsay
N. Ronaldsay Firth
Pierowall
The North Sound
Westray
Start Point
Westray Firth
Sanday
Sanday Sound
Sacquoy Hd
Eday
Rousay
Brough Hd
Eynhallow Sd
Egilsay
Wyre
Stronsay
Gairsay
Stronsay Firth
Shapinsay
Mainland
ORKNEY
Shapinsay Sd
Auskerry
Kirkwall
Mull Hd
Stromness
Ward Hill 881
Skaill
Hoy Sd
Ward Hill 1565
Quoyness
St Mary's
Copinsay
Scapa Flow
Rora Hd
Hoy
Burray
Flotta
St Margaret's Hope
South Ronaldsay
Hurliness
S. Walls
PENTLAND FIRTH
Brough Ness
Muckle Skerry
Dunnet Hd
Stroma
John O' Groats
Duncansby Hd
Dunnet
3° W
59°
58°
57°
4°
2°
West from Greenwich

Relief
Feet Metres
3281 1000
1640 500
656 200
328 100
0 Sea Level
66 20
164 50
328 100
656 200
Spot Heights in Feet ▲4406
ATLANTIC
OCEAN
NORTH CHANNEL
IRISH
STRATHCLYDE
NORTHERN IRELAND
ULSTER
REPUBLIC
CONNACHT
ANTRIM
LONDONDERRY
DONEGAL
TYRONE
FERMANAGH
ARMAGH
DOWN
MONAGHAN
LOUTH
MEATH
WESTMEATH
LONGFORD
LEITRIM
SLIGO
ROSCOMMON
MAYO
LOUGH NEAGH
Lough Foyle
Lough Swilly
Lower Lough Erne
Upper Lough Erne
Belfast
Londonderry
Donegal
Sligo
Ballina
Castlebar
Westport
Armagh
Newry
Dundalk
Drogheda
Enniskillen
Omagh
Coleraine
Larne
Bangor
Lisburn
Strangford L.
Ards Peninsula
Carlingford L.
DUNDALK BAY
DONEGAL BAY
CLEW BAY
Malin Head
Bloody Foreland
Erris Hd.
Achill I.
Tory I.
Rathlin I.
Mull of Kintyre
Sound of Islay
Sound of Gigha

IRELAND
MUNSTER
LEINSTER
CLARE
LIMERICK
TIPPERARY
KERRY
CORK
WATERFORD
KILKENNY
LAOIS
CARLOW
WEXFORD
WICKLOW
ST. GEORGE'S CHANNEL
Aran Is. (Galway)
Inishmore
Kilronan
Inishmaan
Inisheer
South Sound
Black Hd.
Ballyvaughan
Kinvara
Gort
Portumna
Birr
Kinnitty
Mountmellick
Monasterevan
Kilcullen
Liffey
Greystones
Newtown Mt Kennedy
Rathnew
Wicklow
Wicklow Hd.
Wicklow Mts.
Lugnaquilla Mt. 3039
Mullaghcleevaun 2788
Slieve Aughty Mts.
Woodford
Ballingarry
Slieve Bloom Mts.
Arderin 1734
Port Laoise
Mountrath
Borris-in-Ossory
Stradbally
Athy
Barrow
Dunlavin
Baltinglass
Rathdrum
Hags Hd.
Liscannor Bay
Ennistymon
Corofin
Slieve Callan 1284
Miltown Malbay
Ennis
Tulla
Tuamgraney
Lough Derg
Borrisokane
Roscrea
Abbeyleix
Ballinakill
Ballickmoyler
Carlow
Castledermot
Rathvilly
Hacketstown
Tullow
Tinahely
Arklow
Coolgreany
Kilmichael Pt.
Clarecastle
Newmarket on Fergus
Glennagalliagh 1748
Slieve Bernagh
Killaloe
Nenagh
Arra Mts. 1517
Moneygall
Devilsbit Mth. 1577
Templemore
Rathdowney
Durrow
Castlecomer
Ballyragget
Leighlinbridge
Silvermines
Silvermines Mts.
Slievekimalta or Keeper Hill 2279
Newport
Slieve Felim Mountains 1524
Cappamore
Urlingford
Thurles
Freshford
Kilkenny
Muine Bheag
Gorey
Donegal Pt.
Kilkee
Doonbeg
Kilrush
Shannon
Limerick
Sixmilebridge
Pallaskenry
Mungret
Patrickswell
Littleton
Slieveardagh Hills 1051
Gowran
Bennettsbridge
Graiguenamanagh
Thomastown
Brandon Hill 1703
Mt. Leinster 2610
Ballycarney
Ferns
Bann
Ballycanew
Cahore Pt.
Kilbaha
Loop Hd.
Mouth of the Shannon
Tarbert
Glin
Askeaton
Adare
Croom
Golden Vale
Golden
Tipperary
Cashel
Kings
Callan
Kells
Enniscorthy
Slaney
Blackwater
Wexford Bay
Ballybunion
Galey
Listowel
Rathkeale
Athea
Sugar Hill 1090
Newcastle West
Ballingarry
Hospital
Emly
Bruree
Bansha
Fethard
Slievenamon 2368
Kilmaganny
Nore
Mullinavat
Clonroche
Castlebridge
Kerry Hd.
Causeway
Tralee Bay
Brandon Bay
Brandon Pt.
Ardfert
Tralee
Fenit
Castlegregory
Stack's Mountains 1170
Glanaruddery Mts.
Abbeyfeale
Dromcolliher
Mullaghareirk Mountains 1341
Rath Luirc
Kilmallock
Kilfinane
Ballyhoura Mts. 1703
Galtymore 3018
Galty Mountains
Cahir
Clonmel
Suir
Carrick-on-Suir
New Ross
Camaross
Taghmon
Wexford
Rosslare
Kilrane
Greenore Pt.
Tuskar Rock
Carnsore Pt.
Clogher Hd.
Dingle
Brandon Mtn. 3127
Beenoskee 2713
Slieve Mish 2796
Castlemaine
Castlemaine Har.
Maine
Castleisland
Newmarket
Kanturk
Newtown
Buttevant
Kildorrery
Mitchelstown
Clogheen
Kilworth Mts.
Knockmealdown Mts.
Knockmealdown 2609
Comeragh Mountains
Monavullagh Mountains 2597
Kilmacthomas
Waterford
Passage East
Dunmore East
Tramore
Duncannon
Wellingtonbridge
Bridgetown
Fethard
Bannow Bay
Forlorn Pt.
Kilmore Quay
Saltee Is.
Hook Hd.
Gt. Blasket I.
Slea Hd.
Inishvickillane
Dingle Bay
Killorglin
Laune
L. Caragh
Carrauntoohil 3414
Macgillycuddy's Reeks
L. Leane
Killarney
Rathmore
Blackwater
Millstreet
Boggeragh Mountains
Musheramore 2118
The Paps 2284
Mallow
Castletownroche
Nagles Mountains 1406
Fermoy
Rathcormack
Bride
Lismore
Tallow
Cappoquin
Dungarvan
Drum Hills
Dungarvan Har.
Helvick Hd.
Stradbally
Dunmanon
Tramore Bay
Waterford Harbour
Canglass Pt.
Coomacarrea 2542
Doulus Hd.
Valentia I.
Cahersiveen
Mullaghanattin 2539
Mangerton 2756
Mountain
Derrynasaggart Mts. 2133
Ballyvourney
Macroom
Sullane
Lee
Ballincollig
Blarney
Cork
Dungourney
Midleton
Youghal
Killeagh
Ardmore
Ardmore Hd.
Mine Hd.
Bray Hd.
Puffin I.
Ballinskelligs Bay
Waterville
Currane
Sneem
Kenmare
Kilgarvan
Ballingeary
Shehy Mountains 1797
Passage West
Cobh
Aghada
Cork Harbour
Knockadoon Hd.
St. Finan's Bay
Bolus Hd.
Gt. Skellig
Hog's Hd.
Eagles Hill 1786
Kenmare River
Coomnadiha 2116
Knockboy 2321
Glengarriff
Caha Mountains
Slieve Miskish
Scariff I.
Coulagh Bay
Cod's Hd.
Ballydonegan
Dursey I.
Dursey Hd.
Crow Hd.
Bantry Bay
Bantry
Bear I.
Black Bull Hd.
Dunmanway
Enniskean
Bandon
Kinsale
Ballinhassig
Timoleague
Clonakilty
Ilen
Kilcrohane 1339
Mount Gabriel
Ballydehob
Skibbereen
Sheep's Hd.
Dunmanus Bay
Skull
Crookhaven
Streek Hd.
Roaringwater Bay
Mizen Hd.
C. Clear
Clear I.
Fastnet Rock
Sherkin I.
Toe Head
Castletownshend
Galley Hd.
Clonakilty Bay
Seven Heads
Courtmacsherry Bay
Old Head of Kinsale
53°
52°
51°
10°
9°
8°
7°
6°
Scale 1:1 400 000
0 10 20 30 40 50 Miles
0 10 20 30 40 50 60 70 80 Kms.
Lambert Conformal Conic Projection

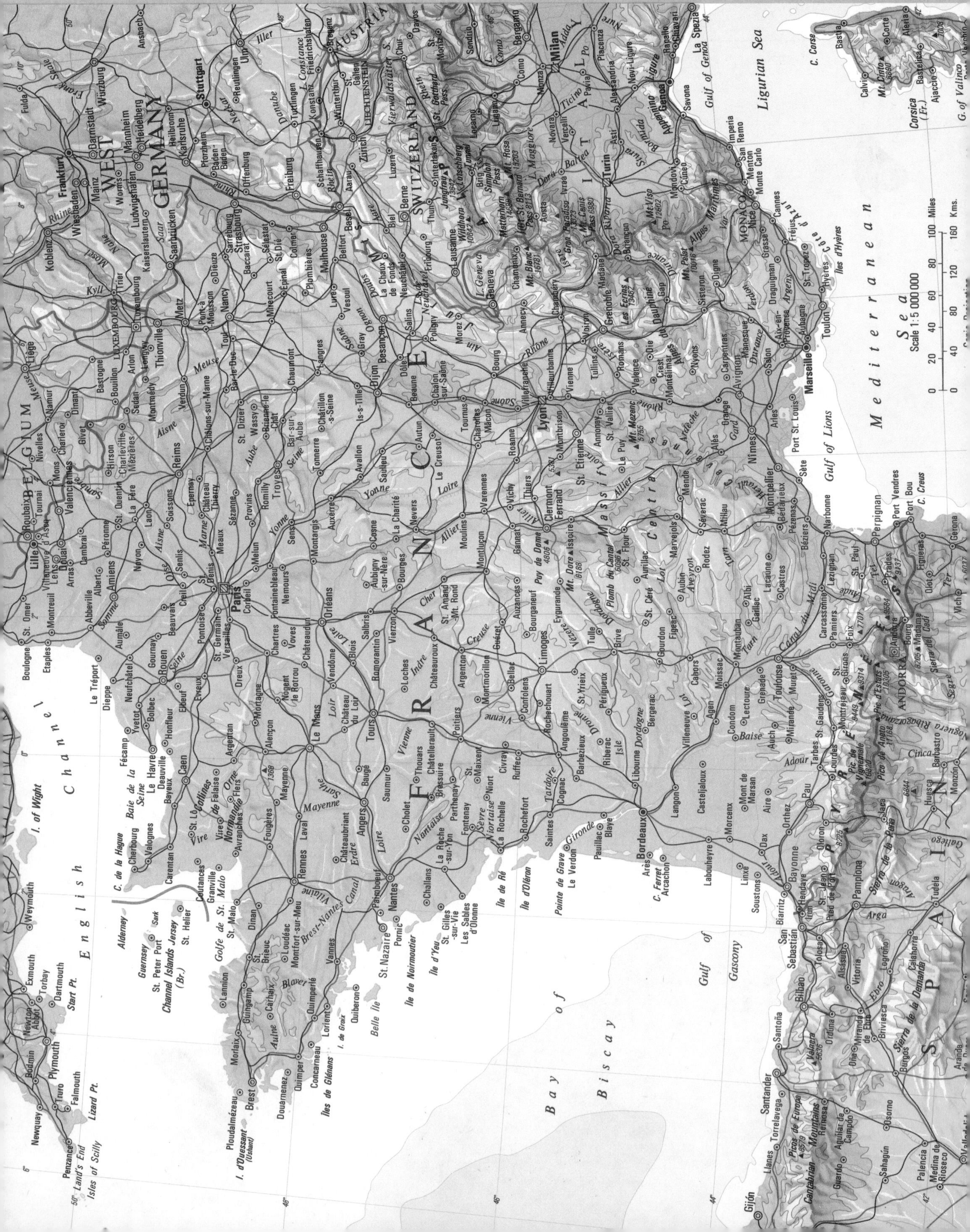
FRANCE
BELGIUM
LUXEMBOURG
WEST GERMANY
SWITZERLAND
LIECHTENSTEIN
AUSTRIA
ITALY
MONACO
ANDORRA
SPAIN
English Channel
Bay of Biscay
Gulf of Gascony
Gulf of Lions
Mediterranean Sea
Ligurian Sea
Gulf of Genoa
Channel Islands (Br.)
Corsica (Fr.)
Massif Central
Paris
Lyon
Marseille
Bordeaux
Toulouse
Nantes
Lille
Strasbourg
Nice
Geneva
Milan
Turin
Genoa
Bilbao
Pamplona
Scale 1:5 000 000
0 20 40 60 80 100 Miles
0 40 80 120 160 Kms.

BAY OF BISCAY
Gulf of Gascony
Gulf of Lions
ATLANTIC OCEAN
MEDITERRANEAN SEA
FRANCE
PYRENEES
ANDORRA
SPAIN
PORTUGAL
MOROCCO
ALGERIA
Cantabrian Mountains
Balearic Islands (Spain)
Majorca (Mallorca)
Minorca (Menorca)
Iviza (Ibiza)
Formentera
Cabrera
Gulf of Valencia
Gulf of San Jorge
Gulf of Cádiz
Strait of Gibraltar
Bay of Setúbal
Costa Brava
Costa del Sol
Sierra Nevada
Sierra Morena
Sierra de Guadarrama
Sierra de Gredos
Serrania de Cuenca
Montes de Toledo
Madrid
Lisbon (Lisboa)
Oporto (Pôrto)
Barcelona
Valencia
Seville
Granada
Málaga
Córdoba
Zaragoza
Bilbao
Algiers (Alger)
Tangier (Tanger)
Gibraltar (Br.)
Ceuta (Sp.)
Melilla (Sp.)
C. Finisterre
C. St Vincent
C. Trafalgar
C. de Gata
C. de la Nao
Tagus
Ebro
Duero
Douro
Guadiana
Guadalquivir
Júcar
Scale 1:5 000 000
0 20 40 60 80 100 Miles
0 40 80 120 160 Kms.
Conic Projection
© Collins ◇ Longman Atlases

Relief

Feet		Metres
16404		5000
9843		3000
6562		2000
3281		1000
1640		500
656		200
0		Sea Level
Land Dep. 656		200
13123		4000
22966		7000

AUSTRIA
Wildspitze 12382
Brenner Pass 4511
Gr. Glockner 12461
SWITZ.
Geneva
Simplon Tunnel
Matterhorn 14688
Mt. Rosa 15203
Mont Blanc 15782
Gt. St. Bernard Pass 8113
Lt. St. Bernard Pass 7179
Gran Paradiso 13323
Bernina 13284
Dolomites
Carnic Alps
Drau
Villach
Klagenfurt
Merano
Bolzano
Trento
Adige
Piave
Triglav 9396
Celje
Ljubljana
Sava
Udine
Gorizia
Trieste
Rijeka
Karlovac
Ogulin
Istra
Krk
Cres
Rovinj
Pula
Lošinj
Pag
Gospić
Dugi Otok
Kornat
Zadar
Šibenik
Clermont Ferrand
Thiers
Roanne
Lyon
Villeurbanne
Mt. Dore 6188
Montbrison
St. Etienne
Loire
Vienne
Rhône
Chamonix
Annecy
FRANCE
Plomb du Cantal 6096
St. Flour
Allier
Le Puy
Isère
Grenoble
Romans
Valence
Les Ecrins 13462
Marvejols
Mende
Sévérac
Millau
Cévennes
Montélimar
Gap
Briançon
Mt. Viso 12602
Alpes Maritimes
Mt. Pelat 10016
Digne
Orange
Alès
Nîmes
Avignon
Durance
Var
Arles
Salon
Montpellier
Pézenas
Béziers
Sète
Aix-en-Provence
Draguignan
Grasse
Aubagne
Marseille
Toulon
Hyères
Iles d'Hyères
Fréjus
St. Tropez
Cannes
Nice
Monte Carlo
MONACO
Menton
San Remo
Imperia
Gulf of Lions
ALPS
Como
Locarno
Maggiore
Monza
Milan
Bergamo
L. Garda
Brescia
Tirano
Novara
Vercelli
Turin
Ticino
Adda
Pavia
Po
Voghera
Asti
Alessandria
Tanaro
Acqui
Cuneo
Mondovì
Savona
Genoa
Rapallo
Chiavari
La Spezia
Gulf of Genoa
Cremona
Piacenza
Verona
Mantua
Vicenza
Padua
Brenta
Treviso
Venice
Gulf of Venice
Parma
Reggio
Modena
Ferrara
Reno
Bologna
Ravenna
Mt. Cimone 7103
Carrara
Massa
Prato
Pisa
Arno
Florence
Faenza
Forlì
SAN MARINO
San Marino
Rimini
Pésaro
Urbino
Senigallia
Iesi
Ancona
Leghorn
Volterra
Siena
Arezzo
Cecina
Piombino
Elba
Pianosa
Grosseto
Ombrone
Amiata 5689
L. Trasimeno
Perugia
Foligno
Macerata
Monte Vettore 8130
Ascoli Piceno
Giglio
Montecristo
Bolsena
Viterbo
Terni
Nera
Teramo
Rieti
L'Aquila
M. Corno 9560
Pescara
Chieti
Civitavecchia
Tiber
Avezzano
Mt. Amaro 9170
Sulmona
Termoli
Rome
Velletri
Frosinone
San Severo
Foggia
Campobasso
Volturno
Benevento
Ofanto
Gaeta
G. of Gaeta
Pontine Is.
Caserta
Ariano
Avellino
Naples
Vesuvius
Ischia
G. of Naples
Capri
Salerno
G. of Salerno
Potenza
Pisciotta
G. of Policastro
APENNINES
ADRIATIC
LIGURIAN SEA
Capraia
C. Corse
Calvi
Bastia
Corsica (Fr.)
Mt. Cinto 8890
Corte
Aleria
Ajaccio
7008
G. of Valinco
Sartène
Pto. Vecchio
Bonifacio
Str. of Bonifacio
Asinara
G. of Asinara
Caprera
C. Falcone
Porto Torres
Sassari
Tempio
Olbia
Alghero
Coghinas
Bosa
Sardinia (Italy)
Macomer
Orosei
Gulf of Orosei
6017
Tirso
C. Mte. Santu
G. of Oristano
Oristano
Arbatax
Mannu
Iglésias
Villaputzu
Cagliari
San Pietro
C. Carbonara
G. of Cagliari
G. of Palmas
C. Spartivento
Minorca
Mahón
TYRRHENIAN SEA
MEDITERRANEAN SEA
Ustica (Italy)
Stromboli 3038
Lipari Is.
Sicily
Marettimo
Trápani
Palermo
Cefalù
Barcellona
Messina
Reggio
Str. of Messina
Favignana
Alcamo
Termini
Nebrodi Mts.
Mt. Etna 10958
Marsala
Adrano
Platani
Enna
Sciacca
Caltanissetta
Catania
Agrigento
Salso
Caltagirone
Licata
Ragusa
Siracusa
Vittória
Módica
C. Passero
Malta Channel
Gozo
MALTA
Malta
Valletta
Pantelleria (Italy)
Linosa
Lampione
Lampedusa (Italy)
Galita
C. de Fer
C. Serrat
Bizerta
Gulf of Tunis
C. Bon
Bejaïa
Akbou
Skikda
Annaba
Tabarka
Mateur
La Calle
Medjerda Mts.
Béja
Tunis
Constantine Mts.
Sétif
Constantine
Medjerda
Wadi Medjerda
Souk Ahras
Le Kef
Nabeul
ALGERIA
TUNISIA
Aïn Beida
Enfida
Batna
Barika
Sousse
Monastir
Thala
W. el Hatob
Kairouan
Msaken
Mahdia
el Abiod
el Arab
Tebessa
W. el Fekka
Biskra
Kasserine
Sbeïtla
42°
40°
38°
36°
6°
8°
10°
12°
14°

HUNGARY
Nagykanizsa
Szekszárd
Hódmezővásárhely
Kaposvár
Baja
Szeged
Makó
Pécs
Subotica
Sombor
Kikinda
Drava
Osijek
Novi Sad
Danube
Tizsa
Brod
Vršac
Ruma
Sava
Šabac
Belgrade
Banja Luka
Doboj
Bosna
Tuzla
Drina
Valjevo
Travnik
YUGOSLAVIA
Sarajevo
Višegrad
Titovo Užice
Kragujevac
Kraljevo
Kruševac
Čvrsnica 7310
Neretva
Mostar
Pljevlja
Durmitor 8274
Tara
Lim
Novi Pazar
Ibar
Kuršumlija
Metković
Nikšić
Peć
Kosovska Mitrovica
Priština
Mljet
Dubrovnik
Titograd
Kotor
Cetinje
Prizren
Bar
L. Shkodër
Shkodër
Drin
8661
Shëngjin
C. Rodonit
C. Palit
Durrës
Tiranë
ALBANIA
Elbasan
Seman
Berat
7930
Ohridsko
Ohrid
Korçë
Vlorë
Vijosë
Str. of Otranto
Kastoria
Smólikas 8639
Pindus
Corfu
Ioánnina
Igoumenitsa
Arta
Préveza
Levkás
Kefallinía
Zákinthos
Ionian Is
Arad
Mureș
Timișoara
Timișul
Lugoj
Deva
Brad
Alba Iulia
White Crișul
Sibiu
Red Tower Pass
Negoiu 8346
Mt. Mindra 8268
Transylvanian Alps
Sighișoara
Odorhei
Sfântu Gheorghe
Brașov
Focșani
Râmnicu Sarat
Buzău
Siret
Prut
Tecuci
Galati
Brăila
Reni
Izmail
U.S.S.R.
Bolgrad
L. Sasyk
Mouths of the Danube
Sulina
Tulcea
St. Gheorghe's Mouth
Portitei Mouth
ROMANIA
Faurei
Ploești
Pitești
Dîmbovița
Tîrgu-Jiu
Olt
Argeș
Ialomita
Bucharest
Cernavodă
Constanța
Călărași
Oltenița
Silistra
Mangalia
Orșova
Iron Gate
Turnu Severin
Slatina
Craiova
Jiu
Caracal
Giurgiu
Ruse
Tolbukhin
Balchik
C. Kaliakra
Požarevac
Negotin
Morava
Zaječar
Timok
Vidin
Calafat
Lom
Corabia
Oryakhovo
Ogosta
Turnu Măgurele
Zimnicea
Svishtov
Razgrad
Kolarovgrad
Varna
Pleven
Niš
Pirot
Leskovac
Balkan Mountains
Vratsa
Iskur
Lovech
Osum
Tŭrnovo
Karnobat
BLACK SEA
Dragoman Pass
Sofia
Botevgrad
7785
Kazanlŭk
Shipka Pass
Sliven
Yambol
Burgas
Dimitrovo (Pernik)
Radomir
Stara Zagora
Tundzha
Trajan's Gate
Elkhovo
BULGARIA
Vranje
Kyustendil
Musala 9597
Plovdiv
Dimitrovgrad
Maritsa
C. Iğneada
Kumanovo
7388
Rhodope Mts.
Khaskovo
Edirne
Kirklareli
Midye
Bosporus
Blagoevgrad
Kočani
Arda
Smolyan
Skopje
Titov Veles
Struma
Luleburgaz
Catalca
Istanbul
Üsküdar
Strumica
Petrich
Mesta
Xanthi
Komotini
Ergene
Tekirdağ
SEA OF MARMARA
Marmara
Prilep
Vardar
Črna
Sérrai
Dráma
Kaválla
Keşan
Alexandroúpolis
Bitola
Prespa L.
Kilkis
Thásos
G. of Saros
Dardanelles
Gallipoli
Bandirma
Bursa
Edhessa
Thessaloníki
Florina
C. Platí
Samothráki
Imroz
Çanakkale
Simav
Kozáni
Aliákmon
Mt. Olympus 9550
G. of Thessaloniki
Singitikos G.
Mt. Áthos 6670
G. of Toronaios
Límnos
Balikesir
5797
Edremit
TURKEY
Ossa 6489
Lárisa
Áyios Evstrátios
AEGEAN SEA
Lésvos
Mitilíni
Ayvalik
Dikili
Bergama
Soma
Akhisar
Tríkkala
Pintos
Vólos
Kardhítsa
Fársala
N. Sporades
Skíros
Psará
G. of Izmir
Manisa
Gediz
Alaşehir
Turgutlu
Izmir
Lamía
Pass of Thermopylae
8235
Parnassos 8061
5718
Khalkís
Euboea
Khíos
Ödemiş
Akhelóös
GREECE
Návpaktos
Mesolóngion
G. of Patras
Gulf of Corinth
Pátras
Marathon
C. Kafirévs
Ándros
Sámos
Aydin
Menderes
Söke
Mégara
Athens
Piraeus
Tínos
Ikaría
Killíni 7795
Corinth
Aiyina
Kéa
Milâs
Muğla
Pírgos
Árgos
Návplion
Kíthnos
Cyclades
Páros
Náxos
Dodecanese
G. of Kerme
Marmaris
Alfiós
Kiparissía
Spárti
Amorgós
Kos
Kalámai
Píloi
Ios
Milos
Rhodes
Thíra
Lindos
Skhiza
G. of Messina
G. of Lakonia
C. Maléa
C. Matapan
Kíthira
SEA OF CRETE
Karpáthos
Andikíthira
C. Spátha
Iráklion
Canea
Réthimnon
Ídhi 8058
Crete
Bari
Monopoli
Brindisi
Táranto
Lecce
Gulf of Taranto
Gallipoli
Otranto
C. Sta Maria di Leuca
Crotone
C. Rizzuto
IONIAN SEA
SEA
Scale 1:5 250 000
0 100 200 Miles
0 100 200 300 Kms.
Conic Projection
© Collins ◇ Longman Atlases

Scale 1:4 000 000
0 20 40 60 80 100 Miles
0 20 40 60 80 100 120 140 160 Kms.
Conic Projection
NORTH SEA
BALTIC SEA
DENMARK
Tönder
Tinglev
Sönderborg
Flensburg
Schleswig
Husum
North Frisian Is
Sylt
Kiel Bay
Langeland
Vordingborg
Nakskov
Lolland
Nyköbing
Falster
Mön
Gedser
Fehmarn
Bornholm
Sassnitz
Rügen
Stralsund
Greifswald
Rostock
Grossenbrode
Oldenburg
Rendsburg
Kiel
Kiel Canal
Neumünster
Lübeck Bay
Itzehoe
Lübeck
Wismar
Heligoland Bay
Heligoland
Cuxhaven
Spiekeroog
Langeoog
Schiermonnikoog
Borkum
East Frisian Is.
Terschelling
Ameland
West Frisian Is.
Wilhelmshaven
Bremerhaven
Elmshorn
Hamburg
Schwerin
Güstrow
Neubrandenburg
Tollense
Peene
Swinoujscie
Wolin
Kołobrzeg
Koszalin
Słupsk
Białogard
Parseta
Szczecinek
Chojnice
Rega
Emden
Leer
Nordenham
Harburg
Leeuwarden
Groningen
Assen
Oldenburg
Delmenhorst
Bremen
Oste
Lüneburg
Elde
L. Müritz
Neustrelitz
Szczecin
Stargard
Ina
Piła
IJsselmeer
NETHERLANDS
WEST GERMANY
Hunte
Weser
Uelzen
Wittenberge
EAST GERMANY
Schwecht
Oder
Havel
Elbe
Eberswalde
Gorzów Wielkopolski
Noteć
Kostrzyn
Warta
POLAND
Poznań
Zwolle
Almelo
Hengelo
Nordhorn
Osnabrück
Ems
Mittelland Canal
Celle
Aller
Stendal
Rathenow
Spandau
Charlottenburg
Berlin
Apeldoorn
Amersfoort
Deventer
Enschede
Rheine
Minden
Hannover
Wolfsburg
Brandenburg
Potsdam
Frankfurt
Fürstenwalde
Arnhem
Herford
Bielefeld
Hildesheim
Braunschweig
Helmstedt
Burg
Magdeburg
Eisenhüttenstadt
Nijmegen
Hameln
Salzgitter
Wolfenbüttel
Schönebeck
Luckenwalde
Gubin
Zielana Góra
Nowa Sól
Leszno
Bocholt
Münster
Ahlen
Detmold
Goslar
Halberstadt
Stassfurt
Dessau
Wittenberg
Spree
Cottbus
Forst
Żary
Głogów
Rhine
Recklinghausen
Bottrop
Hamm
Gütersloh
Paderborn
Lippe
Lippstadt
Solling
Brocken
Quedlinburg
Aschersleben
Bernburg
Köthen
Harz Mts
Oberhausen
Duisburg
Gelsenkirchen
Dortmund
Essen
Bochum
Ruhr
Iserlohn
Göttingen
Eisleben
Halle
Lauchhammer
Hoyerswerda
Neisse
Eindhoven
Maas
Krefeld
Düsseldorf
Hagen
Wuppertal
Nordhausen
Sangerhausen
Merseburg
Leipzig
Riesa
Mönchen-Gladbach
Neuss
Solingen
Korbach
Kassel
Mühlhausen
GERMANY
Bautzen
Görlitz
Legnica
Wrocław
Genk
Heerlen
Rheydt
Cologne (Köln)
Leverkusen
Eisenach
Erfurt
Naumburg
Apolda
Weissenfels
Döbeln
Meissen
Radebeul
Dresden
Jelenia Góra
Świdnica
Maastricht
Aachen
Düren
Porz
Siegen
Sieg
Gotha
Arnstadt
Weimar
Jena
Zeitz
Altenburg
Freital
Pirna
Zittau
Liberec
Wałbrzych
Herstal
Liège
Verviers
Bonn
Siegburg
Euskirchen
Marburg
Thuringian Forest
Rudolstadt
Saale
Gera
Karl Marx Stadt
Děčín
Jablonec nad Nisou
Sudeten Mountains
Nowa Ruda
Westerwald
Wetzlar
Giessen
Fulda
Vogelsberg
Meiningen
Suhl
Greiz
Zwickau
Teplice
Ústí nad Labem
Trutnov
BELGIUM
Neuwied
Koblenz
Eifel
Taunus
Sonneberg
Plauen
Ore Mts
Most
Chomutov
Ohře
Mladá Boleslav
Hradec Králové
Bastogne
Mosel
Wiesbaden
Frankfurt
Hanau
Offenbach
Coburg
Hof
Kladno
Prague (Praha)
Karlovy Vary
Cheb
Labe (Elbe)
Pardubice
Kolín
Hunsrück
Bingen
Mainz
Aschaffenburg
Schweinfurt
Main
Bayreuth
LUX
Trier
Arlon
Luxembourg
Bad Kreuznach
Idar
Worms
Darmstadt
Würzburg
Bamberg
Weiden in der Oberpfalz
Plzeň
Příbram
Sázava
Havlíčkův Brod
Longwy
Kaiserslautern
Odenwald
Mannheim
Heidelberg
Erlangen
Fürth
Nürnberg
Bohemian Forest
CZECHOSLOVAKIA
Thionville
Saarlouis
Ludwigshafen
Speyer
Amberg
Schwandorf
Písek
Vltava
Tábor
Moravian Hts
Jihlava
Metz
Dudweiler
Saarbrücken
Landau
Pirmasens
Ansbach
Třebíč
Brno
Pont-à-Mousson
Dieuze
Wissembourg
Bruchsal
Karlsruhe
Heilbronn
Schwäbisch Hall
Crailsheim
Regensburg
Regen
České Budějovice
Třeboň
Sarre
Rastatt
Pforzheim
Stuttgart
Backnang
Treuchtlingen
Aalen
Heidenheim
Donauworth
Straubing
Znojmo
Nancy
Sarrebourg
Toul
Baden-Baden
Esslingen
Göppingen
Neckar
Ingolstadt
Gmünd
Strasbourg
Reutlingen
Tübingen
Danube
Passau
Baccarat
Offenburg
Black Forest
Swabian Jura
Ulm
Augsburg
Landshut
Krems
FRANCE
Mirecourt
Moselle
St. Dié
Sélestat
Épinal
Colmar
Vosges
Schwenningen
Villingen
Freising
Isar
Dachau
Munich (München)
Inn
Traun
Linz
Danube
St. Pölten
Vienna (Wien)
Plombières
Guebwiller
Memmingen
Tuttlingen
Ginz
Steyr
Baden
Lure
Vesoul
Belfort
Mulhouse
Montbéliard
Freiburg
Singen
Schaffhausen
Ravensburg
Friedrichshafen
Kaufbeuren
Rosenheim
Chiemsee
Gmunden
Salzburg
Wiener Neustadt
Neusiedler
Lörrach
Rhine
Konstanz
L. Constance
Lindau
Kempten
Fussen
Lech
Garmisch Partenkirchen
Kufstein
Teisenberg
Bad Ischl
Dachstein
Enns
Hochschwab
Semmering Pass
Basel
Aarau
Winterthur
Bregenz
Dornbirn
Leoben
Kapfenberg
Doubs
Besançon
La Chaux de Fonds
Zürich
L. Zürich
St. Gallen
Feldkirch
Landeck
Innsbruck
Salzach
AUSTRIA
Szombathely
JURA MTS.
Biel
Neuchâtel
Luzern
Zug
LIECHTENSTEIN
Vaduz
Arlberg Pass
Inn
ALPS
Badgastein
Gross Glockner
Mur
Graz
HUNGARY
Fribourg
L. de Neuchâtel
Berne
SWITZERLAND
Thun
Chur
Davos
Wildspitze
Gran Pilastro
Eisenhut
Spittal
Lienz
Brienz
Interlaken
St. Gotthard P.
Merano
Bressanone
Klagenfurt
Maribor
Mura
Lausanne
Jungfrau
Lötschberg Tunnel
Simplon Tunnel
St. Moritz
Ortles
Villach
Karawanken
Montreux
L. Geneva
Wildhorn
Brig
Bolzano
Dolomites
Piave
Geneva
Martigny
Rhône
Locarno
Sondrio
ITALY
Trento
YUGOSLAVIA
Ljubljana
Varaždin
© Collins • Longman Atlases

Scale 1:2 000 000
0 10 20 30 40 50 60 Miles
0 20 40 60 80 Kms.
Conic Projection
Relief
Feet Metres
16404 5000
9843 3000
6562 2000
3281 1000
1640 500
656 200
0 Sea Level
Land Dep. 656 200
13123 4000
22966 7000
NORTH SEA
West Frisian Islands
East Frisian Is.
Wadden Sea
IJsselmeer
NETHERLANDS
BELGIUM
WEST GERMANY
FRANCE
LUXEMBOURG
GRONINGEN
FRIESLAND
DRENTHE
OVERIJSSEL
GELDERLAND
UTRECHT
NORTH HOLLAND
SOUTH HOLLAND
ZEELAND
NOORD BRABANT
LIMBURG
ANTWERP
FLANDERS
WEST FLANDERS
EAST FLANDERS
BRABANT
LIMBOURG
HAINAUT
LIEGE
NAMUR
ARTOIS
PICARDY
Ardennes
Eifel
Hunsrück
Westerwald
Ruhr
Campine
Hesbaye
Veluwe
Peel
N. E. Polder
E. Flevoland
S. Flevoland
Markerwaard (U.C.)
Amsterdam
Rotterdam
The Hague ('sGravenhage)
Utrecht
Haarlem
Leiden
Groningen
Leeuwarden
Zwolle
Arnhem
Nijmegen
Eindhoven
Tilburg
Breda
Maastricht
Enschede
Hilversum
Apeldoorn
Brussels
Antwerp
Gent
Bruges
Liège
Charleroi
Namur
Mons
Lille
Roubaix
Aachen
Cologne (Köln)
Bonn
Düsseldorf
Essen
Dortmund
Duisburg
Krefeld
Münster
Osnabrück
Oldenburg
Wilhelmshaven
Koblenz
Trier
Luxembourg
Ems
Rhine
Waal
Maas
Meuse
Scheldt
Mosel
Sambre
Oise
© Collins-Longman Atlases

SCANDINAVIA & ICELAND

ICELAND
on the same scale

FAROE IS
on same scale

Scale 1:7 500 000

0 50 100 150 Miles

0 100 200 Kms.

Conic Projection

BLACK SEA
BALTIC SEA
Sea of Azov
Caspian Depression
ADRIATIC SEA
Gulf of Finland
Gulf of Riga
Gulf of Gdańsk
UNION OF SOVIET SOCIALIST REPUBLICS
RUSSIAN SOVIET FEDERAL SOCIALIST REPUBLIC
KAZAKHSTAN SSR
ESTONIA S.S.R.
LATVIA S.S.R.
LITHUANIA S.S.R.
WHITE RUSSIA S.S.R.
UKRAINE S.S.R.
MOLDAVIA S.S.R.
GEORGIA S.S.R.
POLAND
CZECHOSLOVAKIA
HUNGARY
ROMANIA
BULGARIA
YUGOSLAVIA
SWEDEN
FINLAND
DENMARK
CAUCASUS MTS.
Moscow
Leningrad
Kiev
Minsk
Warsaw
Budapest
Bucharest
Sofia
Belgrade
Prague
Berlin
Stockholm
Copenhagen
Scale 1:10 250 000
0 50 100 150 200 250 Miles
0 100 200 300 400 Kms.
Conic Projection
© Collins ◇ Longman Atlases

NORWAY
SWEDEN
FINLAND
POLAND
UNION OF SOVIET
RUSSIAN SOVIET F
KAZAKH S.S.R.
UKRAINE SSR
WHITE RUSSIA SSR
LITHUANIA SSR
LATVIA SSR
ESTONIA SSR
MOLDAVIA SSR
GEORGIA SSR
ARMENIA SSR
AZERBAIJAN SSR
UZBEKISTAN SSR
TURKMENISTAN SSR
KIRGHIZSTAN SSR
TADZHIKISTAN SSR
CZECHOSLOVAKIA
HUNGARY
ROMANIA
WEST GERMANY
EAST GERMANY
TURKEY
IRAQ
IRAN
AFGHANISTAN
SINKIANG
BALTIC SEA
Gulf of Bothnia
G. of Finland
Skagerrak
Kattegat
BARENTS SEA
ARCTIC OCEAN
KARA SEA
White Sea
BLACK SEA
Sea of Azov
CASPIAN SEA
ARAL SEA
Franz Josef Land
Novaya Zemlya
Vaygach
Kolguyev
Kola Pen
Kanin Pen
C. Kanin
Yamal Pen
Gydanskiy
Gulf of Ob
Pechora G.
Baydaratskaya B.
L. Ladoga
L. Onega
Rybinsk Resr
L. Tengiz
Lake Balkhash
L. Zaysan
Kara Bogaz Gol Bay
Mangyshlak Peninsula
Ust Urt Plateau
Caspian Depression
Kirghiz Steppe
West Siberian Plain
Kara Kum
Kyzyl Kum
Caucasus
Ural Mts
Elburz Mts
Zagros Mts
Pamirs
Turfan Depression
Crimea
Bergen
Stavanger
Oslo
Trondheim
Narvik
Göteborg
Stockholm
Norrköping
Malmö
Copenhagen
Luleå
Oulu
Tampere
Helsinki
Tallinn
Tartu
Riga
Kaunas
Klaipeda
Kaliningrad
Gdańsk
Szczecin
Hamburg
Hannover
Berlin
Leipzig
Dresden
Dortmund
Prague
Wrocław
Łódź
Warsaw
Lublin
Cracow
Brest
Vilnius
Minsk
Baranovichi
Pskov
Leningrad
Murmansk
Kirovsk
Petrozavodsk
Arkhangel'sk
Mezen
Naryan Mar
Ust' Tsilma
Vorkuta
Salekhard
Novy Port
Kara
Novgorod
Velikiye Luki
Vitebsk
Mogilev
Smolensk
Bryansk
Gomel
Lvov
Zhitomir
Kiev
Kishinev
Kirovograd
Krivoy Rog
Nikolayev
Odessa
Poltava
Dnepropetrovsk
Kharkov
Zaporozhye
Donetsk
Gorlovka
Makeyevka
Voroshilovgrad
Zhdanov
Taganrog
Rostov
Sevastopol'
Simferopol'
Krasnodar
Tuapse
Armavir
Stavropol'
Batumi
Tbilisi
Yerevan
Kirovabad
Baku
Ordzhonikidze
Groznyy
Astrakhan
Guryev
Fort Shevchenko
Shevchenko
Krasnovodsk
Tabriz
Hamadan
Tehran
Isfahan
Mashhad
Herat
Ashkhabad
Chardzhou
Bukhara
Samarkand
Termez
Dushanbe
Leninabad
Tashkent
Kokand
Namangan
Andizhan
Chimkent
Dzhambul
Turkestan
Frunze
Alma-Ata
Przhevalsk
Kashgar
Yarkand
Urumchi
Moscow
Kalinin
Rybinsk
Cherepovets
Yaroslavl
Vologda
Kostroma
Ivanovo
Vladimir
Orekhovo-Zuyevo
Ryazan
Tula
Orel
Tambov
Voronezh
Gorki
Kirov
Kotlas
Syktyvkar
Troitsko Pechorsk
Kazan
Ulyanovsk
Penza
Syzran
Saratov
Engels
Volgograd
Kuybyshev
Chapayevsk
Chistopol
Bugulma
Izhevsk
Perm
Kungur
Berezniki
Serov
Ufa
Zlatoust
Magnitogorsk
Orenburg
Ural'sk
Aktyubinsk
Orsk
Nizhniy Tagil
Sverdlovsk
Chelyabinsk
Kurgan
Kustanay
Tyumen
Tobolsk
Khanty-Mansiysk
Nizhnevartovsk
Petropavlovsk
Kokchetav
Tselinograd
Karaganda
Omsk
Tatarsk
Pavlodar
Slavgorod
Novosibirsk
Tomsk
Barnaul
Biysk
Prokopyevsk
Semipalatinsk
Leninogorsk
Zyryanovsk
Ayaguz
Zaysan
Balkhash
Aralsk
Novokazalinsk
Karsakpay
Kzyl Orda
Volga
Don
Dnieper
Dniestr
Prut
Desna
Pripet
Dvina
Vistula
N. Dvina
Sukhona
Pechora
Kama
Vyatka
Belaya
Ural
Emba
Tobol
Ishim
Irtysh
Ob
Tavda
Tara
Pur
Taz
Araxes
Syr Darya
Amu Darya
Yarkand
Tarim
Issyk Kul
Elbrus 5633
Kazbek 5036
Mt. Ararat 5165
Demavend 5670
Yaman Tau 1640
Narodnaya 1894
Mt. Belukha 4506
Pik Kommunizma 7495
Pobeda 7439
Kungur 7719
Scale 1 : 20 000 000
0 100 200 300 400 500 miles
0 200 400 600 800 kms
Conic Projection
© Collins • Longman Atlases

Relief
Feet Metres
16404 5000
9843 3000
6562 2000
3281 1000
1640 500
656 200
0 Sea Level
Land Dep.
656 200
13123 4000
22966 7000
Bering Str.
Wrangel I.
De Long Str.
Chuckchee Pen
Gulf of Anadyr
EAST SIBERIAN SEA
New Siberian Is
Novaya Sibiria
Komsomolets
October Revolution
Severnaya Zemlya
Bolshevik
C. Chelyuskin
LAPTEV SEA
Kotelnyy
Bolshoi Lyakhovskiy
Taymyr Peninsula
Byrranga Mts.
Khatangskiy G.
Olenekskiy Gulf
G. of Tona
Nordvik
Ust Olenek
Tiksi
Kazachye
Ambarchik
Anadyr
Koryak Range
Kolyma Range
BERING SEA
Omolon
Kamenskoye
Gizhiga
Gizhiga Gulf
G. of Penzhina
Sredne Kolymskaya
Indigirka
Kolyma
Khatanga
Bulun
Verkhoyansk Range
Cherskogo Range
Mt Pobeda 10325
Mt Chen 8799
Verkhoyansk
Oymyakon
Magadan
Palana
Ukta
Kamchatka Peninsula
Kamen 6672
Putoran Mts
Central Siberian Plateau
Olenek
Anabar
Lena
Yana
Okhotsk
Petropavlovsk Kamchatskiy
SOCIALIST REPUBLICS
Aldan
Markha
Vilyuysk
Yakutsk
Amga
Ust'Maya
Tura
Vilyuy
SEA OF OKHOTSK
Mt Topko 8253
Dzhugdzhur Range
Ayan
Olekminsk
Aldan
Shantar Is
Okha
Kuril Islands
Stony Tunguska
Lower Tunguska
Olekma
Skalistyy 8143
Stanovoy Range
Nikolayevsk-na-Amur
Amgun
Aleksandrovsk Sakhalinskiy
Sakhalin
Poronaysk
Angara
Kirensk
Chuna
Ust Kut
Kansk
Tayshet
Bratsk
Bratsk Resr
Skovorodino
Zeya
Komsomolsk-na-Amur
Uglegorsk
Gulf of Tartary
Sovetskaya Gavan
Yuzhno Sakhalinsk
Tulun
Nizhneudinsk
Vitim
Shilka
Svobodnyy
Amur
Birobidzhan
Khabarovsk
La Perouse Str.
Eastern Sayan
L. Baikal
Yablonovyy Range
Great Khingan Shan
Cheremkhovo
Angarsk
Irkutsk
Ulan-Ude
Chita
Blagoveshchensk
Sikhote Alin Range
Wakkanai
Asahi-dake 7513
Hokkaido
Munku Sardyk 11454
Khöbsögöl Dalai
Petrovsk Zabaykal'skiy
Sungari
Sapporo
Hakodate
CHINA
L. Khanka
Harbin
Ussuriysk
Olga
Vladivostok
Mutankiang
Hachinohe
Ulan Bator
Undur Khan
Kirin
Changchun
SEA OF JAPAN
Niigata
MONGOLIA
INNER MONGOLIA
Gobi
Shenyang
Fushun
Anshan
NORTH KOREA
Pyongyang
SOUTH KOREA
Seoul
Honshu
Tokyo
Yokohama
Fujiyama 12388
Nagoya
Kyoto
Kobe
Osaka
Liaotung Bay
Korea Bay
Lüta
Chiangkiakow
Paotow
Huhehot
Peking
84°
96°
108°
120°
132°
144°
156°
168°
180°

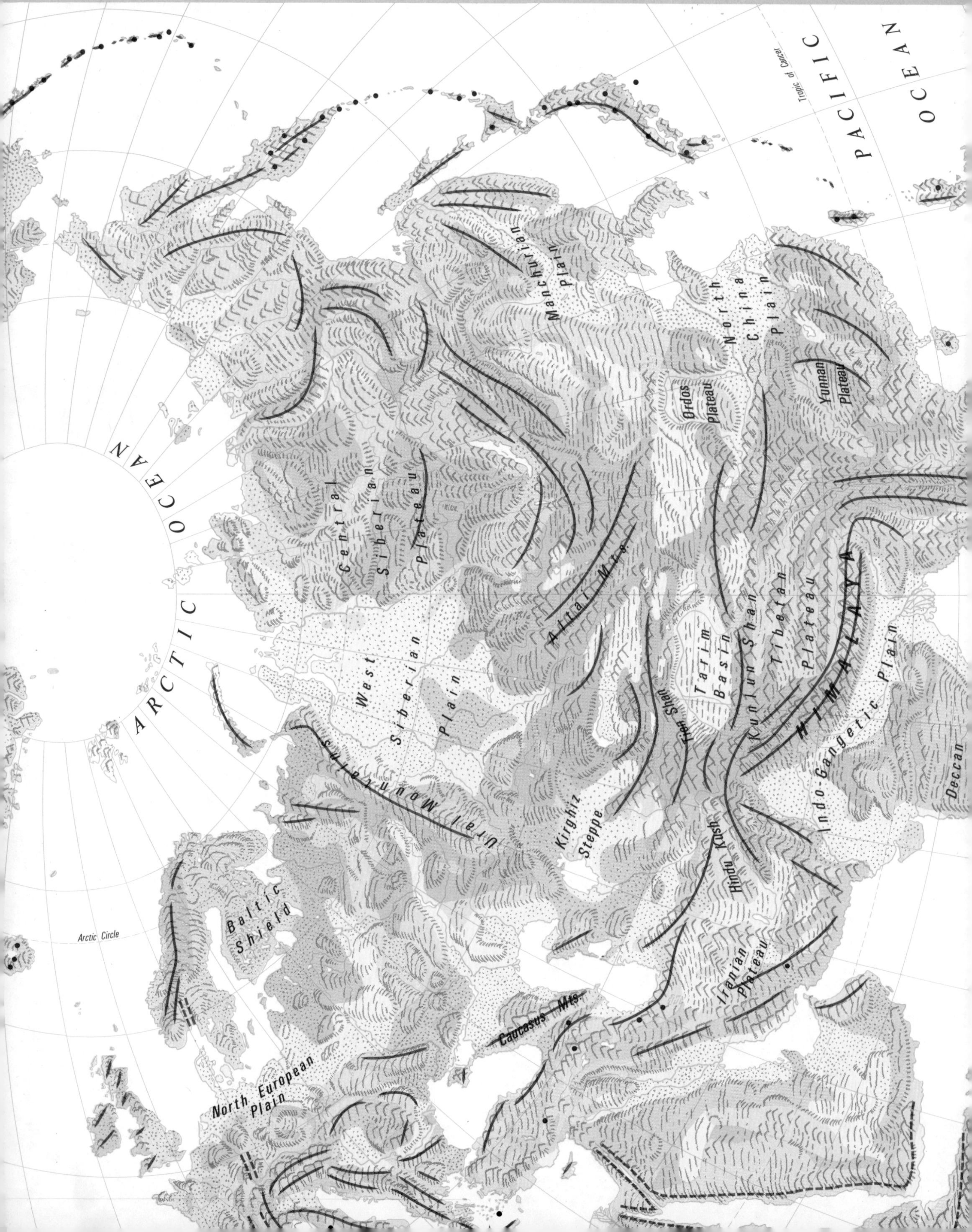

PACIFIC OCEAN
Tropic of Cancer
ARCTIC OCEAN
Arctic Circle
Manchurian Plain
North China Plain
Yunnan Plateau
Ordos Plateau
Central Siberian Plateau
Altai Mts.
West Siberian Plain
Tarim Basin
Kunlun Shan
Tibetan Plateau
HIMALAYA
Indo-Gangetic Plain
Deccan
Tien Shan
Ural Mountains
Kirghiz Steppe
Hindu Kush
Iranian Plateau
Baltic Shield
Caucasus Mts.
North European Plain

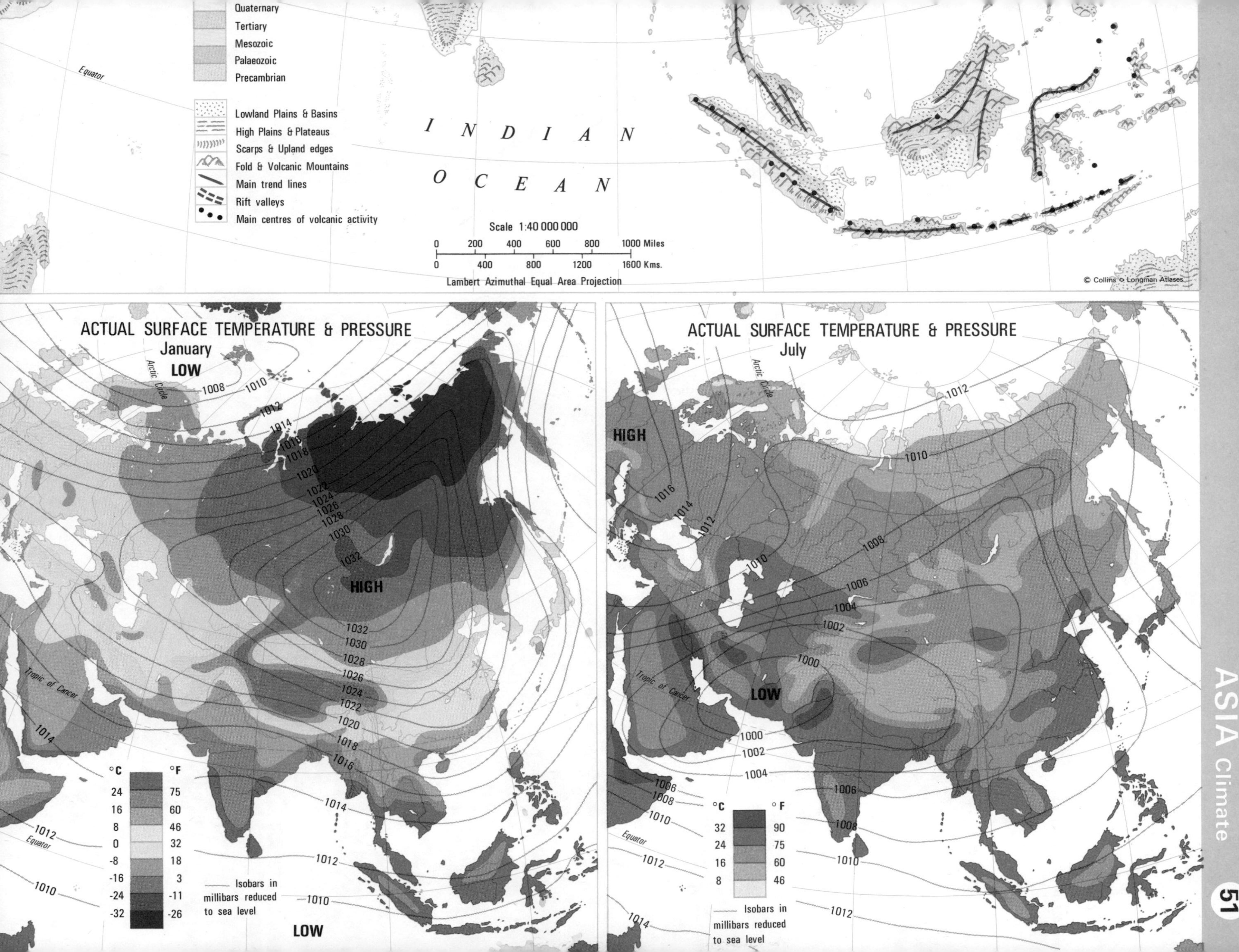

Quaternary
Tertiary
Mesozoic
Palaeozoic
Precambrian
Lowland Plains & Basins
High Plains & Plateaus
Scarps & Upland edges
Fold & Volcanic Mountains
Main trend lines
Rift valleys
Main centres of volcanic activity
INDIAN OCEAN
Equator
Scale 1:40 000 000
0 200 400 600 800 1000 Miles
0 400 800 1200 1600 Kms.
Lambert Azimuthal Equal Area Projection
© Collins-Longman Atlases
ACTUAL SURFACE TEMPERATURE & PRESSURE
January
LOW
HIGH
LOW
Arctic Circle
Tropic of Cancer
Equator
1008 1010 1012 1014 1016 1018 1020 1022 1024 1026 1028 1030 1032
°C 24 16 8 0 -8 -16 -24 -32
°F 75 60 46 32 18 3 -11 -26
Isobars in millibars reduced to sea level
ACTUAL SURFACE TEMPERATURE & PRESSURE
July
HIGH
LOW
Arctic Circle
Tropic of Cancer
Equator
1000 1002 1004 1006 1008 1010 1012 1014 1016
°C 32 24 16 8
°F 90 75 60 46
Isobars in millibars reduced to sea level

PACIFIC OCEAN
ARCTIC OCEAN
ATLANTIC OCEAN
BERING SEA
SEA OF OKHOTSK
SEA OF JAPAN
YELLOW SEA
EAST CHINA SEA
BARENTS SEA
NORWEGIAN SEA
NORTH SEA
BALTIC SEA
CASPIAN SEA
BLACK SEA
ARAL SEA
ARABIAN
SIBERIA
EUROPE
HIMALAYA
ARABIA
Aleutian Is.
Kuril Islands
Hokkaido
Honshu
Kyushu
Shikoku
Ryukyu Is.
Formosa
Luzon
PHILIPPINE IS.
Hainan
Kamchatka Peninsula
Sakhalin
St. Lawrence I.
Koryak Ra.
Kolyma Range
Bering Str.
East Cape
Wrangel I.
Kolyma Plain
Verkhoyansk Range
New Siberian Is.
Lena
Stanovoy Ra.
Yablonovy Range
L. Baikal
Amur
Argun
Great Khingan Mts.
Sungari
Sikhote Alin Range
Gulf of Tartary
Pepi Shan
Korean Str.
G. of Chihli
North China Plain
Hwang Ho
Tsinling Shan
Yangtze Kiang
Nan Ling
Si Kiang
G. of Tongking
Red Basin
Minya Konka 24900
Formosa Str.
Salween
Irrawaddy
Arakan Yo
Khasi Hills
Brahmaputra
Everest 29028
Ganges
Jumna
Narmada
Sutlej
Indus
Thar Desert
Sulaiman Ra.
Gobi
Koko Nor
Nan Shan
Lop Nor
Altin Tagh
Kunlun Shan
Tibetan Plateau
Tarim Basin
Tien Shan
K2 28250
Karakoram Ra.
Pamirs
Hindu Kush
Helmand
Altai Mts.
Yenisei
C. Chelyuskin
Severnaya Zemlya
Taymyr Peninsula
West Siberian Plain
Ob
Irtysh
L. Balkhash
Kirghiz Steppe
Syr Darya
Amu Darya
Turanian Plain
Franz Josef Land
Novaya Zemlya
Spitsbergen
North Cape
Kola Pen.
White Sea
Pechora
Ural Mountains
5373
N. Dvina
Kama
Ural
Volga
Scandinavia
G. of Bothnia
Arctic Circle
L. Ladoga
North European Plain
Central Russian Uplands
Don
Dnieper
Vistula
Carpathians
Danube
Rhine
British Isles
Caucasus
Elbrus 18481
Ararat 16946
Elburz Mts.
Kuh-i-Hazar 14600
Zagros Mts.
Makran
G. of Oman
Persian Gulf
Tigris
Euphrates
Syrian Desert
Jordan
Pontine Mts
Anatolia
Taurus Mts.
Cyprus
Tropic of Cancer
Rub al Khali
Gulf of Aden
Godavari

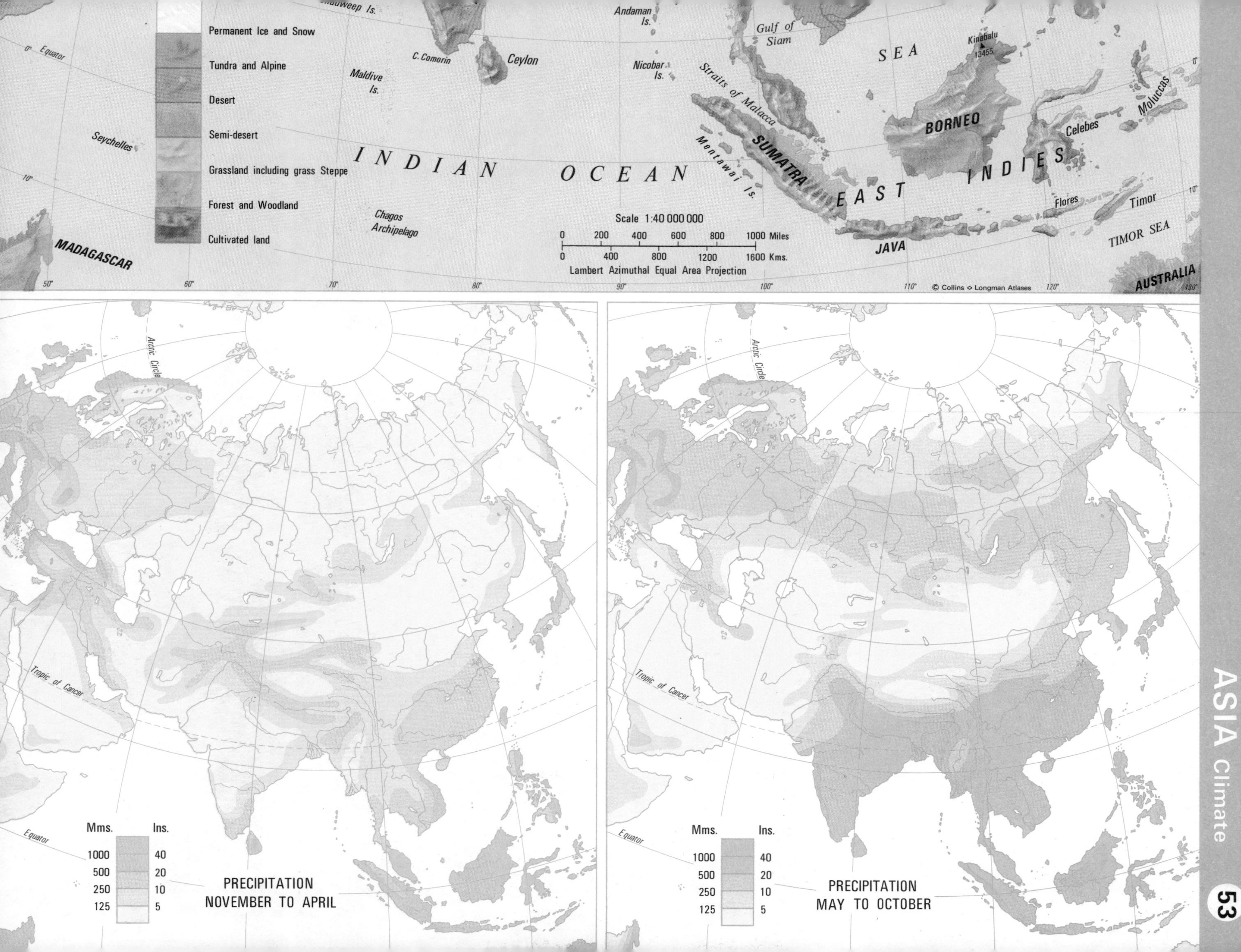
Permanent Ice and Snow
Tundra and Alpine
Desert
Semi-desert
Grassland including grass Steppe
Forest and Woodland
Cultivated land
Seychelles
MADAGASCAR
Equator
Maldive Is.
C. Comorin
Ceylon
Chagos Archipelago
INDIAN OCEAN
Andaman Is.
Nicobar Is.
Gulf of Siam
Straits of Malacca
Mentawai Is.
SUMATRA
SEA
Kinabalu 13455
BORNEO
Celebes
Moluccas
EAST INDIES
Flores
Timor
TIMOR SEA
JAVA
AUSTRALIA
Scale 1:40 000 000
0 200 400 600 800 1000 Miles
0 400 800 1200 1600 Kms.
Lambert Azimuthal Equal Area Projection
© Collins ◇ Longman Atlases
Arctic Circle
Tropic of Cancer
Equator
Mms. Ins.
1000 40
500 20
250 10
125 5
PRECIPITATION NOVEMBER TO APRIL
Arctic Circle
Tropic of Cancer
Equator
Mms. Ins.
1000 40
500 20
250 10
125 5
PRECIPITATION MAY TO OCTOBER

ARCTIC OCEAN
PACIFIC OCEAN
ATLANTIC OCEAN
UNION OF SOVIET SOCIALIST REPUBLICS
MONGOLIA
CHINA
INDIA
TIBET
SINKIANG-UIGHUR
INNER MONGOLIA
JAPAN
KOREA
BURMA
PAKISTAN
AFGHANISTAN
IRAN
IRAQ
SAUDI ARABIA
TURKEY
SYRIA
NEPAL
BANGLADESH
BHUTAN
KASHMIR
YEMEN
SOUTHERN YEMEN
OMAN
QATAR
BAHRAIN
UNION OF ARAB EMIRATES
KUWAIT
JORDAN
LEBANON
ISRAEL
CYPRUS
FINLAND
SWEDEN
NORWAY
DENMARK
POLAND
ROMANIA
BULGARIA
YUGOSLAVIA
HUNGARY
AUSTRIA
CZECHOSLOVAKIA
ITALY
FRANCE
UNITED KINGDOM
REP. OF IRELAND
ICELAND
GREECE
BERING SEA
SEA OF OKHOTSK
SEA OF JAPAN
YELLOW SEA
EAST CHINA SEA
BARENTS SEA
NORWEGIAN SEA
NORTH SEA
BALTIC SEA
BLACK SEA
CASPIAN SEA
ARAL SEA
White Sea
Persian Gulf
Gulf of Aden
Arctic Circle
Tropic of Cancer
Aleutian Is.
Kuril Islands
Hokkaido
Honshu
Shikoku
Kyushu
Ryukyu Is.
Sakhalin
New Siberian Is.
Wrangel I.
Severnaya Zemlya
Franz Josef Land
Novaya Zemlya
Spitsbergen
Bering Str.
St. Lawrence I.
Korea Str.
L. Baikal
L. Balkhash
Lop Nor
Moscow
Leningrad
Helsinki
Stockholm
Oslo
Copenhagen
Berlin
Warsaw
Prague
Vienna
Budapest
Belgrade
Bucharest
Sofia
Istanbul
Ankara
Izmir
Beirut
Damascus
Amman
Jerusalem
Baghdad
Basra
Kuwait
Abadan
Riyadh
Mecca
Aden
Tehran
Isfahan
Tabriz
Mashhad
Kabul
Karachi
Lahore
Delhi
New Delhi
Agra
Bombay
Ahmadabad
Nagpur
Kanpur
Varanasi
Calcutta
Dacca
Katmandu
Lhasa
Mandalay
Hanoi
Kunming
Chungking
Lanchow
Sian
Wuhan
Changsha
Kwangchow
Victoria
HONG KONG (Br.)
Macao (Port.)
Nanking
Shanghai
Tsinan
Tientsin
Peking
Shenyang
Harbin
Lüta
Pyongyang
Seoul
Pusan
Tsingtao
Taipei
TAIWAN (FORMOSA)
Tokyo
Yokohama
Nagoya
Kyoto
Osaka
Kobe
Nagasaki
Hakodate
Vladivostok
Khabarovsk
Komsomolsk-na-Amur
Ulan Bator
Ulan-Ude
Chita
Irkutsk
Krasnoyarsk
Novosibirsk
Tomsk
Omsk
Semipalatinsk
Karaganda
Alma-Ata
Tashkent
Samarkand
Sverdlovsk
Perm
Kuybyshev
Gorki
Volgograd
Saratov
Kharkov
Kiev
Minsk
Riga
Odessa
Sevastopol
Donetsk
Tbilisi
Baku
Astrakhan
Guryev
Krasnovodsk
Murmansk
Arkhangel'sk
Yakutsk
Magadan
Petropavlovsk Kamchatskiy
Anadyr
Verkhoyansk
Nordvik
Dudinka
Urumchi
London
Paris
Brussels
Amsterdam
Bonn
Berne
Dublin
Glasgow

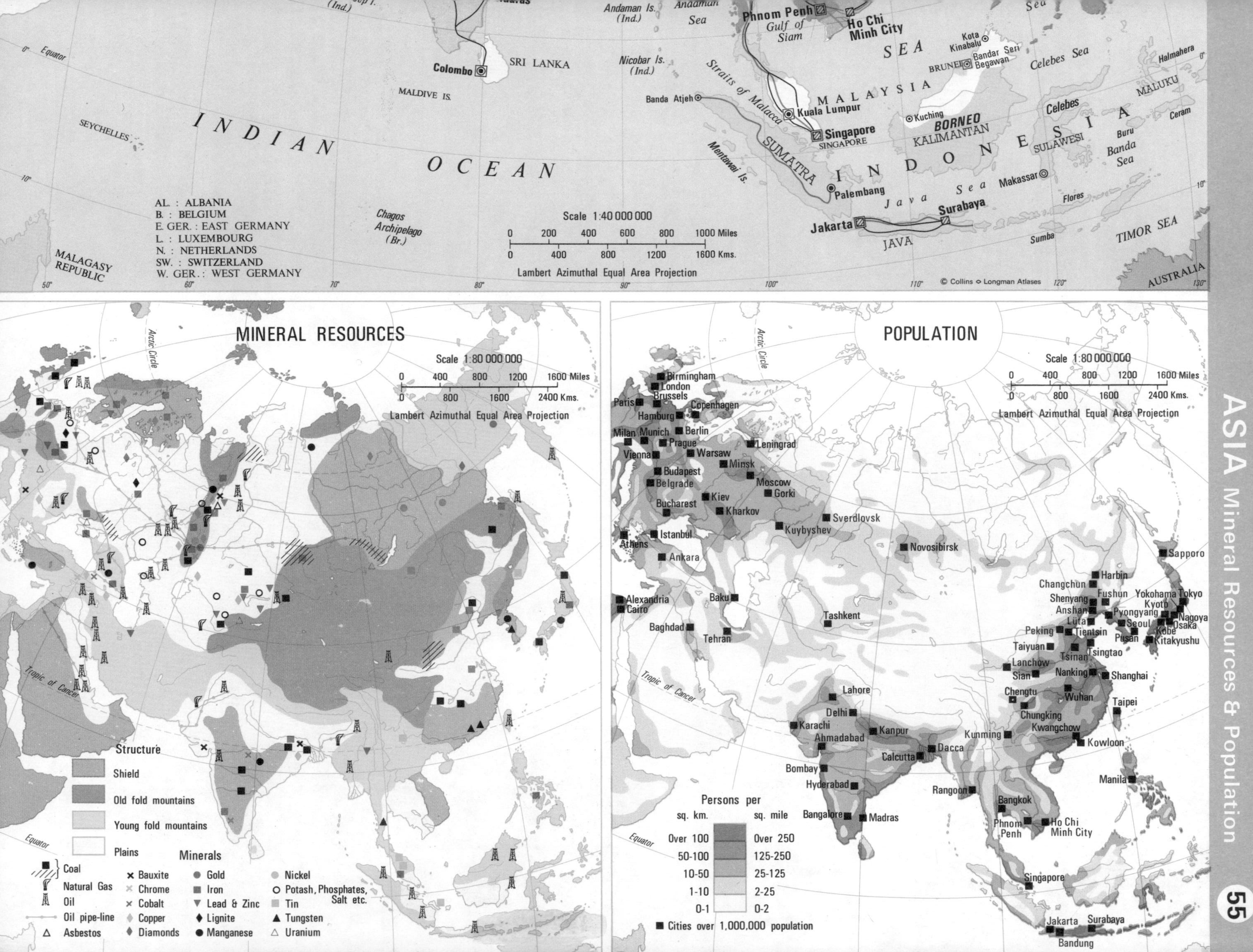
INDIAN OCEAN
SRI LANKA
Colombo
MALDIVE IS.
SEYCHELLES
MALAGASY REPUBLIC
Chagos Archipelago (Br.)
Andaman Is. (Ind.)
Andaman Sea
Nicobar Is. (Ind.)
Banda Atjeh
Straits of Malacca
Mentawai Is.
SUMATRA
Palembang
Phnom Penh
Gulf of Siam
Ho Chi Minh City
SEA
MALAYSIA
Kuala Lumpur
Singapore
SINGAPORE
Kota Kinabalu
BRUNEI
Bandar Seri Begawan
Kuching
BORNEO
KALIMANTAN
INDONESIA
Java Sea
Jakarta
Surabaya
JAVA
Celebes Sea
Celebes
SULAWESI
Makassar
Flores
Sumba
Buru
Banda Sea
Halmahera
MALUKU
Ceram
TIMOR SEA
AUSTRALIA
Equator
AL. : ALBANIA
B. : BELGIUM
E. GER. : EAST GERMANY
L. : LUXEMBOURG
N. : NETHERLANDS
SW. : SWITZERLAND
W. GER. : WEST GERMANY
Scale 1:40 000 000
0 200 400 600 800 1000 Miles
0 400 800 1200 1600 Kms.
Lambert Azimuthal Equal Area Projection
© Collins • Longman Atlases
MINERAL RESOURCES
Scale 1:80 000 000
0 400 800 1200 1600 Miles
0 800 1600 2400 Kms.
Lambert Azimuthal Equal Area Projection
Arctic Circle
Tropic of Cancer
Equator
Structure
Shield
Old fold mountains
Young fold mountains
Plains
Coal
Natural Gas
Oil
Oil pipe-line
Asbestos
Minerals
Bauxite
Chrome
Cobalt
Copper
Diamonds
Gold
Iron
Lead & Zinc
Lignite
Manganese
Nickel
Potash, Phosphates, Salt etc.
Tin
Tungsten
Uranium
POPULATION
Scale 1:80 000 000
0 400 800 1200 1600 Miles
0 800 1600 2400 Kms.
Lambert Azimuthal Equal Area Projection
Arctic Circle
Tropic of Cancer
Equator
Birmingham
London
Brussels
Paris
Copenhagen
Hamburg
Berlin
Milan
Munich
Prague
Vienna
Warsaw
Leningrad
Minsk
Budapest
Belgrade
Moscow
Gorki
Bucharest
Kiev
Kharkov
Sverdlovsk
Kuybyshev
Istanbul
Athens
Ankara
Novosibirsk
Alexandria
Cairo
Baku
Tashkent
Baghdad
Tehran
Sapporo
Harbin
Changchun
Shenyang
Fushun
Anshan
Luta
Yokohama
Tokyo
Kyoto
Pyongyang
Seoul
Nagoya
Osaka
Kobe
Peking
Tientsin
Pusan
Kitakyushu
Taiyuan
Tsinan
Tsingtao
Lanchow
Sian
Nanking
Shanghai
Chengtu
Wuhan
Chungking
Taipei
Kwangchow
Kunming
Kowloon
Lahore
Delhi
Karachi
Kanpur
Ahmadabad
Dacca
Calcutta
Bombay
Hyderabad
Rangoon
Manila
Bangkok
Bangalore
Madras
Phnom Penh
Ho Chi Minh City
Singapore
Jakarta
Surabaya
Bandung
Persons per
sq. km. | sq. mile
Over 100 | Over 250
50-100 | 125-250
10-50 | 25-125
1-10 | 2-25
0-1 | 0-2
Cities over 1,000,000 population

BLACK SEA
Bosporus
Sea of Marmara
Istanbul
Üsküdar
Izmit
Adapazari
Bursa
Bandirma
Gemlik
Gallipoli
Dardanelles
Çanakkale
Tekirdağ
Zonguldak
Bartin
Ereğli
Inebolu
Sinop
Kastamonu
Bafra
Samsun
Çarşamba
Ordu
Ünye
Giresun
Tirebolu
Trabzon
Rize
Artvin
Batumi
Gümüşane
Bayburt
Erzurum
Erzincan
Sivas
Tokat
Amasya
Merzifon
Çorum
Çankiri
Kalecik
Kirikkale
Ankara
Polatli
Eskişehir
Bilecik
Sogut
Kütahya
Balikesir
Edremit
Ayvalik
Manisa
Izmir
Alaşehir
Kula
Uşak
Afyon
Bolvadin
Akşehir
Aydin
Nazilli
Menderes
Denizli
Burdur
Isparta
Eğridir
Eğridir Lake
Beyşehir Lake
Konya
Karaman
Ereğli
Niğde
Aksaray
Nevşehir
Avanos
Kirşehir
Yozgat
Kayseri
Mt Erciyas 12848
Demirkazik 12828
Malatya
Elâziğ
Diyarbakir
Tunceli
Bingöl
Muş
Tatvan
Siirt
Bitlis
Tigris
Euphrates
Maraş
Adiyaman
Gaziantep
Birecik
Urfa
Mardin
Cizre
Nusaybin
Tel Kotchek
Kilis
Adana
Tarsus
Mersin
Osmaniye
Iskenderun
G. of Iskenderun
Antakya
Silifke
Mut
Alanya
Antalya
Fethiye
Gulf of Antalya
Kastellorizon
Rhodes
Milas
Muğla
Kos
Dodecanese
TURKEY
ANATOLIA
TAURUS MOUNTAINS
Pontine Mountains
Kizil
Sakarya
Porsuk
Gediz
Kelkit
Yeşil
GREECE
Thessaloniki
Khalkidhiki
Mt Athos 6670
Kavalla
Xanthi
Komotini
Alexandroupolis
Thasos
Samothraki
G. of Saros
Imroz
Limnos
Volos
AEGEAN SEA
Mitilini
Lésvos
Skíros
Khalkis
Euboea
Athens
Piraeus
Corinth
Khios
Andros
Tinos
Ikaria
Samos
Kea
Cyclades
Paros
Naxos
Milos
Thira
Kárpathos
Kásos
Canea
Réthimnon
Iráklion
CRETE
CYPRUS
C Andreas
C Arnauti
Kyrenia
Nicosia
Famagusta
Mt Olympus 6403
Larnaca
Paphos
Limassol
C Gata
MEDITERRANEAN SEA
Levant
Latakia
Aleppo
Hama
Homs
Tripoli
SYRIA
Raqqa
Deir-ez-Zor
Meyadin
Palmyra
Euphrates
Khabur
LEBANON
Beirut
Zahle
Sidon
Tyre
Damascus
Mt Hermon 9232
Haifa
Nazareth
L. Tiberias
ISRAEL
Tel Aviv-Jaffa
Jerusalem
Jericho
Hebron
Gaza
Beersheba
Dead Sea
Negev
Amman
Zarqa
Mafraq
Jebel ed Druz 5692
JORDAN
Karak
PETRA
Ma'an
Eilat
Aqaba
Gulf of Aqaba
Syrian Desert
J. Aneiza 3068
Ar Rutba
W. Hauran
W. al Ghadaf
W. Arar
Hamad
Ash Shama
Wadi Sirhan
Sakaka
Al Jauf
Jeb. et Tubeiq
W. Fajr
NAFUD
(Great Sandy Desert)
Taima
Hail
Tabuk
J. el-Loz 8461
J. Dibbagh 7706
W. Dama
Al Ula
Safaha
Al Wajh
W. Jizl
W. Hamdh
W. Tubja
Umm Lajj
J. Radhwa 5906
Yanbu
Medina
Hanakiya
Nuqra
Aqlat as Suqur
Muwai Hakran
Hejaz
RED SEA
Ras Banas
Ras Muhammad
Hurghada
Port Safâga
Quseir
G Hamata 6486
Sinai
Plateau of El Tih
G. Katherina 8651
Tor
Abu Zenima
W. el Arish
El 'Arish
Gulf of Suez
Suez
Suez Canal
Bitter Lakes
Port Said
L. Manzala
Damietta
L. Burullus
Nile Delta
Rosetta
Alexandria
Damanhur
El Mahalla el Kubra
El Mansura
Tanta
Zagazig
Ismâ'iliya
El Qantara
Heliopolis
El Giza
Cairo
Pyramids
MEMPHIS
Helwan
Birket Qârûn
El Faiyûm
Beni Suef
Galala
Arabian Plateau
W. Tarfa
Eastern Desert
El Minya
Mallawi
Asyût
Abu Tig
Sohag
Nag' Hammadi
Qena
Upper Egypt
THEBES
Luxor
Isna
Idfu
Aswân
Aswân High Dam
Lake Nasser
Abu Simbel
Nubian Desert
W. 'Allaqi
Wadi Halfa
Lower Egypt
Wadi el Natrûn
EGYPT
El Alamein
Matruh
Sidi Barrani
Buqbuq
Salûm
Bardia
Tobruk
Libyan Plateau
Jaghbub
Qara
Qattara Depression
Siwa Oasis
Siwa
Bawiti
Farafra
Qasr Farafra
Oasis
Libyan Desert
El Qasr
Dakhla Oasis
Kharga Oasis
El Khârga
Tropic of Cancer
LIBYA
SUDAN
Scale 1:9 000 000
0 50 100 150 200 250 Miles
0 100 200 300 400 Kms.

CASPIAN SEA
Kara Bogaz Gol Bay
U. S. S. R.
Turkestan
TURKMENISTAN S.S.R.
KARA KUM
(Black Sand Desert)
CAUCASUS MTS.
AZERBAIJAN S.S.R.
ARMENIA S.S.R.
Apsheron Pen
(92 feet below sea level)
Baku
Sumgait
Derbent
Kirovabad
Kirovakan
Lake Sevan
Stepanakert
Nakhichevan
Alyaty
Salyany
Moghan Steppe
Lenkoran
Krasnovodsk
Krasnovodsk G.
Cheleken
Vyshka
Nebit Dag
Balkhan Ra.
Kum Dag
Kizil Arvat
Yerbent
Ashkhabad
Kopet Range
Lutfabad
Atrek
Gorgan
Bandar e Shah
Gonbad-e-Kavus
Bojnurd
Kuh-i-Aleh
Kuh-i-Shah
Quchan
Mashhad
Kara-Su
Sabzawar
Nishapur
Sultanabad
Mayamey
Shahrud
Damghan
ELBURZ MOUNTAINS
Takht-i-Suleiman 15812
Demavend 18376
Tehran
Tajrish
Semnan
Garmsar
Qom
DASHT-E-KAVIR (Salt Desert)
Kashan
Natanz
Ardistan
Nain
Isfahan
Kuhpayeh
Khur
Tabas
Ferdaus
Bejestan
Kashmar
Torbat-i-Shaikh Jam
Qayen
Birjand
DASHT-E-LUT (Barren Desert)
Kuh-i-Naibandan 9816
I R A N
Kuh-i-Khurunag 10490
Yazd
Bafq
Kuh-i-Darband 8000
Ravar
Zarand
Kerman
Shah Dad
Rafsanjan
Anar
Kuh-i-Masahim 11390
Shahr-i-Babak
Kuh-i-Hazar 14500
Rayen
Kuh-i-Lalehzar 14350
Saidabad
Rahbur
Bam
Rigan
Bazman Kuh 11446
Kuh-i-Shah 8953
Kuh-i-Istin 8164
Nasratabad
Kuh-i-Malik Siah 5390
Zahedan
Seistan
Zabol
Sehkuheh
Hamun-i-Sabari
Dasht-i-Margo
Dasht-i-Zirreh
Kuh-i-Sultan 7654
Saindak
Kuh-i-Taftan 13262
Khwash
Iranshar
Bampur
Magas
Ramishk
Champ
Kuh-i-Ran
Sarbaz
Qasrqand
Geh
Bahao Kalat
Dashtiari
Tump
Chah Bahar
Gwatar
Gwadar
Jask
Makran
Minab
Bandar Abbas
Qishm
Str. of Hormuz
Bandar-e-Lengeh
(Oman)
Tabriz
Marand
Khoi
Ahar
Kuh-i-Savalan 15784
Sarab
Ardabil
Kuh-i-Sahand 12172
Hashtrud
Lake Urmia
Rezaiyeh
Maragheh
Mianeh
Mianduab
Ushnuiyeh
Mahabad
Saqqiz
Zanjan
Qizil Uzun
Heradabad
Bandar-e-Pahlavi
Rasht
Lahijan
Ramsar
Shahsawar
Manjil
Qazvin
Babol
Amol
Sari
Takestan
Bijar
Razan
Sanandaj
Saveh
Hamadan
Malayer
Arak
Kuh-i-Alaband 11010
Kermanshahan
Karand
Shahabad
Bisitun
Nahavand
Burujird
Ilam
Mahallat
Khorramabad
Aligudarz
Golpaigan
Khunsar
Kuh-i-Ushtaran 13352
Daran
Kabir Kuh
Dizful
Kuh-i-Karbush 14089
Zardeh Kuh 14920
Shahr Kord
Julfa
Shushtar
Masjid-i-Sulaiman
Naft Safid
Haft Kel
Ramhormoz
Ahwaz
Karun
ZAGROS MOUNTAINS
Shahreza
Samirum
Kuh-i-Alijuq 12218
Abadeh
Kuh Bul 12017
Deh Bid
Kuh-i-Dinar 14029
Kuh-i-Barm 12050
Behbehan
Gach Saran
Bandar Shahpur
Khorramshahr
Abadan
Abadan I
Bandar Dilam
SHAPUR
Kuh Tasak
PERSEPOLIS
Shiraz
Kazarun
Bandar Rig
Borazjan
Bushire
Firuzabad
Fasa
Istehbanat
Niriz
Jahrom
Furg
Khurmuj
Mand
Kangan
Lar
Gilehdar
Bastak
Ishqanan
Nudushan
Kar Kuh 11519
Shir Kuh 13366
Kharan
Daulatabad
Isfandaqeh
Khanu
Rigmati
Rudan
Sulaimaniya
Kirkuk
Diyala
Khanaqin
Baghdad
IRAQ
Tigris
BABYLON
Al Kut
Hor Sanniya
Ad Diwaniya
Amara
Hor Auda
Al Qurna
An Nasiriya
Samawa
UR
Hor al Hammar
Basra
Shu'aiba
Shamiya Desert
Fao
Bubiyan I
Jahara
KUWAIT
Kuwait
Neutral Territory
Umm-al-Hamir
Burgan
Mina Saud
Wafra
Hafar
Safaniya
PERSIAN GULF
Jubail
Ras Tanura
Uwaina
Qatif
Dammam
Dhahran
BAHRAIN
Muharraq
Manama
Abqaiq
Hasa Oasis
Hofuf
Khor
Dukhan
QATAR
Doha
Al Wakrah
Umm Sa'id
Salwa
Jafura
Zilfi
Majma'a
Ma'qala
Arma Plateau
Ramah
Shaqra
Riyadh
Haradh
Sulaimiya
Ad Dahana
W. Sahba
W. Birq
W. Sirra
Jabrin Oasis
Al Jaub
Qufa
Al Maharadh
Kidan
SAUDI ARABIA
Ad Dahna
Umm-al-Gawein
Sharjah
Dubai
Abu Dhabi
Buraimi
UNION OF ARAB EMIRATES
Western Hajar
Batinah
Sohar
Khaburah
Muscat
Matrah
Sarur
Jebel Akhdar
J. Sham 9900
Eastern Hajar
W. al Ain
W. Batha
Sur
Ras al Hadd
Al Hamra
OMAN
GULF OF OMAN
ARABIAN SEA
Tropic of Cancer
AFGHANISTAN
Herat
Hari
Ghurian
Paropamisus Mts
Safed Koh
Kushka
Kala Nao
Bala Murghab
Maruchak
Doshakh 6920
Adraskand
Farsi
Sabzawar
Harut
Farah
Lar Koh 8400
Tabas
Juwain
Khash
Chakansur
Kala-i-Fath
Helmand
Rudbar
Shelag
Rud-i-Shur
Rud-i-Pusht
Dukhtaran 6765
Koh-i-Koh
Ladis
PAKISTAN
Turtkul
Khiva
Bukhara
Chardzhou
Kara-Kum Canal
Relief
Feet
Metres
16404 5000
9843 3000
6562 2000
3281 1000
1640 500
656 200
0 Sea Level
Land Dep.
656 200
13123 4000
22966 7000
© Collins • Longman Atlases

U.S.S.R.
AFGHANISTAN
IRAN
PAKISTAN
IRAQ
Kuwait
PERSIAN GULF
BAHRAIN
Manama
QATAR
Doha
UNION OF ARAB EMIRATES
NEJD
SAUDI ARABIA
Rub al Khali
OMAN
SOUTHERN YEMEN
ARABIAN SEA
Gulf of Oman
Str. of Hormuz
Tropic of Cancer
Rann of Kutch
G. of Kutch
Gulf of Cambay
GUJARAT
RAJASTHAN
Thar Desert
PUNJAB
HARYANA
JAMMU
KASHMIR
KARNATAKA
KERALA
Hindu Kush
Dasht-e-Lut
Dasht-i-Margo
Baluchistan
Makran
Zagros Mts
Sulaiman Range
Western Ghats
Western Hajar
Eastern Hajar
Karakoram Ra.
Lakshadweep I. (India)
MALDIVE IS.
Arak
Qom
Kashan
Khorramabad
Isfahan
Nain
Dizful
Yazd
Ahwaz
Basra
Khorramshahr
Bandar Shahpur
Abadan
Shatt al Arab
Kuh-i-Dinar
Anar
Bahramabad
Kerman
Shiraz
Bushire
Saidabad
Kuh-i-Hazar
Bam
Lar
Bandar Abbas
Qishm
(Oman)
Jask
Dhahran
Hofuf
Dubai
Abu Dhabi
Buraimi
Khaburah
Muscat
J. Sham
Sur
Ras al Hadd
Masira I
Ras Madraka
Salala
Kuria Muria Is
Qishn
Kushka
Herat
Murghab
Hari
Qayen
Birjand
Farah
Seistan
Helmand
Zahedan
Kuh-i-Taftan
Khwash
Kandahar
Kabul
Khyber Pass
Peshawar
Malakand
Chitral
Gilgit
Nanga Parbat
Islamabad
Rawalpindi
Kohat
Srinagar
Jammu
Mianwali
Sialkot
Gujranwala
Jhelum
Chenab
Dera Ismail Khan
Lahore
Amritsar
Lyallpur
Jullundur
Ferozepore
Ludhiana
Quetta
Loralai
Zhob
Multan
Ravi
Sutlej
Sibi
Kalat
Bahawalpur
Jacobabad
Shikarpur
Sukkur
Khairpur
Indus
Wad
Hingol
Bela
Sarbaz
Turbat
Dasht
Gwadar
Chah Bahar
Gwatar
Hyderabad
Mirpur Khas
Karachi
Bikaner
Sikar
Alwar
Jaipur
Jodhpur
Ajmer
Beawar
Tonk
Kota
Udaipur
Ratlam
Ujjain
Indore
Bhuj
Ahmadabad
Godhra
Vindhya
Narmada
Okha
Jamnagar
Rajkot
Porbandar
Bhavnagar
Junagadh
Veraval
Diu
Baroda
Khandwa
Satpura
Burhanpur
Jalgaon
Tapti
Surat
Dhulia
Malegaon
Daman
Nasik
Aurangabad
Jalna
Godavari
Thana
Bombay
Ahmednagar
Poona
Sholapur
Satara
Bhima
Miraj
Kolhapur
Krishna
Gulbarga
Belgaum
Marmagao
Hubli
Bellary
Tungabhadra
Davangere
Shimoga
Mangalore
Kozhikode
Cochin
Alleppey
Trivandrum
Scale 1:10 000 000
0 50 100 150 200 Miles
0 100 200 300 Kms.
Conic Projection
© Collins ◇ Longman Atlases
Meerut
Amroha
Moradabad
Rampur
Delhi
New Delhi
Ghaziabad
Bulandshahr
Pilibhit
Bareilly
UTTAR PRADESH
Chauka
Budaun
Ganges
Jumna
Aligarh
Shahjahanpur
Mathura
Hathras
Etah
Alwar
Agra
Farrukhabad
Sitapur
Mainpuri
Hardoi
Bara Banki
Bahraich
Firozabad
Ghaghara
Gonda
Dholpur
Etawah
Lucknow
Basti
Gorakhpur
Karauli
Bhind
Unnao
Rae Bareli
Faizabad
(Gogra)
Chambal
Gwalior
Kanpur
Yamuna
Orai
Azamgarh
Muzaffarpur
Darbhanga
Supaul
Hamirpur
Bela
Jaunpur
Ballia
Chapra
Purnea
Datia
Jhansi
Fatehpur
Banda
Ghazipur
Katihar
Berwa
Fathpur
Allahabad
Varanasi
Arrah
Patna
Monghyr
Shivpuri
Lalitpur
Bundelkhand
Satna
Rewa
Mirzapur
Sasaram
Bihar
Gaya
Jamalpur
Bhagalpur
Guna
Bijawar
Mauganj
Bardi
BIHAR
Maihar
Son
Dumka
Rajgarh
Bina
Baghelkhand
Garwah
Daltonganj
Hazaribagh
Sagar
Rihand Dam
Pathari
Murwara
MADHYA PRADESH
Bhopal
Partabpur
Tropic of Cancer
Ranchi
Dhanbad
Purulia
Asansol
Narmada
(Narbada)
Jabalpur
Shahdol
Bankura
Burdwan
Narsimhapur
Mandla
Chota Nagpur
Jamshedpur
Jashpurnagar
Lakhnadon
Porahat
Hoshangabad
Chhindwara
Bilaspur
Sakti
Raigarh
Sundargarh
Kharagpur
Damodar
Howrah
Calcutta
Dum Dum
Sundarbans
Mouths of the Ganges
NEPAL
HIMALAYA
Dhaulagiri
Annapurna
Pokhara
Katmandu
Mt. Everest
Kanchenjunga
Gandak
SIKKIM
Gangtok
Darjeeling
Gyangtse
Kula Kangri
Thimphu
BHUTAN
Siliguri
BENGAL
Jalpaiguri
Cooch Behar
ASSAM
Dhubri
Goalpara
MEGHALAYA
Garo Hills
Saidpur
Rangpur
Dinajpur
Raiganj
Jamalpur
English Bazar
Rajshahi
Bogra
Nasirabad
BANGLADESH
Ganges
Pabna
Berhampore
Kushtia
Dacca
Narayanganj
Krishnanagar
Jessore
Khulna
Barisal

Kunlun Shan
Tibetan Plateau
TIBET
CHINA
TSINGHAI
NINGSIA HUI
SHENSI
Chin Ling Shan
SZECHWAN
KWEICHOW
YUNNAN
Hwang Ho
L. Montcalm
Aling Kangri
Thok Jalung
Gar Dzong
Gartok
Tangra Yum
Ziling Tso
Nam Tso
Bum Tso
Lhasa
Tsetang
Shigatse
Gyangtse
Kula Kangri
Namcha Barwa
Kadusam
Brahmaputra
Tsangpo or
Yalung
Yangtze Kiang
Mekong
Salween
Yushu
Changtu
Paan
Kangting
Minya Konka
Chengtu
Kwanhsien
Yaan
Loshan
Hochwan
Chungking
Luchow
Iping
Sichang
Chaotung
Kweiyang
Anshun
Kunming
Kutsing
Likiang
Chungtien
Tsuyung
Paoshan
Tengchung
Kienshui
Mengtsz
Szemao
Yuan Kiang
Wenshan
Hanchung
Kamet
Nanda Devi
HIMALAYA
NEPAL
Jumla
Dhaulagiri
Mustang
Annapurna
Pokhara
Katmandu
Mt Everest
Kanchenjunga
SIKKIM
Gangtok
Thimphu
BHUTAN
Darjeeling
Siliguri
ASSAM
Sadiya
Dibrugarh
Tezpur
Nowgong
Gauhati
MEGHALAYA
Shillong
NAGALAND
Kohima
MANIPUR
Imphal
Silchar
TRIPURA
Agartala
Patkai Hills
KACHIN STATE
Myitkyina
Mogaung
Bhamo
Katha
Putao
UTTAR PRADESH
Bareilly
Shahjahanpur
Lucknow
Kanpur
Faizabad
Gorakhpur
Allahabad
Varanasi
Mirzapur
Ganges
Yamuna
Ghaghara
Son
Jaunpur
Muzaffarpur
Darbhanga
Patna
Monghyr
Gaya
Bihar
Bhagalpur
BIHAR
Daltonganj
Ranchi
Jamshedpur
Asansol
Purulia
Burdwan
BENGAL
Howrah
Calcutta
Sundarbans
Kharagpur
Balasore
Mouths of the Ganges
Jalpaiguri
Saidpur
Jamalpur
Mymensingh
Sylhet
English Bazar
Berhampore
BANGLADESH
Dacca
Comilla
Khulna
Chittagong
Cox's Bazar
Jabalpur
Bilaspur
Raigarh
Hirakud Res.
Deogarh
Sambalpur
Raipur
Sarangarh
Nagpur
Chanda
ORISSA
Cuttack
Bhubaneswar
Puri
Berhampur
Bolangir
Kanker
Jagdalpur
Jeypore
Indravati
Godavari
Palmyras Pt
Vizianagaram
Vishakhapatnam
Kakinada
Rajahmundry
Kottagudem
Vijayawada
Guntur
Bandar
Eastern Ghats
Kavali
Nellore
Madras
Vellore
Pondicherry
Cuddalore
Karikal
Nagappattinam
Palk Str.
Jaffna
Vavuniya
Trincomalee
Puttalam
Batticaloa
Kandy
Colombo
Galle
SRI LANKA
BAY OF BENGAL
BURMA
SHAN STATE
Mawlaik
Shwebo
Mogok
Lashio
Monywa
Sagaing
Mandalay
Maymyo
Myingyan
Taunggyi
Meiktila
Yamethin
Magwe
Pyinmana
Thayetmyo
Toungoo
KAWTHOOLEI
Prome
Myanaung
Henzada
Pegu
Rangoon
Bassein
Irrawaddy Delta
Irrawaddy
Chindwin
Sittang
Pegu Yoma
Arakan Yoma
Akyab
Kyaukpyu
Ramree I.
Sandoway
C. Negrais
Thaton
Martaban
Moulmein
Ye
Gulf of Martaban
Tavoy
TENASSERIM
Mergui
Mergui Archipelago
ANDAMAN SEA
North
Middle
South
Andaman Islands (India)
Port Blair
Little Andaman
Car Nicobar
Nicobar Islands (India)
Gt Nicobar
INDONESIA
SUMATRA
Banda Atjeh
LAOS
VIETNAM
Hanoi
Haiphong
Cao Bang
Ha Giang
Hokow
Laokay
Lai Chau
Yen Bai
Red
Phong Saly
Sam Neua
Luang Prabang
Ban Houei Sai
Kengtung
Xieng Khouang
Vinh
Vientiane
Nong Khai
Thakhek
Savannakhet
Khemmarat
Udon Thani
M.Khon Kaen
Ubon Ratchathani
Surin
THAILAND
Chiang Rai
Chiang Mai
M.Lampang
Muang Nan
M.Phrae
Uttaradit
Tak
M.Phitsanulok
P. Miang
Nakhon Sawan
Chao Phraya
Nakhon Ratchasima
Ayutthaya
Bangkok
Kanchanaburi
Phet Buri
Chon Buri
Chanthaburi
Battambang
Sisophon
Tonle Sap
KHMER REP.
Pursat
Phnom Penh
Kampot
Prachuap Khiri Khan
Chumphon
Isthmus of Kra
GULF OF SIAM
Surat Thani
Nakhon Si Thammarat
Krabi
Phuket
Ban Kantang
Songkhla
Ban Hat Yai
Kangar
Alor Star
George Town
Penang I.
Tumpat
Kota Bharu
MALAYSIA
Kuala Trengganu
Taiping
Ipoh
Kuala Lipis
Relief
Feet
Metres
16404
5000
9843
3000
6562
2000
3281
1000
1640
500
656
200
0
Sea Level
Land Dep.
656
200
13123
4000
22966
7000
Scale 1:14 000 000
0
100
200
300
400
500 Miles
0
200
400
600
800 Kms.
Conic Projection

CHINA
BURMA
THAILAND
VIETNAM
KHMER REP.
MALAYSIA
WEST
EAST
BRUNEI
SINGAPORE
BORNEO
KALIMANTAN
SUMATRA
JAVA
INDON
SOUTH CHINA SEA
ANDAMAN SEA
INDIAN OCEAN
JAVA SEA
Gulf of Tongking
Gulf of Siam
Gulf of Martaban
Straits of Malacca
HAINAN I.
Nanning
Kwangchow
Swatow
Kowloon
HONG KONG
Victoria (Br.)
Macao (Port.)
Hanoi
Haiphong
Vientiane
Bangkok
Rangoon
Phnom Penh
Ho Chi Minh City
Kuala Lumpur
Singapore
Jakarta
Bandung
Semarang
Surabaya
Medan
Palembang
Scale 1:15 000 000
0 100 200 300 400 500 Miles
0 200 400 600 800 Kms
Bonne Projection
© Collins ◇ Longman Atlases

Relief
Feet Metres
16404 5000
9843 3000
6562 2000
3281 1000
1640 500
656 200
0 Sea Level
Land Dep.
656 200
13123 4000
22966 7000
PACIFIC OCEAN
PHILIPPINES
LUZON
Manila
Quezon City
MINDANAO
Philippine Trench
Cape Johnson Depth 34439
Mariana Islands
Guam
Agana
Saipan
Tinian
Rota
Challenger Depth 36200
Nero Deep 31618
Caroline Islands
(U.S. Trust Territory)
Yap
Palau Is
Koror
Sonsorol
Merir
Tobi
Helen Reef
Mapia Is
Equator
Moro Gulf
Davao G.
Samar
Leyte
Bohol
Negros
Panay
Cebu
Masbate
Catanduanes
CELEBES SEA
Molucca Sea
Talaud Is
Sangihe Is
Morotai
Halmahera
MOLUCCAS
CERAM SEA
BANDA SEA
Ceram
Buru
Ambon
Waigeo
Misoöl
Vogelkop
Teluk Berau
Teluk Irian
Schouten Is
Biak
Japen
IRIAN JAYA
NEW GUINEA
PAPUA NEW GUINEA
Djajapura
Sudirman Mts
Djajawidjaja Mts
Bismarck Sea
Admiralty Is
Manus
Gulf of Papua
Port Moresby
Madang
Lae
Wewak
Aitape
Sepik
Fly
Digoel
Merauke
Kolepom
Aru Is
Kai Is
Tanimbar Is
ARAFURA SEA
Timor
Kupang
Dili
Alor
Wetar
Savu Sea
Torres Str.
Thursday I
Prince of Wales I
C. York
Coral Sea

KAZAKHSTAN S.S.R.
U.S.S.R.
Syr Darya
Balkhash
Kokpekty
Irtysh
Belukha Mt. 14783
Yenisei
Kyzyl
Lake Baikal
Irkutsk
Sayan Mts.
Slyudyanka
Chu
Lake Balkhash
Ayaguz
L. Zaysan
Tarbagatay Range
Aktogay
Zaysan
Kara Irtysh
Ubsa Nur
Ulan Gom
Khöbsögöl Dalai
Ölögey
Hirgis Nur
Altai
Kara Usa Nur
Hovd
Kara Nur
Mörön
Selenga
Bulagan
Chimkent
Dzhambul
Tashkent
Ili
L. Alakol
Uliastaj
UZBEKISTAN SSR
Talasskiy Ala Tau
Frunze
Alma Ata
Ebi Nor
KIRGIZSTAN S.S.R.
Issyk Kul
Leninabad
Namangan
Kokand
Andizhan
Dzungaria
Altai
M O N G O
Altaj
Przhevalsk
Pobedy 24406
Urumchi
TADZHIKISTAN S.S.R.
Dushanbe
Pk. Lenina 23405
Pk. Kommunizma 24590
Artush
T'ien Shan
Aksu
Kucha
Kara-Shahr
Turfan
Turfan Depression -505
Faizabad
AFGHANISTAN
Kashgar
Turkestan
SINKIANG-UIGHUR
Tarim
Baghrash Köl
Hami
16158
Gobi
PAMIRS
Kungur 25325
Yarkand
Hindu Kush
Lop Nor
Chitral
Gilgit
Guma
Takla Makan
Khotan
KANSU
Edsin Gol
NINGSIA
Hsiapa
Malakand
Peshawar
Khyber Pass
KARAKORAM
K2 28250
Charchan
Charkhlik
Ansi
Yümen
Tunchwang
Altyn Tagh
Nan Shan
Indus
18290 Karakoram Pass
23688
Kunlun
PAKISTAN
Islamabad
Rawalpindi
Jhelum
JAMMU AND KASHMIR
Srinagar
KARAKORAM RANGE
Leh
Mangyai
Tatsaitan
Kara Nor
Gujranwala
Jammu
Sialkot
Lahore
Ravi
HIMACHAL PRADESH
Rudok
Wuwei
Ching Hai
TSINGHAI
Sining
Lanchow
Sutlej
Amritsar
Ludhiana
Jullundur
PUNJAB
Aling Kangri 24000
Tibetan Plateau
Simla
Ambala
HARYANA
Gartok
TIBET
Bayan Kara Shan
Hwang Ho
Linsia
Lintan
Lungsi
Tienshui
Joma 22310
Dehra Dun
Saharanpur
Nanda Devi 25645
Meerut
Delhi
New Delhi
Tangla Range
Yangtze Kiang
Yushu
Ziling Tso
C H I N A
HIMALAYA
RAJASTHAN
Jaipur
Mathura
Moradabad
Aligarh
Bareilly
UTTAR PRADESH
Shahjahanpur
Dhaulagiri 26810
Annapurna 26504
Agra
NEPAL
Nam Tso
Changtu
Chambal
Gwalior
Yamuna
Lucknow
Kanpur
Faizabad
Ghaghara
Gorakhpur
Katmandu
Mt. Everest 29028
Kanchenjunga 28168
Shigatse
Gyangtse
Lhasa
Tsangpo or Brahmaputra
Mekong
Salween
Paan
SZECHWAN
Chengtu
Kangting
Loshan
Chungking
Jhansi
Allahabad
Varanasi
Ganges
Muzaffarpur
SIKKIM
Gangtok
Thimphu
Darjeeling
BHUTAN
24900 Minya Konka
Yalung Kiang
Tzekung
Ipin
Luchow
Sagar
Bijawar
Bhopal
Tropic of Cancer
Narmada
INDIA
Murwara
MADHYA PRADESH
Jabalpur
Darbhanga
Patna
Monghyr
Bihar
Gaya
BIHAR
Bhagalpur
Jalpaiguri
Saidpur
Jamalpur
ASSAM
Brahmaputra
Dibrugarh
Sadiya
Tehtsin
Gauhati
Tezpur
MEGHALAYA
Shillong
Putao
Kachin State
NAGALAND
Kohima
KWEICHOW
Kweiyang
Chhindwara
Amraoti
Nagpur
Wardha
Raipur
Ranchi
Jamshedpur
Asansol
BENGAL
BANGLADESH
Sylhet
Silchar
MANIPUR
Imphal
Chindwin
Myitkyina
MAHARASHTRA
Raigarh
Bilaspur
Sarangarh
Dacca
Agartala
TRIPURA
Thaungdut
Tengchung
Paoshan
Kunming
Chanda
Kanker
Sambalpur
Kharagpur
Howrah
Calcutta
Bhatpara
Khulna
Sundarbans
Bhamo
Katha
Mienning
YUNNAN
11483
Hungshui Ho
ORISSA
Indravati
Balasore
Chin Hills
Warangal
Godavari
Jagdalpur
Shubaneswar
Cuttack
Chittagong
Shwebo
Lashio
Kingku
Mengtsz
Berhampur
Puri
Cox's Bazar
Irrawaddy
Arakan Yoma
Mandalay
Red
Laokay
Ha Giang
ANDHRA PRADESH
Myingyan
BURMA
Shan State
Meiktila
Akyab
Phong Saly
Rajahmundry
Kakinada
Vishakhapatnam
Taung-gyi
Kengtung
Yamethin
Hanoi
Guntur
Vijayawada
Bandar
BAY OF BENGAL
Pyinmana
KAWTHOOLEI
Luang Prabang
Xieng Khouang
Nam Dinh
Sandoway
Prome
Pegu Yoma
KAYAH
Chiang Mai
M. Lampang
Mekong
LAOS
VIETNAM
Tharrawaddy
Sittang
THAILAND
Pak Lay
Vinh
Pegu
Uttaradit
Vientiane

U.S.S.R.
HEILUNGKIANG
KIRIN
LIAONING
MONGOLIA
HOPEH
SHANSI
SHANTUNG
HONAN
KIANGSU
ANHWEI
HUPEH
HUNAN
KIANGSI
CHEKIANG
FUKIEN
KWANGTUNG
CHUANG
CHINA
NORTH CHINA PLAIN
NORTH KOREA
SOUTH KOREA
JAPAN
HONSHU
HOKKAIDO
SHIKOKU
KYUSHU
TAIWAN (FORMOSA)
PHILIPPINES
LUZON
HAINAN
HONG KONG (Br.)
Macao (Port.)
SEA OF JAPAN
YELLOW SEA
EAST CHINA SEA
SOUTH CHINA SEA
PACIFIC OCEAN
Gulf of Chihli
Korea Bay
Liaotung Bay
Liaotung Peninsula
Shantung Pen.
Korea Strait
Formosa Strait
Bashi Channel
Luzon Strait
La Perouse Strait
Tropic of Cancer
Great Khingan Shan
Lit. Khingan Shan
Sikhote Alin Range
Great Wall
Amur
Argun
Shilka
Kerulen
Sungari
Hwai Ho
Sangkan Ho
Yangtze Kiang
Tung Ting Hu
Poyang Hu
Si Kiang
Hulun Chih
Khanka
Sakhalin
Kuril Islands
Ryukyu Islands
Osumi Gunto
Oki gunto
Tsushima
Quelpart
Amami
Tokuno
Okinawa
Naha
Miyako
Iriomote
Matsu Is.
Batan Islands
Babuyan Islands
Luichow Peninsula
Chita
Shilka
Borzya
Hailar
Svobodnyy
Blagoveshchensk
Khabarovsk
Birobidzhan
Bikin
Dalnerechensk
Ussuriysk
Vladivostok
Olga
Yuzhno Sakhalinsk
Wakkanai
Asahigawa
Sapporo
Otaru
Muroran
Hakodate
Kushiro
Iturup
Kunashir
Aomori
Hachinohe
Morioka
Akita
Sendai
Yamagata
Niigata
Utsunomiya
Tokyo
Yokohama
Kawasaki
Kanazawa
Toyama
Fujiyama
Gifu
Nagoya
Shizuoka
Hamamatsu
Kyoto
Osaka
Kobe
Amagasaki
Wakayama
Okayama
Hiroshima
Takamatsu
Matsuyama
Shimonoseki
Kitakyushu
Fukuoka
Omuta
Kumamoto
Sasebo
Nagasaki
Kagoshima
Chongjin
Hungnam
Wonsan
Kangnung
Pyongyang
Nampo
Kaesong
Seoul
Inchon
Chonju
Taejon
Taegu
Pusan
Masan
Kwangju
Mokpo
Sayn Shand
Tamsag Bulag
Erhlien
Nunkiang
Pokotu
Pehan
Tsitsihar
Hailun
Ilan
Fuchin
Harbin
Mutankiang
Taonan
Fuyu
Changchun
Kirin
Liaoyuan
Shenyang
Fushun
Penki
Anshan
Yingkow
Antung
Chihfeng
Chinchow
Lüta
Chiangkiakow
Chengte
Huhehot
Peking
Tangshan
Tientsin
Paoting
Ningwu
Taiyuan
Shihkiachwang
Fenyang
Tsinan
Liaochen
Tzepo
Weifang
Yentai
Weihai
Tsingtao
Anyang
Tsining
Tenghsien
Lienyunkang
Sinhailien
Loyang
Chengchow
Kaifeng
Suchow
Tungkwan
Hwaian
Pohsien
Pengpu
Taichow
Nantung
Chinkiang
Nanking
Wusih
Soochow
Shanghai
Kashing
Hofei
Wuhu
Kwanghua
Siangfan
Siangyang
Fengkieh
Ichang
Kiangling
Shasi
Wuhan
Hwangkang
Hwangshih
Anking
Kiukiang
Hangchow
Shaohing
Ningpo
Chuhsien
Lishui
Wenchow
Changteh
Nanchang
Changsha
Siangtan
Shaoyang
Kian
Kienyang
Nanping
Foochow
Changting
Putien
Kanchow
Chuanchow
Changchow
Amoy
Shiukwan
Kweilin
Yingtak
Chaochow
Swatow
Wuchow
Kweiping
Fatshan
Kwangchow
Kowloon
Victoria
Chanchiang
Haikow
Chilung
Taipei
Taichung
Hualien
Taitung
Tainan
Kaohsiung
Aparri
Laoag
Tuguegarao
Ilagan
Relief
Feet
Metres
16 404
5000
9843
3000
6562
2000
3281
1000
1640
500
656
200
0
Sea Level
Land Dep.
656
200
13123
4000
22966
7000
Scale 1:16 000 000
0
100
200
300
400
500 Miles
0
200
400
600
800 Kms.
Conic Projection
© Collins-Longman Atlases

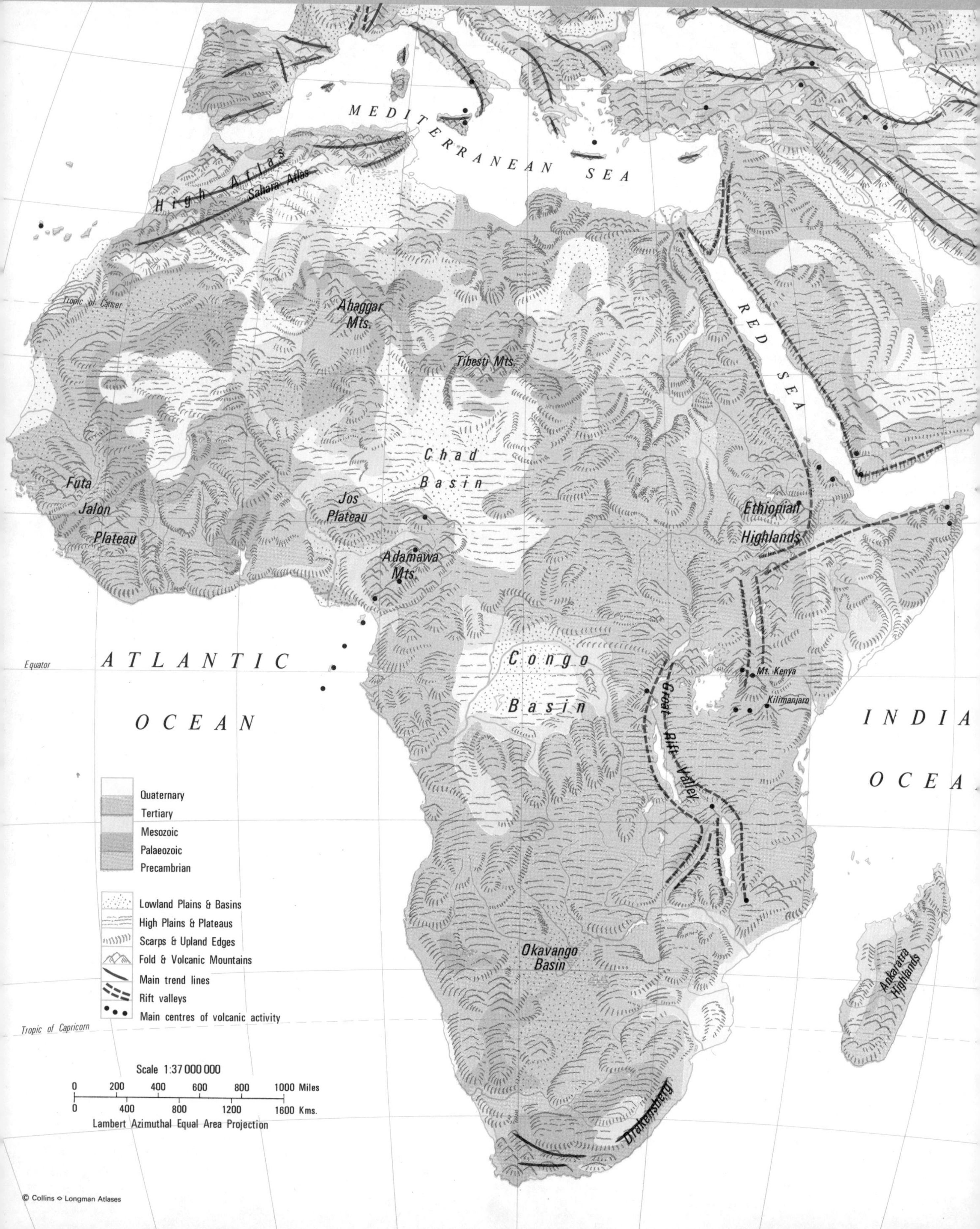

MEDITERRANEAN SEA
High Atlas
Sahara Atlas
Tropic of Cancer
Ahaggar Mts.
Tibesti Mts.
RED SEA
Chad Basin
Futa Jalon Plateau
Jos Plateau
Adamawa Mts.
Ethiopian Highlands
Equator
ATLANTIC OCEAN
Congo Basin
Mt. Kenya
Kilimanjaro
Great Rift Valley
INDIA
OCEA
Quaternary
Tertiary
Mesozoic
Palaeozoic
Precambrian
Lowland Plains & Basins
High Plains & Plateaus
Scarps & Upland Edges
Fold & Volcanic Mountains
Main trend lines
Rift valleys
Main centres of volcanic activity
Okavango Basin
Ankaratra Highlands
Tropic of Capricorn
Scale 1:37 000 000
0 200 400 600 800 1000 Miles
0 400 800 1200 1600 Kms.
Lambert Azimuthal Equal Area Projection
Drakensberg

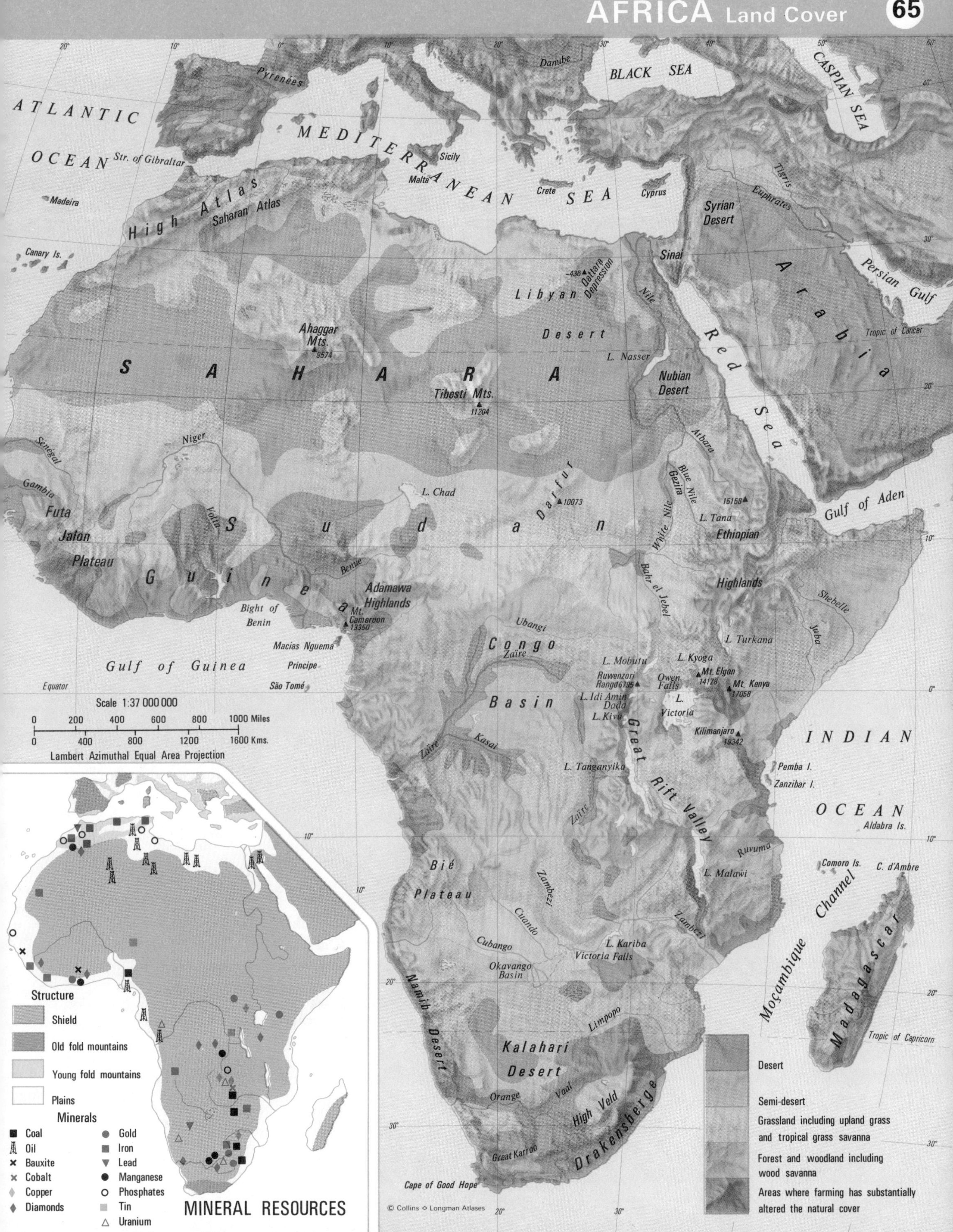
ATLANTIC
OCEAN
MEDITERRANEAN SEA
BLACK SEA
CASPIAN SEA
Pyrenées
Danube
Str. of Gibraltar
Sicily
Malta
Crete
Cyprus
Madeira
High Atlas
Saharan Atlas
Canary Is.
Syrian Desert
Tigris
Euphrates
Sinai
Persian Gulf
Arabia
Tropic of Cancer
Libyan Desert
-436 Qattara Depression
Nile
Red Sea
Ahaggar Mts. 9574
SAHARA
Tibesti Mts. 11204
L. Nasser
Nubian Desert
Niger
Sénégal
Gambia
Atbara
Blue Nile
Gezira
15158
L. Tana
Gulf of Aden
L. Chad
Darfur 10073
Futa Jalon Plateau
Volta
Sudan
White Nile
Ethiopian Highlands
Guinea
Benue
Adamawa Highlands
Bahr el Jebel
Shebelle
Bight of Benin
Mt. Cameroon 13350
Ubangi
Juba
L. Turkana
Macias Nguema
Congo Basin
Zaïre
Principe
São Tomé
Gulf of Guinea
Equator
L. Mobutu
L. Kyoga
Ruwenzori Range 16795
Owen Falls
Mt. Elgon 14178
Mt. Kenya 17058
L. Idi Amin Dada
L. Kiva
L. Victoria
Kilimanjaro 19342
Scale 1:37 000 000
0 200 400 600 800 1000 Miles
0 400 800 1200 1600 Kms.
Lambert Azimuthal Equal Area Projection
Kasai
Great Rift Valley
INDIAN OCEAN
L. Tanganyika
Pemba I.
Zanzibar I.
Aldabra Is.
Ruvuma
Bié Plateau
Zambezi
L. Malawi
Comoro Is.
C. d'Ambre
Moçambique Channel
Cuando
Cubango
L. Kariba
Victoria Falls
Madagascar
Okavango Basin
Namib Desert
Limpopo
Tropic of Capricorn
Kalahari Desert
Orange
Vaal
High Veld
Drakensberge
Great Karroo
Cape of Good Hope
© Collins - Longman Atlases
Desert
Semi-desert
Grassland including upland grass and tropical grass savanna
Forest and woodland including wood savanna
Areas where farming has substantially altered the natural cover
MINERAL RESOURCES
Structure
Shield
Old fold mountains
Young fold mountains
Plains
Minerals
Coal
Oil
Bauxite
Cobalt
Copper
Diamonds
Gold
Iron
Lead
Manganese
Phosphates
Tin
Uranium

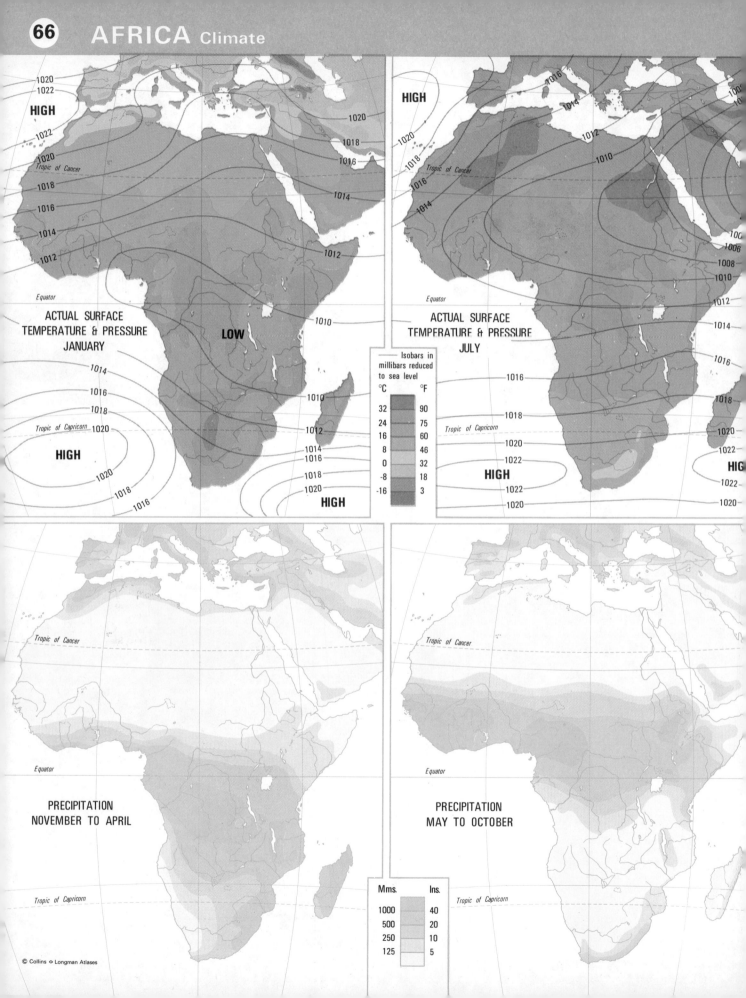

ACTUAL SURFACE TEMPERATURE & PRESSURE JANUARY

ACTUAL SURFACE TEMPERATURE & PRESSURE JULY

Isobars in millibars reduced to sea level

°C	°F
32	90
24	75
16	60
8	46
0	32
-8	18
-16	3

PRECIPITATION NOVEMBER TO APRIL

PRECIPITATION MAY TO OCTOBER

Mms.	Ins.
1000	40
500	20
250	10
125	5

ALGERIA
LIBYA
EGYPT
MOROCCO
WESTERN SAHARA
MAURITANIA
MALI
NIGER
CHAD
SUDAN
ETHIOPIA
NIGERIA
CAMEROON
CENTRAL AFRICAN REPUBLIC
ZAÏRE
CONGO
GABON
KENYA
UGANDA
TANZANIA
ANGOLA
ZAMBIA
RHODESIA
BOTSWANA
SOUTH WEST AFRICA (NAMIBIA)
REPUBLIC OF SOUTH AFRICA
MOCAMBIQUE
MALAWI
MALAGASY REPUBLIC
SOMALI REPUBLIC
TUNISIA
SAUDI ARABIA
TURKEY
IRAN
IRAQ
U.S.S.R.
SPAIN
PORTUGAL
FRANCE
ITALY
YUGOSLAVIA
ROMANIA
BULGARIA
GREECE
ALBANIA
Mediterranean Sea
Black Sea
RED SEA
Gulf of Guinea
ATLANTIC OCEAN
INDIAN OCEAN
Mocambique Channel
Tropic of Cancer
Tropic of Capricorn
Equator
Scale 1:37 000 000
0 200 400 600 800 1000 Miles
0 400 800 1200 1600 Kms.
Lambert Azimuthal Equal Area Projection
POPULATION
Persons per sq. mile
Over 250
125-250
25-125
2-25
0-2
over 1,000,000 population
Longman Atlases

FRANCE
Marseille
Nice
Florence
Sarajevo
Adriatic Sea
ANDORRA
Oporto
Valladolid
Zaragoza
PORTUGAL
SPAIN
Madrid
Barcelona
Corsica (Fr.)
Rome
ITALY
Bari
Naples
Lisbon
Valencia
Majorca
Minorca
Sardinia (It.)
Palma
Iviza
Balearic Islands (Sp.)
Cagliari
MEDITERRANEAN
Seville
Cartagena
Palermo
Messina
Sicily
Catania
Gibraltar (Br.)
Algiers
Bejaïa
Annaba
Bizerta
El Asnam
Tunis
Tangier
Ceuta (Sp.)
Oran
Melilla (Sp.)
Blida
Tell Atlas
Constantine
Kairouan
Sousse
MALTA
Tetuan
Oujda
Sidi-bel-Abbès
Rabat
Fez
Tlemcen
Saharan Atlas
Biskra
Sfax
Meknès
Chott ech Chergui
Djelfa
Chott Melrhir
TUNISIA
Casablanca
Khenifra
G. of Gabes
Gabès
Madeira (Port.)
Safi
MOROCCO
High Atlas
Tendrara
Chott Djerid
Medenine
Aïn Sefra
Touggourt
Tripoli
Misurata
Marrakesh
Toubkal
13661
Ghardaïa
Béchar
Hassi Messaoud
Ouargla
Abadla
Nalut
Gulf of Sirte
Sirte
ATLANTIC OCEAN
Canary Islands (Sp.)
La Palma
Lanzarote
Tenerife
Las Palmas
Gran Canaria
Fuerteventura
Wadi Dra
El Goléa
Ghadames
Tripolitania
Tademait Plateau
ALGERIA
Hun
El Aaiún
Ain Salah
LIBYA
Reggan
Fort Polignac
Sebha
WESTERN SAHARA
Villa Cisneros
Murzuq
Ghat
El Qatrun
Tropic of Cancer
Fdérik
Ahaggar Mts
Mt. Tahat 9574
Tamanrasset
Tummo
C Blanc
Nouadhibou
Djado Plateau
Atar
Bardai
10335
Tibesti
MAURITANIA
Emi Koussi 11204
Nouakchott
Tidjikja
SAHARA
Kidal
Aïr or Azbine
5910
Timbuktu
Bodélé Depression
St. Louis
Gao
MALI
NIGER
Agadès
Senegal
C Verde
Diourbel
Nioro
Dakar
SENEGAL
Kayes
Banjul
GAMBIA
Tambacounda
Mopti
Niamey
Birni N'Konni
Nguigmi
Lake Chad
CHAD
Niger
Maradi
Zinder
Bissau
GUINEA BISSAU
Bamako
San
UPPER VOLTA
Sokoto
Nguru
Yao
Bijagos Archipelago
Futa Jalon
Labé
Ouagadougou
Katsina
Kaura Namoda
Kano
Boké
Sikasso
Maiduguri
N'Djamena
GUINEA
Bobo-Dioulasso
Navrongo
Sansanné-Mango
Zaria
Kankan
Kaduna
Bauchi
Chari
Conakry
Black Volta
White Volta
BENIN
Minna
Jos
Maroua
SIERRA LEONE
Beyla
Tamale
Parakou
Logone
Freetown
NIGERIA
Garoua
Bo
IVORY COAST
Bouaké
GHANA
Ilorin
Ogbomosho
Benue
Savé
Ibadan
Oshogbo
Adamawa Highlands
Sunyani
Lake Volta
Porto-Novo
Makurdi
Ngaoundéré
LIBERIA
Monrovia
Daloa
Kumasi
TOGO
Benin City
Onitsha
Fort Crampel
CENTRAL
Abidjan
Lomé
Cotonou
Lagos
Enugu
Tibati
Accra
Bight of Benin
CAMEROON
Bambari
Sassandra
Sekondi-Takoradi
Warri
Calabar
Mt. Cameroon 13350
Nkongsamba
Carnot
Ft. Sibut
C Palmas
Niger Delta
Port Harcourt
Douala
Sanaga
Bangui
Malabo
Yaoundé
Gulf of Guinea
EQUATORIAL GUINEA
Ubangi
Zaïre
Scale 1:20 000 000
0 100 200 300 400 500 Miles
0 200 400 600 800 Kms.
Principe
Bata
Equator
CONGO
Lambert Azimuthal Equal Area Projection
São Tomé
Libreville
GABON
C Lopez
Lambaréné
40°
30°
20°
10°
0°

BULGARIA
Sofia
Varna
Black Sea
Caucasus Mts
Batumi
Tbilisi
Kara Bogaz Gol Bay
Krasnovodsk
U. S. S. R.
Amu Darya
Bukhara
Chardzhou
Turkestan
Istanbul
Samsun
Baku
Caspian Sea
Thessaloniki
Mt Olympus
9550
Ankara
Bursa
L. Sevan
Yerevan
Mt Ararat
16946
Ashkhabad
Mary
TURKEY
Aegean Sea
Athens
Izmir
Konya
Kayseri
Tuz
Mt Erciyas
12848
Tabriz
15784
Rasht
L. Urmia
L. Van
Kurdistan
Bandar-e-Shah
Mashhad
Elburz Mts
18376
Demavend
Tehran
Kushka
Antalya
Taurus Mts
Adana
Aleppo
Mosul
Herat
Hari
AFGHANISTAN
Rhodes
Iráklion
Crete
Nicosia
CYPRUS
SYRIA
Euphrates
Tigris
Mesopotamia
Homs
Hamadān
Kermānshāhān
Dasht-e-Kavir
(Salt Desert)
SEA
LEBANON
Beirut
Damascus
IRAQ
Baghdad
IRAN
Zagros
Isfahan
Yazd
Dasht-e-Lut
Syrian Desert
Derna
Tobruk
Salûm
Tel Aviv
Jaffa
Amman
Jerusalem
Dead Sea
JORDAN
ISRAEL
Ahwaz
Kermān
Kuh-i-Dinar
14029
Mountains
Alexandria
Port Said
Cairo
Suez Canal
Tanta
El Alamein
Basra
Abadan
Shiraz
Zahedan
KUWAIT
NEUT
Kuwait
Bushire
Jaghbub
Qattara Depression
El Giza
Suez
El Faiyûm
Aqaba
Sinai
Mt Katherina
8651
Al Jauf
An Nafud
Persian Gulf
Bandar Abbas
Makran
Libyan Desert
Hail
Asyût
7173
EGYPT
Qena
Quseir
Luxor
El Khârga
Aswân
Aswân High Dam
L. Nasser
6488
Anaiza
Dhahran
BAHRAIN
QATAR
Hofuf
Dubai
(Oman)
Gulf of Oman
Muscat
SAUDI ARABIA
Riyadh
Medina
HEJAZ
NEJD
Tropic of Cancer
UNION OF ARAB EMIRATES
W. Hajar
E. Hajar
El Jauf
Red Sea
7271
Juddah
Mecca
Wadi Halfa
Nubian Desert
Port Sudan
Suakin
Abu Hamed
Dongola
Karima
Nile
Merowe
Atbara
Ed Damer
ASIR
Tihama
Rub al Khali
OMAN
Salala
Kuria Muria Is
SOUTHERN YEMEN
Hadhramaut
Omdurman
Khartoum
Kassala
Agordat
Massawa
Asmara
Sana
YEMEN
Hodeida
Mukalla
Gulf of Aden
Darfur
SUDAN
Gezira
Wad Medani
Sennar
Aduwa
Ras Dashan
15158
Danakil
Taizz
Al Shaab
Aden
Perim
Assab
Geneina
El Fasher
El Obeid
Kosti
Gondar
Bab el Mandeb
Socotra
(S. Yemen)
C Guardafui
J. Gimbala
10073
Nyala
En Nahud
Er Rahad
Blue Nile
Er Roseires
Tana
FR. TERR. OF AFARS AND ISSAS
Djibouti
Zeila
Berbera
Erigavo
Ethiopian
Birhan
13629
Dessye
ETHIOPIA
El Muglad
White Nile
Malakal
Bahr el Ghazal
Sobat
Ankober
Diredawa
Harar
Hargeisa
Addis Ababa
Highlands
Jimma
Wau
Sudd
Bahr el Jebel
Akobo
RICAN
L. Abaya
Shebelle
SOMALI REPUBLIC
Obbia
Bomu
Zemio
Juba
Monga
Uele
Niangara
Lake Turkana
Buta
Isiro
Pakwach
Albert Nile
Gulu
Iscia Baidoa
Bardera
Juba
Mogadishu
L. Mobutu
Soroti
Mt Elgon
14178
UGANDA
KENYA
Wajir
ZAÏRE
Kisangani
Boyoma Falls
16795
Ruwenzori Ra
Kasese
L. Idi Amin Dada
Kampala
Owen Falls Dam
Jinja
Lake Victoria
Entebbe
Eldoret
Kisumu
Mt Kenya
17058
Garissa
Kismayu
Equator
Relief
Feet
Metres
16404
5000
9843
3000
6562
2000
3281
1000
1640
500
656
200
0
Sea Level
Land Dep.
656
200
13123
4000
22966
7000
© Collins • Longman Atlases

WEST AFRICA

WESTERN SAHARA

MAURITANIA

MALI

SENEGAL

GAMBIA

GUINEA BISSAU

GUINEA

SIERRA LEONE

LIBERIA

IVORY COAST

UPPER VOLTA

GHANA

ATLANTIC OCEAN

S A

SAOU

Nouadhibou

C Blanc

Fdérik

Zouerate

Taoudenni

Atar

Akjoujt

Tidjikja

Nouakchott

Araouane

Méderdra

Bogué

Podor

Dagana

Kaédi

Kiffa

Néma

St. Louis

Sénégal

Louga

Matam

Linguère

Bamba

Bourem

Gourma-Rarous

Timbuktu

Niger

Goundam

Gao

C Verde

Dakar

Rufisque

Thiés

Diourbel

Bakel

Nioro

Nara

Sokolo

Kayes

Douentza

Mopti

Kaolack

Falémé

Baoulé

Djenne

Dori

Banjul

Tambacounda

Gambia

Bafoulabé

Ségou

Bani

Ouahigouya

Bignona

Sédhiou

Kita

San

Ziguinchor

Farim

Kédougou

Satadougou

Kati

Koulikoro

Bamako

Bissau

Bafing

Koutiala

Ouagadougou

Bolamo

Futa Jalon

5042

Yambering

Tinkisso

Bijagos Archipelago

Gaoual

Labé

Siguiri

Bougouni

Bagoe

Black Volta

Red Volta

Boké

Telimélé

Pita

Houndé

Sikasso

Bobo-Dioulasso

Pô

Dabola

Kouroussa

Lawra

Navrongo

UPPER

Boffa

Konkouré

Mamou

Faranah

Kankan

Volta

Sansanné Mango

Kindia

Wa

White Volta

Milo

Odienné

Boundiali

Tamale

Conakry

Forécariah

Kabala

Korhogo

Ferkéssédougou

Kissidougou

Bouna

NORTHERN

Makeni

Port Loko

Rokel

Magburaka

Sefadu

Bole

Freetown

Macenta

Beyla

Touba

Dabakala

Pendembu

Mankono

Bondoukou

Kete Krachi

Bo

Kenema

Nzérékoré

5800

Mt. Nimba

Séguéla

Bouaké

Sewa

Pujehun

Man

BRONG-AHAFO

Sherbro I.

Sunyani

Lake Volta

Bouaflé

ASHANTI

Daloa

Dimbokro

Abengourou

Kumasi

Monrovia

Awaso

Obuasi

EASTERN

Cavally

Gagnoa

Sassandra

Bandama

Agboville

Dunkwa

Koforidua

Enchi

Tano

Kade

Buchanan

Oda

WESTERN

Abidjan

Bingerville

Prestea

CENTRAL

Accra

Winneba

Greenville

Port Bouet

Grand Bassam

Tarkwa

Cape Coast

Sassandra

Axim

Sekondi-Takoradi

C Palmas

Tabou

15° 10° 5° 0° 20°

Relief

Feet	Metres
16 404	5000
9843	3000
6562	2000
3281	1000
1640	500
656	200
0	Sea Level
Land Dep. 656	200
13 123	4000
22 966	7000

Scale 1:10 000 000

0 100 200 300 Miles

0 100 200 300 400 Kms.

Lambert Azimuthal Equal Area Projection

NIGERIA
CENTRAL AFRICAN REPUBLI
CAMEROON
EQUATORIAL GUINEA
GABON
CONGO
ZAÏRE
ANGOLA
SOUTH WEST AFRICA (NAMIBIA)

Gulf of Guinea
Bight of Bonny
ATLANTIC OCEAN

Principe
São Tomé
Equator
C. Lopez

Niger
Aba
Port Harcourt
Bonny
Calabar
Dschang
Foumban
Banganté
Bafia
N'Kongsamba
M'Bangé
Mt. Cameroon 13350
Tiko
Victoria
Douala
Malabo
Edea
Yaoundé
Nyong
Kribi
Ebolowa
Campo
Bata
Bétaré-Oya
Yoko
Sanaga
Bertoua
Batouri
Doumé
Carnot
Berbérati
Kadei
Ekela
M'Baere
Lobaye
Yokadouma
Lomié
Dja
Boumba
Nola
Lopi
Kom
Aïna
Bossembelé
Ft. de Possel
Kouango
Bangui
Zongo
M'Baiki
Libenge
Bosobolo
Mobaye
Bangassou
Rafai
Zemio
Bomu
Bili
Monga
Bondo
Yasanyama
Uele
Gemena
Businga
Ebola
Karawa
Mongala
Budjala
Dua
Komba
Aketi
Buta
Lisala
Bumba
Itimbiri
Tele
Lua
Ubangi
Dongou
Impfondo
Nouvelle Anvers
Busu Djanoa
Lopari
Bongandanga
Basoko
Aruwimi
Yahuma
Isangi
Djolu
Bomongo
Lulonga
Basankusu
EQUATEUR
Bolomba
Befale
Ikelemba
Mbandaka
Giri
Likouala
Sangha
Ouesso
Liouesso
Lengoue
Djouah
Makokou
Mitzic
Ivindo
Libreville
Gabon
Kango
Booué
Ndjolé
Chinchoua
Lambaréné
Port Gentil
Ogowe
Fougamou
Lastoursville
5185
Moanda
Franceville
Mouila
Mbinda
N'Dendé
Setté Cama
Tchibanga
Nyanga
Mayoumba
Banda
Likona
Makoua
Kouyou
Ft. Rousset
Alima
Gamboma
M'Pama
N'Gao
M'Pouya
Djambala
Bolobo
Mushie
Kwamouth
Bandundu
Sibiti
Loudima
Dolisie
Brazzaville
Kinshasa
Malebo Pool
Congo
Ikelemba
Busira
Ingende
Boende
Maringa
Tshuapa
Bokungu
Yapehe
Ubun
Opala
Lomami
Bikoro
L. Tumba
Zaïre
Lokolo
Kiri
Lotoi
Lulaka
Monkoto
Salonga
Lomela
Ikela
Inongo
Mai Ndombe
Lokoro
Kutu
Fimi
Lukenie
Kasai
Oshwe
Dekese
Lodja
Kole
Katako Kombe
KASAI ORIENTAL
BANDUNDU
Kwilu
Lubefu
Ilebo
Basongo
KASAI
Mweka
Lubudi
Sankuru
Lusambo
Luebo
Demba
Dimbelenge
Tshofa
Kananga
Mbuji Mayi
Kabinda
OCCIDENTAL
Tshikapa
Kazumba
Dibaya
Gandajika
Luisa
Mwene Ditu
Kaniama
Lubilash
Luilu
Kapanga
Lulua
Kasai
Kamina
Sandoa
SH
Lubudi
Kenge
Masi-Manimba
Kikwit
Idiofa
Gungu
Bakali
Lukula
Kwango
Popokabaka
Inzia
Feshi
Kwenge
Kasongo-Lunda
Loange
Lovua
Wamba
Kahemba
Portugalia
Vila Verissimo Sarmento
Chiumbe
Luachimo
Caungula
Cuilo
Cachimo
Cuango
LUNDA
Henrique de Carvalho
Cacolo
Malonga
Teixeira de Sousa
Dilolo
Lago Dilolo
Kolwe
Caianda
Nana Candundo
Zambezi
Mwinilunga
Cazombo
Cameia Nat. Park
Luena
Mozico
MOXICO
Lungwebungu
Zambezi
Kabompo
Manyinga
Gago Coutinho
Luanginga
Z
Luena
Mongu
Zambezi
Senanga
Southern Lueti
Kataba
Ngonye Falls
Ngambwe Rapids
Sesheke
Katima Rapids
Chobe
Kasan
Caprivi Strip
Luiana
Andara
Okavango
Utembo
Cubia
Neriquinha
Mavinga
Luengue
Cuito
Cuangar
CUANDO-CUBANGO
Cuando
Longa
Cubango
Cangamba
5098
Menongue
Cuchi
Vila da Ponte
Galangue
Cunene
Plateau
Evale
Roçadas
Vila Pereira de Eça
Ovambo
Cunene
Capelongo
Chibemba
HUILA
Lubango
7464
João de Almeida
Moçâmedes
Porto Alexandre
5905
MOÇÂMEDES
Quilengues
Caconda
5676
Dombe Grande
V. Mariano Machado
Benguela
BENGUELA
Lobito
8597
HUAMBO
Huambo
Bié
V. Silva Porto
BIÉ
Norton de Matos
Vila Teixeira da Silva
Vila Gen. Machado
Vila Luso
Cassai
Vila Nova do Seles
8130
Cela
Andulo
Luando Game Reserve
Novo Redondo
Gabela
Porto Amboim
Quibala
CUANZA SUL
Mussende
Calulo
Nova Gaia
Jombo
Dondo
Cuanza
Malanje
MALANJE
Quela
Duque de Bragança
Falls
Monte Verde
Quicama Nat. Park
Muxima
Luanda
LUANDA
Pta. das Palmeirinhas
Catete
Vila Salazar
CUANZA NORTE
Quibaxi
Dande
Caxito
Camabatela
Uige
UIGE
Ambriz
Loje
Ambrizete
M'bridge
Damba
Sanza Pombo
Tembo Aluma
Quimbele
Maquela do Zombo
São Salvador do Congo
ZAIRE
S. Antonio do Zaire
Banana
Cabinda
Boma
Matadi
Songololo
Lukula
BAS ZAÏRE
Tshela
Zaïre
Necuto
Buco Zau
Pointe Noire
Guilherne Capelo
Ihe
ANGOLA

Relief

Feet	Metres
16404	5000
9843	3000
6562	2000
3281	1000
1640	500
656	200
0	Sea Level
Land Dep. 656	200
13123	4000
22966	7000

Scale 1:10 750 000

0 100 200 300 Miles

0 100 200 300 400 500 Kms.

Lambert Azimuthal Equal Area Projection

SUDAN
ETHIOPIA
SOMALI REP
NORTH
EASTERN
KENYA
UGANDA
ZAÏRE
RWANDA
BURUNDI
TANZANIA
MALAWI
MOÇAMBIQUE
RHODESIA
ZAMBIA
MALAGASY REPUBLIC
INDIAN OCEAN
Moçambique Channel
Comoro Is. (France)
Grande Comore
Mohéli
Anjouan
Île Mayotte
Moroni
Juan de Nova
Equator
Lake Victoria
3720 ft above sea level
Lake Turkana
L. Chamo
L. Mobutu
L. Kyoga
L. George
L. Idi Amin Dada
Lake Kivu
Lake Tanganyika
2534 ft a.s.l.
L. Rukwa
Lake Mweru
Lake Bangweulu
L. Malawi (L. Nyasa)
1550 ft a.s.l.
Lake Kariba
L. Chilwa
L. Chiuta
L. Natron
L. Eyasi
L. Manyara
L. Bisina
EAST RIFT VALLEY
WESTERN
NYANZA
CENTRAL
COAST
WEST LAKE
MARA
MWANZA
SHINYANGA
ARUSHA
KILIMANJARO
TANGA
KIGOMA
TABORA
SINGIDA
DODOMA
RUKWA
MBEYA
IRINGA
MOROGORO
MTWARA
RUVUMA
CABO DELGADO
NIASSA
TETE
ZAMBEZIA
MANICA E SOFALA
Mogadishu
Nairobi
Kampala
Dar es Salaam
Lusaka
Salisbury
Mombasa
Tanga
Zanzibar
Pemba I.
Zanzibar I.
Mafia I.
Pate I.
Mt. Kenya 17058
Kilimanjaro 19342
Mt. Elgon 14178
Meru 14979
Loolmalasin 11969
Ngorongoro Crater
Hanang 11215
Ruwenzori Range 16795
Mt. Karisimbi 14787
Kinyeti 10456
Lotuke 9170
Mt. Nyiru 9203
Mathews' Peak 7792
Mt. Rungwe 9715
Kipengere Range
Nkungwe Mt. 8250
Mitumba Mts.
Muchinga Mts.
Uluguru Mts.
Usambara Mts.
Mulanje Mts.
Nyika Plateau
Masai Steppe
Serengeti Nat. Park
Serengeti Plain
Tsavo National Park
Kabalega Falls Nat. Park
Kabalega Falls
Owen Falls Dam
Kariba Dam
Kafue Dam
Cabora Bassa Dam
Livingstone Memorial
Copper Belt
Kafue Swamp
Aberdare Range
Zambezi
Shire
Ruvuma
Rufiji
Tana
Galana
Juba
Shebelle
Dawa Palma
Ganale Dorya
Lagh Dera
Laga Bor
Bahr el Jebel (Wh. Nile)
Albert Nile
Victoria Nile
Kibali
Uele
Ituri
Lukuga
Luapula
Luangwa
Chambeshi
Great Ruaha
Kilombero
Luwegu
Matandu
Lugenda
Lurio
Messalo
Juba
Mongalla
Maridi
Yei
Loka
Torit
Nagishot
Kapoeta
Murle
Mega
Moyale
Dolo
Belet Wen
Oddur
Lugh Ganana
Iscia Baidoa
Mahaddei Wen
Bardera
Merca
Brava
Afmadu
Kismayu
Wajir
El Wak
Mandera
Marsabit
North Horr
South Horr
Lodwar
Lokitaung
Maralal
Wamba
Archers Post
Isiolo
Mado Gashi
Garissa
Nanyuki
Nyeri
Embu
Muranga
Kitui
Nyahururu
Nakuru
Naivasha
Gilgil
Narok
Ngong
Magadi
Konza
Namanga
Kibwezi
Voi
Taveta
Witu
Lamu
Kipini
Malindi
Kilifi
Kwale
Vanga
Eldoret
Kitale
Kapsabet
Kakamega
Kisumu
Kericho
Sotik
Kisii
Tororo
Mbale
Soroti
Lira
Gulu
Kitgum
Moroto
Arua
Nimule
Kajo Kaji
Rhino Camp
Pakwach
Masindi
Hoima
Butiaba
Fort Portal
Mubende
Jinja
Entebbe
Masaka
Mbarara
Kabale
Kasese
Mbulamuti
Kigali
Biumba
Bujumbura
Gitega
Ngozi
Muyinga
Ruyigi
Rutana
Bururi
Butari
Bukavu
Goma
Rutshuru
Uvira
Fizi
Beni
Bunia
Djugu
Mahagi
Irumu
Mambasa
Wamba
Isiro
Mungbere
Dungu
Faradje
Niangara
Kalemie
Kabambare
Kongolo
Nyunzu
Manono
Moba
Pweto
Mitwaba
Lubumbashi
Kasenga
Bukoba
Kyaka
Musoma
Mwanza
Biharamulo
Nyakanazi
Kibondo
Kahama
Shinyanga
Nzega
Kigoma
Ujiji
Uvinza
Kaliua
Tabora
Tutubu
Tura
Manyoni
Singida
Kondoa
Arusha
Moshi
Same
Mkomazi
Lushoto
Korogwe
Handeni
Pangani
Sadani
Bagamoyo
Dodoma
Kongwa
Mpwapwa
Morogoro
Kilosa
Mikumi
Iringa
Mpanda
Inyonga
Kitunda
Rungwa
Karema
Mtakuja
Kipili
Sumbawanga
Kasanga
Mbala
Chunya
Mbeya
Tunduma
Tukuyu
Njombe
Mahenge
Utete
Mohoro
Kilwa Kivinje
Kilwa Masoko
Liwale
Nachingwea
Masasi
Lindi
Mchinja
Mikindani
Mtwara
Songea
Tunduru
Mbamba Bay
Manda
Cabo Delgado
Palma
Mocimboa da Praia
Mucojo
Quissanga
Ancuabe
Balama
Marrupa
Nungo
Maua
Pemba
Lurio
Ocua
Namapa
Memba
Nacala
Moçambique
Lalaua
Cuamba
Entre Rios
Ribaue
Nampula
Meconta
Chinga
Nametil
Mogincual
Namaponda
Antonio Enes
Alto Molocue
Gilé
Moma
Mocuba
Pebane
Namacurra
Quelimane
Vila da Maganja
Milange
Namarroi
Lichinga
Maniamba
Chitipa
Karonga
Chilumba
Livingstonia
Nkhata Bay
Chintheche
Mzimba
Bandawe
Nkhotakota
Kasungu
Dowa
Salima
Lilongwe
Dedza
Mchinji
Mangochi
Ft. Maguire
Zomba
Blantyre
Ntcheu
Chikwawa
Nsanje
Chiromo
Mulanje
Mkushi
Serenje
Mpika
Kasama
Isoka
Chinsali
Luwingu
Mporokoso
Kawambwa
Mansa
Luena
Mambilima Falls
Mufulira
Sakania
Kabunda
Kitwe
Ndola
Luanshya
Kapiri Mposhi
Kabwe
Mumbwa
Kafue
Mazabuka
Monze
Kariba
Sipolilo
Mt. Darwin
Shamva
Mazoe
Sinoia
Feira
Zumbo
Zambue
Chipata
Lundazi
Petauke
Katete
Vila Vasco da Gama
Furancungo
Vila Coutinho
Chipera
Matope
Magué
Moatize
Tete
Mungari
Chemba
Vila de Sena
Maringue
Chindio
Majunga
Soalala
Marovoay
C. St. André
Ambato Boeni
Besalampy
Mevatanana
Tambohorano
Kandreho
Ranobe
Ikopa

Scale 1:10 750 000

Miles 0 50 100 150 200 250

Kms 0 100 200 300 400

Relief

Feet	Metres
16404	5000
9843	3000
6562	2000
3281	1000
1640	500
656	200
0	Sea Level
Land Dep. 656	200
13123	4000
22966	7000

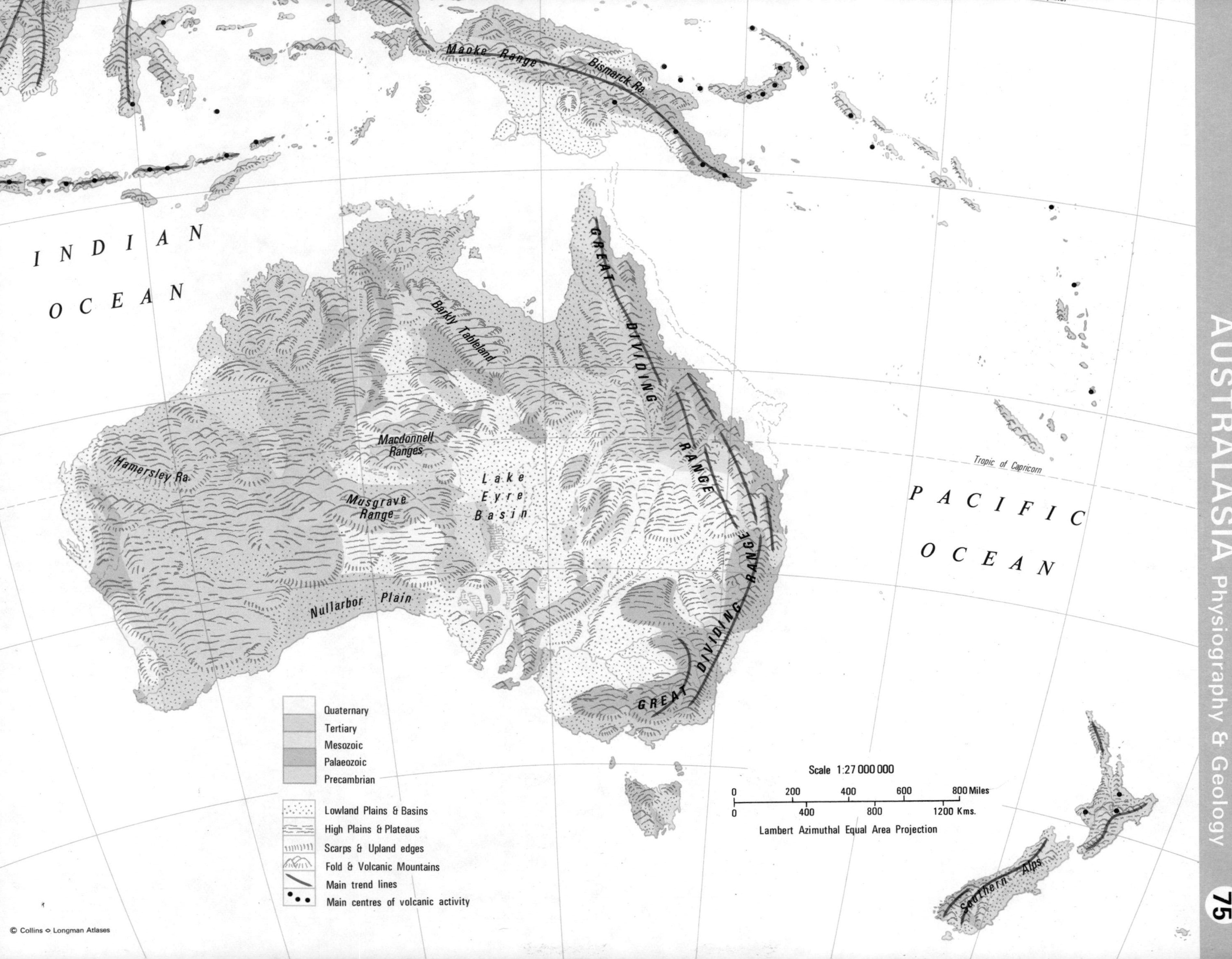
Maoke Range
Bismarck Ra.
INDIAN OCEAN
GREAT DIVIDING RANGE
GREAT DIVIDING RANGE
Barkly Tableland
Macdonnell Ranges
Hamersley Ra.
Lake Eyre Basin
Musgrave Range
Nullarbor Plain
Tropic of Capricorn
PACIFIC OCEAN
Southern Alps
Quaternary
Tertiary
Mesozoic
Palaeozoic
Precambrian
Lowland Plains & Basins
High Plains & Plateaus
Scarps & Upland edges
Fold & Volcanic Mountains
Main trend lines
Main centres of volcanic activity
Scale 1:27 000 000
0 200 400 600 800 Miles
0 400 800 1200 Kms.
Lambert Azimuthal Equal Area Projection

AUSTRALIA Land Cover

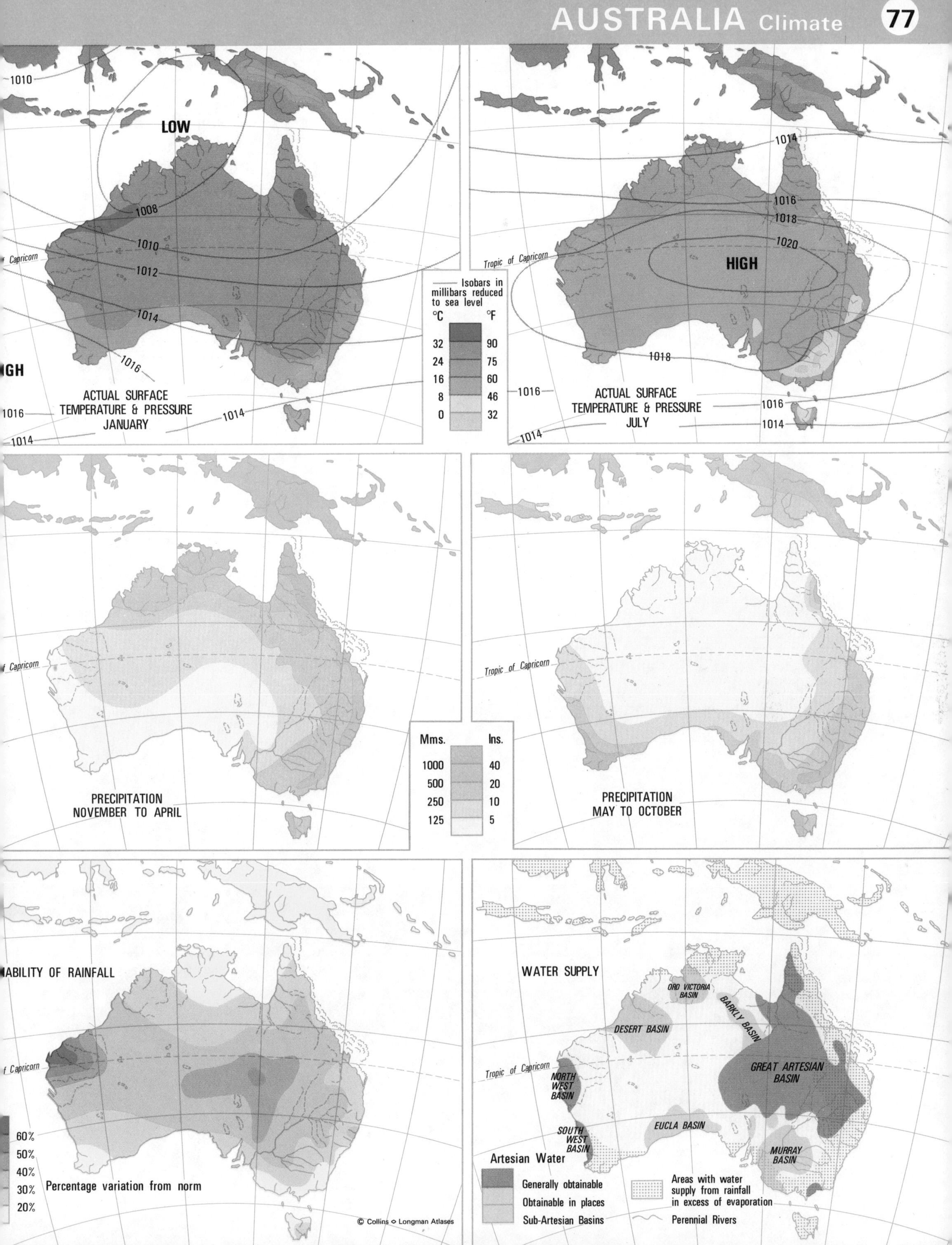
LOW
1010
1008
1010
Capricorn
1012
1014
1016
1016
1014
1014
ACTUAL SURFACE
TEMPERATURE & PRESSURE
JANUARY
Isobars in millibars reduced to sea level
°C °F
32 90
24 75
16 60
8 46
0 32
1014
1016
1018
1020
HIGH
Tropic of Capricorn
1018
1016
1016
1014
1014
ACTUAL SURFACE
TEMPERATURE & PRESSURE
JULY
Capricorn
PRECIPITATION
NOVEMBER TO APRIL
Mms. Ins.
1000 40
500 20
250 10
125 5
Tropic of Capricorn
PRECIPITATION
MAY TO OCTOBER
ABILITY OF RAINFALL
Capricorn
60%
50%
40%
30%
20%
Percentage variation from norm
WATER SUPPLY
ORD VICTORIA BASIN
BARKLY BASIN
DESERT BASIN
Tropic of Capricorn
NORTH WEST BASIN
GREAT ARTESIAN BASIN
EUCLA BASIN
SOUTH WEST BASIN
MURRAY BASIN
Artesian Water
Generally obtainable
Obtainable in places
Sub-Artesian Basins
Areas with water supply from rainfall in excess of evaporation
Perennial Rivers

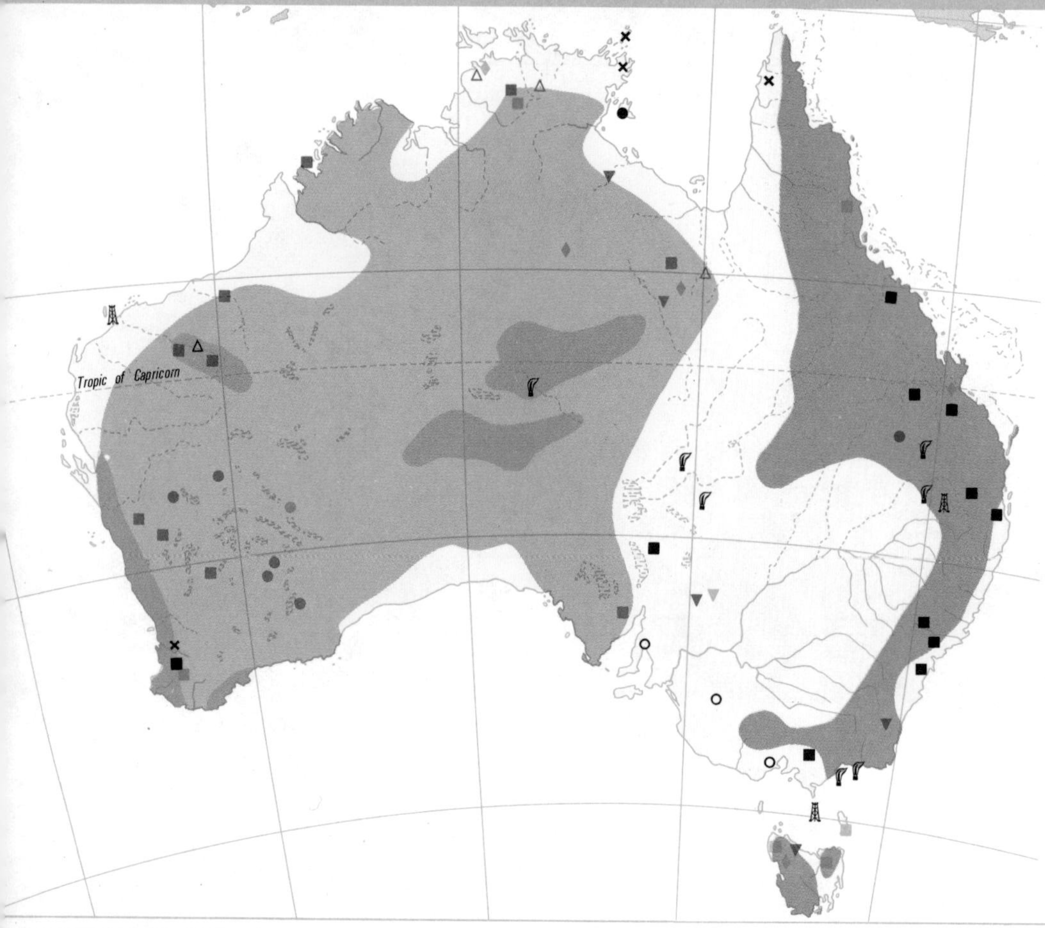

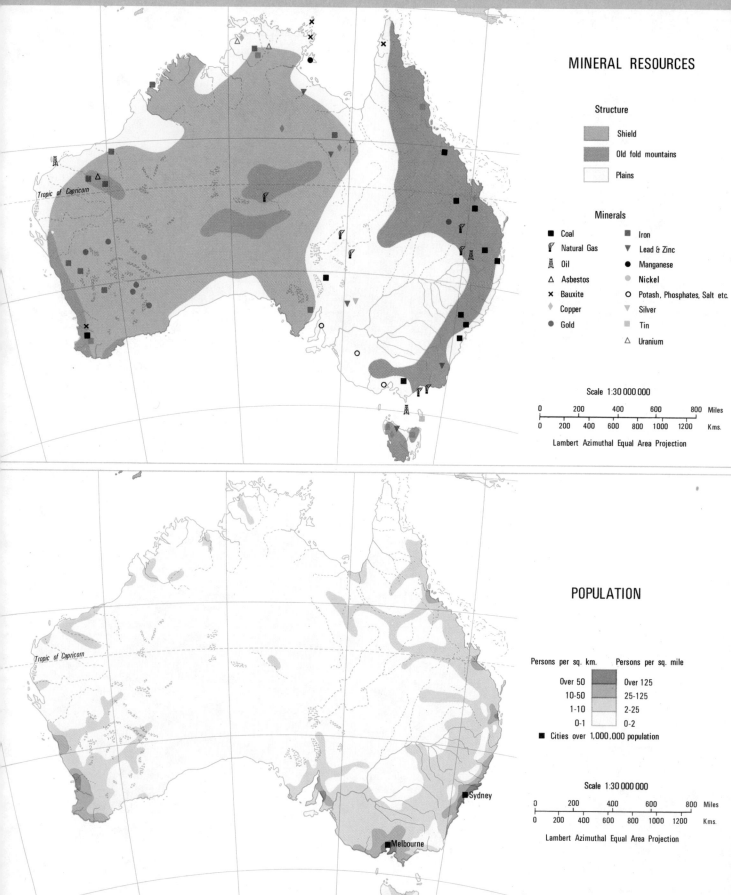

MINERAL RESOURCES

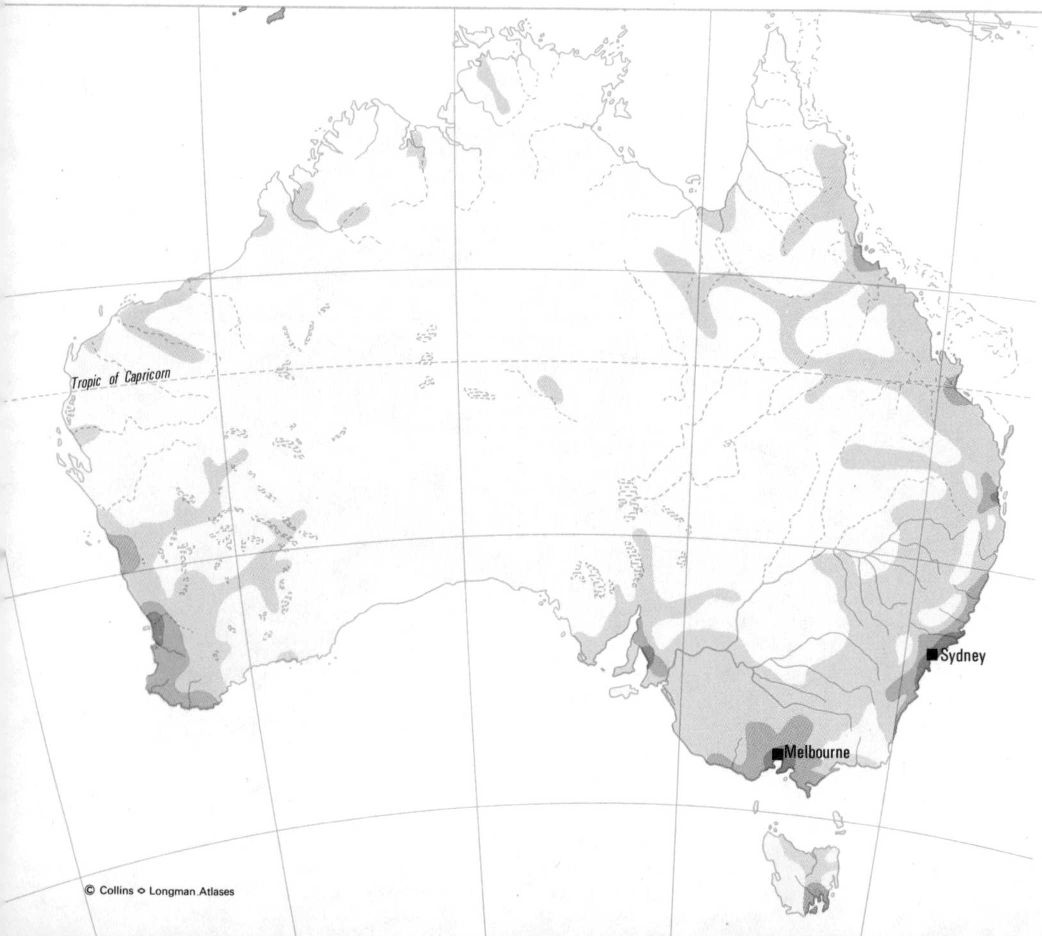

POPULATION

INDONESIA
SULAWESI
Rantekombola 11335
Makassar Strait
Ujung Pandang
Sula Is.
Misoöl
Buru
Ceram
Butung
BANDA SEA
Kabia
FLORES SEA
Wetar
Flores
Aru Is.
Tanimbar Is.
Timor
Sumbawa
Sumba
Roti
ARAFURA SEA
C. Vals
IRIAN JAYA
Djajapura
Maoke Range
Putjak Djaja 16503
NEW GUINEA
Wewak
Sepik
PAPUA NEW GUINEA
Mt Wilhelm 15400
Lae
Admiralty Is.
New Hanover
New Ireland
Bismarck Sea
New Britain
Solomon Sea
Mt. Victoria 13280
Owen Stanley Range
Port Moresby
Gulf of Papua
Torres Strait
C. York
CORAL SEA
Great Barrier Reef
TIMOR SEA
Melville I.
Bathurst I.
Darwin
C. Wessel
C. Arnhem
Groote Eylandt
Gulf of Carpentaria
C. Londonderry
Joseph Bonaparte Gulf
Katherine
Roper
Wyndham
Birdum
Ord
C. Lévêque
King Leopold Ranges
Derby
Broome
Hall's Creek
Eighty Mile Beach
NORTHERN TERRITORY
Tennant Creek
C. Melville
Cooktown
Mitchell
Normanton
Cairns
5287
Flinders
Great Dividing Range
Ingham
Townsville
Bowen
Mount Isa
Hughenden
Port Hedland
Barrow I.
Marble Bar
L. Mackay
Winton
Mackay
Hamersley Range
4024
L. Disappointment
4955
Macdonnell Ranges
Alice Springs
QUEENSLAND
Ashburton
Tropic of Capricorn
L. Amadeus
Barcaldine
Rockhampton
WESTERN AUSTRALIA
AUSTRALIA
Great Artesian Basin
Bundaberg
Gascoyne
Musgrave Ranges
L. Carnegie
Charleville
Murchison
Meekatharra
L. Eyre
Grey Range
Cunnamulla
Brisbane
Toowoomba
Goondiwindi
Warwick
Geraldton
SOUTH AUSTRALIA
4955
L. Torrens
Bourke
L. Moore
Rawlinna
Woomera
Darling
Narrabri
5300
Kalgoorlie
Nullarbor Plain
L. Gairdner
Broken Hill
Nyngan
Cobar
Flinders Range
Ceduna
Port Augusta
NEW SOUTH WALES
Taree
L. Cowan
Whyalla
Maitland
Perth
Fremantle
Great Australian Bight
Lachlan
Newcastle
Murray
Katoomba
Sydney
Esperance
Spencer Gulf
Adelaide
Murrumbidgee
Wollongong
Bunbury
Canberra
Mt. Kosciusko 7316
AUST. CAP. TER.
Albany
C. Leeuwin
Kangaroo I.
Bendigo
Snowy Mts.
VICTORIA
Ballarat
Melbourne
Geelong
C. Howe
TASMAN SEA
INDIAN OCEAN
King I.
Bass Strait
Flinders I.
TASMANIA
Mt. Ossa 5305
Launceston
Hobart
South East C.
Scale 1:20 000 000
0 100 200 300 400 500 Miles
0 200 400 600 800 Kms.
Lambert Azimuthal Equal Area Projection
110° 115° 120° 125° 130° 135° 140° 145° 150°
© Collins Longman Atlases

SOUTHEAST AUSTRALIA

QUEENSLAND

SOUTH AUSTRALIA

NEW SOUTH WALES

VICTORIA

AUST. CAPITAL TERRITORY

TASMANIA

GREAT DIVIDING RANGE

TASMAN SEA

INDIAN OCEAN

Bass Strait

Relief

Feet	Metres
16404	5000
9843	3000
6562	2000
3281	1000
1640	500
656	200
0	Sea Level
Land Dep. 656	200
13123	4000
22966	7000

Scale 1:7 500 000

0 50 100 150 200 Miles

0 100 200 300 Kms.

Lambert Azimuthal Equal Area Projection

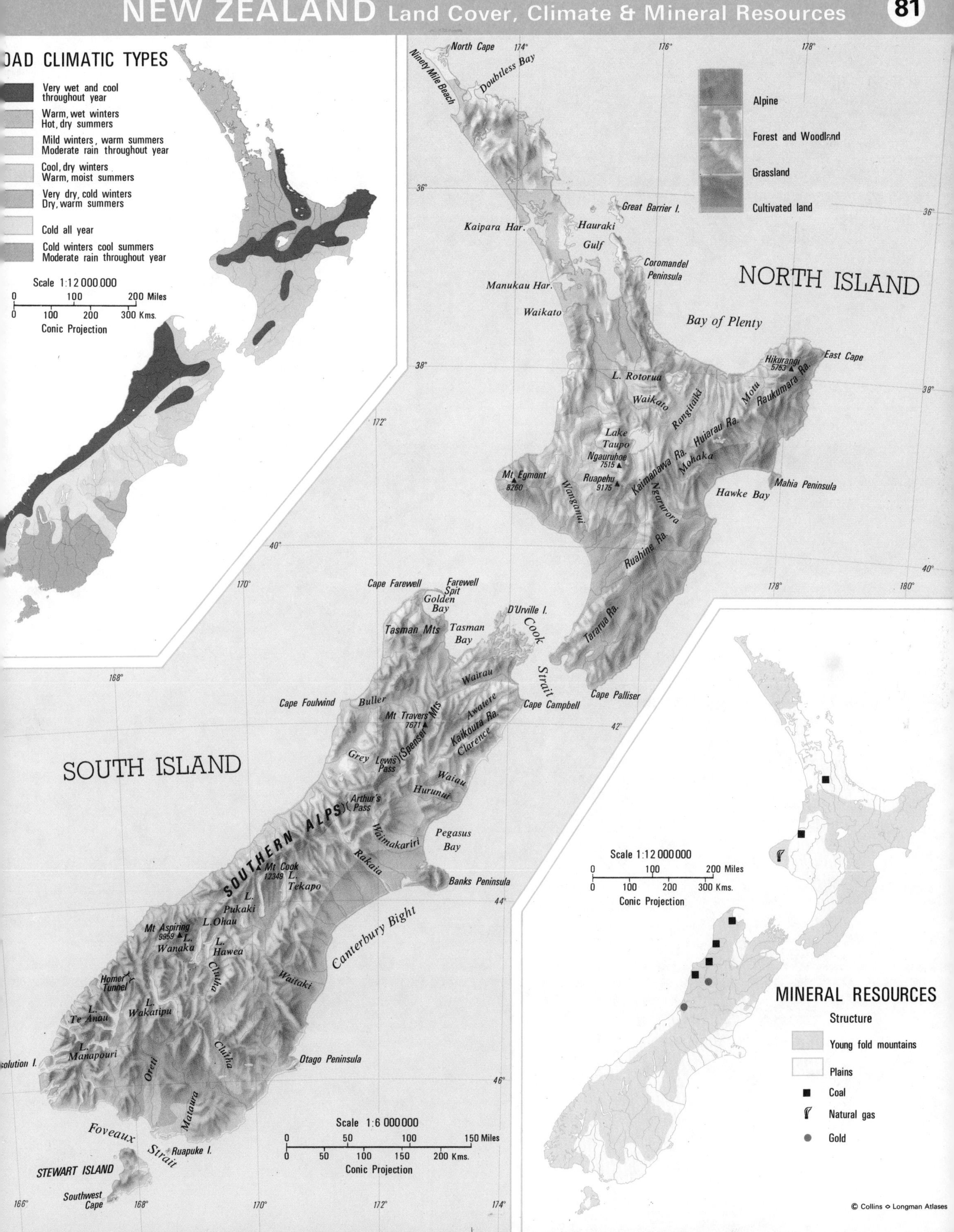

ROAD CLIMATIC TYPES
Very wet and cool throughout year
Warm, wet winters Hot, dry summers
Mild winters, warm summers Moderate rain throughout year
Cool, dry winters Warm, moist summers
Very dry, cold winters Dry, warm summers
Cold all year
Cold winters cool summers Moderate rain throughout year
Scale 1:12 000 000
0 100 200 Miles
0 100 200 300 Kms.
Conic Projection
Alpine
Forest and Woodland
Grassland
Cultivated land
NORTH ISLAND
North Cape
Ninety Mile Beach
Doubtless Bay
Great Barrier I.
Kaipara Har.
Hauraki Gulf
Coromandel Peninsula
Manukau Har.
Waikato
Bay of Plenty
East Cape
Hikurangi 5753
Raukumara Ra.
Motu
L. Rotorua
Waikato
Rangitaiki
Huiarau Ra.
Lake Taupo
Ngauruhoe 7515
Ruapehu 9175
Mt Egmont 8260
Kaimanawa Ra.
Mohaka
Ngaruroro
Wanganui
Mahia Peninsula
Hawke Bay
Ruahine Ra.
Tararua Ra.
Cape Palliser
Cook Strait
D'Urville I.
Cape Farewell
Farewell Spit
Golden Bay
Tasman Mts
Tasman Bay
Wairau
Buller
Cape Foulwind
Cape Campbell
Mt Travers 7671
Spenser Mts
Awatere
Kaikoura Ra.
Clarence
Grey
Lewis Pass
Waiau
Hurunui
Arthur's Pass
SOUTH ISLAND
SOUTHERN ALPS
Waimakariri
Pegasus Bay
Rakaia
Mt Cook 12349
L. Tekapo
Banks Peninsula
L. Pukaki
L. Ohau
Mt Aspiring 9959
L. Wanaka
L. Hawea
Canterbury Bight
Homer Tunnel
Clutha
Waitaki
L. Te Anau
L. Wakatipu
L. Manapouri
Resolution I.
Oreti
Clutha
Otago Peninsula
Mataura
Foveaux Strait
Ruapuke I.
STEWART ISLAND
Southwest Cape
Scale 1:6 000 000
0 50 100 150 Miles
0 50 100 150 200 Kms.
Conic Projection
Scale 1:12 000 000
0 100 200 Miles
0 100 200 300 Kms.
Conic Projection
MINERAL RESOURCES
Structure
Young fold mountains
Plains
Coal
Natural gas
Gold

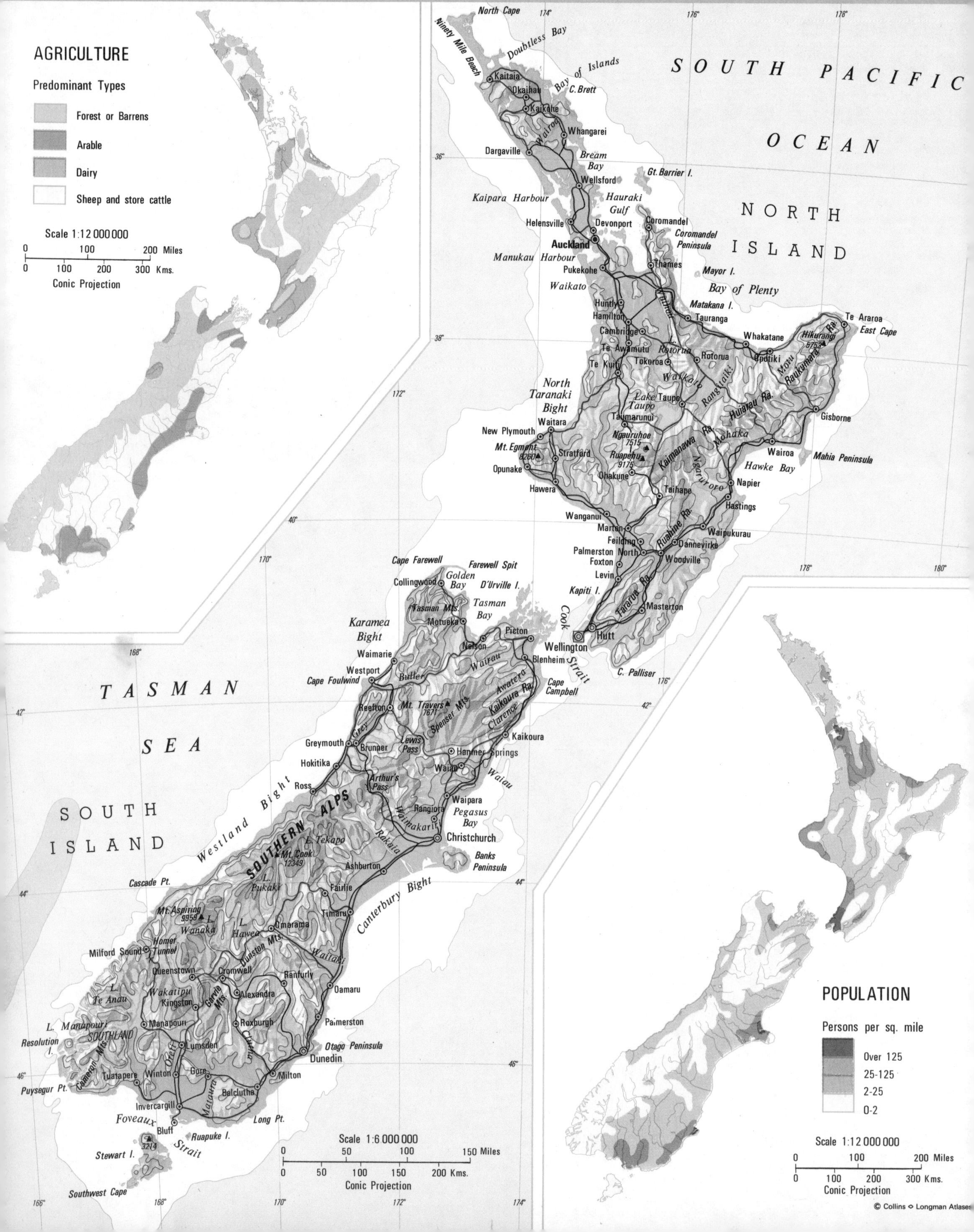

AGRICULTURE

Predominant Types

- Forest or Barrens
- Arable
- Dairy
- Sheep and store cattle

Scale 1:12 000 000

0 100 200 Miles

0 100 200 300 Kms.

Conic Projection

Scale 1:6 000 000

0 50 100 150 Miles

0 50 100 150 200 Kms.

Conic Projection

POPULATION

Persons per sq. mile

- Over 125
- 25-125
- 2-25
- 0-2

Scale 1:12 000 000

0 100 200 Miles

0 100 200 300 Kms.

Conic Projection

ARCTIC OCEAN
PACIFIC OCEAN
ATLANTIC OCEAN
Hudson Bay
Gulf of Mexico
CARIBBEAN SEA
Arctic Circle
Tropic of Cancer
Brooks Range
Alaska Range
Coast Mountains
Rocky Mountains
Canadian Shield
The Great Plains
Cascade Ra.
Coast Range
Great Basin
Sierra Nevada
Ozark Plateau
Appalachian Mts
Blue Ridge
Sierra Madre Occidental
Altiplano Mexicano
Sa. Madre Oriental
Sa. Madre del Sur
Sierra Madre
Tertiary
Mesozoic
Palaeozoic
Precambrian
Lowland Plains & Basins
High Plains & Plateaus
Scarps & Upland Edges
Fold & Volcanic Mountains
Main trend lines
Main centres of volcanic activity
Scale 1:35 000 000
0 200 400 600 800 1000 Miles
0 400 800 1200 1600 Kms.
Bonne Projection

Siberia
ARCTIC OCEAN
Bering Str.
Queen Elizabeth Islands
Ellesmere Island
Melville I.
Devon I.
GREENLAND
Arctic Circle
Iceland
Denmark Str.
Beaufort Sea
Banks I.
Brooks Range
Yukon
Alaska Range
Mt. McKinley 20320
Alaska Pen.
Kodiak I.
Prince of Wales I.
Victoria Island
Baffin Bay
Baffin Island
Davis Strait
C. Farewell
Mt. Logan 19850
Mt. St. Elias 18008
Mackenzie
Gt. Bear Lake
Black
Foxe Basin
Southampton Island
Hudson Strait
C. Chidley
Gt. Slave Lake
ROCKY MOUNTA
Coast Mountains
Ungava Peninsula
Labrador
Queen Charlotte Islands
Peace River Res.
Peace
L. Athabasca
Canadian Shield
Hudson Bay
Nelson
Vancouver I.
Fraser
Mt. Robson 12972
Saskatchewan
Severn
James Bay
Selkirk Mts
The Great
Lake Winnipeg
Albany
Anticosti I.
Gulf of St. Lawrence
Newfoundland
Cape Breton I.
Cascade Range
Mt. Rainier 14408
Columbia
Missouri
L. Superior
St. Lawrence
Green Mts.
Nova Scotia
Snake
Michigan
L. Huron
L. Ontario
Niagara Falls
C. Cod
P

ATLANTIC OCEAN
C. Hatteras
Mt. Mitchell 6684
Tennessee
Ohio
Ozark Plateau
Arkansas
Mississippi
Red
Colorado Plateau
Colorado
Gila
Rio Grande
Guadalupe I.
Lower California
Gulf of California
Tropic of Cancer
C. San Lucas
Sierra Madre Occidental
Altiplano Mexicano
Sierra Madre Oriental
Citlaltepetl 18700
Sierra Madre del Sur
Sierra Madre
Gulf of Mexico
C. Sable
Bahama Islands
Cuba
Hispaniola
Greater Antilles
Jamaica
Yucatan Channel
Yucatan Peninsula
Campeche Bay
Gulf of Honduras
Caribbean Sea
L. Nicaragua
Gulf of Panama
C. San Francisco
Equator
Galapagos Is.
Revilla Gigedo Is.
Clipperton I.
OCEAN
Permanent ice and snow
Tundra and alpine
Forest and woodland
Semi-desert
Desert
Grassland including prairie and savanna
Cultivated land
Scale 1:25 000 000
0 100 200 300 400 500 600 700 Miles
0 200 400 600 800 1000 Kms.
Bonne Projection

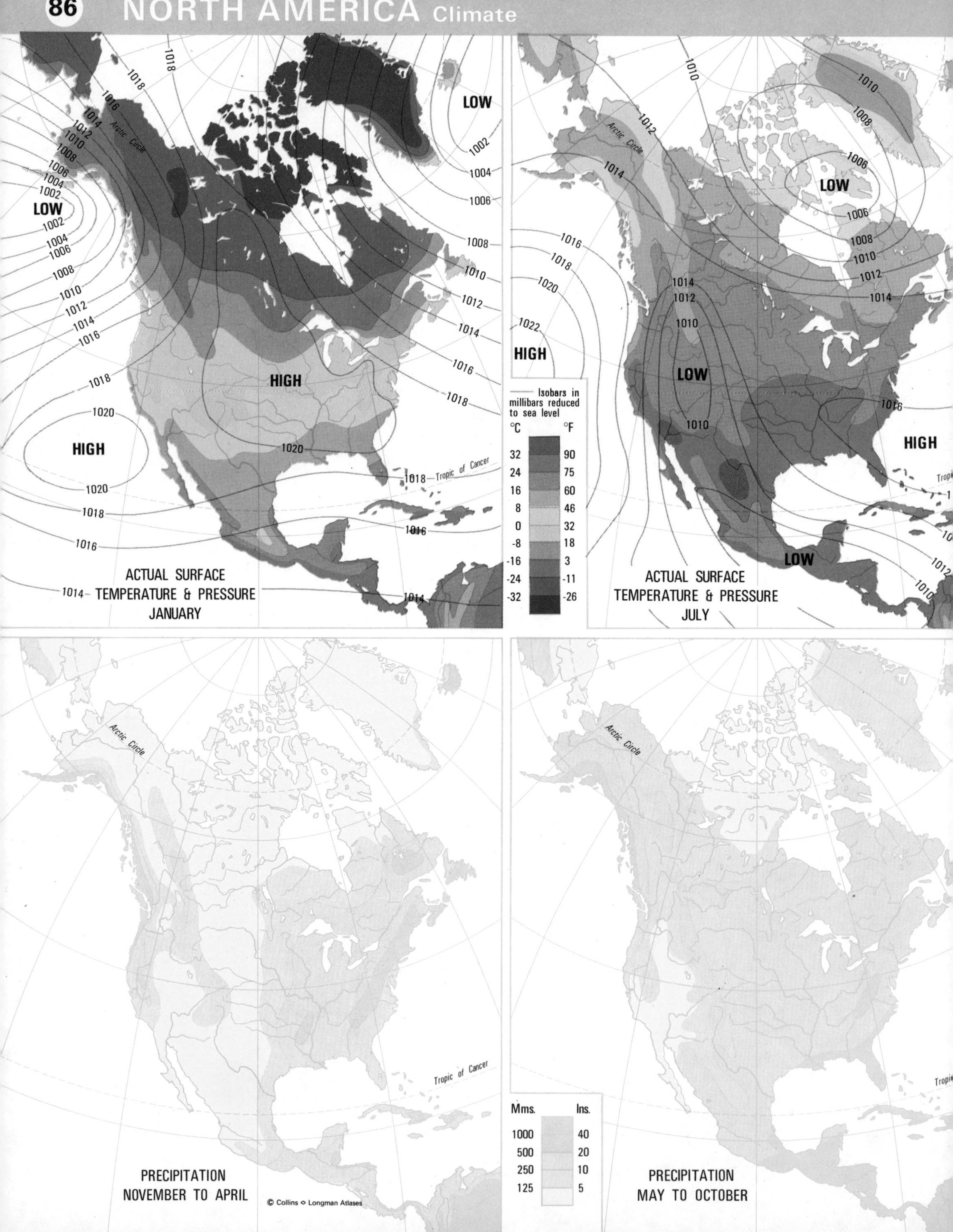
ACTUAL SURFACE
TEMPERATURE & PRESSURE
JANUARY
LOW
HIGH
HIGH
LOW
Arctic Circle
Tropic of Cancer
1002
1004
1006
1008
1010
1012
1014
1016
1018
1020
ACTUAL SURFACE
TEMPERATURE & PRESSURE
JULY
LOW
LOW
HIGH
HIGH
LOW
Isobars in millibars reduced to sea level
°C °F
32 90
24 75
16 60
8 46
0 32
-8 18
-16 3
-24 -11
-32 -26
PRECIPITATION
NOVEMBER TO APRIL
PRECIPITATION
MAY TO OCTOBER
Mms. Ins.
1000 40
500 20
250 10
125 5

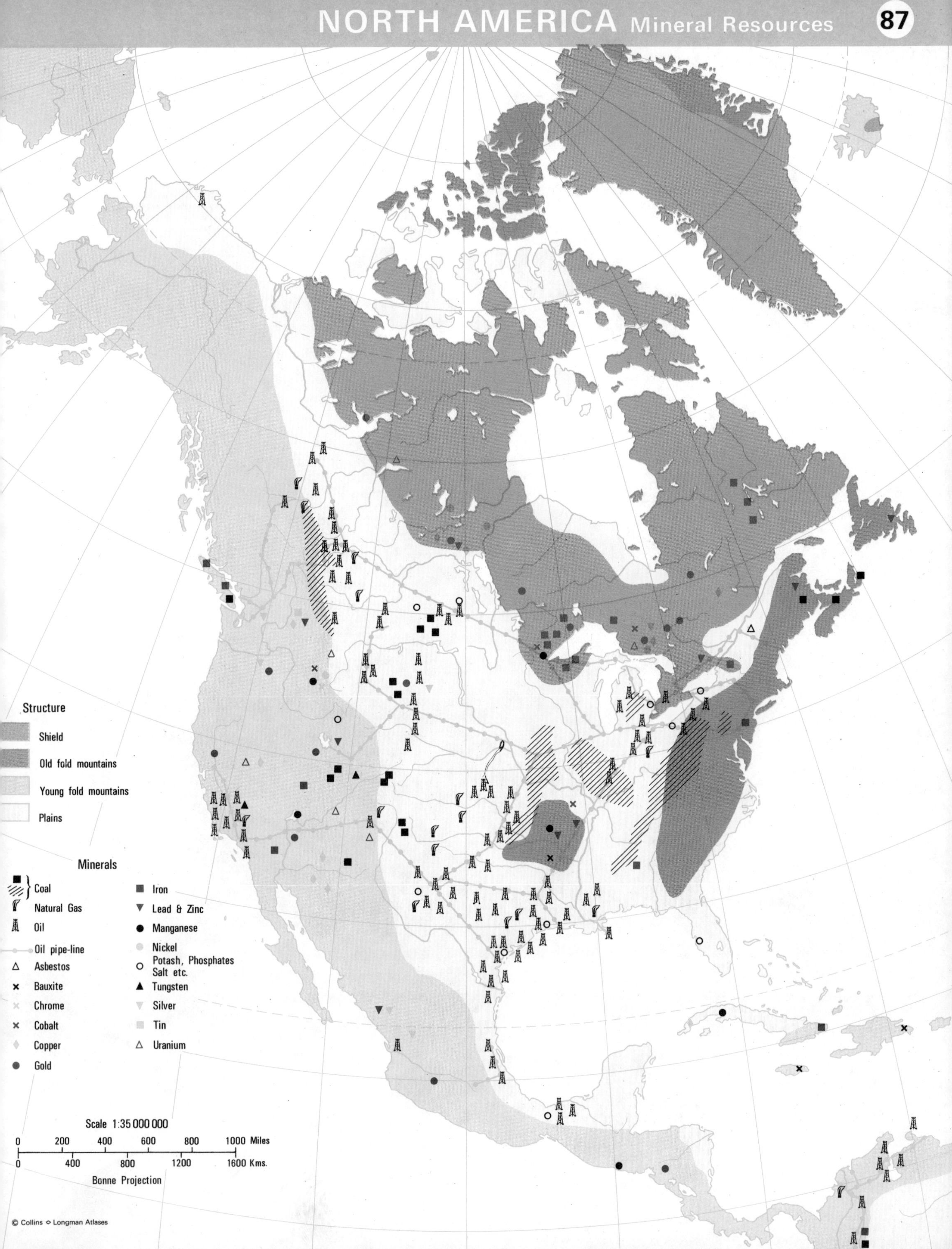
Structure
Shield
Old fold mountains
Young fold mountains
Plains
Minerals
Coal
Natural Gas
Oil
Oil pipe-line
Asbestos
Bauxite
Chrome
Cobalt
Copper
Gold
Iron
Lead & Zinc
Manganese
Nickel
Potash, Phosphates Salt etc.
Tungsten
Silver
Tin
Uranium
Scale 1:35 000 000
0 200 400 600 800 1000 Miles
0 400 800 1200 1600 Kms.
Bonne Projection

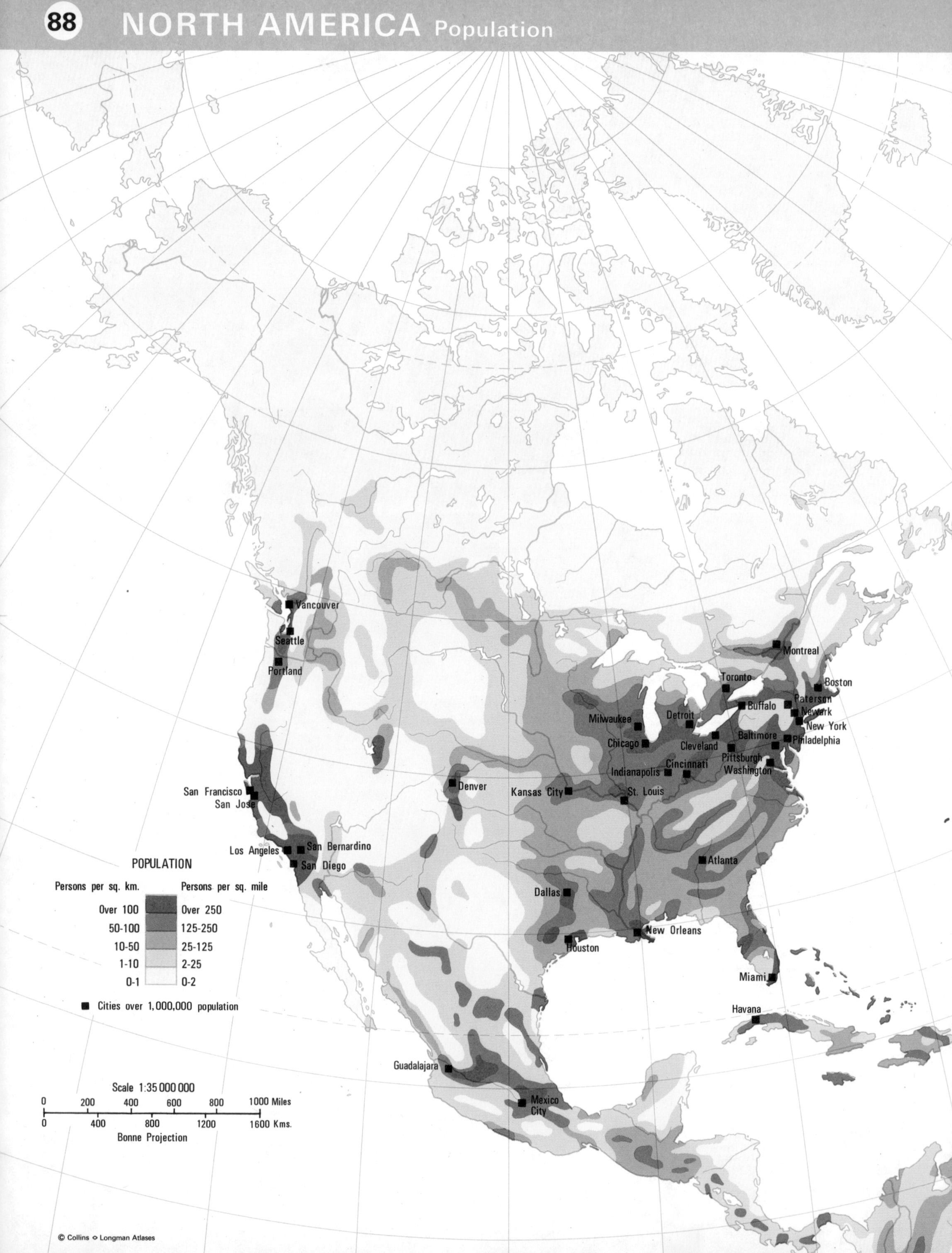
Vancouver
Seattle
Portland
San Francisco
San Jose
Los Angeles
San Bernardino
San Diego
Denver
Kansas City
St. Louis
Dallas
Houston
New Orleans
Milwaukee
Chicago
Detroit
Cleveland
Indianapolis
Cincinnati
Pittsburgh
Washington
Baltimore
Philadelphia
New York
Newark
Paterson
Boston
Buffalo
Toronto
Montreal
Atlanta
Miami
Havana
Guadalajara
Mexico City
POPULATION
Persons per sq. km.
Persons per sq. mile
Over 100
50-100
10-50
1-10
0-1
Over 250
125-250
25-125
2-25
0-2
Cities over 1,000,000 population
Scale 1:35 000 000
0 200 400 600 800 1000 Miles
0 400 800 1200 1600 Kms.
Bonne Projection

U. S. S. R.
ARCTIC OCEAN
GREENLAND (Denmark)
ICELAND
Reykjavik
U.S.A. ALASKA
Fairbanks
Anchorage
Kodiak I.
Bering Strait
St. Lawrence I.
Yukon
Ellesmere Island
Parry Islands
Banks I.
Pr. of Wales I.
Victoria Island
Baffin Bay
Baffin Island
Davis Strait
Godthaab
Arctic Circle
Gt. Bear Lake
Mackenzie
Southampton I.
Hudson Strait
Gt. Slave Lake
L. Athabasca
Peace
Hudson Bay
Churchill
Nelson
Prince Rupert
CANADA
James Bay
Newfoundland
St. John's
Gulf of St. Lawrence
Cape Breton I.
PACIFIC OCEAN
Vancouver I.
Fraser
Edmonton
Saskatchewan
Calgary
Regina
Lake Winnipeg
Albany
Vancouver
Seattle
Portland
Spokane
Columbia
Snake
Missouri
Winnipeg
Quebec
Halifax
Ottawa
Montreal
St. Lawrence
L. Superior
Duluth
Toronto
L. Ontario
Boston
Minneapolis
St. Paul
L. Michigan
L. Huron
Buffalo
Paterson
New York
Milwaukee
Detroit
Cleveland
L. Erie
Pittsburgh
Philadelphia
Gt. Salt Lake
Platte
Omaha
Chicago
Cincinnati
Baltimore
Salt Lake City
Indianapolis
Washington
San Francisco
Colorado
Denver
Kansas City
St Louis
Arkansas
Ohio
UNITED STATES OF AMERICA
ATLANTIC OCEAN
Bermuda
Los Angeles
Oklahoma City
Memphis
Tennessee
Mississippi
San Diego
Phoenix
Albuquerque
Red
Birmingham
Dallas
Tucson
El Paso
Jacksonville
Guadalupe (Mex.)
San Antonio
New Orleans
Mobile
Houston
Rio Grande
Gulf of California
Nassau
BAHAMAS
Tropic of Cancer
Miami
Monterrey
Gulf of Mexico
La Paz
MEXICO
Havana
CUBA
DOMINICAN REP.
Tampico
San Luis Potosi
Mérida
Greater Antilles
HAITI
Port-au-Prince
Santo Domingo
Guadalajara
Kingston
JAMAICA
Revilla Gigedo Is (Mex.)
Veracruz
Mexico City
CARIBBEAN SEA
Belmopan
BELIZE
Scale 1:35 000 000
0 200 400 600 800 1000 Miles
0 400 800 1200 1600 Kms.
Bonne Projection
HONDURAS
Tegucigalpa
GUATEMALA
Guatemala City
NICARAGUA
EL SALVADOR
San Salvador
Managua
San José
PANAMA
CANAL ZONE (U.S.)
Panama City
VENEZUELA
COSTA RICA
COLOMBIA

Hawaiian Islands
(U.S.A.)
PACIFIC OCEAN
Scale 1:20 000 000
WASHINGTON
OREGON
IDAHO
MONTANA
WYOMING
NEVADA
UTAH
COLORADO
CALIFORNIA
ARIZONA
NEW MEXICO
UNITED STATES OF AMERICA
ROCKY MOUNTAINS
PACIFIC OCEAN
MEXICO

CANADA
UNITED STATES OF AMERICA
Sandy L.
Little Grand Rapids
Trout L.
Red Lake
Lac Seul
Sioux Lookout
L. St. Joseph
Eabamet L.
Ogoki
Albany
Moosonee
James Bay
Rupert
Broadback
L. Evans
L. Mistassini
Baie Comeau
Gaspé Pen.
Abitibi
Harricanaw
Chibougamau
Peribonca
St. Lawrence
Rimouski
Campbellton
Bathurst
Pr. Edward I.
Roberval
Saguenay
Chicoutimi-Jonquière
L. St. John
Gouin Resr.
Rivière-du-Loup
Edmundston
Moncton
Fredericton
Truro
Saint John
Digby
Yarmouth
Longlac
Hearst
Missinaibi
Kapuskasing
Cochrane
L. Abitibi
Senneterre
St. Maurice
Quebec
Montmagny
Levis
Presque Isle
L. Nipigon
Kenora
Keewatin
Nipigon
Timmins
Kirkland Lake
Cabonga Resr.
Shawinigan
Trois-Rivières
Thetford Mines
Lake of the Woods
Fort Frances
Trans Canada Highway
Thunder Bay
I. Royale
Michipicoten Harbour
Michipicoten I.
Cobalt
Montreal
Sherbrooke
MAINE
Bangor
Augusta
Bay of Fundy
Grand Marais
L. Superior
Red Lake
Bemidji
Keweenaw Bay
Apostle Is.
Sault Sainte Marie
Sudbury
North Bay
Ottawa
Hull
L. Champlain
Burlington
Montpelier
VERMONT
NEW HAMPSHIRE
Portland
Leech L.
Duluth
Superior
Ashland
Marquette
Ironwood
Iron River
Manistique
Cheboygan
Georgian Bay
Kingston
Concord
Manchester
Fergus Falls
Mille Lacs L.
Rhinelander
Escanaba
MICHIGAN
L. Huron
Owen Sound
Peterborough
Oshawa
NEW YORK
St. Cloud
MINNESOTA
Willmar
Traverse City
Cadillac
Toronto
L. Ontario
Rochester
Utica
Syracuse
Albany
MASS.
Worcester
Boston
C. Cod
Providence
New Bedford
Nantucket I.
St. Paul
Minneapolis
WISCONSIN
Green Bay
Wisconsin Rapids
Winona
Mississippi
L. Michigan
Bay City
Flint
Kitchener
Hamilton
Niagara Falls
St. Catherines
Buffalo
Binghamton
Hudson
CONN.
R.I.
Hartford
New Haven
Winnebago
Muskegon
Grand Rapids
Lansing
London
Detroit
Windsor
Olean
Scranton
Paterson
Jersey City
Bridgeport
Long Island
New York
Worthington
Mason City
Madison
Milwaukee
L. Erie
Erie
Oil City
Williamsport
Allentown
Newark
Trenton
N.J.
Sioux City
Waterloo
Cedar Rapids
IOWA
Rockford
Chicago
Gary
Michigan City
Jackson
Toledo
Cleveland
Youngstown
Akron
PENNSYLVANIA
Harrisburg
Altoona
Philadelphia
Wilmington
Atlantic City
Iowa City
Davenport
Des Moines
Kankakee
Fort Wayne
Mansfield
Pittsburgh
Baltimore
C. May
Delaware Bay
Council Bluffs
Peoria
INDIANA
OHIO
Columbus
Cumberland
Washington D.C.
DEL.
Salisbury
Creston
ILLINOIS
Indianapolis
Dayton
WEST VIRGINIA
MARYLAND
Chesapeake Bay
ATLANTIC OCEAN
Missouri
Quincy
Decatur
Springfield
Hannibal
Terre Haute
Cincinnati
Ohio
Fredericksburg
Charlottesville
St. Joseph
Charleston
Ashland
Richmond
Newport News
Norfolk
Topeka
Kansas City
MISSOURI
Jefferson City
St. Louis
Wabash
Louisville
Frankfort
Lexington
VIRGINIA
Emporia
Evansville
KENTUCKY
Bluefield
Danville
Roanoke
Albemarle Sound
Fort Scott
Rolla
L. Cumberland
Buggs Island L.
Winston-Salem
Greensboro
Raleigh
NORTH CAROLINA
C. Hatteras
Springfield
Cairo
Norris L.
Mt. Mitchell 6684
Neuse
New Bern
Joplin
L. O' The Cherokees
Plateau
Poplar Bluff
Kentucky L.
Nashville
Knoxville
Asheville
Charlotte
Fayetteville
C. Lookout
Tulsa
Ozark
White
Black
TENNESSEE
Appalachian
Allegheny
Wilmington
Muskogee
Fort Smith
Chattanooga
Greenville
Florence
C. Fear
Eufaula Resr.
ARKANSAS
Memphis
Pickwick L.
Tennessee
Guntersville L.
Columbia
SOUTH CAROLINA
Ouachita Mts.
Little Rock
Gadsden
Orangeburg
C. Romain
L. Texoma
Arkansas
Pine Bluff
Tupelo
Atlanta
Resr.
Augusta
Savannah
Charleston
Ouachita
Birmingham
Macon
Ogeechee
Texarkana
Greenville
Tuscaloosa
ALABAMA
Columbus
GEORGIA
Altamaha
Savannah
Dallas
Shreveport
Monroe
MISSISSIPPI
Meridian
Montgomery
Trinity
Tyler
Sabine
Jackson
Hattiesburg
Tombigbee
Alabama
Chattahoochee
Flint
Albany
Waycross
Brunswick
Red
Mississippi
Pearl
Natchez
Dothan
Thomasville
Madison
Okeefenokee Swamp
Jacksonville
St. Augustine
Lufkin
Neches
Alexandria
LOUISIANA
Biloxi
Mobile
Pensacola
Tallahassee
Lake City
Gainesville
Daytona Beach
FLORIDA
Huntsville
Lake Charles
Baton Rouge
Panama City
Apalachee Bay
Mobile Bay
Beaumont
Lafayette
New Orleans
Chandeleur Is.
C. San Blas
Cape Kennedy
Houston
Port Arthur
Morgan City
Galveston Bay
Galveston
Atchafalaya Bay
Mississippi Delta
Orlando
Lakeland
Tampa
St. Petersburg
L. Okeechobee
West Palm Beach
Freeport
Grand Bahama I.
Great Abaco I.
BAHAMAS
Eleuthera I.
Matagorda Bay
Gulf of Mexico
Fort Lauderdale
Miami
The Everglades
Fort Myers
C. Romano
Andros I.
Nassau
New Providence
Cat I.
San Salvador
Relief
Feet
Metres
16404
5000
9843
3000
6562
2000
3281
1000
1640
500
656
200
0
Sea Level
Land Dep.
656
200
13123
4000
22966
7000
Scale 1:12 000 000
0
200
400 Miles
0
200
400
600 Kms.
Bonne Projection
95°
90°
85°
80°
75°
70°
65°
60°
40°
35°
30°
25°

U.S.S.R.
BERING SEA
BEAUFORT SEA
PACIFIC OCEAN
Gulf of Alaska
ALASKA (U.S.A.)
YUKON
BRITISH COLUMBIA
ALBERTA
SASKATCHE
MACKENZIE
NORTHWEST TERRITORIES
ROCKY MOUNTAINS
UNITED STATES
Brooks Range
Endicott Mts
Kuskokwim Mts
Alaska Range
Aleutian Range
Mackenzie Mountains
Selwyn Mountains
Coast Mountains
Cariboo Mts
Selkirk Mts
Bering Str.
Arctic Circle
Norton Sound
Seward Pen.
Bristol Bay
Alaska Pen.
Shelikof Strait
Kodiak I.
Shumagin Is
Nunivak I.
St. Lawrence I.
C. Lisburne
Point Barrow
C. Halkett
Martin Pt
C. Bathurst
Pr. Alfred C.
Amundsen Gulf
Banks Island
Victoria Island
Prince Patrick I.
McClure Strait
Dolphin & Union Str.
Coronation Gulf
Gt. Bear Lake
Gt. Slave Lake
L. Athabasca
Lesser Slave Lake
Churchill Lake
Cree L.
Alexander Archipelago
Chichagof I.
Baranof I.
Pr. of Wales I.
Dixon Entrance
Queen Charlotte Islands
Hecate Str.
Qn. Charlotte Str.
Vancouver Island
Yukon
Porcupine
Peel
Mackenzie
Anderson
Horton
Liard
Stikine
Peace
Athabasca
Fraser
Columbia
Snake
Missouri
Yellowstone
Milk
Big Horn
Mt. McKinley 20320
Mt Logan 19850
Mt St. Elias 18008
Mt Fairweather 15320
Keele Pk 9750
Churchill Pk 9000
Mt Robson 12972
Mt Waddington 13260
Mt Rainier 14408
Borah Pk 12654
Grand Teton 13766
Mt Shasta 14162
Nome
Kotzebue
Wainwright
Barrow
Umiat
Anvik
Aniak
Platinum
Galena
Tanana
Allakaket
Koyukuk
McGrath
Nenana
Fairbanks
Fort Yukon
Anchorage
Talkeetna
Seward
Valdez
Tanacross
Northway
Homer
Kodiak
Naknek
Fort Randall
Scammon Bay
Old Crow
Fort McPherson
Inuvik
Dawson
Mayo Landing
Keno Hill
Carmacks
Whitehorse
Carcross
Skagway
Haines
Juneau
Sitka
Wrangell
Ketchikan
Stewart
Hazelton
Prince Rupert
Kitimat
Watson Lake
Fort Good Hope
Norman Wells
Fort Norman
Wrigley
Fort Simpson
Fort Liard
Fort Nelson
Hay River
Fort Resolution
Fort Reliance
Yellowknife
Coppermine
Fort Chipewyan
Fort Vermilion
Uranium City
Fort St John
Dawson Creek
Peace River
McMurray
Grande Prairie
Athabasca
Prince George
Quesnel
Jasper
Edmonton
Red Deer
Camrose
Lloydminster
North Battleford
Prince Albert
Saskatoon
Rosetown
Drumheller
Calgary
Banff
Kicking Horse Pass
Crowsnest Pass
Kamloops
Revelstoke
Kelowna
Penticton
Nelson
Trail
Cranbrook
Lethbridge
Medicine Hat
Swift Current
Moose Jaw
Vancouver
Nanaimo
Victoria
Seattle
Tacoma
Astoria
Yakima
Spokane
Portland
Eugene
Missoula
Helena
Great Falls
Havre
Butte
Bozeman
Billings
Miles City
Boise
Idaho Falls
Twin Falls
Klamath Falls
Eureka
C. Mendocino
Buffalo
Casper
Trans-Canada
Relief
Feet
Metres
16404 5000
9843 3000
6562 2000
3281 1000
1640 500
656 200
0 Sea Level
Land Dep.
656 200
13123 4000
22966 7000
Scale 1 : 17 000 000
0 100 200 300 400 500 Miles
0 100 200 300 400 500 600 700 800 Kms.
Bonne Projection

Axel Heiberg I.
Nares Strait
C. Parry
Thule
Ellesmere Island
Islands
Devon Island
Cornwallis I.
Resolute
Lancaster Sound
Baffin Bay
Bylot I.
Pond Inlet
Upernavik
GREENLAND
(Denmark)
King Christian IX Land
Mt Forel 11024
Arctic Circle
Angmagssalik
King Frederick VI Coast
Disko Is.
Godhavn
Christianshaab
Somerset Island
Prince of Wales Island
Davis Strait
Home Bay
Penny Highland 8501
C. Dyer
Sukkertoppen
Godthaab
Frederikshaab
Ivigtut
Julianehaab
C. Farewell
Baffin Island
Gulf of Boothia
Spence Bay
Melville Peninsula
Prince Charles I.
Foxe Basin
Pangnirtung
Cumberland Sound
Frobisher Bay
Foxe Channel
NORTHWEST TERRITORIES
Back
Garry L.
Wager Bay
Southampton Island
Hudson Strait
Akpatok I.
C. Chidley
ATLANTIC OCEAN
KEEWATIN
Chesterfield Inlet
Fisher Strait
Sugluk
Wakeham
Ungava Bay
Port-Nouveau Québec
Coats I.
Mansel I.
CANADA
Nain
Hopedale
C. Harrison
Indian Harbour
Fort Chimo
Payne
Koksoak
Leaf
George
Whale
Larch
NEWFOUNDLAND
Eskimo Point
Ottawa Is.
Hudson Bay
Port Harrison
Clearwater Lake
Schefferville
Labrador
Hamilton
North West River
Battle Harbour
C. Bauld
St. Anthony
Seal
Churchill
C. Churchill
C. Tatnam
Port Nelson
York Factory
Nelson
Hayes
Fort Severn
Belcher Is.
Gt. Whale
C. Henrietta Maria
Labrador City
Wabush City
Romaine
Belle Isle Str.
Gander
Bonavista
St. John's
Grand Falls
Newfoundland
Corner Brook
MANITOBA
Winisk
Severn
Fort George
Eastmain
Gagnon
Moisie
Sept Îles
Anticosti I.
Port aux Basques
Gulf of St. Lawrence
Cabot Str.
Cape Breton I.
St. Pierre Miquelon (Fr.)
James Bay
Akimiski I.
Peribonca
Manicouagan
Port Cartier
Baie Comeau
Gaspé
Norway House
Fort Albany
Fort Rupert
Lake Mistassini
QUEBEC
Chibougamau
St. Lawrence
Rimouski
Bathurst
PR EDWARD I.
Charlottetown
Sydney
L. Winnipeg
Albany
Moosonee
ONTARIO
Abitibi
Chicoutimi-Jonquière
NEW BRUNSWICK
NOVA SCOTIA
Sable I.
Red Lake
Hearst
Cochrane
Senneterre
St. Maurice
Roberval
Edmundston
Moncton
Truro
Manitoba
Winnipeg
Portage la Prairie
St Boniface
Morden
Kenora
Sioux Lookout
L. Nipigon
Longlac
Trans Canada Highway
Timmins
Rouyn
Quebec
Levis
St John
Fredericton
Saint John
Halifax
Nipigon
Thunder Bay
Michipicoten Harbour
Kirkland Lake
Cobalt
Trois-Rivières
St Hyacinthe
Sherbrooke
Bangor
Bay of Fundy
Liverpool
Yarmouth
C. Sable
Fort Frances
L. Superior
Sault Sainte Marie
Sudbury
North Bay
Ottawa
Hull
Montreal
L. Champlain
Portland
Grafton
Red
Grand Forks
Duluth
Ironwood
Marquette
Georgian Bay
Kingston
Manchester
Bismarck
Valley City
Fargo
Superior
Manistique
L. Huron
Oshawa
L. Ontario
Syracuse
Utica
Worcester
Boston
C. Cod
Providence
UNITED STATES OF AMERICA
Aberdeen
St Cloud
Minneapolis
St. Paul
Wisconsin
Green Bay
L. Michigan
Owen Sound
Kitchener
Toronto
Rochester
Albany
Hartford
Hudson
New Haven
Long Island
Cadillac
Bay City
Hamilton
St Catherines
Niagara Falls
Buffalo
Scranton
Mississippi
Grand Rapids
London
L. Erie
Erie
Paterson
Newark
New York
Mitchell
Sioux Falls
Mason City
Milwaukee
Madison
Detroit
Windsor
Toledo
Ohio
Philadelphia
Sioux City
Waterloo
Cedar Rapids
Chicago
Gary
Cleveland
Pittsburgh
Baltimore
100°
90°
80°
70°
60°
50°
40°
30°
© Collins ◇ Longman Atlases

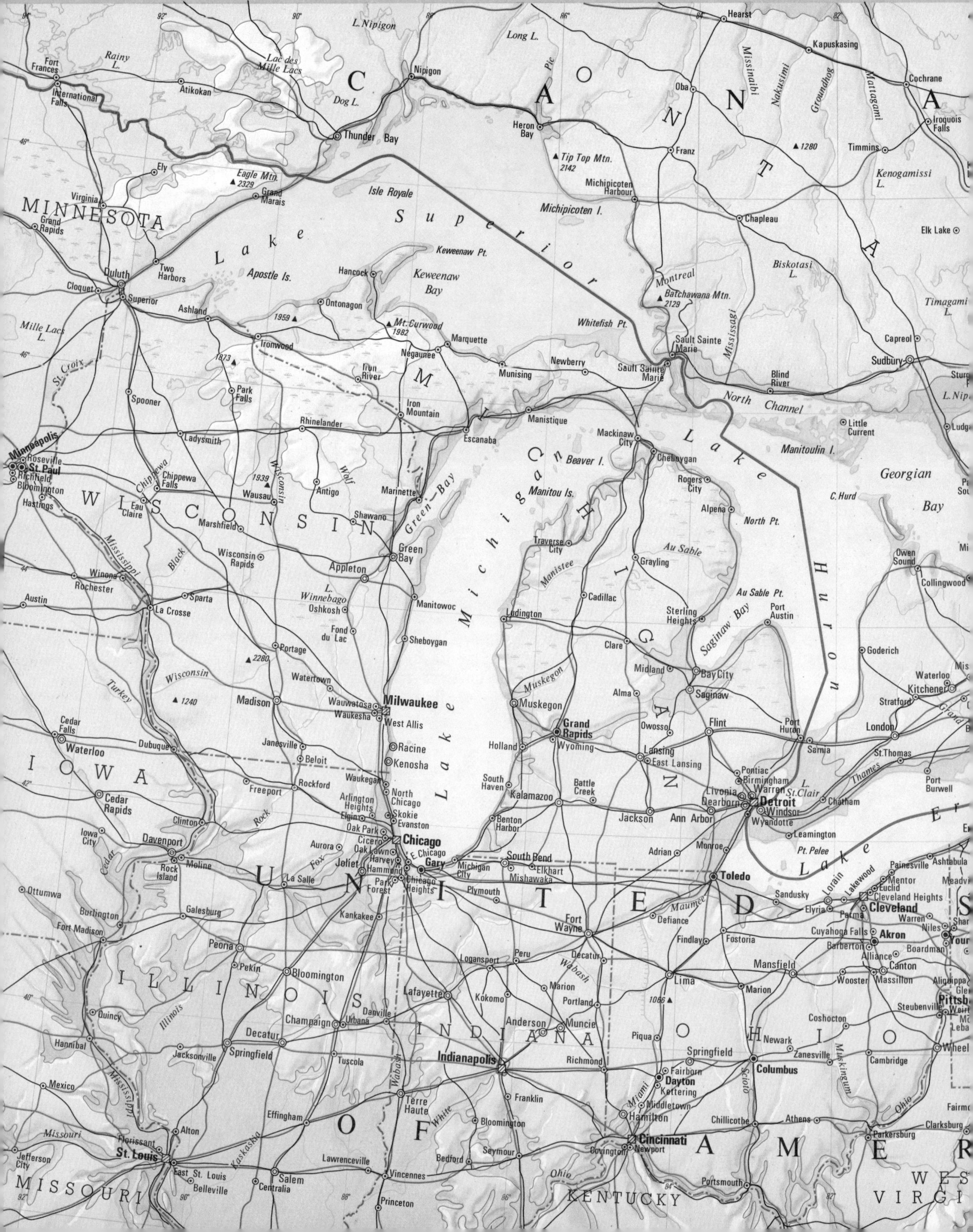

CANADA
UNITED STATES OF AMERICA
MINNESOTA
WISCONSIN
MICHIGAN
IOWA
ILLINOIS
INDIANA
OHIO
MISSOURI
KENTUCKY
Lake Superior
Lake Michigan
Lake Huron
Lake Erie
Georgian Bay
North Channel
Green Bay
Saginaw Bay
L. Nipigon
Lac des Mille Lacs
Rainy L.
Dog L.
Long L.
Isle Royale
Keweenaw Pt.
Keweenaw Bay
Apostle Is.
Michipicoten I.
Whitefish Pt.
Beaver I.
Manitou Is.
Manitoulin I.
North Pt.
Au Sable Pt.
Au Sable
L. Winnebago
Mille Lacs L.
Kenogamissi L.
Biskotasi L.
Timagami L.
Elk Lake
C. Hurd
Pt. Pelee
L. St. Clair
Eagle Mtn. 2329
Tip Top Mtn. 2142
Batchawana Mtn. 2129
Mt. Curwood 1982
1959
1873
1939
2280
1240
1280
1066
Fort Frances
International Falls
Atikokan
Nipigon
Thunder Bay
Heron Bay
Hearst
Kapuskasing
Cochrane
Oba
Iroquois Falls
Timmins
Franz
Michipicoten Harbour
Chapleau
Montreal
Sault Sainte Marie
Capreol
Sudbury
Blind River
Little Current
Ely
Virginia
Grand Rapids
Grand Marais
Two Harbors
Duluth
Cloquet
Superior
Ashland
Ironwood
Ontonagon
Hancock
Marquette
Negaunee
Munising
Newberry
Iron River
Iron Mountain
Manistique
Escanaba
Mackinaw City
Cheboygan
Rogers City
Alpena
Spooner
Park Falls
Rhinelander
Ladysmith
Minneapolis
St. Paul
Roseville
Richfield
Bloomington
Hastings
Chippewa Falls
Eau Claire
Wausau
Antigo
Marinette
Shawano
Marshfield
Wisconsin Rapids
Green Bay
Appleton
Oshkosh
Fond du Lac
Manitowoc
Sheboygan
Winona
Rochester
Austin
Sparta
La Crosse
Portage
Madison
Watertown
Wauwatosa
Waukesha
Milwaukee
West Allis
Janesville
Beloit
Racine
Kenosha
Rockford
Freeport
Waukegan
North Chicago
Arlington Heights
Elgin
Skokie
Evanston
Oak Park
Cicero
Oak Lawn
Chicago
Aurora
Joliet
Harvey
Hammond
E. Chicago
Gary
Park Forest
Chicago Heights
Kankakee
Cedar Falls
Waterloo
Dubuque
Cedar Rapids
Clinton
Iowa City
Davenport
Moline
Rock Island
La Salle
Ottumwa
Burlington
Galesburg
Fort Madison
Peoria
Pekin
Bloomington
Quincy
Hannibal
Champaign
Urbana
Danville
Decatur
Springfield
Jacksonville
Tuscola
Mexico
Effingham
Alton
Florissant
St. Louis
East St. Louis
Belleville
Jefferson City
Salem
Centralia
Lawrenceville
Vincennes
Princeton
Traverse City
Grayling
Cadillac
Ludington
Clare
Sterling Heights
Port Austin
Midland
Bay City
Saginaw
Alma
Muskegon
Grand Rapids
Wyoming
Holland
Owosso
Flint
Lansing
East Lansing
Port Huron
Sarnia
South Haven
Kalamazoo
Battle Creek
Jackson
Ann Arbor
Pontiac
Birmingham
Warren
Livonia
Dearborn
Detroit
Windsor
Wyandotte
Benton Harbor
South Bend
Elkhart
Mishawaka
Michigan City
Plymouth
Adrian
Monroe
Toledo
Sandusky
Leamington
Chatham
Goderich
Owen Sound
Collingwood
Waterloo
Kitchener
Stratford
London
St. Thomas
Port Burwell
Fort Wayne
Defiance
Findlay
Fostoria
Elyria
Lorain
Lakewood
Euclid
Mentor
Painesville
Ashtabula
Cleveland Heights
Cleveland
Parma
Cuyahoga Falls
Akron
Barberton
Warren
Niles
Alliance
Canton
Massillon
Boardman
Wooster
Mansfield
Lima
Marion
Decatur
Logansport
Peru
Kokomo
Marion
Portland
Lafayette
Anderson
Muncie
Indianapolis
Richmond
Piqua
Springfield
Fairborn
Dayton
Kettering
Middletown
Hamilton
Cincinnati
Covington
Newport
Columbus
Newark
Zanesville
Cambridge
Coshocton
Steubenville
Chillicothe
Athens
Parkersburg
Clarksburg
Portsmouth
Terre Haute
Franklin
Bloomington
Seymour
Bedford
Mississippi
Missouri
Illinois
Wisconsin
Rock
Fox
Wabash
White
Ohio
Miami
Scioto
Muskingum
Maumee
Kaskaskia
Turkey
Cedar
Black
Chippewa
St. Croix
Wolf
Manistee
Muskegon
Thames
Grand
Pic
Missinaibi
Nakusimi
Groundhog
Mattagami
Mississagi
88°
86°
84°
82°
90°
92°
94°
48°
46°
44°
42°
40°

Q U E B E C
D A
Waswanipi L.
Gouin Res.
St. Maurice
Amos
Senneterre
Rouyn
Val-d'Or
Ottawa
L. Simard
Cabonga Res.
L. Kempt
Matawin
Baskatong L.
Kipawa L.
Coulonge
Mont Laurier
Mount Tremblant 3176
Maniwaki
Mattawa
Pembroke
Gatineau
R. du Lièvre
Hull
Ottawa
Whitney
Renfrew
Arnprior
Madawaska
Huntsville
Haliburton Highlands
Smith's Falls
Brockville
Ogdensburg
Peterborough
Kingston
Belleville
Picton
Cobourg
Oshawa
L. Simcoe
Scarborough
Toronto
Lake Ontario
St. Lawrence
Cornwall
Valleyfield
Malone
Dolbeau
L. St. John
Chicoutimi-Jonquière
Roberval
Saguenay
Tadoussac
St. Lawrence
Laurentides Mts.
564
La Malbaie
Baie St. Paul
La Tuque
Quebec
Levis
Montmagny
Shawinigan
Trois-Rivières
Joliette
Sorel
Richelieu
Drummondville
Thetford Mines
St. Jérôme
Montreal
Laval
Lachine
Verdun
Jacques-Cartier
St. Hyacinthe
Granby
Farnham
Sherbrooke
Megantic
Megantic Mtn. 3658
Matane
Mont Joli
Rimouski
Mont Blanc 3474
Gaspé Peninsula
Campbellton
Rivière-du-Loup
Edmundston
NEW BRUNSWICK
Big Bald Mtn. 2205
St. Leonard
Grand Falls
Caribou
Presque Isle
Peaked Mtn. 2260
St. John
Allagash
Houlton
Fredericton
Oromocto
Mt. Katahdin 5267
Moosehead L.
White Cap Mtn. 3645
Danforth
Greenville
Caribou Mtn. 3599
Lincoln
St. Stephen
Calais
St. Andrews
Penobscot
M A I N E
Rump Mtn. 3648
Sugarloaf Mtn. 4236
Bangor
Brewer
Grand Manan I.
Waterville
Ellsworth
Augusta
Kennebec
Rockland
Lewistown
Bath
Portland
Sebago L.
Biddeford
Plattsburgh
Lyon Mtn. 3881
L. Champlain
Burlington
Montpelier
Mt. Lafayette 5249
Mt. Washington 6288
Berlin
White Mts.
NEW HAMPSHIRE
VERMONT
Green Mts.
Mt. Marcy 5344
Adirondack Mts.
Snowy Mtn. 3898
L. George
Rutland
Killington Mtn. 4242
Lebanon
Claremont
Connecticut
Winnipesaukee L.
Concord
Portsmouth
Manchester
Watertown
Pulaski
Oswego
Glens Falls
Oneida L.
Rome
Utica
Irondequoit
Greece
Rochester
Niagara Falls
Lockport
Amherst
Depew
Buffalo
Lackawanna
Syracuse
Auburn
Cayuga L.
Seneca L.
Cortland
Ithaca
Oneonta
Amsterdam
Mohawk
Schenectady
Watervliet
Troy
Albany
NEW YORK
Dunkirk
Olean
Jamestown
Alma Hill 2549
Corning
Elmira
Binghamton
Catskill Mts.
Hunter Mtn. 4026
Slide Mtn. 4203
Kingston
Hudson
Taconic Mts.
Keene
Brattleboro
Nashua
Haverhill
Lowell
Lawrence
Gloucester
Beverly
Fitchburg
Lynn
Malden
Medford
Cambridge
Leominster
Boston
Quincy
Pittsfield
MASSACHUSETTS
Framingham
Weymouth
Holyoke
Northampton
Worcester
Brockton
Westfield
Chicopee
Springfield
Woonsocket
Attleboro
Plymouth
C. Cod
Pawtucket
Providence
Taunton
Fall River
New Bedford
Cranston
Warwick
Newport
RHODE ISLAND
Nantucket Sound
Nantucket I.
Martha's Vineyard
Torrington
Hartford
West Hartford
Manchester
East Hartford
New Britain
Waterbury
CONNECTICUT
Meriden
Norwich
Danbury
New Haven
New London
Montauk Pt.
Milford
Fairfield
Bridgeport
Norwalk
Stamford
Greenwich
Mt. Vernon
Yonkers
Long Island
Hempstead
Poughkeepsie
Newburgh
Carbondale
Scranton
Susquehanna
Kingston
Wilkes-Barre
Williamsport
Bloomsburg
Delaware
Paterson
Clifton
East Orange
Jersey City
Newark
New York
Irvington
Elizabeth
Bayonne
Perth Amboy
Long Branch
Kane
Allegheny
Du Bois
PENNSYLVANIA
Kittanning
Sunbury
Hazleton
Pottsville
Allentown
Easton
Bethlehem
State College
Altoona
Lewistown
Reading
Pottstown
New Brunswick
Trenton
Levittown
Harrisburg
Lebanon
3136
Johnstown
Norristown
Lancaster
York
Chester
Philadelphia
Camden
Mt. Davis 3212
Cumberland
Wilmington
Havre de Grace
Hagerstown
Martinsburg
Frederick
Potomac
Baltimore
Parkville
Catonsville
MARYLAND
Annapolis
Rockville
Silver Spring
Arlington
Washington D.C.
Alexandria
VIRGINIA
Bickle Knob 4008
NEW JERSEY
Vineland
Atlantic City
DELAWARE
Dover
Delaware Bay
Wildwood
C. May
Laurel
ATLANTIC OCEAN
UNITED STATES
CANADA
Relief
Feet Metres
16404 5000
9843 3000
6562 2000
3281 1000
1640 500
656 200
0 Sea Level
Land Dep.
656 200
13123 4000
22966 7000
Scale 1:5,000,000
0 50 100 150 200 Miles
0 50 100 150 200 250 300 Kms.
Bonne Projection
© Collins • Longman Atlases
78° 76° 74° 72° 70° 68° 66°
48° 46° 44° 42° 40°

GULF OF MEXICO

PACIFIC OCEAN

Mexican States numbered on map.

1 FEDERAL DISTRICT
2 TLAXCALA
3 AGUASCALIENTES
4 MORELOS

Scale 1:12 500 000

0 100 200 300 400 500 Miles
0 100 200 300 400 500 600 700 800 Kms.

Lambert Azimuthal Equal Area Projection

Relief

Feet	Metres
16404	5000
9843	3000
6562	2000
3281	1000
1640	500
656	200
0	Sea Level
Land Dep.	
656	200
13123	4000
22966	7000

Hamilton
BERMUDA
ATLANTIC
OCEAN
WEST
INDIES
Tropic of Cancer
West Palm Beach
Freeport
Grand Bahama I.
Great Abaco I.
Fort Lauderdale
Miami
New Providence
Nassau
Eleuthera I.
BAHAMAS
Andros I.
Exuma Is.
Cat I.
San Salvador
Rum Cay
Gt. Exuma
Long I.
Samana Cay
Crooked I.
French Cays
Fortune
Mayaguana I.
Acklin's I.
Little Inagua
Great Inagua I.
Caicos Is. (Br.)
Turks Is. (Br.)
Archo de Camagüey
Caibarién
Morón
CAMAGÜEY
Ciego de Avila
Nuevitas
Camagüey
Holguín
Banes
Victoria de las Tunas
Jardines de la Reina
ORIENTE
Bayamo
Manzanillo
S. Luis
Baracoa
Turquino
Sa. Maestra
Guantánamo
6467
Santiago de Cuba
C. Cruz
Cayman Brac
Windward Passage
Tortue
DOMINICAN REPUBLIC
Puerto Plata
Cap Haïtien
Valverde
Gonaïves
Santiago
Samana
G. of Gonâve
St. Marc
La Vega
San Francisco de Macorís
HAITI
Jérémie
Gonâve I.
S. Pedro
La Romana
Azua
Port-au-Prince
8793
S. Cristóbal
Santo Domingo
Saona
Les Cayes
Barahona
Hispaniola
Puerto Rico Trench
27980
PUERTO RICO (U.S.)
Arecibo
San Juan
Mayaguez
Mona
4390
Caguas
Ponce
Vieques
St. Thomas (U.S.)
Tortola (Br.)
Virgin Is.
St. Croix (U.S.)
Anegada (Br.)
Virgin Gorda (Br.)
Anguilla (Br.)
St. Martin Sint Maarten (Fr.-Neth)
Saba (Neth)
Sint Eustatius (Neth.)
St. Kitts (Br.)
Nevis
St. Barthélemy (Fr.)
Barbuda (Br.)
ANTIGUA
St. John's
Montserrat (Br.)
Guadeloupe (Fr.)
Pointe-à-Pitre
4869
Marie Galante (Fr.)
Roseau
Dominica (Br.)
Fort-de-France
Martinique (Fr.)
Castries
St. Lucia (Br.)
St. Vincent (Br.)
Kingstown
BARBADOS
Bridgetown
The Grenadines (Br.)
Carriacou (Br.)
St. George's
Grenada
Leeward Islands
Windward Islands
Lesser Antilles
Greater Antilles
Montego Bay
St. Ann's Bay
Port Antonio
Black River
Kingston
JAMAICA
CARIBBEAN SEA
Aruba (Netherlands)
Curaçao
Bonaire
Willemstad
Paraguaná Pen.
El Cardon
Los Roques
Orchila
La Blanquilla
Margarita I.
Porlamar
Tortuga
Araya Pen.
Carúpano
Paria Pen.
Dragon's Mouth
TOBAGO
Port of Spain
TRINIDAD
S. Fernando
Gulf of Paria
Serpent's Mouth
Orinoco Delta
Guajira Penin.
Riohacha
Gulf of Venezuela
Coro
Sta. Marta
Sa. Nevada de Sta. Marta
Cristóbal Colón
18947
Barranquilla
Soledad
Altagracia
Cabimas
Maracaibo
Lake Maracaibo
Cartagena
Calamar
Arjona
Tucacas
Pto. Cabello
Maracay
La Guaira
Caracas
San Felipe
Barquisimeto
Carora
Valencia
L. Valencia
San Juan de los Morros
Barcelona
Pto. La Cruz
Cumaná
Caripito
Maturín
CANAL ZONE (U.S.)
Colón
Balboa
Panamá City
Gulf of Darien
G. of Uraba
Gulf of Panamá
Archo. de las Perlas
El Real
Magangue
Magdalena
El Banco
Montería
S. Jorge
Sinú
Turbo
Cauca
Atrato
Riosucio
Cordillera Occidental
Sierra de Perijá
Trujillo
Acarigua
Cojedes
Valle
El Tigre
Mérida
Bolívar
16427
Cordillera de Mérida
Barinas
Guanare
VENEZUELA
S. Félix
Barrage
Curiapo
Ciudad Bolívar
Cúcuta
13780
San Cristóbal
Apure
S. Fernando
Arauca
Orinoco
Bucaramanga
Barrancabermeja
Pamplona
12989
COLOMBIA
Bello
Medellín
13396
Cordillera Central
Cordillera Oriental
Malaga
19022
Sa. Nevada de Cocuy
Meta
Puerto Carreño
Caura
Paragua
Caroni
Angel Falls
Cuyuni
GUYANA
80°
75°
70°
65°
60°
30°
25°
20°
15°
10°

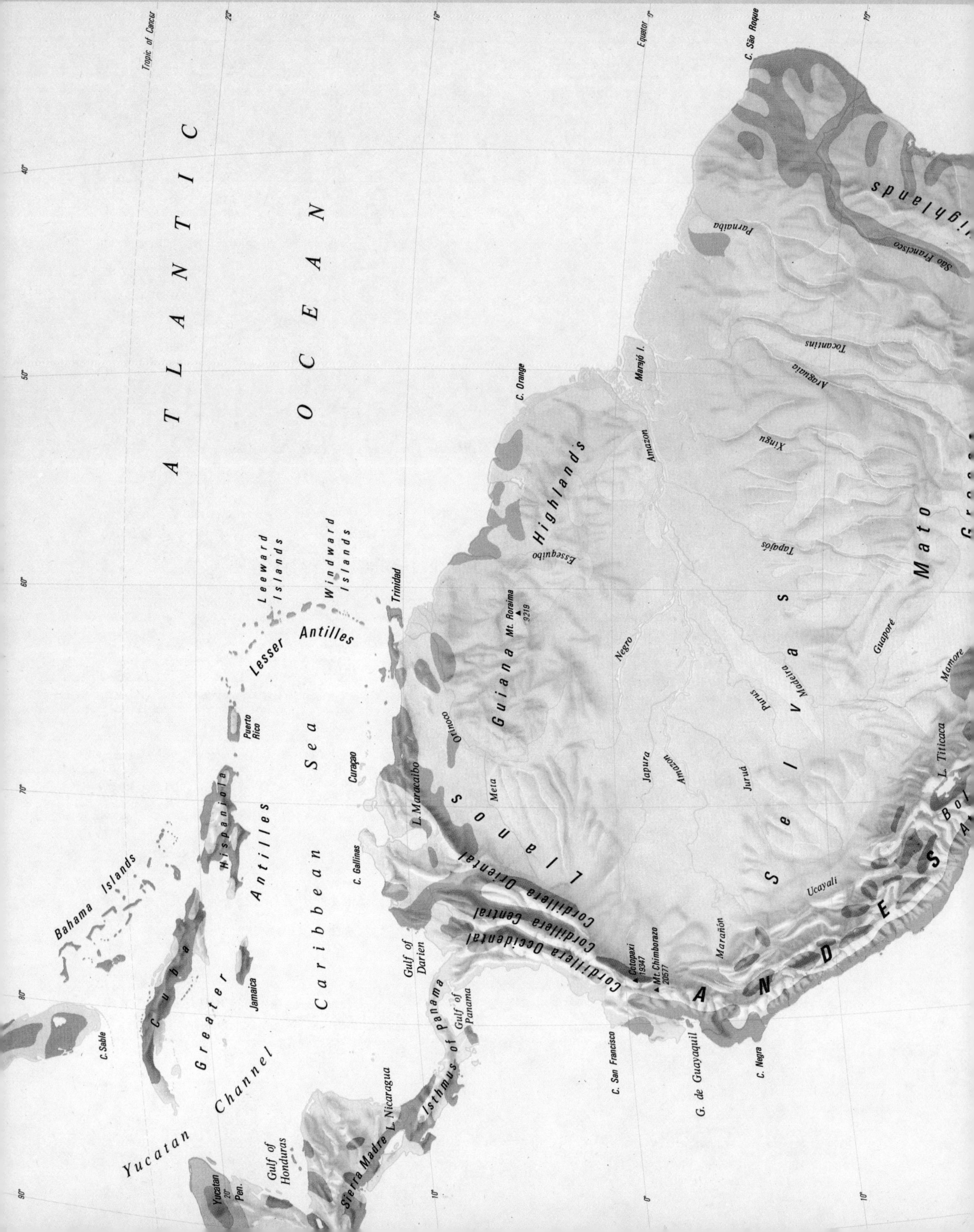

SOUTH AMERICA Land Cover

ATLANTIC OCEAN
Tropic of Cancer
Equator
Caribbean Sea
Bahama Islands
Cuba
Greater Antilles
Hispaniola
Jamaica
Puerto Rico
Lesser Antilles
Leeward Islands
Windward Islands
Trinidad
Curaçao
C. Gallinas
Yucatan Channel
Yucatan Pen.
C. Sable
Gulf of Honduras
Sierra Madre
L. Nicaragua
Isthmus of Panama
Gulf of Panama
Gulf of Darien
L. Maracaibo
Cordillera Oriental
Cordillera Central
Cordillera Occidental
Llanos
Orinoco
Meta
Guiana Highlands
Mt. Roraima 9219
Essequibo
C. Orange
Marajó I.
Amazon
Negro
Japura
Juruá
Purus
Madeira
Tapajós
Xingu
Araguaia
Tocantins
Parnaiba
São Francisco
Highlands
C. São Roque
Guaporé
Mamoré
Mato Grosso
Selvas
L. Titicaca
Bolivia
Ucayali
Marañón
Cotopaxi 19347
Mt. Chimborazo 20577
C. San Francisco
G. de Guayaquil
C. Negra
ANDES

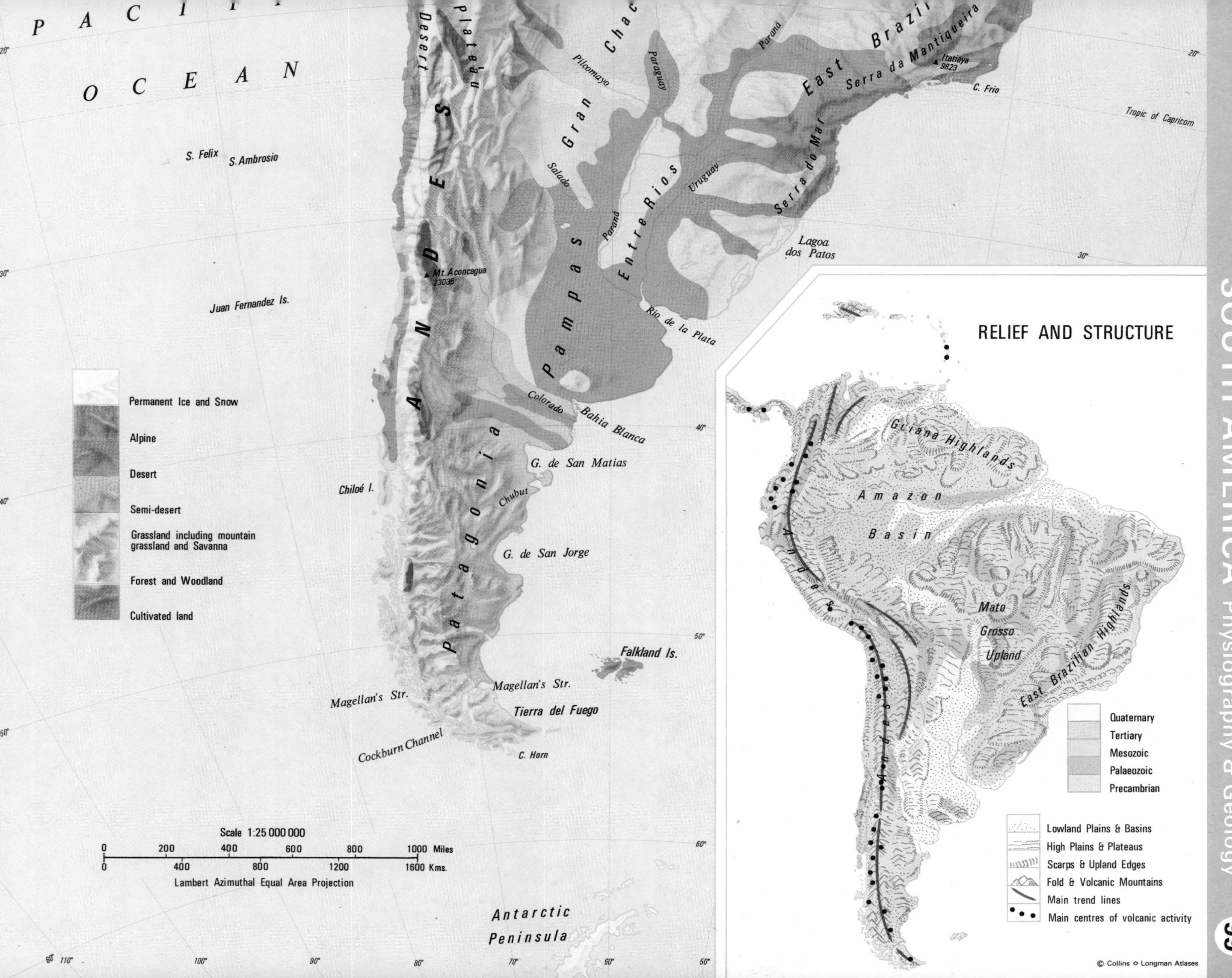
PACIFIC
OCEAN
S. Felix
S. Ambrosio
Juan Fernandez Is.
Chiloé I.
Desert
Plateau
ANDES
Mt. Aconcagua 23035
Gran Chaco
Pilcomayo
Paraguay
Paraná
Uruguay
Entre Rios
Salado
Pampas
Rio de la Plata
Lagoa dos Patos
Serra do Mar
East Brazil
Serra da Mantiqueira
Itatiaya 9823
C. Frio
Tropic of Capricorn
Colorado
Bahia Blanca
G. de San Matias
Chubut
G. de San Jorge
Patagonia
Falkland Is.
Magellan's Str.
Tierra del Fuego
C. Horn
Cockburn Channel
Antarctic
Peninsula
Permanent Ice and Snow
Alpine
Desert
Semi-desert
Grassland including mountain grassland and Savanna
Forest and Woodland
Cultivated land
Scale 1:25 000 000
0 200 400 600 800 1000 Miles
0 400 800 1200 1600 Kms.
Lambert Azimuthal Equal Area Projection
RELIEF AND STRUCTURE
Guiana Highlands
Amazon
Basin
Andes
Mato
Grosso
Upland
East Brazilian Highlands
Quaternary
Tertiary
Mesozoic
Palaeozoic
Precambrian
Lowland Plains & Basins
High Plains & Plateaus
Scarps & Upland Edges
Fold & Volcanic Mountains
Main trend lines
Main centres of volcanic activity

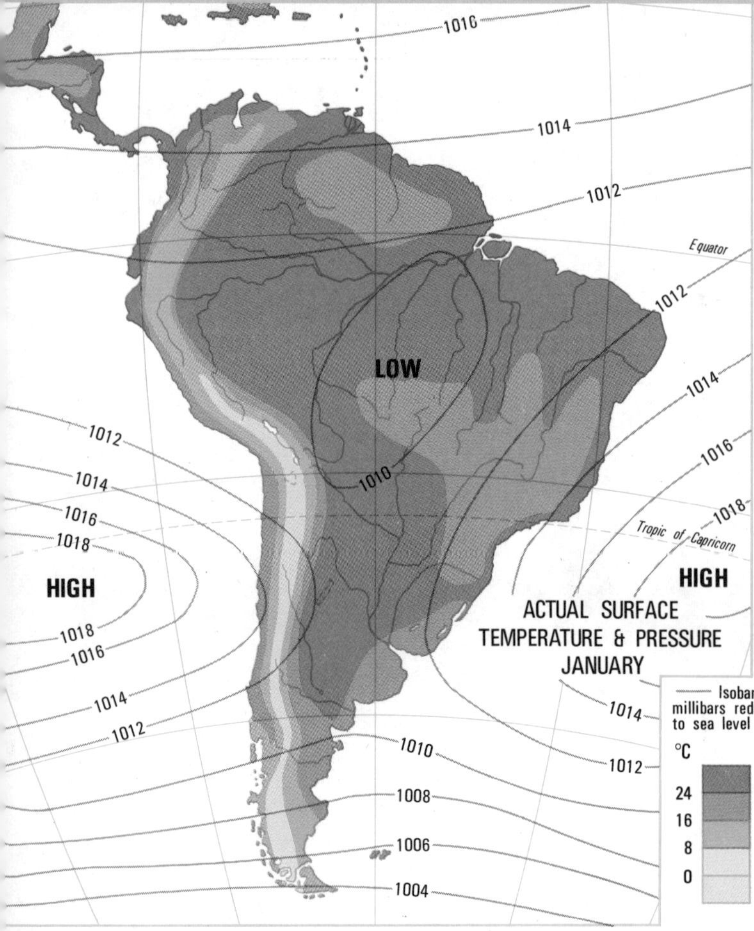

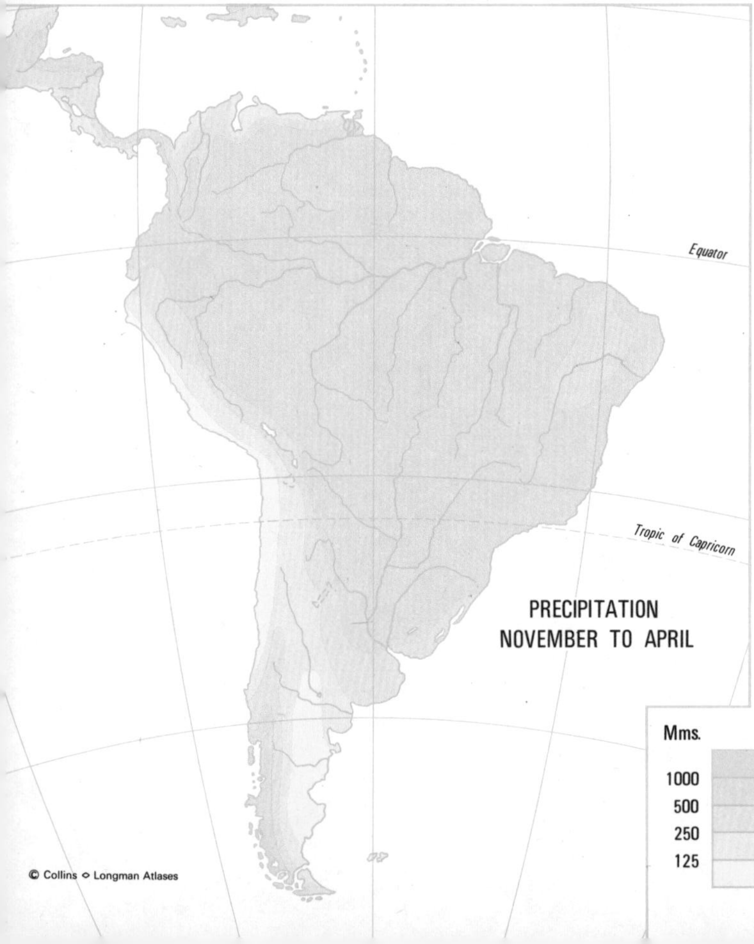

ACTUAL SURFACE TEMPERATURE & PRESSURE JANUARY

LOW
HIGH
HIGH
Equator
Tropic of Capricorn
1016
1014
1012
1010
1008
1006
1004
1018

ACTUAL SURFACE TEMPERATURE & PRESSURE JULY

LOW
HIGH
HIGH
1010
1012
1014
1016
1018
1020
1022

Isobars in millibars reduced to sea level

°C	°F
24	75
16	60
8	46
0	32

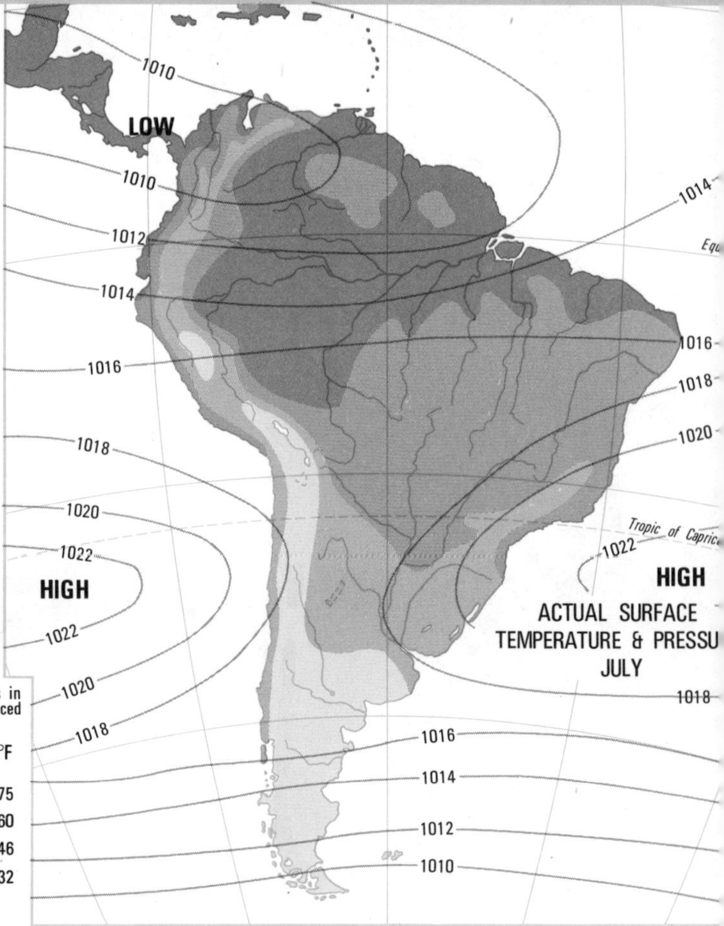

PRECIPITATION NOVEMBER TO APRIL

PRECIPITATION MAY TO OCTOBER

Equator
Tropic of Capricorn

Mms.	Ins.
1000	40
500	20
250	10
125	5

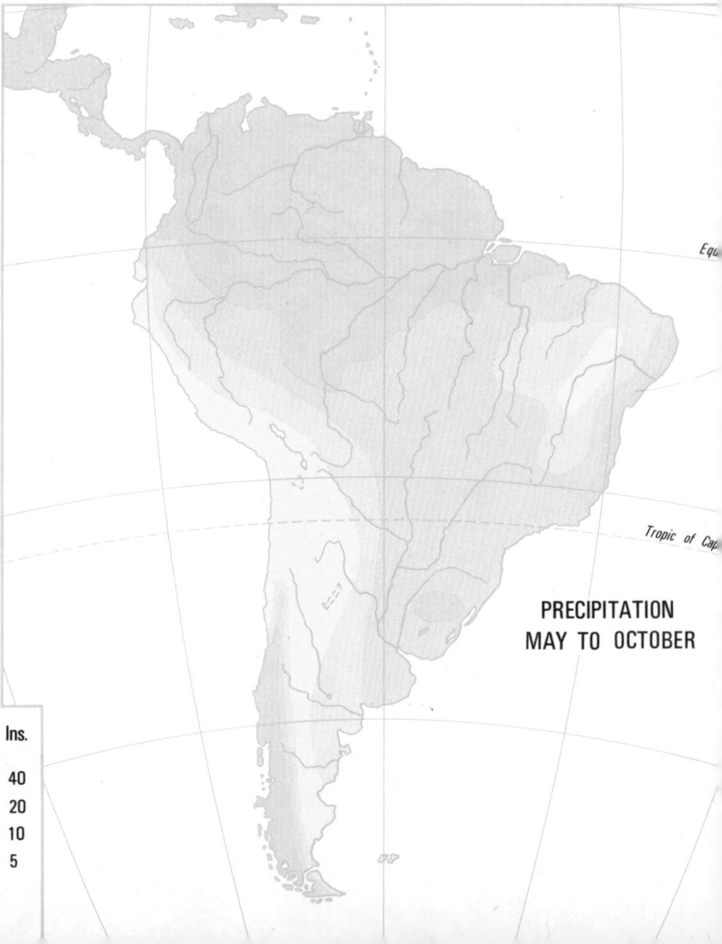

MINERAL RESOURCES
Structure
Shield
Old fold mountains
Young fold mountains
Plains
Coal
Natural Gas
Oil
Oil pipe-line
Minerals
Asbestos
Bauxite
Cobalt
Copper
Gold
Iron
Lead & Zinc
Manganese
Nickel
Phosphates, Potash, Nitrates
Silver
Tin
Scale 1:50 000 000
0 400 800 1200 Miles
0 400 800 1200 1600 Kms.
Lambert Azimuthal Equal Area Projection
Tropic of Capricorn
Equator
Caracas
Medellin
Bogotá
Cali
Lima
Recife
Salvador
Belo Horizonte
Rio de Janeiro
São Paulo
Santiago
Montevideo
Buenos Aires
Tropic of Capricorn
POPULATION
Persons per sq. km.
Persons per sq. mile
Over 100
50-100
10-50
1-10
0-1
Over 250
125-250
25-125
2-25
0-2
Cities over 1 000 000 population
Scale 1:50 000 000
0 400 800 1200 Miles
0 400 800 1200 1600 Kms.
Lambert Azimuthal Equal Area Projection

Havana
CUBA
BAHAMAS
Yucatan Channel
Greater Antilles
HAITI
Port-au-Prince
DOMINICAN REP.
Santo Domingo
PUERTO RICO
San Juan
JAMAICA
Kingston
Lesser Antilles
Leeward Is.
Windward Is.
MEXICO
BELIZE
Belmopan
GUATEMALA
Guatemala City
HONDURAS
Tegucigalpa
San Salvador
EL SALVADOR
NICARAGUA
Managua
L. Nicaragua
COSTA RICA
San José
CANAL ZONE (U.S.)
PANAMA
Panamá City
Caribbean Sea
C. Gallinas
Curaçao
Barranquilla
Cartagena
Maracaibo
L. Maracaibo
Caracas
Ciudad Bolívar
TRINIDAD
Port of Spain
Cúcuta
VENEZUELA
Medellin
Manizales
Bogotá
COLOMBIA
Cali
Orinoco
Georgetown
GUYANA
Essequibo
Paramaribo
SURINAM
Cayenne
GUIANA (Fr.)
Quito
ECUADOR
Guayaquil
Galapagos Is. (Ec.)
Negro
Manaus
Amazon
Iquitos
Tapajós
Xingu
Trans Amazonian Highway
Madeira
Belém
São Luís
Fortaleza
Teresina
Natal
João Pessoa
Recife
Maceió
Aracaju
Salvador
PERU
Pucallpa
Trujillo
Callao
Lima
Cuzco
BRAZIL
Araguaia
Tocantins
São Francisco
L. Titicaca
Arequipa
La Paz
Cochabamba
Santa Cruz
BOLIVIA
Sucre
Cuiabá
Goiânia
Brasília
Arica
Iquique
Paraguay
PARAGUAY
Paraná
Belo Horizonte
Vitória
Ribeirão Prêto
Rio de Janeiro
Niterói
São Paulo
Tropic of Capricorn
Antofagasta
Salta
Asunción
Curitiba
San Miguel de Tucumán
Salado
Uruguay
Florianópolis
CHILE
Pôrto Alegre
Córdoba
Santa Fé
Pelotas
URUGUAY
Valparaíso
Santiago
Mendoza
Rosario
Buenos Aires
Montevideo
Río de la Plata
Juan Fernandez Is. (Chile)
Talca
Concepción
ARGENTINA
Mar del Plata
Bahía Blanca
San Antonio Oeste
G. of San Matias
Puerto Montt
Chiloé I.
Trelew
Comodoro Rivadavia
Falkland Is. (Br.)
Punta Arenas
Tierra del Fuego
PACIFIC OCEAN
ATLANTIC OCEAN
SOUTH ATLANTIC OCEAN
Tropic of Cancer
Equator
Scale 1:35 000 000
0 200 400 600 800 1000 Miles
0 400 800 1200 1600 Kms.
Lambert Azimuthal Equal Area Projection
© Collins ◇ Longman Atlases

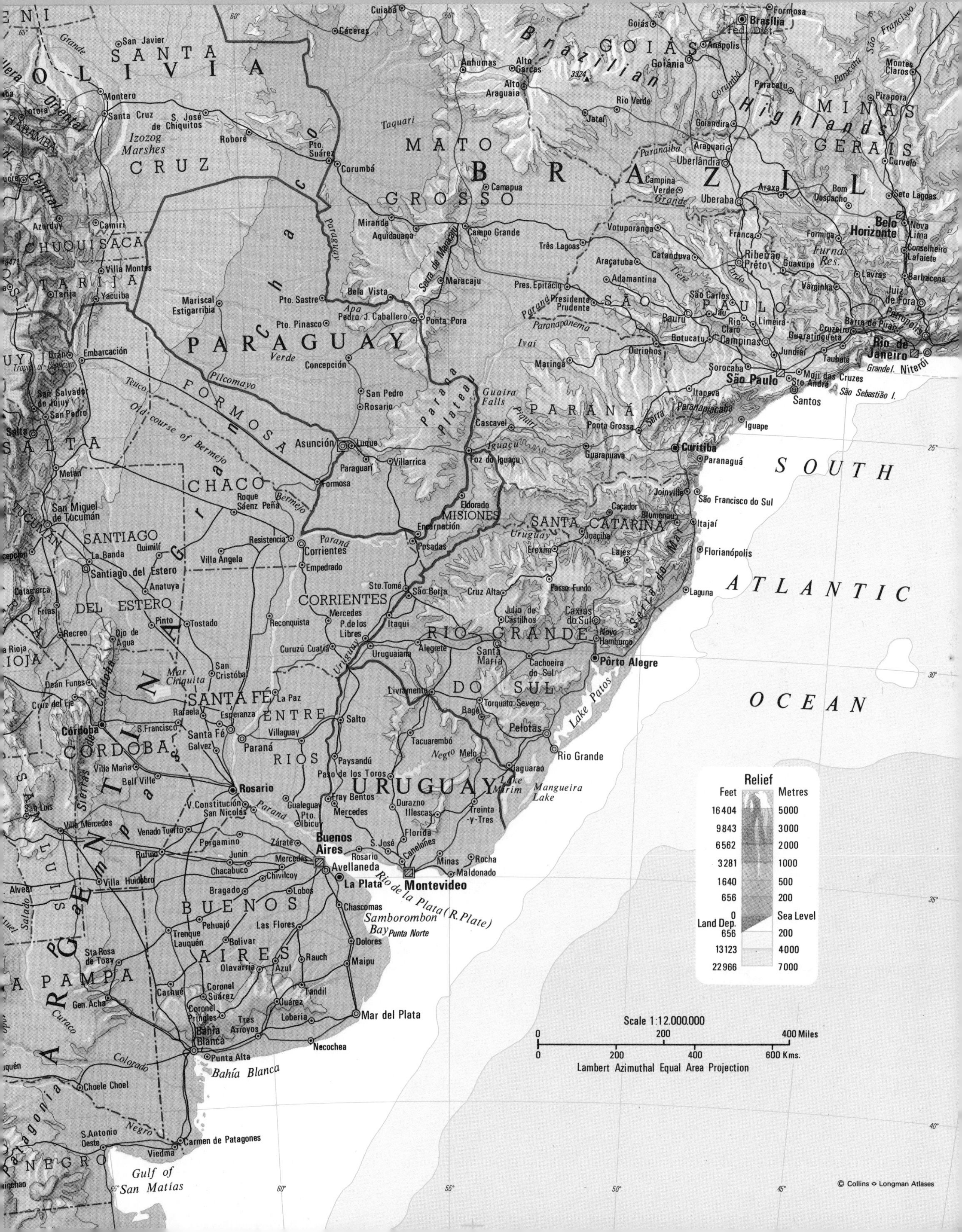

BRAZIL
PARAGUAY
URUGUAY
ARGENTINA
BOLIVIA
SOUTH ATLANTIC OCEAN

SANTA CRUZ
CHUQUISACA
TARIJA
MATO GROSSO
GOIÁS
MINAS GERAIS
SÃO PAULO
PARANÁ
SANTA CATARINA
RIO GRANDE DO SUL
MISIONES
CORRIENTES
ENTRE RIOS
SANTA FÉ
CHACO
FORMOSA
SALTA
SANTIAGO DEL ESTERO
CÓRDOBA
BUENOS AIRES
LA PAMPA
SAN LUIS
RIO NEGRO

Brazilian Highlands
Paraná Plateau
Gran Chaco
Pampas
Patagonia
Izozog Marshes
Serra de Maracaju
Serra do Mar
Sierras de Córdoba
Guaira Falls
Furnas Res.
Mar Chiquita
Lake Patos
Lake Mirim
Mangueira Lake
Samborombon Bay
Punta Norte
Bahía Blanca
Gulf of San Matias
Río de la Plata (R. Plate)
Grande I.
São Sebastião I.
Old course of Bermejo
Tropic of Capricorn
3324

Rivers: Grande, Paraguay, Taquari, Apa, Verde, Pilcomayo, Teuco, Bermejo, Paraná, Uruguay, Iguaçu, Piquiri, Ivaí, Paranapanema, Tietê, Pardo, Paranaíba, Corumbá, Paracatu, São Francisco, Negro, Salado, Colorado, Curaco

Cuiabá, Cáceres, Goiás, Brasília, Fed. Dist., Formosa, Anápolis, Goiânia, Anhumas, Alto Garças, Alto Araguaia, Rio Verde, Jataí, Paracatu, Montes Claros, Pirapora, Goiandira, Araguari, Uberlândia, Curvelo, Campina Verde, Uberaba, Araxá, Bom Despacho, Sete Lagoas, Belo Horizonte, Nova Lima, Conselheiro Lafaiete, Barbacena, Formiga, Lavras, Varginha, Juiz de Fora, Campapua, Miranda, Aquidauana, Campo Grande, Três Lagoas, Votuporanga, Franca, Ribeirão Prêto, Guaxupé, Catanduva, Araçatuba, Adamantina, Maracaju, Bela Vista, Pto. Sastre, Pto. Pinasco, Pedro J. Caballero, Ponta Pora, Pres. Epitácio, Presidente Prudente, São Carlos, Jaú, Bauru, Rio Claro, Limeira, Botucatu, Campinas, Cruzeiro, Guaratinguetá, Barra do Piraí, Petrópolis, Rio de Janeiro, Niterói, Taubaté, Jundiaí, Ourinhos, Maringá, Sorocaba, São Paulo, Moji das Cruzes, Sto. André, Santos, Itapeva, Paranapiacaba, Iguape, Ponta Grossa, Cascavel, Guarapuava, Curitiba, Paranaguá, Foz do Iguaçu, Joinville, São Francisco do Sul, Caçador, Blumenau, Itajaí, Joaçiba, Erexim, Lajes, Florianópolis, Passo Fundo, Laguna, Cruz Alta, Júlio de Castilhos, Caxias do Sul, Novo Hamburgo, Pôrto Alegre, Santa Maria, Cachoeira do Sul, Alegrete, Uruguaiana, Itaqui, São Borja, Santo Tomé, Livramento, Bagé, Torquato Severo, Pelotas, Rio Grande, Jaguarão, Eldorado, Encarnación, Posadas

Montero, Santa Cruz, S. José de Chiquitos, Roboré, San Javier, Pto. Suárez, Corumbá, Camiri, Azurduy, Villa Montes, Tarija, Yacuiba, Mariscal Estigarribia, Concepción, San Pedro, Rosario, Asunción, Luque, Paraguarí, Villarrica

Orán, Embarcación, San Salvador de Jujuy, San Pedro, Salta, Metán, San Miguel de Tucumán, Formosa, Roque Sáenz Peña, Resistencia, Corrientes, Empedrado, Quimilí, La Banda, Santiago del Estero, Villa Angela, Anatuya, Catamarca, Frías, Recreo, Ojo de Agua, Pinto, Tostado, Reconquista, Mercedes, P. de los Libres, Curuzú Cuatiá, La Rioja, San Cristóbal, Deán Funes, Cruz del Eje, Córdoba, Rafaela, Esperanza, Santa Fé, La Paz, Paraná, Villaguay, Salto, S. Francisco, Galvez, Villa María, Bell Ville, Rosario, Paysandú, Tacuarembó, Melo, Paso de los Toros, Fray Bentos, Mercedes, Gualeguay, Pto. Ibicuy, Durazno, Illescas, Treinta y Tres, Florida, Canelones, Minas, Rocha, Maldonado, Montevideo, S. José, Rosario, V. Constitución, San Nicolás, San Luis, Villa Mercedes, Venado Tuerto, Pergamino, Zárate, Buenos Aires, Avellaneda, La Plata, Junín, Mercedes, Rufino, Chacabuco, Chivilcoy, Villa Huidobro, Alvear, Bragado, Lobos, Chascomas, Pehuajó, Las Flores, Dolores, Trenque Lauquén, Bolivar, Sta Rosa de Toay, Rauch, Maipu, Olavarria, Azul, Carhué, Coronel Suárez, Tandil, Gen. Acha, Coronel Pringles, Juárez, Lobería, Mar del Plata, Tres Arroyos, Bahía Blanca, Punta Alta, Necochea, Choele Choel, S. Antonio Oeste, Carmen de Patagones, Viedma

Relief

Feet	Metres
16404	5000
9843	3000
6562	2000
3281	1000
1640	500
656	200
0	Sea Level
Land Dep.	
656	200
13123	4000
22966	7000

Scale 1:12.000.000

0 200 400 Miles
0 200 400 600 Kms.

Lambert Azimuthal Equal Area Projection

65° 60° 55° 50° 45° 25° 30° 35° 40°

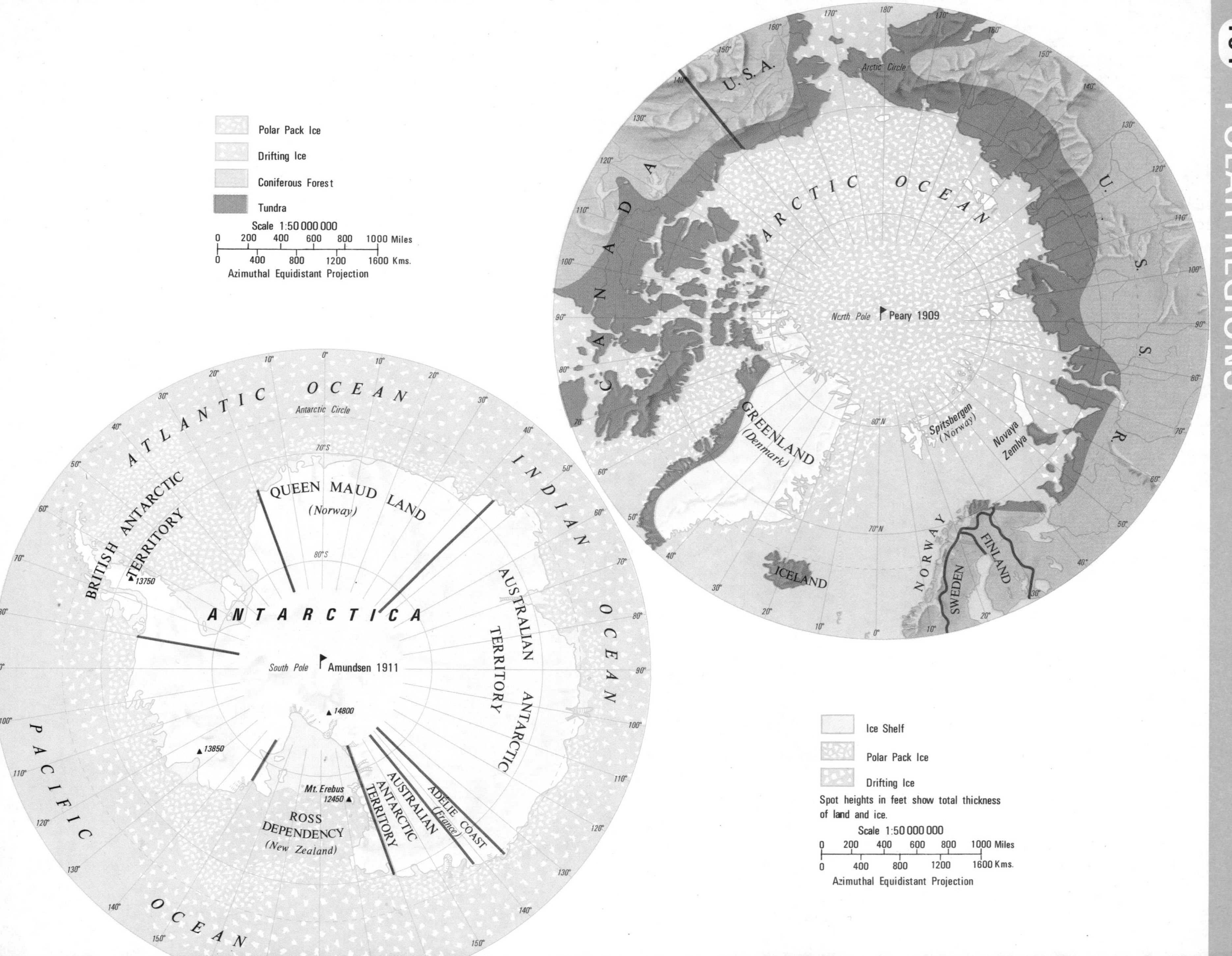

U. S. S. R.
ARCTIC OCEAN
CANADA
U.S.A.
Arctic Circle
North Pole
Peary 1909
Spitsbergen (Norway)
Novaya Zemlya
GREENLAND (Denmark)
ICELAND
NORWAY
SWEDEN
FINLAND
Ice Shelf
Polar Pack Ice
Drifting Ice
Spot heights in feet show total thickness of land and ice.
Scale 1:50 000 000
0 200 400 600 800 1000 Miles
0 400 800 1200 1600 Kms.
Azimuthal Equidistant Projection
Polar Pack Ice
Drifting Ice
Coniferous Forest
Tundra
Scale 1:50 000 000
0 200 400 600 800 1000 Miles
0 400 800 1200 1600 Kms.
Azimuthal Equidistant Projection
ATLANTIC OCEAN
Antarctic Circle
BRITISH ANTARCTIC TERRITORY
13750
QUEEN MAUD LAND (Norway)
INDIAN OCEAN
ANTARCTICA
AUSTRALIAN ANTARCTIC TERRITORY
South Pole
Amundsen 1911
14800
13850
Mt. Erebus 12450
ROSS DEPENDENCY (New Zealand)
AUSTRALIAN ANTARCTIC TERRITORY
ADÉLIE COAST (France)
PACIFIC OCEAN

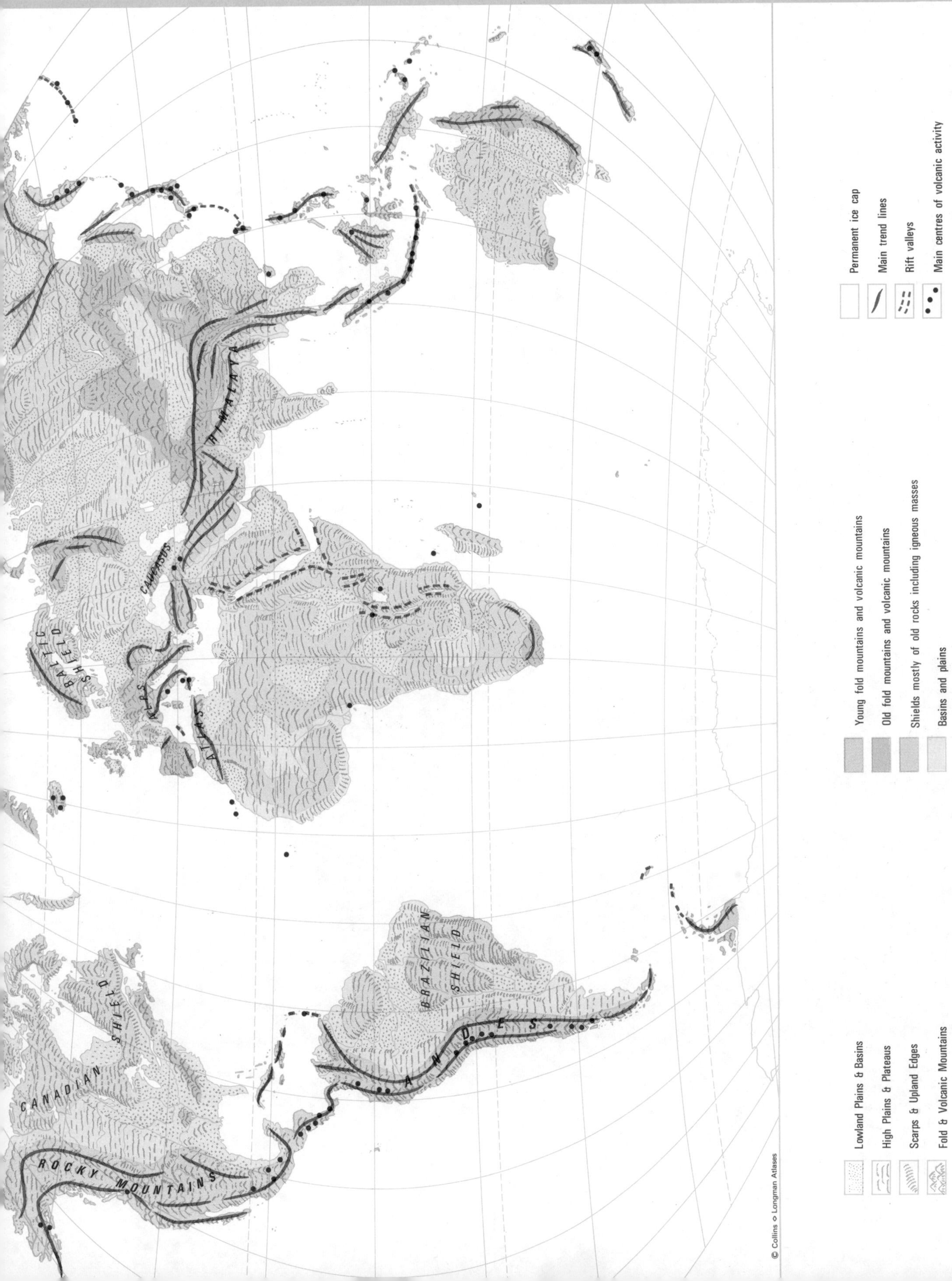

ROCKY MOUNTAINS
CANADIAN SHIELD
BALTIC SHIELD
ALPS
ATLAS
CAUCASUS
HIMALAYA
BRAZILIAN SHIELD
ANDES

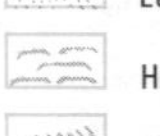

Lowland Plains & Basins
High Plains & Plateaus
Scarps & Upland Edges
Fold & Volcanic Mountains

Young fold mountains and volcanic mountains
Old fold mountains and volcanic mountains
Shields mostly of old rocks including igneous masses
Basins and plains

Permanent ice cap
Main trend lines
Rift valleys
Main centres of volcanic activity

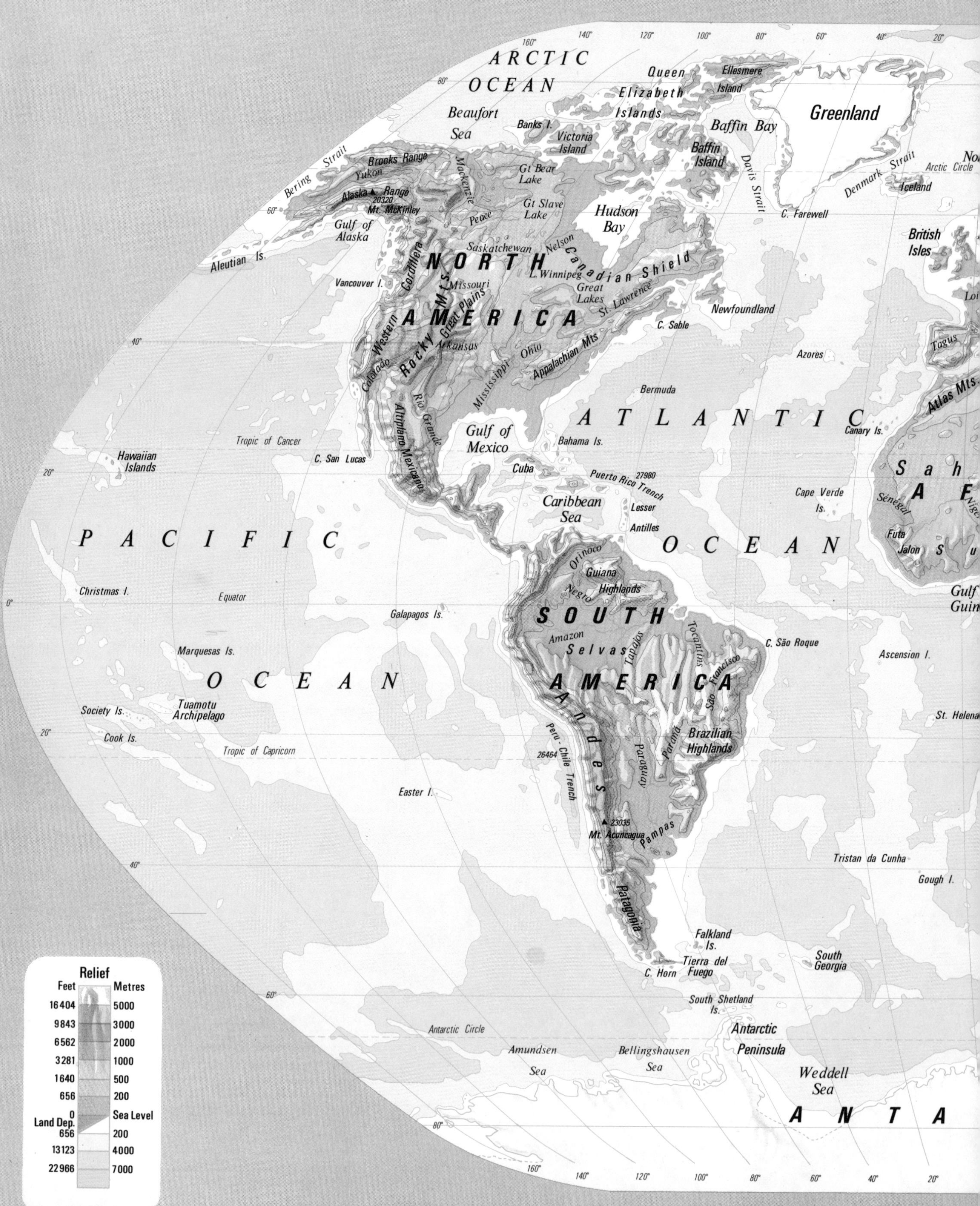
ARCTIC OCEAN
Beaufort Sea
Banks I.
Victoria Island
Queen Elizabeth Islands
Ellesmere Island
Greenland
Baffin Bay
Baffin Island
Davis Strait
Denmark Strait
Arctic Circle
Iceland
C. Farewell
Bering Strait
Brooks Range
Yukon
Alaska Range
20320
Mt. McKinley
Mackenzie
Gt Bear Lake
Gt Slave Lake
Hudson Bay
Peace
Gulf of Alaska
Aleutian Is.
Saskatchewan
Nelson
NORTH AMERICA
Canadian Shield
Vancouver I.
Western Cordillera
Rocky Mts.
Great Plains
Missouri
L. Winnipeg
Great Lakes
St. Lawrence
Newfoundland
C. Sable
British Isles
Arkansas
Colorado
Ohio
Mississippi
Appalachian Mts
Azores
Tagus
Atlas Mts.
Bermuda
Rio Grande
Altiplano Mexicano
Gulf of Mexico
ATLANTIC
Canary Is.
Bahama Is.
Tropic of Cancer
C. San Lucas
Hawaiian Islands
Cuba
Puerto Rico Trench
27980
Cape Verde Is.
Caribbean Sea
Lesser Antilles
Sénégal
PACIFIC
OCEAN
Futa Jalon
Orinoco
Guiana Highlands
Negro
Christmas I.
Equator
Galapagos Is.
SOUTH AMERICA
Amazon
Selvas
Tapajós
Tocantins
C. São Roque
Ascension I.
São Francisco
Marquesas Is.
OCEAN
Andes
Tuamotu Archipelago
Society Is.
St. Helena
Cook Is.
Tropic of Capricorn
Peru-Chile Trench
26464
Paraná
Paraguay
Brazilian Highlands
Easter I.
23035
Mt. Aconcagua
Pampas
Tristan da Cunha
Gough I.
Patagonia
Falkland Is.
Tierra del Fuego
C. Horn
South Georgia
South Shetland Is.
Antarctic Circle
Antarctic Peninsula
Amundsen Sea
Bellingshausen Sea
Weddell Sea
ANTA
Relief
Feet
Metres
16404 5000
9843 3000
6562 2000
3281 1000
1640 500
656 200
0 Sea Level
Land Dep.
656 200
13123 4000
22966 7000

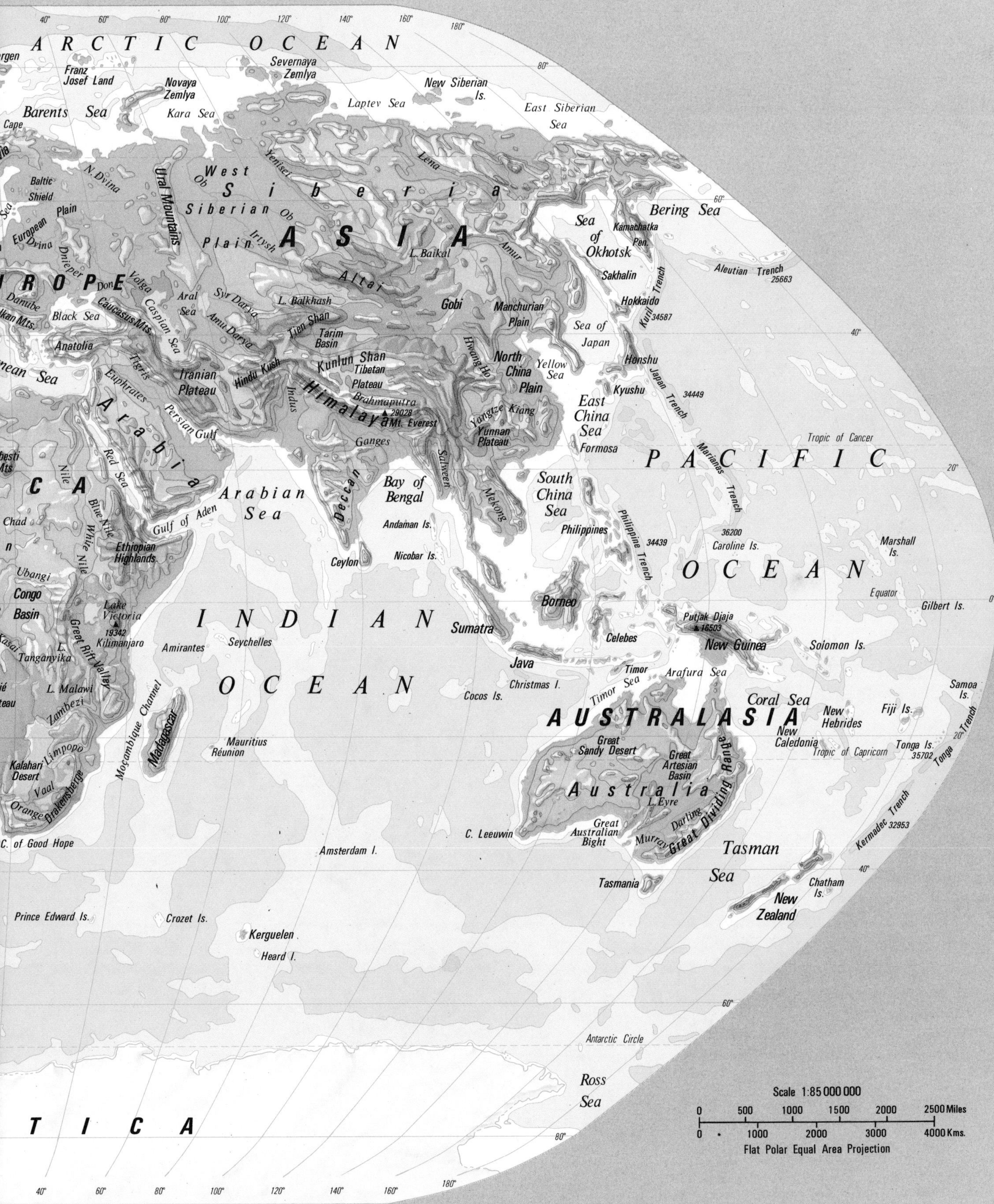
ARCTIC OCEAN
Franz Josef Land
Novaya Zemlya
Severnaya Zemlya
New Siberian Is.
Barents Sea
Kara Sea
Laptev Sea
East Siberian Sea
West Siberian Plain
Siberia
Ural Mountains
Ob
Yenisei
Lena
Irtysh
ASIA
L. Baikal
Bering Sea
Sea of Okhotsk
Kamachatka Pen.
Sakhalin
Aleutian Trench 25663
Kuril Trench 34587
Hokkaido
Baltic Shield
N. Dvina
European Plain
Dvina
Dnieper
Volga
Don
EUROPE
Danube
Black Sea
Caucasus Mts.
Caspian Sea
Aral Sea
Syr Darya
Amu Darya
L. Balkhash
Altai
Gobi
Amur
Manchurian Plain
Sea of Japan
Tien Shan
Tarim Basin
Anatolia
Kunlun Shan
Tibetan Plateau
Hwang Ho
North China Plain
Yellow Sea
Honshu
Kyushu
Japan Trench
34449
Tigris
Euphrates
Iranian Plateau
Hindu Kush
Indus
Himalaya
Brahmaputra
29028 Mt. Everest
Yangtze Kiang
Yunnan Plateau
East China Sea
Formosa
Tropic of Cancer
PACIFIC OCEAN
Arabia
Persian Gulf
Ganges
Red Sea
Nile
Salween
Mariana Trench
Arabian Sea
Deccan
Bay of Bengal
Mekong
South China Sea
Philippines
Philippine Trench
34439
36200
Caroline Is.
Marshall Is.
Gulf of Aden
Blue Nile
White Nile
Chad
Ethiopian Highlands
Andaman Is.
Nicobar Is.
Ceylon
Ubangi
Congo Basin
Lake Victoria
19342 Kilimanjaro
Great Rift Valley
Borneo
Equator
Gilbert Is.
INDIAN OCEAN
Sumatra
Celebes
Putjak Djaja 16503
New Guinea
Solomon Is.
Kasai
L. Tanganyika
Amirantes
Seychelles
Java
Timor
Arafura Sea
Timor Sea
Christmas I.
Cocos Is.
L. Malawi
Zambezi
Moçambique Channel
Madagascar
Coral Sea
AUSTRALASIA
New Hebrides
Fiji Is.
Samoa Is.
New Caledonia
Tonga Is. 35702
Tonga Trench
Tropic of Capricorn
Mauritius
Réunion
Kalahari Desert
Limpopo
Vaal
Orange
Drakensberge
Great Sandy Desert
Great Artesian Basin
Great Dividing Range
Australia
L. Eyre
Darling
Murray
Great Australian Bight
C. Leeuwin
Kermadec Trench 32953
C. of Good Hope
Amsterdam I.
Tasman Sea
Tasmania
Chatham Is.
New Zealand
Prince Edward Is.
Crozet Is.
Kerguelen
Heard I.
Antarctic Circle
Ross Sea
TICA
Scale 1:85 000 000
0 500 1000 1500 2000 2500 Miles
0 1000 2000 3000 4000 Kms.
Flat Polar Equal Area Projection

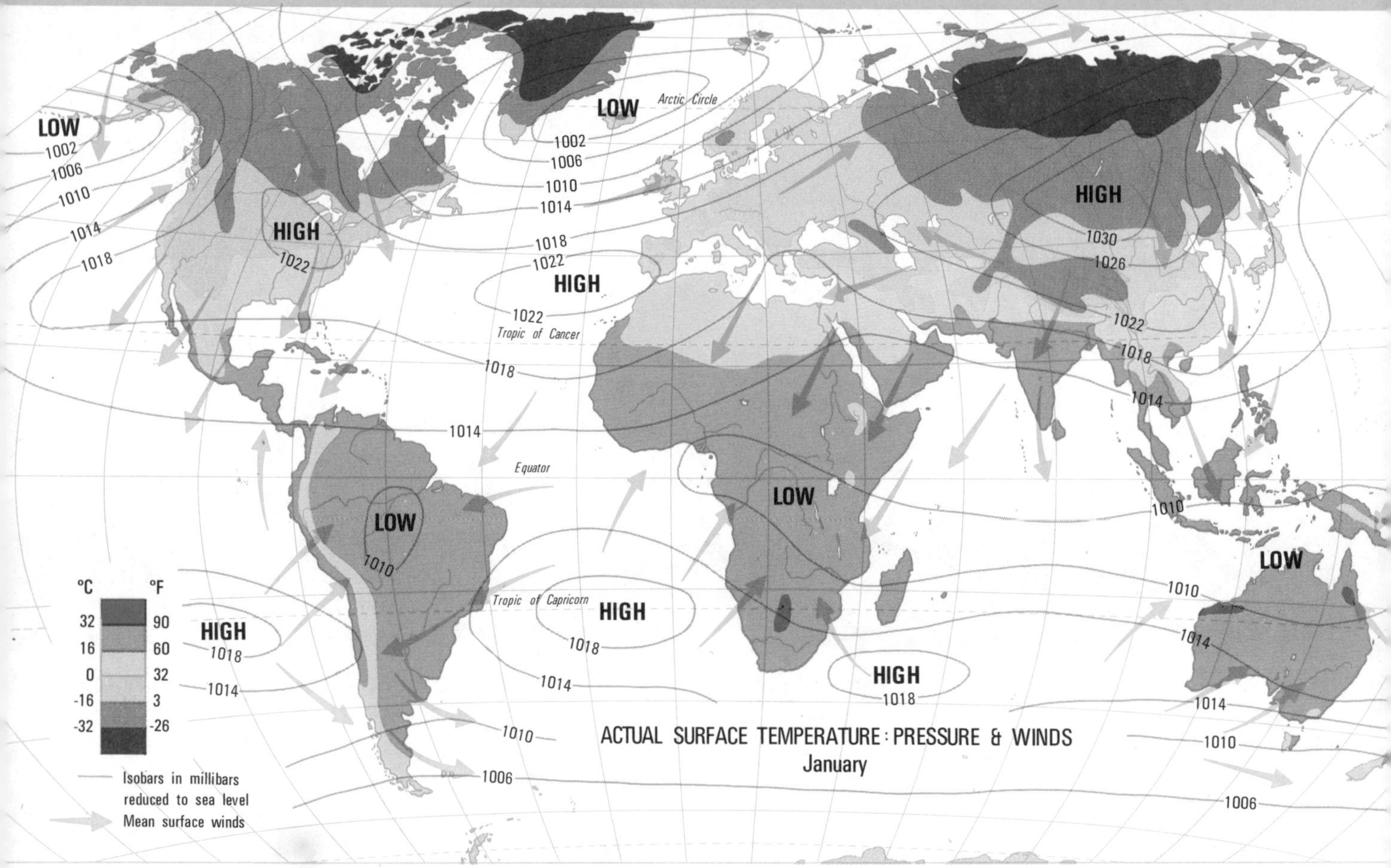

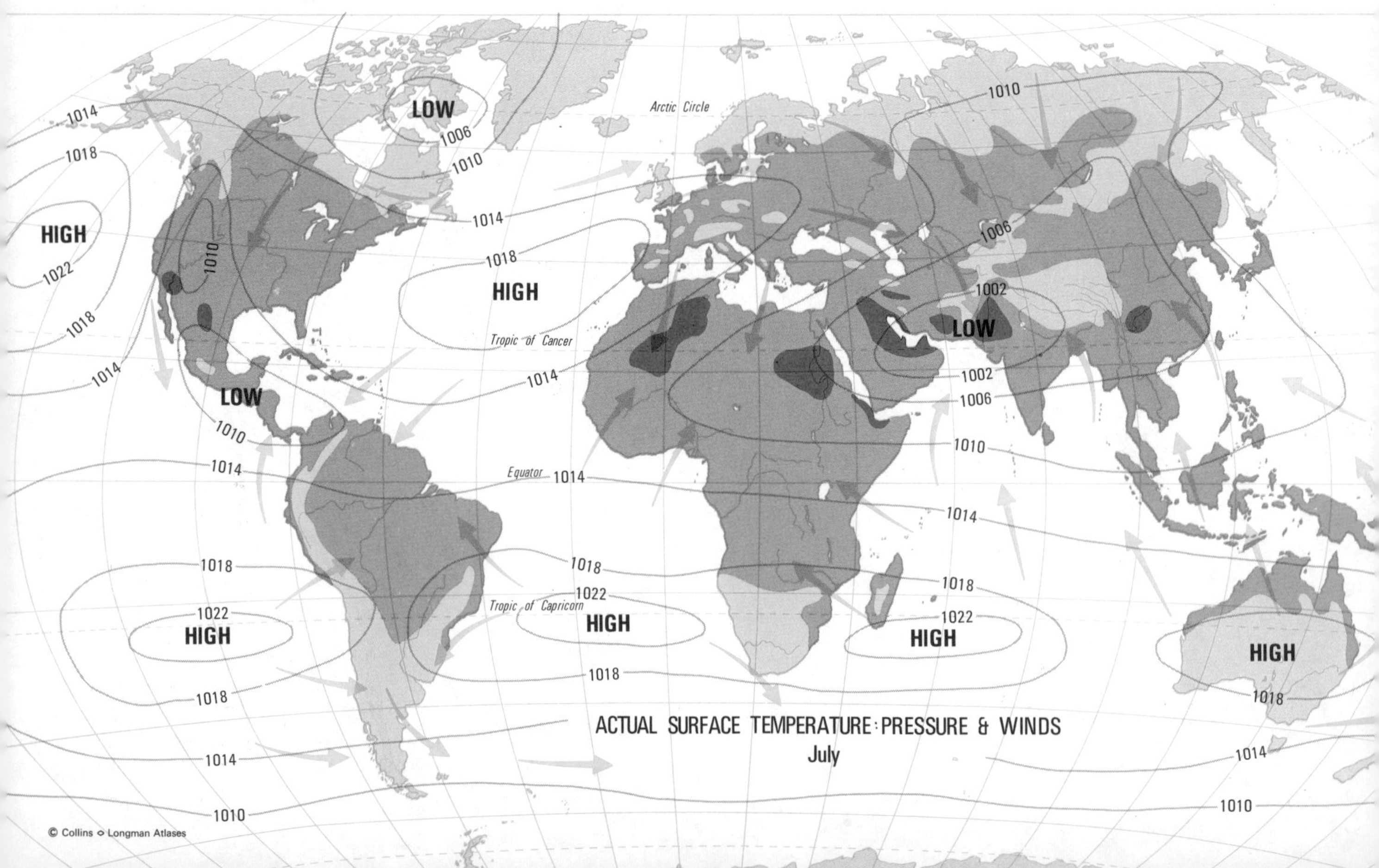

ACTUAL SURFACE TEMPERATURE: PRESSURE & WINDS
January

ACTUAL SURFACE TEMPERATURE: PRESSURE & WINDS
July

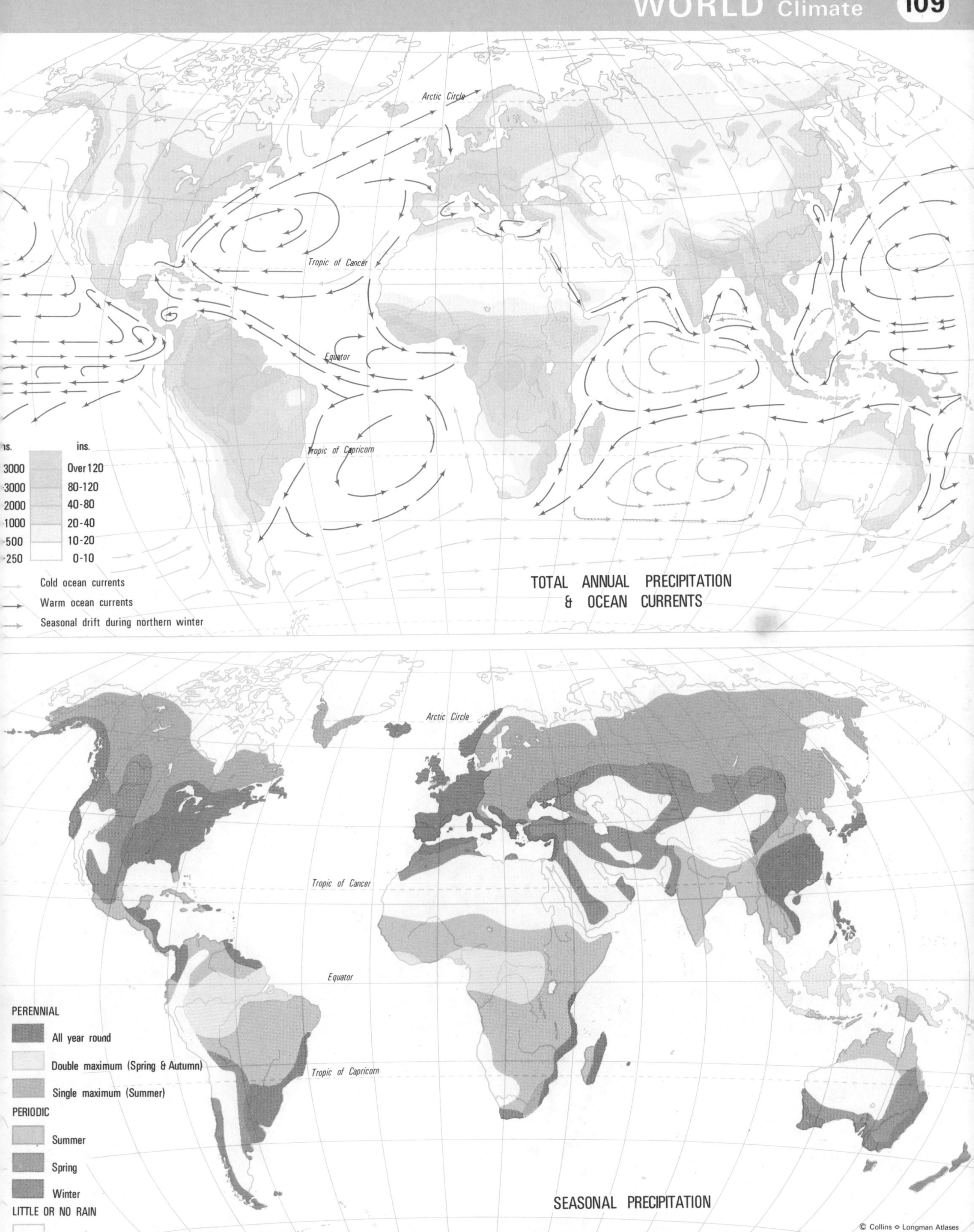

Arctic Circle
Tropic of Cancer
Equator
Tropic of Capricorn
ns.
ins.
3000
Over 120
3000
80-120
2000
40-80
1000
20-40
500
10-20
250
0-10
Cold ocean currents
Warm ocean currents
Seasonal drift during northern winter
TOTAL ANNUAL PRECIPITATION & OCEAN CURRENTS
Arctic Circle
Tropic of Cancer
Equator
Tropic of Capricorn
PERENNIAL
All year round
Double maximum (Spring & Autumn)
Single maximum (Summer)
PERIODIC
Summer
Spring
Winter
LITTLE OR NO RAIN
SEASONAL PRECIPITATION

Reindeer
Arctic Circle
Wheat
Beef Cattle
Fruit
Beef Cattle
Sheep
Dairy Cattle
Beef Cattle
Maize
Wheat
Cotton
Fruit
Cotton
Tropic of Cancer
Sugar
Coffee
Coffee
Coffee
Beef Cattle
Cocoa
Equator
Sheep
Cotton
Beef Cattle
Sugar
Cocoa
Sugar
Beef Cattle
Coffee
Coffee
Tropic of Capricorn
Fruit
Maize
Wheat
Sheep
Dairy Cattle
Wheat
Fruit
Fruit
Fruit
Fruit
Sheep
Sheep
Sheep
Camel
Cattle
Cattle
Oil Palm
Coffee
Cocoa
Cocoa
Oil Palm
Coffee
Scale 1:72 500 000
0 500 1000 1500 Miles
0 500 1000 1500 2000 Kms.
Winkel Projection
Tundra and desert
Forest
Forest with small agricultural communities

Reindeer
Cattle
Wheat
Wheat
Beef Cattle
Maize
Sheep
Sheep
Cotton
Fruit
Fruit
Sheep
Fruit
Wheat
Sheep
Wheat
Cotton
Fruit
Tea
Yak
Rice
Tea
Wheat
Cotton
Rice
Camels
Sheep
Rice
Rice
Cotton
Rice
Cotton
Rice
Coffee
Tea
Rice
Coffee
Rubber
Sheep
Rice
Rubber
Rice
Coffee
Cattle
Tea
Rice
Coffee
Tea
Cattle
Maize
Sugar
Cattle
Sheep
Wheat
Beef
Fruit
Sheep
Fruit
Wheat
Fruit
Dairy Cattle
Sheep
Commercial farming: crops dominant
Commercial farming: animals dominant
Commercial farming: mixed farming and horticulture
Subsistence agriculture, crop based
Subsistence agriculture, animal based
Black names indicate main cash crops and stock, and red names indicate main subsistence crops and stock.

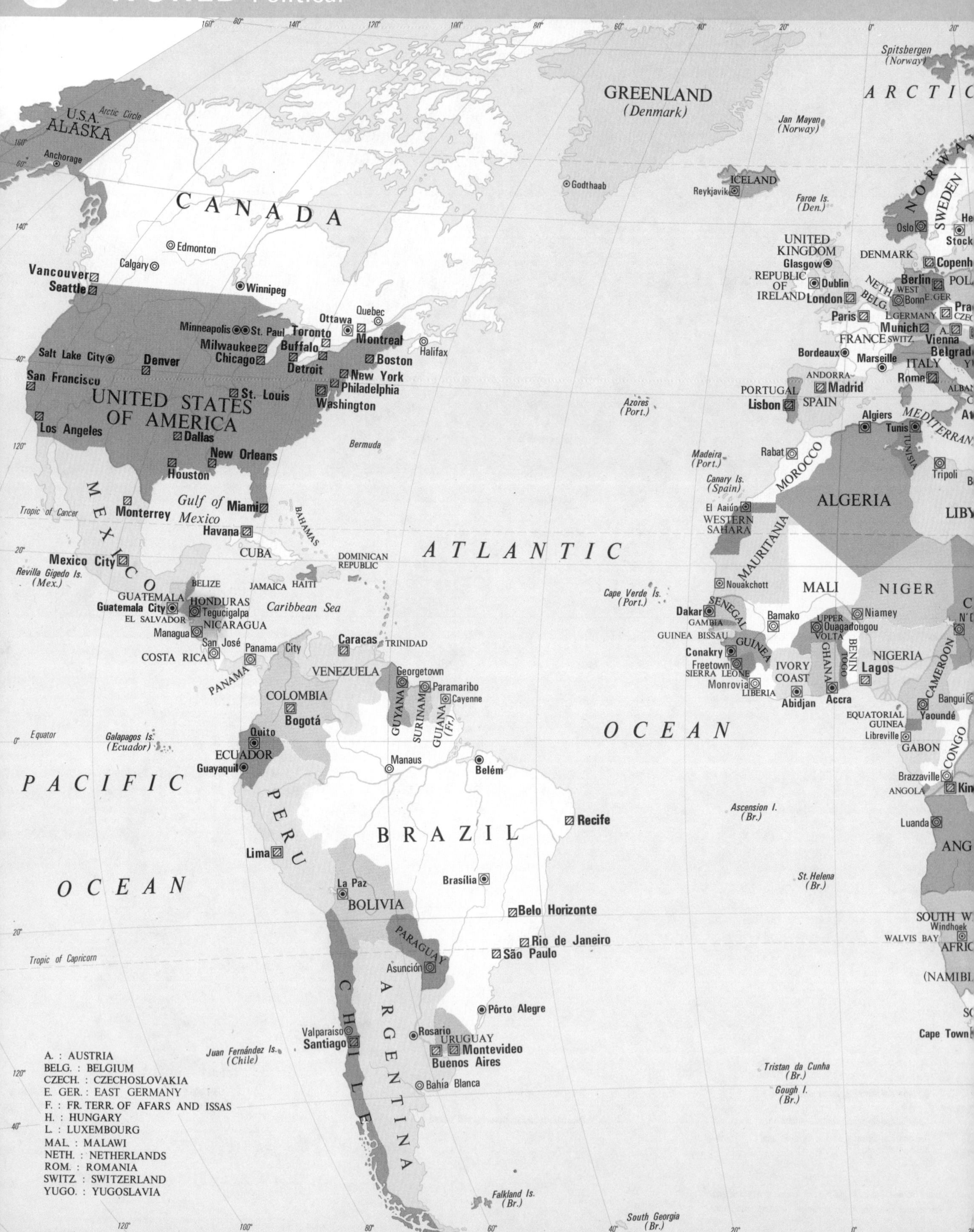

Spitsbergen (Norway)
ARCTIC
GREENLAND (Denmark)
U.S.A. ALASKA
Arctic Circle
Anchorage
Jan Mayen (Norway)
Godthaab
ICELAND
Reykjavik
Faroe Is. (Den.)
NORWAY
SWEDEN
Oslo
CANADA
Edmonton
Calgary
Vancouver
Seattle
Winnipeg
UNITED KINGDOM
Glasgow
DENMARK
Copenh
REPUBLIC OF IRELAND
Dublin
London
NETH.
BELG.
Berlin
WEST GERMANY
Bonn
E. GER
POL.
Paris
L.
Munich
A.
Vienna
FRANCE
SWITZ.
Belgrad
Bordeaux
Marseille
ITALY
ANDORRA
Madrid
Rome
PORTUGAL
Lisbon
SPAIN
Quebec
Ottawa
Minneapolis
St. Paul
Toronto
Montreal
Milwaukee
Buffalo
Halifax
Salt Lake City
Denver
Chicago
Detroit
Boston
San Francisco
New York
Philadelphia
Washington
UNITED STATES OF AMERICA
St. Louis
Los Angeles
Dallas
New Orleans
Houston
Azores (Port.)
Bermuda
Algiers
Tunis
TUNISIA
MEDITERRANEAN
Madeira (Port.)
Rabat
MOROCCO
Tripoli
Canary Is. (Spain)
ALGERIA
LIBYA
El Aaiún
WESTERN SAHARA
MAURITANIA
MEXICO
Monterrey
Tropic of Cancer
Gulf of Mexico
Miami
BAHAMAS
Havana
CUBA
ATLANTIC
DOMINICAN REPUBLIC
Mexico City
Revilla Gigedo Is. (Mex.)
BELIZE
JAMAICA
HAITI
Nouakchott
MALI
NIGER
GUATEMALA
Guatemala City
HONDURAS
Tegucigalpa
Caribbean Sea
EL SALVADOR
NICARAGUA
Managua
Cape Verde Is. (Port.)
Dakar
SENEGAL
GAMBIA
Bamako
UPPER VOLTA
Ouagadougou
Niamey
GUINEA BISSAU
GUINEA
Conakry
Freetown
SIERRA LEONE
Monrovia
LIBERIA
IVORY COAST
Abidjan
GHANA
Accra
TOGO
BENIN
NIGERIA
Lagos
CAMEROON
Yaoundé
Bangui
EQUATORIAL GUINEA
Libreville
GABON
CONGO
Brazzaville
Kin
ANGOLA
Luanda
ANG
San José
COSTA RICA
Panama City
PANAMA
Caracas
TRINIDAD
VENEZUELA
Georgetown
Paramaribo
Cayenne
GUYANA
SURINAM
GUIANA (Fr.)
COLOMBIA
Bogotá
Equator
Galapagos Is. (Ecuador)
Quito
ECUADOR
Guayaquil
OCEAN
Manaus
Belém
PACIFIC
PERU
Ascension I. (Br.)
Recife
BRAZIL
Lima
Brasília
St. Helena (Br.)
OCEAN
La Paz
BOLIVIA
Belo Horizonte
SOUTH WEST AFRICA (NAMIBIA)
Windhoek
WALVIS BAY
PARAGUAY
Rio de Janeiro
São Paulo
Tropic of Capricorn
Asunción
CHILE
ARGENTINA
Pôrto Alegre
Valparaíso
Santiago
Rosario
URUGUAY
Montevideo
Buenos Aires
Cape Town
Juan Fernández Is. (Chile)
Bahía Blanca
Tristan da Cunha (Br.)
Gough I. (Br.)
Falkland Is. (Br.)
South Georgia (Br.)
A. : AUSTRIA
BELG. : BELGIUM
CZECH. : CZECHOSLOVAKIA
E. GER. : EAST GERMANY
F. : FR. TERR. OF AFARS AND ISSAS
H. : HUNGARY
L. : LUXEMBOURG
MAL. : MALAWI
NETH. : NETHERLANDS
ROM. : ROMANIA
SWITZ. : SWITZERLAND
YUGO. : YUGOSLAVIA

UNION OF SOVIET SOCIALIST REPUBLICS
Arkhangel'sk
Gorki
Moscow
Kiev
Kharkov
Sverdlovsk
Omsk
Novosibirsk
Tashkent
Baku
Aral Sea
Caspian Sea
Black Sea
Ankara
TURKEY
SYRIA
LEBANON
ISRAEL
JORDAN
IRAQ
Baghdad
Tehran
IRAN
Kabul
AFGHANISTAN
KASHMIR
Islamabad
Lahore
PAKISTAN
KUWAIT
SAUDI ARABIA
Riyadh
Mecca
BAHRAIN
QATAR
U. OF ARAB EMIRATES
Muscat
OMAN
Red Sea
Sana
YEMEN
SOUTHERN YEMEN
Aden
Karachi
Ahmadabad
Delhi
New Delhi
NEPAL
Katmandu
BHUTAN
INDIA
Calcutta
Dacca
BANGLADESH
Bombay
Hyderabad
Madras
SRI LANKA
Colombo
Lakshadweep Is. (Ind.)
Andaman Is. (Ind.)
Nicobar Is. (Ind.)
MALDIVE ISLANDS
Ulan Bator
MONGOLIA
CHINA
Shenyang
Peking
Chungking
Wuhan
Nanking
Shanghai
Kwangchow
Victoria
HONG KONG (Br.)
NORTH KOREA
Pyongyang
Seoul
SOUTH KOREA
JAPAN
Tokyo
Osaka
Taipei
TAIWAN (FORMOSA)
BURMA
Rangoon
Hanoi
LAOS
Vientiane
THAILAND
Bangkok
VIETNAM
KHMER REP.
Phnom Penh
Ho Chi Minh City
Quezon City
Manila
PHILIPPINES
BRUNEI
Kuala Lumpur
MALAYSIA
Singapore
SINGAPORE
INDONESIA
Jakarta
Surabaya
Christmas I. (Austl.)
Cocos Is. (Austl.)
PAPUA NEW GUINEA
SOLOMON IS
PACIFIC OCEAN
Arctic Circle
Aleutian Is. (U.S.A.)
Tropic of Cancer
Mariana Is. (U.S.A.)
Caroline Is. (U.S.A.)
Equator
New Caledonia (Fr.)
Tropic of Capricorn
AUSTRALIA
Perth
Brisbane
Sydney
Adelaide
Canberra
Melbourne
Auckland
NEW ZEALAND
Wellington
INDIAN OCEAN
Khartoum
SUDAN
Addis Ababa
ETHIOPIA
SOMALI REPUBLIC
Mogadishu
UGANDA
KENYA
Kampala
Nairobi
RWANDA
BURUNDI
TANZANIA
Dar es Salaam
SEYCHELLES
Amirantes (Br.)
Lilongwe
MOCAMBIQUE
MALAGASY REPUBLIC
Tananarive
MAURITIUS
Pretoria
Maputo
SWAZILAND
Johannesburg
Durban
St. Paul (Fr.)
Amsterdam I. (Fr.)
Crozet Is. (Fr.)
Kerguelen (Fr.)
Heard I. (Austl.)
Scale 1:72 500 000
0 500 1000 1500 2000 Miles
0 500 1000 1500 2000 2500 3000 Kms.
Winkel Projection

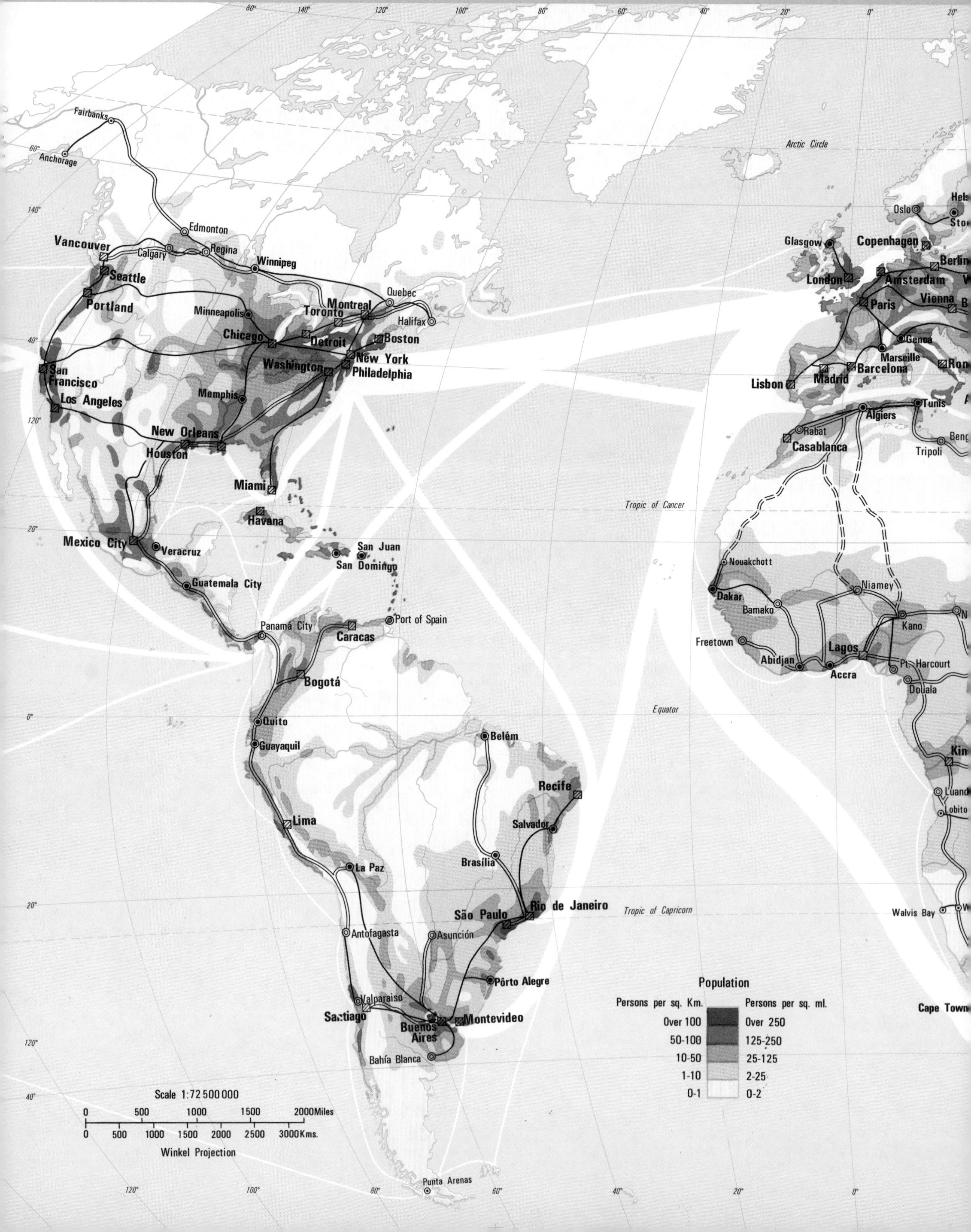

WORLD Population & Communications

Fairbanks
Anchorage
Edmonton
Vancouver
Calgary
Regina
Winnipeg
Seattle
Portland
Quebec
Montreal
Toronto
Minneapolis
Halifax
Chicago
Detroit
Boston
New York
Washington
Philadelphia
San Francisco
Los Angeles
Memphis
New Orleans
Houston
Miami
Havana
Mexico City
Veracruz
San Juan
San Domingo
Guatemala City
Panamá City
Port of Spain
Caracas
Bogotá
Quito
Guayaquil
Belém
Recife
Lima
Salvador
Brasília
La Paz
São Paulo
Rio de Janeiro
Antofagasta
Asunción
Pôrto Alegre
Valparaiso
Santiago
Buenos Aires
Montevideo
Bahía Blanca
Punta Arenas
Arctic Circle
Tropic of Cancer
Equator
Tropic of Capricorn
Oslo
Glasgow
Copenhagen
London
Amsterdam
Berlin
Paris
Vienna
Genoa
Marseille
Barcelona
Madrid
Lisbon
Tunis
Algiers
Rabat
Casablanca
Tripoli
Nouakchott
Dakar
Bamako
Niamey
Kano
Freetown
Abidjan
Accra
Lagos
Pt. Harcourt
Douala
Luanda
Lobito
Walvis Bay
Cape Town

Population

Persons per sq. Km.	Persons per sq. ml.
Over 100	Over 250
50-100	125-250
10-50	25-125
1-10	2-25
0-1	0-2

Scale 1:72 500 000

0 500 1000 1500 2000 Miles

0 500 1000 1500 2000 2500 3000 Kms.

Winkel Projection

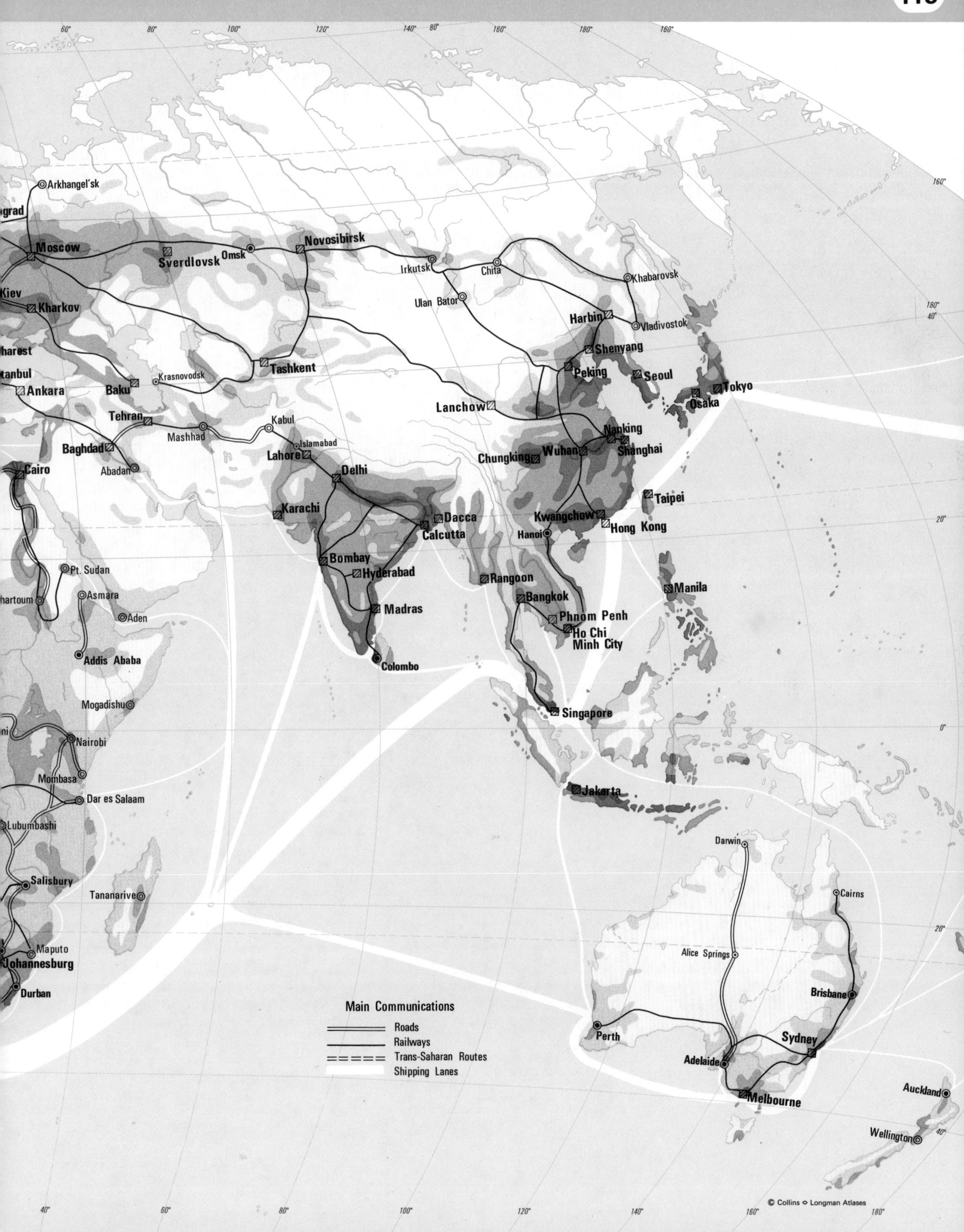

Arkhangel'sk
Moscow
Sverdlovsk
Omsk
Novosibirsk
Irkutsk
Chita
Khabarovsk
Ulan Bator
Kiev
Kharkov
Harbin
Vladivostok
Shenyang
Peking
Seoul
Tashkent
Baku
Krasnovodsk
Ankara
Tokyo
Osaka
Lanchow
Tehran
Mashhad
Kabul
Baghdad
Islamabad
Lahore
Nanking
Shanghai
Chungking
Wuhan
Abadan
Cairo
Delhi
Taipei
Karachi
Dacca
Calcutta
Kwangchow
Hong Kong
Hanoi
Pt. Sudan
Bombay
Hyderabad
Rangoon
Manila
Asmara
Aden
Madras
Bangkok
Phnom Penh
Ho Chi Minh City
Addis Ababa
Colombo
Mogadishu
Singapore
Nairobi
Mombasa
Dar es Salaam
Jakarta
Lubumbashi
Darwin
Salisbury
Tananarive
Cairns
Maputo
Johannesburg
Alice Springs
Durban
Brisbane
Main Communications
Roads
Railways
Trans-Saharan Routes
Shipping Lanes
Perth
Sydney
Adelaide
Melbourne
Auckland
Wellington

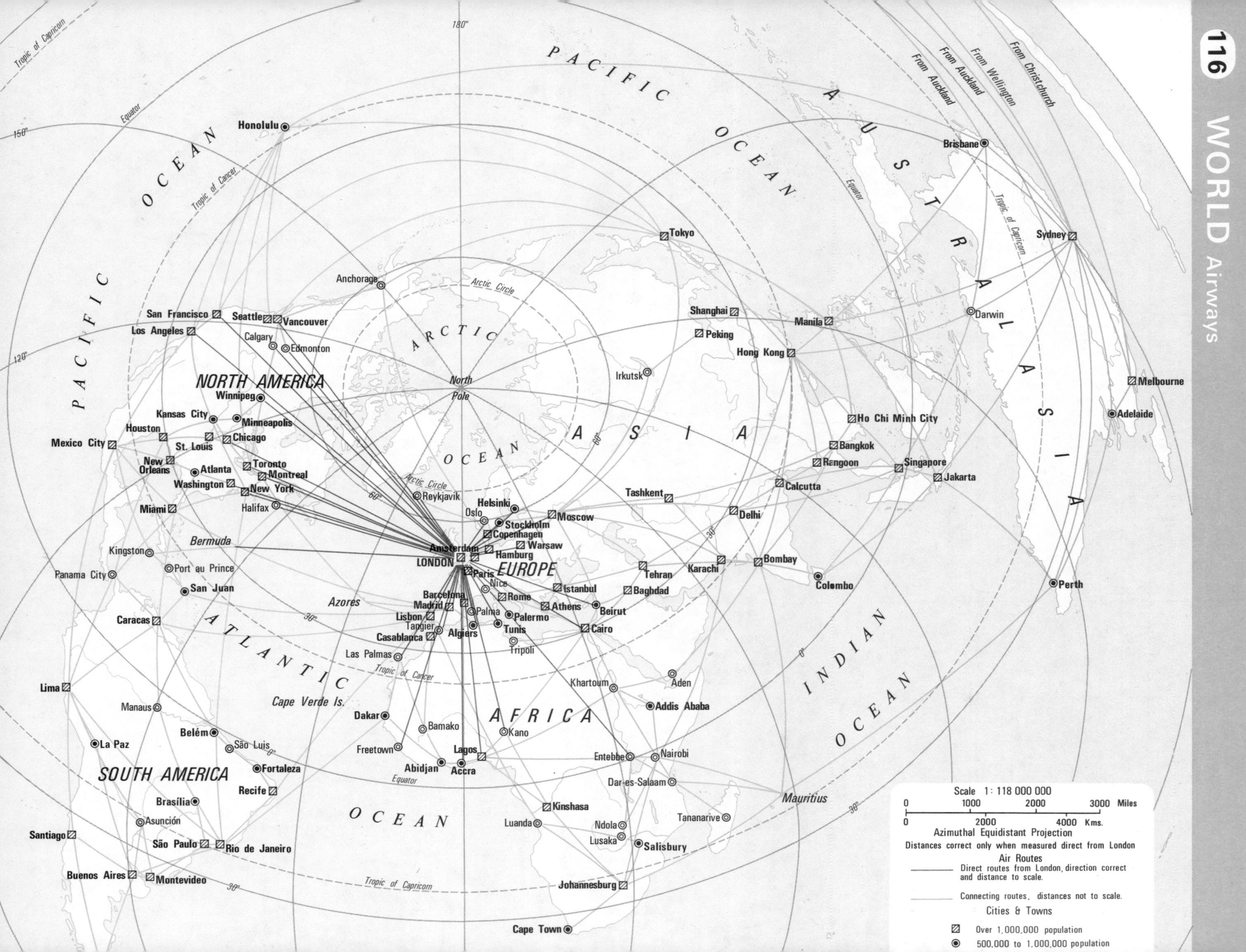
PACIFIC OCEAN
AUSTRALASIA
ASIA
ARCTIC OCEAN
NORTH AMERICA
EUROPE
AFRICA
SOUTH AMERICA
ATLANTIC OCEAN
INDIAN OCEAN
From Christchurch
From Wellington
From Auckland
From Auckland
Tropic of Capricorn
Tropic of Cancer
Equator
Arctic Circle
North Pole
180°
150°
120°
60°
30°
0°
Honolulu
Brisbane
Sydney
Tokyo
Anchorage
San Francisco
Seattle
Vancouver
Los Angeles
Calgary
Edmonton
Shanghai
Peking
Manila
Darwin
Hong Kong
Irkutsk
Melbourne
Adelaide
Winnipeg
Kansas City
Minneapolis
Houston
Chicago
St. Louis
Mexico City
New Orleans
Atlanta
Toronto
Montreal
Washington
New York
Halifax
Miami
Reykjavik
Ho Chi Minh City
Bangkok
Rangoon
Singapore
Jakarta
Calcutta
Tashkent
Delhi
Helsinki
Oslo
Stockholm
Moscow
Copenhagen
Warsaw
Hamburg
Amsterdam
LONDON
Paris
Bermuda
Kingston
Port au Prince
Panama City
San Juan
Nice
Rome
Istanbul
Baghdad
Tehran
Karachi
Bombay
Colombo
Perth
Barcelona
Madrid
Athens
Beirut
Azores
Palma
Palermo
Lisbon
Tangier
Algiers
Tunis
Cairo
Caracas
Casablanca
Tripoli
Las Palmas
Lima
Khartoum
Aden
Addis Ababa
Manaus
Cape Verde Is.
Dakar
Bamako
Kano
La Paz
Belém
São Luís
Freetown
Lagos
Entebbe
Nairobi
Abidjan
Accra
Fortaleza
Recife
Dar-es-Salaam
Mauritius
Brasília
Kinshasa
Asunción
Luanda
Ndola
Tananarive
Santiago
São Paulo
Rio de Janeiro
Lusaka
Salisbury
Buenos Aires
Montevideo
Johannesburg
Cape Town
Scale 1: 118 000 000
0 1000 2000 3000 Miles
0 2000 4000 Kms.
Azimuthal Equidistant Projection
Distances correct only when measured direct from London
Air Routes
Direct routes from London, direction correct and distance to scale.
Connecting routes, distances not to scale.
Cities & Towns
Over 1,000,000 population
500,000 to 1,000,000 population

INDEX

All names in the atlas, except for some of those on the thematic maps, will be found in this index, printed in bold type. Each entry indicates the country or region of the world in which the name is located. This is followed by the number of the most appropriate page on which the name appears—generally the largest scale map. Lastly the latitude and longitude is given. Where the name applies to a very large area of the map these co- ordinates are sometimes omitted. For names that do apply to an area the reference is to the centre of the feature, which will usually also be the position of the name. In the case of rivers the mouth or confluence is always taken as the point of reference. Therefore it is necessary to follow the river upstream from this point to find its name on the map.
Towns listed in the index are not described as such unless the name could be misleading. Thus Whitley Bay is followed by 'town' in italic. Elsewhere, when the name itself does not indicate clearly what it is, a description is always added in italic immediately after. These descriptions have had to be abbreviated in many cases.
Abbreviations used in the index are explained below.

Abbreviations

Afghan.	Afghanistan
Bangla.	Bangladesh
b., **B.**	bay, Bay
Beds.	Bedfordshire
Berks.	Berkshire
Bucks.	Buckinghamshire
Cambs.	Cambridgeshire
c., **C.**	cape, Cape
C.A.R.	Central African Republic
Czech.	Czechoslovakia
d.	internal division eg. county, region, state
Derbys.	Derbyshire
des.	desert
Dom. Rep.	Dominican Republic
D. and G.	Dumfries and Galloway
E. Germany	Eastern Germany
E. Sussex	East Sussex
Equat. Guinea	Equatorial Guinea
est.	estuary
f.	physical feature eg. valley, plain, geographic district or region
F.T.A.I.	French Territory of Afars and Issas
Game Res.	Game Reserve
Glos.	Gloucestershire
G.L.	Greater London
G.M.	Greater Manchester
G.	Gulf
Hants.	Hampshire
H. and W.	Hereford and Worcester
Herts.	Hertfordshire
Humber.	Humberside
i., **I.**, *is.*, **Is.**	island, Island, islands, Islands
I.o.M.	Isle of Man
I.o.W.	Isle of Wight
l., **L.**	lake, Lake
Lancs.	Lancashire
Leics.	Leicestershire
Liech.	Liechtenstein
Lincs.	Lincolnshire
Lux.	Luxembourg
Malagasy Rep.	Malagasy Republic
Mersey.	Merseyside
M.G.	Mid Glamorgan
Mt.	Mount
mtn., **Mtn.**	mountain, Mountain
mts., **Mts.**	mountains, Mountains
Nat. Park	National Park
Neth.	Netherlands
N. Ireland	Northern Ireland
Northants.	Northamptonshire
Northum.	Northumberland
N. Korea	North Korea
N. Vietnam	North Vietnam
N. Yorks.	North Yorkshire
Notts.	Nottinghamshire
Oxon.	Oxfordshire
P.N.G.	Papua New Guinea
pen., **Pen.**	peninsula, Peninsula
Phil.	Philippines
Pt.	Point
Port. Timor	Portuguese Timor
r., **R.**	river, River
Rep. of Ire.	Republic of Ireland
R.S.A.	Republic of South Africa
Resr.	Reservoir
Somali Rep.	Somali Republic
Sd.	Sound
S. Yemen	Southern Yemen
S.G.	South Glamorgan
S. Korea	South Korea
S. Vietnam	South Vietnam
S.W. Africa	South West Africa
S. Yorks.	South Yorkshire
Span. Sahara	Spanish Sahara
Staffs.	Staffordshire
str., **Str.**	strait, Strait
Strath.	Strathclyde
Switz.	Switzerland
T. and W.	Tyne and Wear
U.A.E.	Union of Arab Emirates
U.S.S.R.	Union of Soviet Socialist Republics
U.K.	United Kingdom
U.S.A.	United States of America
U. Volta	Upper Volta
Warwicks.	Warwickshire
W. Germany	Western Germany
W.G.	West Glamorgan
W. Isles	Western Isles
W. Midlands	West Midlands
W. Sussex	West Sussex
W. Yorks.	West Yorkshire
Wilts.	Wiltshire
Yugo.	Yugoslavia

A

Aa *r.* France **29** 51.00N 2.06E
Aachen W. Germany **45** 50.46N 6.06E
Aalen W. Germany **44** 48.50N 10.07E
Äänekoski Finland **46** 62.36N 25.44E
Aarau Switz. **44** 47.24N 8.04E
Aardenburg Neth. **45** 51.16N 3.26E
Aare *r.* Switz. **40** 47.03N 7.18E
Aarschot Belgium **45** 50.59N 4.50E
Aba Nigeria **71** 5.06N 7.21E
Abadan Iran **57** 30.21N 48.15E
Abadan I. Iran **57** 30.10N 48.30E
Abadeh Iran **57** 31.10N 52.40E
Abadla Algeria **68** 31.01N 2.45W
Abakaliki Nigeria **71** 6.17N 8.04E
Abakan U.S.S.R. **49** 53.43N 91.25E
Abaya, L. Ethiopia **69** 6.20N 38.00E
Abbeville France **40** 50.06N 1.51E
Abbeyfeale Rep. of Ire. **39** 52.23N 9.18W
Abbeyleix Rep. of Ire. **39** 52.55N 7.22W
Abbey Town England **32** 54.50N 3.18W
Abbotsbury England **28** 50.40N 2.36W
Abbots Langley England **27** 51.43N 0.25W
Abéché Chad **69** 13.49N 20.49E
Abengourou Ivory Coast **70** 6.42N 3.27W
Åbenrå Denmark **46** 55.03N 9.26E
Abeokuta Nigeria **71** 7.10N 3.26E
Aberayron Wales **30** 52.15N 4.16W
Abercarn Wales **31** 51.39N 3.09W
Aberdare Wales **31** 51.43N 3.27W
Aberdare Range *mts.* Kenya **73** 0.20S 36.40E
Aberdaron Wales **30** 52.48N 4.41W
Aberdeen Scotland **37** 57.08N 2.07W
Aberdeen S. Dak. U.S.A. **90** 45.28N 98.30W
Aberdeen Wash. U.S.A. **90** 46.58N 123.49W
Aberdovey Wales **30** 52.33N 4.03W
Aberfan Wales **31** 51.42N 3.20W
Aberfeldy Scotland **35** 56.37N 3.54W
Aberffraw Wales **30** 53.11N 4.28W
Aberfoyle Scotland **34** 56.11N 4.23W
Abergavenny Wales **30** 51.49N 3.01W
Abergele Wales **30** 53.17N 3.34W
Abernethy Scotland **35** 56.20N 3.19W
Aberporth Wales **30** 52.08N 4.33W
Abersoch Wales **30** 52.50N 4.31W
Abersychan Wales **28** 51.44N 3.03W
Abertillery Wales **31** 51.44N 3.09W
Aberystwyth Wales **30** 52.25N 4.06W
Ab-i-Diz *r.* Iran **57** 31.38N 48.54E
Abidjan Ivory Coast **70** 5.19N 4.01W
Abilene U.S.A. **90** 32.27N 99.45W
Abingdon England **28** 51.40N 1.17W
Abington Scotland **35** 55.29N 3.42W
Abitibi *r.* Canada **91** 51.15N 81.30W
Abitibi, L. Canada **95** 48.40N 79.35W
Abomey Benin **71** 7.14N 2.00E
Abou Deia Chad **71** 11.20N 19.20E
Aboyne Scotland **37** 57.05N 2.48W
Abqaiq Saudi Arabia **57** 25.55N 49.40E
Abrantes Portugal **41** 39.28N 8.12W
Abridge England **27** 51.40N 0.08E
Abu Dhabi U.A.E. **57** 24.27N 54.23E
Abu Hamed Sudan **69** 19.32N 33.20E
Abu Simbel Egypt **56** 22.18N 31.40E
Abu Tig Egypt **56** 27.06N 31.17E
Abu Zenima Egypt **56** 29.03N 33.06E
Acámbaro Mexico **96** 20.01N 101.42W
Acapulco Mexico **96** 16.51N 99.56W
Acarigua Venezuela **97** 9.35N 69.12W
Acatlán Mexico **96** 18.12N 98.02W
Accra Ghana **70** 5.33N 0.15W
Accrington England **32** 53.46N 2.22W
Achahoish Scotland **34** 55.57N 5.30W
à Chairn Bhain, Loch Scotland **36** 58.16N 5.05W
Achill Head Rep. of Ire. **38** 53.59N 10.15W
Achill I. Rep. of Ire. **38** 53.57N 10.00W
Achill Sound *town* Rep. of Ire. **38** 53.56N 9.56W
Achnasheen Scotland **36** 57.34N 5.05W
A'Chràlaig *mtn.* Scotland **36** 57.11N 5.09W
Acklin's I. Bahamas **97** 22.30N 74.10W
Ackworth Moor Top *town* England **33** 53.39N 1.20W
Aconcagua, Mt. S. America **106** 33.00S 70.00W
Acqui Italy **42** 44.41N 8.28E
Acton England **27** 51.31N 0.17W
Adamantina Brazil **103** 21.41S 51.04W
Adamawa Highlands Nigeria/Cameroon **71** 7.05N 12.00E
Adams, Mt. U.S.A. **90** 46.13N 121.29W
Adana Turkey **56** 37.00N 35.19E
Adapazari Turkey **56** 40.45N 30.23E
Adare Rep. of Ire. **39** 52.33N 8.48W
Adda *r.* Italy **40** 45.08N 9.55E
Ad Dahana *des.* Saudi Arabia **57** 26.00N 47.00E
Adderbury England **28** 52.01N 1.19W
Addis Ababa Ethiopia **69** 9.03N 38.42E
Ad Diwaniya Iraq **57** 31.59N 44.57E
Addlestone England **27** 51.22N 0.31W
Adelaide Australia **80** 34.56S 138.36E
Adélie Coast Antarctica **104** 80.00S 140.00E
Aden S. Yemen **69** 12.50N 45.00E
Aden, G. of Indian Oc. **69** 13.00N 50.00E
Adi *i.* Asia **61** 4.10S 133.10E
Adige *r.* Italy **42** 45.10N 12.20E
Adirondack Mts. U.S.A. **95** 44.00N 74.15W
Adiyaman Turkey **56** 37.46N 38.15E
Adlington England **32** 53.37N 2.36W
Admiralty Is. Pacific Oc. **61** 2.30S 147.20E
Adour *r.* France **40** 43.28N 1.35W
Adrano Italy **42** 37.39N 14.49E
Adrar des Iforas *mts.* Algeria **71** 20.00N 2.30E
Adraskand *r.* Afghan. **57** 33.17N 62.08E
Adrian U.S.A. **94** 41.55N 84.01W
Adriatic Sea Med. Sea **42** 42.30N 16.00E
Adur *r.* England **29** 50.50N 0.16W
Aduwa Ethiopia **69** 14.12N 38.56E
Adwick le Street England **33** 53.35N 1.12W
Aegean Sea Med. Sea **43** 39.00N 25.00E
Aeron *r.* Wales **30** 52.14N 4.16W
Afghanistan Asia **58** 34.00N 65.30E
Afif Saudi Arabia **56** 23.53N 42.59E
Afikpo Nigeria **71** 5.53N 7.55E
Afmadu Somali Rep. **73** 0.27N 42.05E
Africa 67
Afyon Turkey **56** 38.46N 30.32E
Agadès Niger **71** 17.00N 7.56E
Agana Asia **61** 13.28N 144.45E
Agartala India **59** 23.49N 91.15E
Agboville Ivory Coast **70** 5.55N 4.15W
Agde France **41** 43.25N 3.30E
Agedabia Libya **68** 30.48N 20.15E
Agen France **40** 44.12N 0.38E
Agger *r.* W. Germany **45** 50.45N 7.06E
Aghada Rep. of Ire. **39** 51.50N 8.13W
Aghda Iran **57** 32.25N 33.38E
Aghleam Rep. of Ire. **38** 54.08N 10.06W
Agnew's Hill N. Ireland **34** 54.51N 5.59W
Agordat Ethiopia **69** 15.35N 37.55E
Agout *r.* France **41** 43.40N 1.40E
Agra India **58** 27.09N 78.00E
Agra *r.* Spain **41** 42.12N 1.43W
Agreda Spain **41** 41.51N 1.55W
Agri *r.* Italy **43** 40.13N 16.45E
Agri Turkey **56** 39.44N 43.04E
Agrigento Italy **42** 37.19N 13.36E
Agrihan *i.* Asia **61** 18.44N 145.39E
Aguascalientes Mexico **96** 21.51N 102.18W
Aguascalientes *d.* Mexico **96** 22.00N 102.00W
Agueda *r.* Spain **41** 41.00N 6.56W
Aguilar de Campóo Spain **40** 42.47N 4.15W
Aguilas Spain **41** 37.25N 1.35W
Agulhas, C. R.S.A. **74** 34.50S 20.00E
Ahaggar Mts. Algeria **71** 24.00N 5.50E
Ahar Iran **57** 38.25N 47.07E
Ahaus W. Germany **45** 52.04N 7.01E
Ahlen W. Germany **44** 51.46N 7.53E
Ahmadabad India **58** 23.03N 72.40E
Ahmednagar India **58** 19.08N 74.48E
Ahr *r.* W. Germany **45** 50.34N 7.16E
Ahwaz Iran **57** 31.17N 48.44E
Aigun China **63** 49.40N 127.10E
Ailette *r.* France **45** 49.35N 3.09E
Ailsa Craig *i.* Scotland **34** 55.15N 5.07W
Ain *r.* France **40** 45.47N 5.12E
Aïna *r.* Gabon **72** 0.38N 12.47E
Ain Beida Algeria **42** 35.50N 7.29E
Ain Salah Algeria **68** 27.12N 2.29E
Aïn Sefra Algeria **68** 32.45N 0.35W
Aïr *mts.* Niger **71** 18.30N 8.30E
Aird Brenish *c.* Scotland **36** 58.08N 7.08W
Airdrie Scotland **35** 55.52N 3.59W
Aire *r.* England **33** 53.42N 0.54W
Aire France **40** 43.39N 0.15W
Airedale *f.* England **32** 53.56N 1.54W
Aisne *r.* France **45** 49.27N 2.51E
Aitape P.N.G. **61** 3.10S 142.17E
Aith Scotland **36** 60.17N 1.23W
Aix-en-Provence France **40** 43.31N 5.27E
Aiyina *i.* Greece **43** 37.43N 23.30E
Ajaccio France **40** 41.55N 8.43E
Ajmer India **58** 26.29N 74.40E
Akbou Algeria **42** 36.26N 4.33E
Aketi Zaïre **72** 2.46N 23.51E
Akhaltsikhe U.S.S.R. **56** 41.37N 42.59E
Akhdar, Jebel *mts.* Libya **69** 32.10N 22.00E
Akhdar, Jebel *mts.* Oman **57** 23.10N 57.25E
Akhdar, Wadi *r.* Saudi Arabia **56** 28.30N 36.48E
Akhelóös Greece **43** 38.20N 21.04E
Akhisar Turkey **43** 38.54N 27.49E
Akimiski I. Canada **93** 53.00N 81.20W
Akita Japan **63** 39.44N 140.05E
Akjoujt Mauritania **70** 19.44N 14.26W
Akkajaure *l.* Sweden **46** 67.40N 17.30E
Akobo *r.* Sudan/Ethiopia **69** 8.30N 33.15E
Akola India **58** 20.40N 77.02E
Akpatok I. Canada **93** 60.30N 68.30W
Akron U.S.A. **94** 41.04N 81.31W
Aksaray Turkey **56** 38.22N 34.02E
Akşehir Turkey **56** 38.22N 31.24E
Aksu China **62** 42.10N 80.00E
Aktogay U.S.S.R. **62** 46.59N 79.42E
Aktyubinsk U.S.S.R. **48** 50.16N 57.13E
Akure Nigeria **71** 7.14N 5.08E
Akureyri Iceland **46** 65.41N 18.04W
Akuse Ghana **70** 6.04N 0.12E
Akyab Burma **59** 20.09N 92.55E
Alabama *d.* U.S.A. **91** 33.00N 87.00W
Alabama *r.* U.S.A. **91** 31.05N 87.55W
Alagez *mtn.* U.S.S.R. **57** 40.32N 44.11E
Al Ain, Wadi *r.* Oman **57** 22.18N 55.35E
Alakol, L. U.S.S.R. **62** 46.00N 81.40E
Alakurtti U.S.S.R. **46** 67.00N 30.23E
Alamagan *i.* Asia **61** 17.35N 145.50E
Alamosa U.S.A. **90** 37.28N 105.54W
Åland Is. Finland **46** 60.20N 20.00E
Alanya Turkey **56** 36.32N 32.02E
Alaşehir Turkey **43** 38.22N 28.29E
Alaska *d.* U.S.A. **92** 65.00N 153.00W
Alaska, G. of U.S.A. **92** 58.45N 145.00W
Alaska Pen. U.S.A. **92** 56.00N 160.00W
Alaska Range *mts.* U.S.A. **92** 62.10N 152.00W
Alazan *r.* U.S.S.R. **57** 41.06N 46.40E
Albacete Spain **41** 39.00N 1.52W
Alba Iulia Romania **43** 46.04N 23.33E
Albania Europe **43** 41.00N 20.00E
Albany Australia **79** 34.57S 117.54E
Albany *r.* Canada **91** 52.10N 82.00W
Albany Ga. U.S.A. **91** 31.37N 84.10W
Albany N.Y. U.S.A. **95** 42.40N 73.49W
Albany Oreg. U.S.A. **90** 44.38N 123.07W
Albemarle Sd. U.S.A. **91** 36.10N 76.00W
Alberche *r.* Spain **41** 40.00N 4.45W
Albert France **40** 50.00N 2.40E
Alberta *d.* Canada **92** 55.00N 115.00W
Albert Canal Belgium **45** 51.00N 5.15E
Albert Nile *r.* Uganda **73** 3.30N 32.00E
Albi France **40** 43.56N 2.08E
Alboran, Isleta de Spain **41** 35.55N 3.10W
Ålborg Denmark **46** 57.03N 9.56E
Albuquerque U.S.A. **90** 35.05N 106.38W
Alburquerque Spain **41** 39.13N 6.59W
Albury Australia **80** 36.03S 146.53E
Alcácer do Sal Portugal **41** 38.22N 8.30W
Alcalá de Chisvert Spain **41** 40.19N 0.13E
Alcalá de Henares Spain **41** 40.28N 3.22W
Alcalá la Real Spain **41** 37.28N 3.55W
Alcamo Italy **42** 37.59N 12.58E
Alcañiz Spain **41** 41.03N 0.09W
Alcaudete Spain **41** 37.35N 4.05W
Alcazar de San Juan Spain **41** 39.24N 3.12W
Alcazarquiver Morocco **41** 35.01N 5.54W
Alcester England **28** 52.13N 1.52W
Alcira Spain **41** 39.10N 0.27W
Alcoy Spain **41** 38.42N 0.29W
Alcubierre, Sierra de *mts.* Spain **41** 41.40N 0.20W
Alcudia Spain **41** 39.51N 3.09E
Aldabra Is. Indian Oc. **67** 9.00S 47.00E
Aldan U.S.S.R. **49** 58.44N 125.22E
Aldan *r.* U.S.S.R. **49** 63.30N 130.00E
Aldbourne England **28** 51.28N 1.38W
Aldbrough England **33** 53.50N 0.07W
Alde *r.* England **29** 52.02N 1.28E
Aldeburgh England **29** 52.09N 1.35E
Alderney *i.* Channel Is. **31** 49.42N 2.11W
Aldershot England **27** 51.15N 0.47W
Aldridge England **28** 52.36N 1.55W
Aldsworth England **28** 51.48N 1.46W
Alegrete Brazil **103** 29.45S 55.46W
Aleksandrovsk Sakhalinskiy U.S.S.R. **49** 50.55N 142.12E
Alençon France **40** 48.25N 0.05E
Aleppo Syria **56** 36.14N 37.10E
Aleria France **40** 42.05N 9.30E
Alès France **40** 44.08N 4.05E
Alessandria Italy **40** 44.55N 8.37E
Alesund Norway **46** 62.28N 6.11E
Aleutian Is. U.S.A. **54** 57.00N 180.00
Aleutian Range *mts.* U.S.A. **92** 58.00N 156.00W
Aleutian Trench Pacific Oc. **107** 50.00N 178.00E
Alexander Archipelago *is.* U.S.A. **92** 56.30N 134.30W
Alexander Bay *town* R.S.A. **74** 28.40S 16.30E
Alexandra New Zealand **82** 45.14S 169.26E
Alexandria Egypt **56** 31.13N 29.55E
Alexandria Scotland **34** 55.59N 4.35W
Alexandria La. U.S.A. **91** 31.19N 92.29W
Alexandria Va. U.S.A. **95** 38.49N 77.06W
Alexandroúpolis Greece **43** 40.50N 25.53E
Alfaro Spain **41** 42.11N 1.45W

Alfiós *r.* Greece **43** 37.37N 21.27E
Alford Scotland **37** 57.14N 2.42W
Alfreton England **33** 53.06N 1.22W
Algeciras Spain **41** 36.08N 5.27W
Alger *see* Algiers Algeria **41**
Algeria Africa **68** 28.00N 2.00E
Al Ghadaf, Wadi *r.* Iraq **56** 32.54N 43.33E
Alghero Italy **42** 40.33N 8.20E
Algiers Algeria **41** 36.50N 3.00E
Algoa B. R.S.A. **74** 33.56S 26.10E
Al Hamra *des.* U.A.E. **57** 22.45N 55.10E
Aliákmon *r.* Greece **43** 40.30N 22.38E
Alicante Spain **41** 38.21N 0.29W
Alice U.S.A. **90** 27.45N 98.06W
Alice Springs *town* Australia **79** 23.42S 133.52E
Aligarh India **58** 27.54N 78.04E
Aligudarz Iran **57** 33.25N 49.38E
Alima *r.* Congo **72** 1.36S 16.35E
Aling Kangri *mtn.* China **59** 32.51N 81.03E
Alingsås Sweden **46** 57.55N 12.30E
Aliquippa U.S.A. **94** 40.38N 80.16W
Aliwal North R.S.A. **74** 30.42S 26.43E
Al Jaub *f.* Saudi Arabia **57** 23.00N 50.00E
Al Jauf Saudi Arabia **56** 29.49N 39.52E
Al Jazi *des.* Iraq **56** 35.00N 41.00E
Al Khurr *r.* Iraq **56** 32.00N 44.15E
Alkmaar Neth. **45** 52.37N 4.44E
Al Kut Iraq **57** 32.30N 45.51E
Allagash *r.* U.S.A. **95** 47.08N 69.10W
Allahabad India **58** 25.57N 81.50E
Allakaket U.S.A. **92** 66.30N 152.45W
Allaqi, Wadi *r.* Egypt **56** 22.55N 33.02E
Allegheny *r.* U.S.A. **95** 40.26N 80.00W
Allegheny Mts. U.S.A. **95** 40.00N 79.00W
Allen *r.* England **35** 54.58N 2.18W
Allen, Lough Rep. of Ire. **38** 54.07N 8.04W
Allentown U.S.A. **95** 40.37N 75.30W
Alleppey India **58** 9.30N 76.22E
Aller *r.* W. Germany **44** 52.43N 9.38E
Alliance Nebr. U.S.A. **90** 42.08N 103.00W
Alliance Ohio U.S.A. **94** 40.56N 81.06W
Allier *r.* France **40** 46.58N 3.04E
Alloa Scotland **35** 56.07N 3.49W
Alma U.S.A. **94** 43.23N 84.40W
Alma-Ata U.S.S.R. **62** 43.19N 76.55E
Almadén Spain **41** 38.47N 4.50W
Al Maharadh *des.* Saudi Arabia **57** 20.00N 52.30E
Alma Hill U.S.A. **95** 42.03N 78.01W
Almansa Spain **41** 38.52N 1.06W
Almanzor, Pico de *mtn.* Spain **41** 40.20N 5.22W
Almanzora *r.* Spain **41** 37.16N 1.49W
Almazán Spain **41** 41.29N 2.31W
Almeirim Portugal **41** 39.12N 8.37W
Almelo Neth. **45** 52.21N 6.40E
Almeria Spain **41** 36.50N 2.26W
Älmhult Sweden **46** 56.32N 14.10E
Al Mira, Wadi *r.* Iraq **56** 32.27N 41.21E
Almond *r.* Scotland **35** 56.25N 3.28W
Almuñécar Spain **41** 36.44N 3.41W
Aln *r.* England **35** 55.23N 1.36W
Alness Scotland **37** 57.42N 4.15W
Alnwick England **35** 55.25N 1.41W
Alor *i.* Indonesia **61** 8.20S 124.30E
Alor Star Malaysia **60** 6.06N 100.23E
Alost Belgium **45** 50.57N 4.03E
Alpena U.S.A. **94** 45.04N 83.27W
Alpes Maritimes *mts.* France **40** 44.07N 7.08E
Alphen Neth. **45** 52.08N 4.40E
Alpine U.S.A. **90** 30.22N 103.40W
Alps *mts.* Europe **44** 47.00N 10.00E
Al Qurna Iraq **57** 31.00N 47.26E
Alsager England **32** 53.07N 2.20W
Alsásua Spain **41** 42.54N 2.10W
Alsh, Loch Scotland **36** 57.15N 5.36W
Al Shaab S. Yemen **69** 12.50N 44.56E
Alston England **32** 54.48N 2.26W
Alta Norway **46** 69.57N 23.10E
Alta *r.* Norway **46** 70.00N 23.15E
Altagraĉia Venezuela **97** 10.44N 71.30W
Altai China **62** 47.48N 88.07E
Altai *mts.* Mongolia **62** 46.30N 93.30E
Altaj Mongolia **62** 46.20N 97.00E
Altamaha *r.* U.S.A. **91** 31.15N 81.23W
Altamura Italy **43** 40.50N 16.32E
Altea Spain **41** 38.37N 0.03W
Altenburg E. Germany **44** 50.59N 12.27E
Altenkirchen W. Germany **45** 50.41N 7.40E
Al Tihama *des.* Saudi Arabia **56** 27.50N 35.30E
Altiplano Mexicano *mts.* N. America **106** 24.00N 105.00W
Altnaharra Scotland **37** 58.16N 4.26W
Alto Araguaia Brazil **103** 17.19S 53.10W
Alto Garcas Brazil **103** 16.57S 53.30W
Alto Molocue Moçambique **73** 15.38S 37.42E
Alton England **28** 51.08N 0.59W
Alton U.S.A. **94** 38.55N 90.10W
Altoona U.S.A. **95** 40.32N 78.23W
Altrincham England **32** 53.25N 2.21W
Altyn Tagh *mts.* China **62** 38.10N 87.50E
Al'Ula Saudi Arabia **56** 26.39N 37.58E
Alva Scotland **35** 56.09N 3.49W
Alva U.S.A. **90** 36.48N 98.40W
Alvarado Mexico **96** 18.49N 95.46W
Älvsbyn Sweden **46** 65.41N 21.00E
Al Wajh Saudi Arabia **56** 26.16N 36.28E
Al Wakrah Qatar **57** 25.09N 51.36E
Alwar India **58** 27.32N 76.35E
Alyaty U.S.S.R. **57** 39.59N 49.20E
Alyth Scotland **35** 56.38N 3.14W
Alzette *r.* Lux. **45** 49.52N 6.07E
Amadeus, L. Australia **79** 24.50S 131.00E
Amadi Sudan **73** 5.32N 30.20E
Amagasaki Japan **63** 34.42N 135.25E
Amami *i.* Japan **63** 28.20N 129.30E
Amara Iraq **57** 31.52N 47.50E
Amarillo U.S.A. **90** 35.14N 101.50W
Amaro, Monte *mtn.* Italy **42** 42.06N 14.04E
Amasya Turkey **56** 40.37N 35.50E
Amazon *r.* Brazil **102** 2.00S 52.00W
Ambala India **58** 30.19N 76.49E
Ambarchik U.S.S.R. **49** 69.39N 162.27E
Ambato-Boeni Malagasy Rep. **73** 16.30S 46.33E
Amberg W. Germany **44** 49.26N 11.52E
Ambergris Cay *i.* Belize **96** 18.00N 87.58W
Amberley England **29** 50.54N 0.33W
Amble England **35** 55.20N 1.34W
Ambleside England **32** 54.26N 2.58W
Ambon Indonesia **61** 4.50S 128.10E
Ambriz Angola **72** 7.54S 13.12E
Ambrizete Angola **72** 7.13S 12.56E
Ameland *i.* Neth. **45** 53.28N 5.48E
Amersfoort Neth. **45** 52.10N 5.23E
Amersham England **27** 51.40N 0.38W
Amesbury England **28** 51.10N 1.46W
Amga U.S.S.R. **49** 60.51N 131.59E
Amga *r.* U.S.S.R. **49** 62.40N 135.20E
Amgun *r.* U.S.S.R. **49** 53.10N 139.47E
Amherst U.S.A. **95** 43.00N 78.45W
Amiata *mtn.* Italy **42** 42.53N 11.37E
Amiens France **40** 49.54N 2.18E
Amirantes *is.* Indian Oc. **113** 6.00S 52.00E
Amlwch Wales **30** 53.24N 4.21W
Amman Jordan **56** 31.57N 35.56E
Ammanford Wales **31** 51.48N 4.00W
Amol Iran **57** 36.26N 52.24E
Amorgós *i.* Greece **43** 36.50N 25.55E
Amos Canada **95** 48.04N 78.08W
Amoy China **63** 24.26N 118.07E
Ampala Honduras **96** 13.16N 87.39W
Ampthill England **29** 52.03N 0.30W
Amraoti India **58** 20.58N 77.50E
Amritsar India **58** 31.35N 74.56E
Amroha India **58** 28.54N 78.14E
Amsterdam Neth. **45** 52.22N 4.54E
Amsterdam U.S.A. **95** 42.56N 74.12W
Amsterdam I. Indian Oc. **113** 37.00S 79.00E
Amu Darya *r.* U.S.S.R. **48** 43.50N 59.00E
Amundsen G. Canada **92** 70.30N 122.00W
Amundsen Sea Antarctica **106** 70.00S 116.00W
Amur *r.* U.S.S.R. **49** 53.17N 140.00E
Anabar *r.* U.S.S.R. **49** 72.40N 113.30E
Anadyr U.S.S.R. **49** 64.40N 177.32E
Anadyr *r.* U.S.S.R. **49** 65.00N 176.00E
Anadyr, G. of U.S.S.R. **49** 64.30N 177.50W
Anaiza Saudi Arabia **57** 26.05N 43.57E
Anambas Is. Indonesia **60** 3.00N 106.10E
Anambra *d.* Nigeria **71** 6.20N 7.25E
Anápolis Brazil **103** 16.19S 48.58W
Anar Iran **57** 30.54N 55.18E
Anatahan *i.* Asia **61** 16.22N 145.38E
Anatolia *f.* Turkey **56** 38.00N 35.00E
Anatuya Argentina **103** 28.26S 62.48W
Anchorage U.S.A. **92** 61.10N 150.00W
Ancona Italy **42** 43.37N 13.33E
Ancroft England **35** 55.42N 2.00W
Ancuabe Moçambique **73** 13.00S 39.50E
Andalsnes Norway **46** 62.33N 7.43E
Andaman Is. India **59** 12.00N 93.00E
Andaman Sea Indian Oc. **59** 11.15N 95.30E
Andara S.W. Africa **74** 18.04S 21.29E
Andernach W. Germany **45** 50.25N 7.24E
Anderson *r.* Canada **92** 69.45N 129.00W
Anderson U.S.A. **94** 40.05N 85.41W
Andes *mts.* S. America **106** 21.00S 68.00W
And Fjord *est.* Norway **46** 69.10N 16.20E
Andhra Pradesh *d.* India **59** 17.00N 79.00E
Andikíthira *i.* Greece **43** 35.52N 23.18E
Andizhan U.S.S.R. **62** 40.48N 72.23E
Andorra *town* Andorra **41** 42.29N 1.31E
Andorra Europe **41** 42.30N 1.32E
Andover England **28** 51.13N 1.29W
Andoy *i.* Norway **46** 69.00N 15.30E
Andreas I.o.M. **32** 54.22N 4.26W
Andreas, C. Cyprus **56** 35.40N 34.35E
Ándros *i.* Greece **56** 37.50N 24.50E
Andros I. Bahamas **91** 24.30N 78.00W
Andujar Spain **41** 38.02N 4.03W
Andulo Angola **72** 11.28S 16.43E
Anécho Togo **71** 6.17N 1.40E
Anegada *i.* Virgin Is. **97** 18.46N 64.24W
Aneiza, Jebel *mtn.* Asia **56** 32.15N 39.19E
Aneto, Pico de *mtn.* Spain **41** 42.40N 0.19E
Angara *r.* U.S.S.R. **49** 58.00N 93.00E
Angarsk U.S.S.R. **49** 52.31N 103.55E
Angaston Australia **80** 34.30S 139.03E
Ange Sweden **46** 62.31N 15.40E
Angel de la Guarda *i.* Mexico **90** 29.10N 113.20W
Angel Falls *f.* Venezuela **97** 5.55N 62.30W
Ängelholm Sweden **46** 56.15N 12.50E
Ångerman Sweden **46** 62.52N 17.45E
Angers France **40** 47.29N 0.32W
Angkor *ruins* Khmer Rep. **60** 13.26N 103.50E
Angle Wales **31** 51.40N 5.03W
Anglesey *i.* Wales **30** 53.16N 4.25W
Angmagssalik Greenland **93** 65.40N 38.00W
Ango Zaïre **72** 4.01N 25.52E
Angola Africa **72** 11.00S 18.00E
Angoulême France **40** 45.40N 0.10E
Aguilar de Campóo Spain **41** 42.55N 4.15W
Anguilla C. America **97** 18.14N 63.05W
Angumu Zaïre **73** 0.10S 27.38E
Anholt W. Germany **45** 51.51N 6.26E
Anhumas Brazil **103** 16.58S 54.43W
Anhwei *d.* China **63** 31.30N 116.45E
Aniak U.S.A. **92** 61.32N 159.40W
Anjouan *i.* Comoro Is. **73** 12.12S 44.28E
Ankara Turkey **56** 39.55N 32.50E
Anking China **63** 30.20N 116.50E
Ankober Ethiopia **69** 9.32N 39.43E
Annaba Algeria **42** 36.55N 7.47E
An Nafud *des.* Saudi Arabia **56** 28.40N 41.30E
An Najaf Iraq **57** 31.59N 44.19E
Annalee *r.* Rep. of Ire. **38** 54.02N 7.25W
Annam Highlands *mts.* Asia **60** 17.40N 105.30E
Annan Scotland **35** 54.59N 3.16W
Annan *r.* Scotland **35** 54.58N 3.16W
Annandale *f.* Scotland **35** 55.12N 3.25W
Annapolis U.S.A. **95** 38.59N 76.30W
Annapurna *mtn.* Nepal **58** 28.34N 83.50E
Ann Arbor U.S.A. **94** 42.18N 83.43W
An Nasiriya Iraq **57** 31.04N 46.16E
Annecy France **40** 45.54N 6.07E
Annfield Plain *town* England **32** 54.42N 1.45W
Annonay France **40** 45.15N 4.40E
Ansbach W. Germany **44** 49.18N 10.36E
Anshan China **63** 41.05N 122.58E
Anshun China **59** 26.02N 105.57E
Ansi China **62** 40.32N 95.57E
Anston England **33** 53.22N 1.13W
Anstruther Scotland **35** 56.14N 2.42W
Antakya Turkey **56** 36.12N 36.10E
Antalya Turkey **56** 36.53N 30.42E
Antalya, G. of Turkey **56** 36.38N 31.00E
Antarctica 104
Antarctic Pen. Antarctica **106** 66.00S 65.00W
An Teallach *mtn.* Scotland **36** 57.48N 5.16W
Antequera Spain **41** 37.01N 4.34W
Anticosti I. Canada **93** 49.20N 63.00W
Antigo U.S.A. **94** 45.10N 89.10W
Antigua C. America **97** 17.09N 61.49W
Antigua Guatemala **96** 14.33N 90.42W
Anti-Lebanon *mts.* Lebanon **56** 34.00N 36.25E
Antofagasta Chile **102** 23.40S 70.23W
Antonio Enes Moçambique **73** 16.10S 39.57E
Antrim N. Ireland **34** 54.43N 6.14W
Antrim *d.* N. Ireland **34** 54.58N 6.20W
Antrim, Mts. of N. Ireland **34** 55.00N 6.10W
Antung China **63** 40.06N 124.25E
Antwerp Belgium **45** 51.13N 4.25E
Antwerp *d.* Belgium **45** 51.16N 4.45E
Anvik U.S.A. **92** 62.38N 160.20W
Anyang China **63** 36.04N 114.20E
Anzhero-Sudzhensk U.S.S.R. **48** 56.10N 86.10E
Aomori Japan **63** 40.50N 140.43E
Aosta Italy **40** 45.43N 7.19E
Apa *r.* Paraguay **103** 22.06S 58.00W
Apalachee B. U.S.A. **91** 29.30N 84.00W
Aparri Phil. **61** 18.22N 121.40E
Apatity U.S.S.R. **46** 67.32N 33.21E
Apeldoorn Neth. **45** 52.13N 5.57E
Apennines *mts.* Italy **42** 42.00N 13.30E
Apolda E. Germany **44** 51.02N 11.31E
Apostle Is. U.S.A. **94** 47.00N 90.30W
Appalachian Mts. U.S.A. **91** 39.30N 78.00W
Appennino Ligure *mts.* Italy **40** 44.33N 8.45E
Appingedam Neth. **45** 53.18N 6.52E
Appleby England **32** 54.35N 2.29W
Appleton U.S.A. **94** 44.17N 88.24W

Apsheron Pen. U.S.S.R. **57** 40.28N 50.00E
Apure *r.* Venezuela **97** 7.44N 66.38W
Aqaba Jordan **56** 29.32N 35.00E
Aqaba, G. of Asia **56** 28.45N 34.45E
Aqlat as Suqur Saudi Arabia **56** 25.50N 42.12E
Aquidauana Brazil **103** 20.27S 55.45W
Aquila Mexico **96** 18.30N 103.50W
Arabia Asia **107** 25.00N 45.00E
Arabian Desert Egypt **56** 28.15N 31.55E
Arabian Sea Asia **58** 16.00N 65.00E
Aracaju Brazil **102** 10.54S 37.07W
Araçatuba Brazil **103** 21.12S 50.24W
Arad Romania **43** 46.12N 21.19E
Arafura Sea Austa. **61** 9.00S 135.00E
Aragon *r.* Spain **41** 42.20N 1.45W
Araguaia *r.* Brazil **102** 5.30S 48.20W
Araguari Brazil **103** 18.38S 48.13W
Arak Iran **57** 34.06N 49.44E
Arakan Yoma *mts.* Burma **59** 20.00N 94.00E
Aral Sea U.S.S.R. **48** 45.00N 60.00E
Aralsk U.S.S.R. **48** 46.56N 61.43E
Aranda de Duero Spain **41** 41.40N 3.41W
Aran Fawddwy *mtn.* Wales **30** 52.48N 3.42W
Aran I. Rep. of Ire. **38** 54.59N 8.27W
Aran Is. Rep. of Ire. **39** 53.07N 9.38W
Aranjuez Spain **41** 40.02N 3.37W
Araouane Mali **70** 18.53N 3.31W
Arapkir Turkey **56** 39.03N 38.29E
Arar, Wadi *r.* Iraq **56** 32.00N 42.30E
Ararat Australia **80** 37.20S 143.00E
Ararat, Mt. Turkey **57** 39.45N 44.15E
Aras *r. see* Araxes Turkey **56**
Arauca *r.* Venezuela **97** 7.20N 66.40W
Araxa Brazil **103** 19.37S 46.50W
Araxes *r.* U.S.S.R. **57** 40.00N 48.28E
Araya Pen. Venezuela **97** 10.30N 64.30W
Arbatax Italy **42** 39.56N 9.41E
Arbroath Scotland **37** 56.34N 2.35W
Arcachon France **40** 44.40N 1.11W
Archers Post Kenya **73** 0.42N 37.40E
Arcila Morocco **41** 35.28N 6.04W
Arctic Ocean 104
Arctic Red *r.* Canada **92** 67.26N 133.48W
Arda *r.* Greece **43** 41.39N 26.30E
Ardabil Iran **57** 38.15N 48.18E
Ardara Rep. of Ire. **38** 54.46N 8.25W
Ardèche *r.* France **40** 44.31N 4.40E
Ardee Rep. of Ire. **38** 53.51N 6.33W
Ardennes *mts.* Belgium **45** 50.10N 5.30E
Ardentinny Scotland **34** 56.03N 4.55W
Arderin *mtn.* Rep. of Ire. **39** 53.02N 7.40W
Ardfert Rep. of Ire. **39** 52.20N 9.48W
Ardglass N. Ireland **38** 54.16N 5.37W
Ardgour *f.* Scotland **36** 56.45N 5.20W
Ardila Spain **41** 38.10N 7.30W
Ardistan Iran **57** 33.22N 52.25E
Ardivachar Pt. Scotland **36** 57.23N 7.26W
Ardlamont Pt. Scotland **34** 55.49N 5.12W
Ardlui Scotland **34** 56.18N 4.43W
Ardmore Rep. of Ire. **39** 51.58N 7.43W
Ardmore Head Rep. of Ire. **39** 51.56N 7.43W
Ardmore Pt. Strath. Scotland **36** 56.39N 6.08W
Ardmore Pt. Strath. Scotland **34** 55.42N 6.01W
Ardnamurchan *f.* Scotland **36** 56.44N 6.00W
Ardnamurchan, Pt. of Scotland **36** 56.44N 6.14W
Ardnave Pt. Scotland **34** 55.54N 6.20W
Ardres France **29** 50.51N 1.59E
Ardrishaig Scotland **34** 56.00N 5.26W
Ardrossan Scotland **34** 55.38N 4.49W
Ards Pen. N. Ireland **38** 54.30N 5.30W
Ardvasar Scotland **36** 57.03N 5.54W
Arecibo Puerto Rico **97** 18.29N 66.44W
Arena, Pt. U.S.A. **90** 38.58N 123.44W
Arendal Norway **46** 58.27N 8.56E
Arequipa Peru **102** 16.25S 72.10W
Arès France **40** 44.47N 1.08W
Arezzo Italy **42** 43.27N 11.52E
Arfak *mtn.* Asia **61** 1.30S 133.50E
Arga *r.* Spain **40** 42.20N 1.44W
Arganda Spain **41** 40.19N 3.26W
Argens *r.* France **40** 43.10N 6.45E
Argentan France **40** 48.45N 0.01W
Argentina S. America **103** 33.30S 64.00W
Argenton France **40** 46.36N 1.30E
Argeş *r.* Romania **43** 44.13N 26.22E
Argos Greece **43** 37.37N 22.45E
Argun *r.* China **63** 53.30N 121.48E
Argyll *f.* Scotland **34** 56.12N 5.15W
Århus Denmark **46** 56.10N 10.13E
Ariano Italy **42** 41.04N 15.00E
Arica Chile **102** 18.30S 70.20W
Ariege *r.* France **41** 43.02N 1.40E
Arinagour Scotland **34** 56.37N 6.31W
Arisaig Scotland **36** 56.55N 5.51W
Arisaig, Sd. of Scotland **36** 56.51N 5.50W
Ariza Spain **41** 41.19N 2.03W
Arizona *d.* U.S.A. **90** 34.00N 112.00W
Arizpe Mexico **96** 30.20N 110.11W
Arjona Colombia **97** 10.14N 75.22W
Arkaig, Loch Scotland **36** 56.58N 5.08W
Arkansas *d.* U.S.A. **91** 35.00N 92.00W
Arkansas *r.* U.S.A. **91** 33.50N 91.00W
Arkansas City U.S.A. **91** 37.03N 97.02W
Arkhangel'sk U.S.S.R. **48** 64.32N 41.10E
Arklow Rep. of Ire. **39** 52.47N 6.10W
Arlberg Pass Austria **44** 47.00N 10.05E
Arles France **40** 43.41N 4.38E
Arlington U.S.A. **95** 38.52N 77.05W
Arlington Heights *town* U.S.A. **94** 42.06N 88.00W
Arlon Belgium **45** 49.41N 5.49E
Armadale Scotland **35** 55.54N 3.41W
Armagh N. Ireland **38** 54.21N 6.41W
Armagh *d.* N. Ireland **38** 54.16N 6.35W
Arma Plateau Saudi Arabia **57** 25.30N 46.30E
Armavir U.S.S.R. **47** 44.59N 41.10E
Armenia Soviet Socialist Republic *d.* U.S.S.R. **57** 40.00N 45.00E
Armentières France **45** 50.41N 2.53E
Armidale Australia **80** 30.32S 151.40E
Armoy N. Ireland **34** 55.07N 6.20W
Arnauti, C. Cyprus **56** 35.06N 32.17E
Arnhem Neth. **45** 52.00N 5.55E
Arnhem, C. Australia **79** 12.10S 137.00E
Arnisdale Scotland **36** 57.08N 5.34W
Arno *r.* Italy **42** 43.43N 10.17E
Arnold England **33** 53.00N 1.08W
Arnprior Canada **95** 45.26N 76.24W
Arnsberg W. Germany **45** 51.24N 8.03E
Arnside England **32** 54.12N 2.49W
Arnstadt E. Germany **44** 50.50N 10.57E
Arrah India **58** 25.34N 84.40E
Ar Ramadi Iraq **56** 33.27N 43.19E
Arra Mts. Rep. of Ire. **39** 52.50N 8.22W
Arran *i.* Scotland **34** 55.35N 5.14W
Arras France **45** 50.17N 2.46E
Arrochar Scotland **34** 56.12N 4.44W
Arrow, Lough Rep. of Ire. **38** 54.03N 8.20W
Ar Rutba Iraq **56** 33.03N 40.18E
Árta Greece **43** 39.10N 20.57E
Arthur's Pass *f.* New Zealand **82** 42.50S 171.45E
Artois *f.* France **45** 50.16N 2.50E
Artush China **62** 38.27N 77.16E
Artvin Turkey **56** 41.12N 41.48E
Arua Uganda **73** 3.02N 30.56E
Aruba *i.* Neth. Antilles **97** 12.30N 70.00W
Aru Is. Indonesia **61** 6.00S 134.30E
Arun *r.* England **28** 50.48N 0.32W
Arundel England **28** 50.52N 0.32W
Arusha Tanzania **73** 3.21S 36.40E
Arusha *d.* Tanzania **73** 4.00S 37.00E
Aruwimi *r.* Zaïre **72** 1.20N 23.36E
Arvagh Rep. of Ire. **38** 53.56N 7.35W
Arvidsjaur Sweden **46** 65.37N 19.10E
Arvika Sweden **46** 59.41N 12.38E
Arzamas U.S.S.R. **47** 55.24N 43.48E
Asahi daki *mtn.* Japan **63** 43.42N 142.54E
Asahigawa Japan **63** 43.50N 142.20E
Asansol India **58** 23.40N 87.00E
Ascension I. Atlantic Oc. **112** 8.00S 14.00W
Aschaffenburg W. Germany **44** 49.58N 9.10E
Aschendorf W. Germany **45** 53.03N 7.20E
Aschersleben E. Germany **44** 51.46N 11.28E
Ascoli Piceno Italy **42** 42.52N 13.36E
Aseda Sweden **46** 57.10N 15.20E
Ash England **27** 51.14N 0.44W
Ash *r.* England **27** 51.48N 0.00
Ashanti *d.* Ghana **70** 6.30N 1.30W
Ashbourne England **32** 53.02N 1.44W
Ashbourne Rep. of Ire. **38** 53.31N 6.25W
Ashburton *r.* Australia **79** 21.15S 115.00E
Ashburton England **31** 50.31N 3.45W
Ashburton New Zealand **82** 43.54S 171.46E
Ashby de la Zouch England **28** 52.45N 1.29W
Ashdown Forest England **29** 51.03N 0.05E
Asheville U.S.A. **91** 35.35N 82.35W
Ashford Kent England **29** 51.08N 0.53E
Ashford Surrey England **27** 51.26N 0.27W
Ashington England **35** 55.11N 1.34W
Ashkhabad U.S.S.R. **57** 37.58N 58.24E
Ashland Wisc. U.S.A. **94** 46.34N 90.45W
Ashland Ky. U.S.A. **91** 38.28N 82.40W
Ash Sham *des.* Saudi Arabia **56** 28.15N 43.05E
Ash Shama *des.* Saudi Arabia **56** 31.20N 38.00E
Ashtabula U.S.A. **94** 41.53N 80.47W
Ashtead England **27** 51.19N 0.18W
Ashton-in-Makerfield England **32** 53.29N 2.39W
Ashton-under-Lyne England **32** 53.30N 2.08W
Asia 54
Asinara *i.* Italy **42** 41.04N 8.18E
Asinara, G. of Med. Sea **42** 41.00N 8.32E
Asir *f.* Saudi Arabia **69** 19.00N 42.00E
Askeaton Rep. of Ire. **39** 52.36N 9.00W
Askern England **33** 53.37N 1.09W
Askersund Sweden **46** 58.55N 14.55E
Asmara Ethiopia **69** 15.20N 38.58E
Aspatria England **32** 54.45N 3.20W
Aspiring, Mt. New Zealand **82** 44.20S 168.45E
Assab Ethiopia **69** 13.01N 42.47E
Assam *d.* India **59** 26.30N 93.00E
Assen Neth. **45** 53.00N 6.34E
Assiniboine, Mt. Canada **90** 50.51N 115.39W
Assynt *f.* Scotland **36** 58.12N 5.08W
Assynt, L. Scotland **36** 58.11N 5.03W
Asti Italy **40** 44.55N 8.13E
Aston Clinton England **27** 51.54N 0.39W
Astorga Spain **41** 42.30N 6.02W
Astoria U.S.A. **90** 46.12N 123.50W
Astrakhan U.S.S.R. **48** 46.22N 48.00E
Asuncion *i.* Asia **61** 19.34N 145.24E
Asunción Paraguay **103** 25.15S 57.40W
Aswân Egypt **56** 24.05N 32.56E
Aswân High Dam Egypt **56** 23.59N 32.54E
Asyût Egypt **56** 27.14N 31.07E
Atakpamé Togo **71** 7.34N 1.14E
Atar Mauritania **70** 20.32N 13.08W
Atbara Sudan **69** 17.42N 34.00E
Atbara *r.* Sudan **69** 17.47N 34.00E
Atchafalaya B. U.S.A. **91** 29.30N 92.00W
Ath Belgium **45** 50.38N 3.45E
Athabasca Canada **92** 54.44N 113.15W
Athabasca *r.* Canada **92** 58.30N 111.00W
Athabasca, L. Canada **92** 59.30N 109.00W
Athboy Rep. of Ire. **38** 53.38N 6.56W
Athea Rep. of Ire. **39** 52.28N 9.19W
Athenry Rep. of Ire. **38** 53.18N 8.45W
Athens Greece **43** 37.59N 23.42E
Athens U.S.A. **94** 39.20N 82.06W
Atherstone England **28** 52.35N 1.32W
Atherton England **32** 53.32N 2.30W
Athleague Rep. of Ire. **38** 53.34N 8.16W
Athlone Rep. of Ire. **38** 53.26N 7.57W
Áthos, Mt. Greece **43** 40.09N 24.19E
Athy Rep. of Ire. **39** 53.00N 7.00W
Atikokan Canada **94** 48.45N 91.38W
Atkarsk U.S.S.R. **47** 51.55N 45.00E
Atlanta U.S.A. **91** 33.45N 84.23W
Atlantic City U.S.A. **95** 39.23N 74.27W
Atlantic Ocean 106
Atlas Mts. Africa **106** 33.00N 4.00W
Atouguia Portugal **41** 39.20N 9.20W
Åtran *r.* Sweden **46** 56.54N 12.30E
Atrato *r.* Colombia **97** 8.15N 76.58W
Atrek *r.* Asia **57** 37.23N 54.00E
Attleboro U.S.A. **95** 41.57N 71.16W
Attleborough England **29** 52.31N 1.01E
Attopeu Laos **60** 14.51N 106.56E
Atuel *r.* Argentina **103** 36.15S 66.45W
Atura Uganda **73** 2.09N 32.22E
Aubagne France **40** 43.17N 5.35E
Aube *r.* France **40** 48.30N 3.37E
Aubigny-sur-Nère France **40** 47.29N 2.26E
Aubin France **40** 44.32N 2.14E
Auburn U.S.A. **95** 42.57N 76.34W
Auch France **40** 43.40N 0.36E
Auchinleck Scotland **34** 55.28N 4.17W
Auchterarder Scotland **35** 56.18N 3.43W
Auchtermuchty Scotland **35** 56.17N 3.15W
Auckland New Zealand **82** 36.55S 174.45E
Aude *r.* France **40** 43.13N 2.20E
Audlem England **32** 52.59N 2.31W
Audruicq France **29** 50.52N 2.05E
Augher N. Ireland **38** 54.26N 7.09W
Aughnacloy N. Ireland **38** 54.25N 7.00W
Augrabies Falls *f.* R.S.A. **74** 28.30S 20.16E
Augsburg W. Germany **44** 48.21N 10.54E
Augusta Ga. U.S.A. **91** 33.29N 82.00W
Augusta Maine U.S.A. **95** 44.17N 69.50W
Aulne *r.* France **40** 48.30N 4.11W
Aultbea Scotland **36** 57.50N 5.35W
Aumâle France **40** 49.46N 1.45E
Aurangabad India **58** 19.52N 75.22E
Aurich W. Germany **45** 53.28N 7.29E
Aurillac France **40** 44.56N 2.26E
Aurora U.S.A. **94** 41.45N 88.20W
Au Sable *r.* U.S.A. **94** 44.25N 83.20W
Au Sable Pt. U.S.A. **94** 44.21N 83.20W
Auskerry *i.* Scotland **37** 59.02N 2.34W
Austin Minn. U.S.A. **94** 43.40N 92.58W
Austin Texas U.S.A. **90** 30.18N 97.47W
Australasia 107
Australia Austa. **79**
Australian Alps *mts.* Australia **80** 36.30S 148.45E
Australian Antarctic Territory Antarctica **104** 73.00S 90.00E
Australian Capital Territory *d.* Australia **80** 35.30S 149.00E
Austria Europe **44** 47.30N 14.00E
Autun France **40** 46.58N 4.18E

Auxerre France **40** 47.48N 3.35E
Auzances France **40** 46.02N 2.29E
Avallon France **40** 47.30N 3.54E
Avanos Turkey **56** 38.44N 34.51E
Aveley England **27** 51.31N 0.15E
Avellaneda Argentina **103** 34.42S 58.20W
Avellino Italy **42** 40.55N 14.46E
Avesnes France **45** 50.08N 3.57E
Avesta Sweden **46** 60.09N 16.10E
Aveyron *r.* France **40** 44.09N 1.10E
Avezzano Italy **42** 42.03N 13.26E
Aviemore Scotland **37** 57.12N 3.50W
Aviero Portugal **41** 40.40N 8.35W
Avignon France **40** 43.56N 4.48E
Avila Spain **41** 40.39N 4.42W
Avon *d.* England **28** 51.35N 2.40W
Avon *r.* Avon England **28** 51.30N 2.43W
Avon *r.* Devon England **31** 50.17N 3.52W
Avon *r.* Dorset England **28** 50.43N 1.45W
Avon *r.* Glos. England **28** 52.00N 2.10W
Avon *r.* Scotland **37** 57.25N 3.23W
Avonmouth England **28** 51.30N 2.42W
Avranches France **40** 48.42N 1.21W
Awaso Ghana **70** 6.20N 2.22W
Awatera *r.* New Zealand **82** 41.37S 174.09E
Awe, Loch Scotland **34** 56.18N 5.24W
Axe *r.* Devon England **31** 50.42N 3.03W
Axe *r.* Somerset England **28** 51.18N 3.00W
Axel Heiberg I. Canada **93** 79.30N 90.00W
Axim Ghana **70** 4.53N 2.14W
Axminster England **28** 50.47N 3.01W
Ayaguz U.S.S.R. **62** 47.59N 80.27E
Ayan U.S.S.R. **49** 56.29N 138.00E
Aycliffe England **33** 54.36N 1.34W
Aydin Turkey **56** 37.52N 27.50E
Áyios Evstrátios *i.* Greece **43** 39.30N 25.00E
Aylesbury England **28** 51.48N 0.49W
Aylesham England **29** 51.14N 1.12E
Aylsham England **29** 52.48N 1.16E
Ayr Scotland **34** 55.28N 4.37W
Ayr *r.* Scotland **34** 55.28N 4.38W
Ayre, Pt. of I.o.M. **32** 54.25N 4.22W
Aysgarth England **32** 54.18N 2.00W
Ayutthaya Thailand **59** 14.25N 100.30E
Ayvalik Turkey **43** 39.19N 26.42E
Azamgarh India **58** 26.03N 83.10E
Azare Nigeria **71** 11.40N 10.08E
Azbine *mts. see* AïrNiger **71**
Azerbaijan Soviet Socialist Republic *d.* U.S.S.R. **57** 40.10N 47.50E
Azores *is.* Atlantic Oc. **112** 39.00N 30.00W
Azov, Sea of U.S.S.R. **47** 46.00N 36.30E
Azua Dom. Rep. **97** 18.29N 70.44W
Azuaga Spain **41** 38.16N 5.40W
Azuero Pen. Panamá **97** 7.30N 80.30W
Azul Argentina **103** 36.46S 59.50W
Azurduy Bolivia **103** 20.00S 64.29W

B

Ba'albek Lebanon **56** 34.00N 36.12E
Baarle-Hertog Neth. **45** 51.26N 4.56E
Babar Is. Indonesia **61** 8.00S 129.30E
Babbacombe B. England **31** 50.30N 3.28W
Bab el Mandeb *str.* Asia **69** 13.00N 43.10E
Babol Iran **57** 36.32N 52.42E
Baboua C.A.R. **71** 5.49N 14.51E
Babuyan Is. Phil. **61** 19.20N 121.30E
Babylon *ruins* Iraq **57** 32.33N 44.25E
Bacau Romania **47** 46.32N 26.59E
Baccarat France **44** 48.27N 6.45E
Back *r.* Canada **93** 66.37N 96.00W
Backnang W. Germany **44** 48.57N 9.26E
Bacolod Phil. **61** 10.38N 122.58E
Bacton England **29** 52.50N 1.29E
Bacup England **32** 53.42N 2.12W
Badajoz Spain **41** 38.53N 6.58W
Badalona Spain **41** 41.27N 2.15E
Baden Austria **44** 48.01N 16.14E
Baden-Baden W. Germany **44** 48.45N 8.15E
Badenoch *f.* Scotland **37** 57.00N 4.10W
Badgastein Austria **44** 47.07N 13.09E
Bad Ischl Austria **44** 47.43N 13.38E
Bad Kreuznach W. Germany **45** 49.51N 7.52E
Baffin B. Canada **93** 74.00N 70.00W
Baffin I. Canada **93** 68.50N 70.00W
Bafia Cameroon **71** 4.39N 11.14E
Bafing *r.* Mali **70** 14.48N 12.10W
Bafoulabé Mali **70** 13.49N 10.50W
Bafq Iran **57** 31.35N 55.21E
Bafra Turkey **56** 41.34N 35.56E
Bafwasende Zaïre **73** 1.09N 27.12E
Bagamoyo Tanzania **73** 6.26S 38.55E
Bagé Brazil **103** 31.22S 54.06W
Baggy Pt. England **31** 51.08N 4.15W
Baghdad Iraq **57** 33.20N 44.26E
Baghelkhand *f.* India **58** 24.20N 82.00E
Bagh nam Faoileann *str.* Scotland **36** 57.23N 7.15W
Baghrash Köl *l.* China **62** 42.00N 87.00E
Bagoé *r.* Mali **70** 12.34N 6.30W
Bagshot England **27** 51.22N 0.42W
Baguio Phil. **61** 16.25N 120.37E
Bahama Is. C. America **106** 25.00N 77.00W
Bahamas C. America **97** 23.30N 75.00W
Bahao Kalat Iran **57** 25.42N 61.28E
Bahawalpur Pakistan **58** 29.24N 71.47E
Bahbah Algeria **41** 35.04N 3.05E
Bahía Blanca Argentina **103** 38.45S 62.15W
Bahraich India **58** 27.35N 81.36E
Bahrain Asia **57** 26.00N 50.35E
Bahramabad Iran **58** 30.24N 56.00E
Bahr Aouk *r.* C.A.R. **71** 8.50N 18.50E
Bahr el Ghazal *r.* Chad **71** 12.26N 15.25E
Bahr el Ghazal *r.* Sudan **69** 9.30N 31.30E
Bahr el Jebel *r.* Sudan **69** 9.30N 30.20E
Bahr Salamat *r.* Chad **71** 9.30N 18.10E
Baie Comeau Canada **91** 49.12N 68.10W
Baie St. Paul Canada **95** 47.27N 70.30W
Baikal, L. U.S.S.R. **62** 53.30N 108.00E
Bailieborough Rep. of Ire. **38** 53.55N 6.59W
Bailleul France **45** 50.44N 2.44E
Bain *r.* England **33** 53.05N 0.12W
Baing Indonesia **61** 10.15S 120.34E
Bairnsdale Australia **80** 37.51S 147.38E
Baise *r.* France **40** 44.15N 0.20E
Baja Hungary **43** 46.12N 18.58E
Bakali *r.* Zaïre **72** 3.58S 17.10E
Bakel Senegal **70** 14.54N 12.26W
Baker Mont. U.S.A. **90** 46.23N 104.16W
Baker Oreg. U.S.A. **90** 44.46N 117.50W
Baker, Mt. U.S.A. **90** 48.48N 121.10W
Bakersfield U.S.A. **90** 35.25N 119.00W
Bakewell England **32** 53.13N 1.40W
Baku U.S.S.R. **57** 40.22N 49.53E
Bala Wales **30** 52.54N 3.36W
Balabac Str. Asia **60** 7.30N 117.00E
Balallan Scotland **36** 58.25N 6.36W
Balama Moçambique **73** 13.19S 38.35E
Bala Murghab Afghan. **57** 35.34N 63.20E
Balashov U.S.S.R. **47** 51.30N 43.10E
Balasore India **59** 21.31N 86.59E
Balaton, L. Hungary **47** 46.55N 17.50E
Balboa Panama Canal Zone **97** 8.37N 79.33W
Balbriggan Rep. of Ire. **38** 53.36N 6.12W
Balchik Bulgaria **43** 43.24N 28.10E
Balclutha New Zealand **82** 46.16S 169.46E
Baldock England **29** 51.59N 0.11W
Balearic Is. Spain **41** 39.30N 2.30E
Balerno Scotland **35** 55.53N 3.10W
Baleshare *i.* Scotland **36** 57.32N 7.22W
Balfron Scotland **34** 56.04N 4.20W
Bali *i.* Indonesia **60** 8.30S 115.05E
Balikesir Turkey **43** 39.38N 27.51E
Balikpapan Indonesia **60** 1.15S 116.50E
Balkan Mts. Bulgaria **43** 42.50N 24.30E
Balkhan Range *mts.* U.S.S.R. **57** 39.38N 54.30E
Balkhash U.S.S.R. **62** 46.51N 75.00E
Balkhash, L. U.S.S.R. **62** 46.40N 75.00E
Balla Rep. of Ire. **38** 53.48N 9.08W
Ballachulish Scotland **34** 56.40N 5.08W
Ballagan Pt. Rep. of Ire. **38** 54.00N 6.07W
Ballaghaderreen Rep. of Ire. **38** 53.54N 8.36W
Ballantrae Scotland **34** 55.06N 5.01W
Ballarat Australia **80** 37.36S 143.58E
Ballater Scotland **37** 57.03N 3.03W
Ballenas B. Mexico **90** 26.40N 113.30W
Ballia India **58** 25.45N 84.09E
Ballickmoyler Rep. of Ire. **39** 52.52N 7.00W
Ballina Rep. of Ire. **38** 54.08N 9.10W
Ballinakill Rep. of Ire. **39** 52.53N 7.20W
Ballinamore Rep. of Ire. **38** 54.03N 7.50W
Ballinasloe Rep. of Ire. **38** 53.20N 8.15W
Ballincollig Rep. of Ire. **39** 51.53N 8.36W
Ballinderry *r.* N. Ireland **34** 54.40N 6.32W
Ballindine Rep. of Ire. **38** 53.40N 8.58W
Ballingarry Limerick Rep. of Ire. **39** 52.28N 8.51W
Ballingarry Tipperary Rep. of Ire. **39** 53.02N 8.02W
Ballingeary Rep. of Ire. **39** 51.50N 9.15W
Ballinhassig Rep. of Ire. **39** 51.48N 8.32W
Ballinlough Rep. of Ire. **38** 53.44N 8.40W
Ballinrobe Rep. of Ire. **38** 53.38N 9.15W
Ballinskelligs B. Rep. of Ire. **39** 51.48N 10.13W
Ballivor Rep. of Ire. **38** 53.31N 6.57W
Balloch Scotland **34** 56.00N 4.36W
Ballybay Rep. of Ire. **38** 54.08N 6.56W
Ballybunion Rep. of Ire. **39** 52.30N 9.40W
Ballycanew Rep. of Ire. **39** 52.36N 6.19W
Ballycarney Rep. of Ire. **39** 52.34N 6.35W
Ballycastle N. Ireland **34** 55.12N 6.15W
Ballyclare N. Ireland **34** 54.45N 6.00W
Ballyconnell Rep. of Ire. **38** 54.06N 7.37W
Ballydehob Rep. of Ire. **39** 51.34N 9.28W
Ballydonegan Rep. of Ire. **39** 51.38N 10.04W
Ballygar Rep. of Ire. **38** 53.32N 8.20W
Ballygawley N. Ireland **38** 54.28N 7.03W
Ballyhaunis Rep. of Ire. **38** 53.45N 8.47W
Ballyhoura Mts. Rep. of Ire. **39** 52.18N 8.31W
Ballyjamesduff Rep. of Ire. **38** 53.52N 7.47W
Ballykelly N. Ireland **34** 55.03N 7.00W
Ballymahon Rep. of Ire. **38** 53.33N 7.47W
Ballymena N. Ireland **34** 54.52N 6.17W
Ballymoe Rep. of Ire. **38** 53.41N 8.29W
Ballymoney N. Ireland **34** 55.04N 6.31W
Ballymore Rep. of Ire. **38** 53.30N 7.42W
Ballymote Rep. of Ire. **38** 54.06N 8.31W
Ballynahinch N. Ireland **38** 54.24N 5.53W
Ballynakill Harbour *est.* Rep. of Ire. **38** 53.34N 10.20W
Ballyquintin Pt. N. Ireland **38** 54.40N 5.30W
Ballyragget Rep. of Ire. **39** 52.47N 7.21W
Ballyshannon Rep. of Ire. **38** 54.30N 8.11W
Ballyvaughan Rep. of Ire. **39** 53.06N 9.09W
Ballyvourney Rep. of Ire. **39** 51.57N 9.10W
Ballywalter N. Ireland **34** 54.33N 5.30W
Balranald Australia **80** 34.37S 143.37E
Balsas *r.* Mexico **96** 18.10N 102.05W
Balta *i.* Scotland **36** 60.44N 0.46W
Baltasound Scotland **36** 60.45N 0.52W
Baltic Sea Europe **46** 56.30N 19.00E
Baltic Shield *f.* Europe **107** 63.00N 30.00E
Baltimore U.S.A. **95** 39.18N 76.38W
Baltinglass Rep. of Ire. **39** 52.56N 6.43W
Baltiysk U.S.S.R. **46** 54.41N 19.59E
Baluchistan *f.* Pakistan **58** 28.00N 66.00E
Bam Iran **57** 29.07N 58.20E
Bamako Mali **70** 12.40N 7.59W
Bamba Mali **70** 17.05N 1.23W
Ba-Mbassa *r.* Chad **71** 11.30N 15.30E
Bamberg W. Germany **44** 49.54N 10.53E
Bambesa Zaïre **72** 3.27N 25.43E
Bambili Zaïre **72** 3.34N 26.07E
Bamburgh England **35** 55.36N 1.41W
Bamenda Cameroon **71** 5.55N 10.09E
Bamenda Highlands Cameroon **71** 6.20N 10.20E
Bampton Devon England **28** 51.00N 3.29W
Bampton Oxon. England **28** 51.44N 1.33W
Bampur Iran **57** 27.13N 60.29E
Bampur *r.* Iran **57** 27.18N 59.02E
Banagher Rep. of Ire. **39** 53.12N 8.00W
Banalia Zaïre **72** 1.33N 25.23E
Banana Zaïre **72** 5.55S 12.27E
Banbasa Nepal **59** 29.00N 80.28E
Banbridge N. Ireland **38** 54.21N 6.17W
Banbury England **28** 52.04N 1.21W
Banchory Scotland **37** 57.03N 2.30W
Banda Gabon **72** 3.47S 11.04E
Banda India **58** 25.28N 80.25E
Banda *i.* Indonesia **61** 4.30S 129.55E
Banda Atjeh Indonesia **60** 5.35N 95.20E
Bandama *r.* Ivory Coast **70** 5.10N 4.59W
Bandar India **59** 16.13N 81.12E
Bandar Abbas Iran **57** 27.10N 56.15E
Bandar Dilam Iran **57** 30.05N 50.11E
Bandar-e-Lengeh Iran **57** 26.34N 54.53E
Bandar-e-Pahlavi Iran **57** 37.26N 49.29E
Bandar-e-Shah Iran **57** 36.55N 54.05E
Bandar Rig Iran **57** 29.30N 50.40E
Bandar Seri Begawan Brunei **60** 4.56N 114.58E
Bandar Shahpur Iran **57** 30.26N 49.03E
Banda Sea Indonesia **61** 5.00S 128.00E
Bandawe Malaŵi **73** 11.57S 34.11E
Bandirma Turkey **43** 40.22N 28.00E
Bandon Rep. of Ire. **39** 51.45N 8.45W
Bandon *r.* Rep. of Ire. **39** 51.43N 8.38W
Bandundu Zaïre **72** 3.20S 17.24E
Bandundu *d.* Zaïre **72** 4.00S 18.30E
Bandung Indonesia **60** 6.57S 107.34E
Banes Cuba **97** 20.59N 75.24W
Banff Canada **90** 51.10N 115.54W
Banff Scotland **37** 57.40N 2.31W
Bangalore India **58** 12.58N 77.35E
Bangangté Cameroon **72** 5.09N 10.29E
Bangassou C.A.R. **72** 4.41N 22.52E
Banggai Is. Indonesia **61** 1.30S 123.10E
Bangka *i.* Indonesia **60** 2.20S 106.10E
Bangkok Thailand **59** 13.45N 100.35E
Bangladesh Asia **58** 24.30N 90.00E
Bangor N. Ireland **34** 54.40N 5.41W
Bangor Rep. of Ire. **38** 54.09N 9.44W
Bangor U.S.A. **95** 44.49N 68.47W
Bangor Wales **30** 53.13N 4.09W
Bangui C.A.R. **71** 4.23N 18.37E
Bangweulu, L. Zambia **73** 11.15S 29.45E
Ban Hat Yai Thailand **60** 7.00N 100.28E
Ban Houei Sai Laos **59** 20.21N 100.26E
Bani *r.* Mali **70** 14.30N 4.15W
Banjak Is. Indonesia **60** 2.15N 97.10E

Banja Luka Yugo. **43** 44.47N 17.10E
Banjarmasin Indonesia **60** 3.22S 114.36E
Banjul Gambia **70** 13.28N 16.39W
Ban Kantang Thailand **59** 7.25N 99.30E
Bankfoot Scotland **35** 56.30N 3.32W
Banks I. Australia **61** 10.15S 142.15E
Banks I. Canada **92** 73.00N 122.00W
Banks Pen. New Zealand **82** 43.45S 173.10E
Banks Str. Australia **80** 40.37S 148.07E
Bankura India **58** 23.14N 87.05E
Ban Me Thuot S. Vietnam **60** 12.41N 108.02E
Bann *r.* N. Ireland **34** 55.10N 6.46W
Bann *r.* Rep. of Ire. **39** 52.33N 6.33W
Bannockburn Rhodesia **74** 20.16S 29.51E
Bannockburn Scotland **35** 56.06N 3.55W
Bannow B. Rep. of Ire. **39** 52.14N 6.48W
Bansha Rep. of Ire. **39** 52.26N 8.04W
Banstead England **27** 51.19N 0.12W
Bantry Rep. of Ire. **39** 51.41N 9.27W
Bantry B. Rep. of Ire. **39** 51.40N 9.40W
Banwy *r.* Wales **30** 52.41N 3.16W
Banyo Cameroon **71** 6.47N 11.50E
Banyuwangi Indonesia **60** 8.12S 114.22E
Baoulé *r.* Mali **70** 13.47N 10.45W
Bapaume France **45** 50.07N 2.51E
Bar Albania **43** 42.05N 19.06E
Bara Banki India **58** 26.56N 81.11E
Baracoa Cuba **97** 20.23N 74.31W
Baradine Australia **80** 30.56S 149.05E
Barahona Dom. Rep. **97** 18.13N 71.07W
Baranof I. U.S.A. **92** 57.05N 135.00W
Baranovichi U.S.S.R. **47** 53.09N 26.00E
Barbacena Brazil **103** 21.13S 43.47W
Barbados C. America **97** 13.20N 59.40W
Barbastro Spain **41** 42.02N 0.07E
Barberton R.S.A. **74** 25.48S 31.03E
Barberton U.S.A. **94** 41.02N 81.37W
Barbezieux France **40** 45.28N 0.09W
Barbuda C. America **97** 17.41N 61.48W
Barcaldine Australia **79** 23.31S 145.15E
Barcellona Italy **42** 38.10N 15.13E
Barcelona Spain **41** 41.25N 2.10E
Barcelona Venezuela **97** 10.08N 64.43W
Bardai Chad **71** 21.21N 16.56E
Bardera Somali Rep. **73** 2.18N 42.18E
Bardi India **58** 24.30N 82.28E
Bardia Libya **56** 31.44N 25.08E
Bardney England **33** 53.13N 0.19W
Bardsey *i.* Wales **30** 52.45N 4.48W
Bardsey Sd. Wales **30** 52.45N 4.48W
Bardu Norway **46** 68.54N 18.20E
Bareilly India **58** 28.20N 79.24E
Barents Sea Arctic Oc. **48** 73.00N 40.00E
Bari Italy **43** 41.08N 16.52E
Barika Algeria **42** 35.25N 5.19E
Barinas Venezuela **97** 8.36N 70.15W
Barisal Bangla. **58** 22.41N 90.20E
Barisan Range *mts.* Indonesia **60** 3.30S 102.30E
Barito *r.* Indonesia **60** 3.35S 114.35E
Bariz Kuh, Jebel *mts.* Iran **57** 28.40N 58.10E
Barking *d.* England **27** 51.32N 0.05E
Barkly West R.S.A. **74** 28.32S 24.32E
Barle *r.* England **31** 51.00N 3.31W
Bar-le-Duc France **40** 48.46N 5.10E
Barletta Italy **42** 41.20N 16.15E
Barmouth Wales **30** 52.44N 4.03W
Barnard Castle *town* England **32** 54.33N 1.55W
Barnaul U.S.S.R. **48** 53.21N 83.15E
Barnes England **27** 51.28N 0.15W
Barnet England **27** 51.39N 0.11W
Barneveld Neth. **45** 52.10N 5.39E
Barnoldswick England **32** 53.55N 2.11W
Barnsley England **33** 53.33N 1.29W
Barnstaple England **31** 51.05N 4.03W
Barnstaple B. England **31** 51.04N 4.20W
Baro Nigeria **71** 8.37N 6.19E
Baroda India **58** 22.19N 73.14E
Barquisimeto Venezuela **97** 10.03N 69.18W
Barra *i.* Scotland **36** 56.59N 7.28W
Barra, Sd. of Scotland **36** 57.04N 7.20W
Barra do Pirai Brazil **103** 22.30S 43.50W
Barra Head Scotland **36** 56.47N 7.36W
Barrancabermeja Colombia **97** 7.06N 73.54W
Barranquilla Colombia **97** 11.00N 74.50W
Barreiro Portugal **41** 38.40N 9.05W
Barrhead Scotland **34** 55.47N 4.24W
Barrie Canada **95** 44.22N 79.42W
Barrington, Mt. Australia **80** 32.03S 151.55E
Barrow *r.* Rep. of Ire. **39** 52.17N 7.00W
Barrow U.S.A. **92** 71.16N 156.50W
Barrow I. Australia **79** 21.40S 115.27E
Barrow-in-Furness England **32** 54.08N 3.15W
Barry Wales **31** 51.23N 3.19W
Barstow U.S.A. **90** 34.55N 117.01W
Bar-sur-Aube France **40** 48.14N 4.43E
Bartin Turkey **56** 41.37N 32.20E
Bartolomeu Dias Moçambique **74** 21.10S 35.09E
Barton on Sea England **28** 50.44N 1.40W
Barton-upon-Humber England **33** 53.41N 0.27W
Barvas Scotland **36** 58.21N 6.31W
Barwon *r.* Australia **80** 30.00S 148.03E
Basankusu Zaïre **72** 1.12N 19.50E
Basel Switz. **44** 47.33N 7.36E
Bashi Channel Asia **63** 21.40N 121.20E
Basilan *i.* Phil. **61** 6.40N 122.10E
Basildon England **27** 51.34N 0.25E
Basingstoke England **28** 51.15N 1.05W
Baskatong L. Canada **95** 46.50N 75.46W
Basoko Zaïre **72** 1.20N 23.36E
Basongo Zaïre **72** 4.23S 20.28E
Basra Iraq **57** 30.33N 47.50E
Bassein Burma **60** 16.45N 94.30E
Bass Rock *i.* Scotland **35** 56.05N 2.38W
Bass Str. Australia **80** 39.45S 146.00E
Bastak Iran **57** 27.15N 54.26E
Bastelica France **40** 42.00N 9.03E
Basti India **58** 26.48N 82.44E
Bastia France **40** 42.41N 9.26E
Bastogne Belgium **45** 50.00N 5.43E
Bas Zaïre *d.* Zaïre **72** 5.15S 14.00E
Bata Equat. Guinea **72** 1.51N 9.49E
Batabanó, G. of Cuba **96** 23.15N 82.30W
Batangas Phil. **61** 13.46N 121.01E
Batan Is. Phil. **61** 20.50N 121.55E
Batchawana Mtn. Canada **94** 46.54N 84.36W
Bath England **28** 51.22N 2.22W
Bath U.S.A. **95** 43.56N 69.50W
Batha *r.* Chad **71** 12.47N 17.34E
Batha, Wadi *r.* Oman **57** 20.01N 59.39E
Bathgate Scotland **35** 55.44N 3.38W
Bathurst Australia **80** 33.27S 149.35E
Bathurst Canada **91** 47.37N 65.40W
Bathurst, C. Canada **92** 70.30N 128.00W
Bathurst I. Australia **79** 11.45S 130.15E
Bathurst I. Canada **93** 76.00N 100.00W
Bathurst Inlet *town* Canada **92** 66.48N 108.00W
Batinah *f.* Oman **57** 24.25N 56.50E
Batjan *i.* Indonesia **61** 0.30S 127.30E
Batley England **32** 53.43N 1.38W
Batna Algeria **42** 35.35N 6.11E
Baton Rouge U.S.A. **91** 30.30N 91.10W
Batouri Cameroon **71** 4.26N 14.27E
Battambang Khmer Rep. **59** 13.06N 103.13E
Battersea England **27** 51.28N 0.10W
Batticaloa Sri Lanka **59** 7.43N 81.42E
Battle England **29** 50.55N 0.30E
Battle Creek *town* U.S.A. **94** 42.20N 85.10W
Battle Harbour Canada **93** 52.16N 55.36W
Battock, Mt. Scotland **37** 56.57N 2.44W
Batu Is. Indonesia **60** 0.30S 98.20E
Batumi U.S.S.R. **56** 41.37N 41.36E
Baturadja Indonesia **60** 4.10S 104.10E
Bauchi Nigeria **71** 10.16N 9.50E
Bauchi *d.* Nigeria **71** 10.40N 10.00E
Baugé France **40** 47.33N 0.06W
Bauld, C. Canada **93** 51.30N 55.45W
Bauru Brazil **103** 22.19S 49.07W
Bautzen E. Germany **44** 51.11N 14.29E
Bavay France **45** 50.18N 3.48E
Bawdsey England **29** 52.01N 1.27E
Bawean *i.* Indonesia **60** 5.50S 112.35E
Bawiti Egypt **56** 28.21N 28.51E
Bawtry England **33** 53.25N 1.01W
Bayamo Cuba **97** 20.23N 76.39W
Bayan Kara Shan *mts.* China **62** 34.00N 97.20E
Bayburt Turkey **56** 40.15N 40.16E
Bay City U.S.A. **94** 43.35N 83.52W
Baydaratskaya B. U.S.S.R. **48** 70.00N 66.00E
Bayeux France **40** 49.16N 0.42W
Bay Is. Honduras **96** 16.10N 86.30W
Bayonne France **40** 43.30N 1.28W
Bayonne U.S.A. **95** 40.39N 74.08W
Bayreuth W. Germany **44** 49.56N 11.35E
Baza Spain **41** 37.30N 2.45W
Bazman Kuh *mtn.* Iran **57** 28.06N 60.00E
Beachport Australia **80** 37.29S 140.01E
Beachy Head England **29** 50.43N 0.15E
Beacon Hill England **28** 51.12N 1.42W
Beacon Hill Wales **30** 52.23N 3.14W
Beaconsfield England **27** 51.37N 0.39W
Beaminster England **28** 50.48N 2.44W
Beare Green England **27** 51.10N 0.18W
Bear I. Rep. of Ire. **39** 51.38N 9.52W
Bearsden Scotland **34** 55.56N 4.20W
Bearsted England **27** 51.17N 0.35E
Beaufort Sea N. America **92** 72.00N 141.00W
Beaufort West R.S.A. **74** 32.21S 22.35E
Beauly Scotland **37** 57.29N 4.29W
Beauly *r.* Scotland **37** 57.29N 4.25W
Beauly Firth *est.* Scotland **37** 57.29N 4.20W
Beaumaris Wales **30** 53.16N 4.07W
Beaumont Belgium **45** 50.14N 4.16E
Beaumont U.S.A. **91** 30.04N 94.06W
Beaune France **40** 47.02N 4.50E
Beauvais France **40** 49.26N 2.05E
Beaver I. U.S.A. **94** 45.40N 85.35W
Beawar India **58** 26.02N 74.20E
Bebington England **32** 53.23N 3.01W
Beccles England **29** 52.27N 1.33E
Béchar Algeria **68** 31.35N 2.17W
Beckenham England **27** 51.24N 0.01W
Beckum W. Germany **45** 51.45N 8.02E
Bedale England **33** 54.18N 1.35W
Bédarieux France **40** 43.35N 3.10E
Beddington England **27** 51.22N 0.08W
Bedford England **29** 52.08N 0.29W
Bedford U.S.A. **94** 38.51N 86.30W
Bedford Levels *f.* England **29** 52.35N 0.08E
Bedfordshire *d.* England **29** 52.04N 0.28W
Bedlington England **35** 55.08N 1.34W
Bedwas Wales **31** 51.36N 3.10W
Bedwellty Wales **31** 51.42N 3.13W
Bedworth England **28** 52.28N 1.29W
Bee, Loch Scotland **36** 57.23N 7.22W
Beenoskee *mtn.* Rep. of Ire. **39** 52.47N 10.04W
Beersheba Israel **56** 31.15N 34.47E
Beeston England **33** 52.55N 1.11W
Beeville U.S.A. **90** 28.25N 97.47W
Befale Zaïre **72** 0.27N 21.01E
Beg, Lough N. Ireland **34** 54.47N 6.29W
Bega Australia **80** 36.41S 149.50E
Begna *r.* Norway **46** 60.06N 10.15E
Behbehan Iran **57** 30.35N 50.17E
Beida Libya **69** 32.50N 21.50E
Beilen Neth. **45** 52.51N 6.31E
Beinn à Ghlò *mtn.* Scotland **37** 56.50N 3.42W
Beinn an Tuirc *mtn.* Scotland **34** 55.24N 5.33W
Beinn Bheigeir *mtn.* Scotland **34** 55.44N 6.08W
Beinn Dearg *mtn.* Scotland **37** 57.47N 4.55W
Beinn Dhorain *mtn.* Scotland **37** 58.07N 3.50W
Beinn Mhor *mtn.* Scotland **36** 57.59N 6.40W
Beinn nam Bad Mor *mtn.* Scotland **37** 58.29N 3.43W
Beinn Resipol *mtn.* Scotland **36** 56.43N 6.38W
Beinn Sgritheall *mtn.* Scotland **36** 57.09N 5.34W
Beinn Tharsuinn *mtn.* Scotland **37** 57.47N 4.21W
Beira Moçambique **74** 19.49S 34.52E
Beirut Lebanon **56** 33.52N 35.30E
Beitbridge Rhodesia **74** 22.10S 30.01E
Beith Scotland **34** 55.45N 4.37W
Béja Tunisia **42** 36.44N 9.12E
Beja Portugal **41** 38.01N 7.52W
Bejaïa Algeria **42** 36.45N 5.05E
Béjar Spain **41** 40.24N 5.45W
Bejestan Iran **57** 34.32N 58.08E
Bela India **58** 25.55N 82.00E
Bela Pakistan **58** 26.12N 66.20E
Belalcázar Spain **41** 38.35N 5.10W
Belang Indonesia **61** 0.58N 124.56E
Bela Vista Brazil **103** 22.05S 56.22W
Bela Vista Moçambique **74** 26.20S 32.40E
Belaya *r.* U.S.S.R. **48** 55.40N 52.30E
Belcher Is. Canada **93** 56.00N 79.00W
Belcoo N. Ireland **38** 54.18N 7.53W
Belém Brazil **102** 1.27S 48.29W
Belen U.S.A. **90** 34.39N 106.48W
Belet Wen Somali Rep. **73** 4.38N 45.12E
Belfast N. Ireland **34** 54.36N 5.57W
Belfast Lough N. Ireland **34** 54.42N 5.45W
Belford England **35** 55.36N 1.48W
Belfort France **44** 47.38N 6.52E
Belgaum India **58** 15.54N 74.36E
Belgium Europe **45** 51.00N 4.30E
Belgorod U.S.S.R. **47** 50.38N 36.36E
Belgorod Dnestrovskiy U.S.S.R. **47** 46.10N 30.19E
Belgrade Yugo. **43** 44.49N 20.28E
Belikh *r.* Syria **56** 35.58N 39.05E
Belitung *i.* Indonesia **60** 3.00S 108.00E
Belize Belize **96** 17.29N 88.20W
Belize C. America **96** 17.00N 88.30W
Bellac France **40** 46.07N 1.04E
Bellary India **58** 15.11N 76.54E
Belleek N. Ireland **38** 54.29N 8.06W
Belle Île France **40** 47.20N 3.10W
Belle Isle Str. Canada **93** 50.45N 58.00W
Bellerive Australia **80** 42.52S 147.21E
Belleville Canada **95** 44.10N 77.22W
Belleville U.S.A. **94** 38.31N 89.59W
Bellingham England **35** 55.09N 2.15W
Bellingham U.S.A. **90** 48.45N 122.29W
Bellingshausen Sea Antarctica **106** 70.00S 84.00W
Bello Colombia **97** 6.20N 75.41W
Bell Rock *i. see* Inchcape Scotland **35**
Bell Ville Argentina **103** 32.35S 62.41W
Belmopan Belize **96** 17.25N 88.46W
Belmullet Rep. of Ire. **38** 54.14N 10.00W
Belo Horizonte Brazil **103** 19.45S 43.54W
Beloit U.S.A. **94** 42.31N 89.04W
Beloye, L. U.S.S.R. **47** 60.12N 37.45E

Belozersk U.S.S.R. **47** 60.00N 37.49E
Belper England **33** 53.02N 1.29W
Beltra, Lough Rep. of Ire. **38** 53.56N 9.26W
Beltsy U.S.S.R. **47** 47.45N 27.59E
Belturbet Rep. of Ire. **38** 54.06N 7.27W
Belukha, Mt. U.S.S.R. **62** 49.46N 86.40E
Belvedere England **27** 51.30N 0.10E
Bembridge England **28** 50.41N 1.04W
Bemidji U.S.A. **91** 47.29N 94.52W
Ben Alder *mtn.* Scotland **37** 56.49N 4.28W
Benalla Australia **80** 36.35S 145.58E
Benavente Spain **41** 42.00N 5.40W
Ben Avon *mtn.* Scotland **37** 57.06N 3.27W
Benbane Head N. Ireland **34** 55.15N 6.29W
Benbecula *i.* Scotland **36** 57.26N 7.18W
Benbulbin *mtn.* Rep. of Ire. **38** 54.22N 8.28W
Ben Chonzie *mtn.* Scotland **35** 56.27N 4.00W
Ben Cruachan *mtn.* Scotland **34** 56.26N 5.18W
Bend U.S.A. **90** 44.04N 121.20W
Bendel *d.* Nigeria **71** 6.10N 6.00E
Bendigo Australia **80** 36.48S 144.21E
Beneraird *mtn.* Scotland **34** 55.04N 4.56W
Benevento Italy **42** 41.07N 14.46E
Bengal *d.* India **58** 23.00N 88.00E
Bengal, B. of Indian Oc. **59** 17.00N 89.00E
Benghazi Libya **68** 32.07N 20.05E
Bengkulu Indonesia **60** 3.46S 102.16E
Ben Griam More *mtn.* Scotland **37** 58.20N 4.02W
Benguela Angola **72** 12.34S 13.24E
Benguela *d.* Angola **72** 12.45S 14.00E
Ben Hee *mtn.* Scotland **37** 58.16N 4.41W
Ben Hiant *mtn.* Scotland **34** 56.42N 6.01W
Ben Hope *mtn.* Scotland **37** 58.24N 4.36W
Ben Horn *mtn.* Scotland **37** 58.07N 4.02W
Ben Hutig *mtn.* Scotland **37** 58.33N 4.31W
Beni *d.* Bolivia **103** 15.50S 65.00W
Beni Zaïre **73** 0.29N 29.27E
Benicarló Spain **41** 40.25N 0.25E
Benin Africa **71** 9.00N 2.30E
Benin, Bight of Africa **71** 5.30N 3.00E
Benin City Nigeria **71** 6.19N 5.41E
Beni-Saf Algeria **41** 35.28N 1.22W
Beni Suef Egypt **56** 29.05N 31.05E
Ben Klibreck *mtn.* Scotland **37** 58.15N 4.22W
Ben Lawers *mtn.* Scotland **34** 56.33N 4.14W
Benllech Wales **30** 53.18N 4.15W
Ben Lomond *mtn.* Scotland **34** 56.12N 4.38W
Ben Lomond *mtn.* Australia **80** 30.04S 151.43E
Ben Loyal *mtn.* Scotland **37** 58.24N 4.26W
Ben Lui *mtn.* Scotland **34** 56.23N 4.49W
Ben Macdhui *mtn.* Scotland **37** 57.04N 3.40W
Ben More *mtn.* Central Scotland **34** 56.23N 4.31W
Ben More *mtn.* Strath. Scotland **34** 56.26N 6.02W
Ben More Assynt *mtn.* Scotland **37** 58.07N 4.52W
Bennane Head Scotland **34** 55.08N 5.00W
Bennettsbridge Rep. of Ire. **39** 52.35N 7.11W
Ben Nevis *mtn.* Scotland **36** 56.48N 5.00W
Benoni R.S.A. **74** 26.12S 28.18E
Ben Rinnes *mtn.* Scotland **37** 57.24N 3.15W
Benton Harbor U.S.A. **94** 42.07N 86.27W
Benue *d.* Nigeria **71** 7.20N 8.00E
Benue *r.* Nigeria **71** 7.52N 6.45E
Ben Vorlich *mtn.* Scotland **34** 56.21N 4.13W
Benwee Head Rep. of Ire. **38** 54.21N 9.48W
Ben Wyvis *mtn.* Scotland **37** 57.40N 4.35W
Beragh N. Ireland **34** 54.34N 7.10W
Berat Albania **43** 40.42N 19.59E
Berbera Somali Rep. **69** 10.28N 45.02E
Berbérati C.A.R. **71** 4.19N 15.51E
Berchem Belgium **45** 50.48N 3.32E
Berdichev U.S.S.R. **47** 49.54N 28.39E
Berdyansk U.S.S.R. **47** 46.45N 36.47E
Berens *r.* Canada **91** 52.25N 97.00W
Berezniki U.S.S.R. **48** 59.26N 57.00E
Bergama Turkey **43** 39.08N 27.10E
Bergamo Italy **40** 45.42N 9.40E
Bergen Norway **46** 60.23N 5.20E
Bergen op Zoom Neth. **45** 51.30N 4.17E
Bergerac France **40** 44.50N 0.29E
Bergheim W. Germany **45** 50.58N 6.39E
Bergisch Gladbach W. Germany **45** 50.59N 7.10E
Berhampore India **58** 24.06N 88.18E
Berhampur India **59** 19.21N 84.51E
Bering Sea N. America/Asia **92** 65.00N 170.00W
Bering Str. U.S.S.R./U.S.A. **92** 65.00N 170.00W
Berkel *r.* Neth. **45** 52.10N 6.12E
Berkhamsted England **27** 51.46N 0.35W
Berkshire *d.* England **28** 51.25N 1.03W
Berkshire Downs *hills* England **28** 51.32N 1.36W
Berlin E. Germany **44** 52.32N 13.25E
Berlin U.S.A. **95** 44.27N 71.13W
Bermagui Australia **80** 36.28S 150.03E
Bermejo *r.* Argentina **103** 26.47S 58.30W
Bermondsey England **27** 51.30N 0.04W
Bermuda Atlantic Oc. **97** 32.18N 64.45W
Bernburg E. Germany **44** 51.49N 11.44E
Berne Switz. **44** 46.57N 7.26E
Berneray *i.* W. Isles Scotland **36** 56.47N 7.38W
Berneray *i.* W. Isles Scotland **36** 57.43N 7.11W
Bernina *mtn.* Italy/Switz. **42** 46.22N 9.57E
Bernkastel W. Germany **45** 49.55N 7.05E
Berri Australia **80** 34.17S 140.36E
Berriedale Scotland **37** 58.11N 3.30W
Berry Head England **31** 50.24N 3.28W
Bertnaghboy B. Rep. of Ire. **38** 53.23N 9.52W
Bertoua Cameroon **71** 4.34N 13.42E
Berwick-upon-Tweed England **35** 55.46N 2.00W
Berwyn *mts.* Wales **30** 52.55N 3.25W
Besalampy Malagasy Rep. **73** 16.53S 44.29E
Besançon France **44** 47.14N 6.02E
Bessarabia *f.* U.S.S.R. **47** 46.30N 28.40E
Betanzos Spain **41** 43.17N 8.13W
Bétaré Oya Cameroon **71** 5.34N 14.09E
Bethal R.S.A. **74** 26.27S 29.28E
Bethersden England **29** 51.08N 0.46E
Bethesda Wales **30** 53.11N 4.03W
Bethlehem R.S.A. **74** 28.15S 28.19E
Bethlehem U.S.A. **95** 40.36N 75.22W
Bethnal Green England **27** 51.32N 0.03W
Béthune France **45** 50.32N 2.38E
Bettyhill Scotland **37** 58.30N 4.14W
Betwa *r.* India **58** 25.48N 80.10E
Betws-y-Coed Wales **30** 53.05N 3.48W
Beult *r.* England **27** 51.13N 0.26E
Beverley England **33** 53.52N 0.26W
Beverly U.S.A. **95** 42.35N 70.52W
Beverwijk Neth. **45** 52.29N 4.40E
Bewcastle England **35** 55.03N 2.45W
Bewcastle Fells *hills* England **35** 55.05N 2.50W
Bewdley England **28** 52.23N 2.19W
Bexhill England **29** 50.51N 0.29E
Bexley England **27** 51.26N 0.10E
Beyla Guinea **70** 8.42N 8.39W
Beysehir L. Turkey **56** 37.47N 31.30E
Bezhetsk U.S.S.R. **47** 57.49N 36.40E
Bezhitsa U.S.S.R. **47** 53.19N 34.17E
Béziers France **40** 43.21N 3.13E
Bhagalpur India **58** 25.14N 85.59E
Bhamo Burma **59** 24.15N 97.15E
Bhatpara India **62** 22.51N 88.31E
Bhavnagar India **58** 21.46N 72.14E
Bhima *r.* India **58** 16.30N 77.10E
Bhind India **58** 26.33N 78.47E
Bhopal India **58** 23.17N 77.28E
Bhubaneswar India **59** 20.15N 85.50E
Bhuj India **58** 23.12N 69.54E
Bhutan Asia **58** 27.20N 90.30E
Biak *i.* Asia **61** 0.55S 136.00E
Białogard Poland **44** 54.00N 16.00E
Białystok Poland **47** 53.09N 23.10E
Biarritz France **40** 43.29N 1.33W
Bicester England **28** 51.53N 1.09W
Bickle Knob *mtn.* U.S.A. **95** 38.56N 79.44W
Bickley England **27** 51.24N 0.03E
Bida Nigeria **71** 9.06N 5.59E
Bidborough England **27** 51.11N 0.14E
Biddeford U.S.A. **95** 43.29N 70.27W
Biddulph England **32** 53.08N 2.11W
Bidean nam Bian *mtn.* Scotland **34** 56.39N 5.02W
Bideford England **31** 51.01N 4.13W
Bideford B. England **31** 51.04N 4.20W
Bié *d.* Angola **72** 12.30S 17.30E
Biel Switz. **44** 47.09N 7.16E
Bielefeld W. Germany **44** 52.02N 8.32E
Bié Plateau *f.* Angola **72** 13.00S 16.00E
Big Bald Mtn. Canada **95** 47.12N 66.25W
Bigbury B. England **31** 50.15N 3.56W
Biggar Scotland **35** 55.38N 3.31W
Biggin Hill *town* England **27** 51.19N 0.04E
Biggleswade England **29** 52.06N 0.16W
Big Horn *r.* U.S.A. **90** 46.05N 107.20W
Bignona Senegal **70** 12.48N 16.18W
Big Snowy Mtn. U.S.A. **90** 46.46N 109.31W
Big Spring *town* U.S.A. **90** 32.15N 101.30W
Bihać Yugo. **42** 44.49N 15.53E
Bihar India **58** 25.13N 85.31E
Bihar *d.* India **58** 24.35N 85.40E
Biharamulo Tanzania **73** 2.34S 31.20E
Bihor *mtn.* Romania **47** 46.26N 22.43E
Bijagos Archipelago *is.* Guinea Bissau **70** 11.30N 16.00W
Bijar Iran **57** 35.52N 47.39E
Bijawar India **58** 24.36N 79.30E
Bikaner India **58** 28.01N 73.22E
Bikin U.S.S.R. **63** 46.52N 134.15E
Bikoro Zaïre **72** 0.45S 18.09E
Bilaspur India **58** 22.03N 82.12E
Bilauktaung Range *mts.* Asia **60** 13.20N 99.30E
Bilbao Spain **41** 43.15N 2.56W
Bilecik Turkey **56** 40.10N 29.59E
Bili *r.* Zaïre **72** 4.09N 22.25E
Billericay England **27** 51.38N 0.25E
Billingham England **33** 54.36N 1.18W
Billings U.S.A. **90** 45.47N 108.30W
Billingshurst England **29** 51.02N 0.28W
Billington England **27** 51.54N 0.39W
Bill of Portland *c.* England **31** 50.32N 2.28W
Bilma Niger **71** 18.46N 12.50E
Biloxi U.S.A. **91** 30.30N 89.00W
Bima *r.* Zaïre **72** 3.24N 25.10E
Bina India **58** 24.09N 78.10E
Binaija *mtn.* Indonesia **61** 3.10S 129.30E
Binche Belgium **45** 50.25N 4.10E
Bindura Rhodesia **74** 17.20S 31.21E
Binga, Mt. Rhodesia **74** 19.47S 33.03E
Bingara Australia **80** 29.51S 150.38E
Bingen W. Germany **45** 49.58N 7.55E
Bingerville Ivory Coast **70** 5.20N 3.53W
Bingham England **33** 52.57N 0.57W
Binghamton U.S.A. **95** 42.06N 75.55W
Bingkor Malaysia **60** 5.26N 116.15E
Bingley England **32** 53.51N 1.50W
Bingöl Turkey **56** 38.54N 40.29E
Bingol Dağlari *mtn.* Turkey **56** 39.21N 41.22E
Binh Dinh Vietnam **60** 13.55N 109.07E
Binjai Indonesia **60** 3.37N 98.25E
Bintan *i.* Indonesia **60** 1.10N 104.30E
Bintulu Malaysia **60** 3.12N 113.01E
Birdum Australia **79** 15.38S 133.12E
Birecik Turkey **56** 37.03N 37.59E
Birhan *mtn.* Ethiopia **69** 11.00N 37.50E
Birjand Iran **57** 32.54N 59.10E
Birkenfeld W. Germany **45** 49.39N 7.10E
Birkenhead England **32** 53.24N 3.01W
Birket Qârûn *l.* Egypt **56** 29.30N 30.40E
Birmingham England **28** 52.30N 1.55W
Birmingham Ala. U.S.A. **91** 33.30N 86.55W
Birmingham Mich. U.S.A. **94** 42.33N 83.12W
Birnin Kebbi Nigeria **71** 12.30N 4.11E
Birni N'Konni Niger **71** 13.49N 5.19E
Birobidzhan U.S.S.R. **63** 48.49N 132.54E
Birq, Wadi *r.* Saudi Arabia **57** 24.08N 47.35E
Birr Rep. of Ire. **39** 53.06N 7.56W
Birreencorragh *mtn.* Rep. of Ire. **38** 53.59N 9.31W
Biscay, B. of France **40** 45.30N 4.00W
Bishop Auckland England **32** 54.40N 1.40W
Bishopbriggs Scotland **34** 55.55N 4.12W
Bishop's Castle England **28** 52.29N 3.00W
Bishop's Lydeard England **28** 51.04N 3.12W
Bishop's Stortford England **27** 51.53N 0.09E
Bishops Waltham England **28** 50.57N 1.13W
Bisina, L. Uganda **73** 1.35N 34.08E
Bisitun Iran **57** 34.22N 47.29E
Biskotasi L. Canada **94** 47.15N 82.15W
Biskra Algeria **42** 34.48N 5.40E
Bisley England **27** 51.20N 0.39W
Bismarck U.S.A. **90** 46.50N 100.48W
Bismarck Range *mts.* P.N.G. **61** 6.00S 145.00E
Bismarck Sea Pacific Oc. **61** 4.00S 146.30E
Bissau Guinea Bissau **70** 11.52N 15.39W
Bistrita *r.* Romania **47** 46.30N 26.54E
Bitburg W. Germany **45** 49.58N 6.31E
Bitlis Turkey **56** 38.23N 42.04E
Bitola Yugo. **43** 41.02N 21.21E
Bitterfontein R.S.A. **74** 31.03S 18.16E
Bitter Lakes Egypt **56** 30.20N 32.50E
Biu Nigeria **71** 10.36N 12.11E
Biumba Rwanda **73** 1.38S 30.02E
Biysk U.S.S.R. **48** 52.35N 85.16E
Bizerta Tunisia **42** 37.17N 9.51E
Black *r.* Vietnam **60** 21.20N 105.45E
Black *r.* Rep. of Ire. **38** 53.50N 7.51W
Black *r.* Ark. U.S.A. **91** 35.30N 91.20W
Black *r.* Wisc. U.S.A. **94** 43.55N 91.20W
Black Bull Head Rep. of Ire. **39** 51.35N 10.03W
Blackburn England **32** 53.44N 2.30W
Black Combe *mtn.* England **32** 54.15N 3.20W
Blackcraig Hill Scotland **34** 55.19N 4.08W
Black Down Hills England **28** 50.55N 3.10W
Blackford Scotland **35** 56.16N 3.48W
Black Forest *f.* W. Germany **44** 48.00N 7.45E
Black Head N. Ireland **34** 54.46N 5.41W
Black Head Rep. of Ire. **39** 53.09N 9.16W
Black Isle *f.* Scotland **37** 57.35N 4.15W
Blackmoor Vale *f.* England **28** 50.55N 2.25W
Black Mtn. Wales **30** 51.52N 3.50W
Black Mts. Wales **30** 51.52N 3.09W
Blackpool England **32** 53.48N 3.03W
Black River *town* Jamaica **97** 18.02N 77.52W
Blackrock Rep. of Ire. **38** 53.18N 6.13W
Black Rock Desert U.S.A. **90** 41.10N 118.45W
Black Sand Desert U.S.S.R. **57** 37.45N 60.00E
Black Sea Europe **47** 43.00N 35.00E
Blacksod B. Rep. of Ire. **38** 54.04N 10.00W
Black Volta *r.* Ghana/U. Volta **70** 8.14N 2.11W
Blackwater *r.* England **29** 51.43N 0.42E
Blackwater *r.* N. Ireland **38** 54.31N 6.36W
Blackwater Rep. of Ire. **39** 52.26N 6.20W
Blackwater *r.* Meath Rep. of Ire. **38** 53.39N 6.41W

Blackwater *r.* Waterford Rep. of Ire. **39** 51.58N 7.52W
Blackwater Resr. Scotland **34** 56.43N 4.58W
Bladnoch *r.* Scotland **34** 54.52N 4.26W
Blaenau Ffestiniog Wales **30** 53.00N 3.57W
Blaenavon Wales **31** 51.46N 3.05W
Blagoevgrad Bulgaria **43** 42.02N 23.04E
Blagoveshchensk U.S.S.R. **63** 50.19N 127.30E
Blair Atholl Scotland **37** 56.46N 3.51W
Blairgowrie Scotland **35** 56.36N 3.21W
Blakeney Pt. England **33** 52.58N 0.57E
Blanc, Cap Mauritania **70** 20.44N 17.05W
Blanc, Mont Canada **95** 48.47N 66.51W
Blanc, Mont Europe **40** 45.50N 6.52E
Blanca, Bahía *b.* Argentina **103** 39.15S 61.00W
Blanchardstown Rep. of Ire. **38** 53.24N 6.23W
Blanche, L. Australia **80** 29.15S 139.40E
Blanco, C. Costa Rica **96** 9.36N 85.06W
Blanco, C. U.S.A. **90** 42.50N 124.29W
Blandford Forum England **28** 50.52N 2.10W
Blankenberge Belgium **45** 51.18N 3.08E
Blantyre Malaŵi **73** 15.46S 35.00E
Blarney Rep. of Ire. **39** 51.56N 8.34W
Blavet *r.* France **40** 47.43N 3.18W
Blaydon England **32** 54.58N 1.42W
Blaye France **40** 45.08N 0.40W
Bleaklow Hill England **32** 53.27N 1.50W
Blenheim New Zealand **82** 41.32S 173.58E
Blessington Rep. of Ire. **39** 53.11N 6.33W
Bletchley England **28** 51.59N 0.45W
Blida Algeria **41** 36.30N 2.50E
Blidworth England **33** 53.06N 1.07W
Blindley Heath England **27** 51.12N 0.04W
Blind River *town* Canada **94** 46.12N 82.59W
Blitta Togo **71** 8.23N 1.06E
Bloemfontein R.S.A. **74** 29.07S 26.14E
Blois France **40** 47.36N 1.20E
Bloody Foreland *c.* Rep. of Ire. **38** 55.09N 8.17W
Bloomington Ind. U.S.A. **94** 39.10N 86.31W
Bloomington Minn. U.S.A. **94** 44.48N 93.19W
Bloomsburg U.S.A. **95** 41.01N 76.27W
Bluefield U.S.A. **91** 37.14N 81.17W
Bluefields Nicaragua **96** 12.00N 83.49W
Blue Mts. Australia **80** 33.30S 150.15E
Blue Mts. U.S.A. **90** 45.00N 118.00W
Blue Nile *r.* Sudan **69** 15.45N 32.25E
Blue Stack Mts. Rep. of Ire. **38** 54.44N 8.09W
Bluff New Zealand **82** 46.38S 168.21E
Blumenau Brazil **103** 26.55S 49.07W
Blyth England **35** 55.07N 1.29W
Blyth *r.* Northum. England **35** 55.08N 1.29W
Blyth *r.* Suffolk England **29** 52.19N 1.36E
Blyth Bridge *town* Scotland **35** 55.42N 3.23W
Blyth Sands England **27** 51.28N 0.33E
Bo Sierra Leone **70** 7.58N 11.45W
Boardman U.S.A. **94** 41.02N 80.40W
Bobo-Dioulasso U. Volta **70** 11.11N 4.18W
Bobruysk U.S.S.R. **47** 53.08N 29.10E
Bocholt W. Germany **45** 51.49N 6.37E
Bochum W. Germany **45** 51.28N 7.11E
Boddam Scotland **37** 57.28N 1.48W
Bodélé Depression *f.* Chad **71** 16.50N 17.10E
Boden Sweden **46** 65.50N 21.44E
Bodenham England **28** 52.09N 2.41W
Bodmin England **31** 50.28N 4.44W
Bodmin Moor England **31** 50.35N 4.35W
Bodö Norway **46** 67.18N 14.26E
Boende Zaïre **72** 0.15S 20.49E
Boffa Guinea **70** 10.12N 14.02W
Bogan Gate *town* Australia **80** 33.08S 147.50E
Bogenfels S.W. Africa **74** 27.23S 15.22E
Boggabilla Australia **80** 28.36S 150.21E
Boggeragh Mts. Rep. of Ire. **39** 52.03N 8.53W
Boghari Algeria **41** 35.55N 2.47E
Bognor Regis England **28** 50.47N 0.40W
Bog of Allen *f.* Rep. of Ire. **38** 53.17N 7.00W
Bogong, Mt. Australia **80** 36.45S 147.21E
Bogor Indonesia **60** 6.34S 106.45E
Bogotá Colombia **102** 4.38N 74.05W
Bogra Bangla. **58** 24.52N 89.28E
Bogué Mauritania **70** 16.40N 14.10W
Bohain France **45** 49.59N 3.28E
Bohemian Forest *mts.* Czech. **44** 49.20N 13.10E
Bohol *i.* Phil. **61** 9.45N 124.10E
Boise U.S.A. **90** 43.38N 116.12W
Bojeador, C. Phil. **61** 18.30N 120.50E
Bojnurd Iran **57** 37.28N 57.20E
Boké Guinea **70** 10.57N 14.13W
Bokn Fjord *est.* Norway **46** 59.15N 5.50E
Bokoro Chad **71** 12.17N 17.04E
Bokungu Zaïre **72** 0.44S 22.28E
Bolamo Guinea Bissau **70** 11.35N 15.30W
Bolangir India **59** 20.41N 83.30E
Bolbec France **40** 49.34N 0.28E
Bole Ghana **70** 9.03N 2.23W
Bolgrad U.S.S.R. **43** 45.42N 28.40E
Bolivar Argentina **103** 36.15S 61.07W
Bolivar *mtn.* Venezuela **97** 7.27N 71.00W
Bolivia S. America **102** 17.00S 65.00W
Bollin *r.* England **32** 53.23N 2.29W
Bollnäs Sweden **46** 61.20N 16.25E
Bolmen *l.* Sweden **46** 57.00N 13.45E
Bolobo Zaïre **72** 2.10S 16.17E
Bologna Italy **42** 44.30N 11.20E
Bologoye U.S.S.R. **47** 57.58N 34.00E
Bolomba Zaïre **72** 0.30N 19.13E
Bolsena, Lago di *l.* Italy **42** 42.36N 11.55E
Bolshevik *i.* U.S.S.R. **49** 78.30N 102.00E
Bolshoi Lyakhovskiy *i.* U.S.S.R. **49** 73.30N 142.00E
Bolsover England **33** 53.14N 1.18W
Bolt Head *c.* England **31** 50.13N 3.48W
Bolton England **32** 53.35N 2.26W
Bolu Turkey **56** 40.45N 31.38E
Bolus Head Rep. of Ire. **39** 51.47N 10.20W
Bolvadin Turkey **56** 38.43N 31.02E
Bolzano Italy **44** 46.30N 11.20E
Boma Zaïre **72** 5.50S 13.03E
Bombala Australia **80** 36.55S 149.16E
Bombay India **58** 18.56N 72.51E
Bom Despacho Brazil **103** 19.46S 45.15W
Bomokandi *r.* Zaïre **73** 3.37N 26.09E
Bomongo Zaïre **72** 1.30N 18.21E
Bomu *r.* C.A.R. **72** 4.08N 22.25E
Bon, C. Tunisia **42** 37.05N 11.02E
Bonaire *i.* Neth. Antilles **97** 12.15N 68.27W
Bonar-Bridge *town* Scotland **37** 57.33N 4.21W
Bonavista Canada **93** 48.38N 53.08W
Bondo Zaïre **72** 3.47N 23.45E
Bondoukou Ivory Coast **70** 8.03N 2.15W
Bone, G. of Indonesia **61** 4.00S 120.50E
Bo'ness Scotland **35** 56.01N 3.36W
Bongandanga Zaïre **72** 1.28N 21.03E
Bonifacio France **42** 41.23N 9.10E
Bonifacio, Str. of Med. Sea **42** 41.18N 9.10E
Bonn W. Germany **45** 50.44N 7.06E
Bonny Nigeria **72** 4.25N 7.15E
Bonny, Bight of Africa **71** 2.58N 7.00E
Bonnyrigg Scotland **35** 55.52N 3.07W
Bontang Indonesia **60** 0.05N 117.31E
Boothia, G. of Canada **93** 70.00N 90.00W
Bootle Cumbria England **32** 54.17N 3.24W
Bootle Mersey. England **32** 53.28N 3.01W
Booué Gabon **72** 0.00 11.58E
Boppard W. Germany **45** 50.13N 7.35E
Borah Peak U.S.A. **90** 44.09N 113.47W
Borås Sweden **46** 57.44N 12.55E
Borazjan Iran **57** 29.14N 51.12E
Bordeaux France **40** 44.50N 0.34W
Borden I. Canada **92** 78.30N 111.00W
Borders *d.* Scotland **35** 55.30N 2.53W
Bordertown Australia **80** 36.18S 140.49E
Bordö *i.* Faroe Is. **46** 62.10N 7.13W
Bordon Camp England **28** 51.06N 0.52W
Borehamwood England **27** 51.40N 0.16W
Boreray *i.* Scotland **36** 57.43N 7.17W
Borgå Finland **46** 60.24N 25.40E
Borgefjell *mtn.* Norway **46** 65.15N 13.50E
Borger U.S.A. **90** 35.39N 101.24W
Borisoglebsk U.S.S.R. **47** 51.23N 42.02E
Borisov U.S.S.R. **47** 54.09N 28.30E
Borken W. Germany **45** 51.50N 6.52E
Borkum W. Germany **45** 53.34N 6.41E
Borkum *i.* W. Germany **45** 53.35N 6.45E
Borlänge Sweden **46** 60.29N 15.25E
Bormida *r.* Italy **40** 45.02N 8.43E
Borneo *i.* Asia **60** 1.00N 114.00E
Bornholm *i.* Denmark **46** 55.02N 15.00E
Borno *d.* Nigeria **71** 12.20N 12.40E
Boroughbridge England **33** 54.06N 1.23W
Borough Green England **27** 51.17N 0.19E
Borris-in-Ossory Rep. of Ire. **39** 52.56N 7.39W
Borrisokane Rep. of Ire. **39** 53.00N 8.08W
Borth Wales **30** 52.29N 4.03W
Borzya U.S.S.R. **63** 50.24N 116.35E
Bosa Italy **42** 40.18N 8.29E
Boscastle England **31** 50.42N 4.42W
Bosna *r.* Yugo. **43** 45.04N 18.27E
Bosobolo Zaïre **72** 4.11N 19.55E
Bosporus *str.* Turkey **43** 41.07N 29.04E
Bossangoa C.A.R. **71** 6.27N 17.21E
Bossembélé C.A.R. **72** 5.10N 17.44E
Bosso Niger **71** 13.43N 13.19E
Boston England **33** 52.59N 0.02W
Boston U.S.A. **95** 42.20N 71.05W
Botany B. Australia **80** 34.04S 151.08E
Botevgrad Bulgaria **43** 42.55N 23.57E
Bothnia, G. of Europe **46** 63.30N 20.30E
Botletle *r.* Botswana **74** 21.06S 24.47E
Botoşani Romania **47** 47.44N 26.41E
Botrange *mtn.* Belgium **45** 50.30N 6.04E
Botswana Africa **74** 22.00S 24.15E
Bottesford England **33** 52.56N 0.48W
Bottrop W. Germany **45** 51.31N 6.55E
Botucatu Brazil **103** 22.52S 48.30W
Bouaflé Ivory Coast **70** 7.01N 5.47W
Bouaké Ivory Coast **70** 7.42N 5.00W
Bouar C.A.R. **71** 5.58N 15.35E
Boufarik Algeria **41** 36.36N 2.54E
Boughton England **33** 53.13N 0.59W
Bougouni Mali **70** 11.25N 7.28W
Bouillon Belgium **40** 49.47N 5.04E
Bouira Algeria **41** 36.22N 3.55E
Boulder U.S.A. **90** 40.02N 105.16W
Boulogne France **40** 50.43N 1.37E
Boumba *r.* Cameroon **71** 2.00N 15.10E
Boumo Chad **71** 9.01N 16.24E
Bouna Ivory Coast **70** 9.19N 2.53W
Boundary Peak *mtn.* U.S.A. **90** 37.51N 118.23W
Boundiali Ivory Coast **70** 9.30N 6.31W
Bourem Mali **70** 16.59N 0.20W
Bourg France **40** 46.12N 5.13E
Bourganeuf France **40** 45.57N 1.44E
Bourges France **40** 47.05N 2.23E
Bourg Madame France **40** 42.26N 1.55E
Bourke Australia **80** 30.09S 145.59E
Bourne England **33** 52.46N 0.23W
Bourne *r.* England **28** 51.04N 1.47W
Bournebridge England **27** 51.37N 0.12E
Bourne End England **27** 51.34N 0.42W
Bournemouth England **28** 50.43N 1.53W
Bovingdon England **27** 51.44N 0.32W
Bowen Australia **79** 20.00S 148.15E
Bowes England **32** 54.31N 2.01W
Bowmore Scotland **34** 55.45N 6.17W
Bowness-on-Solway England **35** 54.57N 3.11W
Boxtel Neth. **45** 51.36N 5.20E
Boyle Rep. of Ire. **38** 53.58N 8.19W
Boyne *r.* Rep. of Ire. **38** 53.43N 6.17W
Boyoma Falls *f.* Zaïre **72** 0.18N 25.32E
Bozeman U.S.A. **90** 45.40N 111.00W
Braan *r.* Scotland **35** 56.34N 3.36W
Brabant *d.* Belgium **45** 50.47N 4.30E
Brac *i.* Yugo. **43** 43.20N 16.38E
Bracadale, Loch Scotland **36** 57.22N 6.30W
Bräcke Sweden **46** 62.44N 15.30E
Bracknell England **27** 51.26N 0.46W
Brad Romania **43** 46.06N 22.48E
Bradano *r.* Italy **43** 40.23N 16.52E
Bradford England **32** 53.47N 1.45W
Bradford-on-Avon England **28** 51.20N 2.15W
Bradwell-on-Sea England **29** 51.44N 0.55E
Bradworthy England **31** 50.54N 4.22W
Brae Scotland **36** 60.24N 1.21W
Braemar Scotland **37** 57.01N 3.24W
Braemar *f.* Scotland **37** 57.02N 3.24W
Braga Portugal **41** 41.32N 8.26W
Bragado Argentina **103** 35.10S 60.29W
Braganca Portugal **41** 41.47N 6.46W
Brahmaputra *r.* Asia **59** 23.50N 89.45E
Brăila Romania **43** 45.18N 27.58E
Brailsford England **32** 52.58N 1.35W
Brain *r.* England **27** 51.47N 0.40E
Braintree England **27** 51.53N 0.32E
Bramley England **27** 51.11N 0.35W
Brampton Canada **95** 43.41N 79.46W
Brampton England **35** 54.56N 2.43W
Brandberg *mtn.* S.W. Africa **74** 21.10S 14.33E
Brandenburg E. Germany **44** 52.25N 12.34E
Brandfort R.S.A. **74** 28.42S 26.28E
Brandon Canada **90** 49.50N 99.57W
Brandon Suffolk England **29** 52.27N 0.37E
Brandon Durham England **32** 54.46N 1.37W
Brandon B. Rep. of Ire. **39** 52.16N 10.05W
Brandon Hill Rep. of Ire. **39** 52.30N 7.00W
Brandon Mtn. Rep. of Ire. **39** 52.14N 10.15W
Brandon Pt. Rep. of Ire. **39** 52.17N 10.11W
Brantford Canada **94** 43.09N 80.17W
Brasília Brazil **103** 15.54S 47.50W
Braşov Romania **43** 45.40N 25.35E
Brass Nigeria **71** 4.20N 6.15E
Bratislava Czech. **47** 48.10N 17.10E
Bratsk U.S.S.R. **49** 56.20N 101.15E
Bratsk Resr. U.S.S.R. **49** 54.40N 103.00E
Brattleboro U.S.A. **95** 42.51N 72.36W
Braunschweig W. Germany **44** 52.15N 10.30E
Braunton England **31** 51.06N 4.09W
Brava Somali Rep. **73** 1.02N 44.02E
Brawley U.S.A. **90** 33.10N 115.30W
Bray *r.* England **31** 50.56N 3.54W
Bray Rep. of Ire. **39** 53.12N 6.07W
Bray Head Kerry Rep. of Ire. **39** 51.53N 10.26W
Bray Head Wicklow Rep. of Ire. **39** 53.11N 6.04W
Brazil S. America **103** 19.00S 50.00W
Brazilian Highlands Brazil **103** 17.02S 50.00W
Brazos *r.* U.S.A. **91** 28.55N 95.20W
Brazzaville Congo **72** 4.14S 15.10E
Breadalbane *f.* Scotland **34** 56.30N 4.20W
Breaksea Pt. Wales **31** 51.24N 3.25W
Bream B. New Zealand **82** 36.00S 174.30E

Brechin Scotland **35** 56.44N 2.40W
Breckland *f.* England **29** 52.28N 0.40E
Brecon Wales **30** 51.57N 3.23W
Brecon Beacons *mts.* Wales **30** 51.53N 3.27W
Breda Neth. **45** 51.35N 4.46E
Bredasdorp R.S.A. **74** 34.32S 20.02E
Brede *r.* England **29** 50.57N 0.44E
Bregenz Austria **44** 47.31N 9.46E
Breidha Fjördhur *est.* Iceland **46** 65.15N 23.00W
Bremen W. Germany **44** 53.05N 8.48E
Bremerhaven W. Germany **44** 53.33N 8.35E
Brendon Hills England **28** 51.05N 3.25W
Brenner Pass Austria/Italy **42** 47.00N 11.30E
Brent *d.* England **27** 51.33N 0.16W
Brenta *r.* Italy **42** 45.25N 12.15E
Brentford England **27** 51.30N 0.18W
Brentwood England **27** 51.38N 0.18E
Brescia Italy **42** 45.33N 10.12E
Breskens Neth. **45** 51.24N 3.34E
Bressanone Italy **44** 46.43N 11.40E
Bressay *i.* Scotland **36** 60.08N 1.05W
Bressay Sd. Scotland **36** 60.08N 1.10W
Bressuire France **40** 46.50N 0.28W
Brest France **40** 48.23N 4.30W
Brest U.S.S.R. **47** 52.08N 23.40E
Brest-Nantes Canal France **40** 47.55N 2.30W
Brett, C. New Zealand **82** 35.15S 174.20E
Brewarrina Australia **80** 29.57S 147.54E
Brewer U.S.A. **95** 44.48N 68.44W
Briançon France **40** 44.53N 6.39E
Bricket Wood *town* England **27** 51.42N 0.20W
Bride I.o.M. **32** 54.23N 4.24W
Bride *r.* Rep. of Ire. **39** 52.05N 7.52W
Bridgend Wales **31** 51.30N 3.35W
Bridge of Allan *town* Scotland **35** 56.09N 3.58W
Bridge of Cally *town* Scotland **35** 56.39N 3.25W
Bridge of Earn *town* Scotland **35** 56.24N 3.25W
Bridgeport U.S.A. **95** 41.12N 73.12W
Bridgetown Barbados **97** 13.06N 59.37W
Bridgetown Rep. of Ire. **39** 52.14N 6.33W
Bridgnorth England **28** 52.33N 2.25W
Bridgwater England **28** 51.08N 3.00W
Bridgwater B. England **28** 51.15N 3.10W
Bridlington England **33** 54.06N 0.11W
Bridlington B. England **33** 54.03N 0.10W
Bridport England **28** 50.43N 2.45W
Brienne-le-Château France **40** 48.24N 4.32E
Brienz Switz. **44** 46.46N 8.02E
Brierfield England **32** 53.49N 2.15W
Brig Switz. **40** 46.19N 8.00E
Brigg England **33** 53.33N 0.30W
Brighouse England **32** 53.42N 1.47W
Bright Australia **80** 36.42S 146.58E
Brightlingsea England **29** 51.49N 1.01E
Brighton England **29** 50.50N 0.09W
Brindisi Italy **43** 40.38N 17.57E
Brisbane Australia **80** 27.30S 153.00E
Bristol England **31** 51.26N 2.35W
Bristol B. U.S.A. **92** 58.00N 158.50W
Bristol Channel England/Wales **31** 51.17N 3.20W
British Antarctic Territory Antarctica **104** 70.00S 50.00W
British Columbia *d.* Canada **92** 55.00N 125.00W
British Isles Europe **106** 54.00N 5.00W
Briton Ferry *town* Wales **31** 51.37N 3.50W
Britstown R.S.A. **74** 30.36S 23.30E
Brive France **40** 45.09N 1.32E
Briviesca Spain **41** 42.33N 3.19W
Brixham England **31** 50.24N 3.31W
Brno Czech. **44** 49.11N 16.39E
Broad B. Scotland **36** 58.15N 6.15W
Broadback *r.* Canada **91** 51.15N 78.55W
Broadford Scotland **36** 57.14N 5.54W
Broad Haven *b.* Rep. of Ire. **38** 54.17N 9.53W
Broad Law *mtn.* Scotland **35** 55.30N 3.21W
Broadstairs England **29** 51.22N 1.27E
Broadstone England **28** 50.45N 2.00W
Broadway England **28** 52.02N 1.51W
Brocken *mtn.* E. Germany **44** 51.50N 10.50E
Brockenhurst England **28** 50.49N 1.34W
Brockham England **27** 51.13N 0.16W
Brockton U.S.A. **95** 42.06N 71.01W
Brockville Canada **95** 44.35N 75.44W
Brod Yugo. **43** 45.09N 18.02E
Brodick Scotland **34** 55.34N 5.09W
Brody U.S.S.R. **47** 50.05N 25.08E
Broken Hill *town* Australia **80** 31.57S 141.30E
Bromley England **27** 51.24N 0.02E
Bromley Common England **27** 51.23N 0.04E
Brompton England **27** 51.24N 0.35E
Bromsgrove England **28** 52.20N 2.03W
Bromyard England **28** 52.12N 2.30W
Brönderslev Denmark **46** 57.16N 9.58E
Brong-Ahafo *d.* Ghana **70** 7.45N 1.30W
Brookes Point *town* Phil. **60** 8.50N 117.52E
Brookmans Park *town* England **27** 51.43N 0.10W
Brooks Range *mts.* U.S.A. **92** 68.50N 152.00W
Brook Street England **27** 51.37N 0.17E
Broom, Loch Scotland **36** 57.52N 5.07W
Broome Australia **79** 17.58S 122.15E
Brora Scotland **37** 58.01N 3.52W
Brora *r.* Scotland **37** 58.00N 3.51W
Brosna *r.* Rep. of Ire. **39** 53.13N 7.58W
Brotton England **33** 54.34N 0.55W
Brough England **32** 54.32N 2.19W
Brough Head Scotland **37** 59.09N 3.19W
Brough Ness *c.* Scotland **37** 58.44N 2.57W
Broughton England **33** 54.26N 1.08W
Broughton Scotland **35** 55.37N 3.25W
Broughton in Furness England **32** 54.17N 3.12W
Brownhills England **28** 52.38N 1.57W
Brownsville U.S.A. **96** 25.54N 97.30W
Brown Willy *hill* England **31** 50.36N 4.36W
Broxbourne England **27** 51.45N 0.01W
Bruay-en-Artois France **45** 50.29N 2.36E
Bruchsal W. Germany **44** 49.07N 8.35E
Brue *r.* England **28** 51.13N 3.00W
Bruernish Pt. Scotland **36** 56.59N 7.22W
Bruges Belgium **45** 51.13N 3.14E
Brühl W. Germany **45** 50.50N 6.55E
Brunei Asia **60** 4.56N 114.58E
Brunner New Zealand **82** 42.28S 171.12E
Brunssun Neth. **45** 50.57N 5.59E
Brunswick U.S.A. **91** 31.09N 81.21W
Bruny I. Australia **80** 43.15S 147.16E
Bruree Rep. of Ire. **39** 52.25N 8.40W
Brussels Belgium **45** 50.50N 4.23E
Bruton England **28** 51.06N 2.28W
Bryansk U.S.S.R. **47** 53.15N 34.09E
Bryher *i.* England **31** 49.57N 6.21W
Bryn Brawd *mtn.* Wales **30** 52.08N 3.54W
Brynmawr Wales **31** 51.48N 3.10W
Bua *r.* Malawi **73** 12.42S 34.15E
Bubiyan I. Kuwait **57** 29.45N 48.15E
Bubye *r.* Rhodesia **74** 22.18S 31.00E
Bucaramanga Colombia **97** 7.08N 73.01W
Buchan *f.* Scotland **37** 57.34N 2.03W
Buchanan Liberia **70** 5.57N 10.02W
Buchan Ness *c.* Scotland **37** 57.28N 1.47W
Bucharest Romania **43** 44.25N 26.06E
Buckfastleigh England **31** 50.28N 3.47W
Buckhaven and Methil Scotland **35** 56.11N 3.03W
Buckhurst Hill England **27** 51.38N 0.03E
Buckie Scotland **37** 57.40N 2.58W
Buckingham England **28** 52.00N 0.59W
Buckinghamshire *d.* England **28** 51.50N 0.48W
Buckley Wales **30** 53.11N 3.04W
Buco Zau Angola **72** 4.46S 12.34E
Budapest Hungary **47** 47.30N 19.03E
Budaun India **58** 28.02N 79.07E
Buddon Ness *c.* Scotland **35** 56.29N 2.42W
Bude England **31** 50.49N 4.33W
Bude B. England **31** 50.50N 4.40W
Budjala Zaïre **72** 2.38N 19.48E
Budleigh Salterton England **28** 50.37N 3.19W
Buea Cameroon **71** 4.09N 9.13E
Buenos Aires Argentina **103** 34.40S 58.25W
Buenos Aires *d.* Argentina **103** 35.00S 61.00W
Buffalo N.Y. U.S.A. **95** 42.52N 78.55W
Buffalo Wyo. U.S.A. **90** 44.21N 106.40W
Bug *r.* Poland **47** 52.29N 21.11E
Bug *r.* U.S.S.R. **47** 46.55N 31.59E
Buggs Island *l.* U.S.A. **91** 36.35N 78.20W
Bugulma U.S.S.R. **48** 54.32N 52.46E
Buie, Loch Scotland **34** 56.20N 5.53W
Builth Wells Wales **30** 52.09N 3.24W
Buitenpost Neth. **45** 53.15N 6.09E
Bujumbura Burundi **73** 3.22S 29.21E
Bukama Zaïre **72** 9.16S 25.52E
Bukavu Zaïre **73** 2.30S 28.49E
Bukhara U.S.S.R. **57** 39.47N 64.26E
Bukittinggi Indonesia **60** 0.18S 100.20E
Bukoba Tanzania **73** 1.20S 31.49E
Bula Indonesia **61** 3.07S 130.27E
Bulagan Mongolia **62** 48.34N 103.12E
Bulan Phil. **61** 12.40N 123.53E
Bulandshahr India **58** 28.30N 77.49E
Bulawayo Rhodesia **74** 20.10S 28.43E
Bulgaria Europe **43** 42.30N 25.00E
Bulkington England **28** 52.29N 1.25W
Buller *r.* New Zealand **82** 41.45S 171.35E
Buller, Mt. Australia **80** 37.11S 146.26E
Bulloo *r.* Australia **80** 27.26S 144.06E
Bultfontein R.S.A. **74** 28.17S 26.10E
Bulun U.S.S.R. **49** 70.50N 127.20E
Bumba Zaïre **72** 2.15N 22.32E
Bum Tso *l.* China **59** 31.30N 91.10E
Bunbury Australia **79** 33.20S 115.34E
Buncrana Rep. of Ire. **38** 55.08N 7.27W
Bundaberg Australia **79** 24.50S 152.21E
Bunde W. Germany **45** 53.12N 7.16E
Bundelkhand *f.* India **58** 24.40N 80.00E
Bundoran Rep. of Ire. **38** 54.28N 8.17W
Bunessan Scotland **34** 56.18N 6.14W
Bungay England **29** 52.27N 1.26E
Bunguran *i.* Indonesia **60** 4.00N 108.20E
Bunguran Selatan *i.* Indonesia **60** 3.00N 108.50E
Buni Nigeria **71** 11.20N 11.59E
Bunia Zaïre **73** 1.30N 30.10E
Buntingford England **29** 51.57N 0.01W
Buol Indonesia **61** 1.12N 121.28E
Buqbuq Egypt **56** 31.30N 25.32E
Bura Coast Kenya **73** 3.30S 38.19E
Buraida Saudi Arabia **57** 26.18N 43.58E
Buraimi U.A.E. **57** 24.15N 55.45E
Burdur Turkey **56** 37.44N 30.17E
Burdwan India **58** 23.15N 87.52E
Bure *r.* England **29** 52.36N 1.44E
Bures England **29** 51.59N 0.46E
Burford England **28** 51.48N 1.38W
Burg E. Germany **44** 52.17N 11.51E
Burgan Kuwait **57** 29.00N 47.53E
Burgas Bulgaria **43** 42.30N 27.29E
Burgess Hill England **29** 50.57N 0.07W
Burghead Scotland **37** 57.42N 3.30W
Burgh Heath England **27** 51.18N 0.12W
Burgh le Marsh England **33** 53.10N 0.15E
Burgos Spain **41** 42.21N 3.41W
Burgsteinfurt W. Germany **45** 52.09N 7.21E
Burgsvik Sweden **46** 57.03N 18.19E
Burhanpur India **58** 21.18N 76.08E
Burias *i.* Phil. **61** 12.50N 123.10E
Burica, Punta Panamá **96** 8.05N 82.50W
Burley U.S.A. **90** 42.32N 113.48W
Burlington Canada **94** 43.19N 79.48W
Burlington Iowa U.S.A. **94** 40.50N 91.07W
Burlington Vt. U.S.A. **95** 44.28N 73.14W
Burma Asia **59** 21.00N 96.30E
Burnham England **27** 51.35N 0.39W
Burnham Beeches England **27** 51.33N 0.39W
Burnham Market England **33** 52.57N 0.43E
Burnham-on-Crouch England **29** 51.37N 0.50E
Burnham-on-Sea England **28** 51.15N 3.00W
Burnie Australia **80** 41.03S 145.55E
Burnley England **32** 53.47N 2.15W
Burntisland Scotland **35** 56.03N 3.15W
Burra Australia **80** 33.40S 138.57E
Burravoe Scotland **36** 60.23N 1.20W
Burray *i.* Scotland **37** 58.51N 2.54W
Burren Junction Australia **80** 30.08S 148.59E
Burriana Spain **41** 30.54N 0.05W
Burrinjuck Resr. Australia **80** 35.00S 148.40E
Burrow Head Scotland **34** 54.41N 4.24W
Burry Port Wales **31** 51.41N 4.17W
Bursa Turkey **43** 40.11N 29.04E
Burscough England **32** 53.37N 2.51W
Burton Agnes England **33** 54.04N 0.18W
Burton Latimer England **28** 52.23N 0.41W
Burton upon Trent England **32** 52.58N 1.39W
Buru *i.* Indonesia **61** 3.30S 126.30E
Burujird Iran **57** 33.54N 48.47E
Burullus, L. Egypt **56** 31.30N 30.45E
Burundi Africa **73** 3.00S 30.00E
Bururi Burundi **73** 3.58S 29.35E
Burwell Cambs. England **29** 52.17N 0.20E
Burwell Lincs. England **33** 53.19N 0.02E
Bury England **32** 53.36N 2.19W
Bury St. Edmunds England **29** 52.15N 0.42E
Bush *r.* N. Ireland **34** 55.13N 6.31W
Bushey England **27** 51.39N 0.22W
Bushire Iran **57** 28.57N 50.52E
Bushmanland *f.* R.S.A. **74** 29.20S 18.45E
Bushmills N. Ireland **34** 55.12N 6.32W
Bushy Park *f.* England **27** 51.25N 0.19W
Businga Zaïre **72** 3.16N 20.55E
Busira *r.* Zaïre **72** 0.05N 18.18E
Bussum Neth. **45** 52.17N 5.10E
Busu Djanoa Zaïre **72** 1.42N 21.23E
Buta Zaïre **72** 2.50N 24.50E
Butari Rwanda **73** 2.38S 29.43E
Bute *i.* Scotland **34** 55.51N 5.07W
Bute, Sd. of Scotland **34** 55.44N 5.10W
Butiaba Uganda **73** 1.48N 31.15E
Butser Hill England **28** 50.58N 0.58W
Butte U.S.A. **90** 46.00N 112.31W
Butterworth Malaysia **60** 5.24N 100.22E
Butterworth R.S.A. **74** 32.20S 28.09E
Buttevant Rep. of Ire. **39** 52.14N 8.41W
Butt of Lewis *c.* Scotland **36** 58.31N 6.15W
Butuan Phil. **61** 8.56N 125.31E
Butung *i.* Indonesia **61** 5.00S 122.50E
Buxton England **32** 53.16N 1.54W
Buy U.S.S.R. **47** 58.23N 41.27E
Buzău Romania **43** 45.10N 26.49E
Buzău *r.* Romania **43** 45.24N 27.48E
Buzi *r.* Moçambique **74** 19.52S 34.00E
Bydgoszcz Poland **47** 53.16N 17.33E
Byfield England **28** 52.10N 1.15W
Byfleet England **27** 51.20N 0.29W

Bylot I. Canada **93** 73.00N 78.30W
Byrock Australia **80** 30.40S 146.25E
Byrranga Mts. U.S.S.R. **49** 74.50N 101.00E
Byske *r.* Sweden **46** 64.58N 21.10E

C

Cabanatuan Phil. **61** 15.30N 120.58E
Cabimas Venezuela **97** 10.26N 71.27W
Cabinda Angola **72** 5.34S 12.12E
Cabo Delgado *d.* Moçambique **73** 12.30S 39.00E
Cabonga Resr. Canada **95** 47.35N 76.40W
Cabora Bassa Dam Moçambique **73** 15.36S 32.41E
Cabot Str. Canada **93** 47.00N 59.00W
Cabrera *i.* Spain **41** 39.08N 2.56E
Cabrera, Sierra *mts.* Spain **41** 42.10N 6.30W
Cabriel *r.* Spain **41** 39.13N 1.07W
Caçador Brazil **103** 26.51S 50.54W
Čačak Yugo. **47** 43.45N 20.22E
Cáceres Brazil **103** 16.05S 57.40W
Cáceres Spain **41** 39.29N 6.23W
Cachimo *r.* Zaïre **72** 7.02S 21.13E
Cachoeira do Sul Brazil **103** 30.03S 52.52W
Cacin *r.* Spain **41** 37.10N 4.01W
Cacolo Angola **72** 10.09S 19.15E
Caconda Angola **72** 13.46S 15.06E
Cader Idris *mtn.* Wales **30** 52.40N 3.55W
Cadi, Sierra del *mts.* Spain **41** 42.12N 1.35E
Cadillac U.S.A. **94** 44.15N 85.23W
Cádiz Spain **41** 36.32N 6.18W
Cádiz, G. of Spain **41** 37.00N 7.10W
Caen France **40** 49.11N 0.22W
Caerleon Wales **31** 51.36N 2.57W
Caernarvon Wales **30** 53.08N 4.17W
Caernarvon B. Wales **30** 53.05N 4.25W
Caerphilly Wales **31** 51.34N 3.13W
Cagayan de Oro Phil. **61** 8.29N 124.40E
Cagliari Italy **42** 39.14N 9.07E
Cagliari, G. of Med. Sea **42** 39.07N 9.15E
Caguas Puerto Rico **97** 18.08N 66.00W
Caha Mts. Rep. of Ire. **39** 51.44N 9.45W
Caherciveen Rep. of Ire. **39** 51.56N 10.13W
Caher I. Rep. of Ire. **38** 53.43N 10.03W
Cahir Rep. of Ire. **39** 52.23N 7.56W
Cahore Pt. Rep. of Ire. **39** 52.34N 6.12W
Cahors France **40** 44.28N 0.26E
Caianda Angola **72** 11.02S 23.29E
Caibarién Cuba **97** 22.31N 79.28W
Caicos Is. C. America **97** 21.30N 72.00W
Cairn *r.* Scotland **35** 55.05N 3.38W
Cairn Gorm *mtn.* Scotland **37** 57.06N 3.39W
Cairngorms *mts.* Scotland **37** 57.04N 3.30W
Cairns Australia **79** 16.51S 145.43E
Cairnsmore of Carsphairn *mtn.* Scotland **34** 55.15N 4.12W
Cairn Table *mtn.* Scotland **35** 55.29N 4.02W
Cairo Egypt **56** 30.03N 31.15E
Cairo U.S.A. **91** 37.02N 89.02W
Caister-on-Sea England **29** 52.38N 1.43E
Caistor England **33** 53.29N 0.20W
Calabar Nigeria **72** 4.56N 8.22E
Calafat Romania **43** 43.59N 22.57E
Calahorra Spain **41** 41.19N 1.58W
Calais France **29** 50.57N 1.52E
Calais U.S.A. **95** 45.11N 67.16W
Calamar Colombia **97** 10.16N 74.55W
Calamian Group *is.* Phil. **61** 12.00N 120.05E
Calamocha Spain **41** 40.54N 1.18W
Calapan Phil. **61** 13.23N 121.10E
Călărăsi Romania **43** 44.11N 27.21E
Calatayud Spain **41** 41.21N 1.39W
Calbayog Phil. **61** 12.04N 124.58E
Calcutta India **58** 22.35N 88.21E
Caldas da Rainha Portugal **41** 39.24N 9.08W
Caldbeck England **32** 54.45N 3.03W
Caldew *r.* England **32** 54.54N 2.55W
Caldy *i.* Wales **31** 51.38N 4.43W
Caledon *r.* R.S.A. **74** 30.35S 26.00E
Calgary Canada **90** 51.05N 114.05W
Cali Colombia **102** 3.24N 76.30W
Caliente U.S.A. **90** 37.36N 114.31W
California *d.* U.S.A. **90** 37.00N 120.00W
California, G. of Mexico **90** 28.30N 112.30W
Callabonna *r.* Australia **80** 29.37S 140.08E
Callabonna, L. Australia **80** 29.47S 140.07E
Callan Rep. of Ire. **39** 52.33N 7.25W
Callander Scotland **34** 56.15N 4.13W
Callanish Scotland **36** 58.12N 6.45W
Callao Peru **102** 12.05S 77.08W
Callington England **31** 50.30N 4.19W
Calne England **28** 51.26N 2.00W
Caltagirone Italy **42** 37.14N 14.30E
Caltanissetta Italy **42** 37.30N 14.05E
Calulo Angola **72** 10.05S 14.56E
Calunga Cameia Angola **72** 11.30S 20.47E
Calvi France **40** 42.34N 8.44E
Calvinia R.S.A. **74** 31.25S 19.47E
Cam *r.* England **29** 52.34N 0.21E
Camabatela Angola **72** 8.20S 15.29E
Camagüey Cuba **97** 21.25N 77.55W
Camagüey *d.* Cuba **97** 21.30N 78.00W
Camagüey, Archipelago de Cuba **97** 22.30N 78.00W
Camapua Brazil **103** 18.34S 54.04W
Camarón, C. Honduras **96** 15.59N 85.00W
Camaross Rep. of Ire. **39** 52.22N 6.44W
Ca Mau, Pointe de *c.* Vietnam **60** 8.30N 104.35E
Cambay, G. of India **58** 20.30N 72.00E
Camberley England **27** 51.21N 0.45W
Camberwell England **27** 51.28N 0.05W
Camborne England **31** 50.12N 5.19W
Cambrai France **45** 50.11N 3.14E
Cambrian Mts. Wales **30** 52.33N 3.33W
Cambridge England **29** 52.13N 0.08E
Cambridge New Zealand **82** 37.53S 175.29E
Cambridge Mass. U.S.A. **95** 42.22N 71.06W
Cambridge Ohio U.S.A. **94** 40.02N 81.36W
Cambridge Bay *town* Canada **92** 69.09N 105.00W
Cambridgeshire *d.* England **29** 52.15N 0.05E
Camden Australia **80** 34.04S 150.40E
Camden *d.* England **27** 51.33N 0.10W
Camden U.S.A. **95** 39.52N 75.07W
Cameia Nat. Park Angola **72** 12.00S 21.30E
Camel *r.* England **31** 50.31N 4.50W
Camelford England **31** 50.37N 4.41W
Cameron Mts. New Zealand **82** 45.50S 167.00E
Cameroon Africa **71** 6.00N 12.30E
Cameroon, Mt. Cameroon **71** 4.20N 9.05E
Camiri Bolivia **103** 20.08S 63.33W
Campbell, C. New Zealand **82** 41.45S 174.15E
Campbellton Canada **95** 48.00N 66.41W
Campbelltown Australia **80** 34.04S 150.49E
Campbeltown Scotland **34** 55.25N 5.36W
Campeche Mexico **96** 19.50N 90.30W
Campeche *d.* Mexico **96** 19.00N 90.00W
Campeche B. Mexico **96** 19.30N 94.00W
Camperdown Australia **80** 38.15S 143.14E
Campinas Brazil **103** 22.54S 47.06W
Campina Verde Brazil **103** 19.36S 49.25W
Campine *f.* Belgium **45** 51.05N 5.00E
Campo Cameroon **71** 2.22N 9.50E
Campo *r.* Cameroon **72** 2.21N 9.51E
Campobasso Italy **42** 41.34N 14.39E
Campo Grande Brazil **103** 20.24S 54.35W
Campo Maior Portugal **41** 39.01N 7.04W
Campsie Fells *hills* Scotland **34** 56.02N 4.15W
Camrose Canada **92** 53.01N 112.48W
Can *r.* England **27** 51.44N 0.28E
Canada N. America **92** 60.00N 105.00W
Canadian *r.* U.S.A. **91** 35.20N 95.40W
Canadian Shield *f.* N. America **106** 50.00N 80.00W
Çanakkale Turkey **43** 40.09N 26.26E
Canal du Midi France **40** 43.18N 2.00E
Canarreos, Archipelago de los Cuba **96** 21.40N 82.30W
Canary Is. Atlantic Oc. **68** 29.00N 15.00W
Canberra Australia **80** 35.18S 149.08E
Candeleda Spain **41** 40.10N 5.14W
Canea Greece **43** 35.30N 24.02E
Canelones Uruguay **103** 34.32S 56.17W
Cangamba Angola **72** 13.40S 19.50E
Canglass Pt. Rep. of Ire. **39** 51.59N 10.15W
Çankiri Turkey **56** 40.35N 33.37E
Canna *i.* Scotland **36** 57.03N 6.30W
Canna, Sd. of Scotland **36** 57.03N 6.27W
Cannes France **40** 43.33N 7.00E
Cannich Scotland **37** 57.20N 4.45W
Cannock England **28** 52.42N 2.02W
Cannock Chase *f.* England **28** 52.45N 2.00W
Canonbie Scotland **35** 55.05N 2.56W
Canon City U.S.A. **90** 38.27N 105.14W
Cantabria, Sierra de *mts.* Spain **41** 42.40N 2.30W
Cantabrian Mts. Spain **41** 42.55N 5.10W
Canterbury England **29** 51.17N 1.05E
Canterbury Bight New Zealand **82** 44.15S 172.00E
Canton U.S.A. **94** 40.48N 81.23W
Canvey England **27** 51.32N 0.35E
Canvey Island England **27** 51.32N 0.34E
Cao Bang Vietnam **59** 22.37N 106.18E
Caoles Scotland **34** 56.32N 6.44W
Caolisport, Loch Scotland **34** 55.54N 5.38W
Cape Barren I. Australia **80** 40.22S 148.15E
Cape Breton I. Canada **93** 46.00N 61.00W
Cape Coast *town* Ghana **70** 5.10N 1.13W
Cape Johnson Depth Pacific Oc. **61** 10.20N 127.20E
Capel England **29** 51.08N 0.18W
Capelongo Angola **72** 14.55S 15.03E
Cape Matifou *town* Algeria **41** 36.51N 3.15E
Cape Province *d.* R.S.A. **74** 31.00S 22.00E
Cape Town R.S.A. **74** 33.56S 18.28E
Cape Verde Is. Atlantic Oc. **112** 17.00N 25.00W
Cap Haitien *town* Haiti **97** 19.47N 72.17W
Cappamore Rep. of Ire. **39** 52.37N 8.21W
Cappoquin Rep. of Ire. **39** 52.09N 7.52W
Capraia *i.* Italy **42** 43.03N 9.50E
Capreol Canada **94** 46.43N 80.56W
Caprera *i.* Italy **42** 41.48N 9.27E
Capri *i.* Italy **42** 40.33N 14.13E
Caprivi Strip *f.* S.W. Africa **74** 17.50S 22.50E
Caquengue Angola **72** 12.23S 22.31E
Cara *i.* Scotland **34** 55.58N 5.45W
Caracal Romania **43** 44.08N 24.18E
Caracas Venezuela **97** 10.35N 66.56W
Caragh, Lough Rep. of Ire. **39** 52.05N 9.51W
Caratasca Lagoon Honduras **96** 15.10N 89.00W
Caravaca Spain **41** 38.06N 1.51W
Carbonara, C. Italy **42** 39.06N 9.32E
Carbondale U.S.A. **95** 41.35N 75.31W
Carbost Scotland **36** 57.27N 6.18W
Carcassonne France **40** 43.13N 2.21E
Carcross Canada **92** 60.11N 134.41W
Cardenas Cuba **96** 23.02N 81.12W
Cardenete Spain **41** 39.46N 1.42W
Cardiff Wales **31** 51.28N 3.11W
Cardigan Wales **30** 52.06N 4.41W
Cardigan B. Wales **30** 52.30N 4.30W
Carentan France **40** 49.18N 1.14W
Carhaix France **40** 48.16N 3.35W
Carhué Argentina **103** 37.10S 62.45W
Caribbean Sea **97** 15.00N 75.00W
Caribou U.S.A. **95** 46.52N 68.01W
Caribou Mtn. U.S.A. **95** 45.26N 70.38W
Caribou Mts. Canada **92** 58.30N 115.00W
Carignan France **45** 49.38N 5.10E
Caripito Venezuela **97** 10.07N 63.07W
Cark Mtn. Rep. of Ire. **38** 54.53N 7.53W
Carlingford Rep. of Ire. **38** 54.03N 6.12W
Carlingford Lough Rep. of Ire. **38** 54.03N 6.09W
Carlisle England **32** 54.54N 2.55W
Carlow Rep. of Ire. **39** 52.50N 6.46W
Carlow *d.* Rep. of Ire. **39** 52.43N 6.50W
Carloway Scotland **36** 58.17N 6.47W
Carlton England **33** 52.58N 1.06W
Carluke Scotland **35** 55.44N 3.51W
Carmacks Canada **92** 62.04N 136.21W
Carmarthen Wales **30** 51.52N 4.20W
Carmarthen B. Wales **31** 51.40N 4.30W
Carmel Head Wales **30** 53.24N 4.35W
Carmen Mexico **96** 18.38N 91.50W
Carmen de Patagones Argentina **103** 40.45S 63.00W
Carmen I. Mexico **96** 18.35N 91.40W
Carmona Spain **41** 37.28N 5.38W
Carmyllie Scotland **35** 56.36N 2.41W
Carnarvon R.S.A. **74** 30.59S 22.08E
Carndonagh Rep. of Ire. **34** 55.15N 7.15W
Carnedd y Filiast *mtn.* Wales **30** 52.56N 3.40W
Carnegie, L. Australia **79** 26.15S 123.00E
Carn Eige *mtn.* Scotland **36** 57.17N 5.07W
Carnew Rep. of Ire. **39** 52.43N 6.31W
Carnforth England **32** 54.08N 2.47W
Carnic Alps *mts.* Austria/Italy **42** 46.40N 12.48E
Car Nicobar *i.* India **60** 9.00N 92.30E
Carn Mòr *mtn.* Scotland **37** 57.14N 3.13W
Càrn na Loine *mtn.* Scotland **37** 57.24N 3.33W
Carnot C.A.R. **71** 4.59N 15.56E
Carnoustie Scotland **35** 56.30N 2.44W
Carnsore Pt. Rep. of Ire. **39** 52.10N 6.21W
Carnwath Scotland **35** 55.43N 3.37W
Carolina R.S.A. **74** 26.05S 30.07E
Caroline Is. Pacific Oc. **61** 7.50N 145.00E
Caroni *r.* Venezuela **97** 8.20N 62.45W
Carora Venezuela **97** 10.12N 70.07W
Carpathian Mts. Europe **47** 48.45N 23.45E
Carpentaria, G. of Australia **79** 14.00S 140.00E
Carpentras France **40** 44.03N 5.03E
Carpio Spain **41** 41.13N 5.07W
Carra, Lough Rep. of Ire. **38** 53.41N 9.15W
Carradale Scotland **34** 55.35N 5.28W
Carrara Italy **42** 44.04N 10.06E
Carrauntoohil *mtn.* Rep. of Ire. **39** 52.00N 9.45W
Carrbridge Scotland **37** 57.17N 3.49W
Carriacou *i.* Grenada **97** 12.30N 61.35W
Carrick *f.* Scotland **34** 55.12N 4.38W
Carrickfergus N. Ireland **34** 54.43N 5.49W
Carrick Forest *hills* Scotland **34** 55.11N 4.29W
Carrickmacross Rep. of Ire. **38** 53.58N 6.43W
Carrick-on-Shannon Rep. of Ire. **38** 53.57N 8.06W
Carrick-on-Suir Rep. of Ire. **39** 52.21N 7.26W
Carron *r.* Highland Scotland **36** 57.25N 5.27W
Carron *r.* Highland Scotland **37** 57.54N 4.23W
Carron, Loch Scotland **36** 57.23N 5.30W
Carrowkeel Rep. of Ire. **34** 55.07N 7.12W
Carrowmore Lough Rep. of Ire. **38** 54.11N 9.47W
Çarşamba Turkey **56** 41.13N 36.43E
Çarşamba *r.* Turkey **56** 37.52N 31.48E
Carse of Gowrie *f.* Scotland **35** 56.25N 3.15W
Carshalton England **27** 51.22N 0.10W
Carson City U.S.A. **90** 39.10N 119.46W

Carsphairn Scotland **34** 55.13N 4.15W
Carstairs Scotland **35** 55.42N 3.41W
Cartagena Colombia **97** 10.24N 75.33W
Cartagena Spain **41** 37.36N 0.59W
Cartago Costa Rica **96** 9.50N 83.52W
Carúpano Venezuela **97** 10.39N 63.14W
Carvin France **45** 50.30N 2.58E
Cary *r.* England **28** 51.10N 3.00W
Casablanca Morocco **68** 33.39N 7.35W
Cascade Pt. New Zealand **82** 44.00S 168.20E
Cascade Range *mts.* U.S.A. **90** 44.00N 144.00W
Cascavel Brazil **103** 24.59S 53.29W
Caserta Italy **42** 41.06N 14.21E
Cashel Rep. of Ire. **39** 52.31N 7.54W
Casino Australia **80** 28.50S 153.02E
Caspe Spain **41** 41.14N 0.03W
Casper U.S.A. **90** 42.50N 106.20W
Caspian Depression *f.* U.S.S.R. **48** 47.00N 48.00E
Caspian Sea U.S.S.R. **48** 42.00N 51.00E
Cassai *r.* Angola **72** 10.38S 22.15E
Cassley *r.* Scotland **37** 57.58N 4.35W
Castaños Mexico **96** 26.48N 101.26W
Casteljaloux France **40** 44.19N 0.06W
Castellón de la Plana Spain **41** 39.59N 0.03W
Castelo Branco Portugal **41** 39.50N 7.30W
Casterton Australia **80** 37.35S 141.25E
Castlebar Rep. of Ire. **38** 53.52N 9.19W
Castlebay *town* Scotland **36** 56.58N 7.30W
Castlebellingham Rep. of Ire. **38** 53.53N 6.24W
Castleblayney Rep. of Ire. **38** 54.08N 6.46W
Castlebridge Rep. of Ire. **39** 52.23N 6.28W
Castle Cary England **28** 51.06N 2.31W
Castlecomer Rep. of Ire. **39** 52.48N 7.14W
Castledawson N. Ireland **34** 54.47N 6.35W
Castlederg N. Ireland **38** 54.42N 7.37W
Castledermot Rep. of Ire. **39** 52.54N 6.52W
Castle Douglas Scotland **35** 54.56N 3.56W
Castlefin Rep. of Ire. **38** 54.48N 7.41W
Castleford England **33** 53.43N 1.21W
Castlegregory Rep. of Ire. **39** 52.16N 10.01W
Castleisland *town* Rep. of Ire. **39** 52.13N 9.28W
Castlemaine Australia **80** 37.05S 144.19E
Castlemaine Rep. of Ire. **39** 52.10N 9.41W
Castlemaine Harbour *est.* Rep. of Ire. **39** 52.08N 9.50W
Castlepollard Rep. of Ire. **38** 53.41N 7.20W
Castlerea Rep. of Ire. **38** 53.45N 8.30W
Castlerock N. Ireland **34** 55.09N 6.47W
Castletown I.o.M. **32** 54.04N 4.38W
Castletownroche Rep. of Ire. **39** 52.10N 8.28W
Castletownshend Rep. of Ire. **39** 51.32N 9.12W
Castlewellan N. Ireland **38** 54.16N 5.57W
Castres France **40** 43.36N 2.14E
Castries St. Lucia **97** 14.01N 60.59W
Catalca Turkey **43** 41.09N 28.29E
Catamarca Argentina **103** 28.28S 65.46W
Catamarca *d.* Argentina **103** 27.40S 67.10W
Catanduanes *i.* Phil. **61** 13.45N 124.20E
Catanduva Brazil **103** 21.03S 49.00W
Catania Italy **42** 37.31N 15.05E
Catanzaro Italy **43** 38.55N 16.35E
Catarman Phil. **61** 12.28N 124.50E
Caterham England **29** 51.17N 0.04W
Catete Angola **72** 9.09S 13.40E
Catford England **27** 51.26N 0.00
Cat I. Bahamas **97** 24.30N 75.30W
Catoche, C. Mexico **96** 21.38N 87.08W
Catonsville U.S.A. **95** 39.17N 76.44W
Catskill Mts. U.S.A. **95** 42.15N 74.15W
Catterick England **32** 54.23N 1.38W
Cauca *r.* Colombia **97** 8.57N 74.30W
Caucasus Mts. U.S.S.R. **47** 43.00N 44.00E
Cauldcleuch Head *mtn.* Scotland **35** 55.18N 2.50W
Caungula Angola **72** 8.26S 18.35E
Caura *r.* Venezuela **97** 7.30N 65.00W
Causeway Rep. of Ire. **39** 52.25N 9.46W
Cavally *r.* Ivory Coast **70** 4.25N 7.39W
Cavan Rep. of Ire. **38** 54.00N 7.22W
Cavan *d.* Rep. of Ire. **38** 53.58N 7.10W
Cavite Phil. **61** 14.30N 120.54E
Cawood England **33** 53.50N 1.07W
Caxias do Sul Brazil **103** 29.14S 51.10W
Caxito Angola **72** 8.32S 13.38E
Cayenne French Guiana **102** 4.55N 52.18W
Cayman Brac *i.* Cayman Is. **97** 19.44N 79.48W
Cayman Is. C. America **97** 19.00N 81.00W
Cayuga L. U.S.A. **95** 42.40N 76.40W
Cazombo Angola **72** 11.54S 22.56E
Cebollera, Sierra de *mts.* Spain **41** 41.58N 2.30W
Cebu Phil. **61** 10.17N 123.56E
Cebu *i.* Phil. **61** 10.15N 123.45E
Cecina Italy **42** 43.18N 10.30E
Cedar *r.* U.S.A. **94** 41.10N 91.25W
Cedar City U.S.A. **90** 37.40N 103.04W
Cedar Falls *town* U.S.A. **94** 42.34N 92.26W
Cedar Rapids *town* U.S.A. **94** 41.59N 91.39W
Cedros I. Mexico **90** 28.15N 115.15W
Ceduna Australia **79** 32.07S 133.42E
Cefalù Italy **42** 38.01N 14.03E
Ceiriog *r.* Wales **30** 52.57N 3.01W
Cela Angola **72** 11.26S 15.05E
Celaya Mexico **96** 20.32N 100.48W
Celebes *i.* Indonesia **61** 2.00S 120.30E
Celebes Sea Indonesia **61** 3.00N 122.00E
Celje Yugo. **42** 46.15N 15.16E
Celle W. Germany **44** 52.37N 10.05E
Cemaes Bay *town* Wales **30** 53.24N 4.27W
Cemaes Head Wales **30** 52.08N 4.42W
Central *d.* Ghana **70** 5.30N 1.10W
Central *d.* Kenya **73** 0.30S 37.00E
Central *d.* Scotland **34** 56.10N 4.20W
Central, Cordillera *mts.* Bolivia **103** 19.00S 65.00W
Central African Republic Africa **68** 6.30N 20.00E
Centralia U.S.A. **94** 38.32N 89.08W
Central Russian Uplands U.S.S.R. **47** 53.00N 37.00E
Central Siberian Plateau *f.* U.S.S.R. **49** 66.00N 108.00E
Ceram *i.* Indonesia **61** 3.10S 129.30E
Ceram Sea Pacific Oc. **61** 2.50S 128.00E
Cerignola Italy **42** 41.17N 15.53E
Cernavodă Romania **43** 44.20N 28.02E
Cerne Abbas England **28** 50.49N 2.29W
Cervera Spain **41** 41.40N 1.16W
Česke Budějovice Czech. **44** 49.00N 14.30E
Cessnock Australia **80** 32.51S 151.21E
Cetinje Yugo. **43** 42.24N 18.55E
Ceuta Spain **41** 35.53N 5.19W
Cevennes *mts.* France **40** 44.25N 4.05E
Ceyhan *r.* Turkey **56** 36.54N 34.58E
Ceylon *i.* Asia **107** 7.00N 81.00E
Chacabuco Argentina **103** 34.40S 60.27W
Chaco *d.* Argentina **103** 26.30S 61.00W
Chad Africa **71** 15.00N 17.00E
Chad, L. Africa **71** 13.30N 14.00E
Chadwell St. Mary England **27** 51.29N 0.22E
Chagford England **31** 50.40N 3.50W
Chagos Archipelago Indian Oc. **55** 7.00S 72.00E
Chah Bahar Iran **57** 25.17N 60.41E
Chakansur Afghan. **57** 31.10N 62.02E
Chalfont St. Giles England **27** 51.39N 0.35W
Chalfont St. Peter England **27** 51.37N 0.33W
Challans France **40** 46.51N 1.52W
Challenger Depth Pacific Oc. **61** 11.19N 142.15E
Châlons-sur-Marne France **40** 48.58N 4.22E
Chalon-sur-Saône France **40** 46.47N 4.51E
Chamai Thailand **60** 8.10N 99.41E
Chambal *r.* India **58** 26.30N 79.20E
Chambéry France **40** 45.34N 5.55E
Chambeshi *r.* Zambia **73** 11.15S 30.37E
Chamo, L. Ethiopia **73** 4.45N 36.53E
Chamonix France **40** 45.55N 6.52E
Champ Iran **57** 26.40N 60.31E
Champaign U.S.A. **94** 40.07N 88.14W
Champlain, L. U.S.A. **95** 44.45N 73.20W
Chanchiang China **63** 21.05N 110.12E
Chanda India **59** 19.58N 79.21E
Chandeleur Is. U.S.A. **91** 29.50N 88.50W
Chandigarh India **58** 30.44N 76.54E
Changchow Fukien China **63** 24.31N 117.40E
Changchun China **63** 43.50N 125.20E
Changkiakow China **63** 41.00N 114.50E
Changsha China **63** 28.10N 113.00E
Changteh China **63** 29.03N 111.35E
Changting China **63** 25.47N 116.17E
Changtu China **62** 31.11N 97.18E
Channel Is. U.K. **31** 49.28N 2.13W
Chanthaburi Thailand **59** 12.38N 102.12E
Chaochow China **63** 23.43N 116.35E
Chao Phraya *r.* Thailand **59** 13.30N 100.25E
Chaotung China **59** 27.30N 103.40E
Chapala, Lago de Mexico **96** 20.00N 103.00W
Chapayevsk U.S.S.R. **47** 52.58N 49.44E
Chapel en le Frith England **32** 53.19N 1.54W
Chapel St. Leonards England **33** 53.14N 0.20E
Chapleau Canada **94** 47.50N 83.24W
Chapra India **58** 23.31N 88.40E
Charchan China **62** 38.08N 85.33E
Charchan *r.* China **62** 40.56N 86.27E
Chard England **28** 50.52N 2.59W
Chardzhou U.S.S.R. **57** 39.09N 63.34E
Chari *r.* Chad **71** 13.00N 14.30E
Charing England **29** 51.12N 0.49E
Charkhlik China **62** 39.00N 88.00E
Charleroi Belgium **45** 50.25N 4.27E
Charleston S.C. U.S.A. **91** 32.48N 79.58W
Charleston W. Va. U.S.A. **91** 38.23N 81.20W
Charlestown Rep. of Ire. **38** 53.57N 8.48W
Charlestown of Aberlour Scotland **37** 57.27N 3.14W
Charleville Australia **79** 26.25S 146.13E
Charleville-Mézières France **45** 49.46N 4.43E
Charlotte U.S.A. **91** 35.05N 80.50W
Charlottenburg W. Germany **44** 52.32N 13.18E
Charlottesville U.S.A. **91** 38.02N 78.29W
Charlottetown Canada **93** 46.14N 63.09W
Charlton Australia **80** 36.18S 143.27E
Charolles France **40** 46.26N 4.17E
Chartres France **40** 48.27N 1.30E
Chascomas Argentina **103** 35.34S 58.00W
Châteaubriant France **40** 47.43N 1.22W
Château du Loir France **40** 47.42N 0.25E
Châteaudun France **40** 48.04N 1.20E
Châteauroux France **40** 46.49N 1.41E
Château Thierry France **40** 49.03N 3.24E
Châtelet Belgium **45** 50.24N 4.32E
Châtellerault France **40** 46.49N 0.33E
Chatham Canada **94** 42.24N 82.11W
Chatham England **27** 51.23N 0.32E
Chatham Is. Pacific Oc. **107** 43.00S 176.00W
Châtillon-s-Seine France **40** 47.52N 4.35E
Chattahoochee *r.* U.S.A. **91** 29.45N 85.00W
Chattanooga U.S.A. **91** 35.01N 85.18W
Chatteris England **29** 52.27N 0.03E
Chauka *r.* India **58** 27.10N 81.28E
Chaumont France **40** 48.07N 5.08E
Chaves Portugal **41** 41.44N 7.28W
Cheadle England **32** 53.24N 2.13W
Cheam England **27** 51.22N 0.13W
Cheb Czech. **44** 50.04N 12.20E
Cheboksary U.S.S.R. **47** 56.08N 47.12E
Cheboygan U.S.A. **94** 45.40N 84.28W
Cheddar England **28** 51.16N 2.47W
Chekiang *d.* China **63** 29.15N 120.00E
Cheleken U.S.S.R. **57** 39.26N 53.11E
Chéliff *r.* Algeria **41** 36.15N 2.05E
Chelmer *r.* England **29** 51.43N 0.40E
Chelmsford England **27** 51.44N 0.28E
Cheltenham England **28** 51.53N 2.07W
Chelyabinsk U.S.S.R. **48** 55.10N 61.25E
Chelyuskin, C. U.S.S.R. **49** 77.20N 106.00E
Chemba Moçambique **73** 17.11S 34.53E
Chen, Mt. U.S.S.R. **49** 65.30N 141.20E
Chenab *r.* Asia **58** 29.26N 71.09E
Chengchow China **63** 34.35N 113.38E
Chengte China **63** 40.48N 118.06E
Chengtu China **62** 30.37N 104.06E
Chepstow Wales **31** 51.38N 2.40W
Cher *r.* France **40** 47.12N 2.04E
Cherbourg France **40** 49.38N 1.37W
Cherchel Algeria **41** 36.36N 2.11E
Cheremkhovo U.S.S.R. **49** 53.08N 103.01E
Cherepovets U.S.S.R. **47** 59.05N 37.55E
Cherkassy U.S.S.R. **47** 49.27N 32.04E
Cherkessk U.S.S.R. **47** 44.14N 42.05E
Chernigov U.S.S.R. **47** 51.30N 31.18E
Chernovtsy U.S.S.R. **47** 48.19N 25.52E
Chernyakhovsk U.S.S.R. **46** 54.36N 12.48E
Cherskogo Range *mts.* U.S.S.R. **49** 65.50N 143.00E
Chertsey England **27** 51.23N 0.27W
Chesapeake B. U.S.A. **91** 38.00N 76.00W
Chesham England **27** 51.43N 0.38W
Cheshire *d.* England **32** 53.14N 2.30W
Cheshunt England **27** 51.43N 0.02W
Chesil Beach *f.* England **28** 50.37N 2.33W
Chess *r.* England **27** 51.38N 0.28W
Chessington England **27** 51.21N 0.18W
Chester England **32** 53.12N 2.53W
Chester U.S.A. **95** 39.50N 75.23W
Chesterfield England **33** 53.14N 1.26W
Chesterfield Inlet *town* Canada **93** 63.00N 91.00W
Chester-le-Street England **33** 54.53N 1.34W
Chetumal Mexico **96** 18.30N 88.17W
Chetumal B. Mexico **96** 18.30N 88.00W
Chew *r.* England **28** 51.25N 2.30W
Chew Magna England **28** 51.21N 2.37W
Cheyenne U.S.A. **90** 41.08N 104.50W
Chhindwara India **58** 22.04N 78.58E
Chiang Mai Thailand **59** 18.48N 98.59E
Chiang Rai Thailand **59** 19.56N 99.51E
Chiapas *d.* Mexico **96** 16.30N 93.00W
Chiavari Italy **40** 44.19N 9.19E
Chibemba Angola **74** 15.43S 14.07E
Chibougamau Canada **91** 49.56N 74.24W
Chibuto Moçambique **74** 24.40S 33.33E
Chicago U.S.A. **94** 41.50N 87.45W
Chicago Heights *town* U.S.A. **94** 41.31N 87.39W
Chichagof I. U.S.A. **92** 57.55N 135.45W
Chichester England **28** 50.50N 0.47W
Chico U.S.A. **90** 39.46N 121.50W
Chicopee U.S.A. **95** 42.09N 72.37W
Chicoutimi-Jonquière Canada **95** 48.26N 71.06W
Chicualacuala Moçambique **74** 22.06S 31.42E
Chiddingstone Causeway *town* England **27** 51.12N 0.08E
Chidley, C. Canada **93** 60.30N 65.00W
Chiemsee *l.* W. Germany **44** 47.55N 12.30E
Chieti Italy **42** 42.22N 14.12E
Chigubo Moçambique **74** 22.38S 33.18E
Chigwell England **27** 51.38N 0.05E
Chihfeng China **63** 41.17N 118.56E
Chihli, G. of China **63** 38.30N 119.30E
Chihuahua Mexico **90** 28.40N 106.06W

Chihuahua *d.* Mexico **96** 28.40N 104.58W
Chikwawa Malaŵi **73** 16.00S 34.54E
Chil *r.* Iran **57** 25.12N 61.30E
Chilapa Mexico **96** 17.31N 99.27W
Chile S. America **102** 30.00S 71.00W
Chillicothe U.S.A. **94** 38.20N 83.00W
Chiloé I. Chile **102** 43.00S 74.00W
Chilpancingo Mexico **96** 17.33N 99.30W
Chiltern Hills England **27** 51.40N 0.53W
Chiltern Hundreds *hills* England **27** 51.37N 0.38W
Chilumba Malaŵi **73** 10.25S 34.18E
Chilung Taiwan **63** 25.10N 121.43E
Chilwa, L. Malaŵi **73** 15.15S 35.45E
Chimay Belgium **45** 50.03N 4.20E
Chimkent U.S.S.R. **62** 42.16N 69.05E
China Asia **62** 33.00N 103.00E
Chinandega Nicaragua **96** 12.35N 87.10W
Chinati Peak U.S.A. **90** 30.05N 104.30W
Chinchoua Gabon **72** 0.00 9.48E
Chinchow China **63** 41.07N 121.06E
Chindio Moçambique **73** 17.46S 35.23E
Chindwin *r.* Burma **62** 21.30N 95.12E
Chinga Moçambique **73** 15.14S 38.40E
Chingford England **27** 51.37N 0.00
Ching Hai *l.* China **62** 36.40N 100.00E
Chingola Zambia **73** 12.29S 27.53E
Chin Hills Burma **62** 22.40N 93.30E
Chinkiang China **63** 32.05N 119.30E
Chin Ling Shan *mts.* China **63** 33.40N 109.00E
Chinsali Zambia **73** 10.33S 32.05E
Chintheche Malaŵi **73** 11.50S 34.13E
Chipata Zambia **73** 13.37S 32.40E
Chipera Moçambique **73** 15.20S 32.35E
Chipinga Rhodesia **74** 20.12S 32.38E
Chippenham England **28** 51.27N 2.07W
Chippewa *r.* U.S.A. **94** 44.23N 92.05W
Chippewa Falls *town* U.S.A. **94** 44.56N 91.25W
Chipping Norton England **28** 51.56N 1.32W
Chipping Ongar England **27** 51.43N 0.15E
Chipping Sodbury England **28** 51.31N 2.23W
Chipstead England **27** 51.18N 0.10W
Chiquita, Mar *l.* Argentina **103** 30.50S 62.30W
Chir *r.* U.S.S.R. **47** 48.34N 42.53E
Chiredzi Rhodesia **74** 21.03S 31.39E
Chiredzi *r.* Rhodesia **74** 21.10S 31.50E
Chiriqui *mtn.* Panamá **96** 8.49N 82.38W
Chiriqui Lagoon Panamá **96** 9.00N 82.00W
Chirnside Scotland **35** 55.48N 2.12W
Chiromo Malaŵi **73** 16.28S 35.10E
Chirripo *mtn.* Costa Rica **96** 9.31N 83.30W
Chislehurst England **27** 51.25N 0.05E
Chistopol U.S.S.R. **47** 55.25N 50.38E
Chiswellgreen England **27** 51.43N 0.24W
Chiswick England **27** 51.29N 0.16W
Chita U.S.S.R. **63** 52.03N 113.35E
Chitipa Malaŵi **73** 9.41S 33.19E
Chitral Pakistan **58** 35.52N 71.58E
Chittagong Bangla. **59** 22.20N 91.48E
Chitterne England **28** 51.12N 2.01W
Chittoor India **59** 13.13N 79.06E
Chiumbe *r.* Zaïre **72** 6.37S 21.04E
Chiuta, L. Malaŵi/Moçambique **73** 14.45S 35.50E
Chivilcoy Argentina **103** 34.55S 60.03W
Chobe *r.* Botswana **72** 17.45S 25.12E
Chobham England **27** 51.21N 0.37W
Choele Choel Argentina **103** 39.16S 65.38W
Chojnice Poland **44** 53.42N 17.32E
Cholet France **40** 47.04N 0.53W
Cholon Vietnam **60** 10.45N 106.39E
Choluteca Honduras **96** 13.16N 87.11W
Choma Zambia **73** 16.51S 27.04E
Chomutov Czech. **44** 50.28N 13.25E
Chon Buri Thailand **59** 13.21N 101.01E
Chongjin N. Korea **63** 41.55N 129.50E
Chonju S. Korea **63** 35.50N 127.05E
Chorley England **32** 53.39N 2.39W
Chorleywood England **27** 51.40N 0.29W
Chorzów Poland **47** 50.19N 18.56E
Chota Nagpur *f.* India **58** 23.30N 84.00E
Chott Djerid *f.* Tunisia **68** 33.30N 8.30E
Chott ech Chergui *f.* Algeria **68** 34.00N 0.30E
Chott Melrhir *f.* Algeria **68** 34.15N 7.00E
Christchurch England **28** 50.44N 1.47W
Christchurch New Zealand **82** 43.33S 172.40E
Christianshaab Greenland **93** 68.50N 51.00W
Christmas I. Indian Oc. **60** 10.30S 105.40E
Christmas I. Pacific Oc. **106** 2.00N 157.00W
Chu *r.* U.S.S.R. **62** 42.30N 76.10E
Chuanchow China **63** 24.57N 118.36E
Chuckchee Pen. U.S.S.R. **49** 66.00N 174.30W
Chudleigh England **31** 50.35N 3.36W
Chudovo U.S.S.R. **47** 59.10N 31.41E
Chuhsien China **63** 28.57N 118.52E
Chuiquimula Guatemala **96** 15.52N 89.50W
Chukai Malaysia **60** 4.16N 103.24E
Chulmleigh England **31** 50.55N 3.52W
Chumphon Thailand **59** 10.35N 99.14E
Chuna *r.* U.S.S.R. **49** 58.00N 94.00E
Chungking China **62** 29.31N 106.35E
Chungtien China **59** 28.00N 99.30E
Chunya Tanzania **73** 8.31S 33.28E
Chuquisaca *d.* Bolivia **103** 21.00S 63.45W
Chur Switz. **44** 46.52N 9.32E
Churchill Canada **93** 58.45N 94.00W
Churchill *r.* Canada **93** 58.20N 94.15W
Churchill, C. Canada **93** 58.50N 93.00W
Churchill L. Canada **92** 56.00N 108.00W
Churchill Peak Canada **92** 58.10N 125.00W
Church Stoke Wales **30** 52.32N 3.04W
Church Stretton England **30** 52.32N 2.49W
Churn *r.* England **28** 51.38N 1.53W
Cicero U.S.A. **94** 41.50N 87.46W
Ciego de Avila Cuba **97** 21.51N 78.47W
Cienfuegos Cuba **97** 22.10N 80.27W
Cieza Spain **41** 38.14N 1.25W
Cifuentes Spain **41** 40.47N 2.37W
Cijara L. Spain **41** 39.20N 4.50W
Cilo, Mt. Turkey **57** 37.30N 44.00E
Cimarron *r.* U.S.A. **91** 36.15N 96.55W
Cimone, Monte *mtn.* Italy **42** 44.12N 10.42E
Cinca *r.* Spain **41** 41.22N 0.20W
Cincinnati U.S.A. **94** 39.10N 84.30W
Cinderford England **28** 51.49N 2.30W
Ciney Belgium **45** 50.17N 5.06E
Cinto, Mont *mtn.* France **40** 42.23N 8.57E
Cirebon Indonesia **60** 6.46S 108.33E
Cirencester England **28** 51.43N 1.59W
City of London England **27** 51.32N 0.06W
City of Westminster England **27** 51.30N 0.09W
Ciudad Bolívar Venezuela **97** 8.06N 63.36W
Ciudad Camargo Mexico **90** 27.41N 105.10W
Ciudadela Spain **41** 40.00N 3.50E
Ciudad Guerrero Mexico **90** 28.33N 107.28W
Ciudad Ixtepec Mexico **96** 16.32N 95.10W
Ciudad Juárez Mexico **90** 31.42N 106.29W
Ciudad Madera Mexico **96** 22.19N 95.50W
Ciudad Obregon Mexico **90** 27.28N 109.55W
Ciudad Real Spain **41** 38.59N 3.55W
Ciudad Rodrigo Spain **41** 40.36N 6.33W
Ciudad Victoria Mexico **96** 23.43N 99.10W
Civitavecchia Italy **42** 42.06N 11.48E
Civray France **40** 46.09N 0.18E
Civril Turkey **56** 38.18N 29.43E
Cizre Turkey **56** 37.21N 42.11E
Clackmannan Scotland **35** 56.06N 3.46W
Clacton on Sea England **29** 51.47N 1.10E
Clane Rep. of Ire. **38** 53.18N 6.42W
Clapham England **27** 51.27N 0.08W
Clara Rep. of Ire. **38** 53.21N 7.37W
Clare Australia **80** 33.50S 138.38E
Clare *d.* Rep. of Ire. **39** 52.52N 8.55W
Clare *r.* Rep. of Ire. **38** 53.17N 9.04W
Clare U.S.A. **94** 43.49N 84.47W
Clarecastle Rep. of Ire. **39** 52.49N 8.58W
Claregalway Rep. of Ire. **38** 53.21N 8.57W
Clare I. Rep. of Ire. **38** 53.48N 10.00W
Claremont U.S.A. **95** 43.23N 72.21W
Claremorris Rep. of Ire. **38** 53.44N 9.00W
Clarence *r.* New Zealand **82** 42.10S 173.55E
Clarke I. Australia **80** 40.30S 148.10E
Clarksburg U.S.A. **94** 39.16N 80.22W
Clatteringshaws Loch Scotland **34** 55.30N 4.25W
Claudy N. Ireland **34** 54.54N 7.09W
Clay Cross England **33** 53.11N 1.26W
Clay Head I.o.M. **32** 54.12N 4.23W
Clayton U.S.A. **90** 36.27N 103.12W
Clear, C. Rep. of Ire. **39** 51.25N 9.32W
Clear I. Rep. of Ire. **39** 51.26N 9.30W
Clearwater L. Canada **93** 56.10N 74.30W
Cleator Moor *town* England **32** 54.30N 3.32W
Clee Hills England **28** 52.25N 2.37W
Cleethorpes England **33** 53.33N 0.02W
Cleobury Mortimer England **28** 52.23N 2.28W
Clermont Ferrand France **40** 45.47N 3.05E
Clevedon England **28** 51.26N 2.52W
Cleveland *d.* England **33** 54.37N 1.08W
Cleveland *f.* England **33** 54.30N 0.55W
Cleveland U.S.A. **94** 41.30N 81.41W
Cleveland Heights *town* U.S.A. **94** 41.30N 81.35W
Cleveland Hills England **33** 54.25N 1.10W
Cleveleys England **32** 53.52N 3.01W
Clew B. Rep. of Ire. **38** 53.50N 9.47W
Cliffe England **27** 51.28N 0.30E
Clifton U.S.A. **95** 40.52N 74.09W
Clinton U.S.A. **94** 41.51N 90.12W
Clisham *mtn.* Scotland **36** 57.58N 6.50W
Clitheroe England **32** 53.52N 2.23W
Cloghan Rep. of Ire. **39** 53.13N 7.54W
Clogheen Rep. of Ire. **39** 52.16N 8.00W
Clogher Head Kerry Rep. of Ire. **39** 52.09N 10.28W
Clogher Head Louth Rep. of Ire. **38** 53.47N 6.14W
Clogh Mills N. Ireland **34** 55.00N 6.20W
Clonakilty Rep. of Ire. **39** 51.37N 8.54W
Clonakilty B. Rep. of Ire. **39** 51.35N 8.52W
Clones Rep. of Ire. **38** 54.11N 7.16W
Clonmany Rep. of Ire. **38** 55.16N 7.25W
Clonmel Rep. of Ire. **39** 52.21N 7.44W
Clonmellon Rep. of Ire. **38** 53.40N 7.02W
Clonroche Rep. of Ire. **39** 52.27N 6.45W
Cloppenburg W. Germany **45** 52.52N 8.02E
Cloquet U.S.A. **94** 46.40N 92.30W
Cloud Peak *mtn.* U.S.A. **90** 44.23N 107.11W
Cloughton England **33** 54.20N 0.27W
Clovelly England **31** 51.00N 4.25W
Clovis U.S.A. **90** 34.14N 103.13W
Clowne England **33** 53.18N 1.16W
Cluanie, Loch Scotland **36** 57.08N 5.05W
Cluj Romania **47** 46.47N 23.37E
Clun Forest *f.* England **28** 52.28N 3.10W
Clutha *r.* New Zealand **82** 46.18S 169.05E
Clwyd *d.* Wales **30** 53.07N 3.20W
Clwyd *r.* Wales **30** 53.19N 3.30W
Clwydian Range *mts.* Wales **30** 53.08N 3.15W
Clyde *r.* Scotland **34** 55.58N 4.53W
Clydebank Scotland **34** 55.53N 4.23W
Clydesdale *f.* Scotland **35** 55.41N 3.48W
Coahuila *d.* Mexico **96** 27.00N 103.00W
Coalville England **28** 52.43N 1.21W
Coast *d.* Kenya **73** 3.00S 39.30E
Coast *d.* Tanzania **73** 7.00S 39.00E
Coast Mts. Canada **92** 55.30N 128.00W
Coast Range *mts.* U.S.A. **90** 40.00N 123.00W
Coatbridge Scotland **35** 55.52N 4.02W
Coats I. Canada **93** 62.30N 83.00W
Coatzacoalcos Mexico **96** 18.10N 94.25W
Cobalt Canada **95** 47.24N 79.41W
Cobán Guatemala **96** 15.28N 90.20W
Cobar Australia **80** 31.32S 145.51E
Cobbin's Brook *r.* England **27** 51.40N 0.01W
Cobh Rep. of Ire. **39** 51.50N 8.18W
Cobham Kent England **27** 51.24N 0.25E
Cobham Surrey England **27** 51.20N 0.25W
Cobourg Canada **95** 43.58N 78.11W
Coburg W. Germany **44** 50.15N 10.58E
Cochabamba Bolivia **103** 17.26S 66.10W
Cochabamba *d.* Bolivia **103** 17.42S 65.00W
Cochin India **58** 9.56N 76.15E
Cochrane Canada **94** 49.04N 81.02W
Cockburn Australia **80** 32.05S 141.00E
Cockburnspath Scotland **35** 55.56N 2.22W
Cockermouth England **32** 54.40N 3.22W
Cockernhoe Green England **27** 51.55N 0.20W
Cockfosters England **27** 51.39N 0.09W
Coco *r.* Honduras **96** 14.58N 83.15W
Cocos Is. Indian Oc. **113** 13.00S 96.00E
Cod, C. U.S.A. **95** 42.08N 70.10W
Cod's Head Rep. of Ire. **39** 51.40N 10.06W
Coesfeld W. Germany **45** 51.55N 7.13E
Coevorden Neth. **45** 52.39N 6.45E
Coff's Harbour Australia **80** 30.19S 153.05E
Cofre de Perote *mtn.* Mexico **96** 19.30N 97.10W
Coggeshall England **29** 51.53N 0.41E
Coghinas *r.* Italy **42** 40.57N 8.50E
Cognac France **40** 45.42N 0.19W
Coiba I. Panamá **96** 8.30N 81.45W
Coigach *f.* Scotland **36** 58.00N 5.10W
Coimbatore India **58** 11.00N 76.57E
Coimbra Portugal **41** 40.12N 8.25W
Coin Spain **41** 36.40N 4.45W
Cojedes *r.* Venezuela **97** 7.35N 66.30W
Colac Australia **80** 38.22S 143.38E
Colchester England **29** 51.54N 0.55E
Coldblow England **27** 51.23N 0.11E
Cold Fell *mtn.* England **35** 54.54N 2.37W
Coldingham Scotland **35** 55.53N 2.10W
Coldstream Scotland **35** 55.39N 2.15W
Coleford England **28** 51.46N 2.38W
Coleman Canada **90** 49.38N 114.28W
Coleraine N. Ireland **34** 55.08N 6.40W
Colesberg R.S.A. **74** 30.44S 25.00E
Colgrave Sd. Scotland **36** 60.30N 0.58W
Colima Mexico **96** 18.00N 103.45W
Colima *d.* Mexico **96** 18.00N 103.45W
Colintraive Scotland **34** 55.56N 5.09W
Coll *i.* Scotland **34** 56.38N 6.34W
Collerina Australia **80** 29.22S 146.32E
Collier Law *mtn.* England **32** 54.45N 1.58W
Collier Row England **27** 51.36N 0.09E
Collier Street *town* England **27** 51.11N 0.27E
Collingwood Canada **94** 44.30N 80.14W
Collingwood New Zealand **82** 40.41S 172.41E
Collin Top *mtn.* N. Ireland **34** 54.58N 6.08W
Collon Rep. of Ire. **38** 53.47N 6.30W
Collooney Rep. of Ire. **38** 54.11N 8.29W
Colmar France **44** 48.05N 7.21E
Colmenar Viejo Spain **41** 40.39N 3.46W
Coln *r.* England **28** 51.41N 1.42W
Colne England **32** 53.51N 2.11W

Colne r. Bucks. England 27 51.26N 0.32W
Colne r. Essex England 29 51.50N 0.59E
Colnett, C. Mexico 90 31.00N 116.20W
Colney Heath town England 27 51.43N 0.14W
Cologne W. Germany 45 50.56N 6.57E
Colombia S. America 97 7.00N 74.00W
Colombo Sri Lanka 59 6.55N 79.52E
Colón Panama Canal Zone 97 9.21N 79.54W
Colonsay i. Scotland 34 56.04N 6.13W
Colorado r. Argentina 103 39.50S 62.02W
Colorado r. N. America 90 32.00N 114.58W
Colorado d. U.S.A. 90 39.00N 106.00W
Colorado r. Texas U.S.A. 91 28.30N 96.00W
Colorado Plateau f. U.S.A. 90 35.45N 112.00W
Colorado Springs town U.S.A. 90 38.50N 104.40W
Colsterworth England 33 52.48N 0.37W
Coltishall England 29 52.44N 1.22E
Columbia U.S.A. 91 34.00N 81.00W
Columbia r. U.S.A. 90 46.10N 123.30W
Columbretes, Islas Spain 41 39.50N 0.40E
Columbus Ga. U.S.A. 91 32.28N 84.59W
Columbus Ohio U.S.A. 94 39.59N 83.03W
Colville r. U.S.A. 92 70.06N 151.30W
Colwyn Bay town Wales 30 53.18N 3.43W
Comayagua Honduras 96 14.30N 87.39W
Combe Martin England 31 51.12N 4.02W
Comber N. Ireland 34 54.33N 5.45W
Comeragh Mts. Rep. of Ire. 39 52.17N 7.34W
Comilla Bangla. 59 23.28N 91.10E
Commonwealth Territory d. Australia 80 35.00S 151.00E
Como Italy 40 45.48N 9.04E
Como, L. Italy 42 46.05N 9.17E
Comodoro Rivadavia Argentina 102 45.50S 67.30W
Comorin, C. India 58 8.04N 77.35E
Comoro Is. Africa 73 12.15S 44.00E
Comrie Scotland 35 56.23N 4.00W
Cona r. Scotland 36 56.46N 5.13W
Conakry Guinea 70 9.30N 13.43W
Concarneau France 40 47.53N 3.55W
Concepcion Argentina 103 27.20S 65.35W
Concepción Chile 102 36.50S 73.03W
Concepción Paraguay 103 23.22S 57.26W
Conception, Pt. U.S.A. 90 34.27N 120.26W
Conchos r. Mexico 90 29.34N 104.30W
Concord U.S.A. 95 43.13N 71.34W
Condobolin Australia 80 33.03S 147.11E
Confolens France 40 46.01N 0.40E
Congleton England 32 53.10N 2.12W
Congo Africa 72 1.00S 16.00E
Congo r. see ZaïreZaïre 72
Congo Basin f. Africa 107 0.30N 22.00E
Congresbury England 28 51.20N 2.49W
Coningsby England 33 53.07N 0.09W
Conisbrough England 33 53.29N 1.12W
Coniston England 32 54.22N 3.06W
Coniston Water l. England 32 54.20N 3.05W
Conn, Lough Rep. of Ire. 38 54.01N 9.15W
Connacht d. Rep. of Ire. 38 53.45N 9.05W
Connah's Quay Wales 30 53.13N 3.03W
Connecticut d. U.S.A. 95 41.30N 72.50W
Connecticut r. U.S.A. 95 41.20N 72.19W
Connel Scotland 34 56.27N 5.24W
Connemara f. Rep. of Ire. 38 53.32N 9.56W
Conon r. Scotland 37 57.33N 4.33W
Conselheiro Lafaiete Brazil 103 20.40S 43.48W
Consett England 32 54.52N 1.50W
Con Son Is. Vietnam 60 8.30N 106.30E
Constance, L. Europe 44 47.40N 9.30E
Constanța Romania 43 44.10N 28.31E
Constantina Spain 41 37.54N 5.36W
Constantine Algeria 42 36.22N 6.38E
Constantine Mts. Algeria 42 36.30N 6.35E
Conwy Wales 30 53.17N 3.50W
Conwy r. Wales 30 53.17N 3.49W
Conwy B. Wales 30 53.19N 3.55W
Cooch Behar India 58 26.18N 89.32E
Cook, Mt. New Zealand 82 43.45S 170.12E
Cook Is. Pacific Oc. 106 20.00S 157.00W
Cookstown N. Ireland 34 54.39N 6.46W
Cook Str. New Zealand 82 41.15S 174.30E
Cooktown Australia 79 15.29S 145.15E
Coolah Australia 80 31.48S 149.45E
Coolgreany Rep. of Ire. 39 52.46N 6.15W
Cooma Australia 80 36.15S 149.07E
Coomacarrea mtn. Rep. of Ire. 39 51.58N 10.02W
Coomnadiha mtn. Rep. of Ire. 39 51.46N 9.40W
Coonabarabran Australia 80 31.16S 149.18E
Coonamble Australia 80 30.55S 148.26E
Cooper Creek Australia 80 28.36S 138.00E
Cootamundra Australia 80 34.41S 148.03E
Cootehill Rep. of Ire. 38 54.05N 7.05W
Copán ruins Guatemala 96 14.52N 89.10W
Copeland I. N. Ireland 34 54.40N 5.22W
Copenhagen Denmark 46 55.43N 12.34E
Copinsay i. Scotland 37 58.54N 2.41W
Copper Belt f. Zambia 73 12.40S 28.00E
Coppermine r. Canada 92 67.54N 115.10W
Coppermine town Canada 92 67.49N 115.12W
Coquet r. England 35 55.21N 1.35W
Coquet I. England 35 55.20N 1.30W
Corabia Romania 43 43.45N 24.29E
Coral Sea Pacific Oc. 79 13.00S 148.00E
Corangamite, L. Australia 80 38.10S 143.25E
Corbeil France 40 48.37N 2.29E
Corbridge England 35 54.58N 2.01W
Corby England 28 52.29N 0.41W
Córdoba Argentina 103 31.25S 64.11W
Córdoba d. Argentina 103 32.00S 64.00W
Cordoba Mexico 96 18.55N 96.55W
Cordoba Spain 41 37.53N 4.46W
Córdoba, Sierras de mts. Argentina 103 32.00S 64.10W
Corfu Greece 43 39.37N 19.50E
Corfu i. Greece 43 39.35N 19.50E
Corigliano Italy 43 39.36N 16.31E
Corinna Australia 80 41.38S 145.06E
Corinth Greece 43 37.56N 22.55E
Corinth, G. of Greece 43 38.15N 22.30E
Corinto Nicaragua 96 12.29N 87.14W
Cork Rep. of Ire. 39 51.54N 8.28W
Cork d. Rep. of Ire. 39 52.00N 8.40W
Cork Harbour est. Rep. of Ire. 39 51.50N 8.17W
Corner Brook town Canada 93 48.58N 57.58W
Corning U.S.A. 95 42.10N 77.04W
Corno, Monte mtn. Italy 42 42.29N 13.33E
Cornwall Canada 95 45.02N 74.45W
Cornwall d. England 31 50.26N 4.40W
Cornwallis I. Canada 93 75.00N 95.00W
Coro Venezuela 97 11.27N 69.41W
Corofin Rep. of Ire. 39 52.57N 9.04W
Coromandel New Zealand 82 36.47S 175.32E
Coromandel Pen. New Zealand 82 36.45S 175.30E
Coronation G. Canada 92 68.00N 112.00W
Coronel Pringles Argentina 103 37.56S 61.25W
Coronel Suárez Argentina 103 37.30S 61.52W
Corowa Australia 80 36.00S 146.20E
Corozal Belize 96 18.23N 88.23W
Corpus Christi U.S.A. 91 27.47N 97.26W
Corran Scotland 34 56.43N 5.14W
Corraun Pen. Rep. of Ire. 38 53.45N 9.52W
Corrib, Lough Rep. of Ire. 38 53.26N 9.14W
Corrientes Argentina 103 27.30S 58.48W
Corrientes d. Argentina 103 29.00S 57.30W
Corringham England 27 51.31N 0.28E
Corry U.S.A. 95 41.56N 79.39W
Corryhabbie Hill Scotland 37 57.21N 3.12W
Corryong Australia 80 36.11S 147.58E
Corryvreckan, G. of Scotland 34 56.09N 5.42W
Corse, Cap France 42 43.00N 9.21E
Corsham England 28 51.25N 2.11W
Corsica i. France 40 42.00N 9.10E
Corte France 40 42.18N 9.08E
Cortegana Spain 41 37.55N 6.49W
Cortland U.S.A. 95 42.36N 76.10W
Coruche Portugal 41 38.58N 8.31W
Çorum Turkey 56 40.31N 34.57E
Corumbá Brazil 103 19.00S 57.25W
Corumbá r. Brazil 103 18.15S 48.55W
Corve r. England 28 52.22N 2.42W
Corwen Wales 30 52.59N 3.23W
Cosenza Italy 42 39.17N 16.14E
Coshocton U.S.A. 94 40.16N 81.53W
Cosne France 40 47.25N 2.55E
Costa Brava d. Spain 41 41.30N 3.00E
Costa del Sol d. Spain 41 36.30N 4.00W
Costa Rica C. America 96 10.00N 84.00W
Costelloe Rep. of Ire. 38 53.17N 9.33W
Côte d'Azur f. France 40 43.20N 6.45E
Cothi r. Wales 30 51.51N 4.10W
Cotonou Benin 71 6.24N 2.31E
Cotswold Hills England 28 51.50N 2.00W
Cottbus E. Germany 44 51.43N 14.21E
Cottenham England 29 52.18N 0.08E
Cottingham England 33 53.17N 0.25W
Coucy France 45 49.32N 3.20E
Coulagh B. Rep. of Ire. 39 51.42N 10.00W
Coulonge r. Canada 95 45.55N 76.52W
Coul Pt. Scotland 34 55.47N 6.29W
Coulsdon England 27 51.19N 0.07W
Council Bluffs U.S.A. 91 41.14N 95.54W
Coupar Angus Scotland 35 56.33N 3.17W
Courtmacsherry B. Rep. of Ire. 39 51.37N 8.40W
Courtrai Belgium 45 50.49N 3.17E
Coutances France 40 49.03N 1.29W
Couvin Belgium 45 50.03N 4.30E
Coventry England 28 52.25N 1.31W
Cover r. England 32 54.17N 1.47W
Covilhã Portugal 41 40.17N 7.30W
Covington U.S.A. 94 40.06N 84.21W
Cowal f. Scotland 34 56.05N 5.05W
Cowal, L. Australia 80 33.36S 147.22E
Cowan, L. Australia 79 32.00S 122.00E
Cowbridge Wales 31 51.28N 3.28W
Cowdenbeath Scotland 35 56.07N 3.21W
Cowes England 28 50.45N 1.18W
Cowra Australia 80 33.50S 148.45E
Cox's Bazar Bangla. 59 21.25N 91.59E
Cozumel I. Mexico 96 20.30N 87.00W
Craboon Australia 80 32.02S 149.29E
Cracow Poland 47 50.03N 19.55E
Cradle Mtn. Australia 80 41.40S 145.55E
Cradock R.S.A. 74 32.10S 25.37E
Craigavon N. Ireland 38 54.28N 6.25W
Craignish, Loch Scotland 34 56.10N 5.32W
Crail Scotland 35 56.16N 2.38W
Crailsheim W. Germany 44 49.09N 10.06E
Craiova Romania 43 44.18N 23.46E
Cramlington England 35 55.06N 1.33W
Cranbourne England 27 51.27N 0.42W
Cranbrook Canada 90 49.29N 115.48W
Cranbrook England 29 51.06N 0.33E
Cranham England 27 51.33N 0.16E
Cranleigh England 29 51.08N 0.29W
Cranston U.S.A. 95 41.47N 71.27W
Crati r. Italy 43 39.43N 16.29E
Craughwell Rep. of Ire. 39 53.14N 8.44W
Crawford Scotland 35 55.28N 3.39W
Crawley England 29 51.07N 0.10W
Crays Hill town England 27 51.36N 0.30E
Creach Bheinn mtn. Scotland 34 56.40N 5.29W
Creag Meagaidh mtn. Scotland 37 56.57N 4.38W
Credenhill England 28 52.06N 2.49W
Crediton England 31 50.47N 3.39W
Cree r. Scotland 34 55.03N 4.35W
Creekmouth England 27 51.32N 0.06E
Cree L. Canada 92 57.20N 108.30W
Creeslough Rep. of Ire. 38 55.07N 7.55W
Creetown Scotland 34 54.54N 4.22W
Creggan N. Ireland 34 54.45N 7.02W
Creil France 40 49.16N 2.29E
Cremona Italy 42 45.08N 10.03E
Cres i. Yugo. 42 44.50N 14.20E
Crescent City U.S.A. 90 41.46N 124.13W
Crest France 40 44.44N 5.02E
Creston U.S.A. 91 41.04N 94.20W
Creswell England 33 53.16N 1.12W
Crete i. Greece 43 35.15N 25.00E
Crete, Sea of Med. Sea 43 36.00N 25.00E
Creus, Cabo Spain 41 42.20N 3.19E
Creuse r. France 40 47.00N 0.35E
Crewe England 32 53.06N 2.28W
Crewkerne England 28 50.53N 2.48W
Crianlarich Scotland 34 56.23N 4.37W
Criccieth Wales 30 52.55N 4.15W
Crickhowell Wales 30 51.52N 3.08W
Cricklade England 28 51.38N 1.50W
Crieff Scotland 35 56.23N 3.52W
Criffel mtn. Scotland 35 54.57N 3.38W
Crimea pen. U.S.S.R. 47 45.30N 34.00E
Crinan Scotland 34 56.06N 5.34W
Cristóbal Colón mtn. Colombia 97 10.53N 73.48W
Crna r. Yugo. 43 41.33N 21.58E
Croaghnameal mtn. Rep. of Ire. 38 54.40N 7.57W
Crockham Hill town England 27 51.14N 0.04E
Crocodile r. Transvaal R.S.A. 74 24.11S 26.48E
Crohy Head Rep. of Ire. 38 54.55N 8.28W
Cromarty Scotland 37 57.40N 4.02W
Cromarty Firth est. Scotland 37 57.41N 4.10W
Cromer England 33 52.56N 1.18E
Cromwell New Zealand 82 45.03S 169.14E
Crook England 32 54.43N 1.45W
Crooked I. Bahamas 97 22.45N 74.00W
Crookhaven Rep. of Ire. 39 51.29N 9.45W
Croom Rep. of Ire. 39 52.31N 8.43W
Crosby England 32 53.30N 3.02W
Crosby I.o.M. 32 54.11N 4.34W
Cross Fell mtn. England 32 54.43N 2.28W
Cross Gates Wales 30 52.17N 3.20W
Cross Hands Wales 31 51.48N 4.05W
Crossmolina Rep. of Ire. 38 54.06N 9.20W
Cross River d. Nigeria 71 5.45N 8.25E
Crotone Italy 43 39.05N 17.06E
Crouch r. England 29 51.37N 0.34E
Crowborough England 29 51.03N 0.09E
Crow Head Rep. of Ire. 39 51.35N 10.10W
Crowland England 29 52.41N 0.10W
Crowle England 33 53.36N 0.49W
Crowlin Is. Scotland 36 57.20N 5.50W
Crowsnest Pass Canada 90 49.40N 114.41W
Croxley Green England 27 51.39N 0.27W
Croyde England 31 51.07N 4.13W
Croydon England 27 51.23N 0.06W
Crozet Is. Indian Oc. 113 46.27S 52.00E
Cruden B. Scotland 37 57.24N 1.51W
Crumlin N. Ireland 34 54.38N 6.13W
Crummock Water l. England 32 54.33N 3.19W
Cruz, Cabo Cuba 97 19.52N 77.44W
Cruz Alta Brazil 103 28.38S 53.38W
Cruz del Eje Argentina 103 30.44S 64.45W

Cruzeiro Brazil **103** 22.33S 44.59W
Crymmych Arms Wales **30** 51.59N 4.40W
Cuamba Moçambique **73** 14.48S 36.32E
Cuando *r.* Africa **74** 18.30S 23.32E
Cuando-Cubango *d.* Angola **72** 16.00S 20.00E
Cuangar Angola **74** 17.34S 18.39E
Cuango *r. see* Kwango Zaïre **72**
Cuanza *r.* Angola **72** 9.20S 13.09E
Cuanza Norte *d.* Angola **72** 8.45S 15.00E
Cuanza Sul *d.* Angola **72** 11.00S 15.00E
Cuba C. America **97** 22.00N 79.00W
Cubango *r. see* Okavango Angola **72**
Cubia *r.* Angola **72** 16.00S 21.46E
Cuchi *r.* Angola **72** 15.23S 17.12E
Cuckfield England **29** 51.00N 0.08W
Cuckmere *r.* England **29** 50.45N 0.09E
Cúcuta Colombia **97** 7.55N 72.31W
Cuddalore India **59** 11.43N 79.46E
Cuenca Spain **41** 40.04N 2.07W
Cuenca, Serrania de *mts.* Spain **41** 40.25N 2.00W
Cuernavaca Mexico **96** 18.57N 99.15W
Cuffley England **27** 51.42N 0.06W
Cuiabá Brazil **103** 15.32S 56.05W
Cuilcagh Mtn. Rep. of Ire. **38** 54.12N 7.50W
Cuillin Hills Scotland **36** 57.12N 6.13W
Cuilo *r. see* Kwilu Zaïre **72**
Cuito *r.* Angola **72** 18.01S 20.50E
Culdaff Rep. of Ire. **34** 55.17N 7.10W
Culemborg Neth. **45** 51.57N 5.14E
Culgoa *r.* Australia **80** 29.54S 145.31E
Cullen Scotland **37** 57.41N 2.50W
Cullera Spain **41** 39.10N 0.15W
Cullin, Lough Rep. of Ire. **38** 53.59N 9.19W
Cullompton England **28** 50.52N 3.23W
Culm *r.* England **28** 50.46N 3.30W
Culross Scotland **35** 56.03N 3.35W
Culvain *mtn.* Scotland **36** 56.57N 5.16W
Culzean B. Scotland **34** 55.21N 4.50W
Cumaná Venezuela **97** 10.29N 64.12W
Cumberland U.S.A. **95** 39.40N 78.47W
Cumberland *r.* U.S.A. **91** 37.16N 88.25W
Cumberland, L. U.S.A. **91** 37.00N 85.00W
Cumberland Sd. Canada **93** 65.00N 65.30W
Cumbernauld Scotland **35** 55.57N 4.00W
Cumbraes *is.* Scotland **34** 55.45N 4.57W
Cumbria *d.* England **32** 54.30N 3.00W
Cumbrian Mts. England **32** 54.32N 3.05W
Cuminestown Scotland **37** 57.32N 2.20W
Cumnock Scotland **34** 55.27N 4.15W
Cunene *r.* Angola **72** 17.15S 11.50E
Cúneo Italy **40** 44.22N 7.32E
Cunnamulla Australia **80** 28.04S 145.40E
Cunninghame *f.* Scotland **34** 55.40N 4.30W
Cupar Scotland **35** 56.19N 3.01W
Curaçao *i.* Neth. Antilles **97** 12.15N 69.00W
Curaco *r.* Argentina **103** 38.45S 65.10W
Curiapo Venezuela **97** 8.33N 61.05W
Curitiba Brazil **103** 25.24S 49.16W
Currane, Lough Rep. of Ire. **39** 51.50N 10.07W
Curuzú Cuatiá Argentina **103** 29.50S 58.05W
Curvelo Brazil **103** 18.45S 44.27W
Curwood, Mt. U.S.A. **94** 46.42N 88.14W
Cushendall N. Ireland **34** 55.06N 6.05W
Cushendun N. Ireland **34** 55.07N 6.03W
Cuttack India **59** 20.26N 85.56E
Cuxhaven W. Germany **44** 53.52N 8.42E
Cuyahoga Falls *town* U.S.A. **94** 41.08N 81.27W
Cuyuni *r.* Guyana **97** 6.10N 58.50W
Cuzco Peru **102** 13.42S 72.10W
Čvrsnica *mtn.* Yugo. **43** 43.35N 17.33E
Cwmbran Wales **31** 51.39N 3.01W
Cyclades *is.* Greece **43** 37.00N 25.00E
Cyprus Asia **56** 35.00N 33.00E
Cyrenaica *f.* Libya **69** 31.00N 22.10E
Czechoslovakia Europe **44** 49.30N 15.00E
Czestochowa Poland **47** 50.49N 19.07E

D

Dabakala Ivory Coast **70** 8.19N 4.24W
Dabola Guinea **70** 10.48N 11.02W
Dacca Bangla. **58** 23.42N 90.22E
Dachau W. Germany **44** 48.15N 11.26E
Dachstein *mtn.* Austria **44** 47.29N 13.36E
Daer Resr. Scotland **35** 55.21N 3.37W
Daet Phil. **61** 14.07N 122.58E
Dagana Senegal **70** 16.28N 15.35W
Dagenham England **27** 51.33N 0.08E
Dagupan Phil. **61** 16.02N 120.21E
Daingean Rep. of Ire. **39** 53.18N 7.19W
Dakar Senegal **70** 14.38N 17.27W
Dakhla Oasis Egypt **56** 25.30N 29.00E
Dal *r.* Sweden **46** 60.38N 17.05E
Da Lat Vietnam **60** 11.56N 108.25E
Dalbeattie Scotland **35** 54.55N 3.49W
Dalby Australia **80** 27.11S 151.12E
Dalkeith Scotland **35** 55.54N 3.04W
Dallas U.S.A. **91** 32.47N 96.48W
Dalmally Scotland **34** 56.25N 4.58W
Dalmatia *f.* Yugo. **43** 43.30N 17.00E
Dalmellington Scotland **34** 55.19N 4.24W
Dalnerechensk U.S.S.R. **63** 45.55N 133.45E
Daloa Ivory Coast **70** 6.56N 6.28W
Dalry D. and G. Scotland **34** 55.07N 4.10W
Dalry Strath. Scotland **34** 55.43N 4.43W
Daltonganj India **58** 24.02N 84.07E
Dalton-in-Furness England **32** 54.10N 3.11W
Dalwhinnie Scotland **37** 56.56N 4.15W
Dama, Wadi *r.* Saudi Arabia **56** 27.04N 35.48E
Daman India **58** 20.25N 72.58E
Damanhûr Egypt **56** 31.03N 30.28E
Damar *i.* Indonesia **61** 7.10S 128.30E
Damascus Syria **56** 33.30N 36.19E
Damaturu Nigeria **71** 11.49N 11.50E
Damba Angola **72** 6.44S 15.17E
Damghan Iran **57** 36.09N 54.22E
Damh, Loch Scotland **36** 57.29N 5.33W
Damietta Egypt **56** 31.26N 31.48E
Dammam Saudi Arabia **57** 26.23N 50.08E
Damodar *r.* India **58** 22.55N 88.30E
Dampier Str. Pacific Oc. **61** 0.30S 130.50E
Danakil *f.* Ethiopia **69** 13.00N 41.00E
Da Nang Vietnam **60** 16.04N 108.14E
Danbury England **27** 51.44N 0.33E
Danbury U.S.A. **95** 41.24N 73.26W
Dande *r.* Angola **72** 8.30S 13.23E
Dandenong Australia **80** 37.59S 145.14E
Danforth U.S.A. **95** 45.42N 67.52W
Danli Honduras **96** 14.02N 86.30W
Dannevirke New Zealand **82** 40.12S 176.08E
Danube *r.* Europe **43** 45.26N 29.38E
Danube, Mouths of the *f.* Romania **43** 45.05N 29.45E
Danville Ill. U.S.A. **94** 40.09N 87.37W
Danville Va. U.S.A. **91** 36.34N 79.25W
Daran Iran **57** 33.00N 50.27E
Darbhanga India **58** 26.10N 85.54E
Dardanelles *str.* Turkey **43** 40.15N 26.30E
Darent *r.* England **27** 51.29N 0.13E
Dar es Salaam Tanzania **73** 6.51S 39.18E
Dar es Salaam *d.* Tanzania **73** 6.45S 39.10E
Darfur *mts.* Sudan **69** 12.30N 24.00E
Dargaville New Zealand **82** 35.57S 173.53E
Darhan Suma Mongolia **62** 49.34N 106.23E
Darien, G. of Colombia **97** 9.20N 77.00W
Darjeeling India **58** 27.02N 88.20E
Darling *r.* Australia **80** 34.05S 141.57E
Darling Downs Australia **80** 28.00S 149.45E
Darlington England **33** 54.33N 1.33W
Darmstadt W. Germany **44** 49.52N 8.30E
Darreh Gaz Iran **57** 37.22N 59.08E
Dart *r.* England **31** 50.24N 3.41W
Dartford England **27** 51.27N 0.14E
Dartmoor Forest *hills* England **31** 50.33N 3.55W
Dartmouth England **31** 50.21N 3.35W
Darton England **33** 53.36N 1.32W
Dartry Mts. Rep. of Ire. **38** 54.23N 8.25W
Darvel Scotland **34** 55.37N 4.17W
Darvel B. Malaysia **60** 4.40N 118.30E
Darwen England **32** 53.42N 2.29W
Darwin Australia **79** 12.23S 130.44E
Dasht *r.* Pakistan **57** 25.07N 61.45E
Dasht-e-Kavir *des.* Iran **57** 34.40N 55.00E
Dasht-e-Lut *des.* Iran **57** 31.30N 58.00E
Dashtiari Iran **57** 25.29N 61.15E
Dasht-i-Margo *des.* Afghan. **57** 30.45N 63.00E
Dasht-i-Zirreh *des.* Afghan. **57** 30.00N 62.00E
Datchet England **27** 51.30N 0.35W
Datia India **58** 25.41N 78.28E
Daugavpils U.S.S.R. **46** 55.52N 26.31E
Daulatabad Iran **57** 28.19N 56.40E
Daun W. Germany **45** 50.11N 6.50E
Dauphin Canada **90** 51.09N 100.05W
Dauphiné, Alpes du *mts.* France **40** 44.35N 5.45E
Davangere India **58** 14.30N 75.52E
Davao Phil. **61** 7.05N 125.38E
Davao G. Phil. **61** 6.30N 126.00E
Davenport U.S.A. **94** 41.32N 90.36W
Daventry England **28** 52.16N 1.10W
David Panamá **96** 8.26N 82.26W
Davis, Mt. U.S.A. **95** 39.47N 79.11W
Davis Str. N. America **93** 66.00N 58.00W
Davos Switz. **44** 46.47N 9.50E
Dawa Palma *r.* Ethiopia **73** 4.10N 42.05E
Dawley England **28** 52.40N 2.29W
Dawlish England **28** 50.34N 3.28W
Dawna Range *mts.* Asia **60** 16.10N 98.30E
Dawros Head Rep. of Ire. **38** 54.50N 8.35W
Dawson Canada **92** 64.04N 139.24W
Dawson Creek *town* Canada **92** 55.44N 120.15W
Dax France **40** 43.43N 1.03W
Dayton U.S.A. **94** 39.45N 84.10W
Daytona Beach *town* U.S.A. **91** 29.11N 81.01W
De Aar R.S.A. **74** 30.39S 24.00E
Dead Sea Jordan **56** 31.25N 35.30E
Deal England **29** 51.13N 1.25E
Deán Funes Argentina **103** 30.25S 64.22W
Dearborn U.S.A. **94** 42.18N 83.14W
Death Valley *f.* U.S.A. **90** 36.00N 116.45W
Deauville France **40** 49.21N 0.04E
Deben *r.* England **29** 52.06N 1.20E
Debenham England **29** 52.14N 1.10E
Debrecen Hungary **47** 47.30N 21.37E
Decatur Ill. U.S.A. **94** 39.51N 88.57W
Decatur Ind. U.S.A. **94** 40.50N 84.57W
Deccan *f.* India **58** 18.30N 77.30E
Děčin Czech. **44** 50.48N 14.15E
Dedza Malaŵi **73** 14.20S 34.24E
Dee *r.* Rep. of Ire. **38** 53.52N 6.21W
Dee *r.* D. and G. Scotland **35** 54.50N 4.05W
Dee *r.* Grampian Scotland **37** 57.07N 2.04W
Dee *r.* Wales **30** 53.13N 3.05W
Deel *r.* Mayo Rep. of Ire. **38** 54.06N 9.17W
Deepcut England **27** 51.19N 0.40W
Deeping Fen *f.* England **29** 52.45N 0.15W
Defiance U.S.A. **94** 41.17N 84.21W
Deh Bid Iran **57** 30.38N 53.12E
Dehra Dun India **59** 30.19N 78.00E
Deinze Belgium **45** 50.59N 3.32E
Deir-ez-Zor Syria **56** 35.20N 40.08E
Dej Romania **47** 47.08N 23.55E
Dekese Zaïre **72** 3.25S 21.24E
Delano U.S.A. **90** 35.45N 119.16W
Delaware *d.* U.S.A. **95** 39.00N 75.30W
Delaware *r.* U.S.A. **95** 39.15N 75.20W
Delaware B. U.S.A. **95** 39.00N 75.05W
Delft Neth. **45** 52.01N 4.23E
Delfzijl Neth. **45** 53.20N 6.56E
Delgado, C. Moçambique **73** 10.45S 40.38E
Delhi India **58** 28.40N 77.14E
Delicias Mexico **90** 28.10N 105.30W
Dellys Algeria **41** 36.57N 3.55E
Delmenhorst W. Germany **44** 53.03N 8.37E
De Long Str. U.S.S.R. **49** 70.00N 178.00E
Del Rio U.S.A. **90** 29.23N 100.56W
Delta U.S.A. **90** 39.22N 112.35W
Delvin Rep. of Ire. **38** 53.37N 7.06W
Demavend *mtn.* Iran **57** 35.47N 52.04E
Demba Zaïre **72** 5.28S 22.14E
Demer *r.* Belgium **45** 50.59N 4.42E
Demirkazik *mtn.* Turkey **56** 37.50N 35.08E
Denbigh Wales **30** 53.11N 3.25W
Den Burg Neth. **45** 53.03N 4.47E
Denby Dale *town* England **32** 53.35N 1.40W
Dendermonde Belgium **45** 51.01N 4.07E
Dendre *r.* Belgium **45** 51.01N 4.07E
Denham England **27** 51.35N 0.31W
Den Helder Neth. **45** 52.58N 4.46E
Denia Spain **41** 38.51N 0.07E
Deniliquin Australia **80** 35.33S 144.58E
Denizli Turkey **56** 37.46N 29.05E
Denmark Europe **46** 56.00N 10.00E
Denmark Str. Greenland/Iceland **106** 66.00N 25.00W
Denny Scotland **35** 56.02N 3.55W
Den Oever Neth. **45** 52.56N 5.01E
Denpasar Indonesia **60** 8.40S 115.14E
Denver U.S.A. **90** 39.45N 104.58W
Deo *r.* Cameroon **71** 8.33N 12.45E
Deogarh India **59** 21.22N 84.45E
Depew U.S.A. **95** 42.54N 78.41W
Deptford England **27** 51.29N 0.03W
Dera Ismail Khan Pakistan **58** 31.51N 70.56E
Derbent U.S.S.R. **57** 42.03N 48.18E
Derby Australia **79** 17.19S 123.38E
Derby England **33** 52.55N 1.28W
Derbyshire *d.* England **33** 52.55N 1.28W
Derg *r.* N. Ireland **38** 54.44N 7.27W
Derg, Lough Donegal Rep. of Ire. **38** 54.37N 7.55W
Derg, Lough Tipperary Rep. of Ire. **39** 52.57N 8.18W
Derna Libya **69** 32.45N 22.39E
Derravaragh, Lough Rep. of Ire. **38** 53.39N 7.23W
Derry *r.* Rep. of Ire. **39** 52.41N 6.40W
Derrynasaggart Mts. Rep. of Ire. **39** 51.58N 9.15W
Derryveagh Mts. Rep. of Ire. **38** 55.00N 8.07W
Dersingham England **33** 52.51N 0.30E
Dervaig Scotland **34** 56.35N 6.11W
Derwent *r.* Australia **80** 42.45S 147.15E
Derwent *r.* Cumbria England **32** 54.38N 3.34W
Derwent *r.* Derbys. England **33** 52.52N 1.19W
Derwent *r.* N. Yorks. England **33** 53.44N 0.57W
Derwent *r.* T. and W. England **32** 54.58N 1.40W
Derwent Water *l.* England **32** 54.35N 3.09W
Desborough England **28** 52.27N 0.50W
Des Moines U.S.A. **91** 41.35N 93.35W
Desna *r.* U.S.S.R. **47** 50.32N 30.37E
Dessau E. Germany **44** 51.51N 12.15E
Dessye Ethiopa **69** 11.05N 39.40E

Desvres France **29** 50.40N 1.50E
Detmold W. Germany **44** 51.56N 8.52E
Detroit U.S.A. **94** 42.23N 83.05W
Dett Rhodesia **74** 18.38S 26.50E
Deurne Belgium **45** 51.13N 4.26E
Deva Romania **43** 45.54N 22.55E
Deventer Neth. **45** 52.15N 6.10E
Deveron *r.* Scotland **37** 57.40N 2.30W
Devilsbit Mtn. Rep. of Ire. **39** 52.50N 7.55W
Devil's Bridge Wales **30** 52.23N 3.50W
Devils Lake *town* U.S.A. **90** 48.08N 98.50W
Devizes England **28** 51.21N 2.00W
Devon *d.* England **31** 50.50N 3.40W
Devon I. Canada **93** 75.00N 86.00W
Devonport Australia **80** 41.09S 146.16E
Devonport New Zealand **82** 36.49S 174.49E
Devrez *r.* Turkey **56** 41.07N 34.25E
Dewsbury England **32** 53.42N 1.38W
Dhahran Saudi Arabia **57** 26.18N 50.08E
Dhanbad India **58** 23.47N 86.32E
Dhaulagiri *mtn.* Nepal **58** 28.39N 83.28E
Dholpur India **58** 26.43N 77.54E
Dhubri India **58** 26.01N 90.00E
Dhulia India **58** 20.52N 74.50E
Dibaya Zaïre **72** 6.31S 22.57E
Dibbagh, Jebel *mtn.* Saudi Arabia **56** 27.51N 35.43E
Dibrugarh India **59** 27.29N 94.56E
Dickinson U.S.A. **90** 46.54N 102.48W
Didcot England **28** 51.36N 1.14W
Die France **40** 44.45N 5.23E
Diekirch Lux. **45** 49.52N 6.10E
Dieppe France **40** 49.55N 1.05E
Dieren Neth. **45** 52.03N 6.06E
Diest Belgium **45** 50.59N 5.03E
Dieuze France **44** 48.49N 6.43E
Digby Canada **91** 44.37N 65.47W
Digne France **40** 44.05N 6.14E
Digoel *r.* Indonesia **61** 7.10S 139.08E
Dijle *r.* Belgium **45** 51.02N 4.25E
Dijon France **40** 47.20N 5.02E
Dikili Turkey **43** 39.05N 26.52E
Dikwa Nigeria **71** 12.01N 13.55E
Dili Port. Timor **61** 8.35S 125.35E
Dillon U.S.A. **90** 45.14N 112.38W
Dilolo Zaïre **72** 10.39S 22.20E
Dimbelenge Zaïre **72** 5.32S 23.04E
Dimbokro Ivory Coast **70** 6.43N 4.46W
Dîmbovita *r.* Romania **43** 44.13N 26.22E
Dimitrovgrad Bulgaria **43** 42.01N 25.34E
Dimitrovo Bulgaria **43** 42.35N 23.03E
Dinagat *i.* Phil. **61** 10.15N 125.30E
Dinajapur Bangla. **58** 25.38N 88.44E
Dinan France **40** 48.27N 2.02W
Dinant Belgium **45** 50.16N 4.55E
Dinaric Alps *mts.* Yugo. **43** 44.00N 16.30E
Dinas Head Wales **30** 52.03N 4.50W
Dinas Mawddwy Wales **30** 52.44N 3.41W
Dingle Rep. of Ire. **39** 52.09N 10.17W
Dingle B. Rep. of Ire. **39** 52.05N 10.12W
Dingwall Scotland **37** 57.35N 4.26W
Diourbel Senegal **70** 14.30N 16.10W
Dipolog Phil. **61** 8.34N 123.28E
Dippin Head Scotland **34** 55.27N 5.05W
Diredawa Ethiopia **69** 9.35N 41.50E
Dirranbandi Australia **80** 28.35S 148.10E
Disappointment, L. Australia **79** 23.30S 122.55E
Disaster B. Australia **80** 37.20S 149.58E
Disko I. Greenland **93** 69.45N 53.00W
Disna *r.* U.S.S.R. **46** 55.30N 28.20E
Diss England **29** 52.23N 1.06E
District of Columbia *d.* U.S.A. **95** 38.55N 77.00W
Ditchling Beacon *hill* England **29** 50.55N 0.08W
Diu India **58** 20.41N 71.03E
Divrigi Turkey **56** 39.23N 38.06E
Dixmude Belgium **45** 51.01N 2.52E
Dixon Entrance *str.* Canada **92** 54.10N 133.30W
Diyala *r.* Iraq **57** 33.13N 44.33E
Diyarbakir Turkey **56** 37.55N 40.14E
Dizful Iran **57** 32.24N 48.27E
Dja *r.* Cameroon **72** 1.38N 16.03E
Djado Niger **71** 21.00N 12.20E
Djado Plateau *f.* Niger **71** 22.00N 12.30E
Djailolo Indonesia **61** 1.05N 127.29E
Djajapura Indonesia **61** 2.28S 160.38E
Djajawidjaja Mts. Asia **61** 4.20S 139.10E
Djambala Congo **72** 2.33S 14.38E
Djelfa Algeria **68** 34.43N 3.14E
Djenne Mali **70** 13.55N 4.31W
Djibouti F.T.A.I. **69** 11.35N 43.11E
Djolu Zaïre **72** 0.35N 22.28E
Djouah *r.* Gabon **72** 1.16N 13.12E
Djougou Benin **71** 9.40N 1.47E
Djugu Zaïre **73** 1.55N 30.31E
Dneprodzerzhinsk U.S.S.R. **47** 48.30N 34.37E
Dnepropetrovsk U.S.S.R. **47** 48.29N 35.00E
Dnestr *r.* U.S.S.R. **47** 46.21N 30.20E
Dnieper *r.* U.S.S.R. **47** 46.30N 32.25E
Dno U.S.S.R. **47** 57.50N 30.00E
Döbeln E. Germany **44** 51.07N 13.07E
Doboj Yugo. **43** 44.44N 18.02E
Dobruja *f.* Romania **47** 44.30N 28.15E
Docking England **33** 52.55N 0.39E
Dodecanese *is.* Greece **43** 37.00N 27.00E
Dodge City U.S.A. **90** 37.45N 100.02W
Dodman Pt. England **31** 50.13N 4.48W
Dodoma Tanzania **73** 6.10S 35.40E
Dodoma *d.* Tanzania **73** 6.00S 36.00E
Doetinchem Neth. **45** 51.57N 6.17E
Dog L. Canada **94** 48.45N 89.30W
Doha Qatar **57** 25.15N 51.34E
Dokkum Neth. **45** 53.20N 6.00E
Dolbeau Canada **95** 48.52N 72.15W
Dôle France **40** 47.05N 5.30E
Dolgellau Wales **30** 52.44N 3.53W
Dolisie Congo **72** 4.09S 12.40E
Dollar Scotland **35** 56.09N 3.41W
Dollart *b.* W. Germany **45** 53.20N 7.10E
Dolo Ethiopia **73** 4.11N 42.03E
Dolomites *mts.* Italy **44** 46.25N 11.50E
Dolores Argentina **103** 36.23S 57.44W
Dolphin and Union Str. Canada **92** 69.20N 118.00W
Dombås Norway **46** 62.05N 9.07E
Dombe Grande Angola **72** 13.00S 13.06E
Dominica C. America **97** 15.30N 61.30W
Dominican Republic C. America **97** 18.00N 70.00W
Dommel *r.* Neth. **45** 51.44N 5.17E
Don *r.* England **33** 53.41N 0.50W
Don *r.* Scotland **37** 57.10N 2.05W
Don *r.* U.S.S.R. **47** 47.06N 39.16E
Donaghadee N. Ireland **34** 54.39N 5.33W
Donald Australia **80** 36.25S 143.04E
Donauworth W. Germany **44** 48.44N 10.48E
Don Benito Spain **41** 38.57N 5.52W
Doncaster England **33** 53.31N 1.09W
Dondo Angola **72** 9.40S 14.25E
Donegal Rep. of Ire. **38** 54.39N 8.06W
Donegal *d.* Rep. of Ire. **38** 54.52N 8.00W
Donegal B. Rep. of Ire. **38** 54.32N 8.18W
Donegal Pt. Rep. of Ire. **39** 52.43N 9.38W
Donets *r.* U.S.S.R. **47** 47.35N 40.55E
Donets Basin *f.* U.S.S.R. **47** 48.20N 38.15E
Donetsk U.S.S.R. **47** 48.00N 37.50E
Donga *r.* Nigeria **71** 8.20N 10.00E
Donggala Indonesia **60** 0.48S 119.45E
Dong Hoi Vietnam **60** 17.32N 106.35E
Dongkala Indonesia **61** 0.12N 120.07E
Dongola Sudan **69** 19.10N 30.27E
Dongou Congo **72** 2.05N 18.00E
Donington England **33** 52.55N 0.12W
Dooega Head Rep. of Ire. **38** 53.55N 10.03W
Doon *r.* Scotland **34** 55.26N 4.38W
Doon, Loch Scotland **34** 55.15N 4.23W
Doonbeg *r.* Rep. of Ire. **39** 52.44N 9.32W
Dora Baltea *r.* Italy **40** 45.08N 8.32E
Dora Riparia *r.* Italy **40** 45.07N 7.45E
Dorchester England **28** 50.52N 2.28W
Dordogne *r.* France **40** 45.03N 0.34W
Dordrecht Neth. **45** 51.48N 4.40E
Dordrecht R.S.A. **74** 31.22S 27.03E
Dore, Mont *mtn.* France **40** 45.32N 2.49E
Dores Scotland **37** 57.23N 4.20W
Dori U. Volta **70** 14.03N 0.02W
Dorking England **27** 51.14N 0.20W
Dormans Land *town* England **27** 51.10N 0.02E
Dornbirn Austria **44** 47.25N 9.46E
Dornie Scotland **36** 57.16N 5.31W
Dornoch Scotland **37** 57.52N 4.02W
Dornoch Firth *est.* Scotland **37** 57.50N 4.04W
Dornum W. Germany **45** 53.39N 7.26E
Dörpen W. Germany **45** 52.58N 7.20E
Dorset *d.* England **28** 50.48N 2.25W
Dorsten W. Germany **45** 51.38N 6.58E
Dortmund W. Germany **45** 51.32N 7.27E
Dortmund-Ems Canal W. Germany **45** 52.20N 7.30E
Doshakh *mtn.* Afghan. **57** 34.04N 61.28E
Dosso Niger **71** 13.03N 3.10E
Dothan U.S.A. **91** 31.12N 85.25W
Douai France **45** 50.22N 3.05E
Douala Cameroon **72** 4.05N 9.47E
Douarnenez France **40** 48.05N 4.20W
Doubs *r.* France **40** 46.57N 5.03E
Doubtless B. New Zealand **82** 35.10S 173.30E
Douentza Mali **70** 14.58N 2.48W
Dough Mtn. Rep. of Ire. **38** 54.20N 8.07W
Douglas I.o.M. **32** 54.09N 4.29W
Douglas Scotland **35** 55.33N 3.51W
Doulus Head Rep. of Ire. **39** 51.57N 10.19W
Doumé Cameroon **72** 4.16N 13.30E
Doumé *r.* Cameroon **72** 4.12N 14.35E
Doune Scotland **35** 56.11N 4.04W
Dounreay Scotland **37** 58.35N 3.42W
Douro *r.* Portugal **41** 41.10N 8.40W
Dove *r.* Derbys. England **32** 52.50N 1.35W
Dove *r.* N. Yorks. England **33** 54.11N 0.55W
Dover England **29** 51.07N 1.19E
Dover U.S.A. **95** 39.10N 75.32W
Dover, Str. of U.K./France **29** 51.00N 1.30E
Dovey *r.* Wales **30** 52.33N 3.56W
Dovrefjell *mts.* Norway **46** 62.05N 9.30E
Dowa Malaŵi **73** 13.40S 33.55E
Down *d.* N. Ireland **34** 54.20N 6.00W
Downham Market England **29** 52.36N 0.22E
Downpatrick N. Ireland **38** 54.21N 5.43W
Downpatrick Head Rep. of Ire. **38** 54.20N 9.22W
Downton England **28** 51.00N 1.44W
Dowra Rep. of Ire. **38** 54.11N 8.02W
Dra, Wadi Morocco **68** 28.40N 11.06W
Drachten Neth. **45** 53.05N 6.06E
Dragoman Pass Bulgaria/Yugo. **43** 42.56N 22.52E
Dragon's Mouth *str.* Trinidad **97** 11.20N 61.00W
Draguignan France **40** 43.32N 6.28E
Drakensberge *mts.* R.S.A. **74** 30.00S 29.00E
Dráma Greece **43** 41.09N 24.11E
Drammen Norway **46** 59.45N 10.15E
Draperstown N. Ireland **34** 54.48N 6.46W
Drau *r.* Austria **43** 46.20N 16.45E
Drava *r.* Yugo. **43** 45.34N 18.56E
Drenthe *d.* Neth. **45** 52.52N 6.30E
Dresden E. Germany **44** 51.03N 13.45E
Dreux France **40** 48.44N 1.23E
Drimnin Scotland **34** 56.37N 5.59W
Drin *r.* Albania **43** 41.45N 19.34E
Drina *r.* Yugo. **43** 44.53N 19.20E
Drogheda Rep. of Ire. **38** 53.43N 6.23W
Droichead Nua Rep. of Ire. **39** 53.11N 6.48W
Droitwich England **28** 52.16N 2.10W
Dromore Tyrone N. Ireland **38** 54.31N 7.28W
Dronfield England **33** 53.18N 1.29W
Dronne *r.* France **40** 44.55N 0.15W
Drumbeg Scotland **36** 58.14N 5.13W
Drumcollogher Rep. of Ire. **39** 52.20N 8.55W
Drumcondra Rep. of Ire. **38** 53.50N 6.40W
Drumheller Canada **90** 51.28N 112.40W
Drum Hills Rep. of Ire. **39** 52.03N 7.42W
Drumlish Rep. of Ire. **38** 53.50N 7.46W
Drummondville Canada **95** 45.52N 72.30W
Drummore Scotland **34** 54.41N 4.54W
Drumnadrochit Scotland **37** 57.20N 4.30W
Drumshanbo Rep. of Ire. **38** 54.03N 8.02W
Druz, Jebel ed *mts.* Syria **56** 32.42N 36.42E
Drymen Scotland **34** 56.04N 4.27W
Dschang Cameroon **72** 5.25N 10.02E
Dua *r.* Zaïre **72** 3.12N 20.55E
Duart Pt. Scotland **34** 56.27N 5.39W
Dubai U.A.E. **57** 25.13N 55.17E
Dubawnt *r.* Canada **93** 62.50N 102.00W
Dubawnt L. Canada **93** 62.50N 102.00W
Dubbo Australia **80** 32.16S 148.41E
Dubh Artach *i.* Scotland **34** 56.08N 6.38W
Dubica Yugo. **43** 45.11N 16.50E
Dublin Rep. of Ire. **38** 53.21N 6.18W
Dublin *d.* Rep. of Ire. **38** 53.20N 6.18W
Dublin B. Rep. of Ire. **38** 53.20N 6.09W
Du Bois U.S.A. **95** 41.06N 78.46W
Dubrovnik Yugo. **43** 42.40N 18.07E
Dubuque U.S.A. **94** 42.31N 90.41W
Duddington England **29** 52.36N 0.32W
Dudinka U.S.S.R. **49** 69.27N 86.13E
Dudley England **28** 52.30N 2.05W
Dudweiler W. Germany **44** 49.16N 7.03E
Duero *r. see* Douro Spain **41**
Duffield England **33** 52.59N 1.30W
Dufftown Scotland **37** 57.27N 3.09W
Dugi Otok *i.* Yugo. **42** 44.04N 15.00E
Duich, L. Scotland **36** 57.15N 5.30W
Duisburg W. Germany **45** 51.26N 6.45E
Duiveland *i.* Neth. **45** 51.39N 4.00E
Dukhan Qatar **57** 25.24N 50.47E
Dukhtaran *mtn.* Iran **57** 30.39N 60.38E
Dulawan Phil. **61** 7.02N 124.30E
Duleek Rep. of Ire. **38** 53.39N 6.24W
Dülmen W. Germany **45** 51.49N 7.17E
Duluth U.S.A. **94** 46.45N 92.10W
Dulverton England **31** 51.02N 3.33W
Dumbarton Scotland **34** 55.57N 4.35W
Dum-Dum India **58** 22.37N 88.25E
Dumfries Scotland **35** 55.04N 3.37W
Dumfries and Galloway *d.* Scotland **35** 55.05N 3.40W
Dumka India **58** 24.17N 87.15E
Dunany Pt. Rep. of Ire. **38** 53.51N 6.15W
Dunbar Scotland **35** 56.00N 2.31W
Dunbeath Scotland **37** 58.14N 3.26W
Dunbeg Rep. of Ire. **38** 55.04N 8.19W
Dunblane Scotland **35** 56.12N 3.59W
Dunboyne Rep. of Ire. **38** 53.26N 6.30W
Duncannon Rep. of Ire. **39** 52.14N 6.57W
Duncansby Head Scotland **37** 58.39N 3.01W
Dunchurch England **28** 52.21N 1.19W

Dundalk Rep. of Ire. **38** 54.01N 6.25W
Dundalk B. Rep. of Ire. **38** 53.55N 6.17W
Dundee R.S.A. **74** 28.10S 30.15E
Dundee Scotland **35** 56.28N 3.00W
Dundrum N. Ireland **38** 54.16N 5.51W
Dundrum Rep. of Ire. **38** 53.18N 6.16W
Dundrum B. N. Ireland **38** 54.12N 5.46W
Dunedin New Zealand **82** 45.52S 170.30E
Dunfermline Scotland **35** 56.04N 3.29W
Dungannon N. Ireland **34** 54.31N 6.47W
Dungarvan Rep. of Ire. **39** 52.06N 7.39W
Dungarvan Harbour *est.* Rep. of Ire. **39** 52.05N 7.36W
Dungeness *c.* England **29** 50.55N 0.58E
Dungiven N. Ireland **34** 54.56N 6.56W
Dungloe Rep. of Ire. **38** 54.57N 8.22W
Dungourney Rep. of Ire. **39** 51.58N 8.06W
Dungu Zaïre **73** 3.40N 28.40E
Dunholme England **33** 53.18N 0.29W
Dunipace Scotland **35** 56.02N 3.45W
Dunkeld Scotland **35** 56.34N 3.36W
Dunkirk France **29** 51.02N 2.23E
Dunkirk U.S.A. **95** 42.29N 79.21W
Dunkwa Central Ghana **70** 5.59N 1.45W
Dún Laoghaire Rep. of Ire. **38** 53.17N 6.09W
Dunlavin Rep. of Ire. **39** 53.04N 6.42W
Dunleer Rep. of Ire. **38** 53.49N 6.24W
Dunmahon Rep. of Ire. **39** 52.09N 7.23W
Dunmanus B. Rep. of Ire. **39** 51.33N 9.45W
Dunmanway Rep. of Ire. **39** 51.43N 9.08W
Dunmore Rep. of Ire. **38** 53.38N 8.45W
Dunmore East Rep. of Ire. **39** 52.10N 7.00W
Dunnet Scotland **37** 58.37N 3.21W
Dunnet B. Scotland **37** 58.38N 3.25W
Dunnet Head Scotland **37** 58.40N 3.23W
Dunoon Scotland **34** 55.57N 4.57W
Dun Rig *mtn.* Scotland **35** 55.34N 3.11W
Duns Scotland **35** 55.47N 2.20W
Dunscore Scotland **35** 55.08N 3.47W
Dunshaughlin Rep. of Ire. **38** 53.30N 6.34W
Dunstable England **29** 51.53N 0.32W
Dunster England **28** 51.11N 3.28W
Dunston Mts. New Zealand **82** 44.45S 169.45E
Dunvegan Scotland **36** 57.26N 6.35W
Dunvegan, Loch Scotland **36** 57.30N 6.40W
Dunvegan Head Scotland **36** 57.31N 6.43W
Duque de Bragança Angola **72** 9.06S 16.11E
Durance *r.* France **40** 43.55N 4.48E
Durango Mexico **96** 24.01N 104.00W
Durango *d.* Mexico **96** 24.01N 104.00W
Durazno Uruguay **103** 33.22S 56.31W
Durban R.S.A. **74** 29.53S 31.00E
Düren W. Germany **45** 50.48N 6.30E
Durham England **33** 54.47N 1.34W
Durham *d.* England **32** 54.42N 1.45W
Durlston Head *c.* England **28** 50.35N 1.58W
Durmitor *mtn.* Yugo. **43** 43.08N 19.03E
Durness Scotland **37** 58.33N 4.45W
Durrës Albania **43** 41.19N 19.27E
Durrow Rep. of Ire. **39** 52.51N 7.25W
Dursey Head Rep. of Ire. **39** 51.35N 10.15W
Dursey I. Rep. of Ire. **39** 51.36N 10.12W
Dursley England **28** 51.41N 2.21W
D'Urville I. New Zealand **82** 40.45S 173.50E
Dushanbe U.S.S.R. **62** 38.38N 68.51E
Düsseldorf W. Germany **45** 51.13N 6.47E
Dvina *r.* U.S.S.R. **46** 57.03N 24.00E
Dyce Scotland **37** 57.12N 2.11W
Dyer, C. Canada **93** 67.45N 61.45W
Dyérem *r.* Cameroon **71** 6.36N 13.10E
Dyfed *d.* Wales **30** 52.00N 4.17W
Dykh Tau *mtn.* U.S.S.R. **47** 43.04N 43.10E
Dymchurch England **29** 51.02N 1.00E
Dyulty *mtn.* U.S.S.R. **57** 41.55N 46.52E
Dzerzhinsk R.S.F.S.R. U.S.S.R. **47** 56.15N 43.30E
Dzerzhinsk White Russia S.S.R. U.S.S.R. **47** 53.40N 27.01E
Dzhambul U.S.S.R. **62** 42.50N 71.25E
Dzhankoi U.S.S.R. **47** 45.40N 34.30E
Dzhugdzhur Range *mts.* U.S.S.R. **49** 57.30N 138.00E
Dzungaria *f.* Asia **62** 44.20N 86.30E

E

Eabamet L. Canada **91** 51.20N 87.30W
Eagle Mtn. U.S.A. **94** 47.50N 90.42W
Eagle Pass *town* U.S.A. **90** 28.44N 100.31W
Eagles Hill Rep. of Ire. **39** 51.48N 10.04W
Ealing England **27** 51.31N 0.20W
Earby England **32** 53.55N 2.08W
Earn *r.* Scotland **35** 56.21N 3.18W
Earn, Loch Scotland **34** 56.23N 4.12W
Easington Durham England **33** 54.47N 1.21W
Easington Humber. England **33** 53.39N 0.08E
Easingwold England **33** 54.08N 1.11W
Easky Rep. of Ire. **38** 54.17N 8.58W
East Anglian Heights *hills* England **29** 52.03N 0.15E
East Barnet England **27** 51.39N 0.09W
Eastbourne England **29** 50.46N 0.18E
Eastbury England **27** 51.36N 0.24W
East C. New Zealand **82** 37.45S 178.30E
East Chicago U.S.A. **94** 41.40N 87.32W
East China Sea Asia **63** 29.00N 125.00E
Eastcote England **27** 51.35N 0.24W
East Dereham England **29** 52.40N 0.57E
Easter I. Pacific Oc. **106** 29.00S 99.00W
Eastern *d.* Ghana **70** 6.20N 0.45W
Eastern *d.* Kenya **73** 0.00 38.00E
Eastern Desert Egypt **56** 28.15N 31.55E
Eastern Ghats *mts.* India **59** 16.30N 80.30E
Eastern Hajar *mts.* Oman **57** 22.45N 58.45E
Eastern Sayan *mts.* U.S.S.R. **49** 53.30N 98.00E
Easter Ross *f.* Scotland **37** 57.46N 4.25W
East European Plain *f.* Europe **47** 57.30N 35.30E
East Flevoland *f.* Neth. **45** 52.30N 5.40E
East Frisian Is. W. Germany **45** 53.45N 7.00E
East Germany Europe **44** 52.15N 12.30E
East Grinstead England **29** 51.08N 0.01W
East Ham England **27** 51.32N 0.04E
East Hartford U.S.A. **95** 41.46N 72.38W
East Horsley England **27** 51.16N 0.26W
East Ilsley England **28** 51.33N 1.15W
Eastington England **28** 51.44N 2.19W
East Kilbride Scotland **34** 55.46N 4.09W
East Lansing U.S.A. **94** 42.45N 84.30W
Eastleigh England **28** 50.58N 1.21W
East Linton Scotland **35** 55.59N 2.39W
East Loch Roag Scotland **36** 58.16N 6.48W
East Loch Tarbert Scotland **36** 57.52N 6.43W
East London R.S.A. **74** 33.00S 27.54E
Eastmain Canada **93** 52.10N 78.30W
Eastmain *r.* Canada **93** 52.10N 78.30W
East Malaysia *d.* Malaysia **60** 4.00N 114.00E
East Markham England **33** 53.16N 0.53W
East Moor *hills* England **33** 53.10N 1.35W
Easton U.S.A. **95** 40.41N 75.13W
East Orange U.S.A. **95** 40.46N 74.14W
East Retford England **33** 53.19N 0.55W
East St. Louis U.S.A. **94** 38.34N 90.04W
East Schelde *est.* Neth. **45** 51.35N 3.57E
East Siberian Sea U.S.S.R. **49** 73.00N 160.00E
East Sussex *d.* England **29** 50.56N 0.12E
East Vlieland Neth. **45** 53.18N 5.04E
Eastwood England **33** 53.02N 1.17W
Eau Claire U.S.A. **94** 44.50N 91.30W
Eauripik *is.* Asia **61** 6.42N 143.04E
Ebbw Vale Wales **28** 51.47N 3.12W
Eberswalde E. Germany **44** 52.50N 13.50E
Ebi Nor *l.* China **62** 45.00N 83.00E
Ebola *r.* Zaïre **72** 3.12N 21.00E
Ebolowa Cameroon **72** 2.56N 11.11E
Ebro *r.* Spain **41** 42.50N 3.59W
Ecclefechan Scotland **35** 55.03N 3.18W
Eccles England **32** 53.29N 2.20W
Eccleshall England **32** 52.52N 2.14W
Echternach Lux. **45** 49.49N 6.25E
Echuca Australia **80** 36.10S 144.20E
Ecija Spain **41** 37.33N 5.04W
Ecuador S. America **102** 2.00S 79.00W
Edam Neth. **45** 52.30N 5.02E
Eday *i.* Scotland **37** 59.11N 2.47W
Ed Damer Sudan **69** 17.37N 33.59E
Eddleston Scotland **35** 55.43N 3.13W
Eddrachillis B. Scotland **36** 58.17N 5.15W
Eddystone *i.* England **31** 50.12N 4.15W
Eddystone Pt. Australia **80** 40.58S 148.12E
Ede Neth. **45** 52.03N 5.40E
Edea Cameroon **72** 3.47N 10.15E
Eden Australia **80** 37.04S 149.54E
Eden *r.* Cumbria England **35** 54.57N 3.02W
Eden *r.* Kent England **27** 51.12N 0.10E
Eden *r.* Scotland **35** 56.22N 2.52W
Edenbridge England **27** 51.12N 0.04E
Edenderry Rep. of Ire. **38** 53.21N 7.05W
Eden Park England **27** 51.23N 0.01W
Ederny N. Ireland **38** 54.32N 7.40W
Edge Hill England **28** 52.08N 1.30W
Edgeworthstown Rep. of Ire. **38** 53.42N 7.38W
Edgware England **27** 51.37N 0.17W
Edhessa Greece **43** 40.47N 22.03E
Edinburgh Scotland **35** 55.57N 3.13W
Edirne Turkey **43** 41.40N 26.35E
Edmonton Canada **92** 53.34N 113.25W
Edmonton England **27** 51.37N 0.02W
Edmundston Canada **95** 47.22N 68.20W
Edremit Turkey **43** 39.35N 27.02E
Edsin Gol *r.* China **62** 42.15N 101.03E
Edwards Plateau *f.* U.S.A. **90** 30.30N 100.30W
Edzell Scotland **37** 56.49N 2.40W
Eeklo Belgium **45** 51.11N 3.34E
Effingham U.S.A. **94** 39.07N 88.33W
Egersund Norway **46** 58.27N 6.01E
Egham England **27** 51.26N 0.34W
Egilsay *i.* Scotland **37** 59.09N 2.56W
Eglington N. Ireland **34** 55.03N 7.10W
Egmont, Mt. New Zealand **82** 39.20S 174.05E
Egremont England **32** 54.28N 3.33W
Eğridir Turkey **56** 37.52N 30.51E
Eğridir L. Turkey **56** 38.04N 30.55E
Egypt Africa **56** 27.00N 29.00E
Eibar Spain **41** 43.11N 2.28W
Eifel *f.* W. Germany **45** 50.10N 6.45E
Eigg *i.* Scotland **36** 56.53N 6.09W
Eigg, Sd. of Scotland **36** 56.51N 6.11W
Eighty Mile Beach *f.* Australia **79** 19.00S 121.00E
Eil, Loch Scotland **36** 56.51N 5.12W
Eilat Israel **56** 29.33N 34.56E
Eildon Resr. Australia **80** 37.10S 146.00E
Eindhoven Neth. **45** 51.26N 5.30E
Eisenach E. Germany **44** 50.59N 10.19E
Eisenhut *mtn.* Austria **44** 47.00N 13.45E
Eisenhüttenstadt E. Germany **44** 52.09N 14.41E
Eishort, Loch Scotland **36** 57.09N 5.58W
Eisleben E. Germany **44** 51.32N 11.33E
Eitorf W. Germany **45** 50.46N 7.27E
Ekeia *r.* Congo **72** 1.40N 16.05E
Eksjo Sweden **46** 57.40N 15.00E
El Aaiún W. Sahara **68** 27.10N 13.11W
El Agheila Libya **68** 30.15N 19.12E
El Alamein Egypt **56** 30.50N 28.57E
Elands *r.* Transvaal R.S.A. **74** 24.55S 29.20E
El'Arish Egypt **56** 31.08N 33.48E
El'Arish, Wadi *r.* Egypt **56** 31.09N 33.49E
El Asnam Algeria **41** 36.20N 1.30E
Elâziğ Turkey **56** 38.41N 39.14E
Elba *i.* Italy **42** 42.47N 10.17E
El Banco Colombia **97** 9.04N 73.59W
Elbasan Albania **43** 41.07N 20.04E
Elbe *r.* W. Germany **44** 53.33N 10.00E
Elbert, Mt. U.S.A. **90** 39.05N 106.27W
Elbeuf France **40** 49.17N 1.01E
Elbistan Turkey **56** 38.14N 37.11E
Elblag Poland **47** 54.10N 19.25E
Elbrus *mtn.* U.S.S.R. **47** 43.21N 42.29E
Elburg Neth. **45** 52.27N 5.50E
Elburz Mts. Iran **57** 36.00N 52.30E
El Cardon Venezuela **97** 11.24N 70.09W
Elche Spain **41** 38.16N 0.41W
Elde *r.* E. Germany **44** 53.17N 12.40E
Eldorado Argentina **103** 26.28S 54.43W
Eldoret Kenya **73** 0.31N 35.17E
Electrostal U.S.S.R. **47** 55.46N 38.30E
Elephant Butte Resr. U.S.A. **90** 33.25N 107.10W
El Escorial Spain **41** 40.34N 4.08W
Eleuthera I. Bahamas **97** 25.00N 76.00W
El Faiyûm Egypt **56** 29.19N 30.50E
El Fasher Sudan **69** 13.37N 25.22E
El Fekka, Wadi *r.* Tunisia **42** 35.25N 9.40E
El Ferrol Spain **41** 43.29N 8.14W
Elgin Scotland **37** 57.39N 3.20W
Elgin U.S.A. **94** 42.03N 88.19W
El Giza Egypt **56** 30.01N 31.12E
Elgol Scotland **36** 57.09N 6.07W
El Goléa Algeria **68** 30.35N 2.51E
Elgon, Mt. Kenya/Uganda **73** 1.07N 34.35E
El Hamad *des.* Asia **56** 31.45N 39.00E
El Hatob, Wadi *r.* Tunisia **42** 35.25N 9.40E
Elie and Earlsferry Scotland **35** 56.11N 2.50W
Elista U.S.S.R. **47** 46.18N 44.14E
Elizabeth U.S.A. **95** 40.40N 74.13W
El Jauf Libya **69** 24.09N 23.19E
El Khârga Egypt **56** 25.27N 30.32E
Elkhart U.S.A. **94** 41.52N 85.56W
Elkhovo Bulgaria **43** 42.10N 26.35E
Elkins U.S.A. **94** 38.56N 79.53W
Elk Lake *town* Canada **94** 47.44N 80.21W
Elko U.S.A. **90** 40.50N 115.46W
Elland England **32** 53.41N 1.49W
Ellen *r.* England **32** 54.42N 3.30W
Ellen, Mt. U.S.A. **90** 38.06N 110.50W
Ellesmere England **32** 52.55N 2.53W
Ellesmere I. Canada **93** 78.00N 82.00W
Ellesmere Port England **32** 53.17N 2.55W
Ellon Scotland **37** 57.22N 2.05W
El Loz, Jebel *mtn.* Saudi Arabia **56** 28.40N 35.20E
Ellsworth U.S.A. **95** 44.34N 68.24W
El Mahalla el Kubra Egypt **56** 30.59N 31.12E
Elmali Turkey **56** 36.43N 29.56E
El Mansûra Egypt **56** 31.03N 31.23E
El Minya Egypt **56** 28.06N 30.45E
Elmira U.S.A. **95** 42.06N 76.50W
Elmshorn W. Germany **44** 53.46N 9.40E
El Muglad Sudan **69** 11.01N 27.50E
El Natrûn, Wadi *f.* Egypt **56** 30.25N 30.18E
El Obeid Sudan **69** 13.11N 30.10E
Eloy U.S.A. **90** 32.45N 111.33W
El Paso U.S.A. **90** 31.45N 106.30W

Elphin Rep. of Ire. **38** 53.50N 8.11W
El Qantara Egypt **56** 30.52N 32.20E
El Qasr Egypt **56** 25.43N 28.54E
El Qatrun Libya **68** 24.55N 14.38E
El Real Panamá **97** 8.06N 77.42W
El Salvador C. America **96** 13.30N 89.00W
Elstead England **27** 51.11N 0.43W
Elstree England **27** 51.39N 0.18W
Eltham England **27** 51.27N 0.04E
El Tigre Venezuela **97** 8.44N 64.18W
El Tîh, Plateau of Egypt **56** 28.50N 34.00E
Elvas Portugal **41** 38.53N 7.10W
Elverum Norway **46** 60.54N 11.33E
El Wak Kenya **73** 2.45N 40.52E
Elwy *r.* Wales **30** 53.17N 3.27W
Ely England **29** 52.24N 0.16E
Ely U.S.A. **94** 47.53N 91.52W
Elyria U.S.A. **94** 41.22N 82.06W
Emba *r.* U.S.S.R. **48** 46.40N 53.30E
Embarcación Argentina **103** 23.15S 64.05W
Embleton England **35** 55.30N 1.37W
Embu Kenya **73** 0.32S 37.28E
Emden W. Germany **45** 53.23N 7.13E
Emerson Canada **91** 49.00N 97.11W
Emi Koussi *mtn.* Chad **71** 19.58N 18.30E
Emlagh Pt. Rep. of Ire. **38** 53.46N 9.45W
Emly Rep. of Ire. **39** 52.28N 8.21W
Emmeloord Neth. **45** 52.43N 5.46E
Emmen Neth. **45** 52.48N 6.55E
Emmerich W. Germany **45** 51.49N 6.16E
Emory Peak U.S.A. **90** 29.15N 103.19W
Empangeni R.S.A. **74** 28.45S 31.54E
Empedrado Argentina **103** 27.59S 58.47W
Emporia U.S.A. **91** 38.24N 96.10W
Ems *r.* W. Germany **45** 53.14N 7.25E
Ems-Jade Canal W. Germany **45** 53.28N 7.40E
Emyvale Rep. of Ire. **38** 54.20N 6.59W
Enard B. Scotland **36** 58.05N 5.20W
Encarnación Paraguay **103** 27.20S 55.50W
Enchi Ghana **70** 5.53N 2.48W
Ende Indonesia **61** 8.51S 121.40E
Endicott Mts. U.S.A. **92** 68.00N 152.00W
Enfida Tunisia **42** 36.08N 10.22E
Enfield England **27** 51.40N 0.05W
Enfield Rep. of Ire. **38** 53.25N 6.52W
Engaño, C. Phil. **61** 18.30N 122.20E
Engels U.S.S.R. **47** 51.30N 46.07E
Enggano *i.* Indonesia **60** 5.20S 102.15E
Enghien Belgium **45** 50.42N 4.02E
Englefield Green England **27** 51.26N 0.36W
English Bazar India **58** 25.00N 88.12E
English Channel France/U.K. **40** 50.15N 1.00W
Enkeldoorn Rhodesia **74** 19.01S 30.53E
Enkhuizen Neth. **45** 52.42N 5.17E
Enköping Sweden **46** 59.38N 17.07E
Enna Italy **42** 37.34N 14.15E
En Nahud Sudan **69** 12.41N 28.28E
Ennell, Lough Rep. of Ire. **38** 53.28N 7.25W
Ennerdale Water *l.* England **32** 54.31N 3.21W
Ennis Rep. of Ire. **39** 52.51N 9.00W
Enniscorthy Rep. of Ire. **39** 52.30N 6.35W
Enniskean Rep. of Ire. **39** 51.45N 8.55W
Enniskerry Rep. of Ire. **39** 53.11N 6.12W
Enniskillen N. Ireland **38** 54.21N 7.40W
Ennistymon Rep. of Ire. **39** 52.56N 9.18W
Enns *r.* Austria **44** 48.14N 14.22E
Enrick *r.* Scotland **37** 57.20N 4.28W
Enschede Neth. **45** 52.13N 6.54E
Ensenada Mexico **90** 31.53N 116.35W
Entebbe Uganda **73** 0.08N 32.29E
Entre Rios *d.* Argentina **103** 31.50S 59.00W
Entre-Rios Moçambique **73** 14.55S 37.09E
Enugu Nigeria **71** 6.20N 7.29E
Epe Neth. **45** 52.21N 5.59E
Epernay France **40** 49.02N 3.58E
Épinal France **44** 48.10N 6.28E
Eport, Loch Scotland **36** 57.30N 7.10W
Epping England **27** 51.42N 0.07E
Epping Forest *f.* England **27** 51.39N 0.03E
Epping Green England **27** 51.43N 0.06E
Epsom England **27** 51.20N 0.16W
Epworth England **33** 53.30N 0.50W
Equateur *d.* Zaïre **72** 0.00 21.00E
Equatorial Guinea Africa **72** 2.00N 10.00E
Erbil Iraq **57** 36.12N 44.01E
Erciyaş, Mt. Turkey **56** 38.33N 35.25E
Erdre *r.* France **40** 47.27N 1.34W
Erebus, Mt. Antarctica **104** 77.40S 167.20E
Ereğli Konya Turkey **56** 37.30N 34.02E
Ereğli Zonguldak Turkey **56** 41.17N 31.26E
Erexim Brazil **103** 27.35S 52.15W
Erft *r.* W. Germany **45** 51.12N 6.45E
Erfurt E. Germany **44** 50.58N 11.02E
Ergani Turkey **56** 38.17N 39.44E
Ergene *r.* Turkey **43** 41.02N 26.22E
Erhlien China **63** 43.50N 112.00E
Eriboll, Loch Scotland **37** 58.28N 4.41W
Ericht, Loch Scotland **37** 56.52N 4.20W
Erie U.S.A. **94** 42.07N 80.05W
Erie, L. Canada/U.S.A. **94** 42.15N 81.00W
Erigavo Somali Rep. **69** 10.40N 47.20E
Eriskay *i.* Scotland **36** 57.04N 7.17W
Erisort, Loch Scotland **36** 58.06N 6.30W
Erith England **27** 51.29N 0.11E
Erkelenz W. Germany **45** 51.05N 6.18E
Erlangen W. Germany **44** 49.36N 11.02E
Ermelo Neth. **45** 52.19N 5.38E
Ermelo R.S.A. **74** 26.32S 29.59E
Erne *r.* Rep. of Ire. **38** 54.30N 8.17W
Er Rahad Sudan **69** 12.42N 30.33E
Errigal Mtn. Rep. of Ire. **38** 55.02N 8.08W
Erris Head Rep. of Ire. **38** 54.19N 10.00W
Er Roseires Sudan **69** 11.52N 34.23E
Erskine Scotland **34** 55.53N 4.27W
Erzincan Turkey **56** 39.44N 39.30E
Erzurum Turkey **56** 39.57N 41.17E
Esbjerg Denmark **46** 55.28N 8.28E
Escanaba U.S.A. **94** 45.47N 87.04W
Esch Lux. **45** 49.31N 5.59E
Eschweiler W. Germany **45** 50.49N 6.16E
Escondido *r.* Nicaragua **96** 11.58N 83.45W
Escuintla Guatemala **96** 14.18N 90.47W
Esha Ness *c.* Scotland **36** 60.29N 1.37W
Esher England **27** 51.23N 0.22W
Eshowe R.S.A. **74** 28.54S 31.28E
Esk *r.* Cumbria England **32** 54.20N 3.24W
Esk *r.* Cumbria England **35** 54.58N 3.02W
Esk *r.* N. Yorks. England **33** 54.29N 0.37W
Eskdale *f.* Scotland **35** 55.13N 3.08W
Eskilstuna Sweden **46** 59.22N 16.31E
Eskimo Point *town* Canada **93** 61.10N 94.15W
Eskişehir Turkey **56** 39.46N 30.30E
Esla *r.* Spain **41** 41.50N 5.48W
Esperance Australia **79** 33.49S 121.52E
Esperanza Argentina **103** 31.29S 61.00W
Espungabera Moçambique **74** 20.28S 32.47E
Essen W. Germany **45** 51.27N 6.57E
Essendon England **27** 51.46N 0.09W
Essequibo *r.* Guyana **102** 6.30N 58.40W
Essex *d.* England **27** 51.46N 0.30E
Esslingen W. Germany **44** 48.45N 9.19E
Estats, Pic d' *mtn.* Spain **40** 42.40N 1.23E
Estepona Spain **41** 36.26N 5.09W
Estevan Canada **90** 49.09N 103.00W
Eston England **33** 54.34N 1.07W
Estonia Soviet Socialist Republic *d.* U.S.S.R. **46** 58.45N 25.30E
Estrêla, Serra da *mts.* Portugal **41** 40.20N 7.40W
Estremoz Portugal **41** 38.50N 7.35W
Etah India **58** 27.33N 78.39E
Etaples France **40** 50.31N 1.39E
Etawah India **58** 26.40N 79.20E
Ethiopia Africa **69** 10.00N 39.00E
Ethiopian Highlands Ethiopia **69** 10.00N 37.00E
Etive, Loch Scotland **34** 56.27N 5.15W
Etna, Mt. Italy **42** 37.43N 14.59E
Etobicoke Canada **95** 43.38N 79.30W
Eton England **27** 51.31N 0.37W
Etosha Game Res. S.W. Africa **74** 18.45S 14.55E
Etosha Pan *f.* S.W. Africa **74** 18.50S 16.30E
Ettelbrück Lux. **45** 49.51N 6.06E
Ettrick *r.* Scotland **35** 55.36N 2.49W
Ettrick Forest *f.* Scotland **35** 55.30N 3.00W
Ettrick Pen *mtn.* Scotland **35** 55.21N 3.16W
Et Tubeiq, Jebel *mts.* Saudi Arabia **56** 29.30N 37.15E
Euboea *i.* Greece **43** 38.30N 23.50E
Euclid U.S.A. **94** 41.34N 81.33W
Eufaula Resr. U.S.A. **91** 35.15N 95.35W
Eugene U.S.A. **90** 44.03N 123.07W
Eugenia, Punta *c.* Mexico **90** 27.50N 115.50W
Eupen Belgium **45** 50.38N 6.04E
Euphrates *r.* Asia **57** 31.00N 47.27E
Eureka U.S.A. **90** 40.49N 124.10W
Euroa Australia **80** 36.46S 145.35E
Europa, Picos de *mts.* Spain **41** 43.10N 4.40W
Europe 18
Europoort Neth. **45** 51.56N 4.08E
Euskirchen W. Germany **45** 50.40N 6.47E
Evale Angola **72** 16.24S 15.50E
Evans, L. Canada **91** 50.55N 77.00W
Evanston U.S.A. **94** 42.02N 87.41W
Evansville U.S.A. **91** 38.02N 87.24W
Evanton Scotland **37** 57.39N 4.21W
Evenlode *r.* England **28** 51.46N 1.21W
Everard, C. Australia **80** 37.50S 149.16E
Evercreech England **28** 51.08N 2.30W
Everest, Mt. Asia **58** 27.59N 86.56E
Evesham England **28** 52.06N 1.57W
Evje Norway **46** 58.36N 7.51E
Evora Portugal **41** 38.34N 7.54W
Evreux France **40** 49.03N 1.11E
Ewe, Loch Scotland **36** 57.48N 5.38W
Ewell England **27** 51.21N 0.15W
Exe *r.* England **31** 50.40N 3.28W
Exeter England **31** 50.43N 3.31W
Exmoor Forest *hills* England **31** 51.08N 3.45W
Exmouth England **28** 50.37N 3.24W
Exuma Is. Bahamas **97** 24.00N 76.00W
Eyasi, L. Tanzania **73** 3.40S 35.00E
Eye England **29** 52.19N 1.09E
Eyemouth Scotland **35** 55.52N 2.05W
Eygurande France **40** 45.40N 2.26E
Eynhallow Sd. Scotland **37** 59.08N 3.05W
Eynort, Loch Scotland **36** 57.13N 7.15W
Eynsford England **27** 51.22N 0.14E
Eyre, L. Australia **79** 28.30S 137.25E
Eyrecourt Rep. of Ire. **39** 53.11N 8.08W

F

Fåborg Denmark **46** 55.06N 10.15E
Fada-N'Gourma U. Volta **70** 12.03N 0.22E
Faenza Italy **42** 44.17N 11.52E
Fagernes Norway **46** 60.59N 9.17E
Fagersta Sweden **46** 59.59N 15.49E
Fairbanks U.S.A. **92** 64.50N 147.50W
Fairborn U.S.A. **94** 39.48N 84.03W
Fairbourne Wales **30** 52.42N 4.03W
Fairfield U.S.A. **95** 41.09N 73.15W
Fair Head N. Ireland **34** 55.13N 6.09W
Fair Isle Scotland **36** 59.32N 1.38W
Fairlie New Zealand **82** 44.05S 170.50E
Fairmont U.S.A. **94** 39.28N 80.08W
Fairweather, Mt. U.S.A. **92** 59.00N 137.30W
Faizabad Afghan. **62** 36.17N 64.49E
Faizabad India **58** 26.46N 82.08E
Fajr, Wadi *r.* Saudi Arabia **56** 30.00N 38.25E
Fakenham England **33** 52.50N 0.51E
Fakfak Asia **61** 2.55S 132.17E
Fal *r.* England **31** 50.14N 4.58W
Falaise France **40** 48.54N 0.11W
Falcarragh Rep. of Ire. **38** 55.08N 8.06W
Falcone, C. Italy **42** 40.57N 8.12E
Falcon Resr. U.S.A. **96** 26.46N 98.55W
Falémé *r.* Senegal **70** 14.55N 12.00W
Falkenberg Sweden **46** 56.55N 12.30E
Falkirk Scotland **35** 56.00N 3.48W
Falkland Scotland **35** 56.15N 3.13W
Falkland Is. S. America **102** 52.00S 60.00W
Fall River *town* U.S.A. **95** 41.42N 71.08W
Falmouth England **31** 50.09N 5.05W
Falmouth B. England **31** 50.06N 5.05W
False B. R.S.A. **74** 34.20S 18.30E
Falster *i.* Denmark **44** 54.30N 12.00E
Falun Sweden **46** 60.37N 15.40E
Famagusta Cyprus **56** 35.07N 33.57E
Fanad Head Rep. of Ire. **38** 55.17N 7.38W
Fannich, Loch Scotland **36** 57.38N 5.00W
Fao Iraq **57** 29.57N 48.30E
Faradje Zaïre **73** 3.45N 29.43E
Farafra Oasis Egypt **56** 27.00N 28.20E
Farah Afghan. **57** 32.23N 62.07E
Farah *r.* Afghan. **57** 31.25N 61.30E
Farallon de Medinilla *i.* Asia **61** 16.01N 146.04E
Farallon de Pajaros *i.* Asia **61** 20.33N 144.59E
Faranah Guinea **70** 10.01N 10.47W
Faraulep *is.* Asia **61** 8.36N 144.33E
Farcet Fen England **29** 52.32N 0.11W
Fareham England **28** 50.52N 1.11W
Farewell, C. Greenland **93** 60.00N 44.20W
Farewell, C. New Zealand **82** 40.30S 172.35E
Farewell Spit *f.* New Zealand **82** 40.30S 173.00E
Fargo U.S.A. **91** 46.52N 96.59W
Farim Guinea Bissau **70** 12.30N 15.09W
Faringdon England **28** 51.39N 1.34W
Farnborough Hants. England **27** 51.17N 0.46W
Farnborough Kent England **27** 51.22N 0.05E
Farncombe England **27** 51.12N 0.37W
Farndon England **32** 53.06N 2.53W
Farne Is. England **35** 55.38N 1.36W
Farnham Canada **95** 45.17N 72.59W
Farnham England **28** 51.13N 0.49W
Farningham England **27** 51.23N 0.15E
Farnworth England **32** 53.33N 2.33W
Faro Portugal **41** 37.01N 7.56W
Faroe Is. Europe **46** 62.00N 7.00W
Fårösund Sweden **46** 57.51N 19.05E
Farrar *r.* Scotland **37** 57.25N 4.39W
Farrukhabad India **58** 27.23N 79.35E
Fársala Greece **43** 39.17N 22.22E
Farsi Afghan. **57** 33.47N 63.12E
Farsund Norway **46** 58.05N 6.49E
Fasa Iran **57** 28.55N 53.38E
Fashven *mtn.* Scotland **37** 58.34N 4.54W
Fastnet Rock *i.* Rep. of Ire. **39** 51.23N 9.37W
Fastov U.S.S.R. **47** 50.08N 29.59E

Fatehpur India **58** 25.56N 80.55E
Fathpur India **58** 25.29N 79.00E
Fatshan China **63** 23.03N 113.08E
Fauldhouse Scotland **35** 55.49N 3.41W
Fauquembergues France **29** 50.35N 2.06E
Faurei Romania **43** 45.04N 27.15E
Faüske Norway **46** 67.17N 15.25E
Faversham England **29** 51.18N 0.54E
Favignana *i.* Italy **42** 37.57N 12.19E
Fawley England **28** 50.49N 1.20W
Faxa Flói *b.* Iceland **46** 64.30N 22.50W
Faxe *r.* Sweden **46** 63.15N 17.15E
Fayetteville U.S.A. **91** 35.03N 78.53W
Fdérik Mauritania **68** 22.30N 12.30W
Fear, C. U.S.A. **91** 33.51N 77.59W
Fécamp France **40** 49.45N 0.23E
Federal Capital Territory *d.* Nigeria **71** 8.50N 7.00E
Federal District *d.* Brazil **103** 15.50S 47.40W
Federal District *d.* Mexico **96** 19.20N 99.10W
Fedorovka U.S.S.R. **47** 47.07N 35.19E
Feeagh, Lough Rep. of Ire. **38** 53.56N 9.35W
Fehmarn *i.* W. Germany **44** 54.30N 11.05E
Feilding New Zealand **82** 40.10S 175.25E
Feira Zambia **73** 15.30S 30.27E
Felanitx Spain **41** 39.27N 3.08E
Feldkirch Austria **44** 47.15N 9.38E
Felixstowe England **29** 51.58N 1.20E
Felsted England **27** 51.52N 0.25E
Feltham England **27** 51.27N 0.25W
Felton England **35** 55.18N 1.42W
Femunden *l.* Norway **46** 62.05N 11.55E
Fengkieh China **63** 31.00N 109.30E
Fenit Rep. of Ire. **39** 52.17N 9.51W
Fenyang China **63** 37.14N 111.43E
Feodosiya U.S.S.R. **47** 45.03N 35.23E
Fer, Cap de Algeria **42** 37.07N 7.10E
Ferbane Rep. of Ire. **39** 53.16N 7.50W
Ferdaus Iran **57** 34.00N 58.10E
Fergus Falls *town* U.S.A. **91** 46.18N 96.00W
Ferkéssédougou Ivory Coast **70** 9.30N 5.10W
Fermanagh *d.* N. Ireland **38** 54.21N 7.40W
Fermoselle Spain **41** 41.19N 6.24W
Fermoy Rep. of Ire. **39** 52.08N 8.17W
Ferndown England **28** 50.48N 1.55W
Ferness Scotland **37** 57.28N 3.45W
Ferns Rep. of Ire. **39** 52.35N 6.31W
Ferozepore India **58** 30.55N 74.38E
Ferrara Italy **42** 44.49N 11.38E
Ferret, Cap France **40** 44.42N 1.16W
Feshi Zaïre **72** 6.08S 18.12E
Fetcham England **27** 51.17N 0.22W
Fethard Tipperary Rep. of Ire. **39** 52.28N 7.42W
Fethard Wexford Rep. of Ire. **39** 52.12N 6.51W
Fethiye Turkey **56** 36.37N 29.06E
Fetlar *i.* Scotland **36** 60.37N 0.52W
Fettercairn Scotland **37** 56.51N 2.35W
Fevzipaşa Turkey **56** 37.07N 36.38E
Fez Morocco **68** 34.05N 5.00W
Ffestiniog Wales **30** 52.58N 3.56W
Ffostrasol Wales **30** 52.06N 4.23W
Fife *d.* Scotland **35** 56.10N 3.10W
Fife Ness *c.* Scotland **35** 56.17N 2.36W
Figeac France **40** 44.32N 2.01E
Figueira da Foz Portugal **41** 40.09N 8.51W
Figueras Spain **41** 42.16N 2.57E
Fiji Is. Pacific Oc. **107** 17.00S 178.00E
Filabusi Rhodesia **74** 20.34S 29.20E
Filey England **33** 54.13N 0.18W
Fimi *r.* Zaïre **72** 3.00S 17.00E
Finchley England **27** 51.37N 0.11W
Findhorn Scotland **37** 57.39N 3.37W
Findhorn *r.* Scotland **37** 57.38N 3.37W
Findlay U.S.A. **94** 41.02N 83.40W
Finisterre, C. Spain **41** 42.54N 9.16W
Finland Europe **46** 64.30N 27.00E
Finland, G. of Finland/U.S.S.R. **46** 60.00N 26.50E
Finlay *r.* Canada **92** 56.30N 124.40W
Finn *r.* Rep. of Ire. **38** 54.50N 7.30W
Finsbury England **27** 51.32N 0.06W
Finschhafen P.N.G. **61** 6.35S 147.51E
Fintona N. Ireland **38** 54.31N 7.19W
Fionn Loch Scotland **36** 57.45N 5.27W
Fionnphort Scotland **34** 56.19N 6.23W
Firozabad India **58** 27.09N 78.24E
Firth of Clyde *est.* Scotland **34** 55.35N 4.53W
Firth of Forth *est.* Scotland **35** 56.05N 3.00W
Firth of Lorne *est.* Scotland **34** 56.20N 5.40W
Firth of Tay *est.* Scotland **35** 56.24N 3.08W
Firuzabad Iran **57** 28.50N 52.35E
Fisher Str. Canada **93** 63.00N 84.00W
Fishguard Wales **30** 51.59N 4.59W
Fishguard B. Wales **30** 52.06N 4.44W
Fitchburg U.S.A. **95** 42.35N 71.50W
Fitful Head Scotland **36** 59.55N 1.23W
Fittri, L. Chad **71** 12.50N 17.30E
Fizi Zaïre **73** 4.18S 28.56E
Flackwell Heath England **27** 51.36N 0.43W
Flagstaff U.S.A. **90** 35.12N 111.38W
Flåm Norway **46** 60.51N 7.08E
Flamborough England **33** 54.07N 0.07W
Flamborough Head England **33** 54.06N 0.05W
Flaming Gorge Resr. U.S.A. **90** 41.10N 109.30W
Flanders *f.* Belgium **45** 50.52N 3.00E
Flanders East *d.* Belgium **45** 51.00N 3.45E
Flanders West *d.* Belgium **45** 51.00N 3.00E
Flathead L. U.S.A. **90** 47.50N 114.05W
Flat Holm *i.* England **28** 51.23N 3.08W
Flattery, C. U.S.A. **90** 48.23N 124.43W
Fleet England **28** 51.16N 0.50W
Fleet *r.* Scotland **37** 57.57N 4.05W
Fleetwood England **32** 53.55N 3.01W
Flekkefjord *town* Norway **46** 58.17N 6.40E
Flen Sweden **46** 59.04N 16.39E
Flensburg W. Germany **44** 54.47N 9.27E
Flers France **40** 48.45N 0.34W
Flimby England **32** 54.42N 3.31W
Flinders *r.* Australia **79** 17.30S 140.45E
Flinders I. Australia **80** 40.00S 148.00E
Flinders Range *mts.* Australia **80** 31.00S 138.30E
Flin Flon Canada **93** 54.47N 101.51W
Flint U.S.A. **94** 43.03N 83.40W
Flint *r.* U.S.A. **91** 30.52N 84.35W
Flint Wales **30** 53.15N 3.07W
Flitwick England **29** 51.59N 0.30W
Flora Norway **46** 61.45N 4.55E
Florence Italy **42** 43.46N 11.15E
Florence U.S.A. **91** 34.12N 79.44W
Florenville Belgium **45** 49.42N 5.19E
Flores *i.* Indonesia **61** 8.40S 121.20E
Flores Sea Indonesia **61** 7.00S 121.00E
Florianópolis Brazil **103** 27.35S 48.31W
Florida Uruguay **103** 34.04S 56.14W
Florida *d.* U.S.A. **91** 29.00N 82.00W
Florida, Straits of U.S.A. **97** 24.00N 81.00W
Florida Keys *is.* U.S.A. **96** 24.30N 81.00W
Florina Greece **43** 40.48N 21.25E
Florissant U.S.A. **94** 38.49N 90.24W
Flotta *i.* Scotland **37** 58.49N 3.07W
Flushing Neth. **45** 51.27N 3.35E
Fly *r.* P.N.G. **61** 8.22S 142.23E
Fochabers Scotland **37** 57.37N 3.07W
Focşani Romania **43** 45.40N 27.12E
Foggia Italy **42** 41.28N 15.33E
Foinaven *mtn.* Scotland **37** 58.24N 4.53W
Foix France **40** 42.57N 1.35E
Folda *est.* Norway **46** 64.45N 11.20E
Foligno Italy **42** 42.56N 12.43E
Folkestone England **29** 51.05N 1.11E
Folkingham England **33** 52.54N 0.24W
Fond du Lac Canada **92** 59.20N 107.09W
Fond du Lac U.S.A. **94** 43.48N 88.27W
Fonseca, G. of Honduras **96** 13.10N 87.30W
Fontainebleau France **40** 48.24N 2.42E
Fontenay France **40** 46.28N 0.48W
Foochow China **63** 26.01N 119.20E
Forbes Australia **80** 33.24S 148.03E
Ford Scotland **34** 56.10N 5.26W
Fordingbridge England **28** 50.56N 1.48W
Forécariah Guinea **70** 9.28N 13.06W
Forel, Mt. Greenland **93** 67.00N 37.00W
Foreland *c.* England **28** 50.42N 1.06W
Foreland Pt. England **31** 51.15N 3.47W
Forest of Atholl *f.* Scotland **37** 56.50N 3.58W
Forest of Bowland *hills* England **32** 53.57N 2.30W
Forest of Dean *f.* England **28** 51.48N 2.32W
Forest of Rossendale *f.* England **32** 53.43N 2.15W
Forest Row England **29** 51.06N 0.03E
Forfar Scotland **35** 56.38N 2.54W
Forli Italy **42** 44.13N 12.02E
Forlorn Pt. Rep. of Ire. **39** 52.10N 6.35W
Formartine *f.* Scotland **37** 57.21N 2.12W
Formby England **32** 53.34N 3.04W
Formby Pt. England **32** 53.34N 3.07W
Formentera *i.* Spain **41** 38.41N 1.30E
Formiga Brazil **103** 20.30S 45.27W
Formosa *d.* Argentina **103** 25.00S 60.00W
Formosa *town* Argentina **103** 26.06S 58.14W
Formosa *i.* Asia **107** 23.00N 121.00E
Formosa *see* Taiwan Asia **63**
Formosa Brazil **103** 15.30S 47.22W
Formosa Str. Asia **63** 25.00N 120.00E
Forres Scotland **37** 57.37N 3.38W
Forssa Finland **46** 60.49N 23.40E
Forst E. Germany **44** 51.46N 14.39E
Forster Australia **80** 32.11S 152.30E
Fort Albany Canada **93** 52.15N 81.35W
Fortaleza Brazil **102** 3.45S 38.35W
Fort Augustus Scotland **37** 57.09N 4.41W
Fort Beaufort R.S.A. **74** 32.47S 26.38E
Fort Chimo Canada **93** 58.10N 68.15W
Fort Chipewyan Canada **92** 58.46N 111.09W
Fort Collins U.S.A. **90** 40.35N 105.05W
Fort Crampel C.A.R. **71** 7.00N 19.10E
Fort-Dauphin Malagasy Rep. **67** 25.01S 47.00E
Fort-de-France Martinique **97** 14.36N 61.05W
Fort de Possel C.A.R. **72** 5.03N 19.14E
Fort Frances Canada **94** 48.37N 93.23W
Fort George Canada **93** 53.50N 79.01W
Fort George *r.* Canada **93** 53.50N 79.00W
Fort Good Hope Canada **92** 66.16N 128.37W
Forth Scotland **35** 55.46N 3.42W
Forth *r.* Scotland **35** 56.06N 3.48W
Fort Lauderdale U.S.A. **91** 26.08N 80.08W
Fort Liard Canada **92** 60.14N 123.28W
Fort Madison U.S.A. **94** 40.38N 91.21W
Fort Maguire Malaŵi **73** 13.38S 34.59E
Fort McPherson Canada **92** 67.29N 134.50W
Fort Myers U.S.A. **91** 26.39N 81.51W
Fort Nelson Canada **92** 58.48N 122.44W
Fort Norman Canada **92** 64.55N 125.29W
Fort Peck Dam U.S.A. **90** 47.55N 106.15W
Fort Peck Resr. U.S.A. **90** 47.55N 107.00W
Fort Polignac Algeria **68** 26.20N 8.20E
Fort Portal Uganda **73** 0.40N 30.17E
Fort Randall U.S.A. **92** 55.10N 162.47W
Fort Reliance Canada **92** 62.45N 109.08W
Fort Resolution Canada **92** 61.10N 113.39W
Fortrose Scotland **37** 57.34N 4.09W
Fort Rousset Congo **72** 0.30S 15.48E
Fort Rupert Canada **93** 51.30N 79.45W
Fort St. John Canada **92** 56.14N 120.55W
Fort Scott U.S.A. **91** 37.52N 94.43W
Fort Severn Canada **93** 56.00N 87.40W
Fort Shevchenko U.S.S.R. **48** 44.31N 50.15E
Fort Sibut C.A.R. **71** 5.46N 19.06E
Fort Simpson Canada **92** 61.46N 121.15W
Fort Smith U.S.A. **91** 35.22N 94.27W
Fortune *i.* Bahamas **97** 22.30N 74.15W
Fortuneswell England **28** 50.33N 2.27W
Fort Vermilion Canada **92** 58.22N 115.59W
Fort Victoria Rhodesia **74** 20.10S 30.49E
Fort Wayne U.S.A. **94** 41.05N 85.08W
Fort William Scotland **36** 56.49N 5.07W
Fort Worth U.S.A. **91** 32.45N 97.20W
Fort Yukon U.S.A. **92** 66.35N 145.20W
Fostoria U.S.A. **94** 41.10N 83.25W
Fougamou Gabon **72** 1.10S 10.31E
Fougères France **40** 48.21N 1.12W
Foula *i.* Scotland **36** 60.08N 2.05W
Foulness I. England **29** 51.35N 0.55E
Foulness Pt. England **29** 51.37N 1.00E
Foulwind, C. New Zealand **82** 41.45S 171.30E
Foumban Cameroon **72** 5.43N 10.50E
Four Elms England **27** 51.14N 0.07E
Foveaux Str. New Zealand **82** 46.40S 168.00E
Fowey England **31** 50.20N 4.39W
Fowey *r.* England **31** 50.22N 4.40W
Fox *r.* U.S.A. **94** 41.19N 88.59W
Foxe Basin *b.* Canada **93** 67.30N 79.00W
Foxe Channel Canada **93** 65.00N 80.00W
Foxford Rep. of Ire. **38** 53.58N 9.08W
Foxton New Zealand **82** 40.27S 175.18E
Foyle *r.* N. Ireland **38** 55.00N 7.20W
Foyle, Lough N. Ireland **34** 55.05N 7.10W
Foz do Iguaçu Brazil **103** 25.33S 54.31W
Framingham U.S.A. **95** 42.18N 71.25W
Framlingham England **29** 52.14N 1.20E
Franca Brazil **103** 20.33S 47.27W
France Europe **40** 47.00N 2.00E
Franceville Gabon **72** 1.38S 13.31E
Francistown Botswana **74** 21.11S 27.32E
Frankfort R.S.A. **74** 27.16S 28.30E
Frankfort U.S.A. **91** 38.11N 84.53W
Frankfurt E. Germany **44** 52.20N 14.32E
Frankfurt W. Germany **44** 50.06N 8.41E
Franklin *d.* Canada **93** 73.00N 100.00W
Franklin U.S.A. **94** 39.29N 86.02W
Franklin D. Roosevelt L. U.S.A. **90** 47.55N 118.20W
Frank Saale *r.* W. Germany **40** 50.00N 8.21E
Franz Canada **94** 48.28N 84.25W
Franz Josef Land *is.* U.S.S.R. **48** 81.00N 54.00E
Fraser *r.* Canada **90** 49.05N 123.00W
Fraserburg R.S.A. **74** 31.55S 21.31E
Fraserburgh Scotland **37** 57.42N 2.00W
Fray Bentos Uruguay **103** 33.10S 58.20W
Fredericia Denmark **46** 55.34N 9.47E
Frederick U.S.A. **95** 39.25N 77.25W
Fredericksburg U.S.A. **91** 38.18N 77.30W
Fredericton Canada **95** 45.57N 66.40W
Frederikshaab Greenland **93** 62.05N 49.30W
Fredrikshavn Denmark **46** 57.28N 10.33E
Fredrikstad Norway **46** 59.15N 10.55E
Freeport Bahamas **97** 26.40N 78.30W
Freeport U.S.A. **94** 42.17N 89.38W
Freetown Sierra Leone **70** 8.30N 13.17W
Freiburg W. Germany **44** 48.00N 7.52E
Freilingen W. Germany **45** 50.33N 7.50E
Freising W. Germany **44** 48.24N 11.45E

Freital E. Germany **44** 51.00N 13.40E
Fréjus France **40** 43.26N 6.44E
Fremantle Australia **79** 32.07S 115.44E
French Cays *is.* Bahamas **97** 21.31N 72.14W
Frenchman's Cap *mtn.* Australia **80** 42.27S 145.54E
French Territory of Afars and Issas Africa **69** 12.00N 42.50E
Frenda Algeria **41** 35.04N 1.03E
Freshford Rep. of Ire. **39** 52.44N 7.23W
Fresno U.S.A. **90** 36.41N 119.57W
Freycinet Pen. Australia **80** 42.10S 148.18E
Frias Argentina **103** 28.35S 65.06W
Fribourg Switz. **44** 46.50N 7.10E
Friedrichshafen W. Germany **44** 47.39N 9.29E
Friern Barnet England **27** 51.37N 0.09W
Friesland *d.* Neth. **45** 53.05N 5.45E
Friesoythe W. Germany **45** 53.02N 7.52E
Frimley England **27** 51.19N 0.44W
Frinton England **29** 51.50N 1.16E
Frisa, Loch Scotland **34** 56.33N 6.05W
Frobisher B. Canada **93** 63.00N 66.45W
Frobisher Bay *town* Canada **93** 63.45N 68.30W
Frodsham England **32** 53.17N 2.45W
Fro Havet *est.* Norway **46** 63.55N 9.05E
Frome England **28** 51.16N 2.17W
Frome *r.* England **28** 50.41N 2.05W
Frome, L. Australia **80** 30.45S 139.45E
Frosinone Italy **42** 41.36N 13.21E
Fröya *i.* Norway **46** 63.45N 8.30E
Frunze U.S.S.R. **62** 42.53N 74.46E
Fuchin China **63** 47.15N 131.59E
Fuchow China **63** 28.03N 116.15E
Fuday *i.* Scotland **36** 57.03N 7.23W
Fuerte *r.* Mexico **90** 25.42N 109.20W
Fuerteventura *i.* Canary Is. **68** 28.20N 14.10W
Fujiyama *mtn.* Japan **63** 35.20N 138.30E
Fukien *d.* China **63** 26.30N 118.00E
Fukuoka Japan **63** 33.39N 130.21E
Fulda W. Germany **44** 50.35N 9.41E
Fulham England **27** 51.29N 0.13W
Fumay France **45** 49.59N 4.42E
Fundy, B. of N.America **91** 44.30N 66.30W
Funen *i.* Denmark **46** 55.15N 10.30E
Funzie Scotland **36** 60.35N 0.48W
Furancungo Moçambique **73** 14.51S 33.38E
Furg Iran **57** 28.19N 55.10E
Furnas Resr. Brazil **103** 21.00S 46.00W
Furneaux Group *is.* Australia **80** 40.15S 148.15E
Furnes Belgium **45** 51.04N 2.40E
Fürstenau W. Germany **45** 52.32N 7.41E
Fürstenwalde E. Germany **44** 52.22N 14.04E
Fürth W. Germany **44** 49.28N 11.00E
Fushun China **63** 41.51N 123.53E
Fussen W. Germany **44** 47.35N 10.43E
Futa Jalon *f.* Guinea **70** 11.30N 12.30W
Fuyu China **63** 45.12N 124.49E
Fyfield England **27** 51.45N 0.16E
Fyne, Loch Scotland **34** 55.55N 5.23W
Fyvie Scotland **37** 57.26N 2.24W

G

Gabela Angola **72** 10.52S 14.24E
Gabes Tunisia **68** 33.52N 10.06E
Gabes, G. of Tunisia **68** 34.00N 11.00E
Gabon Africa **72** 0.00 12.00E
Gabon *r.* Gabon **72** 0.15N 10.00E
Gaborone Botswana **74** 24.45S 25.55E
Gabriel, Mt. Rep. of Ire. **39** 51.34N 9.34W
Gach Saran Iran **57** 30.13N 50.49E
Gadsden U.S.A. **91** 34.00N 86.00W
Gaeta Italy **42** 41.13N 13.35E
Gaeta, G. of Med. Sea **42** 41.05N 13.30E
Gaferut *i.* Asia **61** 9.14N 145.23E
Gagnoa Ivory Coast **70** 6.04N 5.55W
Gagnon Canada **93** 51.56N 68.16W
Gago Coutinho Angola **72** 14.02S 21.35E
Gaillac France **40** 43.54N 1.53E
Gainesville U.S.A. **91** 29.37N 82.31W
Gainford England **32** 54.34N 1.44W
Gainsborough England **33** 53.23N 0.46W
Gairdner, L. Australia **79** 31.30S 136.00E
Gairloch Scotland **36** 57.43N 5.40W
Gairloch, Loch Scotland **36** 57.43N 5.43W
Gairsay *i.* Scotland **37** 59.05N 2.58W
Galala Plateau Egypt **56** 29.00N 32.10E
Galana *r.* Kenya **73** 3.12S 40.09E
Galangue Angola **72** 13.40S 16.00E
Galapagos Is. Ecuador **102** 0.20S 91.00W
Galashiels Scotland **35** 55.37N 2.49W
Galati Romania **43** 45.27N 27.59E
Galena U.S.A. **92** 64.43N 157.00W
Galesburg U.S.A. **94** 40.58N 90.22W
Galey *r.* Rep. of Ire. **39** 52.26N 9.37W
Galita *i.* Tunisia **42** 37.31N 8.55E
Gallan Head Scotland **36** 58.14N 7.01W
Galle Sri Lanka **59** 6.01N 80.13E
Gállego *r.* Spain **41** 41.40N 0.55W
Galley Head Rep. of Ire. **39** 51.32N 8.57W
Gallinas, C. Colombia **102** 12.20N 71.30W
Gallípoli Italy **43** 40.02N 18.01E
Gallipoli Turkey **43** 40.25N 26.31E
Gällivare Sweden **46** 67.10N 20.40E
Galloway *f.* Scotland **34** 55.00N 4.28W
Gallup U.S.A. **90** 35.32N 108.46W
Galong Australia **80** 34.37S 148.34E
Galston Scotland **34** 55.36N 4.23W
Galt Canada **94** 43.21N 80.19W
Galtby Finland **46** 60.08N 21.33E
Galtymore *mtn.* Rep. of Ire. **39** 52.22N 8.13W
Galty Mts. Rep. of Ire. **39** 52.20N 8.10W
Galveston U.S.A. **91** 29.17N 94.48W
Galveston B. U.S.A. **91** 29.40N 94.40W
Galvez Argentina **103** 32.03S 61.14W
Galway Rep. of Ire. **38** 53.17N 9.04W
Galway *d.* Rep. of Ire. **38** 53.25N 9.00W
Galway B. Rep. of Ire. **39** 53.12N 9.07W
Gambia Africa **70** 13.10N 16.00W
Gambia *r.* Gambia **70** 13.28N 15.55W
Gamboma Congo **72** 1.50S 15.58E
Ganale Dorya *r.* Ethiopia **73** 4.13N 42.04E
Gandajika Zaïre **72** 6.46S 23.58E
Gandak *r.* India **58** 25.35N 85.20E
Gander Canada **93** 48.58N 54.34W
Gandia Spain **41** 38.59N 0.11W
Ganges *r.* India **58** 23.30N 90.25E
Ganges, Mouths of the India/Bangla. **58** 22.00N 89.35E
Gangtok India **58** 27.20N 88.39E
Gannat France **40** 46.06N 3.11E
Gannett Peak *mtn.* U.S.A. **90** 43.10N 109.38W
Gao Mali **70** 16.19N 0.09W
Gaoual Guinea **70** 11.44N 13.14W
Gap France **40** 44.33N 6.05E
Gara, Lough Rep. of Ire. **38** 53.57N 8.27W
Gard *r.* France **40** 43.52N 4.40E
Garda, L. Italy **42** 45.40N 10.40E
Gar Dzong China **59** 32.10N 79.59E
Garelochhead Scotland **34** 56.05N 4.49W
Garforth England **33** 53.48N 1.22W
Garies R.S.A. **74** 30.30S 18.00E
Garioch *f.* Scotland **37** 57.18N 2.30W
Garissa Kenya **73** 0.27S 39.49E
Garlieston Scotland **34** 54.46N 4.22W
Garmisch Partenkirchen W. Germany **44** 47.30N 11.05E
Garmouth Scotland **37** 57.40N 3.07W
Garmsar Iran **57** 35.15N 52.21E
Garo Hills India **58** 25.30N 90.30E
Garonne *r.* France **40** 45.00N 0.37W
Garoua Cameroon **71** 9.17N 13.22E
Garrison Resr. U.S.A. **90** 47.30N 102.20W
Garroch Head Scotland **34** 55.43N 5.02W
Garron Pt. N. Ireland **34** 55.03N 5.57W
Garry, Loch Scotland **37** 57.05N 4.55W
Garry L. Canada **93** 66.00N 100.00W
Garstang England **32** 53.53N 2.47W
Garth Wales **30** 52.08N 3.32W
Garthorpe England **33** 53.40N 0.42W
Gartok China **62** 32.00N 80.20E
Garvagh N. Ireland **34** 54.58N 6.42W
Garvão Portugal **41** 37.42N 8.21W
Garve Scotland **37** 57.37N 4.41W
Garvellachs *i.* Scotland **34** 56.15N 5.45W
Garvie Mts. New Zealand **82** 45.15S 169.00E
Garwah India **58** 24.11N 83.47E
Gary U.S.A. **94** 41.34N 87.20W
Gascony, G. of France **40** 44.00N 2.40W
Gascoyne *r.* Australia **79** 25.00S 113.40E
Gaspé Canada **93** 48.50N 64.30W
Gaspé Pen. Canada **95** 48.30N 66.45W
Gata, C. Cyprus **56** 34.33N 33.03E
Gata, Cabo de Spain **41** 36.45N 2.11W
Gata, Sierra de *mts.* Spain **41** 40.20N 6.30W
Gatehouse of Fleet Scotland **34** 54.53N 4.12W
Gateshead England **32** 54.57N 1.35W
Gatineau *r.* Canada **95** 45.25N 75.43W
Gatooma Rhodesia **74** 18.16S 29.55E
Gatun L. Canal Zone **97** 9.20N 80.00W
Gauhati India **59** 26.05N 91.55E
Gauja *r.* U.S.S.R. **46** 57.10N 24.17E
Gavá Spain **41** 41.18N 2.00E
Gävle Sweden **46** 60.41N 17.10E
Gawler Australia **80** 34.38S 138.44E
Gaya India **58** 24.48N 85.00E
Gaya Niger **71** 11.53N 3.31E
Gaydon England **28** 52.11N 1.27W
Gaza Egypt **56** 31.30N 34.28E
Gaza *d.* Moçambique **74** 23.30S 33.00E
Gaziantep Turkey **56** 37.04N 37.21E
Gdańsk Poland **46** 54.22N 18.38E
Gdańsk, G. of Poland **47** 54.45N 19.15E
Gdov U.S.S.R. **46** 58.48N 27.52E
Gdynia Poland **46** 54.31N 18.30E
Geal Chàrn *mtn.* Scotland **37** 57.06N 3.30W
Gebze Turkey **56** 40.48N 29.26E
Gediz *r.* Turkey **43** 38.37N 26.47E
Gedser Denmark **44** 54.35N 11.57E
Geel Belgium **45** 51.10N 5.00E
Geelong Australia **80** 38.10S 144.26E
Geh Iran **57** 26.14N 60.15E
Geidam Nigeria **71** 12.55N 11.55E
Geilenkirchen W. Germany **45** 50.58N 6.08E
Gelderland *d.* Neth. **45** 52.05N 6.00E
Geldern W. Germany **45** 51.31N 6.19E
Geleen Neth. **45** 50.58N 5.51E
Gelligaer Wales **31** 51.40N 3.18W
Gelsenkirchen W. Germany **45** 51.30N 7.05E
Gemas Malaysia **60** 2.35N 102.35E
Gembloux Belgium **45** 50.34N 4.42E
Gemena Zaïre **72** 3.14N 19.48E
Gemlik Turkey **56** 40.26N 29.10E
Geneina Sudan **69** 13.27N 22.30E
General Acha Argentina **103** 37.25S 64.38W
General Alvear Argentina **103** 34.59S 67.40W
Geneva Switz. **44** 46.13N 6.09E
Geneva, L. Switz. **44** 46.30N 6.30E
Genichesk U.S.S.R. **47** 46.10N 34.49E
Genil *r.* Spain **41** 37.42N 5.20W
Genk Belgium **44** 50.58N 5.30E
Genoa Italy **40** 44.24N 8.54E
Genoa, G. of Italy **40** 44.12N 8.55E
Gent Belgium **45** 51.02N 3.42E
George *r.* Canada **93** 58.30N 66.00W
George R.S.A. **74** 33.57S 22.28E
George, L. Australia **80** 35.07S 149.22E
George, L. Uganda **73** 0.00 30.10E
George, L. U.S.A. **95** 43.30N 73.30W
George Town Australia **80** 41.04S 146.48E
Georgetown Cayman Is. **96** 19.20N 81.23W
Georgetown Guyana **102** 6.46N 58.10W
George Town Malaysia **60** 5.30N 100.16E
Georgia *d.* U.S.A. **91** 33.00N 83.00W
Georgia, Str. of Canada **90** 49.15N 123.45W
Georgian B. Canada **94** 45.15N 80.45W
Georgia Soviet Socialist Republic *d.* U.S.S.R. **56** 42.00N 43.30E
Gera E. Germany **44** 50.51N 12.11E
Geraardsbergen Belgium **45** 50.47N 3.53E
Geraldton Australia **79** 28.49S 114.36E
Germiston R.S.A. **74** 26.15S 28.10E
Gerona Spain **41** 41.59N 2.49E
Gerrards Cross England **27** 51.35N 0.34W
Getafe Spain **41** 40.18N 3.44W
Gete *r.* Belgium **45** 50.58N 5.07E
Geyve Turkey **56** 40.32N 30.18E
Gezira *f.* Sudan **69** 14.30N 33.00E
Ghadames Libya **68** 30.10N 9.30E
Ghaghara *r.* India **58** 25.45N 84.50E
Ghana Africa **70** 8.00N 1.00W
Ghanzi Botswana **74** 21.34S 21.42E
Ghardaïa Algeria **68** 32.20N 3.40E
Ghat Libya **68** 24.59N 10.11E
Ghazaouet Algeria **41** 35.10N 1.50W
Ghaziabad India **58** 28.37N 77.30E
Ghazipur India **58** 25.36N 83.36E
Ghurian Afghan. **57** 34.20N 61.25E
Gialo Libya **69** 29.00N 21.30E
Giant's Causeway *f.* N. Ireland **34** 55.14N 6.32W
Gibraltar Europe **41** 36.07N 5.22W
Gibraltar, Str. of Africa/Europe **41** 36.00N 5.25W
Gibraltar Pt. England **33** 53.05N 0.20E
Giessen W. Germany **44** 50.35N 8.42E
Gieten Neth. **45** 53.01N 6.45E
Gifford Scotland **35** 55.55N 2.45W
Gifu Japan **63** 35.27N 136.46E
Gigha *i.* Scotland **34** 55.41N 5.44W
Gigha, Sd. of Scotland **34** 55.40N 5.41W
Giglio *i.* Italy **42** 42.21N 10.53E
Gijón Spain **41** 43.32N 5.40W
Gila *r.* U.S.A. **90** 32.45N 114.30W
Gilbert Is. Pacific Oc. **107** 2.00S 175.00E
Gilé Moçambique **73** 16.10S 38.17E
Gilehdar Iran **57** 27.36N 52.42E
Gilgandra Australia **80** 31.42S 148.40E
Gilgil Kenya **73** 0.29S 36.19E
Gilgit Jammu and Kashmir **58** 35.54N 74.20E
Gilgunnia Australia **80** 32.25S 146.04E
Gill, Lough Rep. of Ire. **38** 54.15N 8.14W
Gillingham Dorset England **28** 51.02N 2.17W
Gillingham Kent England **27** 51.24N 0.33E
Gilsland England **35** 54.59N 2.34W
Gimbala, Jebel *mtn.* Sudan **69** 13.00N 24.20E
Ginz *r.* W. Germany **44** 48.28N 10.18E
Gippsland *f.* Australia **80** 37.40S 147.00E
Giresun Turkey **56** 40.55N 38.25E
Giri *r.* Zaïre **72** 0.30N 17.58E
Gironde *r.* France **40** 45.35N 1.00W

Girvan Scotland **34** 55.15N 4.51W
Gisborne New Zealand **82** 38.41S 178.02E
Gitega Burundi **73** 3.25S 29.58E
Giurgiu Romania **43** 43.52N 25.58E
Givet France **45** 50.08N 4.49E
Gizhiga U.S.S.R. **49** 62.00N 160.34E
Gizhiga G. U.S.S.R. **49** 61.00N 158.00E
Gjövik Norway **46** 60.47N 10.41E
Glacier Peak *mtn.* U.S.A. **90** 48.07N 121.06W
Glamis Scotland **35** 56.37N 3.01W
Glan *r.* W. Germany **45** 49.46N 7.43E
Glanamman Wales **31** 51.49N 3.54W
Glanaruddery Mts. Rep. of Ire. **39** 52.19N 9.27W
Glandorf W. Germany **45** 52.05N 8.00E
Glanton England **35** 55.25N 1.53W
Glasgow Scotland **34** 55.52N 4.15W
Glasgow U.S.A. **90** 48.12N 106.37W
Glas Maol *mtn.* Scotland **37** 56.52N 3.22W
Glass, Loch Scotland **37** 57.43N 4.30W
Glasson England **32** 54.00N 2.49W
Glastonbury England **28** 51.09N 2.42W
Glazov U.S.S.R. **47** 58.09N 52.42E
Glen *r.* England **29** 52.50N 0.06W
Glen Affric *f.* Scotland **36** 57.15N 5.03W
Glen Almond *f.* Scotland **35** 56.28N 3.48W
Glenanane Rep. of Ire. **38** 53.37N 9.40W
Glénans, Îles de France **40** 47.43N 3.57W
Glenarm N. Ireland **34** 54.57N 5.58W
Glen Cannich *f.* Scotland **36** 57.19N 5.03W
Glen Clova *f.* Scotland **37** 56.48N 3.01W
Glen Coe *f.* Scotland **34** 56.40N 5.03W
Glendive U.S.A. **90** 47.08N 104.42W
Glen Dochart *f.* Scotland **34** 56.25N 4.30W
Glen Dye *f.* Scotland **37** 56.58N 2.34W
Glenelg Scotland **36** 57.13N 5.37W
Glenelly *r.* N. Ireland **34** 54.45N 7.19W
Glen Esk *f.* Scotland **37** 56.53N 2.46W
Glen Etive *f.* Scotland **34** 56.37N 5.01W
Glenfinnan Scotland **36** 56.53N 5.27W
Glengarriff Rep. of Ire. **39** 51.45N 9.33W
Glen Garry *f.* Highland Scotland **36** 57.03N 5.04W
Glen Garry *f.* Tayside Scotland **37** 56.47N 4.02W
Glengormley N. Ireland **34** 54.40N 5.59W
Glen Head Rep. of Ire. **38** 54.44N 8.46W
Glen Innes Australia **80** 29.42S 151.45E
Glen Kinglass *f.* Scotland **34** 56.29N 5.03W
Glenluce Scotland **34** 54.53N 4.48W
Glen Lyon *f.* Scotland **34** 56.36N 4.15W
Glen Mòr *f.* Scotland **37** 57.15N 4.30W
Glen More *f.* Scotland **34** 56.25N 5.48W
Glennagalliagh *mtn.* Rep. of Ire. **39** 52.49N 8.32W
Glen Orchy *f.* Scotland **34** 56.28N 4.50W
Glen Orrin *f.* Scotland **37** 57.30N 4.45W
Glen Prosen *f.* Scotland **37** 56.45N 3.05W
Glenrothes Scotland **35** 56.12N 3.10W
Glen Roy *f.* Scotland **37** 56.58N 4.47W
Glens Falls *town* U.S.A. **95** 43.17N 73.41W
Glenshaw U.S.A. **94** 40.31N 79.57W
Glenshee *f.* Scotland **37** 56.45N 3.25W
Glen Spean *f.* Scotland **37** 56.53N 4.40W
Glenties Rep. of Ire. **38** 54.47N 8.17W
Glen Tilt *f.* Scotland **37** 56.50N 3.45W
Glenwhappen Rig *mtn.* Scotland **35** 55.33N 3.30W
Glin Rep. of Ire. **39** 52.34N 9.17W
Glittertind *mtn.* Norway **46** 61.30N 8.20E
Głogów Poland **44** 51.40N 16.06E
Glomma *r.* Norway **46** 59.15N 10.55E
Glossop England **32** 53.27N 1.56W
Gloucester England **28** 51.52N 2.15W
Gloucester U.S.A. **95** 42.37N 70.41W
Gloucestershire *d.* England **28** 51.45N 2.00W
Glyncorrwg Wales **31** 51.40N 3.39W
Glyn Neath Wales **31** 51.45N 3.37W
Gmünd Austria **44** 48.47N 14.59E
Gmunden Austria **44** 47.56N 13.48E
Gniezno Poland **47** 52.32N 17.32E
Goa *d.* India **58** 15.30N 74.00E
Goalpara India **58** 26.10N 90.38E
Goat Fell *mtn.* Scotland **34** 55.37N 5.12W
Gobabis S.W. Africa **74** 22.30S 18.58E
Gobi *des.* Asia **62** 43.30N 103.30E
Godalming England **27** 51.11N 0.37W
Godavari *r.* India **59** 16.40N 82.15E
Goderich Canada **94** 43.43N 81.43W
Godhavn Greenland **93** 69.20N 53.30W
Godhra India **58** 22.49N 73.40E
Godmanchester England **29** 52.19N 0.11W
Godrevy Pt. England **31** 50.15N 5.25W
Godstone England **27** 51.15N 0.04W
Godthaab Greenland **93** 64.10N 51.40W
Gogra *r. see* Ghaghara India **58**
Goiandira Brazil **103** 18.06S 48.07W
Goiânia Brazil **103** 16.43S 49.18W
Goiás Brazil **103** 15.57S 50.07W
Goiás *d.* Brazil **103** 16.00S 50.10W
Göksun Turkey **56** 38.03N 36.30E
Gol Norway **46** 60.43N 8.55E
Gola I. Rep. of Ire. **38** 55.05N 8.21W
Golden Canada **90** 51.19N 116.58W
Golden Rep. of Ire. **39** 52.30N 7.59W
Golden B. New Zealand **82** 40.45S 172.50E
Golden Vale *f.* Rep. of Ire. **39** 52.30N 8.07W
Golders Green England **27** 51.35N 0.12W
Golfito Costa Rica **96** 8.42N 83.10W
Golspie Scotland **37** 57.58N 3.58W
Golyshi U.S.S.R. **47** 58.26N 45.28E
Goma Zaïre **73** 1.37S 29.10E
Gombe Nigeria **71** 10.17N 11.20E
Gombe *r.* Tanzania **73** 4.43S 31.30E
Gomel U.S.S.R. **47** 52.25N 31.00E
Gómez Palacio Mexico **96** 25.39N 103.30W
Gomshall England **27** 51.13N 0.25W
Gonaives Haiti **97** 19.29N 72.42W
Gonâve, G. of Haiti **97** 19.20N 73.00W
Gonâve I. Haiti **97** 18.50N 73.00W
Gonbad-e-Kavus Iran **57** 37.15N 55.11E
Gonda India **58** 27.08N 81.58E
Gondar Ethiopia **69** 12.39N 37.29E
Gongola *d.* Nigeria **71** 8.40N 11.30E
Gongola *r.* Nigeria **71** 9.30N 12.06E
Good Hope, C. of R.S.A. **74** 34.20S 18.25E
Goodooga Australia **80** 29.08S 147.30E
Goodwin Sands *f.* England **29** 51.16N 1.31E
Goole England **33** 53.42N 0.52W
Goondiwindi Australia **80** 28.30S 150.17E
Goose L. U.S.A. **90** 41.55N 120.25W
Göppingen W. Germany **44** 48.43N 9.39E
Gorakhpur India **58** 26.45N 83.23E
Gordon Scotland **35** 55.41N 2.34W
Gore New Zealand **82** 46.06S 168.58E
Gorebridge Scotland **35** 55.51N 3.02W
Gorey Rep. of Ire. **39** 52.40N 6.19W
Gorgan Iran **57** 36.50N 54.29E
Gorgan *r.* Iran **57** 37.00N 54.00E
Gori U.S.S.R. **57** 41.59N 44.05E
Gorinchem Neth. **45** 51.50N 4.59E
Goring England **28** 51.32N 1.08W
Gorizia Italy **42** 45.58N 13.37E
Gorki U.S.S.R. **47** 56.20N 44.00E
Görlitz E. Germany **44** 51.09N 15.00E
Gorlovka U.S.S.R. **47** 48.17N 38.05E
Gorm, Loch Scotland **34** 55.48N 6.25W
Gorongosa *r.* Moçambique **74** 20.29S 34.36E
Gorontalo Indonesia **61** 0.33N 123.05E
Gorseinon Wales **31** 51.40N 4.03W
Gort Rep. of Ire. **39** 53.04N 8.49W
Gortin N. Ireland **38** 54.43N 7.15W
Gorzów Wielkopolski Poland **44** 52.42N 15.12E
Gosford Australia **80** 33.25S 151.18E
Gosforth England **35** 55.02N 1.35W
Goslar W. Germany **44** 51.54N 10.25E
Gospić Yugo. **42** 4.34N 15.23E
Gosport England **28** 50.48N 1.08W
Göta Canal Sweden **46** 57.50N 11.50E
Göteborg Sweden **46** 57.45N 12.00E
Gotha E. Germany **44** 50.57N 10.43E
Gotland *i.* Sweden **46** 57.30N 18.30E
Gottingen W. Germany **44** 51.32N 9.57E
Gouda Neth. **45** 52.01N 4.43E
Gough I. Atlantic Oc. **112** 41.00S 10.00W
Gouin Resr. Canada **95** 48.40N 74.45W
Goulburn Australia **80** 34.47S 149.43E
Goundam Mali **70** 17.27N 3.39W
Gourdon France **40** 44.45N 1.22E
Gouré Niger **71** 13.59N 10.15E
Gourma-Rarous Mali **70** 16.58N 1.50W
Gournay France **40** 49.29N 1.44E
Gourock Scotland **34** 55.58N 4.49W
Gourock Range *mts.* Australia **80** 35.45S 149.25E
Gower *pen.* Wales **31** 51.37N 4.10W
Gowna, Lough Rep. of Ire. **38** 53.50N 7.34W
Gowran Rep. of Ire. **39** 52.38N 7.04W
Gozo *i.* Malta **42** 36.03N 14.16E
Gracias á Dios, Cabo *c.* Honduras/Nicaragua **96** 15.00N 83.10W
Grafton Australia **80** 29.40S 152.56E
Grafton U.S.A. **91** 48.28N 97.25W
Grahamstown R.S.A. **74** 33.19S 26.32E
Graiguenamanagh Rep. of Ire. **39** 52.33N 6.57W
Grain England **29** 51.28N 0.43E
Grampian *d.* Scotland **37** 57.22N 2.35W
Grampian Highlands Scotland **37** 56.55N 4.00W
Grampound England **31** 50.18N 4.54W
Granada Nicaragua **96** 11.58N 85.59W
Granada Spain **41** 37.10N 3.35W
Granard Rep. of Ire. **38** 53.47N 7.30W
Granby Canada **95** 45.23N 72.44W
Gran Canaria *i.* Canary Is. **68** 28.00N 15.30W
Gran Chaco *f.* S. America **103** 23.20S 60.00W
Grand *r.* Canada **94** 42.53N 79.35W
Grand Bahama I. Bahamas **97** 26.35N 78.00W
Grand Bassam Ivory Coast **70** 5.14N 3.45W
Grand Canal Rep. of Ire. **38** 53.21N 6.14W
Grand Canyon *f.* U.S.A. **90** 36.15N 113.00W
Grand Canyon *town* U.S.A. **90** 36.04N 112.07W
Grand Cayman *i.* Cayman Is. **96** 19.20N 81.30W
Grande *r.* Brazil **103** 20.00S 51.00W
Grande Comore *i.* Comoro Is. **73** 11.35S 43.20E
Grande I. Brazil **103** 23.15S 44.30W
Grande Prairie *town* Canada **92** 55.10N 118.52W
Grand Falls *town* New Brunswick Canada **95** 47.02N 67.46W
Grand Falls *town* Newfoundland Canada **93** 48.57N 55.40W
Grand Forks U.S.A. **91** 47.57N 97.05W
Grand Fort Philippe France **29** 51.00N 2.06E
Grand Island *town* U.S.A. **90** 40.56N 98.21W
Grand Junction U.S.A. **90** 39.04N 108.33W
Grand Manan I. Canada **95** 44.45N 66.45W
Grand Marais U.S.A. **94** 47.45N 90.20W
Grândola Portugal **41** 38.10N 8.34W
Grand Rapids *town* Mich. U.S.A. **94** 42.57N 85.40W
Grand Rapids *town* Minn. U.S.A. **94** 47.13N 93.31W
Grand Teton *mtn.* U.S.A. **90** 43.45N 110.50W
Grand Union Canal England **27** 52.37N 0.30W
Graney, Lough Rep. of Ire. **39** 52.59N 8.40W
Grangemouth Scotland **35** 56.01N 3.44W
Grange-over-Sands England **32** 54.12N 2.55W
Granite Peak *mtn.* U.S.A. **90** 45.10N 109.50W
Grankulla Finland **46** 60.12N 24.45E
Granóllers Spain **41** 41.37N 2.18E
Gran Paradiso *mtn.* Italy **42** 45.31N 7.15E
Gran Pilastro *mtn.* Italy **44** 46.58N 11.44E
Grantham England **33** 52.55N 0.39W
Grantown-on-Spey Scotland **37** 57.20N 3.38W
Grants Pass *town* U.S.A. **90** 42.26N 123.20W
Granville France **40** 48.50N 1.35W
Graskop R.S.A. **74** 24.55S 30.50E
Grasse France **40** 43.40N 6.56E
Grave Neth. **45** 51.45N 5.45E
Grave, Pointe de France **40** 45.35N 1.04W
Gravelines France **29** 50.59N 2.08E
Gravesend England **27** 51.27N 0.24E
Gravir Scotland **36** 58.03N 6.26W
Gray France **40** 47.27N 5.35E
Grayling U.S.A. **94** 44.40N 84.43W
Grays England **27** 51.29N 0.20E
Graz Austria **44** 47.05N 15.22E
Great Abaco I. Bahamas **97** 26.30N 77.00W
Great Artesian Basin *f.* Australia **79** 26.30S 143.02E
Great Australian Bight Australia **79** 33.20S 130.00E
Great Baddow England **27** 51.43N 0.29E
Great Bardfield England **29** 51.57N 0.26E
Great Barrier I. New Zealand **82** 36.15S 175.30E
Great Barrier Reef *f.* Australia **79** 16.30S 146.30E
Great Basin *f.* U.S.A. **90** 39.00N 115.30W
Great Bear L. Canada **92** 66.00N 120.00W
Great Bend *town* U.S.A. **90** 38.22N 98.47W
Great Bernera *i.* Scotland **36** 58.13N 6.50W
Great Blasket I. Rep. of Ire. **39** 52.05N 10.32W
Great Bookham England **27** 51.16N 0.20W
Great Chesterford England **29** 52.04N 0.11E
Great Coates England **33** 53.34N 0.05W
Great Coco *i.* Burma **60** 14.10N 93.25E
Great Dividing Range *mts.* Australia **80** 33.00S 151.00E
Great Driffield England **33** 54.01N 0.26W
Great Dunmow England **27** 51.53N 0.22E
Great Eccleston England **32** 53.51N 2.52W
Greater Antilles *is.* C. America **97** 17.00N 70.00W
Greater London *d.* England **27** 51.31N 0.06W
Greater Manchester *d.* England **32** 53.30N 2.18W
Great Exuma I. Bahamas **97** 23.00N 76.00W
Great Falls *town* U.S.A. **90** 47.30N 111.16W
Great Fish *r.* S.W. Africa **74** 28.07S 17.10E
Great Harwood England **32** 53.48N 2.24W
Great Inagua I. Bahamas **97** 21.00N 73.20W
Great Irgiz *r.* U.S.S.R. **47** 52.00N 47.20E
Great Karas Mts. S.W. Africa **74** 27.30S 18.45E
Great Karroo *f.* R.S.A. **74** 32.50S 22.30E
Great Khingan Shan *mts.* China **63** 50.00N 122.10E
Great L. Australia **80** 41.50S 146.43E
Great Lakes N. America **106** 47.00N 83.00W
Great Malvern England **28** 52.07N 2.19W
Great Missenden England **27** 51.43N 0.43W
Great Nama Land *f.* S.W. Africa **74** 25.30S 17.30E
Great Nicobar *i.* India **59** 7.00N 93.50E
Great Ormes Head Wales **30** 53.20N 3.52W
Great Ouse *r.* England **33** 52.47N 0.23E
Great Plains *f.* N. America **106** 45.00N 107.00W
Great Rift Valley *f.* Africa **107** 7.00S 33.00E
Great Ruaha *r.* Tanzania **73** 7.55S 37.52E
Great St. Bernard Pass Italy/Switz. **40** 45.52N 7.11E
Great Salt L. U.S.A. **90** 41.10N 112.40W
Great Sandy Desert Australia **107** 22.00S 125.00E
Great Sandy Desert Saudi Arabia **56** 28.40N 41.30E
Great Shelford England **29** 52.09N 0.08E
Great Shunner Fell *mtn.* England **32** 54.22N 2.12W
Great Skellig *i.* Rep. of Ire. **39** 51.46N 10.33W

Great Slave L. Canada **92** 61.30N 114.20W
Great Stour *r.* England **29** 51.19N 1.15E
Great Torrington England **31** 50.57N 4.09W
Great Whale *r.* Canada **93** 55.28N 77.45W
Great Whernside *mtn.* England **32** 54.09N 1.59W
Great Yarmouth England **29** 52.40N 1.45E
Great Zab *r.* Iraq **57** 35.37N 43.20E
Gredos, Sierra de *mts.* Spain **41** 40.18N 5.20W
Greece Europe **43** 39.00N 22.00E
Greece U.S.A. **95** 43.14N 77.38W
Greeley U.S.A. **90** 40.26N 104.43W
Green *r.* U.S.A. **90** 38.20N 109.53W
Green B. U.S.A. **94** 45.00N 87.30W
Green Bay *town* U.S.A. **94** 44.32N 88.00W
Greencastle Rep. of Ire. **34** 55.12N 6.59W
Greenhithe England **27** 51.28N 0.17E
Greenland N. America **93** 68.00N 45.00W
Greenlaw Scotland **35** 55.43N 2.28W
Green Lowther *mtn.* Scotland **35** 55.23N 3.45W
Green Mts. U.S.A. **95** 43.30N 73.00W
Greenock Scotland **34** 55.57N 4.45W
Greenore Pt. Rep. of Ire. **39** 52.14N 6.19W
Greensboro U.S.A. **91** 36.03N 79.50W
Greenstone Pt. Scotland **36** 57.55N 5.37W
Greenville Liberia **70** 5.01N 9.03W
Greenville Maine U.S.A. **95** 45.28N 69.36W
Greenville Miss. U.S.A. **91** 33.23N 91.03W
Greenville S.C. U.S.A. **91** 34.52N 82.25W
Greenwich *d.* England **27** 51.28N 0.00
Greenwich U.S.A. **95** 41.02N 73.37W
Gregory, L. Australia **80** 28.55S 139.00E
Greifswald E. Germany **44** 54.06N 13.24E
Greiz E. Germany **44** 50.40N 12.11E
Grenå Denmark **46** 56.25N 10.53E
Grenada C. America **97** 12.15N 61.45W
Grenade France **40** 43.47N 1.10E
Grenoble France **40** 45.11N 5.43E
Greta *r.* England **32** 54.09N 2.37W
Gretna Scotland **35** 55.00N 3.04W
Grey *r.* New Zealand **82** 42.28S 171.13E
Greyabbey N. Ireland **34** 54.32N 5.35W
Greymouth New Zealand **82** 42.28S 171.12E
Grey Range *mts.* Australia **80** 28.30S 142.15E
Greystones Rep. of Ire. **39** 53.09N 6.04W
Gribbin Head England **31** 50.19N 4.41W
Griffith Australia **80** 34.18S 146.04E
Grim, C. Australia **80** 40.45S 144.45E
Griminish Pt. Scotland **36** 57.40N 7.29W
Grimsay *i.* Scotland **36** 57.29N 7.14W
Grimsby England **33** 53.35N 0.05W
Grimsvötn *mtn.* Iceland **46** 64.30N 17.10W
Griqualand East *f.* R.S.A. **74** 30.30S 29.00E
Griqualand West *f.* R.S.A. **74** 28.55S 22.50E
Gris Nez, Cap France **29** 50.52N 1.35E
Grodno U.S.S.R. **47** 53.40N 23.50E
Groenlo Neth. **45** 52.02N 6.36E
Groix, Île de France **40** 47 38N 3.26N
Gröningen Neth. **45** 53.13N 6.35E
Gröningen *d.* Neth. **45** 53.15N 6.45E
Groomsport N. Ireland **34** 54.41N 5.37W
Groot *r.* Cape Province R.S.A. **74** 33.57S 25.00E
Groote Eylandt *i.* Australia **79** 14.00S 136.30E
Grootfontein S.W. Africa **74** 19.32S 18.05E
Grootlaagte *r.* Botswana **74** 20.50S 22.05E
Grosnez Pt. Channel Is. **31** 49.15N 2.15W
Grossenbrode W. Germany **44** 54.23N 11.07E
Grosseto Italy **42** 42.46N 11.08E
Gross Glockner *mtn.* Austria **44** 47.05N 12.50E
Grote Nete *r.* Belgium **45** 51.07N 4.20E
Groundhog *r.* Canada **94** 48.45N 82.00W
Grove Park England **27** 51.24N 0.03E
Groznyy U.S.S.R. **47** 43.21N 45.42E
Grumeti *r.* Tanzania **73** 2.05S 33.45E
Gruting Voe *b.* Scotland **36** 60.12N 1.32W
Guadalajara Mexico **96** 20.30N 103.20W
Guadalajara Spain **41** 40.37N 3.10W
Guadalete *r.* Spain **41** 36.37N 6.15W
Guadalmena *r.* Spain **41** 38.00N 3.50W
Guadalquivir *r.* Spain **41** 36.50N 6.20W
Guadalupe Mexico **96** 25.41N 100.15W
Guadalupe, Sierra de *mts.* Spain **41** 39.30N 5.25W
Guadalupe I. Mexico **90** 29.00N 118.25W
Guadarrama *r.* Spain **41** 39.55N 4.10W
Guadarrama, Sierra de *mts.* Spain **41** 41.00N 3.50W
Guadeloupe C. America **97** 16.20N 61.40W
Guadiana *r.* Spain **41** 37.10N 8.36W
Guadix Spain **41** 37.19N 3.08W
Guaira Falls *f.* Brazil **103** 24.00S 54.10W
Guajira Pen. Colombia **97** 12.00N 72.00W
Gualeguay Argentina **103** 33.10S 59.14W
Guam *i.* Pacific Oc. **61** 13.30N 144.40E
Guanajuato Mexico **96** 21.00N 101.16W
Guanajuato *d.* Mexico **96** 21.01N 101.00W
Guanare *r.* Venezuela **97** 8.20N 67.50W
Guane Cuba **96** 22.13N 84.07W
Guantánamo Cuba **97** 20.09N 75.14W
Guarapuava Brazil **103** 25.22S 51.28W
Guaratingueta Brazil **103** 22.49S 45.09W
Guarda Portugal **41** 40.32N 7.17W
Guardafui, C. Somali Rep. **69** 12.00N 51.30E
Guardo Spain **41** 42.47N 4.50W
Guatemala C. America **96** 15.40N 90.00W
Guatemala City Guatemala **96** 14.38N 90.22W
Guaxupe Brazil **103** 21.17S 46.44W
Guayaquil Ecuador **102** 2.13S 80.05W
Guaymas Mexico **90** 27.59N 110.54W
Gubin Poland **44** 51.59N 14.42E
Gudermes U.S.S.R. **47** 43.22N 46.06E
Guebwiller France **44** 47.55N 7.13E
Guecho Spain **41** 43.21N 3.01W
Guelph Canada **94** 43.34N 80.16W
Guéret France **40** 46.10N 1.52E
Guernsey *i.* Channel Is. **31** 49.27N 2.35W
Guerrero *d.* Mexico **96** 18.00N 100.00W
Guguan *i.* Asia **61** 17.20N 145.51E
Guiana S. America **102** 3.00N 53.00W
Guiana Highlands S. America **106** 4.00N 60.00W
Guildford England **27** 51.14N 0.35W
Guildtown Scotland **35** 56.28N 3.25W
Guilherne Capelo Ihe Angola **72** 5.11S 12.10E
Guinea Africa **70** 10.30N 11.30W
Guinea, G. of Africa **71** 3.00N 3.00E
Guinea Bissau Africa **70** 11.30N 15.00W
Güines Cuba **96** 22.50N 82.02W
Guînes France **29** 50.51N 1.52E
Guingamp France **40** 48.34N 3.09W
Guisborough England **33** 54.32N 1.02W
Guise France **45** 49.54N 3.39E
Guiseley England **32** 53.53N 1.42W
Gujarat *d.* India **58** 22.45N 71.30E
Gujranwala Pakistan **58** 32.06N 74.11E
Gulbarga India **58** 17.22N 76.47E
Gulbin Ka *r.* Nigeria **71** 11.35N 4.10E
Gulgong Australia **80** 32.20S 149.49E
Gullane Scotland **35** 56.02N 2.49W
Gulpaigan Iran **57** 33.23N 50.18E
Gulu Uganda **73** 2.46N 32.21E
Guma China **62** 37.30N 78.20E
Gümüşane Turkey **56** 40.26N 39.26E
Guna India **58** 24.39N 77.18E
Gundagai Australia **80** 35.07S 148.05E
Gungu Zaïre **72** 5.43S 19.20E
Gunnedah Australia **80** 30.59S 150.15E
Guntersville L. U.S.A. **91** 34.35N 86.00W
Guntur India **59** 16.20N 80.27E
Gunung Balu *mtn.* Indonesia **60** 3.00N 116.00E
Gurnard's Head *c.* England **31** 50.12N 5.35W
Gürün Turkey **56** 38.44N 37.15E
Guryev U.S.S.R. **48** 47.00N 52.00E
Gusau Nigeria **71** 12.12N 6.40E
Güstrow E. Germany **44** 53.48N 12.11E
Gutcher Scotland **36** 60.40N 1.00W
Gütersloh W. Germany **44** 51.54N 8.22E
Guyana S. America **97** 6.00N 60.00W
Guyhirn England **29** 52.37N 0.05E
Gwabegar Australia **80** 30.34S 149.00E
Gwadar Pakistan **57** 25.09N 62.21E
Gwai Rhodesia **74** 19.15S 27.42E
Gwai *r.* Rhodesia **74** 18.00S 26.47E
Gwalior India **58** 26.12N 78.09E
Gwanda Rhodesia **74** 20.59S 29.00E
Gwatar Iran **57** 25.10N 61.31E
Gweebarra B. Rep. of Ire. **38** 54.52N 8.28W
Gwelo Rhodesia **74** 19.25S 29.50E
Gwent *d.* Wales **31** 51.44N 3.00W
Gwynedd *d.* Wales **30** 53.00N 4.00W
Gyangtse China **58** 29.00N 89.40E
Gydanskiy Pen. U.S.S.R. **48** 70.00N 78.30E
Györ Hungary **47** 47.41N 17.40E

H

Haapajärvi Finland **46** 63.45N 25.20E
Haapamäki Finland **46** 62.15N 24.25E
Haapsalu U.S.S.R. **46** 58.58N 23.32E
Haarlem Neth. **45** 52.22N 4.38E
Habbaniya Iraq **56** 33.22N 43.35E
Hachinohe Japan **63** 40.30N 141.30E
Hacketstown Rep. of Ire. **39** 52.52N 6.35W
Hackney *d.* England **27** 51.33N 0.03W
Haddington Scotland **35** 55.57N 2.47W
Hadejia Nigeria **71** 12.30N 10.03E
Hadejia *r.* Nigeria **71** 12.47N 10.44E
Haderslev Denmark **46** 55.15N 9.30E
Hadfield England **32** 53.28N 1.59W
Hadhramaut *d.* S. Yemen **69** 16.30N 49.30E
Hadleigh England **29** 52.03N 0.58E
Hafar Saudi Arabia **57** 28.28N 46.00E
Hafnarfjördhur Iceland **46** 64.04N 21.58W
Haft Kel Iran **57** 31.28N 49.35E
Hagen W. Germany **45** 51.22N 7.27E
Hagerstown U.S.A. **95** 33.39N 77.44W
Ha Giang Vietnam **59** 22.50N 104.58E
Hags Head Rep. of Ire. **39** 52.56N 9.29W
Haifa Israel **56** 32.49N 34.59E
Haikow China **63** 20.05N 110.25E
Hail Saudi Arabia **56** 27.31N 41.45E
Hailar China **63** 49.15N 119.41E
Hailsham England **29** 50.52N 0.17E
Hailun China **63** 47.29N 126.58E
Hailuoto *i.* Finland **46** 65.00N 24.50E
Hainan *i.* China **60** 18.30N 109.40E
Hainaut *d.* Belgium **45** 50.30N 3.45E
Haines U.S.A. **92** 59.11N 135.23W
Haiphong Vietnam **59** 20.50N 106.41E
Haiti C. America **97** 19.00N 73.00W
Hakari Turkey **57** 37.36N 43.45E
Hakodate Japan **63** 41.46N 140.44E
Halberstadt E. Germany **44** 51.54N 11.04E
Halden Norway **46** 59.08N 11.13E
Halesowen England **28** 52.27N 2.02W
Halesworth England **29** 52.21N 1.30E
Haliburton Highlands Canada **95** 45.10N 78.30W
Halifax Canada **93** 44.38N 63.35W
Halifax England **32** 53.43N 1.51W
Halil *r.* Iran **58** 27.35N 58.44E
Halkett, C. U.S.A. **92** 71.00N 152.00W
Halkirk Scotland **37** 58.30N 3.30W
Halladale *r.* Scotland **37** 58.34N 3.54W
Halle Belgium **45** 50.45N 4.14E
Halle E. Germany **44** 51.28N 11.58E
Hallow England **28** 52.14N 2.15W
Hallsberg Sweden **46** 59.05N 15.07E
Hall's Creek *town* Australia **79** 18.17S 127.44E
Hallstavik Sweden **46** 60.06N 18.42E
Halmahera *i.* Indonesia **61** 0.45N 128.00E
Halmstad Sweden **46** 56.41N 12.55E
Hälsingborg Sweden **46** 56.05N 12.45E
Halstead England **29** 51.57N 0.39E
Haltern W. Germany **45** 51.45N 7.10E
Haltia Tunturi *mtn.* Norway **46** 69.20N 21.10E
Haltwhistle England **35** 54.58N 2.27W
Ham Scotland **36** 6.08N 2.04W
Hama Syria **56** 35.09N 36.44E
Hamadān Iran **57** 34.47N 48.33E
Hamamatsu Japan **63** 34.42N 137.42E
Hamar Norway **46** 60.47N 10.55E
Hamata, Gebel *mtn.* Egypt **56** 24.11N 35.01E
Hamble England **28** 50.52N 1.19W
Hambleton England **33** 53.46N 1.11W
Hambleton Hills England **33** 54.15N 1.11W
Hamborn W. Germany **45** 51.29N 6.46E
Hamburg W. Germany **44** 53.33N 10.00E
Hamdh, Wadi *r.* Saudi Arabia **56** 25.49N 36.37E
Hämeenlinna Finland **46** 61.00N 24.25E
Hameln W. Germany **44** 52.06N 9.21E
Hamersley Range *mts.* Australia **79** 22.00S 118.00E
Hami China **62** 42.40N 93.30E
Hamilton Australia **80** 37.45S 142.04E
Hamilton Bermuda **97** 32.18N 64.48W
Hamilton Canada **94** 43.15N 79.50W
Hamilton *r.* Canada **93** 53.20N 60.00W
Hamilton New Zealand **82** 37.46S 175.18E
Hamilton Scotland **35** 55.46N 4.10W
Hamilton U.S.A. **94** 39.23N 84.33W
Hamina Finland **46** 60.33N 27.15E
Hamirpur India **58** 25.57N 80.08E
Hamm W. Germany **45** 51.40N 7.49E
Hammerfest Norway **46** 70.40N 23.44E
Hammersmith *d.* England **27** 51.30N 0.14W
Hammond U.S.A. **94** 39.48N 88.37W
Hamoir Belgium **45** 50.25N 5.32E
Hampshire *d.* England **28** 51.03N 1.20W
Hampshire Downs *hills* England **28** 51.18N 1.25W
Hampstead England **27** 51.33N 0.11W
Hampton England **27** 51.25N 0.22W
Hamrin, Jabal *mts.* Iraq **57** 34.40N 44.10E
Hamstreet England **29** 51.03N 0.52E
Hamun-i-Sabari *l.* Iran **57** 31.24N 61.16E
Hanakiya Saudi Arabia **56** 24.53N 40.30E
Hanang *mtn.* Tanzania **73** 4.30S 35.21E
Hanau W. Germany **44** 50.08N 8.56E
Hanchung China **59** 33.10N 107.02E
Hancock U.S.A. **94** 47.08N 88.34W
Handa *i.* Scotland **36** 58.23N 5.12W
Handeni Tanzania **73** 5.25S 38.04E
Hangchow China **63** 30.10N 120.07E
Hangö Finland **46** 59.50N 23.00E
Han Kiang *r.* China **63** 30.45N 114.24E
Hanmer Springs *town* New Zealand **82** 42.34S 172.46E
Hannibal U.S.A. **94** 39.41N 91.20W
Hanningfield Water England **27** 51.38N 0.28E
Hannover W. Germany **44** 52.23N 9.44E
Hannut Belgium **45** 50.40N 5.05E
Hanoi Vietnam **59** 21.01N 105.52E
Hanover R.S.A. **74** 31.05S 24.27E

Hanworth England **27** 51.26N 0.23W
Haparanda Sweden **46** 65.50N 24.10E
Haradh Saudi Arabia **57** 24.12N 49.08E
Harar Ethiopia **69** 9.20N 42.10E
Harbin China **63** 45.45N 126.41E
Harburg W. Germany **44** 53.27N 9.58E
Hardanger Fjord *est.* Norway **46** 60.15N 6.25E
Hardanger Vidda *f.* Norway **46** 60.20N 8.00E
Harderwijk Neth. **45** 52.21N 5.37E
Harding R.S.A. **74** 30.36S 29.55E
Hardoi India **58** 27.23N 80.06E
Harefield England **27** 51.36N 0.28W
Haren W. Germany **45** 52.48N 7.15E
Hargeisa Somali Rep. **69** 9.31N 44.02E
Hari *r.* Afghan. **57** 35.42N 61.12E
Hari *r.* Indonesia **60** 1.00S 104.15E
Haringey *d.* England **27** 51.36N 0.06W
Harlech Wales **30** 52.52N 4.08W
Harleston England **29** 52.25N 1.18E
Harlingen Neth. **45** 53.10N 5.25E
Harlington England **27** 51.29N 0.25W
Harlow England **27** 51.47N 0.08E
Harmerhill England **32** 52.48N 2.45W
Harney Basin *f.* U.S.A. **90** 43.20N 119.00W
Härnösand Sweden **46** 62.37N 17.55E
Harold Hill England **27** 51.36N 0.12E
Haroldswick Scotland **36** 60.47N 0.50W
Harold Wood England **27** 51.35N 0.12E
Harpenden England **27** 51.49N 0.22W
Harricanaw *r.* Canada **91** 51.05N 79.45W
Harris *i.* Scotland **36** 57.50N 6.55W
Harris, Sd. of Scotland **36** 57.43N 7.05W
Harrisburg U.S.A. **95** 40.17N 76.54W
Harrismith R.S.A. **74** 28.16S 29.08E
Harrison, C. Canada **93** 55.00N 58.00W
Harrogate England **33** 53.59N 1.32W
Harrow England **27** 51.35N 0.21W
Harrow on the Hill England **27** 51.34N 0.21W
Harstad Norway **46** 68.48N 16.30E
Hartford U.S.A. **95** 41.45N 72.42W
Hartington England **32** 53.08N 1.49W
Hartland England **31** 50.59N 4.29W
Hartland Pt. England **31** 51.01N 4.32W
Hartlepool England **33** 54.42N 1.11W
Hartley England **27** 51.23N 0.18E
Hartley Rhodesia **74** 18.04S 30.06E
Harud *r.* Afghan. **57** 31.36N 61.12E
Harvey U.S.A. **94** 41.38N 87.40W
Harwich England **29** 51.56N 1.18E
Haryana *d.* India **58** 29.15N 76.00E
Harz Mts. E. Germany/W. Germany **44** 51.40N 10.55E
Hasa Oasis Saudi Arabia **57** 25.37N 49.40E
Hase *r.* W. Germany **45** 52.42N 7.17E
Hashtrud Iran **57** 37.29N 47.05E
Haslemere England **28** 51.05N 0.41W
Haslingden England **32** 53.43N 2.20W
Hasselt Belgium **45** 50.56N 5.20E
Hassi Messaoud Algeria **68** 31.53N 5.43E
Hässleholm Sweden **46** 56.09N 13.45E
Hastings England **29** 50.51N 0.36E
Hastings New Zealand **82** 39.39S 176.52E
Hastings U.S.A. **94** 44.43N 92.50W
Hatfield Australia **80** 33.53S 143.47E
Hatfield England **27** 51.46N 0.13W
Hatherleigh England **31** 50.49N 4.04W
Hathersage England **32** 53.20N 1.39W
Hathras India **58** 27.36N 78.02E
Hatteras, C. U.S.A. **91** 35.14N 75.31W
Hattiesburg U.S.A. **91** 31.25N 89.19W
Hatton England **32** 52.52N 1.40W
Haugesund Norway **46** 59.25N 5.16E
Hauki Vesi *l.* Finland **46** 62.10N 28.30E
Hauraki G. New Zealand **82** 36.30S 175.00E
Hauran, Wadi *r.* Iraq **56** 33.57N 42.35E
Haut Zaïre *d.* Zaïre **73** 2.00N 27.00E
Havana Cuba **96** 23.07N 82.25W
Havana *d.* Cuba **96** 23.07N 82.25W
Havant England **28** 50.51N 0.59W
Havel *r.* E. Germany **44** 52.51N 11.57E
Haverfordwest Wales **31** 51.48N 4.59W
Haverhill England **29** 52.06N 0.27E
Haverhill U.S.A. **95** 42.47N 71.07W
Havering England **27** 51.34N 0.14E
Havlickuv Brod Czech. **44** 49.38N 15.35E
Havre U.S.A. **90** 48.34N 109.45W
Havre de Grace U.S.A. **95** 39.33N 76.06W
Hawaii *d.* U.S.A. **90** 21.00N 156.00W
Hawaii *i.* Hawaii U.S.A. **90** 19.30N 155.30W
Hawaiian Is. U.S.A. **90** 21.00N 157.00W
Hawea, L. New Zealand **82** 44.30S 169.15E
Hawera New Zealand **82** 39.35S 174.19E
Hawes England **32** 54.18N 2.12W
Hawes Water *l.* England **32** 54.30N 2.45W
Hawick Scotland **35** 55.25N 2.47W
Hawke, C. Australia **80** 32.12S 152.33E
Hawke B. New Zealand **82** 39.18S 177.15E
Hawkhurst England **29** 51.02N 0.31E
Hawthorne U.S.A. **90** 38.13N 118.37W
Hay Australia **80** 34.31S 144.31E
Haydon Bridge England **35** 54.58N 2.14W
Hayes *r.* Canada **93** 57.00N 92.30W
Hayes England **27** 51.31N 0.25W
Hayle England **31** 50.12N 5.25W
Hay-on-Wye Wales **30** 52.04N 3.09W
Hay River *town* Canada **92** 60.51N 115.42W
Haywards Heath *f.* England **29** 51.00N 0.05W
Hazaribagh India **58** 24.00N 85.23E
Hazelton Canada **92** 55.16N 127.18W
Hazlemere England **27** 51.39N 0.42W
Hazleton U.S.A. **95** 40.58N 75.59W
Heacham England **33** 52.55N 0.30E
Headcorn England **27** 51.11N 0.37E
Headford Rep. of Ire. **38** 53.28N 9.08W
Heads of Ayr *c.* Scotland **34** 55.26N 4.42W
Heanor England **33** 53.01N 1.20W
Heard I. Indian Oc. **113** 53.07S 73.20E
Hearst Canada **94** 49.42N 83.40W
Heath End England **28** 51.21N 1.08W
Heathfield England **29** 50.58N 0.18E
Hebden Bridge *town* England **32** 53.45N 2.00W
Hebel Australia **80** 28.55S 147.49E
Hebrides *is.* U.K. **18** 58.00N 7.00W
Hebron Jordan **56** 31.32N 35.06E
Hecate Str. Canada **92** 53.00N 131.00W
Hechtel Belgium **45** 51.07N 5.22E
Heckington England **33** 52.59N 0.18W
Hedon England **33** 53.44N 0.11W
Heemstede Neth. **45** 52.21N 4.38E
Heerde Neth. **45** 52.23N 6.02E
Heerenveen Neth. **45** 52.57N 5.55E
Heerlen Neth. **45** 50.53N 5.59E
Heidelberg W. Germany **44** 49.25N 8.42E
Heidenheim W. Germany **44** 48.41N 10.10E
Heilbron R.S.A. **74** 27.17S 27.58E
Heilbronn W. Germany **44** 49.08N 9.14E
Heilungkiang *d.* China **63** 47.00N 109.00E
Heinola Finland **46** 61.13N 26.05E
Heinsberg W. Germany **45** 51.04N 6.06E
Hejaz *f.* Saudi Arabia **56** 26.00N 37.30E
Hekla, Mt. Iceland **46** 64.00N 19.45W
Helena U.S.A. **90** 46.35N 112.00W
Helen Reef *i.* Asia **61** 2.43N 131.46E
Helensburgh Scotland **34** 56.01N 4.44W
Helensville New Zealand **82** 36.40S 174.28E
Heligoland *i.* W. Germany **44** 54.10N 7.51E
Heligoland B. W. Germany **44** 54.00N 8.15E
Heliopolis Egypt **56** 30.06N 31.20E
Hellendoorn Neth. **45** 52.24N 6.29E
Hellevoetsluis Neth. **45** 51.49N 4.08E
Hellifield England **32** 54.00N 2.13W
Hellín Spain **41** 38.31N 1.43W
Helmand *r.* Asia **58** 31.10N 61.20E
Helmond Neth. **45** 51.28N 5.40E
Helmsdale Scotland **37** 58.07N 3.40W
Helmsley England **33** 54.15N 1.20W
Helmstedt W. Germany **44** 52.14N 11.01E
Helsingör Denmark **46** 56.03N 12.38E
Helsinki Finland **46** 60.08N 25.00E
Helston England **31** 50.07N 5.17W
Helvellyn *mtn.* England **32** 54.31N 3.00W
Helvick Head Rep. of Ire. **39** 52.03N 7.32W
Helwân Egypt **56** 29.51N 31.20E
Hemel Hempstead England **27** 51.46N 0.28W
Hempstead U.S.A. **95** 40.42N 73.37W
Hemsworth England **33** 53.37N 1.21W
Henares *r.* Spain **41** 40.26N 3.35W
Hendaye France **40** 43.22N 1.46W
Hendon England **27** 51.35N 0.14W
Hendrik Verwoerd Dam R.S.A. **74** 31.00S 26.00E
Henfield England **29** 50.56N 0.17W
Hengelo Neth. **45** 52.16N 6.46E
Henley-on-Thames England **28** 51.32N 0.53W
Henrietta Maria, C. Canada **93** 55.00N 82.15W
Henrique de Carvalho Angola **72** 9.38S 20.20E
Henty Australia **80** 35.30S 147.03E
Henzada Burma **59** 17.38N 95.35E
Herat Afghan. **57** 34.21N 62.10E
Herauabad Iran **57** 37.36N 48.36E
Hérault *r.* France **40** 43.17N 3.28E
Hereford England **28** 52.04N 2.43W
Hereford and Worcester *d.* England **28** 52.08N 2.30W
Herford W. Germany **44** 52.07N 8.40E
Herma Ness *c.* Scotland **36** 60.50N 0.54W
Hermidale Australia **80** 31.33S 146.44E
Hermon, Mt. Lebanon **56** 33.24N 35.52E
Hermosillo Mexico **90** 29.15N 110.59W
Herne W. Germany **45** 51.32N 7.12E
Herne Bay *town* England **29** 51.23N 1.10E
Herning Denmark **46** 56.08N 9.00E
Heron Bay *town* Canada **94** 48.41N 86.26W
Herrick Australia **80** 41.04S 147.53E
Herstal Belgium **45** 50.14N 5.38E
Hertford England **27** 51.48N 0.05W
Hertfordshire *d.* England **29** 51.51N 0.05W
Hesbaye *f.* Belgium **45** 50.32N 5.07E
Hessle England **33** 53.44N 0.28W
Heston England **27** 51.29N 0.23W
Heswall England **30** 53.20N 3.06W
Hetton-le-Hole England **33** 54.19N 1.26W
Hexham England **35** 54.58N 2.06W
Hextable England **27** 51.25N 0.12E
Heysham England **32** 54.03N 2.53W
Heywood England **32** 53.36N 2.13W
Hidalgo *d.* Mexico **96** 20.50N 98.30W
Hidalgo Sabinas Mexico **96** 26.33N 100.10W
Hieradhsvotn *r.* Iceland **46** 65.45N 18.50W
Higham England **27** 51.25N 0.29E
Higham Ferrers England **28** 52.18N 0.36W
High Atlas *mts.* Morocco **68** 32.00N 5.50W
High Bentham England **32** 54.08N 2.31W
Highland *d.* Scotland **36** 57.42N 5.00W
High Peak *mtn.* England **32** 53.22N 1.48W
High Willhays *mtn.* England **31** 50.41N 4.00W
Highworth England **28** 51.38N 1.42W
High Wycombe England **27** 51.38N 0.46W
Hiiumaa *i.* U.S.S.R. **46** 58.50N 22.30E
Hikurangi *mtn.* New Zealand **82** 37.50S 178.10E
Hildesheim W. Germany **44** 52.09N 9.58E
Hilla Iraq **57** 32.28N 44.29E
Hillingdon England **27** 51.32N 0.27W
Hill of Fare Scotland **37** 57.06N 2.33W
Hill of Fearn *town* Scotland **37** 57.47N 3.57W
Hillston Australia **80** 33.30S 145.33E
Hillswick Scotland **36** 60.28N 1.30W
Hilo Hawaii U.S.A. **90** 19.42N 155.04W
Hilpsford Pt. England **32** 54.02N 3.10W
Hilversum Neth. **45** 52.14N 5.12E
Himachal Pradesh *d.* India **58** 31.45N 77.30E
Himalaya *mts.* Asia **58** 29.00N 84.00E
Hinckley England **28** 52.33N 1.21W
Hindhead England **28** 51.06N 0.42W
Hindmarsh, L. Australia **80** 36.03S 141.53E
Hindu Kush *mts.* Asia **58** 36.40N 70.00E
Hingol *r.* Pakistan **58** 25.25N 65.32E
Hinnoy *i.* Norway **46** 68.30N 16.00E
Hirakud Resr. India **59** 21.32N 83.55E
Hirgis Nur *l.* Mongolia **62** 49.20N 93.40E
Hiroshima Japan **63** 34.23N 132.27E
Hirson France **45** 49.56N 4.05E
Hirwaun Wales **31** 51.43N 3.30W
Hispaniola *i.* C. America **97** 19.00N 71.00W
Histon England **29** 52.15N 0.05E
Hit Iraq **56** 33.38N 42.50E
Hitchin England **29** 51.57N 0.16W
Hitra *i.* Norway **46** 63.30N 8.50E
Hjälmaren *l.* Sweden **46** 59.10N 15.45E
Hjörring Denmark **46** 57.28N 9.59E
Hlotse Lesotho **74** 28.52S 28.03E
Ho Ghana **70** 6.38N 0.38E
Hoarusib *r.* S.W. Africa **74** 19.05S 12.36E
Hobart Australia **80** 42.54S 147.18E
Hobro Denmark **46** 56.39N 9.49E
Ho Chi Minh City Vietnam **60** 10.46N 106.43E
Hochschwab *mts.* Austria **44** 47.37N 15.08E
Hochwan China **59** 30.00N 106.15E
Hockley Heath England **28** 52.21N 1.46W
Hodder *r.* England **32** 53.50N 2.26W
Hoddesdon England **27** 51.46N 0.01W
Hodeida Yemen **69** 14.50N 42.58E
Hódmezövásárhely Hungary **43** 46.26N 20.21E
Hodnet England **32** 52.51N 2.35W
Hoehuetenango Guatemala **96** 15.19N 91.26W
Hof W. Germany **44** 50.19N 11.56E
Hofei China **63** 31.55N 117.18E
Hofn Iceland **46** 64.16N 15.10W
Hofors Sweden **46** 60.34N 16.17E
Hofsjökull *mtn.* Iceland **46** 64.50N 19.00W
Hofuf Saudi Arabia **57** 25.20N 49.34E
Hog's Back *hill* England **27** 51.14N 0.39W
Hog's Head Rep. of Ire. **39** 51.47N 10.13W
Hoima Uganda **73** 1.25N 31.22E
Hokitika New Zealand **82** 42.42S 170.59E
Hokkaido *i.* Japan **63** 43.30N 143.20E
Hokow China **59** 22.39N 103.57E
Holbeach England **33** 52.48N 0.01E
Holbrook Australia **80** 35.46S 147.20E
Holbrook U.S.A. **90** 34.58N 110.00W
Holderness *f.* England **33** 53.45N 0.05W
Holguín Cuba **97** 20.54N 76.15W
Holkham B. England **33** 53.00N 0.45E
Holland U.S.A. **94** 42.46N 86.06W
Holland Fen *f.* England **33** 53.02N 0.12W
Hollesley B. England **29** 52.02N 1.33E
Holmes Chapel England **32** 53.13N 2.21W
Holme upon Spalding Moor England **33** 53.50N 0.47W
Holmfirth England **32** 53.34N 1.48W
Holstebro Denmark **46** 56.22N 8.38E

Holsworthy England **31** 50.48N 4.21W
Holt England **33** 52.55N 1.04E
Holten Neth. **45** 52.18N 6.26E
Holwerd Neth. **45** 53.22N 5.54E
Holyhead Wales **30** 53.18N 4.38W
Holyhead B. Wales **30** 53.22N 4.40W
Holy I. England **35** 55.41N 1.47W
Holy I. Scotland **34** 55.32N 5.04W
Holy I. Wales **30** 53.15N 4.38W
Holyoke U.S.A. **95** 42.12N 72.37W
Holywell Wales **30** 53.17N 3.13W
Holywood N. Ireland **34** 54.38N 5.50W
Home B. Canada **93** 69.00N 66.00W
Homer U.S.A. **92** 59.40N 151.37W
Homer Tunnel New Zealand **82** 44.40S 168.15E
Homoine Moçambique **74** 23.45S 35.09E
Homs Syria **56** 34.44N 36.43E
Honan *d.* China **63** 33.45N 113.00E
Hondo *r.* Mexico **96** 18.33N 88.22W
Honduras C. America **96** 14.30N 87.00W
Honduras, G. of Carib. Sea **96** 16.20N 87.30W
Hönefoss Norway **46** 60.10N 10.16E
Honfleur France **40** 49.25N 0.14E
Hong Kong Asia **60** 22.30N 114.10E
Honiton England **28** 50.48N 3.13W
Honolulu Hawaii U.S.A. **90** 21.19N 157.50W
Honshu *i.* Japan **63** 36.00N 138.00E
Hoogeveen Neth. **45** 52.44N 6.29E
Hoogezand Neth. **45** 53.10N 6.47E
Hoogstade Belgium **45** 50.59N 2.42E
Hook England **28** 51.17N 0.55W
Hook Head Rep. of Ire. **39** 52.07N 6.55W
Hook of Holland Neth. **45** 51.59N 4.08E
Hoopstad R.S.A. **74** 27.50S 25.55E
Hoorn Neth. **45** 52.38N 5.03E
Hoover Dam U.S.A. **90** 36.01N 114.45W
Hope, Loch Scotland **37** 58.27N 4.38W
Hopedale Canada **93** 55.30N 60.10W
Hopeh *d.* China **63** 39.20N 117.15E
Hopetoun Australia **80** 35.43S 142.20E
Hopetown R.S.A. **74** 29.37S 24.05E
Hor Al Hammar *l.* Iraq **57** 30.50N 47.00E
Hor Auda *l.* Iraq **57** 31.36N 46.53E
Horbury England **33** 53.41N 1.33W
Horde W. Germany **45** 51.29N 7.30E
Horley England **27** 51.11N 0.11W
Hormuz, Str. of Asia **57** 26.35N 56.20E
Horn, C. S. America **106** 55.00S 67.00W
Hornavan *l.* Sweden **46** 66.15N 17.40E
Horncastle England **33** 53.13N 0.08W
Hornchurch England **27** 51.34N 0.13E
Horn Head Rep. of Ire. **38** 55.13N 7.59W
Hornsea England **33** 53.55N 0.10W
Hornsey England **27** 51.35N 0.08W
Hor Sanniya *l.* Iraq **57** 31.52N 46.50E
Horsell England **27** 51.20N 0.35W
Horsens Denmark **46** 55.53N 9.53E
Horsforth England **33** 53.50N 1.39W
Horsham Australia **80** 36.45S 142.15E
Horsham England **29** 51.04N 0.20W
Horten Norway **46** 59.25N 10.30E
Horton *r.* Canada **92** 70.00N 127.00W
Horton Bucks. England **27** 51.53N 0.40W
Horton Surrey England **27** 51.21N 0.18W
Horwich England **32** 53.37N 2.33W
Hose Range *mts.* Malaysia **60** 1.30N 114.10E
Hoshangabad India **58** 22.44N 77.45E
Hoshiarpur India **58** 31.30N 75.59E
Hospital *town* Rep. of Ire. **39** 52.29N 8.26W
Hospitalet Spain **41** 41.20N 2.06E
Hotazel R.S.A. **74** 27.18S 22.54E
Hoting Sweden **46** 64.08N 16.15E
Houghton-le-Spring England **33** 54.51N 1.28W
Houlton U.S.A. **95** 46.09N 67.50W
Houndé U. Volta **70** 11.34N 3.31W
Hounslow England **27** 51.29N 0.22W
Hourn, Loch Scotland **36** 57.06N 5.33W
Houston U.S.A. **91** 29.45N 95.25W
Hovd Mongolia **62** 46.40N 90.45E
Hove England **29** 50.50N 0.10W
Hoveton England **29** 52.45N 1.23E
Hovingham England **33** 54.10N 0.59W
Howden England **33** 53.45N 0.52W
Howe, C. Australia **80** 37.30S 149.59E
Howitt, Mt. Australia **80** 37.15S 146.40E
Howmore Scotland **36** 57.18N 7.23W
Howrah India **58** 22.35N 88.20E
Howth Rep. of Ire. **38** 53.23N 6.06W
Hoy *i.* Scotland **37** 58.51N 3.17W
Hoyerswerda E. Germany **44** 51.28N 14.17E
Hoylake England **32** 53.24N 3.11W
Hoy Sd. Scotland **37** 58.55N 3.20W
Hradec Králové Czech. **44** 50.13N 15.50E
Hsiapachen China **62** 40.52N 107.04E
Huab *r.* S.W. Africa **74** 20.45S 13.27E
Huajuápam Mexico **96** 17.50N 97.48W
Hualien Taiwan **63** 24.00N 121.39E
Huambo *d.* Angola **72** 12.30S 15.45E
Huambo Angola **72** 12.47S 15.44E
Hubli India **58** 15.20N 75.14E
Hucknall England **33** 53.03N 1.12W
Hucqueliers France **29** 50.34N 1.55E
Huddersfield England **32** 53.38N 1.49W
Hudiksvall Sweden **46** 61.45N 17.10E
Hudson *r.* U.S.A. **95** 40.45N 74.00W
Hudson B. Canada **93** 58.00N 86.00W
Hudson Str. Canada **93** 62.00N 70.00W
Hué Vietnam **60** 16.28N 107.35E
Huelva Spain **41** 37.15N 6.56W
Huelva *r.* Spain **41** 37.25N 6.00W
Huércal Overa Spain **41** 37.23N 1.56W
Huesca Spain **41** 42.02N 0.25W
Hughenden Australia **79** 20.50S 144.10E
Hugh Town England **31** 49.55N 6.19W
Huhehot China **63** 40.49N 111.37E
Huiarau Range *mts.* New Zealand **82** 38.20S 177.15E
Huila *d.* Angola **72** 15.30S 15.30E
Huixtla Mexico **96** 15.09N 92.30W
Hull Canada **95** 45.26N 75.45W
Hull *r.* England **33** 53.44N 0.23W
Hullbridge England **27** 51.37N 0.36E
Hultsfred Sweden **46** 57.30N 15.50E
Hulun Chih *l.* China **63** 49.00N 117.20E
Humansdorp R.S.A. **74** 34.01S 24.45E
Humber *r.* England **33** 53.40N 0.12W
Humberside *d.* England **33** 53.48N 0.35W
Hume, L. Australia **80** 36.05S 147.10E
Humphreys Peak *mtn.* U.S.A. **90** 35.21N 111.41W
Hun Libya **68** 29.06N 15.57E
Húna Flói *b.* Iceland **46** 65.45N 20.50W
Hunan *d.* China **63** 27.30N 111.30E
Hungary Europe **47** 47.30N 19.00E
Hungerford Australia **80** 29.00S 144.26E
Hungerford England **28** 51.25N 1.30W
Hungnam N. Korea **63** 39.49N 127.40E
Hungshui Ho *r.* China **63** 23.20N 110.04E
Hunse *r.* Neth. **45** 53.20N 6.18E
Hunsrück *mts.* W. Germany **45** 49.44N 7.05E
Hunstanton England **33** 52.57N 0.30E
Hunte *r.* W. Germany **44** 52.30N 8.19E
Hunter Mtn. U.S.A. **95** 42.10N 74.14W
Huntingdon England **29** 52.20N 0.11W
Huntly New Zealand **82** 37.35S 175.10E
Huntly Scotland **37** 57.27N 2.47W
Huntsville Canada **95** 45.20N 79.14W
Huntsville U.S.A. **91** 30.43N 95.34W
Hunyani *r.* Moçambique **74** 15.35S 30.30E
Huon Pen. P.N.G. **61** 6.00S 147.00E
Hupeh *d.* China **63** 31.15N 112.15E
Hurd, C. Canada **94** 45.14N 81.44W
Hurghada Egypt **56** 27.17N 33.47E
Hurliness Scotland **37** 58.47N 3.13W
Huron U.S.A. **90** 44.22N 98.12W
Huron, L. Canada/U.S.A. **94** 45.00N 82.30W
Hursley England **28** 51.01N 1.23W
Hurst Green England **27** 51.14N 0.00
Husavik Iceland **46** 66.03N 17.17W
Husbands Bosworth England **28** 52.27N 1.03W
Huskvarna Sweden **46** 57.47N 14.15E
Husum W. Germany **44** 54.29N 9.04E
Hutchinson U.S.A. **90** 38.03N 97.56W
Hutt New Zealand **82** 41.12S 174.54E
Hutton Cranswick England **33** 53.57N 0.27W
Huy Belgium **45** 50.31N 5.14E
Hvar *i.* Yugo. **43** 43.10N 16.45E
Hvita *r.* Iceland **46** 64.33N 21.45W
Hwaian Kiangsu China **63** 33.30N 119.20E
Hwai Ho *r.* China **63** 32.58N 118.18E
Hwang Ho *r.* China **63** 37.55N 118.46E
Hwangkang China **63** 30.40N 114.50E
Hwangshih China **63** 30.13N 115.05E
Hyde England **32** 53.26N 2.06W
Hyde Park *f.* England **27** 51.31N 0.12W
Hyderabad India **59** 17.22N 78.26E
Hyderabad Pakistan **58** 25.23N 68.24E
Hyères France **40** 43.07N 6.08E
Hyères, Îles d' France **40** 43.01N 6.25E
Hyndman Peak U.S.A. **90** 43.46N 113.55W
Hynish Scotland **34** 56.26N 6.55W
Hynish B. Scotland **34** 56.28N 6.52W
Hythe Hants. England **28** 50.51N 1.24W
Hythe Kent England **29** 51.04N 1.05E
Hyvinkää Finland **46** 60.37N 24.50E

I

Ialomita *r.* Romania **43** 44.41N 27.52E
Iar Connacht *f.* Rep. of Ire. **38** 53.21N 9.22W
Iaşi Romania **47** 47.09N 27.38E
Ibadan Nigeria **71** 7.23N 3.56E
Ibar *r.* Yugo. **43** 43.44N 20.44E
Ibbenbüren W. Germany **45** 52.17N 7.44E
Ibi Nigeria **71** 8.11N 9.44E
Ibina *r.* Zaïre **73** 1.00N 28.40E
Ibiza Spain **41** 38.55N 1.30E
Ibiza *i. see* Iviza Spain **41**
Ibstock England **28** 52.42N 1.23W
Iceland Europe **46** 64.45N 18.00W
Ichang China **63** 30.43N 111.22E
Ickenham England **27** 51.34N 0.26W
Idah Nigeria **71** 7.05N 6.45E
Idaho *d.* U.S.A. **90** 45.00N 115.00W
Idaho Falls *town* U.S.A. **90** 43.30N 112.01W
Idar W. Germany **45** 49.43N 7.19E
Idfu Egypt **56** 24.58N 32.50E
Ídhi *mtn.* Greece **43** 35.13N 24.45E
Idi Amin Dada, L. Uganda/Zaïre **73** 0.30S 29.30E
Idiofa Zaïre **72** 4.58S 19.38E
Idrigill Pt. Scotland **36** 57.20N 6.35W
Iesi Italy **42** 43.32N 13.15E
Ifalik *is.* Asia **61** 7.15N 144.27E
Ife Western Nigeria **71** 7.33N 4.34E
Ighil Izane Algeria **41** 35.45N 0.30E
Iglésias Italy **42** 39.18N 8.32E
Iğneada, C. Turkey **43** 41.50N 28.05E
Igoumenitsa Greece **43** 39.32N 20.14E
Iguaçu *r.* Brazil **103** 25.33S 54.35W
Iguala Mexico **96** 18.21N 99.31W
Igualada Spain **41** 41.35N 1.37E
Iguape Brazil **103** 24.44S 47.31W
Ii *r.* Finland **46** 65.17N 25.15E
Iisalmi Finland **46** 63.34N 27.08E
Ijebu Ode Nigeria **71** 6.47N 3.54E
IJmuiden Neth. **45** 52.28N 4.37E
IJssel *r.* Overijssel Neth. **45** 52.34N 5.50E
IJssel *r.* South Holland Neth. **45** 51.54N 4.32E
IJsselmeer *l.* Neth. **45** 52.45N 5.20E
Ijzer *r.* Belgium **45** 51.09N 2.44E
Ikaría *i.* Greece **43** 37.35N 26.10E
Ikela Zaïre **72** 1.06S 23.04E
Ikelemba Congo **72** 1.15N 16.38E
Ikelemba *r.* Zaïre **72** 0.08N 18.19E
Ikomba Tanzania **73** 9.09S 32.20E
Ikopa *r.* Malagasy Rep. **73** 16.00S 46.22E
Ilagan Phil. **61** 17.07N 121.53E
Ilam Iran **57** 33.27N 46.27E
Ilan China **63** 46.22N 129.31E
Ilaro Nigeria **71** 6.53N 3.03E
Ilchester England **28** 51.00N 2.41W
Ilebo Zaïre **72** 4.20S 20.35E
Ilen *r.* Rep. of Ire. **39** 51.53N 9.20W
Ilesha Western Nigeria **71** 7.39N 4.38E
Ilford England **27** 51.33N 0.06E
Ilfracombe England **31** 51.13N 4.08W
Ili *r.* U.S.S.R. **62** 45.00N 74.20E
Iligan Phil. **61** 8.12N 124.13E
Ilkeston England **33** 52.59N 1.19W
Ilkley England **32** 53.56N 1.49W
Iller *r.* W. Germany **40** 48.29N 10.03E
Illescas Uruguay **103** 33.34S 55.20W
Illinois *d.* U.S.A. **94** 40.15N 89.15W
Illinois *r.* U.S.A. **94** 38.56N 90.27W
Ilminster England **28** 50.55N 2.56W
Iloilo Phil. **61** 10.45N 122.33E
Ilorin Nigeria **71** 8.32N 4.34E
Imala Moçambique **73** 14.39S 39.34E
Imandra, L. U.S.S.R. **46** 67.30N 32.45E
Imatra Finland **46** 61.14N 28.50E
Immingham England **33** 53.37N 0.12W
Imo *d.* Nigeria **71** 5.30N 7.20E
Imperia Italy **40** 43.53N 8.00E
Imperial Dam U.S.A. **90** 33.01N 114.25W
Impfondo Congo **72** 1.36N 17.58E
Imphal India **59** 24.47N 93.55E
Imroz *i.* Turkey **43** 40.10N 25.51E
Ina *r.* Poland **44** 53.32N 14.38E
Inari *l.* Finland **46** 69.00N 28.00E
Inca Spain **41** 39.43N 2.54E
Incesu Turkey **56** 38.39N 35.12E
Inchard, Loch Scotland **36** 58.27N 5.05W
Inchcape *i.* Scotland **35** 56.27N 2.24W
Inchfree B. Rep. of Ire. **38** 55.03N 8.23W
Inchkeith *i.* Scotland **35** 56.02N 3.08W
Inchnadamph Scotland **36** 58.08N 4.58W
Inchon S. Korea **63** 37.30N 126.38E
Indaal, Loch Scotland **34** 55.45N 6.20W
Indals *r.* Sweden **46** 62.30N 17.20E
Inderagiri *r.* Indonesia **60** 0.30S 103.08E
India Asia **59** 23.00N 78.30E
Indiana *d.* U.S.A. **94** 40.00N 86.05W
Indianapolis U.S.A. **94** 39.45N 86.10W
Indian Harbour Canada **93** 54.25N 57.20W
Indian Ocean 107
Indigirka *r.* U.S.S.R. **49** 71.00N 148.45E
Indonesia Asia **60** 6.00S 118.00E
Indore India **58** 22.42N 75.54E

Indravati *r.* India **59** 18.45N 80.16E
Indre *r.* France **40** 47.16N 0.06W
Indus *r.* Pakistan **58** 24.00N 67.33E
Inebolu Turkey **56** 41.57N 33.45E
Infiesto Spain **41** 43.21N 5.21W
Ingatestone England **27** 51.41N 0.22E
Ingende Zaïre **72** 0.17S 18.58E
Ingham Australia **79** 18.35S 146.12E
Ingleborough *mtn.* England **32** 54.10N 2.23W
Ingleton England **32** 54.09N 2.29W
Ingolstadt W. Germany **44** 48.46N 11.27E
Inhambane Moçambique **74** 23.51S 35.29E
Inhambane *d.* Moçambique **74** 22.20S 34.00E
Inharrime Moçambique **74** 24.29S 35.01E
Inishark *i.* Rep. of Ire. **38** 53.37N 10.18W
Inishbofin *i.* Donegal Rep. of Ire. **38** 55.10N 8.10W
Inishbofin *i.* Galway Rep. of Ire. **38** 53.38N 10.14W
Inisheer *i.* Rep. of Ire. **39** 53.04N 9.32W
Inishkea *i.* Rep. of Ire. **38** 54.08N 10.13W
Inishmaan *i.* Rep. of Ire. **39** 53.06N 9.36W
Inishmore *i.* Rep. of Ire. **39** 53.08N 9.43W
Inishmurray *i.* Rep. of Ire. **38** 54.26N 8.40W
Inishowen Head Rep. of Ire. **34** 55.09N 6.56W
Inishowen Pen. Rep. of Ire. **34** 55.08N 7.20W
Inishturk *i.* Rep. of Ire. **38** 53.43N 10.08W
Inishvickillane *i.* Rep. of Ire. **39** 52.02N 10.36W
Inn *r.* Europe **44** 48.33N 13.26E
Innellan Scotland **34** 55.54N 4.58W
Inner Hebrides *is.* Scotland **36** 56.50N 6.45W
Innerleithen Scotland **35** 55.37N 3.04W
Inner Mongolia *d.* China **63** 41.30N 112.00E
Inner Sd. Scotland **36** 57.30N 5.55W
Innsbruck Austria **44** 46.17N 11.25E
Inny *r.* England **31** 50.35N 4.17W
Inny *r.* Rep. of Ire. **39** 51.51N 10.10W
Inongo Zaïre **72** 1.55S 18.20E
Inowrocław Poland **47** 52.49N 18.12E
Insch Scotland **37** 57.21N 2.36W
Interlaken Switz. **44** 46.42N 7.52E
International Falls *town* U.S.A. **94** 48.38N 93.26W
Inuvik Canada **92** 68.16N 133.40W
Inveraray Scotland **34** 56.24N 5.05W
Inver B. Rep. of Ire. **38** 54.36N 8.20W
Inverbervie Scotland **37** 56.51N 2.17W
Invercargill New Zealand **82** 46.26S 168.21E
Inverell Australia **80** 29.46S 151.10E
Invergordon Scotland **37** 57.42N 4.10W
Inverie Scotland **36** 57.03N 5.41W
Inverkeithing Scotland **35** 56.02N 3.25W
Invermoriston Scotland **37** 57.13N 4.38W
Inverness Scotland **37** 57.27N 4.15W
Inverurie Scotland **37** 57.17N 2.23W
Inyangani *mtn.* Rhodesia **74** 18.18S 32.54E
Inyonga Tanzania **73** 6.43S 32.02E
Inzia *r.* Zaïre **72** 3.47S 17.57E
Ioánnina Greece **43** 39.39N 20.49E
Iona *i.* Scotland **34** 56.20N 6.25W
Iona, Sd. of Scotland **34** 56.19N 6.24W
Ionian Is. Greece **43** 38.45N 20.00E
Ionian Sea Med. Sea **43** 38.30N 18.45E
Ios *i.* Greece **43** 36.42N 25.20E
Iowa *d.* U.S.A. **91** 42.00N 93.00W
Iowa City U.S.A. **94** 41.39N 91.31W
Iping China **58** 28.50N 104.35E
Ipoh Malaysia **60** 4.36N 101.02E
Ipswich Australia **80** 27.38S 152.40E
Ipswich England **29** 52.04N 1.09E
Iquique Chile **102** 20.15S 70.00W
Iquitos Peru **102** 3.51S 73.30W
Iráklion Greece **43** 35.20N 25.08E
Iran Asia **57** 32.00N 54.30E
Iranian Plateau *f.* Asia **107** 33.00N 55.00E
Iran Range *mts.* Malaysia **60** 3.20N 115.00E
Iranshar Iran **57** 27.14N 60.42E
Irapuato Mexico **96** 20.40N 101.40W
Iraq Asia **56** 33.00N 44.00E
Irazu *mtn.* Costa Rica **96** 9.59N 83.52W
Ireland's Eye *i.* Rep. of Ire. **38** 53.25N 6.05W
Irian Jaya *d.* Indonesia **61** 4.00S 138.00E
Iringa Tanzania **73** 7.49S 35.39E
Iringa *d.* Tanzania **73** 8.30S 35.00E
Iriomote *i.* Japan **63** 24.30N 124.00E
Irish Sea U.K./Rep. of Ire. **38** 53.30N 5.40W
Irkutsk U.S.S.R. **62** 52.18N 104.15E
Iron-Bridge England **28** 52.38N 2.30W
Irondequoit U.S.A. **95** 43.12N 77.36W
Iron Gate *f.* Romania/Yugo. **43** 44.40N 22.30E
Iron Mountain *town* U.S.A. **94** 45.51N 88.05W
Iron Mts. Rep. of Ire. **38** 54.10N 7.56W
Iron River *town* U.S.A. **94** 46.05N 88.38W
Ironwood U.S.A. **94** 46.25N 90.08W
Iroquois Falls *town* Canada **94** 48.47N 80.41W
Irrawaddy *r.* Burma **59** 17.45N 95.25E
Irrawaddy Delta Burma **59** 16.30N 95.20E
Irthing *r.* England **35** 54.55N 2.50W
Irthlingborough England **28** 52.20N 0.37W
Irtysh *r.* U.S.S.R. **48** 61.00N 68.40E
Irumu Zaïre **73** 1.29N 29.48E
Irun Spain **41** 43.20N 1.48W
Irvine Scotland **34** 55.37N 4.40W
Irvine *r.* Scotland **34** 55.37N 4.41W
Irvine B. Scotland **34** 55.36N 4.42W
Irvinestown N. Ireland **38** 54.29N 7.40W
Irvington U.S.A. **95** 40.43N 74.15W
Isabelia, Cordillera *mts.* Nicaragua **96** 13.30N 85.00W
Isafjördhur Iceland **46** 66.05N 23.06W
Isangi Zaïre **72** 0.48N 24.03E
Isar *r.* W. Germany **44** 48.48N 12.57E
Ischia *i.* Italy **42** 40.43N 13.54E
Iscia Baidoa Somali Rep. **73** 3.08N 43.34E
Isère *r.* France **40** 45.02N 4.54E
Iserlohn W. Germany **45** 51.23N 7.42E
Isfahan Iran **57** 32.42N 51.40E
Isfandaqeh Iran **57** 28.39N 57.13E
Ishim *r.* U.S.S.R. **48** 57.50N 71.00E
Ishqanan Iran **57** 27.10N 53.38E
Isiolo Kenya **73** 0.20N 37.36E
Isiro Zaïre **73** 2.50N 27.40E
Iskenderun Turkey **56** 36.37N 36.08E
Iskenderun, G. of Turkey **56** 36.40N 35.50E
Iskilip Turkey **56** 40.45N 34.28E
Iskŭr *r.* Bulgaria **43** 43.42N 24.27E
Isla *r.* Scotland **37** 56.32N 3.22W
Islamabad Pakistan **58** 33.40N 73.08E
Island Magee *pen.* N. Ireland **34** 54.48N 5.44W
Islands, B. of New Zealand **82** 35.15S 174.15E
Islay *i.* Scotland **34** 55.45N 6.20W
Islay, Sd. of Scotland **34** 55.50N 6.06W
Isle *r.* France **40** 45.02N 0.08W
Isle of Axholme *f.* England **33** 53.32N 0.50W
Isle of Ely *f.* England **29** 52.25N 0.11E
Isle of Man U.K. **32** 54.15N 4.30W
Isle of Oxney *f.* England **29** 51.02N 0.44E
Isle of Portland *f.* England **28** 50.32N 2.25W
Isle of Purbeck *f.* England **28** 50.40N 2.05W
Isle of Thanet *f.* England **29** 51.22N 1.20E
Isle of Whithorn *town* Scotland **34** 54.43N 4.22W
Isle of Wight *d.* England **28** 50.40N 1.17W
Isleworth England **27** 51.28N 0.20W
Islington *d.* England **27** 51.33N 0.06W
Ismâ'ilîa Egypt **56** 30.36N 32.15E
Isna Egypt **56** 25.16N 32.30E
Isoka Zambia **73** 10.06S 32.39E
Isparta Turkey **56** 37.46N 30.32E
Israel Asia **56** 32.00N 34.50E
Isser *r.* Algeria **41** 36.20N 3.28E
Issoire France **40** 45.33N 3.15E
Is-sur-Tille France **40** 47.30N 5.10E
Issyk Kul *l.* U.S.S.R. **62** 43.30N 77.20E
Istanbul Turkey **43** 41.02N 28.58E
Istehbanat Iran **57** 29.05N 54.03E
Isthmus of Kra Thailand **59** 10.10N 99.00E
Istra *pen.* Yugo. **42** 45.12N 13.55E
Itajaí Brazil **103** 26.50S 48.39W
Italy Europe **42** 43.00N 12.00E
Itapeva Brazil **103** 23.59S 48.59W
Itaqui Brazil **103** 29.07S 56.33W
Itchen *r.* England **28** 50.55N 1.23W
Iterup *i.* U.S.S.R. **63** 44.00N 147.30E
Ithaca U.S.A. **95** 42.26N 76.30W
Ithon *r.* Wales **30** 52.12N 3.26W
Itimbiri *r.* Zaïre **72** 2.02N 22.47E
Ituri *r.* Zaïre **73** 1.45N 27.06E
Itzehoe W. Germany **44** 53.56N 9.32E
Ivai *r.* Brazil **103** 23.20S 53.40W
Ivalo Finland **46** 68.41N 27.30E
Ivalo *r.* Finland **46** 68.45N 27.36E
Ivanhoe Australia **80** 32.56S 144.22E
Ivano-Frankovsk U.S.S.R. **47** 48.55N 24.42E
Ivanovo U.S.S.R. **47** 57.00N 41.00E
Iver England **27** 51.31N 0.30W
Ivigtut Greenland **93** 61.10N 48.00W
Ivindo Gabon **72** 0.02S 12.13E
Ivinghoe England **27** 51.51N 0.39W
Iviza *i.* Spain **41** 39.00N 1.23E
Ivory Coast Africa **70** 8.00N 5.30W
Ivrea Italy **40** 45.28N 7.52E
Ivybridge England **31** 50.24N 3.56W
Iwo Nigeria **71** 7.38N 4.11E
Ixworth England **29** 52.18N 0.50E
Izabal, L. Guatemala **96** 15.30N 89.00W
Izhevsk U.S.S.R. **48** 56.49N 53.11E
Izmail U.S.S.R. **43** 45.20N 28.50E
Izmir Turkey **43** 38.24N 27.09E
Izmir, G. of Med. Sea **43** 38.30N 26.45E
Izmit Turkey **56** 40.48N 29.55E
Izozog Marshes *f.* Bolivia **103** 18.30S 62.05W

J

Jabalón *r.* Spain **41** 38.55N 4.07W
Jabalpur India **58** 23.10N 79.59E
Jablonec nad Nisou Czech. **44** 50.44N 15.10E
Jabrin Oasis Saudi Arabia **57** 23.15N 49.15E
Jaca Spain **41** 42.34N 0.33W
Jackson Mich. U.S.A. **94** 42.15N 84.24W
Jackson Miss. U.S.A. **91** 32.20N 90.11W
Jacksonville Fla. U.S.A. **91** 30.20N 81.40W
Jacksonville Ill. U.S.A. **94** 39.44N 90.14W
Jacobabad Pakistan **58** 28.16N 68.30E
Jacques-Cartier Canada **95** 45.31N 73.31W
Jade B. W. Germany **45** 53.30N 8.12E
Jaén Spain **41** 37.46N 3.48W
Jaffa, C. Australia **80** 36.58S 139.39E
Jaffna Sri Lanka **59** 9.38N 80.02E
Jafura *des.* Saudi Arabia **57** 24.40N 50.20E
Jagdalpur India **59** 19.04N 82.05E
Jaghbub Libya **56** 29.42N 24.38E
Jaguarao Brazil **103** 32.30S 53.25W
Jahara Kuwait **57** 29.20N 47.41E
Jahrom Iran **57** 28.30N 53.30E
Jaipur India **58** 26.53N 75.50E
Jakarta Indonesia **60** 6.08S 106.45E
Jakobstad Finland **46** 63.41N 22.40E
Jalapa Mexico **96** 19.45N 96.48W
Jalgaon India **58** 21.01N 75.39E
Jalisco *d.* Mexico **96** 21.00N 103.00W
Jalna India **58** 19.50N 75.58E
Jalón *r.* Spain **41** 41.47N 1.02W
Jalpaiguri India **58** 26.30N 88.50E
Jamaica C. America **97** 18.00N 77.00W
Jamalpur Bangla. **58** 24.54N 89.57E
Jamalpur India **58** 25.19N 86.30E
Jamdena *i.* Asia **61** 7.30S 131.00E
James *r.* U.S.A. **91** 42.50N 97.15W
James B. Canada **91** 52.00N 80.00W
Jamestown Australia **80** 33.12S 138.38E
Jamestown N. Dak. U.S.A. **90** 46.54N 98.42W
Jamestown N.Y. U.S.A. **95** 42.05N 79.15W
Jammu and Kashmir *d.* Pakistan **58** 36.00N 75.00W
Jammu and Kashmir *d.* India **58** 33.30N 76.00W
Jamnagar India **58** 22.28N 70.06E
Jämsänkoski Finland **46** 61.54N 25.10E
Jamshedpur India **58** 22.47N 86.12E
Janda, Lago de Spain **41** 36.15N 5.50W
Jandula *r.* Spain **41** 38.08N 4.08W
Janesville U.S.A. **94** 42.42N 89.02W
Jan Mayen *i.* Arctic Oc. **112** 71.00N 9.00W
Japan Asia **63** 36.00N 136.00E
Japan, Sea of Asia **63** 40.00N 135.00E
Japan Trench Pacific Oc. **107** 30.00N 142.00E
Japen *i.* Indonesia **61** 1.45S 136.10E
Jarama *r.* Spain **41** 40.27N 3.32W
Jardines de la Reina *is.* Cuba **97** 20.30N 79.00W
Jarrahi *r.* Iran **57** 30.40N 48.23E
Jarrow England **33** 54.59N 1.28W
Järvenpää Finland **46** 60.29N 25.06E
Jashpurnagur India **58** 22.52N 84.14E
Jask Iran **57** 25.40N 57.45E
Jasper Canada **92** 52.55N 118.05W
Jataí Brazil **103** 17.58S 51.45W
Játiva Spain **41** 39.00N 0.32W
Jau Brazil **103** 22.11S 48.35W
Jaunpur India **58** 25.44N 82.41E
Java *i.* Indonesia **60** 7.30S 110.00E
Java Sea Indonesia **60** 5.00S 111.00E
Jebba Nigeria **71** 9.11N 4.49E
Jedburgh Scotland **35** 55.29N 2.33W
Jefferson, Mt. U.S.A. **90** 38.47N 116.58W
Jefferson City U.S.A. **94** 38.33N 92.10W
Jelenia Góra Poland **44** 50.55N 15.45E
Jelgava U.S.S.R. **46** 56.39N 23.40E
Jena E. Germany **44** 50.56N 11.35E
Jérémie Haiti **97** 18.40N 74.09W
Jerez de la Frontera Spain **41** 36.41N 6.08W
Jericho Jordan **56** 31.51N 35.27E
Jerilderie Australia **80** 35.23S 145.41E
Jersey *i.* Channel Is. **31** 49.13N 2.08W
Jersey City U.S.A. **95** 40.44N 74.04W
Jerusalem Israel/Jordan **56** 31.47N 35.13E
Jessore Bangla. **58** 23.10N 89.12E
Jever W. Germany **45** 53.34N 7.54E
Jeypore India **59** 18.51N 82.41E
Jhansi India **58** 25.27N 78.34E
Jhelum *r.* Pakistan **58** 31.04N 72.10E
Jihlava Czech. **44** 49.24N 15.35E
Jimma Ethiopia **69** 7.39N 36.47E
Jinja Uganda **73** 0.27N 33.10E
Jinotepe Nicaragua **96** 11.50N 86.10W
Jiu *r.* Romania **43** 43.44N 23.52E
Jizl, Wadi *r.* Saudi Arabia **56** 25.37N 38.20E
Joaçiba Brazil **103** 27.05S 51.31W
João de Almeida Angola **72** 15.10S 13.32E

João Pessoa Brazil **102** 7.06S 34.53W
Jódar Spain **41** 37.50N 3.21W
Jodhpur India **58** 26.18N 73.08E
Joensuu Finland **46** 62.35N 29.46E
Jogjakarta Indonesia **60** 7.48S 110.24E
Johannesburg R.S.A. **74** 26.10S 28.02E
John O'Groats Scotland **37** 58.39N 3.02W
Johnstone Scotland **34** 55.50N 4.30W
Johnston's Pt. Scotland **34** 55.22N 5.31W
Johnstown U.S.A. **95** 40.20N 78.56W
Johore Bahru Malaysia **60** 1.29N 103.40E
Joinville Brazil **103** 26.20S 48.49W
Jokkmokk Sweden **46** 66.37N 19.50E
Jökulsá á Brú *r.* Iceland **46** 65.33N 14.23W
Jökulsá á Fjöllum *r.* Iceland **46** 66.05N 16.32W
Joliet U.S.A. **94** 41.32N 88.05W
Joliette Canada **95** 46.02N 73.27W
Jolo *i.* Phil. **61** 5.55N 121.20E
Joma *mtn.* China **59** 33.45N 93.08E
Jombo *r.* Angola **72** 10.20S 16.37E
Jönköping Sweden **46** 57.45N 14.10E
Joplin U.S.A. **91** 37.04N 94.31W
Jordan Asia **56** 31.00N 36.00E
Jordan *r.* Asia **56** 31.47N 35.31E
Jos Nigeria **71** 9.54N 8.53E
Joseph Bonaparte G. Australia **79** 14.00S 128.30E
Jos Plateau *f.* Nigeria **71** 10.00N 9.00E
Jotunheimen *mts.* Norway **46** 61.30N 9.00E
Joyce's Country *f.* Rep. of Ire. **38** 53.33N 9.36W
Juan Fernandez Is. Chile **102** 34.00S 80.00W
Juárez Argentina **103** 37.40S 59.48W
Juba *r.* Somali Rep. **73** 0.20S 42.40E
Juba Sudan **73** 4.50N 31.35E
Jubail Saudi Arabia **57** 27.59N 49.40E
Júcar *r.* Spain **41** 39.10N 0.15W
Juchitán Mexico **96** 20.04N 104.06W
Juddah Saudi Arabia **69** 21.30N 39.10E
Juist *i.* W. Germany **45** 53.43N 7.00E
Juiz de Fora Brazil **103** 21.47S 43.23W
Jujuy *d.* Argentina **103** 23.00S 66.00W
Julfa Iran **57** 32.40N 51.39E
Juliana Canal Neth. **45** 51.00N 5.48E
Julianehaab Greenland **93** 60.45N 46.00W
Jülich W. Germany **45** 50.55N 6.21E
Julio de Castilhos Brazil **103** 29.13S 53.40W
Jullundur India **58** 31.18N 75.40E
Jumet Belgium **45** 50.27N 4.27E
Jumla Nepal **59** 29.17N 82.10E
Jumna *r. see* Yamuna India **58**
Junagadh India **58** 21.32N 70.32E
Junction City U.S.A **91** 39.02N 96.51W
Jundiaí Brazil **103** 23.10S 46.54W
Juneau U.S.A. **92** 58.20N 134.20W
Junee Australia **80** 34.51S 147.40E
Jungfrau *mtn.* Switz. **44** 46.30N 8.00E
Junin Argentina **103** 34.34S 60.55W
Jura *i.* Scotland **34** 55.58N 5.55W
Jura, Sd. of Scotland **34** 56.00N 5.45W
Jura Mts. Europe **44** 46.55N 6.45E
Jurby Head I.o.M. **32** 54.22N 4.33W
Juticalpa Honduras **96** 14.45N 86.12W
Juwain Afghan. **57** 31.43N 61.39E
Jyväskylä Finland **46** 62.16N 25.50E

K

K2 *mtn.* Asia **62** 35.53N 76.32E
Kabaena *i.* Indonesia **61** 5.25S 122.00E
Kabala Sierra Leone **70** 9.40N 11.36W
Kabale Uganda **73** 1.13S 30.00E
Kabalega Falls *f.* Uganda **73** 2.17N 31.46E
Kabalega Falls Nat. Park Uganda **73** 2.15N 31.45E
Kabalo Zaïre **73** 6.02S 27.00E
Kabambare Zaïre **73** 4.40S 27.41E
Kabba Nigeria **71** 7.50N 6.07E
Kabia *i.* Indonesia **61** 6.07S 120.28E
Kabinda Zaïre **72** 6.10S 24.29E
Kabir Kuh *mts.* Iran **57** 33.00N 47.00E
Kabompo *r.* Zambia **72** 14.17S 23.15E
Kabongo Zaïre **72** 7.22S 25.34E
Kabul Afghan. **58** 34.30N 69.10E
Kabunda Zaïre **73** 12.27S 29.15E
Kabwe Zambia **73** 14.27S 28.25E
Kacha Kuh *mts.* Iran **57** 29.30N 61.20E
Kachin State *d.* Burma **59** 25.30N 96.30E
Kade Ghana **70** 6.08N 0.51W
Kadei *r.* C.A.R. **71** 3.28N 16.05E
Kadiyevka U.S.S.R. **47** 48.34N 38.40E
Kaduna Nigeria **71** 10.28N 7.25E
Kaduna *d.* Nigeria **71** 11.00N 7.35E
Kaduna *r.* Nigeria **71** 8.45N 5.45E
Kadusam *mtn.* China **59** 28.30N 96.45E
Kaedi Mauritania **70** 16.12N 13.32W
Kafanchan Nigeria **71** 9.38N 8.20E
Kafirévs, C. Greece **43** 38.11N 24.30E
Kafo *r.* Uganda **73** 1.40N 32.07E
Kafue Zambia **73** 15.40S 28.13E
Kafue *r.* Zambia **73** 15.53S 28.55E
Kafue Dam Zambia **73** 15.40S 27.10E
Kafue Nat. Park Zambia **72** 15.30S 25.35E
Kağizman Turkey **56** 40.08N 43.07E
Kagoshima Japan **63** 31.37N 130.32E
Kahama Tanzania **73** 3.48S 32.38E
Kahemba Zaïre **72** 7.20S 19.00E
Kaiama Nigeria **71** 9.37N 4.03E
Kaifeng China **63** 34.47N 114.20E
Kai Is. Indonesia **61** 5.45S 132.55E
Kaikohe New Zealand **82** 35.25S 173.49E
Kaikoura New Zealand **82** 42.24S 173.41E
Kaikoura Range *mts.* New Zealand **82** 42.00S 173.40E
Kaimana Asia **61** 3.39S 133.44E
Kaimanawa Range *mts.* New Zealand **82** 37.10S 176.15E
Kaipara Harbour New Zealand **82** 36.30S 174.00E
Kairouan Tunisia **42** 35.40N 10.04E
Kaiserslautern W. Germany **45** 49.27N 7.47E
Kaitaia New Zealand **82** 35.08S 173.18E
Kaitum *r.* Sweden **46** 67.30N 21.00E
Kajaani Finland **46** 64.14N 27.37E
Kajan *r.* Indonesia **60** 2.47N 117.46E
Kajo Kaji Sudan **73** 3.56N 31.40E
Kakamas R.S.A. **74** 28.45S 20.33E
Kakamega Kenya **73** 0.21N 34.47E
Kakhovskoye Resr. U.S.S.R. **47** 47.30N 34.00E
Kakinada India **59** 16.59N 82.20E
Kalahari Desert Botswana **74** 23.30S 22.00E
Kalahari Gemsbok Nat. Park R.S.A. **74** 25.30S 20.30E
Kala-i-Fath Afghan. **57** 30.32N 61.52E
Kalámai Greece **43** 37.02N 22.05E
Kalamazoo U.S.A. **94** 42.17N 85.36W
Kala Nao Afghan. **57** 34.58N 63.04E
Kalat Iran **57** 37.02N 59.46E
Kalat Pakistan **58** 29.01N 66.38E
Kalecik Turkey **56** 40.06N 33.22E
Kalehe Zaïre **73** 2.05S 28.53E
Kalemie Zaïre **73** 5.57S 29.10E
Kalgoorlie Australia **79** 30.49S 121.29E
Kaliakra, C. Bulgaria **43** 43.23N 28.29E
Kalima Zaïre **73** 2.35S 26.34E
Kalimantan *d.* Indonesia **60** 1.00S 113.00E
Kalinin U.S.S.R. **47** 56.47N 35.57E
Kaliningrad U.S.S.R. **46** 54.40N 20.30E
Kalispell U.S.A. **90** 48.12N 114.19W
Kalisz Poland **47** 51.46N 18.02E
Kaliua Tanzania **73** 5.08S 31.50E
Kalix *r.* Sweden **46** 65.50N 23.10E
Kalkfontein Botswana **74** 22.08S 20.53E
Kalla Vesi *l.* Finland **46** 62.45N 28.00E
Kallsjön *l.* Sweden **46** 63.30N 13.00E
Kalmar Sweden **46** 56.39N 16.20E
Kalomo Zambia **73** 16.55S 26.29E
Kaluga U.S.S.R. **47** 54.31N 36.16E
Kalundborg Denmark **46** 55.42N 11.06E
Kama *r.* U.S.S.R. **48** 55.30N 52.00E
Kamchatka Pen. U.S.S.R. **49** 56.00N 160.00E
Kamen *mtn.* U.S.S.R. **49** 68.40N 94.20E
Kamenskoye U.S.S.R. **49** 62.31N 165.15E
Kamensk-Shakhtinskiy U.S.S.R. **47** 48.20N 40.16E
Kames Scotland **34** 55.54N 5.15W
Kamet *mtn.* China **59** 31.03N 79.25E
Kamina Zaïre **72** 8.46S 24.58E
Kamloops Canada **90** 50.39N 120.24W
Kampala Uganda **73** 0.19N 32.35E
Kampar *r.* Indonesia **60** 0.20N 102.55E
Kampen Neth. **45** 52.33N 5.55E
Kampot Khmer Rep. **59** 10.37N 104.11E
Kamyshin U.S.S.R. **47** 50.05N 45.24E
Kana *r.* Rhodesia **74** 18.28S 27.03E
Kananga Zaïre **72** 5.53S 22.26E
Kanazawa Japan **63** 36.35N 136.38E
Kanchanaburi Thailand **59** 14.08N 99.31E
Kanchenjunga *mtn.* Asia **58** 27.44N 88.11E
Kanchow China **63** 25.52N 114.51E
Kandahar Afghan. **58** 31.36N 65.47E
Kandalaksha U.S.S.R. **46** 67.09N 32.31E
Kandalakskaya G. U.S.S.R. **46** 66.30N 34.00E
Kandangan Indonesia **60** 2.50S 115.15E
Kandi Benin **71** 11.05N 2.59E
Kandira Turkey **56** 41.05N 30.08E
Kandos Australia **80** 32.53S 149.59E
Kandreho Malagasy Rep. **73** 17.33S 46.00E
Kandy Sri Lanka **59** 7.18N 80.43E
Kane U.S.A. **95** 41.40N 78.48W
Kangan Iran **57** 27.50N 52.07E
Kangar Malaysia **59** 6.27N 100.12E
Kangaroo I. Australia **80** 35.45S 137.30E
Kangean Is. Indonesia **60** 7.00S 115.45E
Kangnŭng S. Korea **63** 37.30N 129.02E
Kango Gabon **72** 0.15N 10.14E
Kangting China **59** 30.05N 102.04E
Kaniama Zaïre **72** 7.32S 24.11E
Kanin, C. U.S.S.R. **48** 68.50N 43.30E
Kanin Pen. U.S.S.R. **48** 68.00N 45.00E
Kankakee U.S.A. **94** 41.08N 87.52W
Kankan Guinea **70** 10.22N 9.11W
Kanker India **59** 20.17N 81.30E
Kano Nigeria **71** 12.00N 8.31E
Kano *d.* Nigeria **71** 12.00N 9.00E
Kanpur India **58** 26.27N 80.14E
Kansas *d.* U.S.A. **90** 38.00N 99.00W
Kansas City U.S.A. **91** 39.02N 94.33W
Kansk U.S.S.R. **49** 56.11N 95.20E
Kanturk Rep. of Ire. **39** 52.10N 8.54W
Kanye Botswana **74** 24.59S 25.19E
Kaohsiung Taiwan **61** 22.36N 120.17E
Kaoko Veld *f.* S.W. Africa **74** 18.30S 13.30E
Kaolack Senegal **70** 14.09N 16.08W
Kaoma Zambia **72** 14.55S 24.58E
Kapanga Zaïre **72** 8.22S 22.37E
Kapfenberg Austria **44** 47.27N 15.18E
Kapiri Mposhi Zambia **73** 13.59S 28.40E
Kapiti I. New Zealand **82** 40.50S 174.50E
Kapoeta Sudan **73** 4.50N 33.35E
Kaposvár Hungary **43** 46.22N 17.47E
Kapsabet Kenya **73** 0.12N 35.05E
Kapuas *r.* Indonesia **60** 0.05N 111.25E
Kapuskasing Canada **94** 49.25N 82.26W
Kara U.S.S.R. **48** 69.12N 65.00E
Kara Bogaz Gol B. U.S.S.R. **57** 41.20N 53.40E
Karabuk Turkey **56** 41.12N 32.36E
Karachi Pakistan **58** 24.51N 67.02E
Karaganda U.S.S.R. **48** 49.53N 73.07E
Kara Irtysh *r.* U.S.S.R. **62** 48.00N 84.20E
Karak Jordan **56** 31.11N 35.42E
Karakelong *i.* Indonesia **61** 4.20N 126.50E
Karakoram Pass Asia **59** 35.53N 77.51E
Karakoram Range *mts.* Jammu and Kashmir **58** 35.30N 76.30E
Kara Kum *des.* U.S.S.R. **57** 37.45N 60.00E
Kara-Kum Canal U.S.S.R. **57** 37.30N 65.48E
Karaman Turkey **56** 37.11N 33.13E
Karamea Bight *b.* New Zealand **82** 41.15S 171.30E
Karamürsel Turkey **56** 40.42N 29.37E
Karand Iran **57** 34.16N 46.15E
Kara Nor *l.* China **62** 38.20N 97.40E
Kara Nur *l.* Mongolia **62** 48.10N 93.30E
Karasburg S.W. Africa **74** 28.00S 18.43E
Kara Sea U.S.S.R. **48** 73.00N 65.00E
Kara-Shahr China **62** 42.00N 86.30E
Karasjok Norway **46** 69.27N 25.30E
Kara-Su *r.* Iran **57** 35.58N 56.25E
Karauli India **58** 26.30N 77.00E
Kara Usa Nor *l.* Mongolia **62** 48.10N 92.10E
Karawa Zaïre **72** 3.12N 20.20E
Karawanken *mts.* Austria **44** 46.20N 14.50E
Karbala Iraq **57** 32.37N 44.03E
Kardhítsa Greece **43** 39.22N 21.59E
Karema Tanzania **73** 6.50S 30.25E
Karhula Finland **46** 60.31N 26.50E
Kariba Rhodesia **74** 16.32S 28.50E
Kariba, L. Rhodesia/Zambia **74** 16.50S 28.00E
Kariba Dam Rhodesia/Zambia **73** 16.15S 28.55E
Karibib S.W. Africa **74** 21.59S 15.51E
Karikal India **59** 10.58N 79.50E
Karima Sudan **69** 18.32N 31.48E
Karis Finland **46** 60.05N 23.40E
Karisimbi, Mt. Zaïre/Rwanda **73** 1.31S 29.25E
Karkheh *r.* Iran **57** 31.45N 47.52E
Karkinitskiy, G. of U.S.S.R. **47** 45.50N 32.45E
Karkkila Finland **46** 60.32N 24.10E
Kar Kuh *mtn.* Iran **57** 31.37N 53.47E
Karl Marx Stadt E. Germany **44** 50.50N 12.55E
Karlovac Yugo. **42** 45.30N 15.34E
Karlovy Vary Czech. **44** 50.14N 12.53E
Karlsborg Sweden **46** 58.32N 14.32E
Karlshamn Sweden **46** 56.10N 14.50E
Karlskoga Sweden **46** 59.19N 14.33E
Karlskrona Sweden **46** 56.10N 15.35E
Karlsruhe W. Germany **44** 49.00N 8.24E
Karlstad Sweden **46** 59.24N 13.32E
Karmöy *i.* Norway **46** 59.15N 5.05E
Karnataka *d.* India **58** 14.45N 76.00E
Karnobat Bulgaria **43** 42.40N 27.00E
Karonga Malaŵi **73** 9.54S 33.55E
Karpáthos *i.* Greece **43** 35.35N 27.08E
Kars Turkey **56** 40.35N 43.05E
Karsakpay U.S.S.R. **48** 47.47N 66.43E
Karun *r.* Iran **57** 30.25N 48.12E
Kasai *r.* Zaïre **72** 3.10S 16.13E
Kasai Occidental *d.* Zaïre **72** 5.00S 21.30E
Kasai Oriental *d.* Zaïre **72** 5.00S 24.00E
Kasama Zambia **73** 10.10S 31.11E
Kasane Botswana **74** 17.50S 25.05E
Kasanga Tanzania **73** 8.27S 31.10E
Kasempa Zambia **72** 13.28S 25.48E

Kasese Uganda **73** 0.07N 30.06E
Kashan Iran **57** 33.59N 51.31E
Kashgar China **62** 39.29N 76.02E
Kashing China **63** 30.40N 120.50E
Kashmar Iran **57** 35.12N 58.26E
Kaskaskia U.S.A. **94** 38.30N 89.15W
Kasongo Zaïre **73** 4.32S 26.33E
Kasongo-Lunda Zaïre **72** 6.30S 16.47E
Kásos *i.* Greece **56** 35.22N 26.57E
Kassala Sudan **69** 15.24N 36.30E
Kassel W. Germany **44** 51.18N 9.30E
Kasserine Tunisia **42** 35.15N 8.44E
Kastamonu Turkey **56** 41.22N 33.47E
Kastellorizon *i.* Greece **56** 36.08N 29.32E
Kastoria Greece **43** 40.32N 21.15E
Kasungu Malaŵi **73** 13.04S 33.29E
Kataba Zambia **72** 16.12S 25.05E
Katahdin, Mt. U.S.A. **95** 45.55N 68.57W
Katako Kombe Zaïre **72** 3.27S 24.21E
Katete Zambia **73** 14.08S 31.50E
Katha Burma **59** 24.11N 96.20E
Katherina, Gebel *mtn.* Egypt **56** 28.30N 33.57E
Katherine Australia **79** 14.29S 132.20E
Kati Mali **70** 12.41N 8.04W
Katihar India **58** 25.33N 87.34E
Katima Rapids *f.* Zambia **72** 17.15S 24.20E
Katmandu Nepal **58** 27.42N 85.19E
Katonga *r.* Uganda **73** 0.03N 30.15E
Katoomba Australia **80** 33.42S 150.23E
Katowice Poland **47** 50.15N 18.59E
Katrine, Loch Scotland **34** 56.15N 4.30W
Katrineholm Sweden **46** 58.59N 16.15E
Katsina Nigeria **71** 13.00N 7.32E
Katsina Ala Nigeria **71** 7.10N 9.30E
Katsina Ala *r.* Nigeria **71** 7.50N 8.58E
Kattegat *str.* Denmark/Sweden **46** 57.00N 11.20E
Katwijk aan Zee Neth. **45** 52.13N 4.27E
Kauai *i.* Hawaii U.S.A. **90** 22.05N 159.30W
Kaufbeuren W. Germany **44** 47.53N 10.37E
Kauhajoki Finland **46** 62.26N 21.10E
Kauhava Finland **46** 63.06N 23.05E
Kaunas U.S.S.R. **46** 54.52N 23.55E
Kaura Namoda Nigeria **71** 12.39N 6.38E
Kavali India **59** 14.55N 80.01E
Kaválla Greece **43** 40.56N 24.24E
Kawambwa Zambia **73** 9.47S 29.10E
Kawasaki Japan **63** 35.32N 139.41E
Kawimbe Zambia **73** 8.50S 31.31E
Kawthoolei *d.* Burma **59** 19.00N 96.30E
Kayah Burma **62** 18.20N 97.00E
Kayes Mali **70** 14.26N 11.28W
Kayseri Turkey **56** 38.42N 35.28E
Kazachye U.S.S.R. **49** 70.46N 136.15E
Kazakhstan Soviet Socialist Republic *d.* U.S.S.R. **47** 48.00N 48.00E
Kazan U.S.S.R. **47** 55.45N 49.10E
Kazanlŭk Bulgaria **43** 42.38N 25.26E
Kazarun Iran **57** 29.35N 51.39E
Kazbek *mtn.* U.S.S.R. **47** 42.42N 44.30E
Kazumba Zaïre **72** 6.30S 22.02E
Kéa *i.* Greece **43** 37.36N 24.20E
Keady N. Ireland **38** 54.15N 6.43W
Keal, Loch na Scotland **34** 56.28N 6.04W
Kearney U.S.A. **90** 40.42N 99.04W
Kebbi *r.* Nigeria **68** 11.22N 4.10E
Kebnekaise *mtn.* Sweden **46** 67.55N 18.30E
Kebock Head Scotland **36** 58.02N 6.22W
Kecskemet Hungary **47** 46.56N 19.43E
Kediri Indonesia **60** 7.55S 112.01E
Kédougou Senegal **70** 12.35N 12.09W
Keele Peak *mtn.* Canada **92** 63.15N 129.50W
Keen, Mt. Scotland **37** 56.58N 2.56W
Keene U.S.A. **95** 42.55N 72.17W
Keeper Hill Rep. of Ire. **39** 52.45N 8.17W
Keetmanshoop S.W. Africa **74** 26.36S 18.08E
Keewatin Canada **91** 49.46N 94.30W
Keewatin *d.* Canada **93** 67.00N 90.00W
Kefallinía *i.* Greece **43** 38.15N 20.33E
Keflavik Iceland **46** 64.01N 22.35W
Kei *r.* R.S.A. **74** 32.40S 28.22E
Keighley England **32** 53.52N 1.54W
Keitele *l.* Finland **46** 62.59N 26.00E
Keith Scotland **37** 57.32N 2.57W
Kelberg W. Germany **45** 50.17N 6.56E
Kelkit *r.* Turkey **56** 40.46N 36.32E
Kelloselkä Finland **46** 66.55N 28.50E
Kells Kilkenny Rep. of Ire. **39** 52.32N 7.18W
Kells Meath Rep. of Ire. **38** 53.44N 6.53W
Kelowna Canada **90** 49.50N 119.29W
Kelsall England **32** 53.14N 2.44W
Kelso Scotland **35** 55.36N 2.26W
Kelvedon England **29** 51.50N 0.43E
Kelvedon Hatch England **27** 51.40N 0.16E
Kemaliye Turkey **56** 39.16N 38.29E
Kemerovo U.S.S.R. **48** 55.25N 86.10E
Kemi Finland **46** 65.45N 24.12E
Kemi *r.* Finland **46** 55.47N 24.28E
Kemijärvi Finland **46** 66.40N 27.21E
Kempsey Australia **80** 31.05S 152.50E
Kempston England **29** 52.07N 0.30W
Kempt, L. Canada **95** 47.30N 74.15W
Kempten W. Germany **44** 47.44N 10.19E
Kemsing England **27** 51.18N 0.14E
Ken, Loch Scotland **35** 55.02N 4.04W
Kendal Australia **80** 31.28S 152.40E
Kendal England **32** 54.19N 2.44W
Kendari Indonesia **61** 3.57S 122.36E
Kenema Sierra Leone **70** 7.57N 11.11W
Kenge Zaïre **72** 4.56S 17.04E
Kengtung Burma **59** 21.16N 99.39E
Kenhardt R.S.A. **74** 29.19S 21.08E
Kenilworth England **28** 52.22N 1.35W
Kenmare Rep. of Ire. **39** 51.53N 9.36W
Kenmare *r.* Rep. of Ire. **39** 51.47N 9.52W
Kenmore Scotland **35** 56.35N 4.00W
Kennebec *r.* U.S.A. **95** 43.55N 69.49W
Kennedy, C. U.S.A. **91** 28.28N 80.28W
Kennet *r.* England **28** 51.28N 0.57W
Kennington England **29** 51.10N 0.54E
Kenogamissi L. Canada **94** 48.10N 81.35W
Keno Hill *town* Canada **92** 63.58N 135.22W
Kenora Canada **91** 49.47N 94.26W
Kenosha U.S.A. **94** 42.34N 87.50W
Kensington and Chelsea *d.* England **27** 51.29N 0.12W
Kent *d.* England **29** 51.12N 0.40E
Kentford England **29** 52.16N 0.30E
Kentucky *d.* U.S.A. **91** 38.00N 85.00W
Kentucky L. U.S.A. **91** 36.15N 88.00W
Kenya Africa **73** 1.00N 38.00E
Kenya, Mt. Kenya **73** 0.10S 37.19E
Kerala *d.* India **58** 10.30N 76.30E
Kerang Australia **80** 35.42S 143.59E
Kerch U.S.S.R. **47** 45.22N 36.27E
Kerch Str. U.S.S.R. **47** 45.15N 36.35E
Kerguelen *i.* Indian Oc. **113** 49.30S 69.30E
Kericho Kenya **73** 0.22S 35.19E
Kerintji *mtn.* Indonesia **60** 1.45S 101.20E
Kerkrade Neth. **45** 50.52N 6.02E
Kerloch *mtn.* Scotland **37** 56.59N 2.30W
Kermadec Trench Pacific Oc. **107** 33.00S 176.00W
Kermān Iran **57** 30.18N 57.05E
Kermānshāhān Iran **57** 34.19N 47.04E
Kerme, G. of Turkey **43** 36.52N 27.53E
Kerpen W. Germany **45** 50.52N 6.42E
Kerrera *i.* Scotland **34** 56.24N 5.33W
Kerry *d.* Rep. of Ire. **39** 52.07N 9.35W
Kerry Head Rep. of Ire. **39** 52.24N 9.56W
Kerulen *r.* Mongolia **63** 48.45N 117.00E
Keşan Turkey **43** 40.50N 26.39E
Kessingland England **29** 52.25N 1.41E
Keswick England **32** 54.35N 3.09W
Ketapang Indonesia **60** 1.50S 110.02E
Ketchikan U.S.A. **92** 55.25N 131.40W
Kete Krachi Ghana **70** 7.50N 0.03W
Kettering England **28** 52.24N 0.44W
Kettering U.S.A. **94** 39.42N 84.11W
Kew England **27** 51.29N 0.18W
Keweenaw B. U.S.A. **94** 47.00N 88.15W
Keweenaw Pt. U.S.A. **94** 47.23N 87.42W
Key, Lough Rep. of Ire. **38** 54.00N 8.15W
Keyingham England **33** 53.42N 0.07W
Keynsham England **28** 51.25N 2.30W
Key West U.S.A. **96** 24.34N 81.48W
Keyworth England **33** 52.52N 1.08W
Khabarovsk U.S.S.R. **63** 48.32N 135.08E
Khabur *r.* Syria **56** 35.07N 40.30E
Khaburah Oman **57** 23.58N 57.10E
Khairpur Pakistan **58** 27.30N 68.50E
Khalkidhiki *pen.* Greece **56** 40.30N 23.25E
Khalkis Greece **43** 38.27N 23.36E
Khanaqin Iraq **57** 34.22N 45.22E
Khandwa India **58** 21.49N 76.23E
Khanka, L. U.S.S.R. **63** 45.00N 132.30E
Khanty-Mansiysk U.S.S.R. **48** 61.00N 69.00E
Khanu Iran **57** 27.55N 57.45E
Kharagpur India **58** 22.23N 87.22E
Kharan *r.* Iran **57** 27.37N 58.48E
Kharga Oasis Egypt **56** 25.00N 30.40E
Kharkov U.S.S.R. **47** 50.00N 36.15E
Kharovsk U.S.S.R. **47** 59.67N 40.07E
Khartoum Sudan **69** 15.33N 32.35E
Khash *r.* Afghan. **57** 31.12N 62.00E
Khaskovo Bulgaria **43** 41.57N 25.33E
Khatanga U.S.S.R. **49** 71.50N 102.31E
Khatangskiy G. U.S.S.R. **49** 75.00N 112.10E
Khemmarat Thailand **59** 16.04N 105.10E
Khenifra Morocco **68** 33.00N 5.40W
Kherson U.S.S.R. **47** 46.39N 32.38E
Khíos Greece **56** 38.23N 26.07E
Khíos *i.* Greece **43** 38.23N 26.04E
Khirsan *r.* Iran **57** 31.29N 48.53E
Khiva U.S.S.R. **57** 41.25N 60.49E
Khmelnitskiy U.S.S.R. **47** 49.25N 26.49E
Khmer Republic Asia **60** 12.00N 105.00E
Khöbsögöl Dalai *l.* Mongolia **62** 51.00N 100.30E
Khoi Iran **57** 38.32N 45.02E
Khomas-Hochland *mts.* S.W. Africa **74** 22.45S 16.20E
Khoper *r.* U.S.S.R. **47** 49.35N 42.17E
Khor Qatar **57** 25.39N 51.32E
Khorramabad Iran **57** 33.29N 48.21E
Khorramshahr Iran **57** 30.26N 48.09E
Khotan China **62** 37.07N 79.57E
Khotin U.S.S.R. **47** 48.30N 26.31E
Khulna Bangla. **58** 22.49N 89.34E
Khunsar Iran **57** 33.12N 50.20E
Khur Iran **57** 33.47N 55.06E
Khurmuj Iran **57** 28.40N 51.20E
Khwash Iran **57** 28.14N 61.15E
Khyber Pass Asia **58** 34.06N 71.05E
Kialing Kiang *r.* China **59** 29.33N 106.30E
Kian China **63** 27.08N 115.00E
Kiangling China **63** 30.20N 112.20E
Kiangsi *d.* China **63** 27.25N 115.20E
Kiangsu *d.* China **63** 34.00N 119.00E
Kibali *r.* Zaïre **73** 3.37N 28.38E
Kibombo Zaïre **72** 3.58S 25.57E
Kibondo Tanzania **73** 3.35S 30.41E
Kibungu Rwanda **73** 2.10S 30.31E
Kibwezi Kenya **73** 2.28S 37.57E
Kicking Horse Pass Canada **90** 51.28N 116.23W
Kidal Mali **71** 18.27N 1.25E
Kidan *des.* Saudi Arabia **57** 22.20N 54.20E
Kidderminster England **28** 52.24N 2.13W
Kidsgrove England **32** 53.06N 2.15W
Kidwelly Wales **31** 51.44N 4.20W
Kiel W. Germany **44** 54.20N 10.08E
Kiel B. W. Germany **44** 54.30N 10.30E
Kiel Canal W. Germany **44** 53.54N 9.12E
Kielder Forest *hills* England **35** 55.15N 2.30W
Kienshui China **59** 23.57N 102.45E
Kienyang Fukien China **63** 27.20N 117.50E
Kiev U.S.S.R. **47** 50.28N 30.29E
Kiffa Mauritania **70** 16.38N 11.28W
Kigali Rwanda **73** 1.59S 30.05E
Kigoma Tanzania **73** 4.52S 29.36E
Kigoma *d.* Tanzania **73** 4.45S 30.00E
Kigosi *r.* Tanzania **73** 4.37S 31.29E
Kikinda Yugo. **43** 45.51N 20.30E
Kikori P.N.G. **61** 7.25S 144.13E
Kikwit Zaïre **72** 5.02S 18.51E
Kil Sweden **46** 59.30N 13.20E
Kilbaha Rep. of Ire. **39** 52.35N 9.52W
Kilbeggan Rep. of Ire. **38** 53.22N 7.31W
Kilberry Head Scotland **34** 55.47N 5.38W
Kilbirnie Scotland **34** 55.45N 4.41W
Kilbrannan Sd. Scotland **34** 55.37N 5.25W
Kilchrenan Scotland **34** 56.21N 5.11W
Kilcock Rep. of Ire. **38** 53.25N 6.43W
Kilcreggan Scotland **34** 55.59N 4.50W
Kilcrohane Rep. of Ire. **39** 51.35N 9.42W
Kilcullen Rep. of Ire. **39** 53.08N 6.46W
Kildare Rep. of Ire. **39** 53.10N 6.55W
Kildare *d.* Rep. of Ire. **39** 53.10N 6.50W
Kildonan Rhodesia **74** 17.15S 30.44E
Kildorrery Rep. of Ire. **39** 52.14N 8.26W
Kilfinan Scotland **34** 55.58N 5.18W
Kilfinane Rep. of Ire. **39** 52.21N 8.28W
Kilgarvan Rep. of Ire. **39** 51.54N 9.28W
Kilifi Kenya **73** 3.30S 39.50E
Kilimanjaro *d.* Tanzania **73** 3.45S 37.40E
Kilimanjaro *mtn.* Tanzania **73** 3.02S 37.20E
Kilis Turkey **56** 36.43N 37.07E
Kilkee Rep. of Ire. **39** 52.41N 9.40W
Kilkeel N. Ireland **38** 54.04N 6.00W
Kilkelly Rep. of Ire. **38** 53.52N 8.52W
Kilkenny Rep. of Ire. **39** 52.39N 7.16W
Kilkenny *d.* Rep. of Ire. **39** 52.35N 7.15W
Kilkhampton England **31** 50.53N 4.29W
Kilkieran B. Rep. of Ire. **38** 53.20N 9.42W
Kilkis Greece **43** 40.59N 22.51E
Killala Rep. of Ire. **38** 54.13N 9.14W
Killala B. Rep. of Ire. **38** 54.15N 9.10W
Killaloe Rep. of Ire. **39** 52.47N 8.28W
Killamarsh England **33** 53.19N 1.19W
Killard Pt. N. Ireland **38** 54.41N 5.31W
Killarney Rep. of Ire. **39** 52.04N 9.32W
Killary Harbour *est.* Rep. of Ire. **38** 53.38N 9.56W
Killchianaig Scotland **34** 56.01N 5.47W
Killeagh Rep. of Ire. **39** 51.56N 8.00W
Killearn Scotland **34** 56.03N 4.22W
Killeshandra Rep. of Ire. **38** 54.01N 7.33W
Killin Scotland **34** 56.29N 4.19W
Killington Mtn. U.S.A. **95** 43.36N 72.49W
Killingworth England **35** 55.02N 1.32W
Killíni *mtn.* Greece **43** 37.56N 22.22E
Killorglin Rep. of Ire. **39** 52.07N 9.45W
Killucan Rep. of Ire. **38** 53.30N 7.09W
Killybegs Rep. of Ire. **38** 54.38N 8.27W

Killyleagh N. Ireland **38** 54.24N 5.39W
Kilmacolm Scotland **34** 55.55N 4.38W
Kilmacthomas Rep. of Ire. **39** 52.12N 7.26W
Kilmaganny Rep. of Ire. **39** 52.26N 7.21W
Kilmallock Rep. of Ire. **39** 52.24N 8.35W
Kilmaluag Scotland **36** 57.41N 6.19W
Kilmarnock Scotland **34** 55.37N 4.30W
Kilmartin Scotland **34** 56.18N 5.28W
Kilmar Tor *hill* England **31** 50.34N 4.29W
Kilmichael Pt. Rep. of Ire. **39** 52.44N 6.09W
Kilmore Australia **80** 37.18S 144.58E
Kilmore Quay Rep. of Ire. **39** 52.11N 6.34W
Kilnaleck Rep. of Ire. **38** 53.51N 7.20W
Kilninver Scotland **34** 56.21N 5.30W
Kilombero *r.* Tanzania **73** 8.30S 37.28E
Kilosa Tanzania **73** 6.49S 37.00E
Kilrane Rep. of Ire. **39** 52.15N 6.21W
Kilrea N. Ireland **34** 54.57N 6.35W
Kilronan Rep. of Ire. **39** 53.08N 9.41W
Kilrush Rep. of Ire. **39** 52.39N 9.30W
Kilsyth Scotland **35** 55.59N 4.04W
Kiltimagh Rep. of Ire. **38** 53.51N 9.00W
Kilwa Kivinje Tanzania **73** 8.45S 39.21E
Kilwa Masoko Tanzania **73** 8.55S 39.31E
Kilwinning Scotland **34** 55.40N 4.41W
Kilworth Mts. Rep. of Ire. **39** 52.14N 8.12W
Kimberley R.S.A. **74** 28.45S 24.46E
Kimbolton England **29** 52.17N 0.23W
Kimito *i.* Finland **46** 60.05N 22.30E
Kimpton England **27** 51.52N 0.18W
Kinabalu *mtn.* Malaysia **60** 6.10N 116.40E
Kinbrace Scotland **37** 58.15N 3.56W
Kincardine Scotland **35** 56.04N 3.44W
Kinder Scout *hill* England **32** 53.23N 1.53W
Kindia Guinea **70** 10.03N 12.49W
Kindu Zaïre **72** 3.00S 25.56E
Kineshma U.S.S.R. **47** 57.28N 42.08E
Kingairloch *f.* Scotland **34** 56.36N 5.35W
Kingarth Scotland **34** 55.46N 5.03W
King Christian Ninth Land *f.* Greenland **93** 68.20N 37.00W
King Frederik Sixth Coast *f.* Greenland **93** 63.00N 44.00W
Kinghorn Scotland **35** 56.04N 3.11W
King I. Australia **80** 39.50S 144.00E
Kingisepp U.S.S.R. **46** 58.12N 22.30E
Kingku China **62** 23.29N 100.19E
King Leopold Ranges *mts.* Australia **79** 17.00S 125.30E
Kings *r.* Rep. of Ire. **39** 52.32N 7.12W
Kingsbridge England **31** 50.17N 3.46W
Kingsbury England **27** 51.35N 0.16W
Kingsclere England **28** 51.20N 1.14W
Kingscourt Rep. of Ire. **38** 53.54N 6.49W
Kingsdown England **29** 51.21N 0.17E
Kings Langley England **27** 51.43N 0.28W
Kingsley Dam U.S.A. **90** 41.15N 101.30W
King's Lynn England **29** 52.45N 0.25E
Kingsthorne England **28** 51.59N 2.43W
Kingston Australia **80** 36.50S 139.50E
Kingston Canada **95** 44.14N 76.30W
Kingston Jamaica **97** 17.58N 76.48W
Kingston New Zealand **82** 45.21S 168.44E
Kingston N.Y. U.S.A. **95** 41.55N 74.00W
Kingston Penn. U.S.A. **95** 41.15N 75.52W
Kingston upon Hull England **33** 53.45N 0.20W
Kingston-upon-Thames England **27** 51.25N 0.17W
Kingstown St. Vincent **97** 13.12N 61.14W
Kingswood Avon England **28** 51.27N 2.29W
Kingswood Surrey England **27** 51.17N 0.12W
Kings Worthy England **28** 51.06N 1.18W
Kington England **28** 52.12N 3.02W
Kingussie Scotland **37** 57.05N 4.04W
King William's Town R.S.A. **74** 32.53S 27.24E
Kingyang China **62** 36.06N 107.49E
Kinloch Scotland **36** 57.00N 6.17W
Kinlochewe Scotland **36** 57.36N 5.18W
Kinlochleven Scotland **34** 56.43N 4.58W
Kinloch Rannoch Scotland **34** 56.42N 4.11W
Kinnairds Head Scotland **37** 57.42N 2.00W
Kinnegad Rep. of Ire. **38** 53.28N 7.08W
Kinnitty Rep. of Ire. **39** 53.06N 7.45W
Kinross Scotland **35** 56.13N 3.27W
Kinsale Rep. of Ire. **39** 51.42N 8.32W
Kinshasa Zaïre **72** 4.18S 15.18E
Kintore Scotland **37** 57.14N 2.21W
Kintyre *pen.* Scotland **34** 55.35N 5.35W
Kinvara Rep. of Ire. **39** 53.08N 8.56W
Kinyeti *mtn.* Sudan **73** 3.56N 32.52E
Kiparissía Greece **43** 37.15N 21.40E
Kipawa L. Canada **95** 46.55N 79.00W
Kipengere Range *mts.* Tanzania **73** 9.15S 34.15E
Kipili Tanzania **73** 7.30S 30.39E
Kipini Kenya **73** 2.31S 40.32E
Kippen Scotland **34** 56.08N 4.11W
Kippure *mtn.* Rep. of Ire. **39** 53.11N 6.20W
Kipushi Zaïre **73** 11.46S 27.15E
Kirensk U.S.S.R. **49** 57.45N 108.00E
Kirghizstan Soviet Socialist Republic *d.* U.S.S.R. **62** 41.30N 75.00E
Kirgiz Steppe *f.* U.S.S.R. **48** 49.28N 57.07E
Kiri Zaïre **72** 1.23S 19.00E
Kirikkale Turkey **56** 39.51N 33.32E
Kirin China **63** 43.53N 126.35E
Kirin *d.* China **63** 43.00N 127.30E
Kirkbean Scotland **35** 54.55N 3.36W
Kirkbride England **35** 54.54N 3.12W
Kirkburton England **32** 53.36N 1.42W
Kirkby England **32** 53.29N 2.54W
Kirkby in Ashfield England **33** 53.06N 1.15W
Kirkby Lonsdale England **32** 54.13N 2.36W
Kirkbymoorside *town* England **33** 54.16N 0.56W
Kirkby Stephen England **32** 54.27N 2.23W
Kirkcaldy Scotland **35** 56.07N 3.10W
Kirkcolm Scotland **34** 54.58N 5.05W
Kirkconnel Scotland **35** 55.23N 4.01W
Kirkcowan Scotland **34** 54.55N 4.36W
Kirkcudbright Scotland **35** 54.50N 4.03W
Kirkcudbright B. Scotland **35** 54.47N 4.05W
Kirkenes Norway **46** 69.44N 30.05E
Kirkham England **32** 53.47N 2.52W
Kirkintilloch Scotland **34** 55.57N 4.10W
Kirkland Lake *town* Canada **94** 48.10N 80.02W
Kirklareli Turkey **43** 41.44N 27.12E
Kirk Michael I.o.M. **32** 54.17N 4.35W
Kirkmichael Scotland **35** 56.44N 3.31W
Kirkmuirhill Scotland **35** 55.40N 3.55W
Kirkoswald England **32** 54.46N 2.41W
Kirkuk Iraq **57** 35.28N 44.26E
Kirkwall Scotland **37** 58.59N 2.58W
Kirn W. Germany **45** 49.47N 7.28E
Kirov R.S.F.S.R. U.S.S.R. **47** 58.38N 49.38E
Kirov R.S.F.S.R. U.S.S.R. **47** 53.59N 34.20E
Kirovabad U.S.S.R. **57** 40.39N 46.20E
Kirovakan U.S.S.R. **57** 40.49N 44.30E
Kirovograd U.S.S.R. **47** 48.31N 32.15E
Kirovsk U.S.S.R. **46** 67.37N 33.39E
Kirriemuir Scotland **35** 56.41N 3.01W
Kirşehir Turkey **56** 39.09N 34.08E
Kirton England **33** 52.56N 0.03W
Kiruna Sweden **46** 67.53N 20.15E
Kisangani Zaïre **72** 0.33N 25.14E
Kishinev U.S.S.R. **47** 47.00N 28.50E
Kishorn, Loch Scotland **36** 57.21N 5.40W
Kisii Kenya **73** 0.40S 34.44E
Kislovodsk U.S.S.R. **47** 43.56N 42.44E
Kismayu Somali Rep. **73** 0.25S 42.31E
Kissidougou Guinea **70** 9.48N 10.08W
Kistna *r. see* KrishnaIndia **58**
Kisumu Kenya **73** 0.07S 34.47E
Kita Mali **70** 13.04N 9.29W
Kitakyushu Japan **63** 33.52N 130.49E
Kitale Kenya **73** 1.01N 35.01E
Kitchener Canada **94** 43.27N 80.30W
Kitgum Uganda **73** 3.17N 32.54E
Kíthira *i.* Greece **43** 36.15N 23.00E
Kíthnos *i.* Greece **43** 37.25N 24.25E
Kitimat Canada **92** 54.05N 128.38W
Kitinen *r.* Finland **46** 67.16N 27.30E
Kittanning U.S.A. **95** 40.49N 79.31W
Kitui Kenya **73** 1.22S 38.01E
Kitunda Tanzania **73** 6.48S 33.17E
Kitwe Zambia **73** 12.50S 28.04E
Kiukiang China **63** 29.41N 116.03E
Kivu *d.* Zaïre **73** 3.00S 27.00E
Kivu, L. Rwanda/Zaïre **73** 2.00S 29.10E
Kizil *r.* Turkey **56** 41.45N 35.57E
Kizil Arvat U.S.S.R. **57** 39.00N 56.23E
Kizlyar U.S.S.R. **47** 43.51N 46.43E
Kladno Czech. **44** 50.10N 14.05E
Klagenfurt Austria **44** 46.38N 14.20E
Klaipeda U.S.S.R. **46** 55.43N 21.07E
Klamath Falls *town* U.S.A. **90** 42.14N 121.47W
Klar *r.* Sweden **46** 59.25N 13.25E
Kleve W. Germany **45** 51.47N 6.11E
Klin U.S.S.R. **47** 56.20N 36.45E
Klintehamn Sweden **46** 57.24N 18.14E
Klintsy U.S.S.R. **47** 52.45N 32.15E
Klipplaat R.S.A. **74** 33.02S 24.20E
Klöfta Norway **46** 60.04N 11.06E
Knap, Pt. of Scotland **34** 55.53N 5.41W
Knapdale *f.* Scotland **34** 55.53N 5.32W
Knaphill *town* England **27** 51.19N 0.37W
Knaresborough England **33** 54.01N 1.29W
Knebworth England **27** 51.52N 0.12W
Knighton Wales **30** 52.21N 3.02W
Knin Yugo. **42** 44.02N 16.10E
Knockadoon Head Rep. of Ire. **39** 51.52N 7.52W
Knockalongy *mtn.* Rep. of Ire. **38** 54.12N 8.45W
Knockboy *mtn.* Rep. of Ire. **39** 51.48N 9.27W
Knock Hill Scotland **37** 57.35N 2.47W
Knocklayd *mtn.* N. Ireland **34** 55.09N 6.15W
Knockmealdown *mtn.* Rep. of Ire. **39** 52.13N 7.53W
Knockmealdown Mts. Rep. of Ire. **39** 52.15N 7.55W
Knottingley England **33** 53.42N 1.15W
Knoxville U.S.A. **91** 36.00N 83.57W
Knoydart *f.* Scotland **36** 57.03N 5.38W
Knutsford England **32** 53.18N 2.22W
Knysna R.S.A. **74** 34.03S 23.03E
Kobe Japan **63** 34.40N 135.12E
Koblenz W. Germany **45** 50.21N 7.36E
Kobroör *i.* Indonesia **61** 6.10S 134.30E
Kočani Yugo. **43** 41.55N 22.24E
Kodiak U.S.A. **92** 57.49N 152.30W
Kodiak I. U.S.A. **92** 57.00N 153.50W
Koffiefontein R.S.A. **74** 29.22S 24.58E
Koforidua Ghana **70** 6.01N 0.12W
Köge Denmark **46** 55.28N 12.12E
Kohat Pakistan **58** 33.37N 71.30E
Kohima India **59** 25.40N 84.08E
Kohtla-Järve U.S.S.R. **47** 59.28N 27.20E
Kokand U.S.S.R. **62** 40.33N 70.55E
Kokchetav U.S.S.R. **48** 53.18N 69.25E
Kokenau Asia **61** 4.42S 136.25E
Kokkola Finland **46** 63.50N 23.10E
Kokomo U.S.A. **94** 40.30N 86.09W
Kokon Selka Finland **46** 61.30N 29.30E
Kokpekty U.S.S.R. **62** 48.45N 82.25E
Koksoak *r.* Canada **93** 58.30N 68.15W
Kokstad R.S.A. **74** 30.32S 29.25E
Kola U.S.S.R. **46** 68.53N 33.01E
Kolaka Indonesia **61** 4.04S 121.38E
Kola Pen. U.S.S.R. **48** 67.00N 38.00E
Kolar India **59** 13.10N 78.10E
Kolari Finland **46** 67.22N 23.50E
Kolarovgrad Bulgaria **43** 43.15N 26.55E
Kolding Denmark **46** 55.29N 9.30E
Kole Zaïre **72** 3.28S 22.29E
Kolea Algeria **41** 36.42N 2.46E
Kolepom *i.* Indonesia **61** 8.00S 138.30E
Kolguyev *i.* U.S.S.R. **48** 69.00N 49.00E
Kolhapur India **58** 16.43N 74.15E
Kolín Czech. **44** 50.02N 15.10E
Köln *see* Cologne W. Germany **45**
Koło Poland **47** 52.12N 18.37E
Kołobrzeg Poland **44** 54.10N 15.35E
Kolomna U.S.S.R. **47** 55.05N 38.45E
Kolomyia U.S.S.R. **47** 48.31N 25.00E
Kolwezi Zaïre **72** 10.44S 25.28E
Kolyma *r.* U.S.S.R. **49** 68.50N 161.00E
Kolyma Range *mts.* U.S.S.R. **49** 63.00N 160.00E
Kom *r.* Cameroon **72** 2.20N 10.38E
Komadugu Gana *r.* Nigeria **71** 13.06N 12.23E
Komadugu Yobe *r.* Niger/Nigeria **71** 13.43N 13.19E
Komatipoort R.S.A. **74** 25.25S 31.55E
Komba Zaïre **72** 2.52N 24.03E
Kommunarsk U.S.S.R. **47** 48.30N 38.47E
Kommunizma, Peak *mtn.* U.S.S.R. **62** 38.39N 72.01E
Komotini Greece **43** 41.07N 25.26E
Komsomolets *i.* U.S.S.R. **49** 80.20N 96.00E
Komsomolsk-na-Amur U.S.S.R. **49** 50.32N 136.59E
Kondoa Tanzania **73** 4.54S 35.49E
Kongolo Zaïre **73** 5.20S 27.00E
Kongsberg Norway **46** 59.42N 9.39E
Kongsvinger Norway **46** 60.13N 11.59E
Kongwa Tanzania **73** 6.13S 36.28E
Konkouré *r.* Guinea **70** 9.55N 13.45W
Konotop U.S.S.R. **47** 51.15N 33.14E
Konstanz W. Germany **44** 47.40N 9.10E
Kontagora Nigeria **71** 10.24N 5.22E
Kontcha Cameroon **71** 7.59N 12.15E
Kontum Vietnam **60** 14.23N 108.00E
Konya Turkey **56** 37.51N 32.30E
Konza Kenya **73** 1.45S 37.07E
Kopet Range *mts.* Asia **57** 38.00N 58.00E
Ko Phangan *i.* Thailand **60** 9.50N 100.00E
Köping Sweden **46** 59.31N 16.01E
Korbach W. Germany **44** 51.16N 8.53E
Korçe Albania **43** 40.37N 20.45E
Korčula *i.* Yugo. **43** 42.56N 16.53E
Korea B. Asia **63** 39.00N 124.00E
Korea Str. Asia **63** 35.00N 129.20E
Korhogo Ivory Coast **70** 9.22N 5.31W
Kornat *i.* Yugo. **42** 43.48N 15.20E
Korogwe Tanzania **73** 5.10S 38.35E
Koror *i.* Asia **61** 7.30N 134.30E
Korosten U.S.S.R. **47** 51.00N 28.30E
Korsor Denmark **46** 55.19N 11.09E
Koryak Range *mts.* U.S.S.R. **49** 62.20N 171.00E
Kos *i.* Greece **43** 36.48N 27.10E
Ko Samui *i.* Thailand **60** 9.30N 100.00E
Kosciusko, Mt. Australia **80** 36.28S 148.17E
Košice Czech. **47** 48.44N 21.15E
Kosovska-Mitrŏvica Yugo. **43** 42.54N 20.51E
Kossovo U.S.S.R. **47** 52.40N 25.18E
Koster R.S.A. **74** 25.52S 26.54E
Kosti Sudan **69** 13.11N 32.38E
Kostroma U.S.S.R. **47** 57.46N 40.59E
Kostrzyn Poland **44** 52.24N 17.11E

Koszalin Poland **44** 54.10N 16.10E
Kota India **58** 25.11N 75.58E
Kota Bharu Malaysia **60** 6.07N 102.15E
Kota Kinabalu Malaysia **60** 5.59N 116.04E
Kotelnich U.S.S.R. **47** 58.20N 48.10E
Kotelnikovo U.S.S.R. **47** 47.39N 43.08E
Kotelnyy *i.* U.S.S.R. **49** 75.30N 141.00E
Köthen E. Germany **44** 51.46N 11.59E
Kotka Finland **46** 60.26N 26.55E
Kotlas U.S.S.R. **48** 61.15N 46.28E
Kotor Yugo. **43** 42.28N 18.47E
Kottagudem India **59** 17.32N 80.39E
Kotuy *r.* U.S.S.R. **49** 71.40N 103.00E
Kotzebue U.S.A. **92** 66.51N 162.40W
Kouango C.A.R. **72** 5.00N 20.04E
Koulikoro Mali **70** 12.55N 7.31W
Kouroussa Guinea **70** 10.40N 9.50W
Koutiala Mali **70** 12.20N 5.23W
Kouvola Finland **46** 60.54N 26.45E
Kouyou *r.* Congo **72** 0.40S 16.37E
Kovel U.S.S.R. **47** 51.12N 24.48E
Kovrov U.S.S.R. **47** 56.23N 41.21E
Kowloon Hong Kong **63** 22.20N 114.15E
Koyukuk *r.* U.S.A. **92** 64.50N 157.30W
Kozan Turkey **56** 37.27N 35.47E
Kozáni Greece **43** 40.18N 21.48E
Kozhikode India **58** 11.15N 75.45E
Krabi Thailand **59** 8.04N 98.52E
Kragero Norway **46** 58.54N 9.25E
Kragujevac Yugo. **43** 44.01N 20.55E
Kraljevo Yugo. **43** 43.44N 20.41E
Kramatorsk U.S.S.R. **47** 48.43N 37.33E
Kramfors Sweden **46** 62.55N 17.50E
Kranskop R.S.A. **74** 29.12S 30.51E
Krasnodar U.S.S.R. **47** 45.02N 39.00E
Krasnograd U.S.S.R. **47** 49.22N 35.28E
Krasnovodsk U.S.S.R. **57** 40.01N 53.00E
Krasnovodsk G. U.S.S.R. **57** 39.50N 53.15E
Krasnoyarsk U.S.S.R. **49** 56.05N 92.46E
Kratie Khmer Rep. **60** 12.30N 106.03E
Krefeld W. Germany **45** 51.20N 6.32E
Kremenchug U.S.S.R. **47** 49.00N 33.25E
Krems Austria **44** 48.25N 15.36E
Kribi Cameroon **71** 2.56N 9.56E
Krishna *r.* India **59** 16.00N 81.00E
Krishnanagar India **58** 23.22N 88.32E
Kristiansand Norway **46** 58.08N 7.59E
Kristianstad Sweden **46** 56.02N 14.10E
Kristiansund Norway **46** 63.15N 7.55E
Kristinehamn Sweden **46** 59.17N 14.09E
Kristinestad Finland **46** 62.16N 21.20E
Krivoy Rog U.S.S.R. **47** 47.55N 33.24E
Krk *i.* Yugo. **42** 45.04N 14.36E
Kronshtadt U.S.S.R. **46** 60.00N 29.40E
Kroonstad R.S.A. **74** 27.40S 27.15E
Kruger Nat. Park R.S.A. **74** 24.10S 31.36E
Krugersdorp R.S.A. **74** 26.06S 27.46E
Kruševac Yugo. **43** 43.34N 21.20E
Kuala Lipis Malaysia **60** 4.11N 102.00E
Kuala Lumpur Malaysia **60** 3.08N 101.42E
Kuala Trengganu Malaysia **60** 5.10N 103.10E
Kuandang Indonesia **61** 0.53N 122.58E
Kuantan Malaysia **60** 3.50N 103.19E
Kuba U.S.S.R. **57** 41.23N 48.33E
Kuban *r.* U.S.S.R. **47** 45.20N 37.17E
Kucha China **62** 41.43N 82.58E
Kuching Malaysia **60** 1.32N 110.20E
Kudat Malaysia **60** 6.45N 116.47E
Kufstein Austria **44** 47.36N 12.11E
Kuh Bul *mtn.* Iran **57** 30.48N 52.45E
Kuh-i-Alaband *mtn.* Iran **57** 34.09N 50.48E
Kuh-i-Aleh *mts.* Iran **57** 37.15N 57.30E
Kuh-i-Alijuq *mtn.* Iran **57** 31.27N 51.43E
Kuh-i-Barm *mtn.* Iran **57** 30.21N 52.00E
Kuh-i-Binalud *mts.* Iran **57** 36.15N 59.00E
Kuh-i-Darband *mtn.* Iran **57** 31.33N 57.08E
Kuh-i-Dinar *mtn.* Iran **57** 30.45N 51.39E
Kuh-i-Hazar *mtn.* Iran **57** 29.30N 57.18E
Kuh-i-Istin *mtn.* Iran **57** 31.18N 60.03E
Kuh-i-Karbush *mtn.* Iran **57** 32.36N 50.02E
Kuh-i-Kargiz *mts.* Iran **57** 33.25N 51.40E
Kuh-i-Khurunag *mtn.* Iran **57** 32.10N 54.38E
Kuh-i-Lalehzar *mtn.* Iran **57** 29.26N 56.48E
Kuh-i-Malik Siah *mtn.* Iran **57** 29.52N 60.55E
Kuh-i-Masahim *mtn.* Iran **57** 30.26N 55.08E
Kuh-i-Naibandan *mtn.* Iran **57** 32.25N 57.30E
Kuh-i-Ran *mtn.* Iran **57** 26.46N 58.15E
Kuh-i-Sahand *mtn.* Iran **57** 37.37N 46.27E
Kuh-i-Savalan *mtn.* Iran **57** 38.15N 47.50E
Kuh-i-Shah *mtn.* Iran **57** 31.38N 59.16E
Kuh-i-Shah *mts.* Iran **57** 37.00N 58.00E
Kuh-i-Sultan *mtn.* Pakistan **57** 29.10N 62.48E
Kuh-i-Taftan *mtn.* Iran **57** 28.38N 61.08E
Kuh-i-Ushtaran *mtn.* Iran **57** 33.18N 49.15E
Kuhpayeh Iran **57** 32.42N 52.25E
Kuh Tasak *mtn.* Iran **57** 29.51N 51.52E
Kula Turkey **56** 38.33N 28.38E
Kula Kangri *mtn.* China **58** 28.15N 90.34E
Kuma *r.* U.S.S.R. **47** 44.50N 46.55E
Kumai Indonesia **60** 2.45S 111.44E
Kumamoto Japan **63** 32.50N 130.42E
Kumanovo Yugo. **43** 42.08N 21.40E
Kumasi Ghana **70** 6.45N 1.35W
Kumba Cameroon **71** 4.39N 9.26E
Kum Dag U.S.S.R. **57** 39.14N 54.33E
Kunashir *i.* U.S.S.R. **63** 44.25N 146.00E
Kundelungu Mts. Zaïre **73** 9.30S 27.50E
Kungur *mtn.* China **62** 38.40N 75.30E
Kungur U.S.S.R. **48** 57.27N 56.50E
Kunlun Shan *mts.* China **62** 36.40N 88.00E
Kunming China **59** 25.04N 102.41E
Kuopio Finland **46** 62.51N 27.30E
Kupa *r.* Yugo. **42** 45.30N 16.20E
Kupang Indonesia **61** 10.13S 123.38E
Kupyansk U.S.S.R. **47** 49.41N 37.37E
Kur *r.* Iran **57** 29.40N 53.17E
Kura *r.* U.S.S.R. **57** 39.18N 49.22E
Kurdistan *f.* Asia **57** 37.00N 43.30E
Kurgan U.S.S.R. **48** 55.20N 65.20E
Kuria Muria Is. Oman **58** 17.30N 56.00E
Kuril Is. U.S.S.R. **63** 46.00N 150.30E
Kuril Trench Pacific Oc. **107** 46.00N 150.00E
Kurlovski U.S.S.R. **47** 55.26N 40.40E
Kurnool India **59** 15.51N 78.01E
Kursk U.S.S.R. **47** 51.45N 36.14E
Kurskiy G. U.S.S.R. **46** 55.00N 21.00E
Kuršumlija Yugo. **43** 43.09N 21.16E
Kuruman R.S.A. **74** 27.28S 23.27E
Kuruman *r.* R.S.A. **74** 27.00S 20.40E
Kushiro Japan **63** 42.58N 144.24E
Kushk Afghan. **57** 34.52N 62.29E
Kushka U.S.S.R. **57** 35.14N 62.15E
Kushtia Bangla. **58** 23.45N 89.07E
Kuskokwim Mts. U.S.A. **92** 62.50N 156.00W
Kustanay U.S.S.R. **48** 53.15N 63.40E
Kusten Canal W. Germany **45** 53.05N 7.46E
Kütahya Turkey **56** 39.25N 29.56E
Kutaisi U.S.S.R. **47** 42.15N 42.44E
Kutch, G. of India **58** 22.30N 69.30E
Kutsing China **59** 25.32N 103.47E
Kutu Zaïre **72** 2.42S 18.09E
Kuusamo Finland **46** 65.57N 29.15E
Kuwait Asia **57** 29.20N 47.40E
Kuwait *town* Kuwait **57** 29.20N 48.00E
Kuybyshev U.S.S.R. **47** 53.10N 50.15E
Kuybyshev Resr. U.S.S.R. **47** 55.00N 49.00E
Kuyto, L. U.S.S.R. **46** 65.10N 31.00E
Kuznetsk U.S.S.R. **47** 53.08N 46.36E
Kwale Kenya **73** 4.20S 39.25E
Kwamouth Zaïre **72** 3.11S 16.16E
Kwangchow China **60** 23.20N 113.30E
Kwanghua China **63** 32.30N 111.50E
Kwangju S. Korea **63** 35.07N 126.52E
Kwango *r.* Zaïre **72** 3.20S 17.23E
Kwangsi-Chuang *d.* China **63** 23.50N 109.00E
Kwangtung China **63** 23.30N 114.30E
Kwanhsien China **59** 30.59N 103.40E
Kwara *d.* Nigeria **71** 8.20N 5.35E
KwaZulu *f.* R.S.A. **74** 28.10S 31.30E
Kweichow *d.* China **59** 27.00N 106.00E
Kweilin China **63** 25.21N 110.11E
Kweiping China **63** 23.20N 110.04E
Kweiyang China **59** 26.35N 106.40E
Kwenge *r.* Zaïre **72** 4.53S 18.47E
Kwilu *r.* Zaïre **72** 3.18S 17.22E
Kwoka *mtn.* Indonesia **61** 1.30S 132.30E
Kyaka Tanzania **73** 1.16S 31.27E
Kyakhta U.S.S.R. **62** 50.22N 106.30E
Kyaukpyu Burma **59** 19.28N 93.30E
Kyle *f.* Scotland **34** 55.33N 4.28W
Kyleakin Scotland **36** 57.16N 5.44W
Kyle of Durness *est.* Scotland **37** 58.32N 4.50W
Kyle of Lochalsh *town* Scotland **36** 57.17N 5.43W
Kyle of Tongue *est.* Scotland **37** 58.27N 4.26W
Kyles of Bute *str.* Scotland **34** 55.55N 5.12W
Kyll *r.* W. Germany **45** 49.48N 6.42E
Kyluchevskaya *mtn.* U.S.S.R. **49** 56.00N 160.30E
Kyminjoki *r.* Finland **46** 60.30N 27.00E
Kyoga, L. Uganda **73** 1.30N 33.00E
Kyogle Australia **80** 28.36S 152.59E
Kyoto Japan **63** 35.02N 135.45E
Kyrenia Cyprus **56** 35.20N 33.20E
Kyushu *i.* Japan **63** 32.50N 130.50E
Kyustendil Bulgaria **43** 42.18N 22.39E
Kyyjärvi Finland **46** 63.02N 24.34E
Kyzyl U.S.S.R. **62** 51.42N 94.28E
Kyzyl Kum *des.* U.S.S.R. **48** 42.00N 64.30E
Kzyl Orda U.S.S.R. **48** 44.52N 65.28E

L

La Banda Argentina **103** 27.44S 64.14W
La Bañeza Spain **41** 42.17N 5.55W
La Barca Mexico **96** 20.20N 102.33W
La Bassée France **45** 50.32N 2.49E
Labe *r. see* Elbe Czech. **44**
Labé Guinea **70** 11.17N 12.11W
La Blanquilla *i.* Venezuela **97** 11.53N 64.38W
Labouheyre France **40** 44.13N 0.55W
Labrador *f.* Canada **93** 54.00N 61.30W
Labrador City Canada **93** 52.54N 66.50W
Labuan *i.* Malaysia **60** 5.20N 115.15E
La Calle Algeria **42** 36.54N 8.25E
La Carolina Spain **41** 38.16N 3.36W
Lacaune France **40** 43.42N 2.41E
La Ceiba Honduras **96** 15.45N 86.45W
La Charité France **40** 47.11N 3.01E
La Chaux de Fonds Switz. **44** 47.07N 6.51E
Lachine Canada **95** 45.27N 73.41W
Lachlan *r.* Australia **80** 34.21S 143.58E
Lackan Resr. Rep. of Ire. **39** 53.09N 6.31W
Lackawanna U.S.A. **95** 42.49N 78.49W
La Coruña Spain **41** 43.22N 8.24W
La Crosse U.S.A. **94** 43.48N 91.04W
La Demanda, Sierra de *mts.* Spain **41** 42.10N 3.20W
Ladis Iran **57** 28.57N 61.18E
Ladismith R.S.A. **74** 33.30S 21.15E
Ladoga, L. U.S.S.R. **46** 61.00N 32.00E
Ladybrand R.S.A. **74** 29.12S 27.27E
Ladysmith R.S.A. **74** 28.34S 29.47E
Ladysmith U.S.A. **94** 45.27N 91.07W
Lae P.N.G. **61** 6.45S 146.30E
La Estrada Spain **41** 42.40N 8.30W
Lafayette Ind. U.S.A. **94** 40.25N 86.54W
Lafayette La. U.S.A. **91** 30.12N 92.18W
Lafayette, Mt. U.S.A. **95** 44.10N 71.38W
La Fère France **45** 49.40N 3.22E
Lafiagi Nigeria **71** 8.50N 5.23E
La Fuente de San Esteban Spain **41** 40.48N 6.15W
Laga Bor *r.* Somali Rep. **73** 0.32N 42.05E
Lagan *r.* N. Ireland **34** 54.37N 5.44W
Lagan *r.* Sweden **46** 56.35N 12.55E
Lågen *r.* Norway **46** 60.10N 11.28E
Lagg Scotland **34** 55.57N 5.50W
Laggan, Loch Scotland **37** 56.57N 4.30W
Laggan B. Scotland **34** 55.41N 6.18W
Lago Dilolo *town* Angola **72** 11.27S 22.03E
Lagos Mexico **96** 21.21N 101.55W
Lagos Nigeria **71** 6.27N 3.28E
Lagos *d.* Nigeria **71** 6.32N 3.30E
Lagos Portugal **41** 37.05N 8.40W
La Guaira Venezuela **97** 10.38N 66.55W
Laguna Brazil **103** 28.29S 48.45W
Laguna Dam U.S.A. **90** 32.55N 114.25W
Lahad Datu Malaysia **60** 5.05N 118.20E
La Hague, Cap de France **40** 49.44N 1.56W
Lahat Indonesia **60** 3.46S 103.32E
Lahijan Iran **57** 37.12N 50.00E
Lahn *r.* W. Germany **45** 50.18N 7.36E
Lahnstein W. Germany **45** 50.17N 7.38E
Lahore Pakistan **58** 31.34N 74.22E
Lahti Finland **46** 61.00N 25.40E
Lai Chad **71** 9.22N 16.14E
Lai Chau Vietnam **59** 22.05N 103.03E
Laidon England **27** 51.34N 0.26E
Laidon, Loch Scotland **34** 56.39N 4.38W
Lainio *r.* Sweden **46** 67.26N 22.37E
Lairg Scotland **37** 58.01N 4.25W
Lajes Brazil **103** 27.48S 50.20W
La Junta U.S.A. **90** 37.59N 103.34W
Lagh Dera *r.* Somali Rep. **73** 0.01S 42.45E
Lake Cargelligo *town* Australia **80** 33.19S 146.23E
Lake Charles *town* U.S.A. **91** 30.13N 93.13W
Lake City U.S.A. **91** 30.05N 82.40W
Lake District *f.* England **32** 54.30N 3.10W
Lakeland *town* U.S.A. **91** 28.02N 81.59W
Lakeview U.S.A. **90** 42.13N 120.21W
Lakewood U.S.A. **94** 41.29N 81.50W
Lakhnadon India **58** 22.34N 79.38E
Lakonia, G. of Med. Sea **43** 36.35N 22.42E
Lakse Fjord *est.* Norway **46** 70.40N 26.50E
Lakselv Norway **46** 70.03N 25.06E
Lakshadweep Is. Indian Oc. **58** 11.00N 72.00E
Lalaua Moçambique **73** 14.20S 38.30E
La Libertad El Salvador **96** 13.28N 89.20W
La Línea Spain **41** 36.10N 5.21W
Lalitpur India **58** 24.42N 78.24E
La Louvière Belgium **45** 50.29N 4.11E
La Malbaie Canada **95** 47.39N 70.11W
Lamar U.S.A. **90** 38.04N 102.37W
Lambaréné Gabon **72** 0.40S 10.15E
Lambay I. Rep. of Ire. **38** 53.29N 6.01W
Lambeth *d.* England **27** 51.27N 0.07W
Lambourn England **28** 51.31N 1.31W

Lamego Portugal **41** 41.05N 7.49W
Lameroo Australia **80** 35.20S 140.33E
Lamía Greece **43** 38.53N 22.25E
Lamlash Scotland **34** 55.32N 5.08W
Lammermuir *f.* Scotland **35** 55.50N 2.25W
Lammermuir Hills Scotland **35** 55.51N 2.40W
Lamotrek *i.* Asia **61** 7.28N 146.23E
Lampedusa *i.* Italy **42** 35.30N 12.35E
Lampeter Wales **30** 52.06N 4.06W
Lampione *i.* Italy **42** 35.33N 12.18E
Lamu Kenya **73** 2.20S 40.54E
La Nao, Cabo de Spain **41** 38.42N 0.15E
Lanark Scotland **35** 55.41N 3.47W
Lancashire *d.* England **32** 53.53N 2.30W
Lancaster England **32** 54.03N 2.48W
Lancaster U.S.A. **95** 40.01N 76.19W
Lancaster Sd. Canada **93** 74.00N 85.00W
Lanchow China **62** 36.01N 103.45E
Landau W. Germany **44** 49.12N 8.07E
Landeck Austria **44** 47.09N 10.35E
Land's End *c.* England **31** 50.03N 5.45W
Landshut W. Germany **44** 48.31N 12.10E
Landskrona Sweden **46** 55.53N 12.50E
Lanesborough Rep. of Ire. **38** 53.40N 8.00W
Langanes *c.* Iceland **46** 66.30N 14.30W
Langavat, Loch Scotland **36** 58.04N 6.45W
Langeland *i.* Denmark **44** 54.50N 10.50E
Langeoog *i.* W. Germany **45** 53.46N 7.30E
Langholm Scotland **35** 55.09N 3.00W
Langkawi *i.* Malaysia **60** 6.20N 99.30E
Langness *c.* I.o.M. **32** 54.03N 4.37W
Langon France **40** 44.33N 0.14W
Langöy *i.* Norway **46** 68.50N 15.00E
Langport England **28** 51.02N 2.51W
Langres France **40** 47.53N 5.20E
Langsa Indonesia **60** 4.28N 97.59E
Långseleån *r.* Sweden **46** 63.30N 16.53E
Lang Son Vietnam **60** 21.50N 106.55E
Langstrothdale Chase *hills* England **32** 54.13N 2.15W
Lannion France **40** 48.44N 3.27W
Lansing U.S.A. **94** 42.44N 84.34W
Lanzarote *i.* Canary Is. **68** 29.00N 13.55W
Laoag Phil. **61** 18.14N 120.36E
Laois *d.* Rep. of Ire. **39** 53.00N 7.20W
Laokay Vietnam **59** 22.30N 104.00E
Laon France **45** 49.34N 3.37E
Laos Asia **60** 19.00N 104.00E
La Palma *i.* Canary Is. **68** 28.50N 18.00W
La Palma Spain **41** 37.23N 6.33W
La Pampa *d.* Argentina **103** 37.30S 65.50W
La Paz Argentina **103** 30.45S 59.36W
La Paz Bolivia **102** 16.30S 68.10W
La Peña, Sierra de *mts.* Spain **41** 42.30N 0.50W
La Perouse Str. U.S.S.R. **49** 45.50N 142.30E
Lapford England **31** 50.52N 3.49W
Lapland *f.* Sweden/Finland **46** 68.10N 24.00E
La Plata Argentina **103** 34.58S 57.55W
La Plata, Rio de *est.* S. America **103** 35.15S 56.45W
Lappa Järvi *l.* Finland **46** 63.05N 23.30E
Lappeenranta Finland **46** 61.04N 28.05E
Laptev Sea U.S.S.R. **49** 74.30N 125.00E
L'Aquila Italy **42** 42.22N 13.25E
Lar Iran **57** 27.37N 54.16E
Larache Morocco **41** 35.12N 6.10W
Laramie U.S.A. **90** 41.20N 105.38W
Larbert Scotland **35** 56.02N 3.51W
Larch *r.* Canada **93** 57.40N 69.30W
Laredo U.S.A. **90** 27.32N 99.22W
Largo Ward Scotland **35** 56.15N 2.52W
Largs Scotland **34** 55.48N 4.52W
La Rioja Argentina **103** 29.26S 66.50W
La Rioja *d.* Argentina **103** 29.40S 67.00W
Lárisa Greece **43** 39.36N 22.24E
Lark *r.* England **29** 52.26N 0.20E
Larkhall Scotland **35** 55.45N 3.59W
Lar Koh *mtn.* Afghan. **57** 32.25N 62.36E
Larnaca Cyprus **56** 34.54N 33.39E
Larne N. Ireland **34** 54.51N 5.49W
Larne Lough N. Ireland **34** 54.50N 5.47W
La Roche Belgium **45** 50.11N 5.35E
La Rochelle France **40** 46.10N 1.10W
La Roche-sur-Yon France **40** 46.40N 1.25W
La Rocque Pt. Channel Is. **31** 49.09N 2.05W
La Roda Spain **41** 39.13N 2.10W
La Romana Dom. Rep. **97** 18.27N 68.57W
La Ronge Canada **92** 55.07N 105.18W
Larvik Norway **46** 59.04N 10.02E
La Sagra *mtn.* Spain **41** 37.58N 2.35W
La Salle U.S.A. **94** 41.20N 89.06W
Las Cruces U.S.A. **90** 32.18N 106.47W
La Seine, Baie de France **40** 49.40N 0.30W
Las Flores Argentina **103** 36.03S 59.08W
Lashio Burma **59** 22.58N 97.48E
Las Palmas Canary Is. **68** 28.08N 15.27W
Las Perlas, Archipelago de Panamá **97** 8.45N 79.30W
La Spezia Italy **40** 44.07N 9.49E
Lastoursville Gabon **72** 0.50S 12.47E
Lastovo *i.* Yugo. **43** 42.45N 16.52E
Las Vegas U.S.A. **90** 36.10N 115.10W
Las Villas *d.* Cuba **97** 22.00N 80.00W
Latakia Syria **56** 35.31N 35.47E
La Tuque Canada **95** 47.26N 72.47W
Latvia Soviet Socialist Republic *d.* U.S.S.R. **46** 57.00N 25.00E
Lauchhammer E. Germany **44** 51.30N 13.48E
Lauder Scotland **35** 55.43N 2.45W
Lauderdale *f.* Scotland **35** 55.43N 2.42W
Laugharne Wales **31** 51.45N 4.28W
Launceston Australia **80** 41.25S 147.07E
Launceston England **31** 50.38N 4.21W
Laune *r.* Rep. of Ire. **39** 52.08N 9.45W
Laurel U.S.A. **95** 38.22N 75.34W
Laurencekirk Scotland **37** 56.50N 2.29W
Laurencetown Rep. of Ire. **39** 53.15N 8.12W
Laurentides Mts. Canada **95** 47.40N 71.40W
Lauritsala Finland **46** 61.05N 28.20E
Lausanne Switz. **44** 46.32N 6.39E
Laut *i.* Indonesia **60** 3.45S 116.20E
Lauterecken W. Germany **45** 49.39N 7.36E
Lavagh More *mtn.* Rep. of Ire. **38** 54.45N 8.07W
Laval Canada **95** 45.33N 73.44W
Laval France **40** 48.04N 0.45W
La Vega Dom. Rep. **97** 19.15N 70.33W
Lavernock Pt. Wales **31** 51.25N 3.10W
Lavras Brazil **103** 21.15S 44.59W
Lawers Scotland **34** 56.32N 4.10W
Lawra Ghana **70** 10.40N 2.49W
Lawrence U.S.A. **95** 42.41N 71.12W
Lawrenceville U.S.A. **94** 38.44N 87.42W
Laxey I.o.M. **32** 54.14N 4.24W
Laxford, Loch Scotland **36** 58.25N 5.06W
Lea *r.* England **27** 51.30N 0.00
Leach *r.* England **28** 51.41N 1.39W
Leadburn Scotland **35** 55.47N 3.14W
Leader *r.* Scotland **35** 55.37N 2.40W
Leadhills Scotland **35** 55.25N 3.46W
Leaf *r.* Canada **93** 58.47N 70.06W
Leamington Canada **94** 42.03N 82.35W
Leane, Lough Rep. of Ire. **39** 52.03N 9.35W
Leatherhead England **27** 51.18N 0.20W
Lebanon Asia **56** 34.00N 36.00E
Lebanon N.H. U.S.A. **95** 43.39N 72.17W
Lebanon Penn. U.S.A. **95** 40.21N 76.25W
Lebork Poland **46** 54.32N 17.43E
Lebrija Spain **41** 36.55N 6.10W
Le Cateau France **45** 50.07N 3.33E
Lecce Italy **43** 40.21N 18.11E
Lech *r.* W. Germany **44** 48.45N 10.51E
Le Chesne France **45** 49.31N 4.46E
Lechlade England **28** 51.42N 1.40W
Le Creusot France **40** 46.48N 4.27E
Lectoure France **40** 43.56N 0.38E
Ledbury England **28** 52.03N 2.25W
Ledesma Spain **41** 41.05N 6.00W
Lee *r.* Rep. of Ire. **39** 51.53N 8.25W
Leech L. U.S.A. **91** 47.10N 94.30W
Leeds England **33** 53.48N 1.34W
Leek England **32** 53.07N 2.02W
Leer W. Germany **45** 53.14N 7.27E
Leeton Australia **80** 34.33S 146.24E
Leeuwarden Neth. **45** 53.12N 5.48E
Leeuwin, C. Australia **79** 34.00S 115.00E
Leeward Is. C. America **97** 18.00N 61.00W
Legaspi Phil. **61** 13.10N 123.45E
Legges Tor *mtn.* Australia **80** 41.32S 147.41E
Leghorn Italy **42** 43.33N 10.18E
Leipzig E. Germany **48** 51.20N 12.20E
Legnica Poland **44** 51.12N 16.10E
Leh Jammu and Kashmir **58** 34.09N 77.35E
Le Havre France **40** 49.30N 0.06E
Leicester England **28** 52.39N 1.09W
Leicestershire *d.* England **28** 52.29N 1.10W
Leiden Neth. **45** 52.10N 4.30E
Leie *r.* Belgium **45** 51.03N 3.44E
Leigh G.M. England **32** 53.30N 2.33W
Leigh Kent England **27** 51.12N 0.13E
Leigh Creek *town* Australia **80** 30.31S 138.25E
Leighlinbridge Rep. of Ire. **39** 52.44N 6.59W
Leighton Buzzard England **28** 51.55N 0.39W
Leinster *d.* Rep. of Ire. **39** 53.05N 7.00W
Leinster, Mt. Rep. of Ire. **39** 52.38N 6.47W
Leipzig E. Germany **44** 51.20N 12.20E
Leiston England **29** 52.13N 1.35E
Leith Scotland **35** 55.59N 2.09W
Leith Hill England **27** 51.11N 0.21W
Leitrim *d.* Rep. of Ire. **38** 54.08N 8.00W
Leixlip Rep. of Ire. **38** 53.22N 6.31W
Lek *r.* Neth. **45** 51.55N 4.29E
Le Kef Algeria **42** 36.10N 8.40E
Lelystad Neth. **45** 52.32N 5.29E
Le Mans France **40** 48.01N 0.10E
Lemmer Neth. **45** 52.50N 5.43E
Lemmon U.S.A. **90** 45.56N 102.00W
Len *r.* England **27** 51.16N 0.31E
Lena *r.* U.S.S.R. **49** 72.00N 127.10E
Lenadoon Pt. Rep. of Ire. **38** 54.18N 9.04W
Lengerich W. Germany **45** 52.12N 7.52E
Lengoue *r.* Congo **72** 1.15S 16.42E
Lenina, Peak *mtn.* U.S.S.R. **62** 40.14N 69.40E
Leninabad U.S.S.R. **62** 40.14N 69.40E
Leninakan U.S.S.R. **57** 40.47N 43.49E
Leningrad U.S.S.R. **47** 59.55N 30.25E
Leninogorsk U.S.S.R. **48** 50.23N 83.32E
Leninsk Kuznetskiy U.S.S.R. **48** 54.44N 86.13E
Lenkoran U.S.S.R. **57** 38.45N 48.50E
Lenne *r.* W. Germany **45** 51.24N 7.30E
Lennoxtown Scotland **34** 55.59N 4.12W
Lens France **45** 50.26N 2.50E
Leoben Austria **44** 47.23N 15.06E
Leominster England **28** 52.15N 2.43W
Leominster U.S.A. **95** 42.31N 71.45W
León Mexico **96** 21.10N 101.42W
León Nicaragua **96** 12.24N 86.52W
Léon Spain **41** 42.35N 5.34W
Le Puy France **40** 45.03N 3.54E
Le Quesnoy France **45** 50.15N 3.39E
Lérida Spain **41** 41.37N 0.38E
Lerma Spain **41** 42.02N 3.46W
Lerwick Scotland **36** 60.09N 1.09W
Les Cayes Haiti **97** 18.15N 73.46W
Les Ecréhou *is.* Channel Is. **31** 49.17N 1.56W
Les Ecrins *mtn.* France **40** 44.50N 6.20E
Leskovac Yugo. **43** 43.00N 21.56E
Leslie Scotland **35** 56.13N 3.13W
Lesmahagow Scotland **35** 55.38N 3.54W
Lesotho Africa **74** 29.00S 28.00E
Les Sables d'Olonne France **40** 46.30N 1.47W
Lesser Antilles *is.* C. America **97** 13.00N 65.00W
Lesser Slave L. Canada **92** 55.30N 115.00W
Lesser Sunda Is. Indonesia **60** 8.30S 118.00E
Lessines Belgium **45** 50.43N 3.50E
Lésvos *i.* Greece **43** 39.10N 26.16E
Leszno Poland **44** 51.51N 16.35E
Letchworth England **29** 51.58N 0.13W
Lethbridge Canada **90** 49.43N 112.48W
Leti Is. Indonesia **61** 8.20S 128.00E
Le Tréport France **40** 50.04N 1.22E
Letterkenny Rep. of Ire. **38** 54.56N 7.45W
Leuser *mtn.* Indonesia **60** 3.50N 97.10E
Leuze Belgium **45** 50.36N 3.37E
Leven England **33** 53.54N 0.18W
Leven Scotland **35** 56.12N 3.00W
Leven, Loch Scotland **35** 56.13N 3.23W
Lévêque, C. Australia **79** 16.25S 123.00E
Leverburgh Scotland **36** 57.46N 7.00W
Le Verdon France **40** 45.33N 1.04W
Leverkusen W. Germany **45** 51.02N 6.59E
Levin New Zealand **82** 40.37S 175.18E
Levis Canada **95** 46.47N 71.12W
Levittown U.S.A. **95** 40.10N 74.50W
Levkás *i.* Greece **43** 38.44N 20.37E
Lew *r.* England **31** 50.50N 4.05W
Lewes England **29** 50.53N 0.02E
Lewis *i.* Scotland **36** 58.10N 6.40W
Lewisham *d.* England **27** 51.27N 0.01W
Lewis Pass *f.* New Zealand **82** 42.30S 172.15E
Lewistown Maine U.S.A. **95** 44.05N 70.15W
Lewistown Penn. U.S.A. **95** 40.37N 77.36W
Lexington U.S.A. **91** 38.02N 84.30W
Leyburn England **32** 54.19N 1.50W
Leydsdorp R.S.A. **74** 23.59S 30.30E
Leyland England **32** 53.41N 2.42W
Leysdown-on-Sea England **29** 51.23N 0.57E
Leyte *i.* Phil. **61** 10.40N 124.50E
Leyton England **27** 51.34N 0.01W
Lezignan France **40** 43.12N 2.46E
Lhasa China **59** 29.41N 91.10E
Lhokseumawe Indonesia **60** 5.09N 97.09E
Liane *r.* France **29** 50.43N 1.35E
Liaocheng China **63** 36.29N 115.55E
Liaoning *d.* China **63** 41.30N 123.00E
Liaotung B. China **63** 40.20N 121.00E
Liaotung Pen. China **63** 40.00N 122.50E
Liaoyuan China **63** 42.53N 125.10E
Liard *r.* Canada **92** 61.56N 120.35W
Libenge Zaïre **72** 3.39N 18.39E
Liberal U.S.A. **90** 37.03N 100.56W
Liberec Czech. **44** 50.48N 15.05E
Liberia Africa **70** 6.30N 9.30W
Liberia Costa Rica **96** 10.39N 85.28W
Libourne France **40** 44.55N 0.14W
Libreville Gabon **72** 0.25N 9.30E
Libya Africa **68** 26.30N 17.00E
Libyan Desert Africa **69** 25.00N 26.10E
Libyan Plateau Africa **56** 30.45N 26.00E
Licata Italy **42** 37.07N 13.58E
Lichanga Moçambique **73** 13.09S 35.17E
Lichfield England **28** 52.40N 1.50W

Lichtenburg R.S.A. 74 26.09S 26.11E
Liddel Water r. England 35 54.58N 3.00W
Liddesdale f. Scotland 35 55.10N 2.50W
Lidköping Sweden 46 58.30N 13.10E
Liechtenstein Europe 44 47.08N 9.35E
Liège Belgium 45 50.38N 5.35E
Liège d. Belgium 45 50.32N 5.35E
Lieksa Finland 46 63.13N 30.01E
Lienyunkang China 63 34.42N 119.28E
Lienz Austria 44 46.51N 12.50E
Liepāja U.S.S.R. 46 56.30N 21.00E
Lier Belgium 45 51.08N 4.35E
Liévin France 45 50.27N 2.49E
Lièvre, R. du Canada 95 45.29N 75.33W
Liffey r. Rep. of Ire. 38 53.21N 6.14W
Lifford Rep. of Ire. 38 54.50N 7.31W
Lightning Ridge town Australia 80 29.25S 147.59E
Lightwater England 27 51.21N 0.37W
Ligurian Sea Med. Sea 42 43.30N 9.00E
Lihue Hawaii U.S.A. 90 21.59N 159.23W
Likasi Zaïre 73 10.58S 26.50E
Likiang China 59 26.50N 100.15E
Likona r. Congo 72 0.11N 16.25E
Likouala r. Congo 72 0.51S 17.17E
Lille France 45 50.39N 3.05E
Lillehammer Norway 46 61.06N 10.27E
Lillers France 45 50.34N 2.29E
Lilleström Norway 46 59.58N 11.05E
Lilongwe Malaŵi 73 13.58S 33.49E
Lim r. Yugo. 43 43.45N 19.13E
Lima Peru 102 12.06S 76.03W
Lima r. Portugal 41 41.40N 8.50W
Lima U.S.A. 94 40.43N 84.06W
Limassol Cyprus 56 34.40N 33.03E
Limavady N. Ireland 34 55.03N 6.57W
Limbourg Belgium 45 50.36N 5.57E
Limbourg d. Belgium 45 51.00N 5.30E
Limburg d. Neth. 45 51.15N 5.45E
Limeira Brazil 103 22.34S 47.25W
Limerick Rep. of Ire. 39 52.40N 8.37W
Limerick d. Rep. of Ire. 39 52.40N 8.37W
Lim Fjord est. Denmark 46 56.55N 9.10E
Límnos i. Greece 43 39.55N 25.14E
Limoges France 40 45.50N 1.15E
Límon Costa Rica 96 10.00N 83.01W
Limpopo r. Moçambique 74 25.14S 33.33E
Limpsfield England 27 51.16N 0.02E
Lina Saudi Arabia 57 28.48N 43.45E
Linares Mexico 96 24.54N 99.38W
Linares Spain 41 38.05N 3.38W
Lincoln England 33 53.14N 0.32W
Lincoln Maine U.S.A. 95 45.23N 68.30W
Lincoln Nebr. U.S.A. 91 40.49N 96.41W
Lincoln Edge hills England 33 53.13N 0.31W
Lincolnshire d. England 33 53.14N 0.32W
Lincoln Wolds hills England 33 53.22N 0.08W
Lindau W. Germany 44 47.33N 9.41E
Lindenborg Denmark 46 55.56N 10.03E
Lindesnes c. Norway 46 58.00N 7.05E
Lindi Tanzania 73 10.00S 39.41E
Lindi r. Zaïre 72 0.30N 25.06E
Lindos Greece 43 36.05N 28.02E
Lingen W. Germany 45 52.32N 7.19E
Lingfield England 27 51.11N 0.01W
Lingga i. Indonesia 60 0.20S 104.30E
Linguère Senegal 70 15.22N 15.11W
Linköping Sweden 46 58.25N 15.35E
Linlithgow Scotland 35 55.58N 3.36W
Linney Head Wales 31 51.37N 5.05W
Linnhe, Loch Scotland 34 56.35N 5.25W
Linosa i. Italy 42 35.52N 12.50E
Linsia China 62 35.31N 103.08E
Linslade England 28 51.55N 0.40W
Lintan China 62 34.39N 103.40E
Linton England 29 52.06N 0.19E
Linxe France 40 43.56N 1.10W
Linz Austria 44 48.19N 14.18E
Lions, G. of France 40 43.12N 4.15E
Liouesso Congo 72 1.12N 15.47E
Lipari Is. Italy 42 38.35N 14.45E
Lipetsk U.S.S.R. 47 52.37N 39.36E
Liphook England 28 51.05N 0.49W
Lippe r. W. Germany 45 51.38N 6.37E
Lippstadt W. Germany 44 51.41N 8.20E
Lira Uganda 73 2.15N 32.55E
Lisala Zaïre 72 2.13N 21.37E
Lisboa see Lisbon Portugal 41
Lisbon Portugal 41 38.44N 9.08W
Lisburn N. Ireland 38 54.30N 6.03W
Lisburne, C. U.S.A. 92 69.00N 165.50W
Liscannor B. Rep. of Ire. 39 52.55N 9.24W
Lishui China 63 28.30N 119.59E
Liskeard England 31 50.27N 4.29W
Liski U.S.S.R. 47 51.00N 39.30E
Lismore Australia 80 28.48S 153.17E
Lismore Rep. of Ire. 39 52.08N 7.57W
Lismore i. Scotland 34 56.31N 5.30W
Lisnaskea N. Ireland 38 54.16N 7.28W
Liss England 28 51.03N 0.53W
Listowel Rep. of Ire. 39 52.27N 9.30W
Litang r. China 59 28.09N 101.30E
Lithgow Australia 80 33.30S 150.09E
Lithuania Soviet Socialist Republic d. U.S.S.R. 46 55.00N 23.50E
Little Andaman i. India 59 10.50N 92.38E
Little Cayman i. Cayman Is. 97 19.40N 80.00W
Little Chalfont England 27 51.39N 0.33W
Little Coco i. Burma 60 13.50N 93.10E
Little Current town Canada 94 45.57N 81.56W
Little Fen f. England 29 52.18N 0.30E
Little Grand Rapids town Canada 91 52.00N 95.01W
Littlehampton England 29 50.48N 0.32W
Little Inagua i. Bahamas 97 21.30N 73.00W
Little Karroo f. R.S.A. 74 33.40S 21.30E
Little Khingan Shan mts. China 63 48.40N 128.30E
Little Loch Broom l. Scotland 36 57.53N 5.20W
Little Nicobar i. Asia 60 8.00N 93.30E
Little Ouse r. England 29 52.34N 0.20E
Littleport England 29 52.27N 0.18E
Little Rock town U.S.A. 91 34.42N 92.17W
Little St. Bernard Pass France/Italy 42 45.40N 6.53E
Little Thurrock England 27 51.28N 0.20E
Littleton Rep. of Ire. 39 52.39N 7.44W
Little Zab r. Iraq 57 35.15N 43.27E
Liuchow China 63 24.17N 109.15E
Livermore, Mt. U.S.A. 90 30.39N 104.11W
Liverpool Canada 93 44.03N 64.43W
Liverpool England 32 53.25N 3.00W
Liverpool B. England 32 53.30N 3.10W
Liverpool Plains f. Australia 80 31.20S 150.00E
Liverpool Range mts. Australia 80 31.45S 150.45E
Livingston Scotland 35 55.54N 3.31W
Livingstone Zambia 72 17.40S 25.50E
Livingstonia Malaŵi 73 10.35S 34.10E
Livonia U.S.A. 94 42.25N 83.23W
Livramento Brazil 103 30.52S 55.30W
Liwale Tanzania 73 9.47S 38.00E
Lizard England 31 49.58N 5.12W
Lizard Pt. England 31 49.57N 5.15W
Ljubljana Yugo. 44 46.04N 14.28E
Ljungan r. Sweden 46 62.20N 17.19E
Ljungby Sweden 46 56.49N 13.55E
Ljusdal Sweden 46 61.49N 16.09E
Ljusnan r. Sweden 46 61.15N 17.08E
Ljusnarsberg Sweden 46 59.48N 14.57E
Llanbedr Wales 30 52.40N 4.07W
Llanberis Wales 30 53.07N 4.07W
Llanbister Wales 30 52.22N 3.19W
Llandeilo Wales 30 51.54N 4.00W
Llandovery Wales 30 51.59N 3.49W
Llandrillo Wales 30 52.55N 3.25W
Llandrindod Wells Wales 30 52.15N 3.23W
Llandudno Wales 30 53.19N 3.49W
Llandyssul Wales 30 52.03N 4.20W
Llanelli Wales 31 51.41N 4.11W
Llanerchymedd Wales 30 53.20N 4.22W
Llanes Spain 41 43.25N 4.45W
Llanfair-ar-y-bryn Wales 30 52.04N 3.43W
Llanfair Caereinion Wales 30 52.39N 3.20W
Llanfairfechan Wales 30 53.15N 3.58W
Llanfihangel-Ystrad Wales 30 52.11N 4.11W
Llanfyllin Wales 30 52.47N 3.17W
Llangadfan Wales 30 52.41N 3.28W
Llangadog Wales 30 51.56N 3.53W
Llangefni Wales 30 53.15N 4.20W
Llangollen Wales 30 52.58N 3.10W
Llangynog Wales 30 52.50N 3.24W
Llanidloes Wales 30 52.28N 3.31W
Llanos f. Venezuela 97 8.30N 67.00W
Llanrhystyd Wales 30 52.19N 4.09W
Llanrwst Wales 30 53.08N 3.48W
Llantrisant Wales 31 51.33N 3.23W
Llantwit Major Wales 31 51.24N 3.29W
Llanuwchllyn Wales 30 52.52N 3.41W
Llanwrtyd Wells Wales 30 52.06N 3.39W
Llanybyther Wales 30 52.04N 4.10W
Llerena Spain 41 38.14N 6.00W
Lleyn Pen. Wales 30 52.50N 4.35W
Lloydminster Canada 92 53.18N 110.00W
Loange r. Zaïre 72 4.18S 20.05E
Loanhead Scotland 35 55.53N 3.09W
Lobatse Botswana 74 25.11S 25.40E
Lobaye r. C.A.R. 71 3.40N 18.35E
Loberia Argentina 103 38.08S 58.48W
Lobito Angola 72 12.20S 13.34E
Lobos Argentina 103 35.11S 59.08W
Locarno Switz. 44 46.10N 8.48E
Lochaber f. Scotland 37 56.55N 4.55W
Lochailort Scotland 36 56.50N 5.40W
Lochaline Scotland 34 56.32N 5.47W
Lochboisdale town Scotland 36 57.09N 7.19W
Lochbuie Scotland 34 56.22N 5.52W
Lochcarron Scotland 36 57.25N 5.36W
Lochdonhead Scotland 34 56.26N 5.41W
Lochearnhead Scotland 34 56.23N 4.17W
Lochem Neth. 45 52.10N 6.25E
Loches France 40 47.08N 1.00E
Lochgelly Scotland 35 56.08N 3.19W
Lochgilphead Scotland 34 56.02N 5.26W
Lochgoilhead Scotland 34 56.10N 4.54W
Lochinver Scotland 36 58.09N 5.15W
Lochmaben Scotland 35 55.08N 3.27W
Lochmaddy town Scotland 36 57.36N 7.10W
Lochnagar mtn. Scotland 37 56.57N 3.15W
Lochranza Scotland 34 55.42N 5.18W
Lochwinnoch Scotland 34 55.48N 4.38W
Lochy r. Scotland 36 56.50N 5.05W
Lochy, Loch Scotland 37 56.58N 4.55W
Lockerbie Scotland 35 55.07N 3.21W
Lockport U.S.A. 95 43.11N 78.39W
Loc Ninh Vietnam 60 11.55N 106.35E
Loddon r. England 28 51.30N 0.53W
Lodja Zaïre 72 3.29S 23.33E
Lodwar Kenya 73 3.06N 35.38E
Łódź Poland 47 51.49N 19.28E
Lofoten is. Norway 46 68.15N 13.50E
Loftus England 33 54.33N 0.52W
Logan, Mt. Canada 92 60.45N 140.00W
Logansport U.S.A. 94 40.45N 86.25W
Logone r. Cameroon/Chad 71 12.10N 15.00E
Logroño Spain 41 42.28N 2.26W
Loimaa Finland 46 60.50N 23.05E
Loir r. France 40 47.29N 0.32E
Loire r. France 40 47.18N 2.00W
Loja Spain 41 37.10N 4.09W
Loje r. Angola 72 7.52S 13.08E
Loka Sudan 73 4.18N 31.00E
Lokeren Belgium 45 51.06N 3.59E
Lokitaung Kenya 73 4.15N 35.45E
Lokoja Nigeria 71 7.49N 6.44E
Lokolo r. Zaïre 72 0.45S 19.36E
Lokoro r. Zaïre 72 1.40S 18.29E
Lolland i. Denmark 44 54.50N 11.30E
Lom Bulgaria 43 43.49N 23.13E
Lomami r. Zaïre 72 0.45N 24.10E
Lombok i. Indonesia 60 8.30S 116.20E
Lomé Togo 71 6.10N 1.21E
Lomela Zaïre 72 2.15S 23.15E
Lomela r. Zaïre 72 0.14S 20.45E
Lomié Cameroon 71 3.09N 13.35E
Lomond, Loch Scotland 34 56.07N 4.36W
Lomża Poland 47 53.11N 22.04E
London Canada 94 42.58N 81.15W
London England 27 51.32N 0.06W
London Colney England 27 51.44N 0.18W
Londonderry N. Ireland 34 55.00N 7.21W
Londonderry d. N. Ireland 34 55.00N 7.00W
Londonderry, C. Australia 79 13.58S 126.55E
Long, Loch Scotland 34 56.05N 4.52W
Longa r. Angola 72 16.15S 19.07E
Longa i. Scotland 36 57.44N 5.48W
Long Beach town U.S.A. 90 33.57N 118.15W
Long Bennington England 33 52.59N 0.45W
Longbenton England 35 55.02N 1.33W
Long Branch U.S.A. 95 40.17N 73.59W
Long Ditton England 27 51.23N 0.20W
Long Eaton England 33 52.54N 1.16W
Longford Australia 80 41.25S 147.02E
Longford Rep. of Ire. 38 53.44N 7.48W
Longford d. Rep. of Ire. 38 53.42N 7.45W
Longhorsley England 35 55.15N 1.46W
Longhoughton England 35 55.26N 1.36W
Long I. Bahamas 97 23.00N 75.00W
Long I. U.S.A. 95 40.50N 73.20W
Long L. Canada 94 49.40N 86.45W
Longlac town Canada 91 49.47N 86.34W
Long Mtn. England 28 52.40N 3.05W
Longniddry Scotland 35 55.58N 2.53W
Long Pt. Canada 94 42.33N 80.04W
Long Pt. New Zealand 82 46.35S 169.35E
Longridge England 32 53.50N 2.37W
Longs Peak U.S.A. 90 40.16N 105.37W
Long Sutton England 33 52.47N 0.09E
Longtown England 35 55.01N 2.58W
Longwy France 45 49.32N 5.46E
Long Xuyen Vietnam 60 10.23N 105.25E
Löningen W. Germany 45 52.44N 7.46E
Looe England 31 50.51N 4.26W
Lookout, C. U.S.A. 91 34.34N 76.34W
Loolmalasin mtn. Tanzania 73 3.00S 35.45E
Loop Head Rep. of Ire. 39 52.33N 9.56W
Lopari r. Zaïre 72 1.20N 20.22E
Lopez, C. Gabon 72 0.36S 8.40E
Lopi Congo 72 2.57N 2.47E
Lop Nor l. China 62 40.30N 90.30E
Lopp Havet est. Norway 46 70.30N 21.00E
Lorain U.S.A. 94 41.28N 82.11W
Loralai Pakistan 58 30.20N 68.41E

Lorca Spain **41** 37.40N 1.41W
Lordsburg U.S.A. **90** 32.22N 108.43W
Lorient France **40** 47.45N 3.21W
Lörrach W. Germany **44** 47.37N 7.40E
Los Angeles U.S.A. **90** 34.00N 118.17W
Los Blancos Spain **41** 37.37N 0.48W
Loshan China **59** 29.34N 103.42E
Lošinj *i.* Yugo. **42** 44.36N 14.20E
Los Libres, Punta de *c.* Argentina **103** 29.40S 57.06W
Los Roques *i.* Venezuela **97** 12.00N 67.00W
Lossie *r.* Scotland **37** 57.43N 3.18W
Lossiemouth Scotland **37** 57.43N 3.18W
Lostwithiel England **31** 50.24N 4.41W
Lot *r.* France **40** 44.17N 0.22E
Lothian *d.* Scotland **35** 55.50N 3.00W
Lotoi *r.* Zaïre **72** 1.30S 18.30E
Lotsani *r.* Botswana **74** 22.41S 28.06E
Lotschberg Tunnel Switz. **44** 46.25N 7.53E
Lotta *r.* U.S.S.R. **46** 68.36N 31.06E
Lotuke *mtn.* Sudan **73** 4.10N 33.46E
Loudéac France **40** 48.11N 2.45W
Loudima Congo **72** 4.06S 13.05E
Louga Senegal **70** 15.37N 16.13W
Loughborough England **33** 52.47N 1.11W
Loughor *r.* Wales **31** 51.41N 4.04W
Loughrea Rep. of Ire. **39** 53.12N 8.35W
Loughros More B. Rep. of Ire. **38** 54.48N 8.32W
Loughton England **27** 51.39N 0.03E
Louisburgh Rep. of Ire. **38** 53.46N 9.49W
Louisiana *d.* U.S.A. **91** 31.00N 92.30W
Louis Trichardt R.S.A. **74** 23.01S 29.43E
Louisville U.S.A. **91** 38.13N 85.45W
Lourdes France **40** 43.06N 0.02W
Louth Australia **80** 30.34S 145.09E
Louth England **33** 53.23N 0.00
Louth *d.* Rep. of Ire. **38** 53.55N 6.30W
Louvain Belgium **45** 50.53N 4.45E
Lovat *r.* U.S.S.R. **47** 58.06N 31.37E
Lovech Bulgaria **43** 43.08N 24.44E
Lovoi *r.* Zaïre **73** 8.14S 26.40E
Lovua *r.* Zaïre **72** 6.08S 20.35E
Lowa *r.* Kivu Zaïre **72** 1.25S 25.55E
Lowell U.S.A. **95** 42.38N 71.19W
Lower California *pen.* Mexico **90** 30.00N 115.00W
Lower Egypt *f.* Egypt **56** 30.30N 31.00E
Lower Lough Erne N. Ireland **38** 54.28N 7.48W
Lower Nazeing England **27** 51.43N 0.03E
Lower Tunguska *r.* U.S.S.R. **49** 65.50N 88.00E
Lowestoft England **29** 52.29N 1.44E
Lowick England **35** 55.39N 1.58W
Lowicz Poland **47** 52.06N 19.55E
Lowther Hills Scotland **35** 55.20N 3.40W
Loxton Australia **80** 34.38S 140.38E
Loyal, Loch Scotland **37** 58.23N 4.21W
Lua *r.* Zaïre **72** 2.45N 18.28E
Lualaba *r.* Zaïre **72** 0.18N 25.32E
Luama *r.* Zaïre **73** 4.45S 26.55E
Luanchimo *r.* Zaïre **72** 6.32S 20.57E
Luanda Angola **72** 8.50S 13.20E
Luanda *d.* Angola **72** 9.00S 13.30E
Luando Game Res. Angola **72** 11.00S 17.45E
Luang Prabang Laos **60** 19.53N 102.10E
Luangwa *r.* Central Zambia **73** 15.32S 30.28E
Luanshya Zambia **73** 13.09S 28.24E
Luapula *r.* Zambia **73** 9.25S 28.36E
Luarca Spain **41** 43.33N 6.31W
Lubango Angola **72** 14.52S 13.30E
Lubbock U.S.A. **90** 33.35N 101.53W
Lübeck W. Germany **44** 53.52N 10.40E
Lübeck B. W. Germany **44** 54.05N 11.00E
Lubefu *r.* Zaïre **72** 4.05S 23.00E
Lubilash *r.* Zaïre **72** 4.59S 23.25E
Lublin Poland **47** 51.18N 22.31E
Lubny U.S.S.R. **47** 50.01N 33.00E
Lubudi Zaïre **72** 9.57S 25.59E
Lubudi *r.* Kasai Occidental Zaïre **72** 4.00S 21.23E
Lubudi *r.* Shaba Zaïre **72** 9.13S 25.40E
Lubumbashi Zaïre **73** 11.44S 27.29E
Lubutu Zaïre **73** 0.48S 26.19E
Lucan Rep. of Ire. **38** 53.21N 6.27W
Luce, Water of *r.* Scotland **34** 54.52N 4.49W
Luce B. Scotland **34** 54.45N 4.47W
Lucena Spain **41** 37.25N 4.29W
Lučenec Czech. **47** 48.20N 19.40E
Lucero Mexico **90** 30.50N 106.30W
Luchow China **59** 28.25N 105.20E
Luckenwalde E. Germany **44** 52.05N 13.11E
Lucknow India **58** 26.50N 80.54E
Lüdenscheid W. Germany **45** 51.13N 7.36E
Lüderitz S.W. Africa **74** 26.38S 15.10E
Ludgate Canada **94** 45.54N 80.32W
Ludgershall England **28** 51.15N 1.38W
Ludhiana India **58** 30.56N 75.52E
Lüdinghausen W. Germany **45** 51.46N 7.27E
Ludington U.S.A. **94** 43.58N 86.27W
Ludlow England **28** 52.23N 2.42W
Ludvika Sweden **46** 60.08N 15.14E
Ludwigshafen W. Germany **44** 49.29N 8.27E
Luebo Zaïre **72** 5.16S 21.27E
Luena *r.* Angola **72** 12.30S 22.37E
Luena Zambia **73** 10.40S 30.21E
Luena *r.* Western Zambia **72** 14.47S 23.05E
Luengue *r.* Angola **72** 16.58S 21.15E
Luenha *r.* Moçambique **74** 16.29S 33.40E
Lufira *r.* Zaïre **73** 8.15S 26.30E
Lufkin U.S.A. **91** 31.21N 94.47W
Luga U.S.S.R. **47** 58.42N 29.49E
Luga *r.* U.S.S.R. **46** 59.40N 28.15E
Lugano Switz. **40** 46.01N 8.57E
Lugenda *r.* Moçambique **73** 11.23S 38.30E
Lugg *r.* England **28** 52.01N 2.38W
Lugh Ganana Somali Rep. **73** 3.49N 42.34E
Lugnaquilla Mtn. Rep. of Ire. **39** 52.58N 6.28W
Lugo Spain **41** 43.00N 7.33W
Lugoj Romania **43** 45.42N 21.56E
Luiana Angola **72** 17.08S 22.59E
Luiana *r.* Angola **72** 17.28S 23.02E
Luichart, Loch Scotland **37** 57.36N 4.45W
Luichow Pen. China **63** 20.40N 109.30E
Luilaka *r.* Zaïre **72** 0.15S 19.00E
Luilu *r.* Zaïre **72** 6.22S 23.53E
Luing *i.* Scotland **34** 56.14N 5.38W
Luiro *r.* Finland **46** 67.22N 27.30E
Luisa Zaïre **72** 7.15S 22.27E
Lukala Zaïre **72** 5.23S 13.02E
Lukanga Swamp *f.* Zambia **73** 14.15S 27.30E
Lukenie *r.* Zaïre **72** 2.43S 18.12E
Lukuga *r.* Zaïre **73** 5.37S 26.58E
Lukula *r.* Zaïre **72** 4.15S 17.59E
Luleå Sweden **46** 65.35N 22.10E
Luleburgaz Turkey **43** 41.25N 27.23E
Lulonga *r.* Zaïre **72** 0.42N 18.26E
Lulua *r.* Zaïre **72** 5.03S 21.07E
Lumsden New Zealand **82** 45.45S 168.27E
Lumsden Scotland **37** 57.17N 2.53W
Lunan B. Scotland **35** 56.38N 2.30W
Lund Sweden **46** 55.42N 13.10E
Lunda *d.* Angola **72** 9.30S 20.00E
Lundazi Zambia **73** 12.19S 33.11E
Lundi *r.* Rhodesia **74** 21.16S 32.20E
Lundy *i.* England **31** 51.10N 4.41W
Lune *r.* England **32** 54.03N 2.49W
Lüneburg W. Germany **44** 53.15N 10.24E
Lunga *r.* Zambia **73** 14.28S 26.27E
Lungsi China **62** 35.00N 105.00E
Lungwebungu *r.* Zambia **72** 14.20S 23.15E
Luninets U.S.S.R. **47** 52.18N 26.50E
Lunna Ness *c.* Scotland **36** 60.27N 1.03W
Luofo Zaïre **73** 0.12S 29.15E
Luque Paraguay **103** 25.15S 57.32W
Lure France **44** 47.42N 6.30E
Lurgan N. Ireland **38** 54.28N 6.21W
Lurio Moçambique **73** 13.30S 40.30E
Lurio *r.* Moçambique **73** 13.32S 40.31E
Lusaka Zambia **73** 15.20S 28.14E
Lusambo Zaïre **72** 4.59S 23.26E
Lushoto Tanzania **73** 4.48S 38.20E
Lusiti *r.* Moçambique **74** 20.00S 33.51E
Lusk Rep. of Ire. **38** 53.32N 6.12W
Lusk U.S.A. **90** 42.47N 104.26W
Luss Scotland **34** 56.06N 4.38W
Lüta China **63** 38.53N 121.37E
Lutfabad U.S.S.R. **57** 37.32N 59.17E
Luton England **27** 51.53N 0.25W
Lutterworth England **28** 52.28N 1.12W
Luvua *r.* Zaïre **73** 6.45S 27.00E
Luwegu *r.* Tanzania **73** 8.30S 37.28E
Luwingu Zambia **73** 10.13S 30.05E
Luxembourg *d.* Belgium **45** 49.58N 5.30E
Luxembourg Europe **45** 49.50N 6.15E
Luxembourg *town* Lux. **45** 49.37N 6.08E
Luxor Egypt **56** 24.41N 32.24E
Luzern Switz. **44** 47.03N 8.17E
Luzon *i.* Phil. **61** 17.50N 121.00E
Luzon Str. Pacific Oc. **61** 20.20N 122.00E
Lvov U.S.S.R. **47** 49.50N 24.00E
Lyallpur Pakistan **58** 31.25N 73.09E
Lybster Scotland **37** 58.18N 3.18W
Lycksele Sweden **46** 64.34N 18.40E
Lyd *r.* England **31** 50.38N 4.18W
Lydd England **29** 50.57N 0.56E
Lydda Israel **56** 31.57N 34.54E
Lydenburg R.S.A. **74** 25.10S 30.29E
Lydney England **28** 51.43N 2.32W
Lyell, Mt. U.S.A. **90** 37.45N 119.18W
Lyme B. England **28** 50.40N 2.55W
Lyme Regis England **28** 50.44N 2.57W
Lyminge England **29** 51.07N 1.06E
Lymington England **28** 50.46N 1.32W
Lympstone England **28** 50.39N 3.25W
Lyndhurst England **28** 50.53N 1.33W
Lynher *r.* England **31** 50.23N 4.18W
Lynn U.S.A. **95** 42.29N 70.57W
Lynn Lake *town* Canada **93** 56.51N 101.01W
Lynton England **31** 51.14N 3.50W
Lyon France **40** 45.46N 4.50E
Lyon *r.* Scotland **35** 56.37N 3.59W
Lyon Mtn. U.S.A. **95** 4444N 73.56W
Lysekil Sweden **46** 58.16N 11.26E
Lytham St. Anne's England **32** 53.45N 3.01W
Lyubertsy U.S.S.R. **47** 55.38N 37.58E

M

Maamakeogh *mtn.* Rep. of Ire. **38** 54.17N 9.29W
Maamtrasna *mtn.* Rep. of Ire. **38** 53.37N 9.35W
Maamturk Mts. Rep. of Ire. **38** 53.32N 9.42W
Ma'an Jordan **56** 30.11N 35.43E
Maas *r.* Neth. **45** 51.44N 4.42E
Maaseik Belgium **45** 51.08N 5.48E
Maastricht Neth. **45** 50.51N 5.42E
Mablethorpe England **33** 53.21N 0.14E
Macao Asia **60** 22.13N 113.36E
Macclesfield England **32** 53.16N 2.09W
Macdonnell Ranges *mts.* Australia **79** 23.30S 132.00E
Macduff Scotland **37** 57.40N 2.29W
Maceió Brazil **102** 9.34S 35.47W
Macenta Guinea **70** 8.31N 9.32W
Macerata Italy **42** 43.18N 13.30E
Macgillycuddy's Reeks *mts.* Rep. of Ire. **39** 52.00N 9.43W
Macheke Rhodesia **74** 18.05S 31.51E
Machrihanish Scotland **34** 55.25N 5.44W
Machynlleth Wales **30** 52.35N 3.51W
Mackay Australia **79** 21.10S 149.10E
Mackay, L. Australia **79** 22.30S 128.58E
Mackenzie *d.* Canada **92** 65.00N 115.00W
Mackenzie *r.* Canada **92** 69.20N 134.00W
Mackenzie King I. Canada **92** 77.30N 112.00W
Mackenzie Mts. Canada **92** 64.00N 130.00W
Mackinaw City U.S.A. **94** 45.47N 84.43W
Mackinnon Road *town* Kenya **73** 3.50S 39.03E
Maclean Australia **80** 29.27S 153.14E
Maclear R.S.A. **74** 31.05S 28.22E
Macleod's Tables *mtn.* Scotland **36** 57.25N 6.45W
Macloutsie *r.* Botswana **74** 22.15S 29.00E
Macnean, Lough N. Ireland **38** 54.19N 7.56W
Macomer Italy **42** 40.16N 8.45E
Mâcon France **40** 46.18N 4.50E
Macon U.S.A. **91** 32.47N 83.37W
Macpherson Range *mts.* Australia **80** 28.15S 153.00E
Macquarie *r.* Australia **80** 41.08S 146.52E
Macroom Rep. of Ire. **39** 51.54N 8.58W
Madagascar *i.* Africa **107** 20.00S 45.00E
Madang P.N.G. **61** 5.14S 145.45E
Madawaska *r.* Canada **95** 45.35N 76.25W
Madeira *i.* Atlantic Oc. **68** 32.45N 17.00W
Madeira *r.* Brazil **102** 3.50S 58.30W
Madhya Pradesh *d.* India **59** 23.00N 79.30E
Madison Fla. U.S.A. **91** 30.29N 83.39W
Madison Wisc. U.S.A. **94** 43.04N 89.22W
Madiun Indonesia **60** 7.37S 111.33E
Mado Gashi Kenya **73** 0.40N 39.11E
Madras India **59** 13.05N 80.18E
Madre, Sierra *mts.* Mexico **96** 16.00N 93.00W
Madre del Sur, Sierra *mts.* Mexico **96** 17.00N 100.00W
Madre Lagoon Mexico **96** 25.00N 97.30W
Madre Occidental, Sierra *mts.* Mexico **96** 24.00N 103.00W
Madre Oriental, Sierra *mts.* Mexico **96** 24.00N 99.00W
Madrid Spain **41** 40.25N 3.43W
Madukani Tanzania **73** 3.57S 35.49E
Madura *i.* Indonesia **60** 7.00S 113.30E
Madurai India **59** 9.55N 78.07E
Maesteg Wales **31** 51.36N 3.40W
Maestra, Sierra *mts.* Cuba **97** 20.10N 76.30W
Mafeking R.S.A. **74** 25.53S 25.39E
Mafeteng Lesotho **74** 29.49S 27.14E
Mafia I. Tanzania **73** 7.50S 39.50E
Mafraq Jordan **56** 32.20N 36.12E
Magadan U.S.S.R. **49** 59.38N 150.50E
Magadi Kenya **73** 1.53S 36.18E
Magangue Colombia **97** 9.14N 74.46W
Magas Iran **57** 27.08N 61.36E
Magburaka Sierra Leone **70** 8.44N 11.57W
Magdalena *r.* Colombia **97** 10.56N 74.58W
Magdalena Mexico **90** 30.38N 110.59W
Magdeburg E. Germany **44** 52.08N 11.36E
Mageröya *i.* Norway **46** 71.00N 25.50E
Maggiore, L. Italy **40** 45.57N 8.37E
Maghera N. Ireland **34** 54.51N 6.41W
Magherafelt N. Ireland **34** 54.45N 6.38W
Maghull England **32** 53.31N 2.56W
Magnitogorsk U.S.S.R. **48** 53.28N 59.06E
Magude Moçambique **74** 25.02S 32.40E
Magué Moçambique **73** 15.46S 31.42E

Magwe Burma **59** 20.10N 95.00E
Mahabad Iran **57** 36.44N 45.44E
Mahaddei Wen Somali Rep. **73** 2.58N 45.32E
Mahagi Zaïre **73** 2.16N 30.59E
Mahalapye Botswana **74** 23.05S 26.51E
Mahallat Iran **57** 33.54N 50.28E
Mahanadi *r.* India **59** 20.17N 86.43E
Maharashtra *d.* India **58** 20.00N 77.00E
Mahdia Tunisia **42** 35.28N 11.01E
Mahenge Tanzania **73** 8.46S 36.38E
Mahia Pen. New Zealand **82** 37.10S 178.30E
Mahón Spain **41** 39.55N 4.18E
Maidenhead England **27** 51.32N 0.44W
Maiden Newton England **28** 50.46N 2.35W
Maidens Scotland **34** 55.20N 4.49W
Maidstone England **27** 51.17N 0.32E
Maiduguri Nigeria **71** 11.53N 13.16E
Maihar India **58** 24.14N 80.50E
Maiko *r.* Zaïre **72** 0.15N 25.35E
Main *r.* N. Ireland **34** 54.43N 6.19W
Main *r.* W. Germany **44** 50.00N 8.19E
Main Barrier Range *mts.* Australia **80** 31.25S 141.25E
Mai Ndombe *l.* Zaïre **72** 2.00S 18.20E
Maine *r.* Rep. of Ire. **39** 52.09N 9.44W
Maine *d.* U.S.A. **95** 45.00N 69.00W
Mainland *i.* Orkney Is. Scotland **37** 59.00N 3.10W
Mainland *i.* Shetland Is. Scotland **37** 60.15N 1.22W
Mainpuri India **58** 27.14N 79.01E
Mainz W. Germany **44** 50.00N 8.16E
Maipu Argentina **103** 36.52S 57.52W
Maitland Australia **80** 32.33S 151.33E
Maja *i.* Indonesia **60** 1.05S 109.25E
Majene Indonesia **60** 3.33S 118.59E
Majma'a Saudi Arabia **57** 25.52N 45.25E
Majorca *i.* Spain **41** 39.35N 3.00E
Majuba Hill R.S.A. **74** 27.30S 29.50E
Majunga Malagasy Rep. **73** 15.50S 46.20E
Makarikari Salt Pan *f.* Botswana **74** 20.50S 25.45E
Makassar Str. Indonesia **60** 3.00S 118.00E
Makeni Sierra Leone **70** 8.57N 12.02W
Makeyevka U.S.S.R. **47** 48.01N 38.00E
Makó Hungary **43** 46.13N 20.30E
Makokou Gabon **72** 0.38N 12.47E
Makoua Congo **72** 0.01S 15.40E
Makran *f.* Asia **57** 26.30N 61.20E
Makurdi Nigeria **71** 7.44N 8.35E
Malabo Equat. Guinea **71** 3.45N 8.48E
Malacca Malaysia **60** 2.14N 102.14E
Malacca, Straits of Indian Oc. **60** 3.00N 100.30E
Málaga Colombia **97** 6.44N 72.45W
Málaga Spain **41** 36.43N 4.25W
Malagasy Republic Africa **73** 17.00S 46.00E
Malahide Rep. of Ire. **38** 53.27N 6.10W
Malakal Sudan **69** 9.31N 31.40E
Malakand Pakistan **58** 34.34N 71.57E
Malang Indonesia **60** 7.59S 112.45E
Malanje Angola **72** 9.36S 16.21E
Malanje *d.* Angola **72** 9.00S 17.00E
Mälaren *l.* Sweden **46** 59.30N 17.00E
Malatya Turkey **56** 38.22N 38.18E
Malaŵi Africa **73** 12.00S 34.00E
Malaŵi, L. Africa **73** 12.00S 34.30E
Malayer Iran **57** 34.19N 48.51E
Malaysia Asia **60** 5.00N 110.00E
Malbork Poland **47** 54.02N 19.01E
Malden England **27** 51.23N 0.15W
Malden U.S.A. **95** 42.24N 71.04W
Maldive Is. Indian Oc. **58** 6.20N 73.00E
Maldon England **29** 51.43N 0.41E
Maldonado Uruguay **103** 34.57S 54.59W
Maléa, C. Greece **43** 36.27N 23.11E
Malebo Pool *f.* Zaïre **72** 4.15S 15.25E
Malegaon India **58** 20.32N 74.38E
Mali Africa **70** 17.30N 2.30E
Malili Indonesia **61** 2.38S 121.06E
Malin Rep. of Ire. **34** 55.18N 7.15W
Malindi Kenya **73** 3.14S 40.08E
Malines Belgium **45** 51.01N 4.28E
Malin Head Rep. of Ire. **38** 55.23N 7.24W
Malin More Rep. of Ire. **38** 54.42N 8.48W
Mallacoota Australia **80** 37.34S 149.43E
Mallaig Scotland **36** 57.00N 5.50W
Mallawi Egypt **56** 27.44N 30.50E
Mallorca *i. see* MajorcaSpain **41**
Mallow Rep. of Ire. **39** 52.08N 8.39W
Malmédy Belgium **45** 50.25N 6.02E
Malmesbury England **28** 51.35N 2.05W
Malmesbury R.S.A. **74** 33.28S 18.43E
Malmö Sweden **46** 55.35N 13.00E
Malone U.S.A. **95** 44.52N 74.19W
Malonga Zaïre **72** 10.26S 23.10E
Målöy Norway **46** 61.57N 5.06E
Malta Europe **42** 35.55N 14.25E
Malta *i.* Malta **42** 35.55N 14.25E
Malta Channel Med. Sea **42** 36.20N 14.45E
Maltby England **33** 53.25N 1.12W
Malton England **33** 54.09N 0.48W
Maluku *d.* Indonesia **61** 4.00S 129.00E
Malvern Hills England **28** 52.05N 2.16W
Mambasa Zaïre **73** 1.20N 29.05E
Mamberamo *r.* Asia **61** 1.45S 137.25E
Mambéré *r.* C.A.R. **71** 3.30N 16.08E
Mambilima Falls *town* Zambia **73** 10.32S 28.45E
Mamfe Cameroon **71** 5.46N 9.18E
Mamou Guinea **70** 10.24N 12.05W
Mamudju Indonesia **60** 2.41S 118.55E
Man Ivory Coast **70** 7.31N 7.37W
Manacle Pt. England **31** 50.04N 5.05W
Manacor Spain **41** 39.32N 3.12E
Manado Indonesia **61** 1.30N 124.58E
Managua Nicaragua **96** 12.06N 86.18W
Managua, L. Nicaragua **96** 12.10N 86.30W
Manama Bahrain **57** 26.12N 50.36E
Manapouri New Zealand **82** 45.35S 167.38E
Manapouri, L. New Zealand **82** 45.30S 167.00E
Manastir Turkey **56** 37.33N 31.37E
Manaus Brazil **102** 3.06S 60.00W
Manchester England **32** 53.30N 2.15W
Manchester Conn. U.S.A. **95** 41.47N 72.31W
Manchester N.H. U.S.A. **95** 42.59N 71.28W
Manchuria *f.* China **63** 46.00N 125.00E
Manchurian Plain *f.* Asia **107** 42.00N 122.00E
Mand *r.* Iran **57** 28.09N 51.16E
Manda Iringa Tanzania **73** 10.30S 34.37E
Mandal Norway **46** 58.02N 7.30E
Mandala Peak Asia **61** 4.45S 140.15E
Mandalay Burma **59** 21.57N 96.04E
Mandal Gobi Mongolia **62** 45.40N 106.10E
Mandara Mts. Nigeria/Cameroon **71** 10.30N 13.30E
Mandla India **58** 22.35N 80.28E
Manfredonia Italy **42** 41.38N 15.54E
Mangalia Romania **43** 43.48N 28.30E
Mangalore India **58** 12.54N 74.51E
Mangerton Mtn. Rep. of Ire. **39** 51.58N 9.30W
Mangochi Malaŵi **73** 14.29S 35.15E
Mangotsfield England **28** 51.29N 2.29W
Mangueira L. Brazil **103** 33.15S 52.50W
Mangyai China **62** 37.52N 91.26E
Mangyshlak Pen. U.S.S.R. **48** 44.00N 52.30E
Manhiça Moçambique **74** 25.23S 32.49E
Maniamba Moçambique **73** 12.30S 35.05E
Manica e Sofala *d.* Moçambique **73** 17.30S 34.00E
Manicouagan *r.* Canada **93** 49.00N 68.13W
Manila Phil. **61** 14.36N 120.59E
Maninga *r.* Zambia **72** 13.28S 24.25E
Manipur *d.* India **59** 25.00N 93.40E
Manisa Turkey **43** 38.37N 27.28E
Manistee *r.* U.S.A. **94** 44.17N 85.45W
Manistique U.S.A. **94** 45.58N 86.17W
Manitoba *d.* Canada **93** 54.00N 96.00W
Manitoba, L. Canada **90** 51.35N 99.00W
Manitou Is. U.S.A. **94** 45.05N 86.05W
Manitoulin I. Canada **94** 45.50N 82.15W
Manitowoc U.S.A. **94** 44.04N 87.40W
Maniwaki Canada **95** 46.22N 75.58W
Manizales Colombia **102** 5.30N 75.38W
Manjil Iran **57** 36.44N 49.29E
Mankono Ivory Coast **70** 8.01N 6.09W
Manly Australia **80** 33.47S 151.17E
Mannar, G. of India/Sri Lanka **59** 8.20N 79.00E
Mannheim W. Germany **44** 49.30N 8.28E
Mannin B. Rep. of Ire. **38** 53.28N 10.06W
Manningtree England **29** 51.56N 1.03E
Mannu *r.* Italy **42** 39.16N 9.00E
Manokwari Asia **61** 0.53S 134.05E
Manono Zaïre **73** 7.18S 27.24E
Manorhamilton Rep. of Ire. **38** 54.18N 8.10W
Manosque France **40** 43.50N 5.47E
Manresa Spain **41** 41.43N 1.50E
Mansa Zambia **73** 11.10S 28.52E
Mansel I. Canada **93** 62.00N 80.00W
Mansfield Australia **80** 37.04S 146.04E
Mansfield England **33** 53.08N 1.12W
Mansfield U.S.A. **94** 40.46N 82.31W
Mänttä Finland **46** 62.00N 24.40E
Mantua Italy **42** 45.09N 10.47E
Manukau Harbour New Zealand **82** 37.10S 174.00E
Manus *i.* Pacific Oc. **61** 2.00S 147.00E
Manyara, L. Tanzania **73** 3.40S 35.50E
Manych *r.* U.S.S.R. **47** 47.14N 40.20E
Manych Gudilo, L. U.S.S.R. **47** 46.20N 42.45E
Manyoni Tanzania **73** 5.46S 34.50E
Manzala, L. Egypt **56** 31.20N 32.00E
Manzanares Spain **41** 39.00N 3.23W
Manzanillo Cuba **97** 20.21N 77.21W
Manzini Swaziland **74** 26.30S 31.22E
Maoke Range *mts.* Indonesia **61** 4.00S 137.30E
Mapai Moçambique **74** 22.51S 32.00E
Mapia Is. Asia **61** 1.00N 134.15E
Maputo Moçambique **74** 25.58S 32.35E
Maputo *d.* Moçambique **74** 26.00S 32.30E
Ma'qala Saudi Arabia **57** 26.29N 47.20E
Maquela do Zombo Angola **72** 6.06S 15.12E
Maquinchao Argentina **103** 41.19S 68.47W
Mar *f.* Scotland **37** 57.07N 3.03W
Mar, Serra do *mts.* Brazil **103** 28.00S 49.30W
Mara *d.* Tanzania **73** 1.45S 34.30E
Mara *r.* Tanzania **73** 1.30S 33.52E
Maracaibo Venezuela **97** 10.44N 71.37W
Maracaibo, L. Venezuela **97** 10.00N 71.30W
Maracaju Brazil **103** 21.38S 55.10W
Maracaju, Serra de *mts.* Brazil **103** 21.00S 55.05W
Maracay Venezuela **97** 10.20N 67.28W
Maradi Niger **71** 13.29N 7.10E
Maragheh Iran **57** 37.25N 46.13E
Maralal Kenya **73** 1.15N 36.48E
Marand Iran **57** 38.25N 45.50E
Marandellas Rhodesia **74** 18.05S 31.42E
Marapi *mtn.* Indonesia **60** 0.20S 100.45E
Maraş Turkey **56** 37.34N 36.54E
Marathon Greece **43** 38.10N 23.59E
Marazion England **31** 50.08N 5.29W
Marbella Spain **41** 36.31N 4.53W
Marble Bar Australia **79** 21.16S 119.45E
Marburg W. Germany **44** 50.49N 8.36E
March England **29** 52.33N 0.05E
Marche Belgium **45** 50.13N 5.21E
Marchena Spain **41** 37.20N 5.24W
Marcy, Mt. U.S.A. **95** 44.07N 73.56W
Mar del Plata Argentina **103** 38.00S 57.32W
Marden England **27** 51.11N 0.30E
Mardin Turkey **56** 37.19N 40.43E
Maree, Loch Scotland **36** 57.41N 5.28W
Marettimo *i.* Italy **42** 37.58N 12.05E
Margarita I. Venezuela **97** 11.00N 64.00W
Margate England **29** 51.23N 1.24E
Mariana Is. Asia **61** 15.00N 145.00E
Marianao Cuba **96** 23.03N 82.29W
Marianas Trench Pacific Oc. **107** 19.00N 146.00E
Maribor Yugo. **44** 46.35N 15.40E
Marico *r.* Botswana **74** 24.15S 26.48E
Maridi Sudan **73** 4.55N 29.30E
Marie Galante *i.* Guadeloupe **97** 16.00N 61.15W
Mariehamn Finland **46** 60.05N 19.55E
Mariental S.W. Africa **74** 24.36S 17.59E
Mariestad Sweden **46** 58.44N 13.50E
Mariga *r.* Nigeria **71** 9.37N 5.55E
Marinette U.S.A. **94** 45.06N 87.38W
Maringá Brazil **103** 23.36S 52.02W
Maringa *r.* Zaïre **72** 1.13N 19.50E
Maringue Moçambique **74** 17.55S 34.24E
Marinha Grande Portugal **41** 39.45N 8.55W
Marion Ind. U.S.A. **94** 40.33N 85.40W
Marion Ohio U.S.A. **94** 40.35N 83.08W
Mariscal Estigarribia Paraguay **103** 22.03S 60.35W
Maritsa *r.* Turkey **43** 41.00N 26.15E
Markaryd Sweden **46** 56.26N 13.35E
Markerwaard *f.* Neth. **45** 52.30N 5.15E
Market Deeping England **29** 52.40N 0.20W
Market Drayton England **32** 52.55N 2.30W
Market Harborough England **28** 52.29N 0.55W
Market Rasen England **33** 53.24N 0.20W
Market Weighton England **33** 53.52N 0.04W
Markha *r.* U.S.S.R. **49** 63.37N 119.00E
Markinch Scotland **35** 56.12N 3.09W
Markyate England **27** 51.51N 0.28W
Marlborough England **28** 51.26N 1.44W
Marlborough Downs *hills* England **28** 51.28N 1.48W
Marle France **45** 49.44N 3.47E
Marlow England **27** 51.35N 0.48W
Marlpit Hill *town* England **27** 51.13N 0.04E
Marmagao India **58** 15.26N 73.50E
Marmara *i.* Turkey **43** 40.38N 27.37E
Marmara, Sea of Turkey **43** 40.45N 28.15E
Marmaris Turkey **43** 36.50N 28.17E
Marne *r.* France **40** 48.50N 2.25E
Maroua Cameroon **71** 10.35N 14.20E
Marovoay Malagasy Rep. **73** 16.05S 46.35E
Marple England **32** 53.23N 2.05W
Marquesas Is. Pacific Oc. **106** 9.00S 139.00W
Marquette U.S.A. **94** 46.33N 87.23W
Marquise France **29** 50.48N 1.42E
Marrakesh Morocco **68** 31.49N 8.00W
Marrawah Australia **80** 40.57S 144.44E
Marrupa Moçambique **73** 13.10S 37.30E
Marsabit Kenya **73** 2.20N 37.59E
Marsala Italy **42** 37.48N 12.27E
Marsden England **32** 53.36N 1.55W
Marseille France **40** 43.18N 5.22E
Marshall Is. Pacific Oc. **107** 8.00N 172.00E
Marshfield England **28** 51.28N 2.19W
Marshfield U.S.A. **94** 44.40N 90.11W
Marshland Fen *f.* England **29** 52.40N 0.18E
Marske-by-the-Sea England **33** 54.35N 1.00W
Martaban, G. of Burma **59** 15.10N 96.30E
Martelange Belgium **45** 49.50N 5.44E
Martés, Sierra *mts.* Spain **41** 39.10N 1.00W
Martha's Vineyard *i.* U.S.A. **95** 41.25N 70.35W

Martigny Switz. **44** 46.07N 7.05E
Martinique C. America **97** 14.40N 61.00W
Martin Pt. U.S.A. **92** 70.10N 143.50W
Martinsburg U.S.A. **95** 39.28N 77.59W
Marton New Zealand **82** 40.04S 175.25E
Maruchak Afghan. **57** 35.50N 63.08E
Marum Neth. **45** 53.06N 6.16E
Marvejols France **40** 44.33N 3.18E
Mary U.S.S.R. **69** 37.42N 61.54E
Maryborough Australia **80** 37.05S 143.47E
Maryland *d.* U.S.A. **91** 39.00N 76.30W
Maryport England **32** 54.43N 3.30W
Masai Steppe *f.* Tanzania **73** 4.30S 37.00E
Masaka Uganda **73** 0.20S 31.46E
Masan S. Korea **63** 35.10N 128.35E
Masasi Tanzania **73** 10.43S 38.48E
Masbate *i.* Phil. **61** 12.00N 123.30E
Mascara Algeria **41** 35.20N 0.09E
Maseru Lesotho **74** 29.19S 27.29E
Masham England **32** 54.15N 1.40W
Mashhad Iran **57** 36.16N 59.34E
Mashonaland *f.* Rhodesia **74** 18.20S 32.00E
Masi-Manimba Zaïre **72** 4.47S 17.54E
Masindi Uganda **73** 1.41N 31.45E
Masira I. Oman **58** 20.30N 58.50E
Masjid-i-Sulaiman Iran **57** 31.59N 49.18E
Mask, Lough Rep. of Ire. **38** 53.38N 9.22W
Mason City U.S.A. **91** 43.10N 93.10W
Massa Italy **42** 44.02N 10.09E
Massachusetts *d.* U.S.A. **95** 43.00N 72.25W
Massangena Moçambique **74** 21.31S 33.03E
Massawa Ethiopia **69** 15.36N 39.29E
Massif Central *mts.* France **40** 45.00N 3.30E
Massif de l'Ouarsenis *mts.* Algeria **41** 35.55N 1.40E
Massillon U.S.A. **94** 40.48N 81.32W
Massinga Moçambique **74** 23.20S 35.25E
Masterton New Zealand **82** 40.57S 175.39E
Masurian Lakes Poland **47** 54.00N 21.45E
Matabeleland *f.* Rhodesia **74** 19.30S 28.15E
Matadi Zaïre **72** 5.50S 13.36E
Matagorda B. U.S.A. **91** 28.30N 96.20W
Matakana I. New Zealand **82** 37.35S 176.15E
Matam Senegal **70** 15.40N 13.18W
Matamoros Mexico **96** 25.33N 103.15W
Matandu *r.* Tanzania **73** 8.44S 39.22E
Matane Canada **95** 48.50N 67.13W
Matanzas Cuba **96** 23.04N 81.35W
Matanzas *d.* Cuba **96** 23.04N 81.35W
Matapan, C. Greece **43** 36.22N 22.28E
Mataró Spain **41** 41.32N 2.72E
Matatiele R.S.A. **74** 30.20S 28.49E
Mataura *r.* New Zealand **82** 46.34S 168.45E
Matawin *r.* Canada **95** 46.56N 72.55W
Matehuala Mexico **96** 23.40N 100.40W
Matera Italy **43** 40.41N 16.36E
Mateur Tunisia **42** 37.02N 9.39E
Mathews Peak *mtn.* Kenya **73** 1.18N 37.20E
Mathura India **58** 27.30N 77.42E
Matlock England **33** 53.08N 1.32W
Mato Grosso *d.* Brazil **103** 19.00S 55.00W
Matope Malaŵi **73** 15.20S 34.57E
Matopo Hills Rhodesia **74** 20.45S 28.30E
Matrah Oman **57** 23.37N 58.33E
Matruh Egypt **56** 31.21N 27.15E
Matsu Is. Taiwan **63** 26.12N 120.00E
Matsuyama Japan **63** 33.50N 132.47E
Mattagami *r.* Canada **94** 49.45N 82.00W
Mattawa Canada **95** 46.19N 58.42W
Matterhorn *mtn.* Switz. **40** 45.58N 7.38E
Maturín Venezuela **97** 9.45N 61.16W
Maubeuge France **45** 50.17N 3.58E
Mauchline Scotland **34** 55.31N 4.23W
Maude Australia **80** 34.27S 144.21E
Mauganj India **58** 24.40N 81.53E
Maughold Head I.o.M. **32** 54.18N 4.19W
Maui *i.* Hawaii U.S.A. **90** 20.45N 156.15W
Maumee *r.* U.S.A. **94** 41.34N 83.41W
Maumere Indonesia **61** 8.35S 122.13E
Maun Botswana **74** 19.52S 23.40E
Mauritania Africa **70** 20.00N 10.00E
Mauritius Indian Oc. **113** 20.10S 58.00E
Mavinga Angola **72** 15.47S 20.21E
Mavuradonha Mts. Rhodesia **74** 16.30S 31.30E
Mawlaik Burma **59** 23.40N 94.26E
May, C. U.S.A. **95** 38.55N 74.55W
May, Isle of Scotland **35** 56.12N 2.32W
Maya Spain **41** 43.12N 1.29W
Mayaguana I. Bahamas **97** 22.30N 73.00W
Mayaguez Puerto Rico **97** 18.13N 67.09W
Mayamey Iran **57** 36.27N 55.40E
Maya Mts. Belize **96** 16.30N 89.00W
Maybole Scotland **34** 55.21N 4.41W
Maydena Australia **80** 42.48S 146.30E
Mayen W. Germany **45** 50.19N 7.14E
Mayenne France **40** 48.18N 0.37W
Mayenne *r.* France **40** 48.18N 0.37W
Mayfield England **29** 51.01N 0.17E
Maykop U.S.S.R. **47** 44.37N 40.48E
Maymyo Burma **59** 22.05N 96.33E
Maynooth Rep. of Ire. **38** 53.23N 6.37W
Mayo *d.* Rep. of Ire. **38** 53.47N 9.07W
Mayo Daga Nigeria **71** 6.59N 11.25E
Mayo Landing Canada **92** 63.45N 135.45W
Mayor I. New Zealand **82** 37.15S 176.15E
Mayotte, Île *i.* Comoro Is. **73** 12.50S 45.10E
Mayoumba Gabon **72** 3.23S 10.38E
Mazabuka Zambia **73** 15.50S 27.47E
Mazatenango Guatemala **96** 14.31N 91.30W
Mažeikiai U.S.S.R. **46** 56.06N 23.06E
Mazoe *r.* Moçambique **73** 16.22S 33.38E
Mazoe Rhodesia **74** 17.30S 31.03E
Mbabane Swaziland **74** 26.20S 31.08E
M'Baere *r.* C.A.R. **72** 3.45N 17.35E
M'Baiki C.A.R. **71** 3.53N 18.01E
Mbala Zambia **73** 8.50S 31.24E
Mbale Uganda **73** 1.04N 34.12E
Mbamba Bay *town* Tanzania **73** 11.18S 34.50E
Mbandaka Zaïre **72** 0.03N 18.21E
M'Bangé Cameroon **72** 4.32N 9.31E
Mbarara Uganda **73** 0.36S 30.40E
Mbeya Tanzania **73** 8.54S 33.29E
Mbeya *d.* Tanzania **73** 8.30S 32.30E
Mbinda Congo **72** 2.11S 12.55E
M'bridge *r.* Angola **72** 7.12S 12.55E
Mbuji Mayi Zaïre **72** 6.08S 23.39E
Mbulamuti Uganda **73** 0.50N 33.05E
McClintock Channel Canada **93** 71.20N 102.00W
McClure Str. Canada **92** 74.30N 116.00W
McConaughy, L. U.S.A. **90** 41.20N 102.00W
McCook U.S.A **90** 40.15N 100.45W
McGrath U.S.A. **92** 62.58N 155.40W
Mchinja Tanzania **73** 9.44S 39.45E
Mchinji Malaŵi **73** 13.48S 32.55E
McKeesport U.S.A. **94** 40.21N 79.52W
McKinley, Mt. U.S.A. **92** 63.00N 151.00W
McMurray Canada **92** 56.45N 111.27W
McSwyne's B. Rep. of Ire. **38** 54.36N 8.26W
Mead, L. U.S.A. **90** 36.10N 114.25W
Meadville U.S.A. **94** 41.38N 80.10W
Mealasta *i.* Scotland **36** 58.05N 7.07W
Meath *d.* Rep. of Ire. **38** 53.32N 6.40W
Meaux France **40** 48.58N 2.54E
Mecca Saudi Arabia **69** 21.26N 39.49E
Meconta Moçambique **73** 15.00S 39.50E
Medan Indonesia **60** 3.35N 98.39E
Médéa Algeria **41** 36.15N 2.48E
Mededsiz *mtn.* Turkey **56** 37.33N 34.38E
Medellín Colombia **97** 6.15N 75.36W
Medenine Tunisia **68** 33.24N 10.25E
Méderdra Mauritania **70** 17.02N 15.41W
Medford U.S.A. **95** 42.25N 71.05W
Medicine Hat Canada **90** 50.03N 110.41W
Medina Saudi Arabia **56** 24.30N 39.35E
Medina del Campo Spain **41** 41.20N 4.55W
Medina de Rioseco Spain **41** 41.53N 5.03W
Mediterranean Sea **68** 37.00N 15.00E
Medjerda, Wadi *r.* Algeria **42** 37.07N 10.12E
Medjerda Mts. Algeria **42** 36.35N 8.20E
Medveditsa *r.* U.S.S.R. **47** 49.35N 42.45E
Medway *r.* England **27** 51.24N 0.31E
Meekatharra Australia **79** 26.35S 118.30E
Meerut India **58** 29.00N 77.42E
Mega Ethiopia **69** 4.02N 38.19E
Megantic Canada **95** 45.34N 70.53W
Megantic Mtn. Canada **95** 45.27N 71.09W
Mégara Greece **43** 38.00N 23.21E
Meghalaya *d.* India **58** 25.30N 91.00E
Meiktila Burma **59** 20.53N 95.54E
Meiningen E. Germany **44** 50.34N 10.25E
Meissala Chad **71** 8.20N 17.40E
Meissen E. Germany **44** 51.10N 13.28E
Meknès Morocco **68** 33.53N 5.37W
Mekong *r.* Asia **60** 10.00N 106.20E
Mekong Delta Vietnam **60** 10.00N 106.20E
Mekongga *mtn.* Indonesia **61** 3.39S 121.15E
Mékrou *r.* Benin **71** 12.20N 2.47E
Melbourn England **29** 52.05N 0.01E
Melbourne Australia **80** 37.45S 144.58E
Melbourne England **33** 52.50N 1.25W
Melfi Chad **71** 11.04N 18.03E
Melfi Italy **42** 40.59N 15.39E
Melilla Spain **41** 35.17N 2.57W
Melitopol U.S.S.R. **47** 46.51N 35.22E
Melksham England **28** 51.22N 2.09W
Mellerud Sweden **46** 58.42N 12.27E
Melmore Pt. Rep. of Ire. **38** 55.15N 7.49W
Melo Uruguay **103** 32.22S 54.10W
Melrose Scotland **35** 55.36N 2.43W
Melsetter Rhodesia **74** 19.48S 32.50E
Meltham England **32** 53.36N 1.52W
Melton Mowbray England **28** 52.46N 0.53W
Melun France **40** 48.32N 2.40E
Melvaig Scotland **36** 57.48N 5.49W
Melville Canada **90** 50.57N 102.49W
Melville, C. Australia **79** 14.02S 144.30E
Melville I. Australia **79** 11.30S 131.00E
Melville I. Canada **92** 75.30N 110.00W
Melville Pen. Canada **93** 68.00N 84.00W
Melvin, Lough N. Ireland **38** 54.26N 8.12W
Memba Moçambique **73** 14.16S 40.30E
Memel *see* Klaipeda U.S.S.R. **47**
Memmingen W. Germany **44** 47.59N 10.11E
Memphis U.S.A. **91** 35.05N 90.00W
Memphis *ruins* Egypt **56** 29.52N 31.12E
Menai Bridge *town* Wales **30** 53.14N 4.11W
Menai Str. Wales **30** 53.17N 4.20W
Mendawai *r.* Indonesia **60** 3.17S 113.20E
Mende France **40** 44.32N 3.30E
Menderes *r.* Turkey **43** 37.30N 27.05E
Mendip Hills England **28** 51.15N 2.40W
Mendocino, C. U.S.A. **90** 40.26N 124.24W
Mendoza Argentina **102** 34.00S 68.52W
Mendoza *d.* Argentina **103** 34.00S 67.40W
Mengtsz China **59** 23.20N 103.21E
Menin Belgium **45** 50.48N 3.07E
Menindee Australia **80** 32.23S 142.30E
Menjapa *mtn.* Indonesia **60** 1.00N 116.20E
Menongue Angola **72** 14.40S 17.41E
Menorca *i. see* MinorcaSpain **41**
Mentawai Is. Indonesia **60** 2.50S 99.00E
Menteith, L. of Scotland **34** 56.10N 4.18W
Menton France **40** 43.47N 7.30E
Mentor U.S.A. **94** 41.42N 81.22W
Meon *r.* England **28** 50.49N 1.15W
Meopham Station England **27** 51.23N 0.22E
Meppel Neth. **45** 52.42N 6.12E
Meppen W. Germany **45** 52.42N 7.17E
Merano Italy **44** 46.41N 11.10E
Merauke Indonesia **61** 8.30S 140.22E
Merca Somali Rep. **73** 1.42N 44.47E
Merced U.S.A. **90** 37.17N 120.29W
Mercedes Buenos Aires Argentina **103** 34.42S 59.30W
Mercedes Corrientes Argentina **103** 29.15S 58.05W
Mercedes San Luis Argentina **103** 33.43S 65.29W
Mercedes Uruguay **103** 33.16S 58.05W
Mere England **28** 51.05N 2.16W
Mergui Burma **59** 12.26N 98.34E
Mergui Archipelago *is.* Burma **59** 11.30N 98.15E
Meribah Australia **80** 34.42S 140.53E
Mérida Mexico **96** 20.59N 89.39W
Mérida Spain **41** 38.55N 6.20W
Mérida Venezuela **97** 8.24N 71.08W
Mérida, Cordillera de *mts.* Venezuela **97** 8.00N 71.30W
Meriden U.S.A. **95** 41.32N 72.48W
Meridian U.S.A. **91** 32.21N 88.42W
Merir *i.* Asia **61** 4.19N 132.18E
Merksem Belgium **45** 51.14N 4.25E
Merowe Sudan **69** 18.30N 31.49E
Merrick *mtn.* Scotland **34** 55.08N 4.29W
Merrygoen Australia **80** 31.51S 149.16E
Merse *f.* Scotland **35** 55.45N 2.15W
Mersea I. England **29** 51.47N 0.58E
Merseburg E. Germany **44** 51.22N 12.00E
Mersey *r.* England **32** 53.22N 2.37W
Merseyside *d.* England **32** 53.28N 3.00W
Mersin Turkey **56** 36.47N 34.37E
Mersing Malaysia **60** 2.25N 103.50E
Merstham England **27** 51.16N 0.09W
Merthyr Tydfil Wales **31** 51.45N 3.23W
Mértola Portugal **41** 37.38N 7.40W
Merton *d.* England **27** 51.25N 0.12W
Meru *mtn.* Tanzania **73** 3.15S 36.44E
Merzifon Turkey **56** 40.52N 35.28E
Merzig W. Germany **45** 49.26N 6.39E
Mesolóngion Greece **43** 38.23N 21.23E
Mesopotamia *f.* Iraq **57** 33.30N 44.30E
Messalo *r.* Moçambique **73** 11.38S 40.27E
Messina Italy **42** 38.13N 15.34E
Messina R.S.A. **74** 22.23S 30.00E
Messina, G. of Med. Sea **43** 36.50N 22.05E
Messina, Str. of Med. Sea **42** 38.10N 15.35E
Mesta *r.* Greece **43** 40.51N 24.48E
Meta *r.* Venezuela **97** 6.10N 67.30W
Metan Argentina **103** 25.30S 64.50W
Metheringham England **33** 53.09N 0.22W
Methven Scotland **35** 56.25N 3.37W
Methwold England **29** 52.30N 0.33E
Metković Yugo. **43** 43.03N 17.38E
Metz France **40** 49.07N 6.11E
Meulaboh Indonesia **60** 4.10N 96.09E
Meuse *r. see* Maas Belgium **45**
Mevagissey England **31** 50.16N 4.48W
Mevatanana Malagasy Rep. **73** 17.06S 46.45E
Mexborough England **33** 53.29N 1.18W
Mexicali Mexico **90** 32.26N 115.30W
Mexico C. America **89** 20.00N 100.00W
Mexico *d.* Mexico **96** 19.45N 99.30W
Mexico U.S.A. **94** 39.10N 91.53W

Mexico, G. of N. America **96** 25.00N 90.00W
Mexico City Mexico **96** 19.25N 99.10W
Meyadin Syria **56** 35.01N 40.28E
Mezen U.S.S.R. **48** 65.50N 44.20E
Mezenc, Mt. France **40** 44.54N 4.11E
Miami U.S.A. **91** 25.45N 80.10W
Miami *r.* U.S.A. **94** 39.07N 84.43W
Mianduab Iran **57** 36.57N 46.06E
Mianeh Iran **57** 37.23N 47.45E
Mianwali Pakistan **58** 32.32N 71.33E
Michigan *d.* U.S.A. **94** 44.50N 85.20W
Michigan, L. U.S.A. **94** 44.00N 87.00W
Michigan City U.S.A. **94** 41.43N 86.54W
Michipicoten Harbour *town* Canada **94** 47.57N 84.55W
Michipicoten I. Canada **94** 47.45N 85.45W
Michoacan *d.* Mexico **96** 19.20N 101.00W
Michurinsk U.S.S.R. **47** 52.54N 40.30E
Middelburg Neth. **45** 51.30N 3.36E
Middelburg Cape Province R.S.A. **74** 31.30S 25.00E
Middelburg Transvaal R.S.A. **74** 25.47S 29.28E
Middlesbrough England **33** 54.34N 1.13W
Middleton England **32** 53.33N 2.12W
Middleton in Teesdale England **32** 54.38N 2.05W
Middleton on the Wolds England **33** 53.56N 0.35W
Middletown U.S.A. **94** 39.31N 84.13W
Middlewich England **32** 53.12N 2.28W
Mid Glamorgan *d.* Wales **31** 51.38N 3.25W
Midhurst England **28** 50.59N 0.44W
Midi, Canal du France **41** 43.18N 2.00W
Midland Canada **94** 44.45N 79.53W
Midland U.S.A. **94** 43.38N 84.14W
Midleton Rep. of Ire. **39** 51.55N 8.10W
Midsomer Norton England **28** 51.17N 2.29W
Midye Turkey **43** 41.37N 28.07E
Mid Yell Scotland **36** 60.31N 1.03W
Mienning China **59** 24.00N 100.10E
Mieres Spain **41** 43.15N 5.46W
Mijares *r.* Spain **41** 39.58N 0.01W
Mikhaylovka U.S.S.R. **47** 50.05N 43.15E
Mikindani Tanzania **73** 10.16S 40.05E
Mikkeli Finland **46** 61.44N 27.15E
Mikumi Tanzania **73** 7.22S 37.00E
Milan Italy **40** 45.28N 9.10E
Milange Moçambique **73** 16.09S 35.44E
Milâs Turkey **43** 37.18N 27.48E
Milborne Port England **28** 50.58N 2.28W
Mildenhall England **29** 52.20N 0.30E
Mildura Australia **80** 34.14S 142.13E
Miles City U.S.A. **90** 46.24N 105.48W
Milford England **27** 51.10N 0.40W
Milford U.S.A. **95** 41.13N 73.04W
Milford Haven *b.* Wales **31** 51.42N 5.05W
Milford Haven *town* Wales **31** 51.43N 5.02W
Milford on Sea England **28** 50.44N 1.36W
Milford Sound *town* New Zealand **82** 44.41S 167.56E
Miliana Algeria **41** 36.20N 2.15E
Milk *r.* U.S.A. **90** 47.55N 106.15W
Millau France **40** 44.06N 3.05E
Mille Lacs, Lac des Canada **94** 48.50N 90.30W
Mille Lacs L. U.S.A. **91** 46.15N 93.40W
Millerovo U.S.S.R. **47** 48.55N 40.25E
Milleur Pt. Scotland **34** 55.01N 5.07W
Mill Hill *town* England **27** 51.37N 0.14W
Millicent Australia **80** 37.36S 140.22E
Millom England **32** 54.13N 3.16W
Millport Scotland **34** 55.45N 4.56W
Millstreet Rep. of Ire. **39** 52.04N 9.05W
Milnathort Scotland **35** 56.14N 3.26W
Milngavie Scotland **34** 55.57N 4.19W
Milnthorpe England **32** 54.14N 2.47W
Milo *r.* Guinea **70** 11.05N 9.05W
Milos *i.* Greece **43** 36.40N 24.26E
Milparinka Australia **80** 29.45S 141.55E
Milton New Zealand **82** 46.08S 169.59E
Milton Abbot England **31** 50.35N 4.16W
Milton Keynes England **28** 52.03N 0.42W
Miltown Malbay Rep. of Ire. **39** 52.51N 9.25W
Milverton England **28** 51.02N 3.15W
Milwaukee U.S.A. **94** 43.03N 87.56W
Minab Iran **57** 27.07N 57.05E
Minas Uruguay **103** 34.20S 55.15W
Mina Saud Kuwait **57** 28.48N 48.24E
Minas Gerais Brazil **103** 18.00S 45.00W
Minatitlán Mexico **96** 17.59N 94.32W
Mindanao *i.* Phil. **61** 7.30N 125.00E
Minden W. Germany **44** 52.18N 8.54E
Mindoro *i.* Phil. **61** 13.00N 121.00E
Mindoro Str. Pacific Oc. **61** 12.30N 120.10E
Mindra, Mt. Romania **43** 45.20N 23.32E
Minehead England **28** 51.12N 3.29W
Mine Head Rep. of Ire. **39** 51.59N 7.35W
Minginish *f.* Scotland **36** 57.15N 6.20W
Mingulay *i.* Scotland **36** 56.48N 7.37W
Minna Nigeria **71** 9.39N 6.32E
Minneapolis U.S.A. **94** 45.00N 93.15W
Minnesota *d.* U.S.A. **91** 46.00N 95.00W
Miño *r.* Spain **41** 42.50N 8.52W
Minorca *i.* Spain **41** 40.00N 4.00E
Minot U.S.A. **90** 48.16N 101.19W
Minsk U.S.S.R. **46** 53.51N 27.30E
Minster England **29** 51.25N 0.50E
Minsterley England **28** 52.38N 2.56W
Mintlaw Scotland **37** 57.31N 2.00W
Minya Konka *mtn.* China **59** 29.30N 101.30E
Miraj India **58** 16.51N 74.42E
Miranda Brazil **103** 20.10S 56.19W
Miranda de Ebro Spain **41** 42.41N 2.57W
Miranda do Douro Portugal **41** 41.30N 6.16W
Mirande France **40** 43.31N 0.25E
Mirandela Portugal **41** 41.28N 7.10W
Mirecourt France **44** 48.18N 6.08E
Miri Malaysia **60** 4.28N 114.00E
Mirim, L. Brazil **103** 33.10S 53.30W
Mirpur Khas Pakistan **58** 25.33N 69.05E
Mirzapur India **58** 25.09N 82.34E
Misbourne *r.* England **27** 51.33N 0.29W
Mishawaka U.S.A. **94** 41.38N 86.10W
Misiones *d.* Argentina **103** 27.00S 54.30W
Miskolc Hungary **47** 48.07N 20.47E
Misoöl *i.* Indonesia **61** 1.50S 130.10E
Missinaibi *r.* Canada **91** 50.50N 81.12W
Mississauga Canada **95** 43.35N 79.37W
Mississippi *d.* U.S.A. **91** 33.00N 90.00W
Mississippi *r.* U.S.A. **94** 28.55N 89.05W
Mississippi Delta U.S.A. **91** 29.00N 89.10W
Missoula U.S.A. **90** 46.52N 114.00W
Missouri *d.* U.S.A. **94** 39.45N 91.30W
Missouri *r.* U.S.A. **94** 38.40N 90.20W
Mistassini, L. Canada **91** 50.45N 73.40W
Misurata Libya **68** 32.24N 15.04E
Mitcham England **27** 51.24N 0.09W
Mitchell *r.* Australia **79** 15.12S 141.40E
Mitchell U.S.A. **90** 43.40N 98.01W
Mitchell, Mt. U.S.A. **91** 35.57N 82.16W
Mitchelstown Rep. of Ire. **39** 52.16N 8.17W
Mitilíni Greece **43** 39.06N 26.34E
Mittelland Canal W. Germany **45** 52.24N 7.52E
Mitumba Mts. Zaïre **73** 3.00S 28.30E
Mitwaba Zaïre **73** 8.32S 27.20E
Mitzic Gabon **72** 0.48N 11.30E
Miyako *i.* Japan **63** 24.45N 125.25E
Mizen Head Rep. of Ire. **39** 51.27N 9.50W
Mjölby Sweden **46** 58.19N 15.10E
Mjösa *l.* Norway **46** 60.50N 10.50E
Mkushi Zambia **73** 13.40S 29.26E
Mladá Boleslav Czech. **44** 50.26N 14.55E
Mljet *i.* Yugo. **43** 42.45N 17.30E
Moamba Moçambique **74** 25.35S 32.13E
Moanda Gabon **72** 1.25S 13.18E
Moate Rep. of Ire. **38** 53.24N 7.45W
Moatize Moçambique **73** 16.04S 33.40E
Moba Zaïre **73** 7.03S 29.42E
Mobaye C.A.R. **72** 4.21N 21.10E
Mobile U.S.A. **91** 30.40N 88.05W
Mobile B. U.S.A. **91** 30.30N 87.50W
Mobridge U.S.A. **90** 45.31N 100.25W
Mobutu, L. Uganda/Zaïre **73** 1.45N 31.00E
Moçambique Africa **74** 21.00S 34.00E
Moçambique *d.* Moçambique **73** 15.00S 39.00E
Moçambique *town* Moçambique **73** 15.00S 40.47E
Moçambique Channel Indian Oc. **73** 16.00S 42.30E
Moçâmedes Angola **72** 15.10S 12.10E
Moçâmedes *d.* Angola **72** 15.00S 12.30E
Mocimboa da Praia Moçambique **73** 11.19S 40.19E
Mocuba Moçambique **73** 16.52S 37.02E
Modane France **40** 45.12N 6.40E
Modbury England **31** 50.21N 3.53W
Modder *r.* R.S.A. **74** 29.03S 23.56E
Modena Italy **42** 44.39N 10.55E
Módica Italy **42** 36.51N 14.51E
Moffat Scotland **35** 55.20N 3.27W
Mogadishu Somali Rep. **73** 2.02N 45.21E
Mogaung Burma **59** 25.20N 97.00E
Moghan Steppe *f.* U.S.S.R. **57** 39.40N 48.30E
Mogilev U.S.S.R. **47** 53.54N 30.20E
Mogincual Moçambique **73** 15.33S 40.29E
Mogok Burma **59** 23.00N 96.40E
Mogomo Moçambique **73** 15.25S 36.45E
Mohaka *r.* New Zealand **82** 39.07S 177.10E
Mohammadia Algeria **41** 35.35N 0.05E
Mohawk *r.* U.S.A. **95** 42.50N 73.40W
Mohéli *i.* Comoro Is. **73** 12.22S 43.45E
Mohill Rep. of Ire. **38** 53.55N 7.53W
Mohoro Tanzania **73** 8.09S 39.07E
Moidart *f.* Scotland **36** 56.48N 5.40W
Mo-i-Rana Norway **46** 66.20N 14.12E
Moisie *r.* Canada **93** 50.15N 66.00W
Moissac France **40** 44.07N 1.05E
Moji das Cruzes Brazil **103** 23.33S 46.14W
Mokpo S. Korea **63** 34.50N 126.25E
Mold Wales **30** 53.10N 3.08W
Moldavia Soviet Socialist Republic *d.* U.S.S.R. **47** 47.30N 28.30E
Molde Norway **46** 62.44N 7.08E
Mole *r.* Devon England **31** 50.59N 3.53W
Mole *r.* Surrey England **27** 51.24N 0.20W
Molepolole Botswana **74** 24.25S 25.30E
Molfetta Italy **43** 41.12N 16.36E
Molina de Aragón Spain **41** 40.50N 1.54W
Moline U.S.A. **94** 41.31N 90.26W
Moliro Zaïre **73** 8.11S 30.29E
Mölndal Sweden **47** 57.40N 12.00E
Molodechno U.S.S.R. **46** 54.16N 26.50E
Molokai *i.* Hawaii U.S.A. **90** 21.20N 157.00W
Molong Australia **80** 33.08S 148.53E
Molopo *r.* R.S.A. **74** 28.30S 20.07E
Molteno R.S.A. **74** 31.24S 26.22E
Moluccas *is.* Indonesia **61** 4.00S 128.00E
Molucca Sea Pacific Oc. **61** 2.00N 126.30E
Moma Moçambique **73** 16.40S 39.10E
Mombasa Kenya **73** 4.04S 39.40E
Mön *i.* Denmark **44** 54.58N 12.20E
Mona *i.* Puerto Rico **97** 18.06N 67.54W
Monach, Sd. of *str.* Scotland **36** 57.34N 7.35W
Monach Is. Scotland **36** 57.32N 7.38W
Monaco Europe **40** 43.40N 7.25E
Monadhliath Mts. Scotland **37** 57.09N 4.08W
Monaghan Rep. of Ire. **38** 54.15N 6.58W
Monaghan *d.* Rep. of Ire. **38** 54.10N 7.00W
Monar, Loch Scotland **36** 57.25N 5.05W
Monasterevan Rep. of Ire. **39** 53.09N 7.05W
Monastir Tunisia **42** 35.35N 10.50E
Monavullagh Mts. Rep. of Ire. **39** 52.14N 7.37W
Monchegorsk U.S.S.R. **46** 67.55N 33.01E
Mönchen-Gladbach W. Germany **45** 51.12N 6.25E
Monclova Mexico **90** 26.55N 101.20W
Moncton Canada **91** 46.10N 64.50W
Mondovi Italy **40** 44.24N 7.48E
Moneygall Rep. of Ire. **39** 52.53N 7.58W
Moneymore N. Ireland **34** 54.42N 6.40W
Monforte Spain **41** 42.32N 7.30W
Monga Zaïre **72** 4.10N 23.00E
Mongala *r.* Zaïre **72** 1.58N 19.55E
Mongalla Sudan **73** 5.12N 31.42E
Monghyr India **58** 25.24N 86.29E
Mongolia Asia **62** 46.30N 104.00E
Mongu Zambia **72** 15.10S 23.09E
Moniaive Scotland **35** 55.12N 3.55W
Monifieth Scotland **35** 56.29N 2.50W
Monkoto Zaïre **72** 1.39S 20.41E
Monmouth Wales **31** 51.48N 2.43W
Monnow *r.* England **28** 51.49N 2.42W
Monongahela *r.* U.S.A. **94** 40.26N 80.00W
Monopoli Italy **43** 40.56N 17.19E
Monroe La. U.S.A. **91** 32.31N 92.06W
Monroe Mich. U.S.A. **94** 41.56N 83.21W
Monrovia Liberia **70** 6.20N 10.46W
Mons Belgium **45** 50.27N 3.57E
Montalbán Spain **41** 40.50N 0.48W
Montana *d.* U.S.A. **90** 47.00N 110.00W
Montargis France **40** 48.00N 2.44E
Montauban France **40** 44.01N 1.20E
Montauk Pt. U.S.A. **95** 41.04N 71.51W
Mont-aux-Sources *mtn.* Lesotho **74** 28.50S 28.50E
Montbéliard France **44** 47.31N 6.48E
Montbrison France **40** 45.37N 4.04E
Montcalm, L. China **59** 34.30N 89.00E
Mont Cenis Pass France **40** 45.15N 6.55E
Montcornet France **45** 49.41N 4.01E
Mont de Marsan *town* France **40** 43.54N 0.30W
Monte Carlo Monaco **40** 43.44N 7.25E
Montecristo *i.* Italy **42** 42.20N 10.19E
Montego Bay *town* Jamaica **97** 18.27N 77.56W
Montélimar France **40** 44.33N 4.45E
Monterey U.S.A. **90** 36.35N 121.55W
Monterey B. U.S.A. **90** 36.45N 122.00W
Montería Colombia **97** 8.45N 75.54W
Montero Bolivia **103** 17.20S 63.15W
Monterrey Mexico **96** 25.40N 100.20W
Monte Santu, C. Italy **42** 40.05N 9.44E
Montes Claros Brazil **103** 16.45S 43.52W
Monte Verde Angola **72** 8.45S 16.50E
Montevideo Uruguay **103** 34.55S 56.10W
Montfort-sur-Meu France **40** 48.08N 1.57W
Montgomery U.S.A. **91** 32.22N 86.20W
Montgomery Wales **30** 52.34N 3.09W
Montijo Portugal **41** 38.42N 8.59W
Montijo Dam Spain **41** 38.52N 6.20W
Mont Joli Canada **95** 48.34N 68.05W
Mont Laurier *town* Canada **95** 46.33N 75.31W
Montluçon France **40** 46.20N 2.36E
Montmagny Canada **95** 46.58N 70.34W
Montmédy France **45** 49.31N 5.21E
Montmorillon France **40** 46.26N 0.52E
Montoro Spain **41** 38.02N 4.23W
Montpelier U.S.A. **95** 44.16N 72.34W
Montpellier France **40** 43.36N 3.53E

Montreal Canada **95** 45.30N 73.36W
Montreal *r.* Canada **94** 47.13N 84.40W
Montrejeau France **40** 43.05N 0.33E
Montreuil France **40** 50.28N 1.46E
Montreux Switz. **44** 46.27N 6.55E
Montrose Scotland **35** 56.43N 2.29W
Montrose U.S.A. **90** 38.29N 107.53W
Montsant, Sierra de *mts.* Spain **41** 41.20N 1.00E
Montserrat *i.* C. America **97** 16.45N 62.14W
Monywa Burma **59** 22.07N 95.11E
Monza Italy **40** 45.35N 9.16E
Monze Zambia **73** 16.16S 27.28E
Monzón Spain **41** 41.52N 0.10E
Moore, L. Australia **79** 29.30S 117.30E
Moorfoot Hills Scotland **35** 55.43N 3.03W
Moorhead U.S.A. **91** 46.51N 96.44W
Moosehead L. U.S.A. **95** 45.45N 69.45W
Moose Jaw Canada **90** 50.23N 105.35W
Moosonee Canada **91** 51.18N 80.40W
Mopti Mali **70** 14.29N 4.10W
Mora Sweden **46** 61.00N 14.30E
Moradabad India **58** 28.50N 78.45E
Morar, Loch Scotland **36** 56.56N 5.40W
Morava *r.* Yugo. **43** 44.43N 21.02E
Moravian Heights *mts.* Czech. **44** 49.30N 15.45E
Moray Firth *est.* Scotland **37** 57.35N 4.00W
Morcenx France **40** 44.02N 0.55W
Morden Canada **93** 49.15N 98.10W
Morden England **27** 51.23N 0.12W
More, Loch Scotland **37** 58.23N 4.51W
Morecambe England **32** 54.03N 2.52W
Morecambe B. England **32** 54.05N 3.00W
Moree Australia **80** 29.29S 149.53E
Morelia Mexico **96** 19.40N 101.11W
Morella Spain **41** 40.37N 0.06W
Morelos *d.* Mexico **96** 18.40N 99.00W
Morena, Sierra *mts.* Spain **41** 38.10N 5.00W
Moretonhampstead England **31** 50.39N 3.45W
Morez France **40** 46.31N 6.02E
Morgan Australia **80** 34.02S 139.40E
Morgan City U.S.A. **91** 29.41N 91.13W
Morie, Loch Scotland **37** 57.44N 4.27W
Morioka Japan **63** 39.43N 141.08E
Morkalla Australia **80** 34.22S 141.10E
Morlaix France **40** 48.35N 3.50W
Morley England **33** 53.45N 1.36W
Morocco Africa **68** 31.00N 5.00W
Moro G. Phil. **61** 6.30N 123.20E
Morogoro Tanzania **73** 6.47S 37.40E
Morogoro *d.* Tanzania **73** 8.30S 37.00E
Morón Cuba **97** 22.08N 78.39W
Mörön Mongolia **62** 49.36N 100.08E
Moroni Comoro Is. **73** 11.40S 43.19E
Morotai *i.* Indonesia **61** 2.10N 128.30E
Moroto Uganda **73** 2.32N 34.41E
Morpeth England **35** 55.10N 1.40W
Morsbach W. Germany **45** 50.52N 7.44E
Mortagne France **40** 48.32N 0.33E
Morte Pt. England **31** 51.12N 4.13W
Mortimer Common England **28** 51.22N 1.05W
Moruya Australia **80** 35.56S 150.06E
Morven *mtn.* Scotland **37** 58.13N 3.42W
Morvern *f.* Scotland **36** 56.37N 5.45W
Morwell Australia **80** 38.14S 146.25E
Moscow U.S.S.R. **47** 55.45N 37.42E
Mosel *r.* W. Germany **45** 50.23N 7.37E
Moselle *r. see* Mosel France/Lux. **45**
Moshi Tanzania **73** 3.20S 37.21E
Mosjöen Norway **46** 65.50N 13.10E
Moskog Norway **46** 61.30N 5.59E
Moskva *r.* U.S.S.R. **47** 55.08N 38.50E
Mosquitia Plain Honduras **96** 15.00N 89.00W
Mosquito Coast *f.* Nicaragua **96** 13.00N 84.00W
Mosquitos, G. of Panamá **96** 9.00N 81.00W
Moss Norway **46** 59.26N 10.41E
Mossbank Scotland **36** 60.27N 1.10W
Mossel Bay *town* R.S.A. **74** 34.12S 22.08E
Mossgiel Australia **80** 33.18S 144.05E
Mossuma *r.* Zambia **72** 15.11S 23.05E
Moss Vale *town* Australia **80** 34.33S 150.20E
Most Czech. **44** 50.31N 13.39E
Mostaganem Algeria **41** 35.54N 0.05E
Mostar Yugo. **43** 43.20N 17.50E
Mosul Iraq **56** 36.21N 43.08E
Motagua *r.* Guatemala **96** 15.56N 87.45W
Motala Sweden **46** 58.34N 15.05E
Motherwell Scotland **35** 55.48N 4.00W
Motu *r.* New Zealand **82** 37.52S 177.37E
Motueka New Zealand **82** 41.08S 173.01E
Mouila Gabon **72** 1.50S 11.02E
Moulamein Australia **80** 35.03S 144.05E
Moulins France **40** 46.34N 3.20E
Moulmein Burma **59** 16.30N 97.40E
Mountain Ash Wales **31** 51.42N 3.22W
Mount Bellew *town* Rep. of Ire. **38** 53.28N 8.30W
Mount Darwin *town* Rhodesia **74** 16.45S 31.39E
Mount Fletcher *town* R.S.A. **74** 30.41S 28.30E
Mount Gambier *town* Australia **80** 37.51S 140.50E
Mount Hagen *town* P.N.G. **61** 5.54S 144.13E
Mount Isa *town* Australia **79** 20.50S 139.29E
Mount Lebanon *town* U.S.A. **94** 40.52N 80.04W
Mountmellick Rep. of Ire. **39** 53.08N 7.21W
Mountnessing England **27** 51.40N 0.21E
Mountrath Rep. of Ire. **39** 53.00N 7.30W
Mount's B. England **31** 50.05N 5.25W
Mourne *r.* N. Ireland **38** 54.50N 7.29W
Mourne Mts. N. Ireland **38** 54.10N 6.02W
Moussoro Chad **71** 13.41N 16.31E
Moville Rep. of Ire. **34** 55.11N 7.03W
Moxico Angola **72** 11.50S 20.05E
Moxico *d.* Angola **72** 13.00S 21.00E
Moy N. Ireland **38** 54.27N 6.43W
Moy *r.* Rep. of Ire. **38** 54.10N 9.09W
Moyale Kenya **73** 3.31N 39.04E
Moyowosi *r.* Tanzania **73** 4.59S 30.58E
Mozdok U.S.S.R. **47** 43.45N 44.43E
Mozyr U.S.S.R. **47** 52.02N 29.10E
M'Pama *r.* Congo **72** 0.59S 15.40E
Mpanda Tanzania **73** 6.21S 31.01E
Mpika Zambia **73** 11.52S 31.30E
Mporokoso Zambia **73** 9.22S 30.06E
M'Pouya Congo **72** 2.38S 16.08E
Mpwapwa Tanzania **73** 6.23S 36.38E
Mrewa Rhodesia **74** 17.35S 31.45E
Msaken Tunisia **42** 35.42N 10.33E
Msta *r.* U.S.S.R. **47** 58.28N 31.20E
Mtakuja Tanzania **73** 7.21S 30.37E
Mtsensk U.S.S.R. **47** 53.18N 36.35E
Mt. Vernon *town* U.S.A. **95** 40.55N 73.51W
Mtwara Tanzania **73** 10.17S 40.11E
Mtwara *d.* Tanzania **73** 10.00S 38.30E
Muang Khon Kaen Thailand **59** 16.25N 102.50E
Muang Lampang Thailand **59** 18.16N 99.30E
Muang Nan Thailand **59** 18.52N 100.42E
Muang Phitsanulok Thailand **59** 16.50N 100.15E
Muang Phrae Thailand **59** 18.07N 100.09E
Muara Indonesia **60** 0.32S 101.20E
Mubende Uganda **73** 0.30N 31.24E
Mubi Nigeria **71** 10.16N 13.17E
Much Hadham England **27** 51.52N 0.04E
Muchinga Mts. Zambia **73** 12.15S 31.00E
Much Wenlock England **28** 52.36N 2.34W
Muck *i.* Scotland **36** 56.50N 6.14W
Muckish Mtn. Rep. of Ire. **38** 55.06N 7.59W
Muckle Roe *i.* Scotland **36** 60.22N 1.26W
Muckle Skerry *i.* Scotland **37** 58.41N 2.53W
Muckno Lough Rep. of Ire. **38** 54.07N 6.43W
Mucojo Moçambique **73** 12.05S 40.26E
Mudgee Australia **80** 32.37S 149.36E
Mudhnib Saudi Arabia **57** 25.52N 44.15E
Muff Rep. of Ire. **34** 55.04N 7.16W
Mufulira Zambia **73** 12.30S 28.12E
Mugia Spain **41** 43.06N 9.14W
Muğla Turkey **43** 37.12N 28.22E
Muharraq Bahrain **57** 26.16N 50.38E
Mühlhausen E. Germany **44** 51.12N 10.27E
Muine Bheag *town* Rep. of Ire. **39** 52.42N 6.58W
Muirkirk Scotland **35** 55.31N 4.04W
Muir of Ord *f.* Scotland **37** 57.31N 4.28W
Mukachevo U.S.S.R. **47** 48.26N 22.45E
Mukah Malaysia **60** 2.56N 112.02E
Mukalla S. Yemen **69** 14.34N 49.09E
Mulanje Mts. Malaŵi **73** 15.57S 35.33E
Mulgrave Is. Australia **61** 10.05S 142.00E
Mulhacén *mtn.* Spain **41** 37.04N 3.22W
Mülheim Nordrhein-Westfalen W. Germany **45** 51.25N 6.50E
Mülheim Nordrhein-Westfalen W. Germany **45** 50.58N 7.00E
Mulhouse France **44** 47.45N 7.21E
Mull *i.* Scotland **34** 56.28N 5.56W
Mull, Sd. of *str.* Scotland **34** 56.32N 5.55W
Mullaghanattin *mtn.* Rep. of Ire. **39** 51.56N 9.51W
Mullaghareirk Mts. Rep. of Ire. **39** 52.19N 9.06W
Mullaghcarn *mtn.* N. Ireland **38** 54.40N 7.14W
Mullaghcleevaun *mtn.* Rep. of Ire. **39** 53.06N 6.25W
Mullaghmore *mtn.* N. Ireland **34** 54.51N 6.51W
Mullaley Australia **80** 31.06S 149.55E
Mullardoch, Loch Scotland **36** 57.19N 5.04W
Mullet Pen. Rep. of Ire. **38** 54.12N 10.04W
Mull Head Orkney Is. Scotland **37** 59.23N 2.53W
Mull Head Orkney Is. Scotland **37** 58.58N 2.42W
Mullinavat Rep. of Ire. **39** 52.22N 7.11W
Mullingar Rep. of Ire. **38** 53.31N 7.21W
Mullion England **31** 50.01N 5.15W
Mull of Galloway *c.* Scotland **34** 54.39N 4.52W
Mull of Kintyre *c.* Scotland **34** 55.17N 5.45W
Mull of Oa *c.* Scotland **34** 55.36N 6.20W
Mulobezi Zambia **72** 16.45S 25.11E
Mulroy B. Rep. of Ire. **38** 55.15N 7.46W
Multan Pakistan **58** 30.10N 71.36E
Multyfarnham Rep. of Ire. **38** 53.37N 7.25W
Mumbles Head Wales **31** 51.35N 3.58W
Mumbwa Zambia **73** 14.57S 27.01E
Muna *i.* Indonesia **61** 5.00S 122.30E
München *see* Munich W. Germany **44**
Muncie U.S.A. **94** 40.11N 85.22W
Mundesley England **33** 52.53N 1.24E
Mundo *r.* Spain **41** 38.20N 1.50W
Mungari Moçambique **73** 17.12S 33.35E
Mungbere Zaïre **73** 2.40N 28.25E
Mungindi Australia **80** 28.58S 148.56E
Mungret Rep. of Ire. **39** 52.38N 8.42W
Munich W. Germany **44** 48.08N 11.35E
Munising U.S.A. **94** 46.24N 86.40W
Munku Sardyk *mtn.* Mongolia **49** 51.45N 100.30E
Munster *d.* Rep. of Ire. **39** 52.10N 8.25W
Münster W. Germany **45** 51.58N 7.37E
Muntok Indonesia **60** 2.04S 105.12E
Muonio Finland **46** 67.52N 23.45E
Muonio *r.* Sweden/Finland **46** 67.13N 23.30E
Mur *r.* Austria **44** 46.40N 16.03E
Mura *r.* Yugo. **44** 46.18N 16.53E
Muranga Kenya **73** 0.43S 37.10E
Murchison *r.* Australia **79** 27.30S 114.10E
Murcia Spain **41** 37.59N 1.08W
Mures *r.* Romania **43** 46.16N 20.10E
Muret France **40** 43.28N 1.19E
Murghab *r.* Afghan. **58** 36.50N 63.00E
Müritz, L. E. Germany **44** 52.25N 12.45E
Murjo *mtn.* Indonesia **60** 6.30S 110.55E
Murle Ethiopia **73** 5.11N 36.09E
Murmansk U.S.S.R. **46** 68.59N 33.08E
Muroran Japan **63** 42.21N 140.59E
Murray *r.* Australia **80** 35.23S 139.20E
Murray Bridge *town* Australia **80** 35.10S 139.17E
Murrumbidgee *r.* Australia **80** 34.38S 143.10E
Murrurundi Australia **80** 31.47S 150.51E
Murtoa Australia **80** 36.40S 142.31E
Murud, Mt. Malaysia **60** 3.45N 115.30E
Murwara India **58** 23.49N 80.28E
Murwillumbah Australia **80** 28.20S 153.24E
Murzuq Libya **68** 25.56N 13.57E
Muş Turkey **56** 38.45N 41.30E
Musala *mtn.* Bulgaria **43** 42.11N 23.35E
Muscat Oman **57** 23.36N 58.37E
Musgrave Ranges *mts.* Australia **79** 26.30S 131.10E
Musheramore *mtn.* Rep. of Ire. **39** 52.01N 8.58W
Mushie Zaïre **72** 2.59S 16.55E
Musi *r.* Indonesia **60** 2.20S 104.57E
Muskegon U.S.A. **94** 43.13N 86.15W
Muskegon *r.* U.S.A. **94** 43.13N 86.20W
Muskingum *r.* U.S.A. **94** 39.25N 81.25W
Muskogee U.S.A. **91** 35.45N 95.21W
Musoma Tanzania **73** 1.31S 33.48E
Musselburgh Scotland **35** 55.57N 3.04W
Mussende Angola **72** 10.33S 16.02E
Mustang Nepal **59** 29.10N 83.55E
Mustjala U.S.S.R. **46** 58.30N 22.10E
Muswellbrook Australia **80** 32.17S 150.55E
Mut Turkey **56** 36.38N 33.27E
Mutankiang China **63** 44.36N 129.42E
Muwai Hakran Saudi Arabia **56** 22.41N 41.37E
Muxima Angola **72** 9.33S 13.58E
Muyinga Burundi **73** 2.48S 30.21E
Muzaffarnagar India **58** 29.28N 77.42E
Muzaffarpur India **58** 26.07N 85.23E
Mwanza Tanzania **73** 2.30S 32.54E
Mwanza *d.* Tanzania **73** 3.00S 32.30E
Mwanza Zaïre **73** 7.51S 26.43E
Mwaya Mbeya Tanzania **73** 9.33S 33.56E
Mweelrea Mts. Rep. of Ire. **38** 53.40N 9.52W
Mweka Zaïre **72** 4.51S 21.34E
Mwene Ditu Zaïre **72** 7.04S 23.27E
Mweru, L. Zaïre/Zambia **73** 9.00S 28.40E
Mwinilunga Zambia **72** 11.44S 24.24E
Myanaung Burma **59** 18.25N 95.10E
Myingyan Burma **59** 21.25N 95.20E
Myitkyina Burma **59** 25.24N 97.25E
Mymensingh Bangla. **58** 24.45N 90.23E
Mynydd Bach *mts.* Wales **30** 52.18N 4.03W
Mynydd Eppynt *mts.* Wales **30** 52.06N 3.30W
Mynydd Prescelly *mts.* Wales **30** 51.58N 4.47W
Myrdal Norway **46** 60.44N 7.08E
Mysen Norway **46** 59.33N 11.20E
Mysore India **58** 12.18N 76.37E
My Tho Vietnam **60** 10.21N 106.21E
Mytishchi U.S.S.R. **47** 55.54N 37.47E
Mzimba Malaŵi **73** 12.00S 33.39E

N

Naas Rep. of Ire. **39** 53.13N 6.41W
Nabeul Tunisia **42** 36.28N 10.44E
Nacala Moçambique **73** 14.30S 40.37E
Nachingwea Tanzania **73** 10.21S 38.46E

Nadder *r.* England **28** 51.05N 1.52W
Naestved Denmark **46** 55.14N 11.47E
Naft Safid Iran **57** 31.38N 49.20E
Naga Phil. **61** 13.36N 123.12E
Nagaland *d.* India **59** 26.10N 94.30E
Nagappattinam India **59** 10.45N 79.50E
Nagasaki Japan **63** 32.45N 129.52E
Nagercoil India **58** 8.11N 77.30E
Nag' Hammadi Egypt **56** 26.04N 32.13E
Nagishot Sudan **73** 4.18N 33.32E
Nagles Mts. Rep. of Ire. **39** 52.06N 8.26W
Nagoya Japan **63** 35.08N 136.53E
Nagpur India **59** 21.10N 79.12E
Nagykanizsa Hungary **43** 46.27N 17.01E
Naha Japan **63** 26.10N 127.40E
Nahavand Iran **57** 34.13N 48.23E
Nahe *r.* W. Germany **45** 49.58N 7.54E
Nahr Ouassel *r.* Algeria **41** 35.30N 2.03E
Nailsworth England **28** 51.41N 2.12W
Nain Canada **93** 56.30N 61.45W
Nain Iran **57** 32.52N 53.05E
Nairn Scotland **37** 57.35N 3.52W
Nairn *r.* Scotland **37** 57.35N 3.51W
Nairobi Kenya **73** 1.17S 36.50E
Naivasha Kenya **73** 0.44S 36.26E
Nakhichevan U.S.S.R. **57** 39.12N 45.24E
Nakhon Phanom Thailand **60** 17.22N 104.45E
Nakhon Ratchasima Thailand **59** 14.59N 102.12E
Nakhon Sawan Thailand **59** 15.35N 100.10E
Nakhon Si Thammarat Thailand **59** 8.29N 100.00E
Naknek U.S.A. **92** 58.45N 157.00W
Nakskov Denmark **44** 54.50N 11.10E
Nakuru Kenya **73** 0.16S 36.04E
Nakusimi *r.* Canada **94** 49.55N 82.00W
Nalchik U.S.S.R. **47** 43.31N 43.38E
Nalon *r.* Spain **41** 43.35N 6.06W
Nalut Libya **68** 31.53N 10.59E
Namaki *r.* Iran **57** 31.02N 55.20E
Namanga Kenya **73** 2.33S 36.48E
Namangan U.S.S.R. **62** 40.59N 71.41E
Namapa Moçambique **73** 13.48S 39.44E
Namaponda Moçambique **73** 15.51S 39.52E
Namarroi Moçambique **73** 15.58S 36.55E
Namcha Barwa *mtn.* China **59** 29.30N 95.10E
Nam Dinh Vietnam **60** 20.25N 106.12E
Nametil Moçambique **73** 15.41S 39.30E
Namibia *see* South West Africa Africa **74**
Namib Desert S.W. Africa **74** 23.30S 15.00E
Namlea Indonesia **61** 3.15S 127.07E
Nampo N. Korea **63** 38.40N 125.30E
Nampula Moçambique **73** 15.09S 39.14E
Namsos Norway **46** 64.28N 11.30E
Nam Tso *l.* China **59** 30.40N 90.30E
Namur Belgium **45** 50.28N 4.52E
Namur *d.* Belgium **45** 50.20N 4.45E
Namurro Moçambique **73** 16.57S 39.06E
Namutoni S.W. Africa **74** 18.49S 16.55E
Namwala Zambia **73** 15.44S 26.25E
Nana Candundo Angola **72** 11.28S 23.01E
Nanaimo Canada **90** 49.08N 123.58W
Nanchang China **63** 28.38N 115.56E
Nanchung China **62** 30.54N 106.06E
Nancy France **44** 48.42N 6.12E
Nanda Devi *mtn.* India **59** 30.21N 79.50E
Nander India **58** 19.11N 77.21E
Nandewar Range *mts.* Australia **80** 30.20S 150.45E
Nanga Parbat *mtn.* Kashmir **58** 35.10N 74.35E
Nanking China **63** 32.00N 118.40E
Nan Ling *mts.* China **63** 25.20N 110.30E
Nanning China **60** 22.50N 108.19E
Nanping China **63** 26.40N 118.07E
Nan Shan *mts.* China **62** 38.30N 99.20E
Nanshan Is. Asia **60** 10.30N 116.00E
Nantaise *r.* France **40** 47.12N 1.35W
Nantes France **40** 47.14N 1.35W
Nantucket I. U.S.A. **95** 41.16N 70.00W
Nantucket Sd. U.S.A. **95** 41.30N 70.15W
Nantung China **63** 32.05N 120.59E
Nantwich England **32** 53.05N 2.31W
Nanyuki Kenya **73** 0.01N 37.03E
Napier New Zealand **82** 39.29S 176.58E
Naples Italy **42** 40.50N 14.14E
Naples, G. of Med. Sea **42** 40.42N 14.15E
Nar *r.* England **29** 52.45N 0.24E
Nara Mali **70** 15.13N 7.20W
Naracoorte Australia **80** 36.58S 140.46E
Narayanganj Bangla. **58** 23.36N 90.28E
Narbada *r. see* NarmadaIndia **58**
Narberth Wales **31** 51.48N 4.45W
Narbonne France **40** 43.11N 3.00E
Nare Head England **31** 50.12N 4.55W
Nares Str. Canada **93** 78.30N 75.00W
Narmada *r.* India **58** 21.40N 73.00E
Narodnaya *mtn.* U.S.S.R. **48** 65.00N 61.00E
Narok Kenya **73** 1.04S 35.54E
Narooma Australia **80** 36.15S 150.06E
Narrabri Australia **80** 30.20S 149.49E
Narrandera Australia **80** 34.36S 146.34E
Narran L. Australia **80** 29.40S 147.25E
Narromine Australia **80** 32.17S 148.20E
Narsimhapur India **58** 22.58N 79.15E
Narva U.S.S.R. **46** 59.22N 28.17E
Narva *r.* U.S.S.R. **46** 59.30N 28.00E
Narvik Norway **46** 68.26N 17.25E
Naryan Mar U.S.S.R. **48** 67.37N 53.02E
Nasarawa Nigeria **71** 8.35N 7.44E
Nash Pt. Wales **31** 51.25N 3.35W
Nashua U.S.A. **95** 42.44N 71.28W
Nashville U.S.A. **91** 36.10N 86.50W
Nasik India **58** 20.00N 73.52E
Nasratabad Iran **57** 29.54N 59.58E
Nassau Bahamas **97** 25.03N 77.20W
Nasser, L. Egypt **56** 22.40N 32.00E
Nässjö Sweden **46** 57.39N 14.40E
Natal Brazil **102** 5.46S 35.15W
Natal Indonesia **60** 0.35N 99.07E
Natal *d.* R.S.A. **74** 28.30S 31.00E
Natanz Iran **57** 33.30N 51.57E
Natchez U.S.A. **91** 31.22N 91.24W
Natitingou Benin **71** 10.17N 1.19E
Natron, L. Tanzania **73** 2.18S 36.05E
Naumburg E. Germany **44** 51.09N 11.48E
Nava *r.* Zaïre **73** 1.45N 27.06E
Navalmoral de la Mata Spain **41** 39.54N 5.33W
Navan Rep. of Ire. **38** 53.39N 6.42W
Nave *i.* Scotland **34** 55.55N 6.20W
Navenby England **33** 53.07N 0.32W
Naver *r.* Scotland **37** 58.32N 4.14W
Naver, Loch Scotland **37** 58.17N 4.20W
Návpaktos Greece **43** 38.24N 21.49E
Návplion Greece **43** 37.33N 22.47E
Navrongo Ghana **70** 10.51N 1.03W
Náxos *i.* Greece **43** 37.03N 25.30E
Nayarit *d.* Mexico **96** 21.30N 104.00W
Nayland England **29** 51.59N 0.52E
Nazareth Israel **56** 32.41N 35.16E
Nazas *r.* Mexico **96** 25.34N 103.25W
Nazilli Turkey **56** 37.55N 28.20E
N'Dendé Gabon **72** 2.20S 11.23E
N'Djamena Chad **71** 12.10N 14.59E
Ndjolé Gabon **72** 0.07S 10.45E
Ndola Zambia **73** 13.00S 28.35E
Neagh, Lough N. Ireland **34** 54.36N 6.25W
Neath Wales **31** 51.39N 3.49W
Neath *r.* Wales **31** 51.39N 3.50W
Nebit Dag U.S.S.R. **57** 39.31N 54.24E
Nebraska *d.* U.S.A. **90** 41.30N 100.00W
Nebrodi Mts. Italy **42** 37.53N 14.32E
Neches *r.* U.S.A. **91** 29.55N 93.50W
Neckar *r.* W. Germany **44** 49.32N 8.26E
Necochea Argentina **103** 38.31S 58.46W
Necuto Angola **72** 4.55S 12.38E
Needham Market England **29** 52.09N 1.02E
Needles U.S.A. **90** 34.51N 114.36W
Neerpelt Belgium **45** 51.13N 5.28E
Nefyn Wales **30** 52.55N 4.31W
Negaunee U.S.A. **94** 46.31N 87.37W
Negev *des.* Israel **56** 30.42N 34.55E
Negoiu *mtn.* Romania **43** 45.36N 24.32E
Negotin Yugo. **43** 44.14N 22.33E
Negrais, C. Burma **59** 16.00N 94.30E
Negro *r.* Argentina **103** 41.00S 62.48W
Negro *r.* Brazil **102** 3.30S 60.05W
Negro *r.* Uruguay **103** 33.27S 58.20W
Negros *i.* Phil. **61** 10.00N 123.00E
Neisse *r.* Poland/E. Germany **44** 52.05N 14.42E
Nejd *d.* Saudi Arabia **56** 25.00N 45.00E
Neksö Denmark **46** 55.04N 15.09E
Nellore India **59** 14.29N 80.00E
Nelson Canada **90** 49.29N 117.17W
Nelson England **32** 53.50N 2.14W
Nelson *r.* Canada **93** 57.00N 93.20W
Nelson New Zealand **82** 41.18S 173.17E
Nelson U.S.A. **90** 35.30N 113.16W
Nelson, C. Australia **80** 38.27S 141.35E
Nelspruit R.S.A. **74** 25.30S 30.58E
Néma Mauritania **70** 16.32N 7.12W
Neman *r.* U.S.S.R. **46** 55.23N 21.15E
Nemours France **40** 48.16N 2.41E
Nenagh Rep. of Ire. **39** 52.52N 8.13W
Nenana U.S.A. **92** 64.35N 149.20W
Nene *r.* England **33** 52.49N 0.12E
Nepal Asia **58** 28.00N 84.30E
Nephin *mtn.* Rep. of Ire. **38** 54.01N 9.23W
Nephin Beg *mtn.* Rep. of Ire. **38** 54.02N 9.38W
Nephin Beg Range *mts.* Rep. of Ire. **38** 54.00N 9.37W
Nera *r.* Italy **42** 42.33N 12.43E
Neretva *r.* Yugo. **43** 43.02N 17.28E
Neriquinha Angola **72** 15.50S 21.40E
Nero Deep Pacific Oc. **61** 12.40N 145.50E
Nes Neth. **45** 53.27N 5.46E
Ness *f.* Scotland **36** 58.26N 6.15W
Ness, Loch Scotland **37** 57.16N 4.30W
Neston England **30** 53.17N 3.03W
Netherlands Europe **45** 52.00N 5.30E
Nether Stowey England **28** 51.10N 3.10W
Neto *r.* Italy **43** 39.12N 17.08E
Neubrandenburg E. Germany **44** 53.33N 13.16E
Neuchâtel Switz. **44** 47.00N 6.56E
Neuchâtel, Lac de Switz. **44** 46.55N 6.55E
Neuenhaus W. Germany **45** 52.30N 6.58E
Neufchâteau Belgium **45** 49.51N 5.26E
Neufchâtel France **40** 49.44N 1.26E
Neumünster W. Germany **44** 54.06N 9.59E
Neuquén Argentina **103** 38.55S 68.55W
Neuse *r.* U.S.A. **91** 35.04N 77.04W
Neusiedler, L. Austria **44** 47.52N 16.45E
Neuss W. Germany **45** 51.12N 6.42E
Neustrelitz E. Germany **44** 53.22N 13.05E
Neutral Territory Asia **57** 29.05N 45.40E
Neuwied W. Germany **45** 50.26N 7.28E
Nevada *d.* U.S.A. **90** 39.00N 117.00W
Nevada, Sierra *mts.* Spain **41** 37.04N 3.20W
Nevada, Sierra *mts.* U.S.A. **90** 37.30N 119.00W
Nevada de Cocuy, Sierra *mts.* Colombia **97** 6.15N 72.00W
Nevada de Santa Marta, Sierra *mts.* Colombia **97** 11.00N 73.30W
Nevel U.S.S.R. **47** 56.00N 29.59E
Nevers France **40** 47.00N 3.09E
Nevertire Australia **80** 31.52S 147.47E
Nevis *i.* C. America **97** 17.11N 62.35W
Nevis, Loch Scotland **36** 56.59N 5.40W
Nevşehir Turkey **56** 38.38N 34.43E
New Addington England **27** 51.21N 0.00
New Alresford England **28** 51.06N 1.10W
Newark N.J. U.S.A. **95** 40.44N 74.11W
Newark Ohio U.S.A. **94** 40.03N 82.25W
Newark-on-Trent England **33** 53.06N 0.48W
New Bedford U.S.A. **95** 41.38N 70.55W
New Bern U.S.A. **91** 35.05N 77.04W
Newberry U.S.A. **94** 46.22N 85.30W
Newbiggin-by-the-Sea England **35** 55.11N 1.30W
Newbridge on Wye Wales **30** 52.13N 3.27W
New Britain *i.* P.N.G. **79** 6.00S 150.00E
New Britain U.S.A. **95** 41.40N 72.47W
New Brunswick *d.* Canada **93** 47.00N 66.00W
New Brunswick U.S.A. **95** 40.29N 74.27W
Newburgh Fife Scotland **35** 56.21N 3.15W
Newburgh Grampian Scotland **37** 57.19N 2.01W
Newburgh U.S.A. **95** 41.30N 74.00W
Newbury England **28** 51.24N 1.19W
New Caledonia *i.* Pacific Oc. **107** 22.00S 165.00E
Newcastle Australia **80** 32.55S 151.46E
Newcastle N. Ireland **38** 54.13N 5.53W
New Castle U.S.A. **94** 41.00N 80.22W
Newcastle U.S.A. **90** 43.52N 104.14W
Newcastle Emlyn Wales **30** 52.02N 4.29W
Newcastleton Scotland **35** 55.21N 2.49W
Newcastle-under-Lyme England **32** 53.02N 2.15W
Newcastle upon Tyne England **35** 54.58N 1.36W
Newcastle West Rep. of Ire. **39** 52.26N 9.04W
New Cumnock Scotland **34** 55.24N 4.11W
New Deer Scotland **37** 57.31N 2.11W
New Delhi India **58** 28.37N 77.13E
New England Range *mts.* Australia **80** 30.00S 152.00E
Newent England **28** 51.56N 2.24W
New Forest *f.* England **28** 50.50N 1.35W
Newfoundland *d.* Canada **93** 55.00N 60.00W
Newfoundland *i.* Canada **93** 48.30N 56.00W
New Galloway Scotland **34** 55.05N 4.09W
New Guinea *i.* Austa. **61** 5.00S 140.00E
Newham *d.* England **27** 51.32N 0.03E
New Hampshire *d.* U.S.A. **95** 43.50N 71.45W
New Hanover *i.* Pacific Oc. **79** 2.00S 150.00E
Newhaven England **29** 50.47N 0.04E
New Haven U.S.A. **95** 41.18N 72.55W
New Hebrides *is.* Pacific Oc. **107** 16.00S 167.00E
New Holland England **33** 53.42N 0.22W
New Hythe England **27** 51.18N 0.27E
New Ireland *i.* P.N.G. **79** 2.30S 151.30E
New Jersey *d.* U.S.A. **95** 39.50N 74.45W
New London U.S.A. **95** 41.21N 72.06W
Newmarket England **29** 52.15N 0.23E
Newmarket Rep. of Ire. **39** 52.13N 9.00W
Newmarket-on-Fergus Rep. of Ire. **39** 52.46N 8.55W
New Mexico *d.* U.S.A **90** 34.00N 106.00W
New Mills England **32** 53.23N 2.00W
Newmilns Scotland **34** 55.37N 4.20W
Newnham England **28** 51.48N 2.27W
New Norfolk Australia **80** 42.46S 147.02E
New Orleans U.S.A. **91** 30.00N 90.03W
New Pitsligo Scotland **37** 57.35N 2.12W
New Plymouth New Zealand **82** 39.03S 174.04E
Newport Essex England **29** 51.58N 0.13E
Newport Hants. England **28** 50.43N 1.18W
Newport Salop England **30** 52.47N 2.22W
Newport Mayo Rep. of Ire. **38** 53.53N 9.34W
Newport Tipperary Rep. of Ire. **39** 52.42N 8.25W

Newport Ky. U.S.A. **94** 39.05N 84.27W
Newport R.I. U.S.A. **95** 41.30N 71.19W
Newport Dyfed Wales **30** 52.01N 4.51W
Newport Gwent Wales **31** 51.34N 2.59W
Newport News U.S.A. **91** 36.59N 76.26W
Newport-on-Tay Scotland **35** 56.27N 2.56W
Newport Pagnell England **28** 52.05N 0.42W
New Providence *i.* Bahamas **97** 25.03N 77.25W
Newquay England **31** 50.24N 5.06W
New Quay Wales **30** 52.13N 4.22W
New Radnor Wales **30** 52.15N 3.10W
New Rochelle U.S.A. **95** 40.55N 73.47W
New Romney England **29** 50.59N 0.58E
New Ross Rep. of Ire. **39** 52.24N 6.57W
Newry N. Ireland **38** 54.11N 6.21W
New Scone Scotland **35** 56.25N 3.25W
New Siberian Is. U.S.S.R. **49** 76.00N 144.00E
New South Wales *d.* Australia **80** 33.45S 147.00E
Newton Abbot England **31** 50.32N 3.37W
Newton-le-Willows England **32** 53.28N 2.38W
Newton Mearns Scotland **34** 55.46N 4.18W
Newtonmore Scotland **37** 57.04N 4.08W
Newton Stewart Scotland **34** 54.57N 4.29W
Newtown Rep. of Ire. **39** 52.20N 8.48W
Newtown Wales **30** 52.31N 3.19W
Newtownabbey N. Ireland **34** 54.39N 5.57W
Newtownards N. Ireland **34** 54.35N 5.41W
Newtown Butler N. Ireland **38** 54.12N 7.22W
Newtown Cunningham Rep. of Ire. **38** 54.59N 7.31W
Newtown Forbes Rep. of Ire. **38** 53.45N 7.50W
Newtown Hamilton N. Ireland **38** 54.12N 6.36W
Newtown Mount Kennedy Rep. of Ire. **39** 53.06N 6.07W
Newtownstewart N. Ireland **38** 54.43N 7.25W
New York U.S.A. **95** 40.40N 73.50W
New York *d.* U.S.A. **95** 42.50N 75.50W
New Zealand Austa. **82** 41.00S 175.00E
Neyland Wales **31** 51.43N 4.58W
Nezhin U.S.S.R. **47** 51.03N 31.54E
Ngambwe Rapids *f.* Zambia **72** 17.08S 24.10E
Ngami, L. Botswana **74** 20.25S 23.00E
Ngamiland *f.* Botswana **74** 20.00S 22.30E
N'Gao Congo **72** 2.28S 15.40E
Ngaoundéré Cameroon **71** 7.20N 13.35E
Ngaruroro *r.* New Zealand **82** 39.34S 176.54E
Ngauruhoe *mtn.* New Zealand **82** 37.10S 175.35E
Ngong Kenya **73** 1.22S 36.40E
Ngonye Falls *f.* Zambia **72** 16.35S 23.39E
Ngorongoro Crater *f.* Tanzania **73** 3.13S 35.32E
Ngozi Burundi **73** 2.52S 29.50E
Nguigmi Niger **71** 14.00N 13.11E
Nguru North-Eastern Nigeria **71** 12.53N 10.30E
Nhamacurra Moçambique **73** 17.35S 37.00E
Nhandugue *r.* Moçambique **74** 19.45S 34.40E
Nha Trang Vietnam **60** 12.15N 109.10E
Nhill Australia **80** 36.20S 141.40E
Niagara Falls *town* U.S.A. **95** 43.06N 79.04W
Niamey Niger **71** 13.32N 2.05E
Niangara Zaïre **73** 3.47N 27.54E
Niapa *mtn.* Indonesia **60** 2.45N 117.30E
Nias *i.* Indonesia **60** 1.05N 97.30E
Niassa *d.* Moçambique **73** 13.00S 36.30E
Nicaragua C. America **96** 13.00N 85.00W
Nicaragua, L. Nicaragua **96** 11.30N 85.30W
Nicastro Italy **42** 38.58N 16.16E
Nice France **40** 43.42N 7.16E
Nicobar Is. India **59** 8.00N 94.00E
Nicosia Cyprus **56** 35.11N 33.23E
Nicoya, G. of Costa Rica **96** 9.30N 85.00W
Nicoya Pen. Costa Rica **96** 10.30N 85.30W
Nidd *r.* England **33** 54.01N 1.12W
Nidderdale *f.* England **32** 54.07N 1.50W
Nidelva *r.* Norway **46** 58.26N 8.44E
Niers *r.* Neth. **45** 51.43N 5.56E
Nieuwpoort Belgium **45** 51.08N 2.45E
Niğde Turkey **56** 37.58N 34.42E
Niger Africa **68** 17.00N 9.30E
Niger *d.* Nigeria **71** 9.50N 6.00E
Niger *r.* Nigeria **71** 4.15N 6.05E
Niger Delta Nigeria **71** 4.00N 6.10E
Nigeria Africa **71** 9.00N 9.00E
Niigata Japan **63** 37.58N 139.02E
Nijmegen Neth. **45** 51.50N 5.52E
Nikel U.S.S.R. **46** 69.20N 29.44E
Nikiniki Indonesia **61** 9.49S 124.29E
Nikki Benin **71** 9.55N 3.18E
Nikolayev U.S.S.R. **47** 46.57N 32.00E
Nikolayevsk-na-Amur U.S.S.R. **49** 53.20N 140.44E
Niksar Turkey **56** 40.35N 36.59E
Nikšić Yugo. **43** 42.48N 18.56E
Nila *i.* Indonesia **61** 6.45S 129.30E
Nile *r.* Egypt **56** 31.30N 30.25E
Nile Delta Egypt **56** 31.00N 31.00E
Niles U.S.A. **94** 41.11N 80.46W
Nilgiri Hills India **58** 11.30N 77.30E
Nimba, Mt. Guinea **70** 7.35N 8.28W
Nîmes France **42** 43.50N 4.21E
Nimmitabel Australia **80** 36.32S 149.19E
Nimule Sudan **73** 3.35N 32.04E
Ninety Mile Beach *f.* Australia **80** 38.07S 147.30E
Ninety Mile Beach *f.* New Zealand **82** 34.45S 173.00E
Nineveh *ruins* Iraq **56** 36.24N 43.08E
Ningpo China **63** 29.54N 121.33E
Ningsia Hui *d.* China **59** 34.00N 104.30E
Ningwu China **63** 39.00N 112.19E
Ninove Belgium **45** 50.50N 4.02E
Niobrara *r.* U.S.A. **90** 42.45N 98.10W
Nioro Mali **70** 15.12N 9.35W
Niort France **40** 46.19N 0.27W
Nipigon Canada **94** 49.02N 88.26W
Nipigon, L. Canada **94** 48.40N 88.30W
Nipissing, L. Canada **94** 46.15N 79.45W
Niriz Iran **57** 29.12N 54.17E
Niš Yugo. **43** 43.20N 21.54E
Nishapur Iran **57** 36.13N 58.49E
Niterói Brazil **103** 22.54S 43.06W
Nith *r.* Scotland **35** 55.00N 3.35W
Nithsdale *f.* Scotland **35** 55.15N 3.48W
Niut *mtn.* Indonesia **60** 1.00N 110.00E
Nivelles Belgium **45** 50.36N 4.20E
Nizamabad India **59** 18.40N 78.05E
Nizhneudinsk U.S.S.R. **49** 54.55N 99.00E
Nizhniy Tagil U.S.S.R. **48** 58.00N 60.00E
Njombe Tanzania **73** 9.20S 34.47E
Njombe *r.* Tanzania **73** 7.02S 35.55E
Njoro Tanzania **73** 5.16S 36.30E
Nkhata Bay *town* Malaŵi **73** 11.37S 34.20E
Nkhotakota Malaŵi **73** 12.55S 34.19E
Nkongsamba Cameroon **71** 4.59N 9.53E
Nkungwe Mt. Tanzania **73** 6.15S 29.54E
Nogales Mexico **90** 31.20N 111.00W
Nogent le Rotrou France **40** 48.19N 0.50E
Noguera Ribagorzana *r.* Spain **41** 41.27N 0.25E
Noirmoutier, Île de *i.* France **40** 47.00N 2.15W
Nokia Finland **46** 61.29N 23.31E
Nola C.A.R. **71** 3.28N 16.08E
Noma Omuramba *r.* Botswana **74** 19.20S 22.05E
Nome U.S.A. **92** 64.30N 165.30W
Nong Khai Thailand **59** 17.50N 102.46E
Nongoma R.S.A. **74** 27.54S 31.40E
Noord Brabant *d.* Neth. **45** 51.37N 5.00E
Noorvik U.S.A. **92** 66.50N 161.14W
Noranda Canada **95** 48.16N 79.03W
Nord *d.* France **29** 50.49N 2.21E
Norddeich W. Germany **45** 53.35N 7.10E
Norden W. Germany **45** 53.34N 7.13E
Nordenham W. Germany **44** 53.30N 8.29E
Norderney *i.* W. Germany **45** 53.45N 7.15E
Nord Fjord *est.* Norway **46** 61.50N 6.00E
Nordhausen E. Germany **44** 51.31N 10.48E
Nordhorn W. Germany **45** 52.27N 7.05E
Nordvik U.S.S.R. **49** 73.40N 110.50E
Nore *r.* Rep. of Ire. **39** 52.25N 6.58W
Norfolk *d.* England **29** 52.39N 1.00E
Norfolk U.S.A. **91** 36.54N 76.18W
Norfolk Broads *f.* England **29** 52.43N 1.35E
Norham England **35** 55.43N 2.10W
Norilsk U.S.S.R. **49** 69.21N 88.02E
Normandie, Collines de *hills* France **40** 48.50N 0.40W
Normandy England **27** 51.15N 0.38W
Normanton Australia **79** 17.40S 141.05E
Normanton England **33** 53.41N 1.26W
Norman Wells Canada **92** 65.19N 126.46W
Nörresundby Denmark **46** 57.05N 9.52E
Norris L. U.S.A. **91** 36.20N 83.55W
Norristown U.S.A. **95** 40.07N 75.20W
Norrköping Sweden **46** 58.35N 16.10E
Norrtälje Sweden **46** 59.46N 18.43E
Norte, Punta *c.* Argentina **103** 36.08S 56.50W
Northallerton England **33** 54.20N 1.26W
Northam England **31** 51.02N 4.13W
North America **89**
Northampton England **28** 52.14N 0.54W
Northampton U.S.A. **95** 42.19N 72.38W
Northamptonshire *d.* England **28** 52.18N 0.55W
Northaw England **27** 51.43N 0.09W
North Ballachulish Scotland **36** 56.42N 5.11W
North Battleford Canada **92** 52.47N 108.19W
North Bay *town* Canada **95** 46.20N 79.28W
North Bend U.S.A. **90** 43.26N 124.14W
North Berwick Scotland **35** 56.04N 2.43W
North Beveland *f.* Neth. **45** 51.35N 3.45E
North C. New Zealand **82** 34.28S 173.00E
North C. Norway **46** 71.10N 25.45E
North Canadian *r.* U.S.A. **91** 35.30N 95.45W
North Carolina *d.* U.S.A. **91** 35.30N 79.00W
North Channel Canada **94** 46.05N 83.00W
North Channel U.K. **34** 55.15N 5.52W
North Chicago U.S.A. **94** 42.18N 87.52W
North China Plain *f.* China **63** 34.30N 117.00E
North Dakota *d.* U.S.A. **90** 47.00N 100.00W
North Donets *r.* U.S.S.R. **47** 49.08N 37.28E
North Dorset Downs *hills* England **28** 50.46N 2.25W
North Downs *hills* England **29** 51.18N 0.40E
North Dvina *r.* U.S.S.R. **48** 64.40N 40.50E
North Eastern *d.* Kenya **73** 1.00N 40.00E
North East Polder *f.* Neth. **45** 52.45N 5.45E
Northern *d.* Ghana **70** 9.00N 1.30W
Northern Ireland U.K. **38** 54.40N 6.45W
Northern Territory *d.* Australia **79** 20.00S 133.00E
North Esk *r.* Scotland **37** 56.45N 2.25W
North European Plain *f.* Europe **107** 56.00N 27.00E
Northfleet England **27** 51.27N 0.20E
North Foreland *c.* England **29** 51.23N 1.26E
North Frisian Is. W. Germany **44** 54.30N 8.00E
North Harris *f.* Scotland **36** 57.58N 6.52W
North Holland *d.* Neth. **45** 52.37N 4.50E
North Horr Kenya **73** 3.19N 37.00E
North I. New Zealand **82** 39.00S 175.00E
Northiam England **29** 50.59N 0.39E
North Korea Asia **63** 40.00N 128.00E
North Kyme England **33** 53.04N 0.17W
Northleach England **28** 51.49N 1.50W
North Platte U.S.A. **90** 41.09N 100.45W
North Platte *r.* U.S.A. **90** 41.09N 100.55W
North Pt. U.S.A. **94** 45.02N 83.17W
North Ronaldsay *i.* Scotland **37** 59.23N 2.26W
North Ronaldsay Firth *est.* Scotland **37** 59.20N 2.25W
North Sd. Rep. of Ire. **39** 53.11N 9.34W
North Sea Europe **18** 56.00N 5.00E
North Somercotes England **33** 53.28N 0.08E
North Sporades *is.* Greece **43** 39.00N 24.00E
North Taranaki Bight *b.* New Zealand **82** 38.45S 174.15E
North Tawton England **31** 50.48N 3.55W
North Tidworth England **28** 51.14N 1.40W
North Tolsta Scotland **36** 58.20N 6.13W
North Truchas Peak *mtn.* U.S.A. **90** 35.58N 105.48W
North Tyne *r.* England **35** 54.59N 2.08W
North Uist *i.* Scotland **36** 57.35N 7.20W
Northumberland *d.* England **35** 55.12N 2.00W
North Walsham England **29** 52.49N 1.22E
Northway U.S.A. **92** 62.58N 142.00W
North Weald Bassett England **27** 51.42N 0.12E
North West Highlands Scotland **36** 57.30N 5.15W
North West River *town* Canada **93** 53.30N 60.10W
Northwest Territories *d.* Canada **93** 66.00N 95.00W
Northwich England **32** 53.16N 2.30W
Northwood England **27** 51.36N 0.25W
North York Canada **95** 43.44N 79.26W
North York Moors *hills* England **33** 54.21N 0.50W
North Yorkshire *d.* England **33** 54.14N 1.14W
Norton England **33** 54.08N 0.47W
Norton de Matos Angola **72** 12.20S 14.45E
Norton Sound *b.* U.S.A. **92** 63.50N 164.00W
Norwalk U.S.A. **95** 41.07N 73.25W
Norway Europe **46** 65.00N 13.00E
Norway House *town* Canada **93** 53.59N 97.50W
Norwegian Sea Europe **54** 65.00N 5.00E
Norwich England **29** 52.38N 1.17E
Norwich U.S.A. **95** 41.32N 72.05W
Noss, I. of Scotland **36** 60.08N 1.01W
Noss Head Scotland **37** 58.28N 3.03W
Nossob *r.* R.S.A./Botswana **74** 26.54S 20.39E
Noteć *r.* Poland **44** 52.44N 15.26E
Nottingham England **33** 52.57N 1.10W
Nottinghamshire *d.* England **33** 53.10N 1.00W
Notwani *r.* Botswana **74** 23.14S 27.30E
Nouadhibou Mauritania **70** 20.54N 17.01W
Nouakchott Mauritania **68** 18.09N 15.58W
Noup Head Scotland **37** 59.20N 3.04W
Nouvelle Anvers Zaïre **72** 1.38N 19.10E
Nova Gaia Angola **72** 10.09S 17.35E
Nova Lima Brazil **103** 20.00S 43.51W
Novara Italy **40** 45.27N 8.37E
Nova Scotia *d.* Canada **93** 45.00N 64.00W
Nova Sofala Moçambique **74** 20.09S 34.42E
Novaya Ladoga U.S.S.R. **47** 60.09N 32.15E
Novaya Siberia *i.* U.S.S.R. **49** 75.20N 148.00E
Novaya Zemlya *i.* U.S.S.R. **48** 74.00N 56.00E
Novelda Spain **41** 38.24N 0.45W
Novgorod U.S.S.R. **47** 58.30N 31.20E
Novi-Ligure Italy **40** 44.46N 8.47E
Novi Pazar Yugo. **43** 43.08N 20.28E
Novi Sad Yugo. **43** 45.16N 19.52E
Novocherkassk U.S.S.R. **47** 47.25N 40.05E
Novograd Volynskiy U.S.S.R. **47** 50.34N 27.32E
Novogrudok U.S.S.R. **47** 53.35N 25.50E
Novo Hamburgo Brazil **103** 29.37S 51.07W
Novokazalinsk U.S.S.R. **48** 45.48N 62.06E
Novokuznetsk U.S.S.R. **48** 53.45N 87.12E
Novomoskovsk U.S.S.R. **47** 54.06N 38.15E
Novo Redondo Angola **72** 11.11S 13.52E
Novorossiysk U.S.S.R. **47** 44.44N 37.46E
Novoshakhtinsk U.S.S.R. **47** 47.46N 39.55E
Novosibirsk U.S.S.R. **48** 55.04N 82.55E
Novy Port U.S.S.R. **48** 67.38N 72.33E
Nowa Ruda Poland **44** 50.34N 16.30E
Nowa Sól Poland **44** 51.49N 15.41E
Nowgong India **59** 26.20N 92.41E

Nowra Australia **80** 34.54S 150.36E
Nowy Sącz Poland **47** 49.39N 20.40E
Noyon France **45** 49.35N 3.00E
Nsanje Malaŵi **73** 16.55S 35.12E
Nsukka Nigeria **71** 6.51N 7.29E
Ntcheu Malaŵi **73** 14.50S 34.45E
Nuanetsi *r.* Moçambique **74** 22.42S 31.45E
Nuanetsi Rhodesia **74** 21.22S 30.45E
Nubian Desert Sudan **69** 21.00N 34.00E
Nudushan Iran **57** 32.03N 53.33E
Nueces *r.* U.S.A. **91** 27.55N 97.30W
Nueva Gerona Cuba **96** 21.53N 82.49W
Nuevitas Cuba **97** 21.34N 77.18W
Nuevo Laredo Mexico **90** 27.30N 99.30W
Nuevo Leon *d.* Mexico **96** 26.00N 99.00W
Nukha U.S.S.R. **57** 41.12N 47.10E
Nullarbor Plain *f.* Australia **79** 31.30S 128.00E
Nuneaton England **28** 52.32N 1.29W
Nungo Moçambique **73** 13.25S 37.45E
Nunivak I. U.S.A. **92** 60.00N 166.30W
Nunkiang China **63** 49.10N 125.15E
Nuqra Saudi Arabia **56** 25.35N 41.28E
Nure *r.* Italy **40** 45.06N 9.50E
Nurmes Finland **46** 63.32N 29.10E
Nürnberg W. Germany **44** 49.27N 11.05E
Nusaybin Turkey **56** 37.05N 41.11E
Nuweveld Mts. R.S.A. **74** 32.00S 21.50E
Nyahururu Kenya **73** 0.04N 36.22E
Nyakanazi Tanzania **73** 3.05S 31.16E
Nyala Sudan **69** 12.01N 24.50E
Nyamandhlovu Rhodesia **74** 19.50S 28.15E
Nyanga *r.* Gabon **72** 3.00S 10.17E
Nyanza *d.* Kenya **73** 0.30S 34.30E
Nyanza Rwanda **73** 2.20S 29.42E
Nyasa, L. *see* Malaŵi, L. Africa **73**
Nybro Sweden **46** 56.44N 15.55E
Nyeri Kenya **73** 0.22S 36.56E
Nyika Plateau *f.* Malaŵi **73** 10.25S 33.50E
Nyiru, Mt. Kenya **73** 2.06N 36.44E
Nyköbing Falster Denmark **44** 54.47N 11.53E
Nyköbing Thisted Denmark **46** 56.49N 8.50E
Nyköping Sweden **46** 58.45N 17.03E
Nylstroom R.S.A. **74** 24.42S 28.20E
Nymagee Australia **80** 32.05S 146.20E
Nynäshamn Sweden **46** 58.54N 17.55E
Nyngan Australia **80** 31.34S 147.14E
Nyong *r.* Cameroon **71** 3.15N 9.55E
Nyons France **40** 44.22N 5.08E
Nyunzu Zaïre **73** 5.55S 28.00E
Nzega Tanzania **73** 4.13S 33.09E
N'zérékoré Guinea **70** 7.49N 8.48W

O

Oadby England **28** 52.37N 1.07W
Oahe Resr. U.S.A. **90** 45.45N 100.20W
Oahu *i.* Hawaii U.S.A. **90** 21.30N 158.00W
Oakengates England **28** 52.42N 2.29W
Oakham England **28** 52.40N 0.43W
Oakland U.S.A. **90** 37.50N 122.15W
Oak Lawn U.S.A. **94** 41.42N 87.45W
Oak Park *town* U.S.A. **94** 41.52N 87.47W
Oakville Canada **95** 43.27N 79.41W
Oamaru New Zealand **82** 45.07S 170.58E
Oasis *d.* Algeria **71** 22.00N 6.00E
Oaxaca Mexico **96** 17.05N 96.41W
Oaxaca *d.* Mexico **96** 17.30N 97.00W
Ob *r.* U.S.S.R. **48** 66.50N 69.00E
Ob, G. of U.S.S.R. **48** 68.30N 74.00E
Oba Canada **94** 49.04N 84.07W
Oban Scotland **34** 56.26N 5.28W
Obbia Somali Rep. **69** 5.20N 48.30E
Oberhausen W. Germany **45** 51.28N 6.51E
Obi *i.* Indonesia **61** 1.45S 127.30E
Obo C.A.R. **73** 5.18N 26.28E
Obuasi Ghana **70** 6.15N 1.36W
Ocaña Spain **41** 39.57N 3.30W
Occidental, Cordillera *mts.* Colombia **97** 7.00N 76.15W
Ochil Hills Scotland **35** 56.16N 3.25W
Ock *r.* England **28** 51.40N 1.18W
Ocotlán Mexico **96** 20.21N 102.42W
October Revolution *i.* U.S.S.R. **49** 79.30N 96.00E
Ocua Moçambique **73** 13.37S 39.42E
Oda Ghana **70** 5.55N 0.56W
Odádhahraun *mts.* Iceland **46** 65.00N 17.30W
Odda Norway **46** 60.03N 6.45E
Oddur Somali Rep. **73** 4.11N 43.52E
Ödemis Turkey **43** 38.12N 28.00E
Odense Denmark **46** 55.24N 10.25E
Odenwald *mts.* W. Germany **44** 49.40N 9.20E
Oder *r.* Europe **44** 53.30N 14.36E
Odessa U.S.A. **90** 31.50N 102.23W
Odessa U.S.S.R. **47** 46.30N 30.46E
Odienné Ivory Coast **70** 9.36N 7.32W
Odorhei Romania **43** 46.18N 25.18E
Odzi *r.* Rhodesia **74** 19.49S 32.15E
Ofanto *r.* Italy **42** 41.22N 16.12E
Offaly *d.* Rep. of Ire. **39** 53.15N 7.30W
Offenbach W. Germany **44** 50.06N 8.46E
Offenburg W. Germany **44** 48.29N 7.57E
Ogbomosho Nigeria **71** 8.05N 4.11E
Ogden U.S.A. **90** 41.14N 111.59W
Ogdensburg U.S.A. **95** 44.42N 75.31W
Ogeechee *r.* U.S.A. **91** 32.54N 81.05W
Ognon *r.* France **40** 47.20N 5.37E
Ogoja Nigeria **71** 6.40N 8.45E
Ogoki *r.* Canada **91** 51.00N 84.30W
Ogosta *r.* Bulgaria **43** 43.44N 23.51E
Ogowe *r.* Gabon **72** 1.00S 9.05E
Ogulin Yugo. **42** 45.17N 15.14E
Ogun *d.* Nigeria **71** 6.50N 3.20E
Ohakune New Zealand **82** 39.24S 175.25E
Ohio *d.* U.S.A. **94** 40.10N 82.20W
Ohio *r.* U.S.A. **94** 37.07N 89.10W
Ohře *r.* Czech. **44** 50.32N 14.08E
Ohrid Yugo. **43** 41.06N 20.48E
Ohridsko, L. Albania/Yugo. **43** 41.00N 20.43E
Oich *r.* Scotland **37** 57.04N 4.46W
Oich, Loch Scotland **37** 57.04N 4.46W
Oil City U.S.A. **95** 41.26N 79.44W
Oise *r.* France **40** 49.00N 2.10E
Ojocaliente Mexico **96** 22.35N 102.18W
Ojo de Agua Argentina **103** 29.30S 63.44W
Oka *r.* U.S.S.R. **47** 56.09N 43.00E
Okahandja S.W. Africa **74** 21.59S 16.58E
Okaihau New Zealand **82** 35.18S 173.47E
Okanogan *r.* U.S.A. **90** 47.45N 120.05W
Okavango *r.* Botswana **74** 18.30S 22.04E
Okavango Basin *f.* Botswana **74** 19.30S 23.00E
Okayama Japan **63** 34.40N 133.54E
Okeechobee, L. U.S.A. **91** 27.00N 80.45W
Okeefenoke Swamp *f.* U.S.A. **91** 30.40N 82.40W
Okehampton England **31** 50.44N 4.01W
Okement *r.* England **31** 50.50N 4.04W
Okere *r.* Uganda **73** 1.37N 33.53E
Okha India **58** 22.29N 69.09E
Okha U.S.S.R. **49** 53.35N 142.50E
Okhotsk U.S.S.R. **49** 59.20N 143.15E
Okhotsk, Sea of U.S.S.R. **49** 55.00N 150.00E
Oki gunto *is.* Japan **63** 36.30N 133.20E
Okinawa *i.* Japan **63** 26.30N 128.00E
Okipoko *r.* S.W. Africa **74** 18.40S 16.03E
Okitipupa Nigeria **71** 6.31N 4.50E
Oklahoma *d.* U.S.A. **91** 35.00N 97.00W
Oklahoma City U.S.A. **91** 35.28N 97.33W
Öland *i.* Sweden **46** 56.50N 16.50E
Olary Australia **80** 32.18S 140.19E
Olavarria Argentina **103** 36.57S 60.20W
Olbia Italy **42** 40.55N 9.29E
Old Crow Canada **92** 67.34N 139.43W
Oldenburg Niedersachsen West W. Germany **45** 53.08N 8.13E
Oldenburg Schleswig Holstein W. Germany **44** 54.17N 10.52E
Oldenzaal Neth. **45** 52.19N 6.55E
Old Fletton England **29** 52.34N 0.14W
Oldham England **32** 53.33N 2.08W
Old Head of Kinsale *c.* Rep. of Ire. **39** 51.37N 8.33W
Oldmeldrum Scotland **37** 57.20N 2.20W
Old Rhine *r.* Neth. **45** 52.14N 4.26E
Old Windsor England **27** 51.28N 0.35W
Olean U.S.A. **95** 42.05N 78.26W
Olekma *r.* U.S.S.R. **49** 60.20N 120.30E
Olekminsk U.S.S.R. **49** 60.25N 120.00E
Olenek U.S.S.R. **49** 68.38N 112.15E
Olenek *r.* U.S.S.R. **49** 73.00N 120.00E
Olenekskiy G. U.S.S.R. **49** 74.00N 120.00E
Oléron, Île d' *i.* France **40** 45.55N 1.16W
Olga U.S.S.R. **63** 43.46N 135.14E
Olhão Portugal **41** 37.01N 7.50W
Olifants *r.* Cape Province R.S.A. **74** 31.43S 18.10E
Olifants *r.* Transvaal R.S.A. **74** 24.08S 32.40E
Olifants *r.* S.W. Africa **74** 25.28S 19.23E
Olivares Spain **41** 39.45N 2.21W
Olney England **28** 52.09N 0.42W
Ölögey Mongolia **62** 48.54N 90.00E
Olomouc Czech. **47** 49.38N 17.15E
Oloron France **40** 43.12N 0.35W
Olot Spain **41** 42.11N 2.30E
Olpe W. Germany **45** 51.02N 7.52E
Olsztyn Poland **47** 53.48N 20.29E
Oltenița Romania **43** 44.05N 26.31E
Oltet *r.* Romania **43** 44.13N 24.28E
Olympus, Mt. Cyprus **56** 34.55N 32.52E
Olympus, Mt. Greece **43** 40.04N 22.20E
Omagh N. Ireland **38** 54.36N 7.20W
Omaha U.S.A. **91** 41.15N 96.00W
Oman Asia **58** 22.30N 57.30E
Oman, G. of Asia **57** 25.00N 58.00E
Omarama New Zealand **82** 44.29S 169.59E
Omaruru S.W. Africa **74** 21.28S 15.56E
Ombrone *r.* Italy **42** 42.40N 11.00E
Omdurman Sudan **69** 15.37N 32.59E
Ommen Neth. **45** 52.32N 6.25E
Omolon *r.* U.S.S.R. **49** 68.50N 158.30E
Omsk U.S.S.R. **48** 55.00N 73.22E
Omuramba Omatako *r.* S.W. Africa **74** 17.59S 20.32E
Omuta Japan **63** 33.02N 130.26E
Oña Spain **41** 42.44N 3.25W
Onda Spain **41** 39.58N 0.16W
Ondangua S.W. Africa **74** 17.59S 16.02E
Ondo *d.* Nigeria **70** 7.10N 5.20E
Onega, L. U.S.S.R. **48** 62.00N 35.30E
Oneida L. U.S.A. **95** 43.13N 75.55W
Oneonta U.S.A. **95** 42.28N 75.04W
Onitsha Nigeria **71** 6.10N 6.47E
Onslow Village England **27** 51.14N 0.36W
Onstwedde Neth. **45** 53.04N 7.02E
Ontario *d.* Canada **94** 47.00N 80.40W
Ontario, L. N. America **95** 43.40N 78.00W
Ontonagon U.S.A. **94** 46.52N 89.18W
Oosterhout Neth. **45** 51.38N 4.50E
Oosthuizen Neth. **45** 52.33N 5.00E
Oostmalle Belgium **45** 51.18N 4.45E
Opala Zaïre **72** 0.42S 24.15E
Opole Poland **47** 50.40N 17.56E
Oporto Portugal **41** 41.09N 8.37W
Opotiki New Zealand **82** 38.00S 177.18E
Opunake New Zealand **82** 39.27S 173.52E
Oradea Romania **47** 47.03N 21.55E
Orai India **58** 26.00N 79.26E
Oran Algeria **41** 35.45N 0.38W
Orán Argentina **103** 23.07S 64.16W
Orange Australia **80** 33.19S 149.10E
Orange France **40** 44.08N 4.48E
Orange *r.* R.S.A. **74** 28.43S 16.30E
Orangeburg U.S.A. **91** 33.28N 80.53W
Orange Free State *d.* R.S.A. **74** 29.00S 26.30E
Oranjemond S.W. Africa **74** 28.38S 16.24E
Oranmore Rep. of Ire. **39** 53.17N 8.52W
Orbost Australia **80** 37.42S 148.30E
Orchies France **45** 50.28N 3.15E
Orchila *i.* Venezuela **97** 11.52N 66.10W
Orchy *r.* Scotland **34** 56.25N 5.02W
Ord *r.* Australia **79** 15.30S 128.30E
Ordu Turkey **56** 41.00N 37.52E
Orduna Spain **41** 43.00N 3.00W
Ordzhonikidze U.S.S.R. **47** 43.02N 44.43E
Örebro Sweden **46** 59.17N 15.13E
Oregon *d.* U.S.A. **90** 44.00N 120.00W
Öregrund Sweden **46** 60.20N 18.30E
Orekhovo Zuyevo U.S.S.R. **47** 55.47N 39.00E
Orel U.S.S.R. **47** 52.58N 36.04E
Ore Mts. E. Germany **44** 50.30N 12.50E
Orenburg U.S.S.R. **48** 51.50N 55.00E
Orense Spain **41** 42.20N 7.52W
Ore Sund *str.* Denmark **46** 56.00N 12.30E
Oreti *r.* New Zealand **82** 46.27S 168.14E
Orford England **29** 52.06N 1.31E
Orford Ness *c.* England **29** 52.05N 1.36E
Oriental, Cordillera *mts.* Bolivia **103** 17.00S 65.00W
Oriental, Cordillera *mts.* Colombia **97** 6.30N 74.30W
Oriente *d.* Cuba **97** 20.30N 75.30W
Orihuela Spain **41** 38.05N 0.56W
Orinoco *r.* Venezuela **97** 9.00N 61.30W
Orinoco Delta *f.* Venezuela **97** 9.00N 61.30W
Orissa *d.* India **59** 20.15N 84.00E
Oristano Italy **42** 39.53N 8.36E
Oristano, G. of Med. Sea **42** 39.50N 8.30E
Ori Vesi *l.* Finland **46** 62.20N 29.30E
Orizaba Mexico **96** 18.51N 97.08W
Orkney Is. *d.* Scotland **37** 59.00N 3.00W
Orlando U.S.A. **91** 28.33N 81.21W
Orléans France **40** 47.54N 1.54E
Ormiston Scotland **35** 55.55N 2.56W
Ormskirk England **32** 53.35N 2.53W
Orne *r.* France **40** 49.17N 0.10W
Ornsay *i.* Scotland **36** 57.08N 5.49W
Ornsköldsvik Sweden **46** 63.19N 18.45E
Oromocto Canada **95** 45.50N 66.28W
Oronsay *i.* Scotland **34** 56.01N 6.14W
Orosei Italy **42** 40.23N 9.40E
Orosei, G. of Med. Sea **42** 40.15N 9.45E
Oroville U.S.A. **90** 48.57N 119.27W
Orpington England **27** 51.23N 0.06E
Orrin *r.* Scotland **37** 57.33N 4.29W
Orsett England **27** 51.31N 0.23E
Orsha U.S.S.R. **47** 54.30N 30.23E
Orsk U.S.S.R. **48** 51.13N 58.35E
Orșova Romania **43** 44.42N 22.22E
Orthez France **40** 43.29N 0.46W
Ortles *mtn.* Italy **44** 46.30N 10.30E
Oryakhovo Bulgaria **43** 43.42N 23.58E
Osaka Japan **63** 34.40N 135.30E
Osa Pen. Costa Rica **96** 8.20N 83.30W
Oshawa Canada **95** 43.53N 78.51W

Oshkosh U.S.A. **94** 44.01N 88.32W
Oshogbo Nigeria **71** 7.50N 4.35E
Oshwe Zaïre **72** 3.27S 19.32E
Osijek Yugo. **43** 45.35N 18.43E
Oskarshamn Sweden **46** 57.16N 16.25E
Oskol *r.* U.S.S.R. **47** 49.08N 37.10E
Oslo Norway **46** 59.56N 10.45E
Oslo Fjord *est.* Norway **46** 59.30N 10.30E
Osmancik Turkey **56** 40.58N 34.50E
Osmaniye Turkey **56** 37.04N 36.15E
Osnabrück W. Germany **45** 52.17N 8.03E
Osorno Spain **41** 42.24N 4.22W
Oss Neth. **45** 51.46N 5.31E
Ossa *mtn.* Greece **43** 39.47N 22.41E
Ossa, Mt. Australia **80** 41.52S 146.04E
Osse *r.* Nigeria **71** 5.55N 5.15E
Ossett England **33** 53.40N 1.35W
Ostashkov U.S.S.R. **47** 57.09N 33.10E
Oste *r.* W. Germany **44** 53.10N 9.40E
Ostend Belgium **45** 51.13N 2.55E
Österdal *r.* Sweden **46** 61.03N 14.30E
Österö *i.* Faroe Is. **46** 62.10N 7.00W
Östersund Sweden **46** 63.10N 14.40E
Östhammar Sweden **46** 60.15N 18.25E
Ostrava Czech. **47** 49.50N 18.15E
Ostrov U.S.S.R. **46** 57.22N 28.22E
Ostrów Mazowiecka Poland **47** 52.50N 21.51E
Osŭm *r.* Bulgaria **43** 43.41N 24.51E
Osumi gunto *is.* Japan **63** 30.30N 130.40E
Osuna Spain **41** 37.14N 5.06W
Oswego U.S.A. **95** 43.27N 76.31W
Oswestry England **30** 52.52N 3.03W
Otago Pen. New Zealand **82** 45.48S 170.45E
Otaru Japan **63** 43.14N 140.59E
Otavi S.W. Africa **74** 19.39S 17.20E
Otford England **27** 51.19N 0.12E
Oti *r.* Ghana **70** 8.43N 0.10E
Otjiwarongo S.W. Africa **74** 20.29S 16.36E
Otley England **32** 53.54N 1.41W
Otra *r.* Norway **46** 58.10N 8.00E
Otranto Italy **43** 40.09N 18.30E
Otranto, Str. of Med. Sea **43** 40.10N 19.00E
Otta Norway **46** 61.46N 9.33E
Ottawa Canada **95** 45.25N 75.43W
Ottawa *r.* Canada **95** 45.23N 73.55W
Ottawa Is. Canada **93** 59.50N 80.00W
Otter *r.* England **31** 50.38N 3.19W
Otterburn England **35** 55.14N 2.10W
Ottery St. Mary England **31** 50.45N 3.16W
Ottumwa U.S.A. **94** 41.02N 92.26W
Otway, C. Australia **80** 38.51S 143.34E
Ouachita *r.* U.S.A. **91** 33.10N 92.10W
Ouachita Mts. U.S.A. **91** 34.40N 94.30W
Ouagadougou U. Volta **70** 12.20N 1.40W
Ouahigouya U. Volta **70** 13.31N 2.21W
Ouargla Algeria **68** 32.00N 5.16E
Oudenarde Belgium **45** 50.50N 3.37E
Oudtshoorn R.S.A. **74** 33.35S 22.12E
Ouerk *r.* Algeria **41** 35.15N 2.15E
Ouessant, Ile d' *i.* France **40** 48.28N 5.05W
Ouesso Congo **72** 1.38N 16.03E
Ouezzane Morocco **41** 34.52N 5.35W
Oughter, Lough Rep. of Ire. **38** 54.01N 7.28W
Oughterard Rep. of Ire. **38** 53.27N 9.22W
Ouham *r.* Chad **71** 9.15N 18.13E
Oujda Morocco **68** 34.41N 1.45W
Oulu Finland **46** 65.02N 25.27E
Oulu *r.* Finland **46** 65.04N 25.23E
Oulu Järvi *l.* Finland **46** 64.30N 27.00E
Ounas *r.* Finland **46** 66.33N 25.37E
Oundle England **29** 52.28N 0.28W
Our *r.* Lux. **45** 49.53N 6.16E
Ourinhos Brazil **103** 23.00S 49.54W
Ourthe *r.* Belgium **45** 50.38N 5.36E
Ouse *r.* E. Sussex England **29** 50.46N 0.03E
Ouse *r.* Humber. England **33** 53.41N 0.42W
Outer Hebrides *is.* Scotland **36** 57.40N 7.35W
Outjo S.W. Africa **74** 20.08S 16.08E
Out Skerries *is.* Scotland **36** 60.20N 0.45W
Outwell England **29** 52.36N 0.15E
Ouyen Australia **80** 35.06S 142.22E
Ovambo *f.* S.W. Africa **74** 17.45S 16.00E
Overath W. Germany **45** 50.56N 7.18E
Overflakkee *i.* Neth. **45** 51.45N 4.08E
Overijssel *d.* Neth. **45** 52.25N 6.30E
Overton England **28** 51.15N 1.15W
Overton Wales **30** 52.58N 2.56W
Overuman *l.* Sweden **46** 66.06N 14.40E
Oviedo Spain **41** 43.21N 5.50W
Owel, Lough Rep. of Ire. **38** 53.34N 7.24W
Owen Falls Dam Uganda **73** 0.30N 33.07E
Oweniny *r.* Rep. of Ire. **38** 54.08N 9.51W
Owenkillew *r.* N. Ireland **34** 54.43N 7.23W
Owen Sound *town* Canada **94** 44.34N 80.56W
Owen Stanley Range *mts.* P.N.G. **79** 9.30S 148.00E
Owerri Nigeria **71** 5.29N 7.02E
Owo Nigeria **71** 7.10N 5.39E
Owosso U.S.A. **94** 43.00N 84.11W
Oxelösund Sweden **46** 58.40N 17.10E
Oxford England **28** 51.45N 1.15W
Oxfordshire *d.* England **28** 51.46N 1.10W
Oxley Australia **80** 34.11S 144.10E
Oxley's Peak *mtn.* Australia **80** 31.48S 150.17E
Oxshott England **27** 51.19N 0.20W
Oxted England **27** 51.16N 0.01E
Oykel *r.* Scotland **37** 57.53N 4.21W
Oykel Bridge *town* Scotland **37** 57.57N 4.44W
Oymyakon U.S.S.R. **49** 63.30N 142.44E
Oyo Nigeria **71** 7.50N 3.55E
Oyo *d.* Nigeria **71** 8.10N 3.40E
Oyster B. Australia **80** 42.10S 148.10E
Ozamiz Phil. **61** 8.09N 123.59E
Ozark Plateau U.S.A. **91** 36.00N 93.35W

P

Paan China **59** 30.02N 99.01E
Paarl R.S.A. **74** 33.45S 18.58E
Pabbay *i.* W. Isles Scotland **36** 57.46N 7.14W
Pabbay *i.* W. Isles Scotland **36** 56.51N 7.35W
Pabna Bangla. **58** 24.00N 89.15E
Pachuca Mexico **96** 20.10N 98.44W
Pacific Ocean 106
Padang Indonesia **60** 0.55S 100.21E
Paddington England **27** 51.31N 0.12W
Paddock Wood England **29** 51.11N 0.23E
Paderborn W. Germany **44** 51.43N 8.44E
Padre I. U.S.A. **91** 27.00N 97.20W
Padstow England **31** 50.33N 4.57W
Padua Italy **42** 45.27N 11.52E
Pag *i.* Yugo. **42** 44.28N 15.00E
Pagai Selatan *i.* Indonesia **60** 3.00S 100.30E
Pagai Utara *i.* Indonesia **60** 2.40S 100.10E
Pagan *i.* Asia **61** 18.08N 145.46E
Pager *r.* Uganda **73** 3.05N 32.28E
Pahala Hawaii U.S.A. **90** 19.12N 155.28W
Paible Scotland **36** 57.35N 7.27W
Paijänne *l.* Finland **46** 61.30N 25.30E
Paimboeuf France **40** 47.14N 2.01W
Painesville U.S.A. **94** 41.43N 81.15W
Painswick England **28** 51.47N 2.11W
Paisley Scotland **34** 55.50N 4.26W
Pakanbaru Indonesia **60** 0.33N 101.20E
Pakhoi China **60** 21.39N 109.10E
Pakistan Asia **58** 30.00N 70.00E
Pak Lay Laos **60** 18.10N 101.24E
Pakse Laos **60** 15.05N 105.50E
Pakwach Uganda **73** 2.27N 31.18E
Palana U.S.S.R. **49** 59.05N 159.59E
Palapye Botswana **74** 22.37S 27.06E
Palau Is. Asia **61** 7.00N 134.25E
Palawan *i.* Phil. **60** 9.30N 118.30E
Paldiski U.S.S.R. **47** 59.22N 24.08E
Palembang Indonesia **60** 2.59S 104.50E
Palencia Spain **41** 42.01N 4.34W
Palenque Mexico **96** 17.32N 91.59W
Palermo Italy **42** 38.09N 13.22E
Palit, C. Albania **43** 41.24N 19.23E
Palk Str. India/Sri Lanka **59** 10.00N 79.40E
Pallaskenry Rep. of Ire. **39** 52.39N 8.52W
Palliser, C. New Zealand **82** 41.35S 175.15E
Palma Moçambique **73** 10.48S 40.25E
Palma Spain **41** 39.36N 2.39E
Palma, B. of Spain **41** 39.30N 2.40E
Palma del Rio Spain **41** 37.43N 5.17W
Palmas, C. Liberia **70** 4.30N 7.55W
Palmas, G. of Med. Sea **42** 39.00N 8.30E
Palmeirinhas, Punta das Angola **72** 9.09S 12.58E
Palmerston New Zealand **82** 45.30S 170.42E
Palmerston North New Zealand **82** 40.20S 175.39E
Palmi Italy **42** 38.22N 15.50E
Palm Springs *town* U.S.A. **90** 33.49N 116.34W
Palmyra Syria **56** 34.36N 38.15E
Palmyras Pt. India **59** 20.40N 87.00E
Paloh Indonesia **60** 1.46N 109.17E
Palopo Indonesia **61** 3.01S 120.12E
Pamekasan Indonesia **60** 7.11S 113.50E
Pamiers France **40** 43.07N 1.36E
Pamirs *mts.* U.S.S.R. **62** 37.50N 73.30E
Pampa U.S.A. **90** 35.32N 100.58W
Pampas *f.* Argentina **103** 34.00S 64.00W
Pamplona Colombia **97** 7.24N 72.38W
Pamplona Spain **41** 42.49N 1.39W
Panama C. America **97** 9.00N 80.00W
Panamá, G. of Panama **97** 8.30N 79.00W
Panama Canal Zone C. America **97** 9.10N 79.55W
Panamá City Panama **97** 8.57N 79.30W
Panama City U.S.A. **91** 30.10N 85.41W
Panay *i.* Phil. **61** 11.10N 122.30E
Panevežys U.S.S.R. **46** 55.44N 24.24E
Pangani Tanga Tanzania **73** 5.21S 39.00E
Pangi Zaïre **73** 3.10S 26.38E
Pangkalpinang Indonesia **60** 2.05S 106.09E
Pangnirtung Canada **93** 66.05N 65.45W
Pantano del Esla *l.* Spain **41** 41.40N 5.50W
Pantelleria *i.* Italy **42** 36.48N 12.00E
Paoki China **62** 34.23N 107.16E
Páola Italy **42** 39.21N 16.03E
Paoshan China **59** 25.07N 99.08E
Paoting China **63** 38.54N 115.26E
Paotow China **63** 40.38N 109.59E
Papa Stour *i.* Scotland **36** 60.20N 1.42W
Papa Westray *i.* Scotland **37** 59.22N 2.54W
Papenburg W. Germany **45** 53.05N 7.25E
Paphos Cyprus **56** 34.45N 32.25E
Paps of Jura *mts.* Scotland **34** 55.55N 6.00W
Papua, G. of P.N.G. **61** 8.50S 145.00E
Papua New Guinea Austa. **61** 6.00S 143.00E
Paracatu Brazil **103** 17.14S 46.52W
Paracatu *r.* Brazil **103** 16.30S 45.10W
Paracel Is. Asia **60** 16.20N 112.00E
Paragua *r.* Venezuela **97** 6.45N 63.00W
Paraguaná Pen. Venezuela **97** 12.00N 70.00W
Paraguarí Paraguay **103** 25.36S 57.06W
Paraguay *r.* Argentina **103** 27.30S 58.50W
Paraguay S. America **103** 23.00S 57.00W
Parakou Benin **71** 9.23N 2.40E
Paramaribo Surinam **102** 5.52N 55.14W
Paraná Argentina **103** 31.45S 60.30W
Paraná *r.* Argentina **103** 34.00S 58.30W
Paraná *d.* Brazil **103** 24.30S 52.00W
Paranaguá Brazil **103** 25.32S 48.36W
Paranaiba *r.* Brazil **103** 20.00S 51.00W
Paranapanema *r.* Brazil **103** 22.30S 53.03W
Paranapiacaba, Serra *mts.* Brazil **103** 24.30S 49.15W
Parana Plateau Paraguay **103** 24.32S 55.00W
Pardo *r.* Brazil **103** 20.10S 48.30W
Pardubice Czech. **44** 50.03N 15.45E
Parece Vela *i.* Asia **61** 20.24N 136.02E
Parepare Indonesia **60** 4.03S 119.40E
Paria, G. of Venezuela **97** 10.30N 62.00W
Pariaman Indonesia **60** 0.36S 100.09E
Paria Pen. Venezuela **97** 10.45N 62.30W
Paris France **40** 48.52N 2.20E
Park *f.* Scotland **36** 58.05N 6.32W
Parkano Finland **46** 62.03N 23.00E
Parker Dam U.S.A. **90** 34.25N 114.05W
Parkersburg U.S.A. **94** 39.17N 81.33W
Parkes Australia **80** 33.10S 148.13E
Park Falls *town* U.S.A. **94** 45.57N 90.28W
Park Forest *town* U.S.A. **94** 41.28N 87.40W
Parkville U.S.A. **95** 39.23N 76.32W
Parma Italy **42** 44.48N 10.18E
Parma U.S.A. **94** 41.24N 81.44W
Parnassos *mtn.* Greece **43** 38.33N 22.35E
Pärnu U.S.S.R. **46** 58.28N 24.30E
Pärnu *r.* U.S.S.R. **46** 58.23N 24.32E
Paroo *r.* Australia **80** 31.30S 143.34E
Paropamisus Mts. Afghan. **57** 34.30N 63.30E
Páros *i.* Greece **43** 37.04N 25.11E
Parral Mexico **90** 26.58N 105.40W
Parramatta Australia **80** 33.50S 150.57E
Parrett *r.* England **28** 51.10N 3.00W
Parry, C. Greenland **93** 76.50N 71.00W
Parry Is. Canada **93** 76.00N 102.00W
Parry Sound *town* Canada **94** 45.21N 80.03W
Parseta *r.* Poland **44** 54.12N 15.33E
Partabpur India **58** 23.28N 83.15E
Parthenay France **40** 46.39N 0.14W
Partry Mts. Rep. of Ire. **38** 53.40N 9.30W
Parys R.S.A. **74** 26.55S 27.28E
Pasadena U.S.A. **90** 34.10N 118.09W
Pas de Calais *d.* France **29** 50.30N 2.30E
Paso de los Toros *town* Uruguay **103** 32.45S 56.47W
Passage East *town* Rep. of Ire. **39** 52.14N 7.00W
Passage West *town* Rep. of Ire. **39** 51.52N 8.20W
Passau W. Germany **44** 48.35N 13.28E
Passero, C. Italy **42** 36.40N 15.08E
Pass of Thermopylae Greece **43** 38.47N 22.34E
Passo Fundo Brazil **103** 28.16S 52.20W
Pasvik *r.* Norway **46** 69.45N 30.00E
Patagonia *f.* Argentina **103** 40.20S 67.00W
Pate I. Kenya **73** 2.08S 41.02E
Pateley Bridge *town* England **32** 54.05N 1.45W
Paterson U.S.A. **95** 40.55N 74.10W
Pathari India **58** 23.56N 78.12E
Pathfinder Resr. U.S.A. **90** 42.25N 106.55W
Patiala India **58** 30.21N 76.27E
Patkai Hills Burma **59** 26.30N 95.40E
Patna India **58** 25.37N 85.12E
Patna Scotland **34** 55.22N 4.30W
Patos, L. Brazil **103** 31.00S 51.10W
Pátras Greece **43** 38.15N 21.45E
Patras, G. of Med. Sea **43** 38.15N 21.35E
Patrickswell Rep. of Ire. **39** 52.36N 8.43W
Patrington England **33** 53.41N 0.02W

Patuca r. Honduras **96** 30.48N 84.25W
Pau France **40** 43.18N 0.22W
Pauillac France **40** 45.12N 0.44W
Pavia Italy **40** 45.12N 9.09E
Pavlodar U.S.S.R. **48** 52.21N 76.59E
Pavlograd U.S.S.R. **47** 48.34N 35.50E
Pawtucket U.S.A. **95** 41.53N 71.23W
Payne r. Canada **93** 60.00N 69.45W
Paysandú Uruguay **103** 32.21S 58.05W
Peace r. Canada **92** 59.00N 111.26W
Peace River town Canada **92** 56.15N 117.18W
Peace River Resr. Canada **92** 55.00N 126.00W
Peaked Mtn. Canada **95** 46.34N 68.49W
Peak Hill town Australia **80** 32.47S 148.13E
Peale, Mt. U.S.A. **90** 38.26N 109.14W
Pearl r. U.S.A. **91** 30.15N 89.25W
Pebane Moçambique **73** 17.14S 38.10E
Pec Yugo. **43** 42.40N 20.17E
Pechenga U.S.S.R. **46** 69.28N 31.04E
Pechora r. U.S.S.R. **48** 68.10N 54.00E
Pechora G. U.S.S.R. **48** 69.00N 56.00E
Pecos U.S.A. **96** 31.25N 103.30W
Pecos r. U.S.A. **90** 29.45N 101.25W
Pécs Hungary **43** 46.05N 18.14E
Pedro J. Caballero Paraguay **103** 22.30S 55.44W
Peebinga Australia **80** 34.55S 140.57E
Peebles Scotland **35** 55.39N 3.12W
Peel r. Canada **92** 68.13N 135.00W
Peel I.o.M. **32** 54.14N 4.42W
Peel f. Neth. **45** 51.30N 5.50E
Peel Fell mtn. England/Scotland **35** 55.17N 2.35W
Peene r. E. Germany **44** 53.53N 13.49E
Pegasus B. New Zealand **82** 43.15S 173.00E
Pegu Burma **59** 17.18N 96.31E
Pegu Yoma mts. Burma **59** 18.40N 96.00E
Pegwell B. England **29** 51.18N 1.25E
Pehan China **63** 48.17N 126.33E
Pehuajó Argentina **103** 35.50S 61.50W
Peipus, L. U.S.S.R. **46** 58.30N 27.30E
Pekalongan Indonesia **60** 6.54S 109.37E
Pekin U.S.A. **94** 40.34N 89.40W
Peking China **63** 39.55N 116.25E
Pelat, Mont mtn. France **40** 44.17N 6.41E
Pelee, Pt. Canada **94** 41.45N 82.09W
Peleng i. Indonesia **61** 1.30S 123.10E
Pelly r. Canada **92** 62.50N 137.35W
Pelotas Brazil **103** 31.45S 52.20W
Pematangsiantar Indonesia **60** 2.59N 99.01E
Pemba Moçambique **73** 13.02S 40.30E
Pemba I. Tanzania **73** 5.10S 39.45E
Pembridge England **28** 52.13N 2.54W
Pembroke Canada **95** 45.49N 77.08W
Pembroke Wales **31** 51.41N 4.57W
Penang I. Malaysia **60** 5.30N 100.10E
Peñaranda de Bracamonte Spain **41** 40.54N 5.13W
Penarth Wales **31** 51.26N 3.11W
Peñas, Cabo de Spain **41** 43.42N 5.52W
Pende r. Chad **71** 7.30N 16.20E
Pendembu Eastern Sierra Leone **70** 8.09N 10.42W
Pendine Wales **31** 51.44N 4.33W
Pendle Hill England **32** 53.52N 2.18W
Penganga r. India **59** 18.52N 79.56E
Penge England **27** 51.25N 0.04W
Pengpu China **63** 32.56N 117.27E
Penicuik Scotland **35** 55.49N 3.13W
Penistone England **32** 53.31N 1.38W
Penki China **63** 41.21N 123.45E
Penmaenmawr Wales **30** 53.16N 3.54W
Pennsylvania d. U.S.A. **95** 41.00N 75.45W
Penny Highland Canada **93** 67.10N 66.50W
Penobscot r. U.S.A. **95** 44.34N 68.48W
Penola Australia **80** 37.23S 140.21E
Penonomé Panamá **97** 8.30N 80.20W
Penrhyndeudraeth Wales **30** 52.56N 4.04W
Penrith Australia **80** 33.47S 150.44E
Penrith England **32** 54.40N 2.45W
Penryn England **31** 50.10N 5.07W
Pensacola U.S.A. **91** 30.30N 87.12W
Penticton Canada **90** 49.29N 119.38W
Pentire Pt. England **31** 50.35N 4.55W
Pentland Firth str. Scotland **37** 58.40N 3.00W
Pentland Hills Scotland **35** 55.50N 3.20W
Pen-y-ghent mtn. England **32** 54.10N 2.14W
Pen-y-groes Wales **30** 53.03N 4.18W
Penza U.S.S.R. **47** 53.11N 45.00E
Penzance England **31** 50.07N 5.32W
Penzhina, G. of U.S.S.R. **49** 61.00N 163.00E
Peoria U.S.A. **94** 40.43N 89.38W
Perekop U.S.S.R. **47** 46.10N 33.42E
Pergamino Argentina **103** 33.55S 60.32W
Peribonca r. Canada **91** 48.50N 72.00W
Périgueux France **40** 45.12N 0.44E
Perija, Sierra de mts. Venezuela **97** 9.00N 73.00W
Perim i. Asia **69** 12.40N 43.24E
Perm U.S.S.R. **48** 58.01N 56.10E
Pernik see Dimitrovo Bulgaria **43**
Péronne France **45** 49.56N 2.57E
Perpignan France **40** 42.42N 2.54E
Perranporth England **31** 50.21N 5.09W
Persepolis ruins Iran **57** 29.55N 53.00E
Pershore England **28** 52.07N 2.04W
Persian G. Asia **57** 27.00N 50.00E
Perth Australia **79** 31.58S 115.49E
Perth Scotland **35** 56.24N 3.28W
Perth Amboy U.S.A. **95** 40.32N 74.17W
Peru S. America **102** 10.00S 75.00W
Peru U.S.A. **94** 40.45N 86.04W
Peru-Chile Trench Pacific Oc. **106** 24.00S 74.00W
Perugia Italy **42** 43.06N 12.24E
Péruwelz Belgium **45** 50.32N 3.36E
Pésaro Italy **42** 43.54N 12.54E
Pescara Italy **42** 42.27N 14.13E
Pescara r. Italy **42** 42.28N 14.13E
Peshawar Pakistan **58** 34.01N 71.40E
Petatlán Mexico **96** 17.31N 101.16W
Petauke Zambia **73** 14.16S 31.21E
Peterborough Australia **80** 33.00S 138.51E
Peterborough Canada **95** 44.19N 78.20W
Peterborough England **29** 52.35N 0.14W
Peterhead Scotland **37** 57.30N 1.46W
Peterlee England **35** 54.45N 1.18W
Petersfield England **28** 51.00N 0.56W
Petra ruins Jordan **56** 30.19N 35.26E
Petrich Bulgaria **43** 41.25N 23.13E
Petropavlovsk U.S.S.R. **48** 54.53N 69.13E
Petropavlovsk Kamchatskiy U.S.S.R. **49** 53.03N 158.43E
Petrópolis Brazil **103** 22.30S 43.06W
Petrovsk Zabaykal'skiy U.S.S.R. **49** 51.20N 108.55E
Petrozavodsk U.S.S.R. **48** 61.46N 34.19E
Petworth England **28** 50.59N 0.37W
Pewsey England **28** 51.20N 1.46W
Pézenas France **40** 43.28N 3.25E
Pforzheim W. Germany **44** 48.53N 8.41E
Phan Rang Vietnam **60** 11.35N 109.00E
Phet Buri Thailand **59** 13.01N 99.55E
Philadelphia U.S.A. **95** 40.00N 75.10W
Philippeville Belgium **45** 50.12N 4.32E
Philippine Is. Asia **107** 10.00N 124.00E
Philippines Asia **61** 13.00N 123.00E
Philippine Trench Pacific Oc. **61** 8.45N 127.20E
Philipstown R.S.A. **74** 30.26S 24.28E
Phnom Penh Khmer Rep. **59** 11.35N 104.55E
Phoenix U.S.A. **90** 33.30N 111.55W
Phong Saly Laos **60** 21.40N 102.06E
Phukao Miang mtn. Thailand **59** 16.50N 101.00E
Phuket Thailand **59** 8.00N 98.28E
Phuket i. Thailand **60** 8.10N 98.20E
Phu Quoc i. Khmer Rep. **60** 10.10N 104.00E
Piacenza Italy **42** 45.03N 9.42E
Piangil Australia **80** 35.04S 143.20E
Pianosa i. Italy **42** 42.35N 10.05E
Piave r. Italy **42** 45.33N 12.45E
Pic r. Canada **94** 48.35N 86.17W
Picardy f. France **45** 49.47N 2.45E
Pickering England **33** 54.15N 0.46W
Pickwick L. U.S.A. **91** 35.00N 88.10W
Picton Canada **95** 44.01N 77.09W
Picton New Zealand **82** 41.17S 174.02E
Picton, Mt. Australia **80** 43.10S 146.30E
Piedras Negras Mexico **90** 28.40N 100.32W
Pieksämäki Finland **46** 62.18N 27.10E
Pielinen l. Finland **46** 63.20N 29.50E
Pierowall Scotland **37** 59.19N 3.00W
Pierre U.S.A. **90** 44.23N 100.20W
Pietermaritzburg R.S.A. **74** 29.36S 30.24E
Pietersburg R.S.A. **74** 23.54S 29.23E
Piet Retief R.S.A. **74** 27.00S 30.49E
Pigailoe i. Asia **61** 8.08N 146.40E
Pikes Peak U.S.A. **90** 38.50N 105.03W
Piketberg R.S.A. **74** 32.55S 18.45E
Piła Poland **44** 53.09N 16.44E
Pilcomayo r. Argentina/Paraguay **103** 25.15S 57.43W
Pilgrim's Hatch England **27** 51.37N 0.16E
Pilibhit India **58** 28.37N 79.48E
Pílos Greece **43** 36.55N 21.40E
Pinarbaşi Turkey **56** 38.43N 36.23E
Pinar del Rio Cuba **96** 22.24N 83.42W
Pinar del Rio d. Cuba **96** 22.30N 83.30W
Pindus Mts. Albania/Greece **43** 39.40N 21.00E
Pine Bluff U.S.A. **91** 34.13N 92.00W
Pines, I. of Cuba **96** 21.40N 82.40W
Ping r. Thailand **59** 15.45N 100.10E
Pingliang China **62** 35.25N 107.14E
Pini i. Indonesia **60** 0.10N 98.30E
Pinios r. Greece **43** 37.51N 22.37E
Pinnaroo Australia **80** 35.18S 140.54E
Pinner England **27** 51.36N 0.23W
Pinsk U.S.S.R. **47** 52.08N 26.01E
Pinto Argentina **103** 29.09S 62.38W
Piombino Italy **42** 42.56N 10.30E
Piqua U.S.A. **94** 40.08N 84.14W
Piquiri r. Brazil **103** 24.00S 54.00W
Piraeus Greece **43** 37.56N 23.38E
Pirapora Brazil **103** 17.20S 44.54W
Pirbright England **27** 51.18N 0.39W
Pírgos Greece **43** 37.42N 21.27E
Pirmasens W. Germany **44** 49.12N 7.37E
Pirna E. Germany **44** 50.58N 13.58E
Pirot Yugo. **43** 43.10N 22.32E
Pisa Italy **42** 43.43N 10.24E
Pisciotta Italy **42** 40.08N 15.12E
Pisek Czech. **44** 49.19N 14.10E
Pisuerga r. Spain **41** 41.35N 5.40W
Pita Guinea **70** 11.05N 12.15W
Pitea Sweden **46** 65.19N 21.30E
Piteşti Romania **43** 44.52N 24.51E
Pitlochry Scotland **37** 56.43N 3.45W
Pittenweem Scotland **35** 56.13N 2.44W
Pittsburgh U.S.A. **94** 40.26N 80.00W
Pittsfield U.S.A. **95** 42.27N 73.15W
Plain of Bornu f. Nigeria **71** 12.30N 13.00E
Plains of Ellertrin f. Rep. of Ire. **38** 53.37N 9.11W
Plains of Mayo f. Rep. of Ire. **38** 53.46N 9.05W
Plasencia Spain **41** 40.02N 6.05W
Platani r. Italy **42** 37.24N 13.15E
Plate, R. see la Plata, Rio de Argentina **103**
Plateau d. Nigeria **71** 8.50N 9.00E
Platí, C. Greece **43** 40.26N 23.59E
Platinum U.S.A. **92** 59.00N 161.50W
Platte r. U.S.A. **91** 41.05N 96.50W
Plattsburgh U.S.A. **95** 44.42N 73.29W
Plauen E. Germany **44** 50.29N 12.08E
Plenty, B. of New Zealand **82** 37.40S 176.50E
Pleven Bulgaria **43** 43.25N 24.39E
Pljevlja Yugo. **43** 43.22N 19.22E
Ploeşti Romania **43** 44.57N 26.02E
Plomb du Cantal mtn. France **40** 45.04N 2.45E
Plombières France **44** 47.58N 6.28E
Ploudalmézeau France **40** 48.33N 4.39W
Plovdiv Bulgaria **43** 42.09N 24.45E
Plumtree Rhodesia **74** 20.30S 27.50E
Plym r. England **31** 50.21N 4.06W
Plymouth England **31** 50.23N 4.09W
Plymouth Ind. U.S.A. **94** 41.20N 86.19W
Plymouth Mass. U.S.A. **95** 41.58N 70.40W
Plympton England **31** 50.24N 4.02W
Plzeň Czech. **44** 49.45N 13.22E
Po r. Italy **42** 44.51N 12.30E
Pô U. Volta **70** 11.11N 1.10W
Pobé Benin **71** 7.00N 2.56E
Pobeda, Mt. U.S.S.R. **49** 65.20N 145.50E
Pobedy mtn. China **62** 42.09N 80.12E
Pobla de Segur Spain **41** 42.15N 0.58E
Pocatello U.S.A. **90** 42.53N 112.26W
Pocklington England **33** 53.56N 0.48W
Podolsk U.S.S.R. **47** 55.23N 37.32E
Podor Senegal **70** 16.35N 15.02W
Pods Brook r. England **27** 51.52N 0.33E
Pofadder R.S.A. **74** 29.09S 19.25E
Poh Indonesia **61** 1.00S 122.50E
Pohsien China **63** 33.40N 115.50E
Pointe-à-Pitre Guadeloupe **97** 16.14N 61.32W
Pointe Noire town Congo **72** 4.46S 11.53E
Poitiers France **40** 46.35N 0.20E
Pokhara Nepal **58** 28.14N 83.58E
Poko Zaïre **73** 3.08N 26.51E
Pokotu China **63** 48.45N 121.58E
Poland Europe **47** 52.30N 19.00E
Polatli Turkey **56** 39.34N 32.08E
Polden Hills England **28** 51.07N 2.50W
Polegate England **29** 50.49N 0.15E
Policastro, G. of Med. Sea **42** 40.00N 15.35E
Poligny France **40** 46.50N 4.42E
Pollina mtn. Italy **42** 39.53N 16.11E
Pollnalaght mtn. N. Ireland **38** 54.34N 7.27W
Polperro England **31** 50.19N 4.31W
Poltava U.S.S.R. **47** 49.35N 34.35E
Pombal Portugal **41** 39.55N 8.38W
Ponce Puerto Rico **97** 18.00N 66.40W
Pondicherry India **59** 11.59N 79.50E
Pond Inlet str. Canada **93** 72.30N 75.00W
Ponferrada Spain **41** 42.32N 6.31W
Pongola r. Moçambique **74** 26.13S 32.38E
Ponta Grossa Brazil **103** 25.00S 50.09W
Pont-à-Mousson France **44** 48.55N 6.03E
Ponta Pora Brazil **103** 22.27S 55.39W
Pontardawe Wales **31** 51.44N 3.51W
Pontardulais Wales **31** 51.42N 4.03W
Pontchartrain, L. U.S.A. **96** 30.50N 90.00W
Pontefract England **33** 53.42N 1.19W
Ponteland England **35** 55.03N 1.43W
Ponterwyd Wales **30** 52.25N 3.50W
Pontevedra Spain **41** 42.25N 8.39W
Pontiac U.S.A. **94** 42.39N 83.18W
Pontianak Indonesia **60** 0.05S 109.16E
Pontine Is. Italy **42** 40.56N 12.58E
Pontine Mts. Turkey **56** 40.32N 38.00E
Pontoise France **40** 49.03N 2.05E

Pontrilas England **28** 51.56N 2.53W
Pontypool Wales **31** 51.42N 3.01W
Pontypridd Wales **28** 51.36N 3.21W
Poole England **28** 50.42N 2.02W
Poole B. England **28** 50.40N 1.55W
Poolewe Scotland **36** 57.45N 5.37W
Pooley Bridge *town* England **32** 54.37N 2.49W
Poona India **58** 18.34N 73.58E
Poperinge Belgium **45** 50.51N 2.44E
Poplar England **27** 51.31N 0.01E
Poplar Bluff U.S.A. **91** 36.40N 90.25W
Popocatépetl *mtn.* Mexico **96** 19.02N 98.38W
Popokabaka Zaïre **72** 5.41S 16.40E
Porahat India **58** 22.35N 85.27E
Porbandar India **58** 21.40N 69.40E
Porcupine *r.* U.S.A. **92** 66.25N 145.20W
Pori Finland **46** 61.28N 21.45E
Porkkala Finland **46** 60.00N 24.25E
Porlamar Venezuela **97** 11.01N 63.54W
Porlock England **31** 51.14N 3.36W
Pornic France **40** 47.07N 2.05W
Poronaysk U.S.S.R. **49** 49.13N 142.55E
Porsanger *est.* Norway **46** 70.30N 25.45E
Porsgrunn Norway **46** 59.10N 9.40E
Porsuk *r.* Turkey **56** 39.41N 31.56E
Port Adelaide Australia **80** 34.52S 138.30E
Portadown N. Ireland **38** 54.25N 6.27W
Portaferry N. Ireland **38** 54.23N 5.33W
Portage U.S.A. **94** 43.33N 89.29W
Portage la Prairie *town* Canada **90** 50.01N 98.20W
Portalegre Portugal **41** 39.17N 7.25W
Port Alfred R.S.A. **74** 33.36S 26.54E
Port Angeles U.S.A. **90** 48.06N 123.26W
Port Antonio Jamaica **97** 18.10N 76.27W
Portarlington Rep. of Ire. **39** 53.10N 7.12W
Port Arthur Australia **80** 43.08S 147.50E
Port Arthur U.S.A. **91** 29.55N 93.56W
Port Askaig Scotland **34** 55.51N 6.07W
Port Augusta Australia **79** 32.30S 137.46E
Port-au-Prince Haiti **97** 18.33N 72.20W
Port Austin U.S.A. **94** 44.04N 82.59W
Port aux Basques Canada **93** 47.35N 59.10W
Port Bannatyne Scotland **34** 55.52N 5.04W
Port Blair India **59** 11.40N 92.30E
Port Bou Spain **41** 42.25N 3.09E
Port Bouet Ivory Coast **70** 5.14N 3.58W
Port Burwell Canada **94** 42.39N 80.47W
Port Cartier Canada **93** 50.03N 66.46W
Port Charlotte Scotland **34** 55.45N 6.23W
Port Dinorwic Wales **30** 53.11N 4.12W
Port Elizabeth R.S.A. **74** 33.58S 25.36E
Port Ellen Scotland **34** 55.38N 6.12W
Port Erin I.o.M. **32** 54.05N 4.45W
Port-Eynon Wales **31** 51.33N 4.13W
Port Gentil Gabon **72** 0.40S 8.46E
Port Glasgow Scotland **34** 55.56N 4.40W
Portglenone N. Ireland **34** 54.52N 6.30W
Port Harcourt Nigeria **71** 4.43N 7.05E
Port Harrison Canada **93** 58.25N 78.18W
Porthcawl Wales **31** 51.28N 3.42W
Port Hedland Australia **79** 20.24S 118.36E
Porthmadog Wales **30** 52.55N 4.08W
Port Huron U.S.A. **94** 42.59N 82.28W
Portimão Portugal **41** 37.08N 8.32W
Port Isaac B. England **31** 50.36N 4.50W
Portishead England **28** 51.29N 2.46W
Portiţei Mouth *f.* Romania **43** 44.40N 29.00E
Port Kelang Malaysia **60** 2.57N 101.24E
Port Kembla Australia **80** 34.30S 150.54E
Portknockie Scotland **37** 57.42N 2.52W
Portland Australia **80** 38.21S 141.38E
Portland Ind. U.S.A. **94** 40.25N 84.58W
Portland Maine U.S.A. **95** 43.41N 70.18W
Portland Oreg. U.S.A. **90** 45.32N 122.40W
Portland, C. Australia **80** 40.43S 148.08E
Portland, I. of England **31** 50.32N 2.25W
Port Laoise Rep. of Ire. **39** 53.03N 7.20W
Port Logan Scotland **34** 54.43N 4.57W
Port Loko Sierra Leone **70** 8.50N 12.50W
Port Macquarie Australia **80** 31.28S 152.25E
Portmahomack Scotland **37** 57.49N 3.50W
Portmarnock Rep. of Ire. **38** 53.25N 6.09W
Port Moresby P.N.G. **61** 9.30S 147.07E
Portnacroish Scotland **36** 56.25N 5.22W
Portnaguiran Scotland **36** 58.15N 6.10W
Portnahaven Scotland **34** 55.41N 6.31W
Port Nelson Canada **93** 57.10N 92.35W
Port Nolloth R.S.A. **74** 29.17S 16.51E
Port-Nouveau Québec Canada **93** 58.35N 65.59W
Pôrto *see* Oporto Portugal **41**
Pôrto Alegre Brazil **103** 30.03S 51.10W
Porto Alexandre Angola **72** 15.55S 11.51E
Porto Amboim Angola **72** 10.45S 13.43E
Port of Ness Scotland **36** 58.30N 6.13W
Port of Spain Trinidad **97** 10.38N 61.31W
Pörtom Finland **46** 62.44N 21.35E
Porton England **28** 51.08N 1.44W
Porto-Novo Benin **71** 6.30N 2.47E
Porto Torres Italy **42** 40.49N 8.24E
Porto Vecchio France **40** 41.35N 9.16E
Portpatrick Scotland **34** 54.51N 5.07W
Port Phillip B. Australia **80** 38.05S 144.50E
Port Pirie Australia **80** 33.11S 138.01E
Portreath England **31** 50.15N 5.17W
Portree Scotland **36** 57.24N 6.12W
Portrush N. Ireland **34** 55.12N 6.40W
Port Safâga Egypt **56** 26.45N 33.55E
Port Said Egypt **56** 31.17N 32.18E
Port St. Johns R.S.A. **74** 31.37S 29.32E
Port St. Louis France **40** 43.25N 4.40E
Port Shepstone R.S.A. **74** 30.44S 30.28E
Portskerra Scotland **37** 58.33N 3.55W
Portsmouth England **28** 50.48N 1.06W
Portsmouth N.H. U.S.A. **95** 43.03N 70.47W
Portsmouth Ohio U.S.A. **94** 38.45N 82.59W
Portsoy Scotland **37** 57.41N 2.41W
Portstewart N. Ireland **34** 55.11N 6.43W
Port Sudan Sudan **69** 19.39N 37.01E
Port Talbot Wales **31** 51.35N 3.48W
Portugal Europe **41** 39.30N 8.05W
Portugalia Angola **72** 7.25S 20.43E
Portuguese Timor Austa. **61** 9.00S 126.00E
Portumna Rep. of Ire. **39** 53.06N 8.14W
Port Vendres France **40** 42.31N 3.06E
Port Victoria Kenya **73** 0.07N 34.00E
Port William Scotland **34** 54.46N 4.35W
Porz W. Germany **45** 50.53N 7.05E
Posadas Argentina **103** 27.25S 55.48W
Poso Indonesia **61** 1.23S 120.45E
Postmasburg R.S.A. **74** 28.20S 23.05E
Potchefstroom R.S.A. **74** 26.42S 27.06E
Potenza Italy **42** 40.40N 15.47E
Potgietersrus R.S.A. **74** 24.15S 28.55E
Poti U.S.S.R. **47** 42.11N 41.41E
Potiskum Nigeria **71** 11.40N 11.03E
Potomac *r.* U.S.A. **95** 38.35N 77.00W
Potosí Bolivia **103** 19.34S 65.45W
Potosí *d.* Bolivia **103** 21.50S 66.00W
Potsdam E. Germany **44** 52.24N 13.04E
Potters Bar England **27** 51.42N 0.11W
Potter Street England **27** 51.46N 0.08E
Pottstown U.S.A. **95** 40.15N 75.38W
Pottsville U.S.A. **95** 40.42N 76.13W
Poughkeepsie U.S.A. **95** 41.43N 73.56W
Póvoa de Varzim Portugal **41** 41.22N 8.46W
Povorino U.S.S.R. **47** 51.12N 42.15E
Powder *r.* U.S.A. **90** 46.40N 105.15W
Powell, L. U.S.A. **90** 37.30N 110.45W
Powys *d.* Wales **30** 52.26N 3.26W
Poyang Hu *l.* China **63** 29.05N 116.20E
Poyntzpass N. Ireland **38** 54.16N 6.23W
Požarevac Yugo. **43** 44.38N 21.12E
Poza Rica Mexico **96** 20.34N 97.26W
Poznań Poland **44** 52.25N 16.53E
Pozoblanco Spain **41** 38.23N 4.51W
Prachuap Khiri Khan Thailand **59** 11.50N 99.49E
Prades France **40** 42.38N 2.25E
Prague Czech. **44** 50.05N 14.25E
Praha *see* Prague Czech. **44**
Prato Italy **42** 43.52N 10.50E
Pratt's Bottom England **27** 51.21N 0.06E
Prawle Pt. England **31** 50.12N 3.43W
Preesall England **32** 53.55N 2.58W
Preparis *i.* Burma **60** 14.40N 93.40E
Prescot England **32** 53.27N 2.49W
Prescott U.S.A. **90** 34.34N 112.28W
Presidente Epitácio Brazil **103** 21.56S 52.07W
Presidente Prudente Brazil **103** 22.09S 51.24W
Prespa, L. Albania/Greece/Yugo. **43** 40.53N 21.02E
Presque Isle *town* U.S.A. **95** 46.42N 68.01W
Prestatyn Wales **30** 53.20N 3.24W
Prestea Ghana **70** 5.26N 2.07W
Presteigne Wales **30** 52.17N 3.00W
Preston England **32** 53.46N 2.42W
Prestonpans Scotland **35** 55.57N 3.00W
Prestwick Scotland **34** 55.30N 4.36W
Prestwood England **27** 51.42N 0.43W
Pretoria R.S.A. **74** 25.45S 28.12E
Préveza Greece **43** 38.58N 20.43E
Příbram Czech. **44** 49.42N 14.00E
Prieska R.S.A. **74** 29.40S 22.45E
Prikumsk U.S.S.R. **47** 44.46N 44.10E
Prilep Yugo. **43** 41.20N 21.32E
Priluki U.S.S.R. **47** 50.35N 32.24E
Primorsk U.S.S.R. **46** 60.18N 28.35E
Prince Albert Canada **92** 53.13N 105.45W
Prince Albert R.S.A. **74** 33.15S 22.03E
Prince Alfred C. Canada **92** 74.30N 125.00W
Prince Charles I. Canada **93** 67.50N 76.00W
Prince Edward I. Canada **91** 46.15N 64.00W
Prince Edward Is. Indian Oc. **107** 47.00S 37.00E
Prince Edward Island *d.* Canada **93** 46.15N 63.10W
Prince George Canada **92** 53.55N 122.49W
Prince of Wales, C. U.S.A. **92** 66.00N 168.30W
Prince of Wales I. Australia **61** 10.55S 142.05E
Prince of Wales I. Canada **93** 73.00N 99.00W
Prince of Wales I. U.S.A. **92** 55.00N 132.30W
Prince Patrick I. Canada **92** 77.00N 120.00W
Prince Rupert Canada **92** 54.09N 130.20W
Princes Risborough England **28** 51.43N 0.50W
Princeton U.S.A. **94** 38.21N 87.33W
Princetown England **31** 50.33N 4.00W
Principe *i.* Africa **71** 1.37N 7.27E
Prinzapolca Nicaragua **96** 13.19N 83.35W
Pripet *r.* U.S.S.R. **47** 51.08N 30.30E
Pripet Marshes *f.* U.S.S.R. **47** 52.15N 28.00E
Priština Yugo. **43** 42.39N 21.10E
Prizren Yugo. **43** 42.13N 20.42E
Progreso Mexico **96** 21.20N 89.40W
Prokopyevsk U.S.S.R. **48** 53.55N 86.45E
Prome Burma **59** 18.50N 95.14E
Providence U.S.A. **95** 41.50N 71.25W
Provideniya U.S.S.R. **92** 64.30N 173.11W
Provins France **40** 48.34N 3.18E
Provo U.S.A. **90** 40.15N 111.40W
Prudhoe England **35** 54.58N 1.51W
Prüm W. Germany **45** 50.12N 6.25E
Prüm *r.* W. Germany **45** 49.50N 6.29E
Prut *r.* Romania/U.S.S.R. **43** 45.29N 28.14E
Przemyśl Poland **47** 49.48N 22.48E
Przhevalsk U.S.S.R. **62** 42.31N 78.22E
Psará *i.* Greece **43** 38.34N 25.35E
Psel *r.* U.S.S.R. **47** 49.03N 33.26E
Pskov U.S.S.R. **46** 57.48N 28.00E
Pskov, L. U.S.S.R. **47** 58.00N 28.00E
Pucallpa Peru **102** 7.06S 75.36W
Puddletown England **28** 50.45N 2.21W
Pudsey England **32** 53.47N 1.40W
Puebla Mexico **96** 19.03N 98.10W
Puebla *d.* Mexico **96** 18.30N 98.00W
Pueblo U.S.A. **90** 38.17N 104.38W
Puente Genil Spain **41** 37.24N 4.46W
Puerto Armuelles Panamá **96** 8.19N 82.15W
Puerto Barrios Guatemala **96** 15.41N 88.32W
Puerto Cabello Venezuela **97** 10.29N 68.02W
Puerto Cabezas Nicaragua **96** 14.02N 83.24W
Puerto Carreño Colombia **97** 6.00N 67.35W
Puerto Cortes Honduras **96** 15.50N 87.55W
Puerto de Santa Maria Spain **41** 36.36N 6.14W
Puerto Ibicuy Argentina **103** 33.44S 59.10W
Puerto Juárez Mexico **96** 21.26N 86.51W
Puerto la Cruz Venezuela **97** 10.14N 64.40W
Puertollano Spain **41** 38.41N 4.07W
Puerto Montt Chile **102** 41.28S 73.04W
Puerto Penasco Mexico **90** 31.20N 113.35W
Puerto Pinasco Paraguay **103** 22.36S 57.53W
Puerto Plata Dom. Rep. **97** 19.48N 70.41W
Puerto Princesa Phil. **60** 9.46N 118.45E
Puerto Quepos Costa Rica **96** 9.28N 84.10W
Puerto Rico C. America **97** 18.20N 66.30W
Puerto Rico Trench Atlantic Oc. **97** 19.50N 66.00W
Puerto Sastre Paraguay **103** 22.02S 58.00W
Puerto Suárez Bolivia **103** 18.59S 57.46W
Puffin I. Rep. of Ire. **39** 51.50N 10.25W
Puffin I. Wales **30** 53.18N 4.04W
Pujehun Sierra Leone **70** 7.23N 11.44W
Pukaki, L. New Zealand **82** 44.00S 170.10E
Pukekohe New Zealand **82** 37.12S 174.56E
Pula Yugo. **42** 44.52N 13.53E
Pulaski U.S.A. **95** 43.34N 76.06W
Pulborough England **29** 50.58N 0.30W
Pulog, Mt. Phil. **61** 16.50N 120.50E
Pułtusk Poland **47** 52.42N 21.02E
Pulvar *r.* Iran **57** 29.50N 52.47E
Pumlumon Fawr *mtn.* Wales **30** 52.28N 3.47W
Pumpsaint Wales **30** 52.03N 3.58W
Punjab *d.* India **58** 30.30N 75.15E
Punta Alta *town* Argentina **103** 38.50S 62.00W
Punta Arenas *town* Chile **102** 53.10S 70.56W
Punta Gorda *town* Belize **96** 16.10N 88.45W
Puntarenas Costa Rica **96** 10.00N 84.50W
Pur *r.* U.S.S.R. **48** 67.30N 75.30E
Purfleet England **27** 51.29N 0.15E
Puri India **59** 19.49N 85.54E
Purley England **27** 51.21N 0.07W
Purnea India **58** 25.47N 87.28E
Pursat Khmer Rep. **59** 12.33N 103.55E
Purulia India **58** 23.20N 86.24E
Puru Vesi *l.* Finland **46** 62.00N 29.50E
Pusan S. Korea **63** 35.05N 129.02E
Pushkin U.S.S.R. **47** 59.43N 30.22E
Pustoshka U.S.S.R. **47** 56.20N 29.20E
Putao Burma **59** 27.22N 97.27E
Putien China **63** 25.32N 119.02E
Putjak Djaja *mtn.* Indonesia **61** 4.00S 137.15E
Putney England **27** 51.28N 0.14W
Putoran Mts. U.S.S.R. **49** 68.30N 96.00E
Puttalam Sri Lanka **59** 8.02N 79.50E

Puula Vesi *l.* Finland **46** 63.45N 25.25E
Puy de Dôme *mtn.* France **40** 45.46N 2.56E
Puysegur Pt. New Zealand **82** 46.10S 166.35E
Pweto Zaïre **73** 8.27S 28.52E
Pwllheli Wales **30** 52.53N 4.25W
Pya, L. U.S.S.R. **46** 66.00N 31.00E
Pyasina *r.* U.S.S.R. **49** 73.10N 84.55E
Pyatigorsk U.S.S.R. **47** 44.04N 43.06E
Pyha *r.* Finland **46** 64.30N 24.20E
Pyhä-järvi *l.* Finland **46** 61.00N 22.10E
Pyhajoki Finland **46** 64.28N 24.15E
Pyinmana Burma **59** 19.45N 96.12E
Pyongyang N. Korea **63** 39.00N 125.47E
Pyramid L. U.S.A. **90** 40.00N 119.35W
Pyrénées *mts.* France/Spain **40** 42.40N 0.30E
Pytalovo U.S.S.R. **46** 57.30N 27.57E

Q

Qara Egypt **56** 29.38N 26.30E
Qasr Farafra Egypt **56** 27.05N 28.00E
Qasrqand Iran **57** 26.13N 60.37E
Qatar Asia **57** 25.20N 51.10E
Qatif Saudi Arabia **57** 26.31N 5.00E
Qattara Depression *f.* Egypt **56** 29.40N 27.30E
Qayen Iran **57** 33.44N 59.07E
Qazvin Iran **57** 36.16N 50.00E
Qena Egypt **56** 26.08N 32.42E
Qena, Wadi *r.* Egypt **56** 26.07N 32.42E
Qishm Iran **57** 26.58N 57.17E
Qishm *i.* Iran **57** 26.48N 55.48E
Qishn S. Yemen **58** 15.25N 51.40E
Qizil Uzun *r.* Iran **57** 36.44N 49.27E
Qom Iran **57** 34.40N 50.57E
Quang Ngai Vietnam **60** 15.09N 108.50E
Quang Tri Vietnam **60** 16.46N 107.11E
Quantock Hills England **28** 51.06N 3.12W
Qu'Appelle *r.* Canada **90** 49.40N 99.40W
Quchan Iran **57** 37.04N 58.29E
Queanbeyan Australia **80** 35.24S 149.17E
Quebec Canada **95** 46.50N 71.15W
Quebec *d.* Canada **93** 51.00N 70.00W
Quebrabasa Gorge *f.* Moçambique **73** 15.34S 33.00E
Quedlinburg E. Germany **44** 51.48N 11.09E
Queenborough England **29** 51.24N 0.46E
Queen Charlotte Is. Canada **92** 53.00N 132.30W
Queen Charlotte Str. Canada **92** 51.00N 129.00W
Queen Elizabeth Is. Canada **93** 78.30N 99.00W
Queen Maud G. Canada **93** 68.30N 99.00W
Queen Maud Land Antarctica **104** 74.00S 10.00E
Queensberry *mtn.* Scotland **35** 55.16N 3.36W
Queensferry Scotland **35** 56.01N 3.24W
Queensland *d.* Australia **79** 23.30S 144.00E
Queenstown Australia **80** 42.07S 145.33E
Queenstown New Zealand **82** 45.03S 168.41E
Queenstown R.S.A. **74** 31.54S 26.53E
Quela Angola **72** 9.18S 17.05E
Quelimane Moçambique **73** 17.53S 36.57E
Quelpart *i.* S. Korea **63** 33.20N 126.30E
Que Que Rhodesia **74** 18.55S 29.51E
Querétaro Mexico **96** 20.38N 100.23W
Querétaro *d.* Mexico **96** 21.03N 100.00W
Quesnel Canada **92** 53.03N 122.31W
Quetta Pakistan **58** 30.15N 67.00E
Quezaltenango Guatemala **96** 14.50N 91.30W
Quezon City Phil. **61** 14.59N 121.01E
Qufa *des.* U.A.E. **57** 23.30N 53.30E
Quibala Angola **72** 10.48S 14.56E
Quibaxi Angola **72** 8.34S 14.37E
Quiberon France **40** 47.29N 3.07W
Quicama Nat. Park Angola **72** 9.40S 13.30E
Quilengues Angola **72** 14.09S 14.04E
Quill Lakes Canada **90** 51.50N 104.10W
Quimbele Angola **72** 6.29S 16.25E
Quimilí Argentina **103** 27.35S 62.25W
Quimper France **40** 48.00N 4.06W
Quimperlé France **40** 47.52N 3.33W
Quincy Ill. U.S.A. **94** 39.55N 91.22W
Quincy Mass. U.S.A. **95** 42.14N 71.00W
Quintana Roo *d.* Mexico **96** 19.00N 88.00W
Quinto Spain **41** 41.25N 0.30W
Quirigua *ruins* Guatemala **96** 15.20N 89.25W
Quirindi Australia **80** 31.32S 150.44E
Quissanga Moçambique **73** 12.24S 40.33E
Quissico Moçambique **74** 24.42S 34.44E
Quito Ecuador **102** 0.14S 78.30W
Quoich, Loch Scotland **36** 57.04N 5.15W
Quorn Australia **80** 32.20S 138.02E
Quoyness Scotland **37** 58.54N 3.17W
Quseir Egypt **56** 26.04N 34.15E
Qutur Iran **57** 38.28N 44.25E

R

Raalte Neth. **45** 52.22N 6.17E
Raasay *i.* Scotland **36** 57.25N 6.05W
Raasay, Sd. of Scotland **36** 57.25N 6.05W
Raba Indonesia **60** 8.27S 118.45E
Rabat Morocco **68** 34.02N 6.51W
Racine U.S.A. **94** 42.42N 87.50W
Radcliffe England **32** 53.35N 2.19W
Radebeul E. Germany **44** 51.06N 13.41E
Radhwa, Jebel *mtn.* Saudi Arabia **56** 24.36N 38.18E
Radlett England **27** 51.42N 0.20W
Radom Poland **47** 51.26N 21.10E
Radomir Bulgaria **43** 42.32N 22.56E
Radstock England **28** 51.17N 2.25W
Rae Bareli India **58** 26.14N 81.14E
Rafaela Argentina **103** 31.16S 61.44W
Rafai C.A.R. **72** 4.56N 23.55E
Rafsanjan Iran **57** 30.24N 56.00E
Raglan Wales **31** 51.46N 2.51W
Ragusa Italy **42** 36.56N 14.44E
Rahbur Iran **57** 29.18N 56.56E
Raichur India **58** 16.15N 77.20E
Raiganj India **58** 25.38N 88.11E
Raigarh India **58** 21.53N 83.28E
Rainford England **32** 53.30N 2.48W
Rainham G.L. England **27** 51.31N 0.12E
Rainham Kent England **27** 51.23N 0.36E
Rainier, Mt. U.S.A. **90** 46.52N 121.45W
Rainy L. Canada **94** 48.40N 93.15W
Raipur India **59** 21.16N 81.42E
Raja *mtn.* Indonesia **60** 0.45S 112.45E
Rajahmundry India **59** 17.01N 81.52E
Rajang *r.* Malaysia **60** 2.10N 112.45E
Rajapalaiyam India **58** 9.26N 77.36E
Rajasthan *d.* India **58** 27.00N 74.00E
Rajgarh India **58** 24.01N 76.42E
Rajkot India **58** 22.18N 70.53E
Rajshahi Bangla. **58** 24.24N 88.40E
Rakaia *r.* New Zealand **82** 43.52S 172.13E
Rakvere U.S.S.R. **46** 59.22N 26.28E
Raleigh U.S.A. **91** 35.46N 78.39W
Rama Nicaragua **96** 12.09N 84.15W
Ramah Saudi Arabia **57** 25.33N 47.08E
Rame Head England **31** 50.18N 4.13W
Ramelton Rep. of Ire. **38** 55.02N 7.40W
Ramhormoz Iran **57** 31.14N 49.37E
Ramillies Belgium **45** 50.39N 4.56E
Ramishk Iran **57** 26.52N 58.46E
Râmnicu Sarat Romania **43** 45.24N 27.06E
Ramor, Lough Rep. of Ire. **38** 53.49N 7.05W
Rampur India **58** 28.48N 79.03E
Ramree I. Burma **59** 19.10N 93.40E
Ramsar Iran **57** 36.54N 50.41E
Ramsbottom England **32** 53.38N 2.20W
Ramsey England **29** 52.27N 0.06W
Ramsey I.o.M. **32** 54.19N 4.23W
Ramsey *i.* Wales **30** 51.53N 5.21W
Ramsey B. I.o.M. **32** 54.20N 4.20W
Ramsgate England **29** 51.20N 1.25E
Ranchi India **58** 23.22N 85.20E
Randalstown N. Ireland **34** 54.45N 6.20W
Randers Denmark **46** 56.28N 10.03E
Ranfurly New Zealand **82** 45.08S 170.08E
Rangiora New Zealand **82** 43.18S 172.38E
Rangitaiki *r.* New Zealand **82** 37.55S 176.50E
Rangoon Burma **59** 16.45N 96.20E
Rangpur Bangla. **58** 25.45N 89.21E
Rannoch, Loch Scotland **37** 56.41N 4.20W
Rannoch Moor *f.* Scotland **37** 56.38N 4.40W
Rann of Kutch *f.* India **58** 23.50N 69.50E
Ranobe *r.* Malagasy Rep. **73** 17.20S 44.05E
Rantauparapat Indonesia **60** 2.05N 99.46E
Rantekombola *mtn.* Indonesia **60** 3.30S 119.58E
Rapallo Italy **40** 44.20N 9.14E
Rapid City U.S.A. **90** 44.06N 103.14W
Raqqa Syria **56** 35.57N 39.03E
Ras al Hadd *c.* Oman **57** 22.32N 59.49E
Ras Banas *c.* Egypt **56** 23.54N 35.48E
Ras Dashan *mtn.* Ethiopia **69** 13.20N 38.10E
Rasht Iran **57** 37.18N 49.38E
Ras Madraka *c.* Oman **58** 19.00N 57.55E
Ras Muhammad *c.* Egypt **56** 27.42N 34.13E
Rass Saudi Arabia **56** 25.54N 43.30E
Ras Tanura *c.* Saudi Arabia **57** 26.40N 50.10E
Rastatt W. Germany **44** 48.51N 8.13E
Rathangan Rep. of Ire. **39** 53.13N 7.00W
Rathcoole Rep. of Ire. **38** 53.17N 6.30W
Rathcormack Rep. of Ire. **39** 52.05N 8.18W
Rathdowney Rep. of Ire. **39** 52.51N 7.36W
Rathdrum Rep. of Ire. **39** 52.56N 6.15W
Rathenow E. Germany **44** 52.37N 12.21E
Rathfriland N. Ireland **38** 54.14N 6.10W
Rathkeale Rep. of Ire. **39** 52.30N 8.57W
Rathlin I. N. Ireland **34** 55.17N 6.15W
Rathlin Sd. N. Ireland **34** 55.15N 6.15W
Rath Luirc Rep. of Ire. **39** 52.21N 8.41W
Rathmore Rep. of Ire. **39** 52.05N 9.12W
Rathmullen Rep. of Ire. **38** 55.06N 7.32W
Rathnew Rep. of Ire. **39** 53.01N 6.07W
Rathvilly Rep. of Ire. **39** 52.52N 6.43W
Ratlam India **58** 23.18N 75.06E
Raton U.S.A. **90** 36.54N 104.27W
Rattray Head Scotland **37** 57.37N 1.50W
Rättvik Sweden **46** 60.56N 15.10E
Rauch Argentina **103** 36.45S 59.05W
Raukumara Range *mts.* New Zealand **82** 38.00S 177.45E
Rauma Finland **46** 61.09N 21.30E
Raunds England **29** 52.21N 0.33W
Ravar Iran **57** 31.14N 56.51E
Ravenna Italy **42** 44.25N 12.12E
Ravensburg W. Germany **44** 47.47N 9.37E
Ravi *r.* Pakistan **58** 30.30N 72.13E
Rawalpindi Pakistan **58** 33.40N 73.08E
Rawlinna Australia **79** 31.00S 125.21E
Rawlins U.S.A. **90** 41.46N 107.16W
Rawmarsh England **33** 53.27N 1.20W
Rawtenstall England **32** 53.42N 2.18W
Rayen Iran **57** 29.34N 57.26E
Rayleigh England **27** 51.36N 0.36E
Razan Iran **57** 35.22N 49.02E
Razgrad Bulgaria **43** 43.32N 26.30E
Ré, Ile de *i.* France **40** 46.10N 1.26W
Reading England **28** 51.27N 0.57W
Reading U.S.A. **95** 40.20N 75.55W
Reay Forest *f.* Scotland **37** 58.17N 4.48W
Recife Brazil **102** 8.06S 35.34W
Recklinghausen W. Germany **45** 51.36N 7.11E
Reconquista Argentina **103** 29.08S 59.38W
Recreo Argentina **103** 29.18S 65.05W
Red *r.* Canada **91** 50.30N 96.50W
Red *r.* Vietnam **62** 20.15N 106.25E
Red *r.* U.S.A. **91** 31.10N 92.00W
Red B. N. Ireland **34** 55.04N 6.02W
Red Bluff U.S.A. **90** 40.11N 122.16W
Redbourn England **27** 51.48N 0.24W
Redbridge England **27** 51.35N 0.06E
Redcar England **33** 54.37N 1.04W
Red Deer Canada **92** 52.15N 113.48W
Red Deer *r.* Canada **90** 50.55N 110.00W
Redding U.S.A. **90** 40.35N 122.24W
Redditch England **28** 52.18N 1.57W
Rede *r.* England **35** 55.08N 2.13W
Redhill England **27** 51.14N 0.11W
Red L. U.S.A. **91** 48.00N 95.00W
Red Lake *town* Canada **91** 50.59N 93.40W
Redpoint Scotland **36** 57.39N 5.49W
Redruth England **31** 50.14N 5.14W
Red Sea Africa/Asia **69** 20.00N 39.00E
Red Tower Pass Romania **43** 45.37N 24.17E
Red Volta *r.* Ghana **70** 10.32N 0.31W
Red Wharf B. Wales **30** 53.20N 4.10W
Ree, Lough Rep. of Ire. **38** 53.31N 7.58W
Reedham England **29** 52.34N 1.33E
Reefton New Zealand **82** 42.05S 171.51E
Rega *r.* Poland **44** 54.10N 15.18E
Regen *r.* W. Germany **44** 49.02N 12.03E
Regensburg W. Germany **44** 49.01N 12.07E
Reggan Algeria **68** 26.30N 0.30E
Reggio Calabria Italy **42** 38.07N 15.38E
Reggio Emilia-RomagnaItaly **42** 44.40N 10.37E
Regina Canada **90** 50.30N 104.38W
Rehoboth S.W. Africa **74** 23.18S 17.03E
Reigate England **27** 51.14N 0.13W
Reims France **40** 49.15N 4.02E
Reindeer L. Canada **92** 57.00N 102.20W
Reinosa Mexico **96** 26.09N 97.10W
Reinosa Spain **41** 43.01N 4.09W
Reiss Scotland **37** 58.28N 3.09W
Rembang Indonesia **60** 6.45S 111.22E
Remich Lux. **45** 49.34N 6.23E
Remscheid W. Germany **45** 51.10N 7.11E
Renaix Belgium **45** 50.45N 3.36E
Rendsburg W. Germany **44** 54.19N 9.39E
Renfrew Canada **95** 45.28N 76.44W
Renfrew Scotland **34** 55.52N 4.23W
Rengat Indonesia **60** 0.26S 102.35E
Reni U.S.S.R. **43** 45.28N 28.17E
Renish Pt. Scotland **36** 57.43N 6.58W
Renkum Neth. **45** 51.59N 5.46E
Renmark Australia **80** 34.10S 140.45E
Rennes France **40** 48.06N 1.40W
Reno *r.* Italy **42** 44.36N 12.17E
Reno U.S.A. **90** 39.32N 119.49W
Renvyle Pt. Rep. of Ire. **38** 53.37N 10.04W
Republican *r.* U.S.A. **91** 39.05N 94.50W
Republic of Ireland Europe **39** 53.00N 8.00W
Republic of South Africa Africa **74** 28.30S 24.50E
Requena Spain **41** 39.29N 1.08W
Resistencia Argentina **103** 27.28S 59.00W
Resolute Canada **93** 74.40N 95.00W

Resolution I. New Zealand **82** 45.40S 166.30E
Resort, Loch Scotland **36** 58.03N 6.56W
Rethel France **45** 49.31N 4.22E
Réthimnon Greece **43** 35.22N 24.29E
Réunion *i.* Indian Oc. **107** 22.00S 55.00E
Reus Spain **41** 41.10N 1.06E
Reutlingen W. Germany **44** 48.30N 9.13E
Revelstoke Canada **90** 51.00N 118.12W
Revilla Gigedo Is. Mexico **89** 19.00N 111.00W
Revue *r.* Moçambique **74** 19.58S 34.40E
Rewa India **58** 24.32N 81.18E
Reykjavik Iceland **46** 64.09N 21.58W
Rezaiyeh Iran **57** 37.32N 45.02E
Rēzekne U.S.S.R. **46** 56.30N 27.22E
Rhayader Wales **30** 52.19N 3.30W
Rheden Neth. **45** 52.01N 6.02E
Rheine W. Germany **45** 52.17N 7.26E
Rhenen Neth. **45** 51.58N 5.34E
Rheydt W. Germany **45** 51.10N 6.25E
Rhine *r.* Europe **45** 51.53N 6.03E
Rhinelander U.S.A. **94** 45.39N 89.23W
Rhinns of Kells *hills* Scotland **34** 55.08N 4.21W
Rhinns Pt. Scotland **34** 55.40N 6.29W
Rhino Camp *town* Uganda **73** 2.58N 31.20E
Rhode Island *d.* U.S.A. **95** 43.30N 71.35W
Rhodes Greece **43** 36.24N 28.15E
Rhodes *i.* Greece **43** 36.12N 28.00E
Rhodesia Africa **74** 18.55S 30.00E
Rhodope Mts. Bulgaria **43** 41.35N 24.35E
Rhondda Wales **31** 51.39N 3.30W
Rhondda Valley *f.* Wales **31** 51.38N 3.29W
Rhône *r.* France **40** 43.25N 4.45E
Rhosllanerchrugog Wales **30** 53.03N 3.04W
Rhosneigr Wales **30** 53.14N 4.31W
Rhum *i.* Scotland **36** 57.00N 6.20W
Rhum, Sd. of *str.* Scotland **36** 56.57N 6.15W
Rhyddhywel *mtn.* Wales **30** 52.25N 3.27W
Rhyl Wales **30** 53.19N 3.29W
Riau Is. Indonesia **60** 0.50N 104.00E
Rib *r.* England **27** 51.48N 0.04W
Ribadeo Spain **41** 43.32N 7.04W
Ribauè Moçambique **73** 14.57S 38.27E
Ribble *r.* England **32** 53.45N 2.44W
Ribblesdale *f.* England **32** 54.03N 2.17W
Ribeirão Prêto Brazil **103** 21.09S 47.48W
Riberac France **40** 45.14N 0.22E
Riccall England **33** 53.50N 1.04W
Richelieu *r.* Canada **95** 46.02N 73.03W
Richfield U.S.A. **94** 44.51N 93.17W
Richland U.S.A. **90** 46.20N 119.17W
Richmond England **32** 54.24N 1.43W
Richmond Cape Province R.S.A. **74** 31.25S 23.57E
Richmond Ind. U.S.A. **94** 39.50N 84.51W
Richmond Va. U.S.A. **91** 37.34N 77.27W
Richmond Park *f.* England **27** 51.26N 0.13W
Richmond-upon-Thames England **27** 51.26N 0.17W
Rickmansworth England **27** 51.39N 0.29W
Ridderkirk Neth. **45** 51.53N 4.39E
Riesa E. Germany **44** 51.18N 13.18E
Rieti Italy **42** 42.24N 12.53E
Rift Valley *d.* Kenya **73** 1.00N 36.00E
Riga U.S.S.R. **46** 56.53N 24.08E
Riga, G. of U.S.S.R. **46** 57.30N 23.50E
Rigan Iran **57** 28.40N 58.58E
Rigmati Iran **57** 27.40N 58.11E
Rihand Dam India **58** 24.09N 83.02E
Riihimaki Finland **46** 60.45N 24.45E
Rijeka Yugo. **42** 45.20N 14.25E
Rijswijk Neth. **45** 52.03N 4.22E
Rima, Wadi *r.* Saudi Arabia **56** 26.10N 44.00E
Rimini Italy **42** 44.01N 12.34E
Rimouski Canada **95** 48.27N 68.32W
Ringköbing Denmark **46** 56.06N 8.15E
Ringvassöy *i.* Norway **46** 70.00N 19.00E
Ringwood England **28** 50.50N 1.48W
Rinrawros Pt. Rep. of Ire. **38** 55.01N 8.34W
Rio Claro *town* Brazil **103** 22.19S 47.35W
Rio de Janeiro *town* Brazil **103** 22.53S 43.17W
Rio Grande *town* Brazil **103** 32.03S 52.08W
Rio Grande *r.* Mexico/U.S.A. **96** 25.55N 97.08W
Río Grande *r.* Nicaragua **96** 12.48N 83.30W
Rio Grande do Sul *d.* Brazil **103** 30.15S 53.30W
Riohacha Colombia **97** 11.34N 72.58W
Rio Negro *d.* Argentina **103** 41.15S 67.15W
Riosucio Colombia **97** 7.25N 77.05W
Rio Verde *town* Brazil **103** 17.50S 50.55W
Ripley Derbys. England **33** 53.03N 1.24W
Ripley Surrey England **27** 51.18N 0.29W
Ripon England **33** 54.08N 1.31W
Risca Wales **31** 51.36N 3.06W
Risha, Wadi *r.* Saudi Arabia **57** 25.40N 44.08E
Risor Norway **46** 58.44N 9.15E
Ristikent U.S.S.R. **46** 68.40N 31.47E
Rivas Nicaragua **96** 11.26N 85.50W
Riverhead England **27** 51.17N 0.11E
Riverina *f.* Australia **80** 35.00S 146.00E
Rivers *d.* Nigeria **71** 4.45N 6.35E
Riversdale R.S.A. **74** 34.05S 21.14E
Rivière-du-Loup *town* Canada **95** 47.49N 69.32W
Riyadh Saudi Arabia **57** 24.39N 46.44E
Rize Turkey **56** 41.03N 40.31E
Rizzuto, C. Italy **43** 38.53N 17.06E
Rjukan Norway **46** 59.54N 8.33E
Roanne France **40** 46.02N 4.05E
Roanoke *r.* U.S.A. **91** 36.00N 76.35W
Roaringwater B. Rep. of Ire. **39** 51.32N 9.26W
Robertson R.S.A. **74** 33.48S 19.53E
Roberval Canada **95** 48.31N 72.16W
Robin Hood's Bay *town* England **33** 54.26N 0.31W
Robinvale Australia **80** 34.37S 142.50E
Roboré Bolivia **103** 18.20S 59.45W
Robson, Mt. Canada **92** 53.00N 121.00W
Roca, Cabo de Portugal **41** 38.40N 9.31W
Roçadas Angola **72** 16.31S 15.00E
Roccella Italy **43** 38.19N 16.24E
Rocha Uruguay **103** 34.30S 54.22W
Rochdale England **32** 53.36N 2.10W
Rochechouart France **40** 45.49N 0.50E
Rochefort Belgium **45** 50.10N 5.13E
Rochefort France **40** 45.57N 0.58W
Rochester Kent England **27** 51.22N 0.30E
Rochester Northum. England **35** 55.16N 2.16W
Rochester Minn. U.S.A. **94** 44.01N 92.27W
Rochester N.Y. U.S.A. **95** 43.12N 77.37W
Rochfort Bridge Rep. of Ire. **38** 53.25N 7.19W
Rock *r.* U.S.A. **94** 41.30N 90.35W
Rockford U.S.A. **94** 42.16N 89.06W
Rockhampton Australia **79** 23.22S 150.32E
Rockingham Forest *f.* England **28** 52.30N 0.35W
Rock Island *town* U.S.A. **94** 41.30N 90.34W
Rockland U.S.A. **95** 44.06N 69.08W
Rocklands Resr. Australia **80** 37.13S 141.52E
Rock Springs *town* U.S.A. **90** 41.35N 109.13W
Rockville U.S.A. **95** 39.05N 77.10W
Rocky Mts. N. America **92** 50.00N 114.00W
Rocroi France **45** 49.56N 4.31E
Rodel Scotland **36** 57.44N 6.58W
Roden *r.* England **32** 52.42N 2.36W
Rodez France **40** 44.21N 2.34E
Roding *r.* England **27** 51.31N 0.05E
Rodonit, C. Albania **43** 41.34N 19.25E
Roe *r.* N. Ireland **34** 55.06N 7.00W
Roermond Neth. **45** 51.12N 6.00E
Rogan's Seat *mtn.* England **32** 54.25N 2.05W
Rogers City U.S.A. **94** 45.24N 83.50W
Rokan *r.* Indonesia **60** 2.00N 101.00E
Rokel *r.* Sierra Leone **70** 8.36N 12.55W
Rolla U.S.A. **91** 37.56N 91.55W
Roma *i.* Indonesia **61** 7.45S 127.20E
Romain, C. U.S.A. **91** 33.01N 71.23W
Romaine *r.* Canada **93** 50.20N 63.45W
Romania Europe **47** 46.30N 24.00E
Romano, C. U.S.A. **91** 25.50N 81.42W
Romans France **40** 45.03N 5.03E
Rome Italy **42** 41.54N 12.29E
Rome U.S.A. **95** 43.13N 75.28W
Romford England **27** 51.35N 0.11E
Romilly France **40** 48.31N 3.44E
Romney Marsh *f.* England **29** 51.03N 0.55E
Romorantin France **40** 47.22N 1.44E
Romsey England **28** 51.00N 1.29W
Rona *i.* Scotland **36** 57.33N 5.58W
Ronas Hill Scotland **36** 60.32N 1.26W
Ronas Voe *b.* Scotland **36** 60.31N 1.29W
Ronay *i.* Scotland **36** 57.29N 7.10W
Ronda Spain **41** 36.45N 5.10W
Rönne Denmark **46** 55.07N 14.43E
Roof Butte *mtn.* U.S.A. **90** 36.29N 109.05W
Roosendaal Neth. **45** 51.32N 4.28E
Roper *r.* Australia **79** 14.40S 135.30E
Roque Sáenz Peña Argentina **103** 26.50S 60.28W
Rora Head Scotland **37** 58.52N 3.26W
Röros Norway **46** 62.35N 11.23E
Rosa, Monte Italy/Switz. **40** 45.56N 7.51E
Rosario Argentina **103** 33.00S 60.40W
Rosario Paraguay **103** 24.28S 57.13W
Rosario Uruguay **103** 34.20S 57.26W
Roscommon Rep. of Ire. **38** 53.38N 8.13W
Roscommon *d.* Rep. of Ire. **38** 53.38N 8.11W
Roscrea Rep. of Ire. **39** 52.57N 7.49W
Roseau Dominica **97** 15.18N 61.23W
Roseburg U.S.A. **90** 43.13N 123.21W
Rosehearty Scotland **37** 57.42N 2.07W
Rosenheim W. Germany **44** 47.51N 12.09E
Rosetown Canada **92** 51.34N 107.59W
Rosetta Egypt **56** 31.25N 30.25E
Roseville U.S.A. **94** 44.59N 93.11W
Rosières France **45** 49.49N 2.43E
Roskilde Denmark **46** 55.39N 12.07E
Roslags-Näsby Sweden **46** 59.01N 18.02E
Roslavl U.S.S.R. **47** 53.55N 32.53E
Ross New Zealand **82** 42.54S 170.48E
Rossall Pt. England **32** 53.55N 3.03W
Ross Dependency Antarctica **104** 75.00S 170.00W
Rosses B. Rep. of Ire. **38** 55.01N 8.29W
Rosskeeragh Pt. Rep. of Ire. **38** 54.21N 8.41W
Rosslare Rep. of Ire. **39** 52.17N 6.23W
Rosslea N. Ireland **38** 54.15N 7.12W
Ross of Mull *pen.* Scotland **34** 56.19N 6.10W
Ross-on-Wye England **28** 51.55N 2.36W
Ross Sea Antarctica **107** 73.00S 179.00E
Rostock E. Germany **44** 54.06N 12.09E
Rostov R.S.F.S.R. U.S.S.R. **47** 47.15N 39.45E
Rostov R.S.F.S.R. U.S.S.R. **47** 57.11N 39.23E
Rösvatn *l.* Norway **46** 65.50N 14.00E
Rosyth Scotland **35** 56.03N 3.26W
Rota *i.* Asia **61** 14.10N 145.15E
Rothbury England **35** 55.19N 1.54W
Rothbury Forest *f.* England **35** 55.18N 1.52W
Rother *r.* E. Sussex England **29** 50.56N 0.46E
Rother *r.* W. Sussex England **29** 50.57N 0.32W
Rotherham England **33** 53.26N 1.21W
Rothes Scotland **37** 57.31N 3.13W
Rothesay Scotland **34** 55.50N 5.03W
Rothwell Northants. England **28** 52.25N 0.48W
Rothwell W. Yorks. England **33** 53.46N 1.29W
Roti *i.* Indonesia **61** 10.30S 123.10E
Roto Australia **80** 33.04S 145.27E
Rotorua New Zealand **82** 38.07S 176.17E
Rotorua, L. New Zealand **82** 38.00S 176.00E
Rotterdam Neth. **45** 51.55N 4.29E
Roubaix France **45** 50.42N 3.10E
Rouen France **40** 49.26N 1.05E
Roulers Belgium **45** 50.57N 3.06E
Round Mt. Australia **80** 30.26S 152.15E
Roundup U.S.A. **90** 46.27N 108.34W
Rousay *i.* Scotland **37** 59.10N 3.02W
Rouyn Canada **95** 48.15N 79.00W
Rovaniemi Finland **46** 66.29N 25.40E
Rovinj Yugo. **42** 45.06N 13.39E
Roxburgh New Zealand **82** 45.34S 169.21E
Roxburgh Scotland **35** 55.34N 2.23W
Royale, I. U.S.A. **94** 48.00N 88.45W
Royal Leamington Spa England **28** 52.18N 1.32W
Royal Tunbridge Wells England **29** 51.07N 0.16E
Roydon England **27** 51.46N 0.03E
Roye France **45** 49.42N 2.48E
Royston Herts. England **29** 52.03N 0.01W
Royston S. Yorks. England **33** 53.37N 1.27W
Rozel Channel Is. **31** 49.19N 2.03W
Rtishchevo U.S.S.R. **47** 52.16N 43.45E
Ruabon Wales **30** 53.00N 3.03W
Ruahine Range *mts.* New Zealand **82** 40.00S 176.00E
Ruapehu *mtn.* New Zealand **82** 39.20S 175.30E
Ruapuke I. New Zealand **82** 46.45S 168.30E
Rub al Khali *des.* Saudi Arabia **58** 20.20N 52.30E
Rubha A'Mhàil *c.* Scotland **34** 55.57N 6.08W
Rubha Ardvule *c.* Scotland **36** 57.15N 7.28W
Rubha Coigeach *c.* Scotland **36** 58.06N 5.25W
Rubha Hunish *c.* Scotland **36** 57.42N 6.21W
Rubh'an Dunain *c.* Scotland **36** 57.09N 6.19W
Rubha Réidh *c.* Scotland **36** 57.51N 5.49W
Rubi *r.* Zaïre **72** 2.50N 24.06E
Rudan *r.* Iran **57** 27.02N 56.53E
Rudbar Afghan. **57** 30.10N 62.38E
Ruddstadt E. Germany **44** 50.44N 11.20E
Rud-i-Pusht *r.* Iran **57** 29.09N 58.09E
Rud-i-Shur *r.* Kermā n Iran **57** 31.14N 55.29E
Rud-i-Shur *r.* Khorā sā n Iran **57** 34.05N 60.22E
Rudok China **62** 33.30N 79.40E
Ruffec France **40** 46.02N 0.12E
Rufford England **32** 53.38N 2.50W
Rufiji *r.* Tanzania **73** 8.02S 39.19E
Rufino Argentina **103** 34.16S 62.45W
Rufisque Senegal **70** 14.43N 17.16W
Rugby England **28** 52.23N 1.16W
Rugby U.S.A. **90** 48.24N 99.59W
Rugeley England **32** 52.47N 1.56W
Rügen *i.* E. Germany **44** 54.30N 13.30E
Ruhr *f.* W. Germany **45** 51.22N 7.26E
Ruhr *r.* W. Germany **45** 51.27N 6.41E
Ruislip England **27** 51.35N 0.25W
Rukwa *d.* Tanzania **73** 7.05S 31.25E
Rukwa, L. Tanzania **73** 8.00S 32.20E
Ruma Yugo. **43** 44.59N 19.51E
Rum Cay *i.* Bahamas **97** 23.41N 74.53W
Rumney Wales **31** 51.32N 3.07W
Rump Mtn. U.S.A. **95** 45.12N 71.04W
Runabay Head N. Ireland **34** 55.09N 6.02W
Runcorn England **32** 53.20N 2.44W
Rungwa Singida Tanzania **73** 6.57S 33.35E
Rungwa *r.* Tanzania **73** 7.38S 31.55E
Rungwe Mt. Tanzania **73** 9.10S 33.40E
Rupert *r.* Canada **91** 51.25N 78.45W
Rur *r.* Neth. **45** 51.12N 5.58E
Rusape Rhodesia **74** 18.35S 32.08E
Ruse Bulgaria **43** 43.50N 25.59E
Rush Rep. of Ire. **38** 53.32N 6.06W

Rushden England **28** 52.17N 0.37W
Russian Soviet Federal Socialist Republic *d.* U.S.S.R. **48** 62.00N 80.00E
Rustenburg R.S.A. **74** 25.40S 27.15E
Rutana Burundi **73** 3.58S 30.00E
Rütenbrock W. Germany **45** 52.51N 7.06E
Ruteng Indonesia **61** 8.35S 120.28E
Rutherglen Scotland **34** 55.49N 4.12W
Ruthin Wales **30** 53.07N 3.18W
Rutland U.S.A. **95** 43.37N 72.59W
Rutshuru Zaïre **73** 1.10S 29.26E
Ruvu Coast Tanzania **73** 6.50S 38.42E
Ruvuma *r.* Moçambique/Tanzania **73** 10.30S 40.30E
Ruvuma *d.* Tanzania **73** 10.45S 36.15E
Ruwandiz Iraq **57** 36.38N 44.32E
Ruwenzori Range *mts.* Uganda/Zaïre **73** 0.30N 30.00E
Ruyigi Burundi **73** 3.26S 30.14E
Ruzayevka U.S.S.R. **47** 54.04N 44.55E
Rwanda Africa **73** 2.00S 30.00E
Ryan, Loch Scotland **34** 54.56N 5.02W
Ryazan U.S.S.R. **47** 54.37N 39.43E
Ryazhsk U.S.S.R. **47** 53.40N 40.07E
Rybachi Pen. U.S.S.R. **46** 69.45N 32.30E
Rybinsk U.S.S.R. **47** 58.01N 38.52E
Rybinsk Resr. U.S.S.R. **47** 58.30N 38.25E
Ryde England **28** 50.44N 1.09W
Ryder's Hill England **31** 50.31N 3.53W
Rye England **29** 50.57N 0.46E
Rye *r.* England **33** 54.10N 0.44W
Rye B. England **29** 50.53N 0.48E
Ryton England **35** 54.59N 1.47W
Ryukyu Is. Japan **63** 26.30N 125.00E
Rzeszów Poland **47** 50.04N 22.00E
Rzhev U.S.S.R. **47** 56.15N 34.18E

S

Saale *r.* E. Germany **44** 51.58N 11.53E
Saar *r.* W. Germany **45** 49.43N 6.34E
Saarbrücken W. Germany **44** 49.15N 6.58E
Saarburg W. Germany **45** 49.36N 6.33E
Saaremaa *i.* U.S.S.R. **46** 58.30N 22.30E
Saarijärvi Finland **46** 62.44N 25.15E
Saarlouis W. Germany **44** 49.19N 6.45E
Saba *i.* Neth. Antilles **96** 17.42N 63.26W
Šabac Yugo. **43** 44.45N 19.41E
Sabadell Spain **41** 41.33N 2.07E
Sabana, Archipelago de Cuba **97** 23.30N 80.00W
Sabi *r.* Rhodesia **74** 21.16S 32.20E
Sabinas Mexico **90** 26.33N 101.10W
Sabinas *r.* Mexico **96** 27.31N 100.40W
Sabine *r.* U.S.A. **91** 29.40N 93.50W
Sable, C. Canada **93** 43.30N 65.50W
Sable, C. U.S.A. **96** 25.05N 81.10W
Sable I. Canada **93** 44.00N 60.00W
Sabzawar Afghan. **57** 33.18N 62.05E
Sabzawar Iran **57** 36.13N 57.38E
Sacedón Spain **41** 40.29N 2.44W
Sacquoy Head Scotland **37** 59.12N 3.05W
Sacramento U.S.A. **90** 38.32N 121.30W
Sacramento *r.* U.S.A. **90** 38.05N 122.00W
Sádaba Spain **41** 42.19N 1.10W
Sadani Tanzania **73** 6.00S 38.40E
Saddle Head Rep. of Ire. **38** 54.02N 10.12W
Saddleworth Moor *hills* England **32** 53.32N 1.55W
Sadiya India **59** 27.49N 95.38E
Safaha *des.* Saudi Arabia **56** 26.30N 39.30E
Safaniya Saudi Arabia **57** 28.00N 48.48E
Safed Koh *mtn.* Afghan. **57** 34.15N 63.30E
Säffle Sweden **46** 59.08N 12.55E
Saffron Walden England **29** 52.02N 0.15E
Safi Morocco **68** 32.20N 9.17W
Safonovo U.S.S.R. **47** 55.08N 33.16E
Sagaing Burma **59** 22.00N 96.00E
Sagar India **58** 23.50N 78.44E
Saginaw U.S.A. **94** 43.25N 83.54W
Saginaw B. U.S.A. **94** 44.00N 83.30W
Sagua la Grande Cuba **97** 22.55N 80.05W
Saguenay *r.* Canada **95** 48.10N 69.43W
Sagunto Spain **41** 39.40N 0.17W
Sahagún Spain **41** 42.23N 5.02W
Sahara *des.* Africa **68** 18.00N 12.00E
Saharan Atlas *mts.* Algeria **68** 34.20N 2.00E
Saharanpur India **58** 29.58N 77.33E
Sahba, Wadi *r.* Saudi Arabia **57** 23.48N 49.50E
Saida Algeria **41** 34.50N 0.10E
Saidabad Iran **57** 29.28N 55.43E
Saidpur Bangla. **58** 25.48N 89.00E
Saimaa *l.* Finland **46** 61.20N 28.00E
Saimbeyli Turkey **56** 38.07N 36.08E
Saindak Pakistan **57** 29.16N 61.36E
St. Abb's Head Scotland **35** 55.54N 2.07W
St. Agnes England **31** 50.18N 5.13W
St. Agnes *i.* England **31** 49.53N 6.20W
St. Albans England **27** 51.46N 0.21W
St. Alban's Head England **28** 50.35N 2.04W
St. Aldhelm's Head England **28** 50.35N 2.04W
St. Amand France **45** 50.27N 3.26E
St. Amand-Mt. Rond *town* France **40** 46.43N 2.29E
St. André, Cap Malagasy Rep. **73** 16.10S 44.27E
St. Andrews Canada **95** 45.05N 67.04W
St. Andrews Scotland **35** 56.20N 2.48W
St. Andrews B. Scotland **35** 56.23N 2.43W
St. Ann's Bay *town* Jamaica **97** 18.26N 77.12W
St. Ann's Head Wales **31** 51.41N 5.11W
St. Anthony Canada **93** 51.24N 55.37W
St. Arnaud Australia **80** 36.40S 143.20E
St. Aubin Channel Is. **31** 49.12N 2.10W
St. Augustine U.S.A. **91** 29.54N 81.19W
St. Austell England **31** 50.20N 4.48W
St. Austell B. England **31** 50.16N 4.43W
St. Barthélemy C. America **97** 17.55N 62.50W
St. Bees England **32** 54.29N 3.36W
St. Bees Head England **32** 54.31N 3.39W
St. Blazey England **31** 50.22N 4.48W
St. Boniface Canada **91** 49.58N 97.07W
St. Boswells Scotland **35** 55.35N 2.40W
St. Brides B. Wales **30** 51.48N 5.03W
St. Brieuc France **40** 48.31N 2.45W
St. Catherines Canada **95** 43.10N 79.15W
St. Catherine's Pt. England **28** 50.34N 1.18W
St. Céré France **40** 44.52N 1.53E
St. Christophe *i.* Malagasy Rep. **73** 17.06S 42.53E
St. Clair, L. Canada **94** 42.25N 82.35W
St. Clears Wales **30** 51.48N 4.30W
St. Cloud U.S.A. **91** 45.34N 94.10W
St. Columb Major England **31** 50.26N 4.56W
St. Croix *r.* U.S.A. **94** 44.43N 92.47W
St. Croix *i.* Virgin Is. **97** 17.45N 64.35W
St. David's Wales **30** 51.54N 5.16W
St. David's Head Wales **30** 51.55N 5.19W
St. Denis France **40** 48.56N 2.21E
St. Dié France **44** 48.17N 6.57E
St. Dizier France **40** 48.38N 4.58E
St. Elias, Mt. U.S.A. **92** 60.20N 139.00W
Saintes France **40** 45.44N 0.38W
St. Etienne France **40** 45.26N 4.26E
Saintfield N. Ireland **38** 54.28N 5.50W
St. Fillans Scotland **34** 56.24N 4.07W
St. Finan's B. Rep. of Ire. **39** 51.49N 10.21W
St. Flour France **40** 45.02N 3.05E
St. Gallen Switz. **44** 47.25N 9.23E
St. Gaudens France **40** 43.07N 0.44E
St. George Australia **80** 28.03S 148.30E
St. George's Grenada **97** 12.04N 61.44W
St. George's Channel Rep. of Ire./U.K. **39** 51.30N 6.20W
St. Germain France **40** 48.53N 2.04E
St. Gheorghe's Mouth *est.* Romania **43** 44.51N 29.37E
St. Gilles-sur-Vie France **40** 46.42N 1.56W
St. Girons France **40** 42.59N 1.08E
St. Gotthard Pass Switz. **44** 46.30N 8.55E
St. Govan's Head Wales **31** 51.36N 4.55W
St. Helena *i.* Atlantic Oc. **112** 16.00S 6.00W
St. Helena B. R.S.A. **74** 32.35S 18.00E
St. Helens England **30** 53.28N 2.43W
St. Helier Channel Is. **31** 49.12N 2.07W
St. Hubert Belgium **45** 50.02N 5.22E
St. Hyacinthe Canada **95** 45.38N 72.57W
St. Ives Cambs. England **29** 52.20N 0.05W
St. Ives Cornwall England **31** 50.13N 5.29W
St. Ives B. England **31** 50.14N 5.26W
St. Jean Pied de Port France **40** 43.10N 1.14W
St. Jérôme Canada **95** 45.47N 74.01W
St. John Canada **91** 45.16N 66.03W
St. John *r.* Canada **93** 45.30N 66.05W
St. John, L. Canada **95** 48.40N 72.00W
St. John's Antigua **97** 17.07N 61.51W
St. John's Canada **93** 47.34N 52.41W
St. John's Pt. N. Ireland **38** 54.14N 5.39W
St. John's Pt. Rep. of Ire. **38** 54.34N 8.28W
St. Joseph U.S.A. **91** 39.45N 94.51W
St. Joseph, L. Canada **91** 51.00N 91.05W
St. Just England **31** 50.07N 5.41W
St. Keverne England **31** 50.03N 5.05W
St. Kitts *i.* C. America **97** 17.25N 62.45W
St. Lawrence *r.* Canada **95** 48.45N 68.30W
St. Lawrence, G. of Canada **93** 48.00N 52.00W
St. Lawrence I. U.S.A. **92** 63.00N 170.00W
St. Leonard Canada **95** 47.10N 67.55W
St. Lô France **40** 49.07N 1.05W
St. Louis Senegal **70** 16.01N 16.30W
St. Louis U.S.A. **94** 38.40N 90.15W
St. Lucia C. America **97** 14.05N 61.00W
St. Magnus B. Scotland **36** 60.25N 1.35W
St. Maixent France **40** 46.25N 0.12W
St. Malo France **40** 48.39N 2.00W
St. Malo, Golfe de France **40** 49.20N 2.00W
St. Marc Haiti **97** 19.08N 72.41W
St. Margaret's at Cliffe England **29** 51.10N 1.23E
St. Margaret's Hope Scotland **37** 58.49N 2.57W
St. Martin Channel Is. **31** 49.27N 2.34W
St. Martin C. America **97** 18.05N 63.05W
St. Martin's *i.* England **31** 49.57N 6.16W
St. Mary Channel Is. **31** 49.14N 2.10W
St. Marys Australia **80** 41.33S 148.12E
St. Mary's *i.* England **31** 49.55N 6.16W
St. Mary's Scotland **37** 58.54N 2.55W
St. Mary's Loch Scotland **35** 55.29N 3.12W
St. Maurice *r.* Canada **95** 46.20N 72.30W
St. Mawes England **31** 50.10N 5.01W
St. Moritz Switz. **44** 46.30N 9.51E
St. Nazaire France **40** 47.17N 2.12W
St. Neots England **29** 52.14N 0.16W
St. Nicolas Belgium **45** 51.10N 4.09E
St. Ninian's I. Scotland **36** 59.58N 1.21W
St. Omer France **29** 50.45N 2.15E
St. Pancras England **27** 51.32N 0.08W
St. Paul France **40** 42.49N 2.29E
St. Paul *i.* Indian Oc. **113** 38.44S 77.30E
St. Paul U.S.A. **94** 45.00N 93.10W
St. Paul's Cray England **27** 51.24N 0.06E
St. Peter Port Channel Is. **31** 49.27N 2.32W
St. Petersburg U.S.A. **91** 27.45N 82.40W
St. Pierre-Miquelon *i.* N. America **93** 47.00N 56.15W
St. Pölten Austria **44** 48.13N 15.37E
St. Quentin France **45** 49.51N 3.17E
St. Sampson Channel Is. **31** 49.29N 2.31W
St. Stephen Canada **95** 45.12N 67.18W
St. Thomas Canada **94** 42.46N 81.12W
St. Thomas *i.* Virgin Is. **97** 18.22N 64.57W
St. Trond Belgium **45** 50.49N 5.11E
St. Tropez France **40** 43.16N 6.39E
St. Vallier France **40** 45.11N 4.49E
St. Vincent C. America **97** 13.10N 61.15W
St. Vincent, C. Portugal **41** 37.01N 8.59W
St. Vith Belgium **45** 50.15N 6.08E
St. Wendel W. Germany **45** 49.27N 7.10E
St. Yrieix France **40** 45.31N 1.12E
Saipan *i.* Asia **61** 15.12N 145.43E
Sakaka Saudi Arabia **56** 29.59N 40.12E
Sakania Zaïre **73** 12.44S 28.34E
Sakarya *r.* Turkey **56** 41.08N 30.36E
Sakété Benin **71** 6.45N 2.45E
Sakhalin *i.* U.S.S.R. **63** 50.00N 143.00E
Sakrivier R.S.A. **74** 30.50S 20.26E
Sakti India **58** 22.02N 82.56E
Sal *r.* U.S.S.R. **47** 47.33N 40.40E
Sala Sweden **46** 59.55N 16.38E
Salado *r.* La Pampa Argentina **103** 36.15S 66.45W
Salado *r.* Santa Fé Argentina **102** 32.00S 61.00W
Salado *r.* Mexico **96** 26.46N 98.55W
Salala Oman **58** 17.00N 54.04E
Salamanca Spain **41** 40.58N 5.40W
Salbris France **40** 47.26N 2.03E
Salcombe England **31** 50.14N 3.47W
Saldanha B. R.S.A. **74** 33.00S 17.56E
Sale Australia **80** 38.06S 147.06E
Sale England **32** 53.26N 2.19W
Salekhard U.S.S.R. **48** 66.33N 66.35E
Salem India **59** 11.38N 78.08E
Salem U.S.A. **94** 38.37N 88.58W
Salen Highland Scotland **34** 56.43N 5.46W
Salen Strath. Scotland **34** 56.31N 5.56W
Salerno Italy **42** 40.41N 14.45E
Salerno, G. of Med. Sea **42** 40.30N 14.45E
Salford England **32** 53.30N 2.17W
Salfords England **27** 51.12N 0.12W
Salima Malaŵi **73** 13.45S 34.29E
Salina Cruz Mexico **96** 16.11N 95.12W
Salins France **40** 46.56N 4.53E
Salisbury Rhodesia **74** 17.43S 31.05E
Salisbury England **28** 51.04N 1.48W
Salisbury U.S.A. **91** 38.22N 75.37W
Salisbury Plain *f.* England **28** 51.15N 1.55W
Salmon *r.* U.S.A. **90** 45.50N 116.50W
Salmon River Mts. U.S.A. **90** 44.30N 114.30W
Salo Finland **46** 60.23N 23.10E
Salobreña Spain **41** 36.45N 3.35W
Salon France **40** 43.38N 5.06E
Salonga *r.* Zaïre **72** 0.09S 19.52E
Salop *d.* England **28** 52.35N 2.40W
Salsk U.S.S.R. **47** 46.30N 41.33E
Salso *r.* Italy **42** 37.07N 13.57E
Salt Jordan **56** 32.03N 35.44E
Salta Argentina **103** 24.46S 65.28W
Salta *d.* Argentina **103** 25.05S 65.00W
Saltash England **31** 50.25N 4.13W
Saltburn-by-the-Sea England **33** 54.35N 0.58W
Saltcoats Scotland **34** 55.37N 4.47W
Saltee Is. Rep. of Ire. **39** 52.08N 6.36W
Saltfleet England **33** 53.25N 0.11E
Saltillo Mexico **96** 25.30N 101.00W
Salt Lake City U.S.A. **90** 40.45N 111.55W
Salto Uruguay **103** 31.27S 57.50W
Salton Sea *l.* U.S.A. **90** 33.25N 115.45W
Salûm Egypt **56** 31.31N 25.09E

Salvador Brazil **102** 12.58S 38.20W
Salwa Qatar **57** 24.44N 50.50E
Salween *r.* Burma **59** 16.30N 97.33E
Salyany U.S.S.R. **57** 39.36N 48.59E
Salzach *r.* Austria **44** 48.35N 13.30E
Salzburg Austria **44** 47.54N 13.03E
Salzgitter W. Germany **44** 52.02N 10.22E
Samana Dom. Rep. **97** 19.14N 69.20W
Samana Cay *i.* Bahamas **97** 23.05N 73.45W
Samar *i.* Phil. **61** 11.45N 125.15E
Samarinda Indonesia **60** 0.30S 117.09E
Samarkand U.S.S.R. **48** 39.40N 66.57E
Samarra Iraq **57** 34.13N 43.52E
Samawa Iraq **57** 31.18N 45.18E
Sambalpur India **59** 21.28N 84.04E
Samborombon Bay Argentina **103** 36.00S 56.50W
Sambre *r.* Belgium **45** 50.29N 4.52E
Same Tanzania **73** 4.10S 37.43E
Samer France **29** 50.38N 1.45E
Samirum Iran **57** 31.31N 52.10E
Sam Neua Laos **60** 20.25N 104.04E
Samoa Is. Pacific Oc. **107** 13.00S 171.00W
Sámos *i.* Greece **43** 37.44N 26.45E
Samothráki *i.* Greece **43** 40.26N 25.35E
Sampit Indonesia **60** 2.34S 112.59E
Samsun Turkey **56** 41.17N 36.22E
San Mali **70** 13.21N 4.57W
Sana Yemen **69** 16.02N 49.44E
Sana *r.* Yugo. **42** 45.03N 16.22E
Sanaga *r.* Cameroon **71** 3.35N 9.40E
Sanandaj Iran **57** 35.18N 47.01E
San Antonio U.S.A. **90** 29.25N 98.30W
San Antonio, C. Cuba **96** 21.50N 84.57W
San Antonio, Punta *c.* Mexico **90** 29.45N 115.41W
San Antonio Oeste Argentina **103** 40.45S 65.05W
San Bernardino U.S.A. **90** 34.07N 117.18W
San Blas, C. U.S.A. **91** 29.40N 85.25W
San Carlos Phil. **61** 15.59N 120.22E
San Cristóbal Argentina **103** 30.20S 61.14W
San Cristóbal Dom. Rep. **97** 18.27N 70.07W
San Cristóbal Venezuela **97** 7.46N 72.15W
Sancti Spíritus Cuba **97** 21.55N 79.28W
Sanda *i.* Scotland **34** 55.17N 5.34W
Sandakan Malaysia **60** 5.52N 118.04E
Sanday *i.* Scotland **37** 59.15N 2.33W
Sanday Sd. Scotland **37** 59.11N 2.35W
Sandbach England **32** 53.09N 2.23W
Sandbank Scotland **34** 55.59N 4.58W
Sanderstead England **27** 51.21N 0.05W
Sandgate Australia **80** 27.18S 153.00E
Sandgate England **29** 51.05N 1.09E
San Diego U.S.A. **90** 32.45N 117.10W
Sandling England **27** 51.18N 0.33E
Sandnes Norway **46** 58.51N 5.45E
Sandness Scotland **36** 60.18N 1.38W
Sandö *i.* Faroe Is. **46** 61.50N 6.45W
Sandoa Zaïre **72** 9.41S 22.56E
Sandoway Burma **59** 18.28N 94.20E
Sandown England **28** 50.39N 1.09W
Sandpoint U.S.A. **90** 48.17N 116.34W
Sandray *i.* Scotland **36** 56.53N 7.31W
Sandringham England **33** 52.50N 0.30E
Sandusky U.S.A. **94** 41.27N 82.42W
Sandviken Sweden **46** 60.38N 16.50E
Sandwich England **29** 51.16N 1.21E
Sandwick Scotland **36** 60.00N 1.14W
Sandy England **29** 52.08N 0.18W
Sandy L. Canada **91** 53.00N 93.00W
San Felipe Mexico **90** 31.03N 114.52W
San Felipe Venezuela **97** 10.25N 68.40W
San Felíu de Guixols Spain **41** 41.47N 3.02E
San Félix Venezuela **97** 8.22N 62.37W
San Fernando Phil. **61** 16.39N 120.19E
San Fernando Spain **41** 36.28N 6.12W
San Fernando Trinidad **97** 10.16N 61.28W
San Fernando Venezuela **97** 7.53N 67.15W
San Francisco Argentina **103** 31.29S 62.06W
San Francisco U.S.A. **90** 37.45N 122.27W
San Francisco de Macorís Dom. Rep. **97** 19.19N 70.15W
Sangerhausen E. Germany **44** 51.29N 11.18E
Sangha *r.* Congo **72** 1.10S 16.47E
Sangi *i.* Indonesia **61** 3.30N 125.30E
Sangihe Is. Indonesia **61** 2.45N 125.20E
Sangkan Ho *r.* China **63** 40.23N 115.18E
Sangonera *r.* Spain **41** 37.58N 1.04W
San Javier Bolivia **103** 16.22S 62.38W
San Jorge *r.* Colombia **97** 9.10N 74.40W
San Jorge, G. of Spain **41** 40.50N 1.10E
San José Costa Rica **96** 9.59N 84.04W
San José Guatemala **96** 13.58N 90.50W
San José Uruguay **103** 34.20S 56.42W
San Jose U.S.A. **90** 37.20N 121.55W
San José de Chiquitos Bolivia **103** 17.53S 60.45W
San Juan *r.* Costa Rica **96** 10.50N 83.40W
San Juan Puerto Rico **97** 18.29N 66.08W
San Juan *r.* U.S.A. **90** 37.20N 110.05W
San Juan del Norte Nicaragua **96** 10.58N 83.40W
San Juan de los Morros Venezuela **97** 9.53N 67.23W
San Juan Mts. U.S.A. **90** 37.30N 107.00W
Sankuru *r.* Zaïre **72** 4.20S 20.27E
San Leonardo Spain **41** 41.49N 3.04W
Sanlúcar de Barrameda Spain **41** 36.46N 6.21W
San Lucas, C. N. America **106** 22.50N 110.00W
San Luis Argentina **103** 33.20S 66.23W
San Luis *d.* Argentina **103** 33.00S 66.10W
San Luis Cuba **97** 20.13N 75.50W
San Luis Obispo U.S.A. **90** 35.16N 120.40W
San Luis Potosí Mexico **96** 22.10N 101.00W
San Luis Potosí *d.* Mexico **96** 23.00N 100.00W
San Marino Europe **42** 43.55N 12.27E
San Marino *town* San Marino **42** 43.55N 12.27E
San Matías, G. of Argentina **103** 41.30S 64.00W
San Miguel El Salvador **96** 13.28N 88.10W
San Miguel de Tucumán Argentina **103** 26.47S 65.15W
San Nicolás Argentina **103** 33.25S 60.15W
San Pablo Phil. **61** 13.58N 121.10E
San Pedro Argentina **103** 24.30S 65.00W
San Pedro Dom. Rep. **97** 18.30N 69.18W
San Pedro Mexico **96** 24.50N 102.59W
San Pedro Paraguay **103** 24.08S 57.08W
San Pedro, Punta *c.* Costa Rica **96** 8.30N 83.30W
San Pedro, Sierra de *mts.* Spain **41** 39.20N 6.20W
San Pedro Sula Honduras **96** 15.26N 88.01W
San Pietro *i.* Italy **42** 39.09N 8.16E
Sanquhar Scotland **35** 55.22N 3.56W
San Remo Italy **40** 43.48N 7.46E
San Salvador *i.* Bahamas **97** 24.00N 74.32W
San Salvador El Salvador **96** 13.40N 89.10W
San Salvador de Jujuy Argentina **103** 24.10S 65.18W
Sansanné-Mango Togo **70** 10.23N 0.30E
San Sebastián Spain **41** 43.19N 1.59W
San Severo Italy **42** 41.40N 15.24E
Santa Ana El Salvador **96** 14.00N 79.31W
Santa Barbara U.S.A. **90** 34.25N 119.41W
Santa Catarina *d.* Brazil **103** 27.00S 52.00W
Santa Clara Cuba **97** 22.25N 79.58W
Santa Cruz Bolivia **103** 17.45S 63.14W
Santa Cruz *d.* Bolivia **103** 17.45S 62.00W
Santa Elena, C. Costa Rica **96** 10.54N 85.56W
Santa Fé Argentina **103** 31.38S 60.43W
Santa Fé *d.* Argentina **103** 31.00S 61.00W
Santa Fe U.S.A. **90** 35.41N 105.57W
Santa María Brazil **103** 29.40S 53.47W
Santa Maria U.S.A. **90** 34.56N 120.25W
Santa Maria di Leuca, C. Italy **43** 39.47N 18.24E
Santa Marta Colombia **97** 11.18N 74.10W
Santander Spain **41** 43.28N 3.48W
Santañy Spain **41** 39.20N 3.07E
Santarém Portugal **41** 39.14N 8.40W
Santa Rosa Honduras **96** 14.47N 88.46W
Santa Rosa de Toay Argentina **103** 36.36S 64.15W
Santa Rosalia Mexico **90** 27.20N 112.20W
Santiago Chile **102** 34.00S 70.40W
Santiago Dom. Rep. **97** 19.30N 70.42W
Santiago Panamá **96** 8.08N 80.59W
Santiago de Compostela Spain **41** 42.52N 8.33W
Santiago de Cuba Cuba **97** 20.00N 75.49W
Santiago del Estero Argentina **103** 27.48S 64.15W
Santiago del Estero *d.* Argentina **103** 28.00S 63.50W
Santo André Brazil **103** 23.39S 46.29W
Santo Antonio do Zaire Angola **72** 6.12S 12.25E
Santo Domingo Dom. Rep. **97** 18.30N 69.57W
Santoña Spain **41** 43.27N 3.26W
Santos Brazil **103** 23.56S 46.22W
Santo Tomé Argentina **103** 28.31S 56.03W
San Vicente El Salvador **96** 13.38N 88.42W
Sanza Pombo Angola **72** 7.20S 16.12E
São Borja Brazil **103** 28.35S 56.01W
São Carlos Brazil **103** 22.02S 47.53W
São Francisco *r.* Brazil **102** 10.10S 36.10W
São Francisco do Sul Brazil **103** 26.17S 48.39W
São Luís Brazil **102** 2.44S 44.16W
Saona *i.* Dom. Rep. **97** 18.09N 68.42W
Saône *r.* France **40** 45.46N 4.52E
São Paulo Brazil **103** 23.33S 46.39W
São Paulo *d.* Brazil **103** 22.05S 48.00W
São Roque, C. S. America **106** 5.00S 35.00W
São Salvador do Congo Angola **72** 6.18S 14.16E
São Sebastião I. Brazil **103** 24.00S 45.25W
São Tomé *i.* Africa **72** 0.20N 6.30E
Saoura *d.* Algeria **70** 22.50N 0.10W
Sapporo Japan **63** 43.05N 141.21E
Sapri Italy **42** 40.04N 15.38E
Saqqiz Iran **57** 36.14N 46.15E
Sarab Iran **57** 37.56N 47.35E
Sara Buri Thailand **60** 14.32N 100.53E
Sarajevo Yugo. **43** 43.52N 18.26E
Sarangarh India **59** 21.38N 83.09E
Saransk U.S.S.R. **47** 54.12N 45.10E
Saratov U.S.S.R. **47** 51.30N 45.55E
Saratov Resr. U.S.S.R. **47** 51.00N 46.00E
Sarbaz Iran **57** 26.39N 61.20E
Sardinia *i.* Italy **42** 40.00N 9.00E
Sarek *mtn.* Sweden **46** 67.10N 17.45E
Sarh Chad **71** 9.08N 18.22E
Sari Iran **57** 36.33N 53.06E
Sarigan *i.* Asia **61** 16.43N 145.47E
Sark *i.* Channel Is. **31** 49.26N 2.22W
Sarmi Asia **61** 1.51S 138.45E
Särna Sweden **46** 61.40N 13.10E
Sarnia Canada **94** 42.57N 82.24W
Sarny U.S.S.R. **47** 51.21N 26.31E
Saros, G. of Turkey **43** 40.32N 26.25E
Sarpsborg Norway **46** 59.17N 11.06E
Sarre *r. see* Saar France **44**
Sarrebourg France **44** 48.43N 7.03E
Sarria Spain **41** 42.47N 7.25W
Sartène France **42** 41.38N 8.48E
Sarthe *r.* France **40** 47.29N 0.30W
Sarur Oman **57** 23.25N 58.10E
Sasaram India **58** 24.58N 84.01E
Sasebo Japan **63** 33.10N 129.42E
Saskatchewan *d.* Canada **92** 55.00N 105.00W
Saskatchewan *r.* Canada **93** 53.25N 100.15W
Saskatoon Canada **90** 52.10N 106.40W
Sasovo U.S.S.R. **47** 54.21N 41.58E
Sassandra Ivory Coast **70** 4.58N 6.08W
Sassandra *r.* Ivory Coast **70** 5.00N 6.04W
Sássari Italy **42** 40.43N 8.33E
Sassnitz E. Germany **44** 54.32N 13.40E
Sasyk, L. U.S.S.R. **43** 45.38N 29.38E
Satadougou Mali **70** 12.30N 11.30W
Satara India **58** 17.43N 74.05E
Satna India **58** 24.33N 80.50E
Satpura Range *mts.* India **58** 21.50N 76.00E
Satu Mare Romania **47** 47.48N 22.52E
Sauda Norway **46** 59.38N 6.23E
Saudi Arabia Asia **56** 26.00N 44.00E
Saulieu France **40** 47.17N 4.14E
Sault Sainte Marie Canada **94** 46.32N 84.20W
Sault Sainte Marie U.S.A. **94** 46.29N 84.22W
Saumur France **40** 47.16N 0.05W
Saundersfoot Wales **31** 51.43N 4.42W
Sava *r.* Yugo. **43** 44.50N 20.26E
Savannah U.S.A. **91** 32.09N 81.01W
Savannah *r.* U.S.A. **91** 32.10N 81.00W
Savannakhet Laos **60** 16.34N 104.55E
Savé Benin **71** 8.04N 2.37E
Save *r.* France **41** 43.30N 0.55E
Save *r.* Moçambique **74** 21.00S 35.01E
Saveh Iran **57** 35.00N 50.25E
Savona Italy **40** 44.18N 8.28E
Savonlinna Finland **46** 61.52N 28.51E
Savu Sea Pacific Oc. **61** 9.30S 122.30E
Sawbridgeworth England **27** 51.50N 0.09E
Sawston England **29** 52.07N 0.11E
Sawu *i.* Indonesia **61** 10.30S 121.50E
Saxmundham England **29** 52.13N 1.29E
Saxthorpe England **29** 52.50N 1.09E
Sayan Mts. U.S.S.R. **62** 51.30N 102.00E
Sayn Shand Mongolia **63** 44.58N 110.10E
Sayula Mexico **96** 19.52N 103.36W
Sázava *r.* Czech. **44** 49.53N 14.21E
Sbeitla Tunisia **42** 35.16N 9.10E
Scafell Pike *mtn.* England **32** 54.27N 3.12W
Scalasaig Scotland **34** 56.04N 6.12W
Scalby England **33** 54.18N 0.26W
Scalloway Scotland **36** 60.08N 1.17W
Scalpay *i.* Highland Scotland **36** 57.18N 5.58W
Scalpay *i.* W. Isles Scotland **36** 57.52N 6.40W
Scammon Bay *town* U.S.A. **92** 61.50N 165.35W
Scandinavia *f.* Europe **107** 65.00N 18.00E
Scapa Flow *str.* Scotland **37** 58.53N 3.05W
Scarba *i.* Scotland **34** 56.11N 5.42W
Scarborough Canada **95** 43.44N 79.16W
Scarborough England **33** 54.17N 0.24W
Scariff I. Rep. of Ire. **39** 51.43N 10.16W
Scarinish Scotland **34** 56.30N 6.48W
Scarp *i.* Scotland **36** 58.02N 7.07W
Scavaig, Loch Scotland **36** 57.10N 6.08W
Schaffhausen Switz. **44** 47.42N 8.38E
Schagen Neth. **45** 52.47N 4.47E
Schefferville Canada **93** 54.50N 67.00W
Schelde *r.* Belgium **45** 51.13N 4.25E
Schenectady U.S.A. **95** 42.28N 73.57W
Scheveningen Neth. **45** 52.07N 4.16E
Schiedam Neth. **45** 51.55N 4.25E
Schiehallion *mtn.* Scotland **35** 56.40N 4.08W
Schiermonnikoog *i.* Neth. **45** 53.28N 6.15E
Schleiden W. Germany **45** 50.32N 6.29E
Schleswig W. Germany **44** 54.32N 9.34E
Schönebeck E. Germany **44** 52.01N 11.45E
Schouten Is. Indonesia **61** 0.45S 135.50E
Schouwen *i.* Neth. **45** 51.42N 3.45E
Schwäbish Hall W. Germany **44** 49.07N 9.45E
Schwandorf W. Germany **44** 49.20N 12.07E
Schwaner Mts. Indonesia **60** 0.45S 113.20E
Schwecht E. Germany **44** 53.04N 14.17E

Schweinfurt W. Germany **44** 50.03N 10.16E
Schwelm W. Germany **45** 51.17N 7.18E
Schwenningen W. Germany **44** 48.03N 8.32E
Schwerin E. Germany **44** 53.38N 11.25E
Sciacca Italy **42** 37.31N 13.05E
Scilly, Isles of England **31** 49.55N 6.20W
Scioto *r.* U.S.A. **94** 38.43N 83.00W
Scone Australia **80** 32.01S 150.53E
Scottsbluff U.S.A. **90** 41.52N 103.40W
Scottsdale Australia **80** 41.09S 147.31E
Scourie Scotland **36** 58.20N 5.08W
Scranton U.S.A. **95** 41.25N 75.40W
Scridain, Loch Scotland **34** 56.22N 6.06W
Scunthorpe England **33** 53.35N 0.38W
Seaford England **29** 50.46N 0.08E
Seaham England **33** 54.52N 1.21W
Seahouses England **35** 55.35N 1.38W
Seal *r.* Canada **93** 59.00N 95.00W
Sea Lake *town* Australia **80** 35.31S 142.54E
Seamill Scotland **34** 55.41N 4.52W
Seascale England **32** 54.24N 3.29W
Seaton Cumbria England **32** 54.41N 3.31W
Seaton Devon England **28** 50.43N 3.05W
Seaton Delaval England **35** 55.05N 1.31W
Seattle U.S.A. **90** 47.35N 122.20W
Sebago L. U.S.A. **95** 43.37N 71.20W
Sebastian Vizcaino B. Mexico **90** 28.20N 114.45W
Sebha Libya **68** 27.04N 14.25E
Sebinkarahisar Turkey **56** 40.19N 38.25E
Séda *r.* Portugal **41** 38.55N 7.30W
Sedan France **45** 49.42N 4.57E
Sedbergh England **32** 54.20N 2.31W
Sedgefield England **33** 54.40N 1.27W
Sédhiou Senegal **70** 12.44N 15.30W
Sefadu Sierra Leone **70** 8.41N 10.55W
Ségou Mali **70** 13.28N 6.18W
Segovia Spain **41** 40.57N 4.07W
Segre *r.* Spain **41** 41.25N 0.21E
Séguéla Ivory Coast **70** 7.58N 6.44W
Segura *r.* Spain **41** 38.07N 0.14W
Segura, Sierra de *mts.* Spain **41** 38.00N 2.50W
Sehkuheh Iran **57** 30.45N 61.29E
Seil *i.* Scotland **34** 56.18N 5.33W
Seiland Norway **46** 70.30N 23.00E
Seinäjoki Finland **46** 62.45N 22.55E
Seine *r.* France **40** 49.28N 0.25E
Seistan *f.* Iran **57** 31.00N 61.15E
Sekondi-Takoradi Ghana **70** 4.57N 1.44W
Selaru *i.* Asia **61** 8.15S 131.00E
Selby England **33** 53.47N 1.05W
Sele *r.* Italy **42** 40.30N 14.50E
Selenga *r.* U.S.S.R. **62** 52.20N 106.20E
Sélestat France **44** 48.16N 7.28E
Selkirk Scotland **35** 55.33N 2.51W
Selkirk Mts. Canada/U.S.A. **90** 50.00N 116.30W
Selsdon England **27** 51.21N 0.03W
Selsey England **28** 50.44N 0.47W
Selsey Bill *c.* England **28** 50.44N 0.47W
Selukwe Rhodesia **74** 19.40S 30.00E
Selvas *f.* S. America **106** 7.00S 66.00W
Selwyn Mts. Canada **92** 63.00N 130.00W
Seman *r.* Albania **43** 40.53N 19.25E
Semarang Indonesia **60** 6.58S 110.29E
Seminoe Resr. U.S.A. **90** 42.05N 106.50W
Semipalatinsk U.S.S.R. **48** 50.26N 80.16E
Semliki *r.* Zaïre **73** 1.12N 30.27E
Semmering Pass Austria **44** 47.40N 16.00E
Semnan Iran **57** 35.31N 53.24E
Semois *r.* France **45** 49.53N 4.45E
Semu *r.* Tanzania **73** 3.57S 34.20E
Senanga Zambia **72** 15.52S 23.19E
Send England **27** 51.17N 0.33W
Sendai Japan **63** 38.16N 140.52E
Seneca L. U.S.A. **95** 42.35N 77.07W
Senegal Africa **70** 14.30N 14.30W
Sénégal *r.* Senegal/Mauritania **70** 16.00N 16.28W
Senekal R.S.A. **74** 28.19S 27.38E
Senigallia Italy **42** 43.42N 13.14E
Senja *i.* Norway **46** 69.20N 17.30E
Senlis France **40** 49.12N 2.35E
Sennar Sudan **69** 13.31N 33.38E
Sennen England **31** 50.04N 5.42W
Senneterre Canada **95** 48.24N 77.16W
Sennybridge Wales **30** 51.57N 3.35W
Sens France **40** 48.12N 3.18E
Sentery Zaïre **72** 5.19S 25.43E
Seoul S. Korea **63** 37.30N 127.00E
Sepik *r.* P.N.G. **61** 3.54S 144.30E
Sept Îles *town* Canada **93** 50.13N 66.22W
Seraing Belgium **45** 50.37N 5.33E
Serengeti Nat. Park Tanzania **73** 2.30S 35.00E
Serengeti Plain *f.* Tanzania **73** 3.00S 35.00E
Serenje Zambia **73** 13.12S 30.50E
Sérevac France **42** 44.20N 3.05E
Sergach U.S.S.R. **47** 55.32N 45.27E
Sermate *i.* Indonesia **61** 8.30S 129.00E
Serov U.S.S.R. **48** 59.22N 60.32E
Serowe Botswana **74** 22.25S 26.44E
Serpa Portugal **41** 37.56N 7.36W
Serpent's Mouth *str.* Venezuela **97** 9.50N 61.00W
Serpukhov U.S.S.R. **47** 54.53N 37.25E
Sérrai Greece **43** 41.04N 23.32E
Serrat, C. Tunisia **42** 37.15N 9.12E
Serre *r.* France **45** 49.40N 3.22E
Sese Is. Uganda **73** 0.20S 32.30E
Sesheke Zambia **72** 17.14S 24.22E
Sesimbra Portugal **41** 38.26N 9.06W
Sète France **40** 43.25N 3.43E
Sete Lagoas Brazil **103** 19.29S 44.15W
Sétif Algeria **42** 36.10N 5.26E
Setté Cama Gabon **72** 2.32S 9.46E
Settle England **32** 54.05N 2.18W
Setúbal Portugal **41** 38.31N 8.54W
Setúbal, B. of Portugal **41** 38.20N 9.00W
Seul, Lac *l.* Canada **91** 50.25N 92.15W
Sevan, L. U.S.S.R. **57** 40.22N 45.20E
Sevastopol' U.S.S.R. **47** 44.36N 33.31E
Seven Heads *c.* Rep. of Ire. **39** 51.34N 8.43W
Seven Kings England **27** 51.34N 0.06E
Sevenoaks England **27** 51.16N 0.12E
Séverac France **40** 44.20N 3.05E
Severn *r.* Canada **93** 56.00N 87.40W
Severn *r.* England **28** 51.50N 2.21W
Severnaya Zemlya *is.* U.S.S.R. **49** 80.00N 96.00E
Seville Spain **41** 37.24N 5.59W
Sèvre Niortaise *r.* France **40** 46.35N 1.05W
Sewa *r.* Sierra Leone **70** 7.15N 12.08W
Seward U.S.A. **92** 60.05N 149.34W
Seward Pen. U.S.A. **92** 65.00N 164.10W
Seychelles *is.* Indian Oc. **55** 5.00S 55.00E
Seydhisfjördhur Iceland **46** 65.16N 14.02W
Seymour U.S.A. **94** 38.57N 85.55W
Sézanne France **40** 48.44N 3.44E
Sfântu Gheorghe Romania **43** 45.52N 25.50E
Sfax Tunisia **68** 34.45N 10.43E
'sGravenhage *see* The Hague Neth. **45**
Sgurr Mòr *mtn.* Scotland **36** 57.41N 5.01W
Sgurr na Lapaich *mtn.* Scotland **36** 57.22N 5.04W
Shaba *d.* Zaïre **73** 8.00S 27.00E
Shabani Rhodesia **74** 20.20S 30.05E
Shabunda Zaïre **73** 2.42S 27.20E
Shaftesbury England **28** 51.00N 2.12W
Shahabad Iran **57** 34.08N 46.35E
Shah Dad Iran **57** 30.27N 57.44E
Shahdol India **58** 23.10N 81.26E
Shahjahanpur India **58** 27.53N 79.55E
Shahpur Iran **57** 38.13N 44.50E
Shahreza Iran **57** 32.00N 51.52E
Shahr-i-Babak Iran **57** 30.08N 55.04E
Shahr Kord Iran **57** 32.40N 50.52E
Shahrud Iran **57** 36.25N 55.00E
Shahsawar Iran **57** 36.49N 50.54E
Shaib al Qur *r.* Saudi Arabia **56** 31.02N 42.00E
Shakhty U.S.S.R. **47** 47.43N 40.16E
Shalford England **27** 51.13N 0.35W
Sham, Jebel *mtn.* Oman **57** 23.14N 57.17E
Shamiya Desert Iraq **57** 30.30N 45.30E
Shamley Green England **27** 51.11N 0.30W
Shamva Rhodesia **74** 17.20S 31.38E
Shanghai China **63** 31.13N 121.25E
Shanklin England **28** 50.39N 1.09W
Shannon *r.* Rep. of Ire. **38** 52.39N 8.43W
Shannon, Mouth of the *est.* Rep. of Ire. **39** 52.29N 9.57W
Shansi *d.* China **63** 36.45N 112.00E
Shan State *d.* Burma **59** 21.30N 98.00E
Shantar Is. U.S.S.R. **49** 55.00N 138.00E
Shantung *d.* China **63** 35.45N 117.30E
Shantung Pen. China **63** 37.00N 121.30E
Shaohing China **63** 30.02N 120.35E
Shaoyang China **63** 27.43N 111.24E
Shap England **32** 54.32N 2.40W
Shapinsay *i.* Scotland **37** 59.03N 2.51W
Shapinsay Sd. Scotland **37** 59.01N 2.55W
Shapur *ruins* Iran **57** 29.42N 51.30E
Shaqra Saudi Arabia **57** 25.17N 45.14E
Sharjah U.A.E. **57** 25.20N 55.26E
Sharon U.S.A. **94** 41.16N 80.30W
Shashi *r.* Botswana **74** 22.10S 29.15E
Shasi China **63** 30.16N 112.20E
Shasta, Mt. U.S.A. **90** 41.35N 122.12W
Shatt al Arab *r.* Iraq **57** 30.00N 48.30E
Shawano U.S.A. **94** 44.46N 88.38W
Shawinigan Canada **95** 46.33N 72.45W
Shebelle *r.* Somali Rep. **73** 0.30N 43.10E
Sheboygan U.S.A. **94** 43.46N 87.44W
Shebshi Mts. Nigeria **71** 8.30N 11.45E
Sheeffry Hills Rep. of Ire. **38** 53.41N 9.42W
Sheelin, Lough Rep. of Ire. **38** 53.48N 7.20W
Sheep Haven *b.* Rep. of Ire. **38** 55.12N 7.52W
Sheep's Head Rep. of Ire. **39** 51.33N 9.52W
Sheerness England **29** 51.26N 0.47E
Sheffield England **33** 53.23N 1.28W
Shefford England **29** 52.02N 0.20W
Shehy Mts. Rep. of Ire. **39** 51.47N 9.15W
Shelag *r.* Afghan. **57** 30.18N 61.02E
Shelby U.S.A. **90** 48.30N 111.52W
Shelikof Str. U.S.A. **92** 58.00N 153.45W
Shellharbour Australia **80** 34.35S 150.52E
Shëngjin Albania **43** 41.49N 19.33E
Shenley England **27** 51.43N 0.17W
Shensi *d.* China **63** 35.00N 109.00E
Shenyang China **63** 41.50N 123.26E
Shepparton Australia **80** 36.25S 145.26E
Shepperton England **27** 51.23N 0.28W
Sheppey, Isle of England **29** 51.24N 0.50E
Shepshed England **33** 52.46N 1.17W
Shepton Mallet England **28** 51.11N 2.31W
Shepway England **27** 51.15N 0.33E
Sherborne England **28** 50.56N 2.31W
Sherbro I. Sierra Leone **70** 7.30N 12.50W
Sherbrooke Canada **95** 45.24N 71.54W
Shere England **27** 51.13N 0.28W
Sheridan U.S.A. **90** 44.48N 107.05W
Sheringham England **33** 52.56N 1.11E
Sherkin I. Rep. of Ire. **39** 51.28N 9.25W
Sherman U.S.A. **91** 33.39N 96.35W
Sherridon Canada **93** 57.07N 101.05W
'sHertogenbosch Neth. **45** 51.42N 5.19E
Sherwood Forest *f.* England **33** 53.10N 1.05W
Shetland Is. *d.* Scotland **36** 60.20N 1.15W
Shevchenko U.S.S.R. **48** 43.40N 51.20E
Shiant Is. Scotland **36** 57.54N 6.20W
Shiel, Loch Scotland **36** 56.48N 5.33W
Shiel Bridge *town* Scotland **36** 57.12N 5.26W
Shieldaig Scotland **36** 57.31N 5.40W
Shifnal England **28** 52.40N 2.23W
Shigatse China **59** 29.18N 88.50E
Shihkiachwang China **63** 38.04N 114.28E
Shihtsien China **63** 27.30N 108.20E
Shikarpur Pakistan **58** 27.58N 68.42E
Shikoku *i.* Japan **63** 33.30N 133.30E
Shilbottle England **35** 55.22N 1.43W
Shildon England **32** 54.37N 1.39W
Shilka U.S.S.R. **63** 51.55N 116.01E
Shilka *r.* U.S.S.R. **63** 53.20N 121.10E
Shillong India **59** 25.34N 91.53E
Shimoga India **58** 13.56N 75.31E
Shimonoseki Japan **63** 33.59N 130.58E
Shin, Loch Scotland **37** 58.06N 4.32W
Shinyanga Tanzania **73** 3.40S 33.20E
Shinyanga *d.* Tanzania **73** 3.30S 33.00E
Shipka Pass Bulgaria **43** 42.45N 25.25E
Shipley England **32** 53.50N 1.47W
Shipston on Stour England **28** 52.04N 1.38W
Shipton England **33** 54.01N 1.09W
Shirak Steppe *f.* U.S.S.R. **57** 41.40N 46.20E
Shiraz Iran **57** 29.36N 52.33E
Shire *r.* Moçambique **73** 17.46S 35.20E
Shir Kuh *mtn.* Iran **57** 31.38N 54.07E
Shiukwan China **63** 24.54N 113.33E
Shivpuri India **58** 25.26N 77.39E
Shizuoka Japan **63** 34.59N 138.24E
Shkodër Albania **43** 42.03N 19.30E
Shkoder, L. Albania/Yugo. **43** 42.10N 19.18E
Shoeburyness England **29** 51.31N 0.49E
Sholapur India **58** 17.43N 75.56E
Shoreditch England **27** 51.32N 0.05W
Shoreham-by-Sea England **29** 50.50N 0.17W
Shostka U.S.S.R. **47** 51.53N 33.30E
Shotts Scotland **35** 55.49N 3.48W
Shreveport U.S.A. **91** 32.30N 93.46W
Shrewsbury England **28** 52.42N 2.45W
Shrewton England **28** 51.11N 1.55W
Shu'aiba Iraq **57** 30.30N 47.40E
Shumagin Is. U.S.A. **92** 55.00N 160.00W
Shur *r.* Iran **57** 28.00N 55.45E
Shurab *r.* Iran **57** 31.30N 55.18E
Shushtar Iran **57** 32.04N 48.53E
Shuya U.S.S.R. **47** 56.49N 41.23E
Shwebo Burma **59** 22.35N 95.42E
Sialkot Pakistan **58** 32.29N 74.35E
Siam, G. of Asia **59** 10.30N 101.00E
Sian China **63** 34.16N 108.54E
Siangfan China **63** 32.20N 112.05E
Siang Kiang *r.* Kwangsi-Chuang China **63** 23.25N 110.00E
Siangtan China **63** 27.55N 112.47E
Siangyang China **63** 32.00N 112.00E
Siargao *i.* Phil. **61** 9.55N 126.05E
Siauliai U.S.S.R. **46** 55.51N 23.20E
Šibenik Yugo. **42** 43.45N 15.55E
Siberia *d.* Asia **107** 62.00N 104.00E
Siberut *i.* Indonesia **60** 1.30S 99.00E
Sibi Pakistan **58** 29.31N 67.54E
Sibiti Congo **72** 3.40S 13.24E
Sibiti *r.* Tanzania **73** 3.47S 34.45E
Sibiu Romania **43** 45.47N 24.09E
Sibolga Indonesia **60** 1.42N 98.48E
Sibu Malaysia **60** 2.18N 111.49E

Sichang China **59** 28.00N 102.10E
Sicily *i.* Italy **42** 37.30N 14.00E
Sidcup England **27** 51.26N 0.07E
Sidi Barrani Egypt **56** 31.38N 25.58E
Sidi-bel-Abbès Algeria **41** 35.15N 0.39W
Sidlaw Hills Scotland **35** 56.31N 3.10W
Sidmouth England **28** 50.40N 3.13W
Sidon Lebanon **56** 33.32N 35.22E
Siedlce Poland **47** 52.10N 22.18E
Sieg *r.* W. Germany **45** 50.49N 7.11E
Siegburg W. Germany **45** 50.48N 7.13E
Siegen W. Germany **45** 50.52N 8.02E
Siena Italy **42** 43.19N 11.20E
Sierra Blanca *mtn.* U.S.A. **90** 33.23N 105.49W
Sierra Leone Africa **70** 9.00N 12.00W
Sighişoara Romania **43** 46.13N 24.49E
Sighty Crag *mtn.* England **35** 55.07N 2.38W
Siglufjördhur Iceland **46** 66.09N 18.55W
Signy France **45** 49.42N 4.25E
Sigüenza Spain **41** 41.04N 2.38W
Siguiri Guinea **70** 11.28N 9.07W
Siirt Turkey **56** 37.56N 41.56E
Sikar India **58** 27.33N 75.12E
Sikasso Mali **70** 11.18N 5.38W
Sikhote-Alin Range *mts.* U.S.S.R. **63** 45.20N 136.50E
Si Kiang *r.* China **63** 22.23N 113.20E
Sikkim *d.* India **58** 27.30N 88.30E
Sil *r.* Spain **41** 42.24N 7.15W
Silchar India **59** 24.49N 92.47E
Sileby England **28** 52.44N 1.06W
Silesian Plateau *f.* Poland **47** 50.30N 20.00E
Silgarhi Nepal **59** 29.14N 80.58E
Silifke Turkey **56** 36.22N 33.57E
Siliguri India **58** 26.42N 88.30E
Silistra Bulgaria **43** 44.07N 27.17E
Siljan *l.* Sweden **46** 60.50N 14.40E
Silkeborg Denmark **46** 56.10N 9.39E
Silloth England **35** 54.53N 3.25W
Silsden England **32** 53.55N 1.55W
Silver City U.S.A. **90** 32.47N 108.16W
Silver End England **27** 51.51N 0.38E
Silvermines Rep. of Ire. **39** 52.48N 8.15W
Silvermines Mts. Rep. of Ire. **39** 52.46N 8.17W
Silver Spring *town* U.S.A. **95** 39.00N 77.01W
Silverstone England **28** 52.05N 1.03W
Silverton England **28** 50.49N 3.29W
Simanggang Malaysia **60** 1.10N 111.32E
Simard, L. Canada **95** 47.37N 78.40W
Simav *r.* Turkey **43** 40.24N 28.31E
Simcoe, L. Canada **95** 44.25N 79.20W
Simeulue *i.* Indonesia **60** 2.30N 96.00E
Simferopol' U.S.S.R. **47** 44.57N 34.05E
Simiyu *r.* Tanzania **73** 2.32S 33.25E
Simla India **58** 31.07N 77.09E
Simmern W. Germany **45** 49.59N 7.32E
Simo *r.* Finland **46** 65.38N 24.57E
Simonsbath England **31** 51.07N 3.45W
Simonstown R.S.A. **74** 34.12S 18.26E
Simplon Pass Switz. **40** 46.15N 8.03E
Simplon Tunnel Italy/Switz. **44** 46.20N 8.05E
Simrishamn Sweden **46** 55.35N 14.20E
Sinai *pen.* Egypt **56** 29.00N 34.00E
Sinclair's B. Scotland **37** 58.30N 3.07W
Sines Portugal **41** 37.58N 8.52W
Singapore Asia **60** 1.20N 103.45E
Singapore *town* Singapore **60** 1.20N 103.45E
Singaraja Indonesia **60** 8.06S 115.07E
Singen W. Germany **44** 47.45N 8.50E
Singida Tanzania **73** 4.45S 34.42E
Singida *d.* Tanzania **73** 6.00S 34.30E
Singitikos G. Med. Sea **43** 40.12N 24.00E
Singkep *i.* Indonesia **60** 0.30S 104.20E
Sinhailien China **63** 34.37N 119.10E
Sining China **62** 36.35N 101.55E
Sinj Yugo. **43** 43.42N 16.38E
Sinkiang-Uighur *d.* China **62** 41.15N 87.00E
Sinoia Rhodesia **74** 17.21S 30.13E
Sinop Turkey **56** 42.02N 35.09E
Sint Eustatius *i.* Neth. Antilles **97** 17.33N 63.00W
Sinu *r.* Colombia **97** 9.25N 76.00W
Sioux City U.S.A. **91** 42.30N 96.28W
Sioux Falls *town* U.S.A. **91** 43.34N 96.42W
Sioux Lookout *town* Canada **91** 50.07N 91.54W
Sipolilo Rhodesia **74** 16.43S 30.43E
Sipora *i.* Indonesia **60** 2.10S 99.40E
Sira *r.* Norway **46** 58.13N 6.13E
Siracusa Italy **42** 37.05N 15.17E
Siret *r.* Romania **43** 45.28N 27.56E
Sirhan, Wadi *f.* Saudi Arabia **56** 31.00N 37.30E
Sirra, Wadi *r.* Saudi Arabia **57** 23.10N 44.22E
Sirte Libya **68** 31.10N 16.39E
Sirte, G. of Libya **68** 31.45N 17.50E
Sisak Yugo. **42** 45.30N 16.21E
Sishen R.S.A. **74** 27.47S 23.00E
Sisophon Khmer Rep. **59** 13.37N 102.58E
Sisteron France **40** 44.16N 5.56E
Sitapur India **58** 27.33N 80.40E
Sitka U.S.A. **92** 57.05N 135.20W
Sittang *r.* Burma **59** 17.30N 96.53E
Sittard Neth. **45** 51.00N 5.52E
Sittingbourne England **29** 51.20N 0.43E
Sivas Turkey **56** 39.44N 37.01E
Sivrihisar Turkey **56** 39.29N 31.32E
Siwa Egypt **56** 29.11N 25.31E
Siwa Oasis Egypt **56** 29.10N 25.45E
Sixmilebridge *town* Rep. of Ire. **39** 52.45N 8.47W
Sixmilecross N. Ireland **34** 54.34N 7.08W
Skagen Denmark **46** 57.44N 10.37E
Skagerrak *str.* Denmark/Norway **46** 57.45N 8.55E
Skagway U.S.A. **92** 59.23N 135.20W
Skaill Scotland **37** 58.56N 2.43W
Skalintyy *mtn.* U.S.S.R. **49** 56.00N 130.40E
Skara Sweden **46** 58.23N 13.25E
Skaw Taing *c.* Scotland **36** 60.23N 0.56W
Skeena *r.* Canada **92** 54.10N 129.08W
Skegness England **33** 53.09N 0.20E
Skellefte *r.* Sweden **46** 64.44N 21.07E
Skellefteå Sweden **46** 64.45N 21.00E
Skelmersdale England **32** 53.34N 2.49W
Skelmorlie Scotland **34** 55.51N 4.52W
Skene Sweden **46** 57.30N 12.35E
Skerries Rep. of Ire. **38** 53.35N 6.07W
Skerryvore *i.* Scotland **34** 56.20N 7.05W
Skhiza *i.* Greece **43** 36.42N 21.45E
Ski Norway **46** 59.43N 10.52E
Skibbereen Rep. of Ire. **39** 51.34N 9.16W
Skiddaw *mtn.* England **32** 54.40N 3.09W
Skien Norway **46** 59.14N 9.37E
Skikda Algeria **42** 36.53N 6.54E
Skipness Scotland **34** 56.45N 5.22W
Skipton England **32** 53.57N 2.01W
Skíros *i.* Greece **43** 38.50N 24.33E
Skjálfanda Fljót *r.* Iceland **46** 65.55N 17.30W
Skokholm *i.* Wales **31** 51.42N 5.17W
Skokie U.S.A. **94** 42.01N 87.45W
Skomer *i.* Wales **31** 51.45N 5.18W
Skopje Yugo. **43** 41.58N 21.27E
Skövde Sweden **46** 58.24N 13.52E
Skovorodino U.S.S.R. **49** 54.00N 123.53E
Skreia Norway **46** 60.38N 10.57E
Skull Rep. of Ire. **39** 51.32N 9.33W
Skye *i.* Scotland **36** 57.20N 6.15W
Slagelse Denmark **46** 55.24N 11.23E
Slaidburn England **32** 53.57N 2.28W
Slamat *mtn.* Indonesia **60** 7.10S 109.10E
Slane Rep. of Ire. **38** 53.43N 6.33W
Slaney *r.* Rep. of Ire. **39** 52.21N 6.30W
Slantsy U.S.S.R. **46** 59.09N 28.09E
Slapin, Loch Scotland **36** 57.10N 6.01W
Slatina Romania **43** 44.26N 24.23E
Slave *r.* Canada **92** 51.10N 113.30W
Slavgorod R.S.F.S.R. U.S.S.R. **48** 53.01N 78.37E
Slavgorod W.R.S.S.R. U.S.S.R. **47** 53.25N 31.00E
Slavyansk U.S.S.R. **47** 48.51N 37.36E
Sleaford England **33** 53.00N 0.22W
Slea Head Rep. of Ire. **39** 52.05N 10.27W
Sleat, Pt. of Scotland **36** 57.01N 6.01W
Sleat, Sd. of *str.* Scotland **36** 57.05N 5.48W
Sledmere England **33** 54.04N 0.35W
Sleetmute U.S.A. **92** 61.40N 157.11W
Sleights England **33** 54.26N 0.40W
Sliabh Gaoil *mtn.* Scotland **34** 55.54N 5.30W
Slide Mtn. U.S.A. **95** 42.00N 74.23W
Sliedrecht Neth. **45** 51.48N 4.46E
Slieveardagh Hills Rep. of Ire. **39** 52.39N 7.32W
Slieve Aughty *mtn.* Rep. of Ire. **39** 53.05N 8.37W
Slieve Aughty Mts. Rep. of Ire. **39** 53.05N 8.31W
Slieve Bernagh *mts.* Rep. of Ire. **39** 52.48N 8.35W
Slieve Bloom Mts. Rep. of Ire. **39** 53.03N 7.35W
Slieve Callan *mtn.* Rep. of Ire. **39** 52.51N 9.18W
Slieve Donard *mtn.* N. Ireland **38** 54.11N 5.56W
Slieve Felim Mts. Rep. of Ire. **39** 52.40N 8.16W
Slieve Fyagh *mtn.* Rep. of Ire. **38** 54.12N 9.42W
Slieve Gamph *mts.* Rep. of Ire. **38** 54.06N 8.52W
Slievekimalta *mtn.* Rep. of Ire. **39** 52.45N 8.17W
Slieve Mish *mts.* Rep. of Ire. **39** 52.48N 9.48W
Slieve Miskish *mts.* Rep. of Ire. **39** 51.41N 9.56W
Slievemore *mtn.* Rep. of Ire. **38** 54.01N 10.04W
Slieve Na Calliagh *mtn.* Rep. of Ire. **38** 53.45N 7.06W
Slievenamon *mtn.* Rep. of Ire. **39** 52.25N 7.34W
Slieve Snaght *mtn.* Donegal Rep. of Ire. **38** 55.12N 7.20W
Sligachan Scotland **36** 57.17N 6.10W
Sligo Rep. of Ire. **38** 54.17N 8.28W
Sligo *d.* Rep. of Ire. **38** 54.10N 8.35W
Sligo B. Rep. of Ire. **38** 54.18N 8.40W
Slioch *mtn.* Scotland **36** 57.40N 5.20W
Sliven Bulgaria **43** 42.41N 26.19E
Slobodskoy U.S.S.R. **47** 58.42N 50.10E
Slough England **27** 51.30N 0.35W
Sluch *r.* U.S.S.R. **47** 52.05N 27.52E
Sluis Neth. **45** 51.18N 3.23E
Słupsk Poland **44** 54.28N 17.00E
Slyne Head Rep. of Ire. **38** 53.25N 10.12W
Slyudyanka U.S.S.R. **62** 51.40N 103.40E
Smithfield R.S.A. **74** 30.13S 26.32E
Smith's Falls *town* Canada **95** 44.54N 76.01W
Smöla *i.* Norway **46** 63.20N 8.00E
Smolensk U.S.S.R. **47** 54.49N 32.04E
Smólikas *mtn.* Greece **43** 40.06N 20.55E
Smolyan Bulgaria **43** 41.34N 24.45E
Smorgon U.S.S.R. **47** 54.28N 27.20E
Snaefell *mtn.* I.o.M. **32** 54.16N 4.28W
Snaith England **33** 53.42N 1.01W
Snake *r.* Idaho U.S.A. **90** 43.50N 117.05W
Snake *r.* Wash. U.S.A. **90** 46.15N 119.00W
Snåsa Norway **46** 64.15N 12.23E
Snåsavatn *l.* Norway **46** 64.10N 12.00E
Sneek Neth. **45** 53.03N 5.40E
Sneem Rep. of Ire. **39** 51.50N 9.54W
Sneeuwberg *mtn.* R.S.A. **74** 32.20S 19.10E
Snizort, Loch Scotland **36** 57.35N 6.30W
Snodland England **27** 51.20N 0.27E
Snöhetta *mtn.* Norway **46** 62.15N 9.05E
Snook Pt. England **35** 55.31N 1.35W
Snowdon *mtn.* Wales **30** 53.05N 4.05W
Snowy *r.* Australia **80** 37.49S 148.30E
Snowy Mtn. U.S.A. **95** 43.42N 74.23W
Snowy Mts. Australia **80** 36.25S 145.15E
Soalala Malagasy Rep. **73** 16.08S 45.21E
Soar *r.* England **33** 52.52N 1.17W
Soay *i.* Scotland **36** 57.09N 6.13W
Soay Sd. *str.* Scotland **36** 57.09N 6.16W
Sobat *r.* Sudan/Ethiopia **69** 9.30N 31.30E
Sobernheim W. Germany **45** 49.47N 7.40E
Sochi U.S.S.R. **47** 43.35N 39.46E
Society Is. Pacific Oc. **106** 17.00S 150.00W
Socotra *i.* Indian Oc. **69** 12.30N 54.00E
Sodankylä Finland **46** 67.21N 26.31E
Söderhamn Sweden **46** 61.19N 17.10E
Södertälje Sweden **46** 59.11N 17.39E
Soest W. Germany **45** 51.34N 8.06E
Sofia Bulgaria **43** 42.41N 23.19E
Sogne Fjord *est.* Norway **46** 61.10N 5.50E
Sögüt Turkey **56** 40.02N 30.10E
Sohag Egypt **56** 26.33N 31.42E
Soham England **29** 52.20N 0.20E
Sohar Oman **57** 24.23N 56.43E
Soignies Belgium **45** 50.35N 4.04E
Soissons France **40** 49.23N 3.20E
Söke Turkey **43** 37.46N 27.26E
Sokodé Togo **71** 8.59N 1.11E
Sokol U.S.S.R. **47** 59.28N 40.04E
Sokolo Mali **70** 14.53N 6.11W
Sokoto Nigeria **71** 13.02N 5.15E
Sokoto *d.* Nigeria **71** 11.50N 5.05E
Sokoto *r.* Nigeria **71** 13.05N 5.13E
Soledad Colombia **97** 10.54N 74.58W
Solihull England **28** 52.26N 1.47W
Solingen W. Germany **45** 51.10N 7.05E
Sollas Scotland **36** 57.39N 7.22W
Sollefteå Sweden **46** 63.09N 17.15E
Soller Spain **41** 39.47N 2.41E
Solling *mtn.* W. Germany **44** 51.45N 9.30E
Solomon Is. Austa. **113** 10.00S 160.00E
Solomon Sea Austa. **79** 7.00S 150.00E
Solta *i.* Yugo. **42** 43.23N 16.17E
Solway Firth *est.* England/Scotland **32** 54.50N 3.30W
Solwezi Zambia **73** 12.11S 26.23E
Soma Turkey **43** 39.11N 27.36E
Somabula Rhodesia **74** 19.40S 29.38E
Somali Republic Africa **69** 5.30N 47.00E
Sombor Yugo. **43** 45.48N 19.08E
Somerset *d.* England **28** 51.09N 3.00W
Somerset East R.S.A. **74** 32.44S 25.35E
Somerset I. Canada **93** 73.00N 93.30W
Somerton England **28** 51.03N 2.44W
Somes *r.* Hungary **47** 48.40N 22.30E
Somme *r.* France **40** 50.01N 1.40E
Son *r.* India **58** 25.55N 84.55E
Sönderborg Denmark **44** 54.55N 9.48E
Sondrio Italy **44** 46.11N 9.52E
Songea Tanzania **73** 10.42S 35.39E
Songkhla Thailand **59** 7.13N 100.37E
Songololo Zaïre **72** 5.40S 14.05E
Sonneberg E. Germany **44** 50.22N 11.10E
Sonora *r.* Mexico **90** 28.45N 111.55W
Sonsorol *i.* Asia **61** 5.20N 132.13E
Soochow China **63** 31.21N 120.40E
Sorel Canada **95** 46.03N 73.06W
Soria Spain **41** 41.46N 2.28W
Sorisdale Scotland **34** 56.40N 6.28W
Sor Kvalöy *i.* Norway **46** 69.45N 18.20E
Sorocaba Brazil **103** 23.30S 47.32W
Sorol *i.* Asia **61** 8.09N 140.25E
Sorong Asia **61** 0.50S 131.17E
Soroti Uganda **73** 1.40N 33.37E
Söröya *i.* Norway **46** 70.30N 22.30E
Sorraia *r.* Portugal **41** 39.00N 8.51W

Sorsele Sweden **46** 65.32N 17.34E
Sortavala U.S.S.R. **46** 61.40N 30.40E
Sotik Kenya **73** 0.40S 35.08E
Sotra *i.* Norway **46** 60.20N 5.00E
Souk Ahras Algeria **42** 36.14N 7.59E
Soure Portugal **41** 40.04N 8.38W
Souris *r.* U.S.A. **90** 49.38N 99.35W
Sousse Tunisia **42** 35.48N 10.38E
Soustons France **40** 43.45N 1.19W
Southall England **27** 51.31N 0.23W
Southam England **28** 52.16N 1.24W
South America 102
Southampton England **28** 50.54N 1.23W
Southampton I. Canada **93** 64.30N 84.00W
Southampton Water *est.* England **28** 50.52N 1.21W
South Atlantic Ocean 102
South Australia *d.* Australia **79** 29.00S 135.00E
South Barrule *mtn.* I.o.M. **32** 54.09N 4.41W
South Bend U.S.A. **94** 41.40N 86.15W
South Benfleet England **27** 51.33N 0.34E
South Beveland *f.* Neth. **45** 51.30N 3.50E
Southborough England **29** 51.10N 0.15E
South Brent England **31** 50.26N 3.50W
South Carolina *d.* U.S.A. **91** 34.00N 81.00W
South Cave England **33** 53.46N 0.37W
South Cerney England **28** 51.40N 1.55W
South China Sea Asia **60** 12.30N 115.00E
South Dakota *d.* U.S.A. **90** 44.30N 100.00W
South Dorset Downs *hills* England **28** 50.40N 2.25W
South Downs *hills* England **28** 50.04N 0.34W
South East C. Australia **80** 43.38S 146.48E
Southend Scotland **34** 55.19N 5.38W
Southend-on-Sea England **29** 51.32N 0.43E
Southern Alps *mts.* New Zealand **82** 43.20S 170.45E
Southern Lueti *r.* Zambia **74** 16.16S 23.15E
Southern Uplands *hills* Scotland **35** 55.30N 3.30W
Southern Yemen Asia **69** 16.00N 49.30E
South Esk *r.* Scotland **35** 56.43N 2.32W
South Flevoland *f.* Neth. **45** 52.22N 5.22E
South Foreland *c.* England **29** 51.08N 1.24E
Southgate England **27** 51.38N 0.07W
South Georgia *i.* Atlantic Oc. **106** 54.00S 37.00W
South Glamorgan *d.* Wales **31** 51.27N 3.22W
South-haa Scotland **36** 60.34N 1.17W
South Harris *f.* Scotland **36** 57.49N 6.55W
South Haven U.S.A. **94** 42.25N 86.16W
South Hayling England **28** 50.47N 0.56W
South Holland *d.* Neth. **45** 52.00N 4.30E
South Hornchurch England **27** 51.32N 0.13E
South Horr Kenya **73** 2.10N 36.45E
South I. New Zealand **82** 43.00S 171.00E
South Kirby England **33** 53.35N 1.25W
South Korea Asia **63** 36.00N 128.00E
Southland *f.* New Zealand **82** 45.40S 167.15E
Southminster England **29** 51.40N 0.51E
South Molton England **31** 51.01N 3.50W
South Nahanni *r.* Canada **92** 61.00N 123.20W
South Norwood England **27** 51.24N 0.04W
South Nutfield England **27** 51.14N 0.06W
South Ockendon England **27** 51.32N 0.18E
South Oxhey England **27** 51.38N 0.24W
Southport Australia **80** 27.58S 153.20E
Southport England **32** 53.38N 3.01W
South Ronaldsay *i.* Scotland **37** 58.47N 2.56W
South Saskatchewan *r.* Canada **90** 50.45N 108.30W
South Sd. Rep. of Ire. **39** 53.03N 9.28W
South Shetland Is. Antarctica **106** 62.00S 60.00W
South Shields England **33** 55.00N 1.24W
South Tyne *r.* England **35** 54.59N 2.08W
South Uist *i.* Scotland **36** 57.15N 7.20W
South Walls *i.* Scotland **37** 58.45N 3.07W
Southwark *d.* England **27** 51.30N 0.06W
Southwell England **33** 53.05N 0.58W
South West Africa Africa **74** 22.30S 17.00E
South West C. Australia **80** 43.32S 145.59E
Southwest C. New Zealand **82** 47.15S 167.30E
Southwick England **29** 50.50N 0.14W
Southwold England **29** 52.19N 1.41E
South Woodham Ferrers England **27** 51.39N 0.36E
South Yorkshire *d.* England **33** 53.28N 1.25W
Soutpansberge *mts.* R.S.A. **74** 22.50S 29.30E
Sovetsk U.S.S.R. **46** 55.02N 21.50E
Sovetskaya Gavan U.S.S.R. **49** 48.57N 140.16E
Spa Belgium **45** 50.29N 5.52E
Spain Europe **41** 40.00N 4.00W
Spalding Australia **80** 33.29S 138.40E
Spalding England **33** 52.47N 0.09W
Spandau W. Germany **44** 52.32N 13.13E
Spanish Sahara Africa **70** 2.30N 14.30E
Sparta U.S.A. **94** 43.57N 90.50W
Spárti Greece **43** 37.04N 22.28E
Spartivento, C. Calabria Italy **42** 37.55N 16.04E
Spartivento, C. Sardinia Italy **42** 38.53N 8.51E
Spátha, C. Greece **43** 35.42N 23.43E
Spean Bridge *town* Scotland **37** 56.53N 4.54W
Speke G. Tanzania **73** 2.20S 33.30E
Spence Bay *town* Canada **93** 69.30N 93.20W
Spencer G. Australia **79** 34.30S 136.10E
Spennymoor *town* England **33** 54.43N 1.35W
Spenser Mts. New Zealand **82** 42.15S 172.45E
Sperrin Mts. N. Ireland **34** 54.49N 7.06W
Spey *r.* Scotland **37** 57.40N 3.06W
Spey B. Scotland **37** 57.42N 3.04W
Speyer W. Germany **44** 49.18N 8.26E
Spiekeroog *i.* W. Germany **45** 53.48N 7.45E
Spilsby England **33** 53.10N 0.06E
Spithead *str.* England **28** 50.45N 1.05W
Spitsbergen *is.* Europe **54** 78.00N 17.00E
Spittal Austria **44** 46.48N 13.30E
Split Yugo. **43** 43.32N 16.27E
Spokane U.S.A. **90** 47.40N 117.25W
Spooner U.S.A. **94** 45.50N 91.53W
Spratly I. Asia **60** 8.45N 111.54E
Spree *r.* E. Germany **44** 52.32N 13.15E
Springbok R.S.A. **74** 29.43S 17.55E
Springfield Ill. U.S.A. **94** 39.49N 89.39W
Springfield Mass. U.S.A. **95** 42.07N 72.35W
Springfield Miss. U.S.A. **91** 37.11N 93.19W
Springfield Ohio U.S.A. **94** 39.55N 83.48W
Springfontein R.S.A. **74** 30.16S 25.42E
Springs *town* R.S.A. **74** 26.15S 28.26E
Spurn Head England **33** 53.35N 0.08E
Sredne Kolymskaya U.S.S.R. **49** 67.27N 153.35E
Sri Lanka Asia **59** 7.30N 80.50E
Srinagar Jammu and Kashmir **58** 34.08N 74.50E
Stack's Mts. Rep. of Ire. **39** 52.18N 9.36W
Stadskanaal Neth. **45** 53.02N 6.55E
Stadtkyll W. Germany **45** 50.21N 6.32E
Staffa *i.* Scotland **34** 56.26N 6.21W
Staffin Scotland **36** 57.38N 6.13W
Stafford England **32** 52.49N 2.09W
Staffordshire *d.* England **28** 52.40N 1.57W
Staines England **27** 51.26N 0.31W
Stainforth England **33** 53.37N 1.01W
Stalbridge England **28** 50.57N 2.22W
Stalham England **29** 52.46N 1.31E
Stamford England **29** 52.39N 0.29W
Stamford U.S.A. **95** 41.03N 73.32W
Stamford Bridge *town* England **33** 53.59N 0.53W
Standerton R.S.A. **74** 26.57S 29.14E
Standon England **27** 51.53N 0.02E
Stanford le Hope England **27** 51.31N 0.26E
Stanger R.S.A. **74** 29.20S 31.18E
Stanhope England **32** 54.45N 2.00W
Stanley Australia **80** 40.46S 145.20E
Stanley England **32** 54.53N 1.42W
Stanley Scotland **35** 56.29N 3.28W
Stanmore England **27** 51.38N 0.19W
Stanovoy Range *mts.* U.S.S.R. **49** 56.00N 125.40E
Stanstead Abbots England **27** 51.47N 0.01E
Stansted Mountfitchet England **27** 51.55N 0.12E
Stanthorpe Australia **80** 28.37S 151.52E
Stapleford England **33** 52.56N 1.16W
Staraya Russa U.S.S.R. **47** 58.00N 31.22E
Stara Zagora Bulgaria **43** 42.26N 25.37E
Stargard Poland **44** 53.21N 15.01E
Start B. England **31** 50.17N 3.35W
Start Pt. England **31** 50.13N 3.38W
Start Pt. Scotland **37** 59.17N 2.24W
State College U.S.A. **95** 40.48N 77.52W
Staunton England **28** 51.58N 2.19W
Stavanger Norway **46** 58.58N 5.45E
Staveley England **33** 53.16N 1.20W
Stavelot Belgium **45** 50.23N 5.54E
Staveren Neth. **45** 52.53N 5.21E
Stavropol' U.S.S.R. **47** 45.03N 41.59E
Stavropol Highlands U.S.S.R. **47** 45.00N 42.30E
Stawell Australia **80** 37.05S 142.52E
Staxton England **33** 54.11N 0.26W
Steelpoort R.S.A. **74** 24.48S 30.11E
Steenbergen Neth. **45** 51.36N 4.19E
Steenvorde France **45** 50.49N 2.35E
Steenwijk Neth. **45** 52.47N 6.07E
Steep Holm *i.* England **28** 51.20N 3.06W
Steeping *r.* England **33** 53.06N 0.19E
Steinkjer Norway **46** 64.00N 11.30E
Stellenbosch R.S.A. **74** 33.56S 18.51E
Stenay France **45** 49.29N 5.12E
Stendal E. Germany **44** 52.36N 11.52E
Stepanakert U.S.S.R. **57** 39.48N 46.45E
Stepney England **27** 51.31N 0.04W
Sterling U.S.A. **90** 40.37N 103.13W
Sterling Heights *town* U.S.A. **94** 44.08N 83.52W
Steubenville U.S.A. **94** 40.22N 80.39W
Stevenage England **29** 51.54N 0.11W
Stevenston Scotland **34** 55.39N 4.45W
Stewart Canada **92** 55.56N 130.01W
Stewart I. New Zealand **82** 47.00S 168.00E
Stewarton Scotland **34** 55.41N 4.31W
Stewartstown N. Ireland **34** 54.35N 6.42W
Steyning England **29** 50.54N 0.19W
Steyr Austria **44** 48.04N 14.25E
Stikine *r.* Canada **92** 56.45N 132.30W
Stikine Mts. Canada **92** 59.00N 129.00W
Stilton England **29** 52.29N 0.17W
Stinchar *r.* Scotland **34** 55.06N 5.00W
Stirling Scotland **35** 56.07N 3.57W
Stjördalshalsen Norway **46** 63.30N 10.59E
Stock England **27** 51.40N 0.26E
Stockbridge England **28** 51.07N 1.30W
Stockholm Sweden **46** 59.20N 18.05E
Stockport England **32** 53.25N 2.11W
Stocksbridge England **33** 53.30N 1.36W
Stockton U.S.A. **90** 37.59N 121.20W
Stockton-on-Tees England **33** 54.34N 1.20W
Stoer Scotland **36** 58.12N 5.20W
Stoer, Pt. of Scotland **36** 58.16N 5.23W
Stoke D'Abernon England **27** 51.19N 0.22W
Stoke Newington England **27** 51.34N 0.04W
Stoke-on-Trent England **32** 53.01N 2.11W
Stokesley England **33** 54.27N 1.12W
Stone Kent England **27** 51.27N 0.17E
Stone Staffs. England **32** 52.55N 2.10W
Stonehaven Scotland **37** 56.58N 2.13W
Stony Stratford England **28** 52.04N 0.51W
Stony Tunguska *r.* U.S.S.R. **49** 61.40N 90.00E
Stopsley England **27** 51.54N 0.24W
Stora Lule *r.* Sweden **46** 65.40N 21.48E
Stora Lulevatten *l.* Sweden **46** 67.00N 19.30E
Storavan *l.* Sweden **46** 65.45N 18.10E
Storby Finland **46** 60.14N 19.36E
Stord *i.* Norway **46** 59.50N 5.25E
Store Baelt *str.* Denmark **46** 55.30N 11.00E
Stören Norway **46** 63.03N 10.16E
Stornoway Scotland **36** 58.12N 6.23W
Storsjön *l.* Sweden **46** 63.10N 14.20E
Storuman Sweden **46** 65.05N 17.10E
Storuman *l.* Sweden **46** 65.14N 16.50E
Stotfold England **29** 52.02N 0.13W
Stoughton England **27** 51.15N 0.36W
Stour *r.* Dorset England **28** 50.43N 1.47W
Stour *r.* Kent England **29** 51.19N 1.22E
Stour *r.* Suffolk England **29** 51.56N 1.03E
Stourbridge England **28** 52.28N 2.08W
Stourport-on-Severn England **28** 52.21N 2.16W
Stow Scotland **35** 55.42N 2.52W
Stowmarket England **29** 52.11N 1.00E
Stow on the Wold England **28** 51.55N 1.42W
Strabane N. Ireland **38** 54.50N 7.30W
Strachur Scotland **34** 56.10N 5.04W
Stradbally Laois Rep. of Ire. **39** 53.01N 7.09W
Stradbally Waterford Rep. of Ire. **39** 52.08N 7.29W
Strahan Australia **80** 42.08S 145.21E
Stralsund E. Germany **44** 54.18N 13.06E
Strangford Lough N. Ireland **38** 54.28N 5.35W
Stranorlar Rep. of Ire. **38** 54.48N 7.48W
Stranraer Scotland **34** 54.54N 5.02W
Strasbourg France **44** 48.35N 7.45E
Stratford Canada **94** 43.22N 81.00W
Stratford New Zealand **82** 39.20S 174.18E
Stratford-upon-Avon England **28** 52.12N 1.42W
Strathallan *f.* Scotland **35** 56.14N 3.52W
Strathardle *f.* Scotland **35** 56.42N 3.28W
Strathaven *town* Scotland **35** 55.41N 4.05W
Strath Avon *f.* Scotland **37** 57.21N 3.21W
Strathbogie *f.* Scotland **37** 57.25N 2.55W
Strathclyde *d.* Scotland **34** 55.45N 4.45W
Strathdearn *f.* Scotland **37** 57.17N 4.00W
Strathearn *f.* Scotland **35** 56.20N 3.45W
Strathglass *f.* Scotland **37** 57.25N 4.38W
Strath Halladale *f.* Scotland **37** 58.27N 3.53W
Strath More *f.* Highland Scotland **37** 58.25N 4.38W
Strathmore *f.* Tayside Scotland **37** 56.44N 2.45W
Strathnairn *f.* Scotland **37** 57.23N 4.10W
Strathnaver *f.* Scotland **37** 58.24N 4.12W
Strath of Kildonan *f.* Scotland **37** 58.09N 3.50W
Strathpeffer *town* Scotland **37** 57.34N 4.33W
Strathspey *f.* Scotland **37** 57.25N 3.25W
Strath Tay *f.* Scotland **35** 56.38N 3.41W
Strathy Pt. Scotland **37** 58.35N 4.01W
Stratton England **31** 50.49N 4.31W
Straubing W. Germany **44** 48.53N 12.35E
Straumnes *c.* Iceland **46** 66.30N 23.05W
Streatham England **27** 51.26N 0.07W
Streek Head Rep. of Ire. **39** 51.29N 9.43W
Street England **28** 51.07N 2.43W
Strichen Scotland **37** 57.35N 2.05W
Striven, Loch Scotland **34** 55.57N 5.05W
Strokestown Rep. of Ire. **38** 53.46N 8.08W
Stroma *i.* Scotland **37** 58.41N 3.09W
Stromboli *i.* Italy **42** 38.48N 15.14E
Stromeferry Scotland **36** 57.21N 5.34W
Stromness Scotland **37** 58.57N 3.18W
Strömö *i.* Faroe Is. **46** 62.08N 7.00W
Strömstad Sweden **46** 58.56N 11.11E
Ströms Vattudal *l.* Sweden **46** 63.55N 15.30E
Stronsay *i.* Scotland **37** 59.07N 2.36W
Stronsay Firth *est.* Scotland **37** 59.05N 2.45W

Strontian Scotland **34** 56.42N 5.33W
Strood England **27** 51.24N 0.28E
Stroud England **28** 51.44N 2.12W
Struma *r.* Greece **43** 40.45N 23.51E
Strumble Head Wales **30** 52.03N 5.05W
Strumica Yugo. **43** 41.26N 22.39E
Stryn Norway **46** 61.55N 6.47E
Stryy U.S.S.R. **47** 49.16N 23.51E
Stura *r.* Italy **40** 44.53N 8.38E
Sturgeon Falls *town* Canada **94** 46.22N 79.57W
Sturminster Newton England **28** 50.56N 2.18W
Sturt Desert Australia **80** 28.30S 141.12E
Stuttgart W. Germany **44** 48.47N 9.12E
Styr *r.* U.S.S.R. **47** 52.07N 26.35E
Suakin Sudan **69** 19.04N 37.22E
Subotica Yugo. **43** 46.04N 19.41E
Suchow China **63** 34.17N 117.18E
Suck *r.* Rep. of Ire. **38** 53.16N 8.04W
Sucre Bolivia **103** 19.05S 65.15W
Sudan Africa **69** 14.00N 30.00E
Sudbury Canada **94** 46.30N 81.01W
Sudbury England **29** 52.03N 0.45E
Sudd *f.* Sudan **69** 7.50N 30.00E
Sudeten Mts. Czech./Poland **44** 50.30N 16.30E
Sudirman Mts. Asia **61** 3.50S 136.30E
Suez Egypt **56** 29.59N 32.33E
Suez, G. of Egypt **56** 28.48N 33.00E
Suez Canal Egypt **56** 30.40N 32.20E
Suffolk *d.* England **29** 52.16N 1.00E
Sugar Hill Rep. of Ire. **39** 52.26N 9.11W
Sugarloaf Mtn. U.S.A. **95** 45.02N 70.18W
Sugluk Canada **93** 62.10N 75.40W
Suhl E. Germany **44** 50.37N 10.43E
Suir *r.* Rep. of Ire. **39** 52.17N 7.00W
Sukabumi Indonesia **60** 6.55S 106.50E
Sukadana Indonesia **60** 1.15S 110.00E
Sukaradja Indonesia **60** 2.23S 110.35E
Sukhinichi U.S.S.R. **47** 54.07N 35.21E
Sukhona *r.* U.S.S.R. **18** 61.30N 46.28E
Sukhumi U.S.S.R. **47** 43.01N 41.01E
Sukkertoppen Greenland **93** 65.40N 53.00W
Sukkur Pakistan **58** 27.42N 68.54E
Sulaimaniya Iraq **57** 35.32N 45.27E
Sulaiman Range *mts.* Pakistan **58** 30.50N 70.20E
Sulaimiya Saudi Arabia **57** 24.10N 47.20E
Sula Is. Indonesia **61** 1.50S 125.10E
Sulawesi *d.* Indonesia **61** 2.00S 120.30E
Sulina Romania **43** 45.08N 29.40E
Sullane *r.* Rep. of Ire. **39** 51.53N 8.56W
Sullom Voe *b.* Scotland **36** 60.29N 1.16W
Sulmona Italy **42** 42.04N 13.57E
Sultanabad Iran **57** 36.25N 58.02E
Sulu Archipelago Phil. **61** 5.30N 121.00E
Sulu Sea Pacific Oc. **61** 8.00N 120.00E
Sumatra *i.* Indonesia **60** 2.00S 102.00E
Sumba *i.* Indonesia **60** 9.30S 119.55E
Sumbar *r.* U.S.S.R. **57** 38.00N 55.20E
Sumbawa *i.* Indonesia **60** 8.45S 117.50E
Sumbawanga Tanzania **73** 7.58S 31.36E
Sumburgh Head Scotland **36** 59.51N 1.16W
Sumgait U.S.S.R. **57** 40.35N 49.38E
Summan *f.* Saudi Arabia **57** 27.00N 47.00E
Summer Is. Scotland **36** 58.01N 5.26W
Sumy U.S.S.R. **47** 50.55N 34.49E
Sunart *f.* Scotland **36** 56.44N 5.35W
Sunart, Loch Scotland **36** 56.43N 5.45W
Sunbury England **27** 51.24N 0.25W
Sunbury U.S.A. **95** 40.52N 76.47W
Sundarbans *f.* India/Bangla. **58** 22.00N 89.00E
Sundargarh India **58** 22.04N 84.08E
Sunda Str. Indonesia **60** 6.00S 105.50E
Sundays *r.* R.S.A. **74** 33.49S 25.46E
Sunderland England **35** 54.55N 1.22W
Sundsvall Sweden **46** 62.22N 17.20E
Sungari *r.* China **63** 47.46N 132.30E
Sungurlu Turkey **56** 40.10N 34.23E
Sunninghill *town* England **27** 51.24N 0.39W
Sunyani Ghana **70** 7.22N 2.18W
Suomussalmi Finland **46** 64.52N 29.10E
Suonenjoki Finland **46** 62.40N 27.06E
Supaul India **58** 26.57N 86.15E
Superior U.S.A. **94** 46.42N 92.05W
Superior, L. N. America **94** 48.00N 88.00W
Süphan Dağlari *mtn.* Turkey **56** 38.55N 42.55E
Sur Oman **57** 22.23N 59.32E
Sura U.S.S.R. **47** 53.52N 45.45E
Sura *r.* U.S.S.R. **47** 56.13N 46.00E
Surabaya Indonesia **60** 7.14S 112.45E
Surakarta Indonesia **60** 7.32S 110.50E
Surat Australia **80** 27.10S 149.05E
Surat India **58** 21.10N 72.54E
Surat Thani Thailand **59** 9.03N 99.28E
Surbiton England **27** 51.24N 0.19W
Sûre *r.* Lux. **45** 49.43N 6.31E
Surigao Phil. **61** 9.47N 125.29E
Surin Thailand **59** 14.50N 103.34E
Surinam S. America **102** 4.00N 56.00W
Surrey *d.* England **29** 51.16N 0.30W
Surrey Hill England **27** 51.23N 0.43W
Surtsey *i.* Iceland **46** 63.18N 20.37W
Susquehanna *r.* U.S.A. **95** 39.33N 76.05W
Sutherland R.S.A. **74** 32.24S 20.40E
Sutlej *r.* Pakistan **58** 29.26N 71.09E
Sutton G.L. England **27** 51.22N 0.12W
Sutton Surrey England **27** 51.12N 0.26W
Sutton Bridge England **33** 52.46N 0.12E
Sutton Coldfield England **28** 52.33N 1.50W
Sutton in Ashfield England **33** 53.08N 1.16W
Sutton on Sea England **33** 53.18N 0.18E
Suwanee *r.* U.S.A. **96** 29.15N 82.50W
Svartisen *mtn.* Norway **46** 66.30N 14.00E
Sveg Sweden **46** 62.02N 14.20E
Svendborg Denmark **46** 55.04N 10.38E
Sverdlovsk U.S.S.R. **48** 56.52N 60.35E
Svetogorsk U.S.S.R. **46** 61.07N 28.50E
Svishtov Bulgaria **43** 43.36N 25.23E
Svobodnyy U.S.S.R. **63** 51.24N 128.05E
Svolvaer Norway **46** 68.15N 14.40E
Swabian Jura *mts.* W. Germany **44** 48.20N 9.20E
Swadlincote England **33** 52.47N 1.34W
Swaffham England **29** 52.38N 0.42E
Swakop *r.* S.W. Africa **74** 22.38S 14.30E
Swakopmund S.W. Africa **74** 22.40S 14.34E
Swale *r.* England **33** 54.05N 1.20W
Swanage England **28** 50.36N 1.59W
Swan Hill *town* Australia **80** 35.23S 143.37E
Swanley England **27** 51.24N 0.12E
Swanlinbar Rep. of Ire. **38** 54.12N 7.44W
Swan River *town* Canada **90** 52.06N 101.17W
Swanscombe England **27** 51.26N 0.19E
Swansea Wales **31** 51.37N 3.57W
Swansea B. Wales **31** 51.33N 3.50W
Swarbacks Minn *str.* Scotland **36** 60.22N 1.21W
Swartberg Range *mts.* R.S.A. **74** 33.20S 22.00E
Swatow China **60** 23.23N 116.39E
Swaziland Africa **74** 26.30S 32.00E
Sweden Europe **46** 63.00N 16.00E
Sweetwater U.S.A. **90** 32.37N 100.25W
Swidnica Poland **44** 50.51N 16.29E
Swift Current *town* Canada **90** 50.17N 107.49W
Swilly *r.* Rep. of Ire. **38** 54.57N 7.42W
Swilly, Lough Rep. of Ire. **38** 55.10N 7.32W
Swindon England **28** 51.33N 1.47W
Swinford Rep. of Ire. **38** 53.56N 8.57W
Swinoujscie Poland **44** 53.55N 14.18E
Switzerland Europe **44** 47.00N 8.15E
Swords Rep. of Ire. **38** 53.27N 6.15W
Syderö *i.* Faroe Is. **46** 61.30N 6.50W
Sydney Australia **80** 33.55S 151.10E
Sydney Canada **93** 46.10N 60.10W
Syktyvkar U.S.S.R. **48** 61.42N 50.45E
Sylhet Bangla. **59** 24.53N 91.51E
Sylt *i.* W. Germany **44** 54.50N 8.20E
Syracuse U.S.A. **95** 43.03N 76.10W
Syr Darya *r.* U.S.S.R. **48** 46.00N 61.12E
Syria Asia **56** 35.00N 38.00E
Syrian Desert Asia **56** 32.00N 39.00E
Syzran U.S.S.R. **47** 53.10N 48.29E
Szczecin Poland **44** 53.25N 14.32E
Szczecinek Poland **44** 53.42N 16.41E
Szechwan *d.* China **62** 30.30N 103.00E
Szeged Hungary **43** 46.16N 20.08E
Szekszárd Hungary **43** 46.22N 18.44E
Szemao China **59** 22.50N 101.00E
Szenan China **63** 27.56N 108.22E
Szombathely Hungary **47** 47.12N 16.38E

T

Tabarka Tunisia **42** 36.56N 8.43E
Tabas Khora¯ sa¯ n Iran **57** 32.48N 60.14E
Tabas Khora¯ sa¯ n Iran **57** 33.36N 56.55E
Tabasco *d.* Mexico **96** 18.30N 93.00W
Table B. R.S.A. **74** 33.30S 18.05E
Tabór Czech. **44** 49.25N 14.41E
Tabora Tanzania **73** 5.02S 32.50E
Tabora *d.* Tanzania **73** 5.30S 32.50E
Tabou Ivory Coast **70** 4.28N 7.20W
Tabriz Iran **57** 38.05N 46.18E
Tacloban Phil. **61** 11.15N 124.59E
Tacoma U.S.A. **90** 47.16N 122.30W
Taconic Mts. U.S.A. **95** 42.00N 73.45W
Tacuarembó Uruguay **103** 31.42S 56.00W
Tadcaster England **33** 53.53N 1.16W
Tademait Plateau Algeria **68** 28.45N 2.10E
Tadoussac Canada **95** 48.09N 69.43W
Tadzhikistan Soviet Socialist Republic *d.* U.S.S.R. **62** 39.00N 70.30E
Taegu S. Korea **63** 35.52N 128.36E
Taejon S. Korea **63** 36.20N 127.26E
Tafersit Morocco **41** 35.01N 3.33W
Taganrog U.S.S.R. **47** 47.14N 38.55E
Taganrog, G. of U.S.S.R. **47** 47.00N 38.30E
Taghmon Rep. of Ire. **39** 52.20N 6.40W
Tagus *r.* Portugal **41** 39.00N 8.57W
Tahat, Mt. Algeria **71** 23.30N 5.40E
Taichow China **63** 32.30N 119.50E
Taichung Taiwan **63** 24.09N 120.40E
Taihape New Zealand **82** 39.40S 175.48E
Taima Saudi Arabia **56** 27.37N 38.30E
Tain Scotland **37** 57.48N 4.04W
Tainan Taiwan **61** 23.01N 120.14E
Taipei Taiwan **63** 25.05N 121.32E
Taiping Malaysia **60** 4.54N 100.42E
Taitung Taiwan **63** 22.49N 121.10E
Taivalkoski Finland **46** 65.35N 28.20E
Taiwan Asia **63** 23.30N 121.00E
Taiyuan China **63** 37.50N 112.30E
Taizz Yemen **69** 13.35N 44.02E
Tajan Indonesia **60** 0.02S 110.05E
Tajrish Iran **57** 35.48N 51.20E
Tajuna *r.* Spain **41** 40.10N 3.35W
Tak Thailand **59** 16.47N 99.10E
Takamatsu Japan **63** 34.20N 134.01E
Takeley England **27** 51.52N 0.15E
Takestan Iran **57** 36.02N 49.40E
Takht-i-Suleiman *mtn.* Iran **57** 36.23N 50.59E
Takla Makan *des.* China **62** 38.10N 82.00E
Talasskiy Ala Tau *mts.* U.S.S.R. **62** 42.20N 73.20E
Talaud Is. Indonesia **61** 4.20N 126.50E
Talavera de la Reina Spain **41** 39.58N 4.50W
Talca Chile **102** 36.00S 71.40W
Taldom U.S.S.R. **47** 56.49N 37.30E
Talgarth Wales **30** 51.59N 3.15W
Taliabu *i.* Indonesia **61** 1.50S 124.55E
Talkeetna U.S.A. **92** 62.20N 150.09W
Tallahassee U.S.A. **91** 30.28N 84.19W
Tallinn U.S.S.R. **46** 59.22N 24.48E
Tallow Rep. of Ire. **39** 52.06N 8.01W
Talsi U.S.S.R. **47** 57.18N 22.39E
Tamale Ghana **70** 9.26N 0.49W
Tamanrasset Algeria **71** 22.50N 5.31E
Tamar *r.* England **31** 50.28N 4.13W
Tamatave Malagasy Rep. **67** 18.10S 49.23E
Tamaulipas *d.* Mexico **96** 24.00N 98.20W
Tambacounda Senegal **70** 13.45N 13.40W
Tambohorano Malagasy Rep. **73** 17.40S 43.59E
Tambov U.S.S.R. **47** 52.44N 41.28E
Tambre *r.* Spain **41** 42.50N 8.55W
Tamega *r.* Portugal **41** 41.04N 8.17W
Tamil Nadu *d.* India **59** 11.15N 79.00E
Tampa U.S.A. **91** 27.58N 82.38W
Tampa B. U.S.A. **96** 27.48N 82.15W
Tampere Finland **46** 61.32N 23.45E
Tampico Mexico **96** 22.18N 97.52W
Tamsag Bulag Mongolia **63** 47.10N 117.21E
Tamworth Australia **80** 31.07S 150.57E
Tamworth England **28** 52.38N 1.42W
Tana *r.* Kenya **73** 2.32S 40.32E
Tana Norway **46** 70.26N 28.14E
Tana *r.* Norway **46** 69.45N 28.15E
Tana, L. Ethiopia **69** 12.00N 37.20E
Tanacross U.S.A. **92** 63.12N 143.30W
Tanana U.S.A. **92** 65.11N 152.10W
Tananarive Malagasy Rep. **67** 18.52S 47.30E
Tanaro *r.* Italy **42** 45.01N 8.46E
Tanat *r.* Wales **30** 52.46N 3.07W
Tanderagee N. Ireland **38** 54.22N 6.27W
Tandil Argentina **103** 37.18S 59.10W
Tandjungpandan Indonesia **60** 2.44S 107.36E
Tanga Tanzania **73** 5.07S 39.05E
Tanga *d.* Tanzania **73** 5.20S 38.30E
Tanganyika, L. Africa **73** 6.00S 29.30E
Tanger *see* Tangier Morocco **41**
Tangier Morocco **41** 35.48N 5.45W
Tanglha Range *mts.* China **62** 32.40N 92.30E
Tangra Yum *l.* China **59** 31.00N 86.30E
Tangshan China **63** 39.37N 118.05E
Tanimbar Is. Indonesia **61** 7.50S 131.30E
Tanjung Datu *c.* Malaysia **60** 2.00N 109.30E
Tanjungkarang Indonesia **60** 5.28S 105.16E
Tanjung Puting *c.* Indonesia **60** 3.35S 111.52E
Tanjungredeb Indonesia **60** 2.09N 117.29E
Tanjung Selatan *c.* Indonesia **60** 4.20S 114.45E
Tannu Ola Range *mts.* U.S.S.R. **49** 51.00N 93.30E
Tano *r.* Ghana **70** 5.07N 2.54W
Tanout Niger **71** 14.55N 8.49E
Tanta Egypt **56** 30.48N 31.00E
Tanzania Africa **73** 5.00S 35.00E
Taonan China **63** 45.25N 122.46E
Taoudenni Mali **70** 22.45N 4.00W
Tapachula Mexico **96** 14.54N 92.15W
Tapai Shan *mtn.* China **59** 34.00N 107.40E
Tapajós *r.* Brazil **102** 2.40S 55.00W
Tapti *r.* India **58** 21.05N 72.45E
Taquari *r.* Brazil **103** 19.00S 57.22W

Tara *r.* U.S.S.R. **48** 56.30N 74.40E
Tara *r.* Yugo. **43** 43.23N 18.47E
Tarakan Indonesia **60** 3.20N 117.38E
Tarancón Spain **41** 40.01N 3.01W
Taransay *i.* Scotland **36** 57.53N 7.03W
Taranto Italy **43** 40.28N 17.14E
Taranto, G. of Italy **43** 40.00N 17.20E
Tararua Range *mts.* New Zealand **82** 40.45S 175.30E
Tarbagatay Range *mts.* U.S.S.R. **62** 47.00N 83.00E
Tarbat Ness *c.* Scotland **37** 57.52N 3.46W
Tarbert Rep. of Ire. **39** 52.34N 9.24W
Tarbert Strath. Scotland **34** 55.51N 5.25W
Tarbert W. Isles Scotland **36** 57.54N 6.49W
Tarbert, Loch Scotland **34** 55.48N 5.31W
Tarbes France **40** 43.14N 0.05E
Tarbolton Scotland **34** 55.31N 4.29W
Tardoire *r.* France **40** 45.57N 1.00W
Taree Australia **80** 31.54S 152.26E
Tarfa, Wadi *r.* Egypt **56** 28.36N 30.50E
Tarifa Spain **41** 36.01N 5.36W
Tarija Bolivia **103** 21.33S 64.45W
Tarija *d.* Bolivia **103** 21.30S 64.00W
Tarim *r.* China **62** 41.00N 83.30E
Tarim Basin *f.* Asia **107** 40.00N 83.00E
Tarkwa Ghana **70** 5.16N 1.59W
Tarlac Phil. **61** 15.29N 120.35E
Tarland Scotland **37** 57.08N 2.52W
Tarleton England **32** 53.41N 2.50W
Tarn *r.* France **40** 44.15N 1.15E
Tarnow Poland **47** 50.01N 20.59E
Tarporley England **32** 53.10N 2.42W
Tarragona Spain **41** 41.07N 1.15E
Tarrasa Spain **41** 41.34N 2.00E
Tarsus Turkey **56** 36.52N 34.52E
Tartary, G. of U.S.S.R. **49** 47.40N 141.00E
Tartu U.S.S.R. **46** 58.20N 26.44E
Tashkent U.S.S.R. **62** 41.16N 69.13E
Tasman B. New Zealand **82** 41.00S 173.15E
Tasmania *d.* Australia **80** 42.00S 147.00E
Tasman Mts. New Zealand **82** 41.00S 172.40E
Tasman Pen. Australia **80** 43.08S 147.51E
Tasman Sea Pacific Oc. **107** 38.00S 163.00E
Tatarsk U.S.S.R. **48** 55.14N 76.00E
Tatnam, C. Canada **93** 57.00N 91.00W
Tatsaitan China **62** 37.44N 95.08E
Tatsfield England **27** 51.18N 0.02E
Tatu *r.* China **59** 28.47N 104.40E
Tatvan Turkey **56** 38.31N 42.15E
Taubaté Brazil **103** 23.00S 45.36W
Taumarunui New Zealand **82** 38.53S 175.16E
Taung R.S.A. **74** 27.32S 24.48E
Taung-gyi Burma **59** 20.49N 97.01E
Taunton England **31** 51.01N 3.07W
Taunton U.S.A. **95** 41.54N 71.06W
Taunus *mts.* W. Germany **44** 50.07N 7.48E
Taupo New Zealand **82** 38.42S 176.06E
Taupo, L. New Zealand **82** 38.45S 175.30E
Tauranga New Zealand **82** 37.42S 176.11E
Taurus Mts. Turkey **56** 37.15N 34.15E
Taveta Kenya **73** 3.23S 37.42E
Tavira Portugal **41** 37.07N 7.39W
Tavistock England **31** 50.33N 4.09W
Tavoy Burma **59** 14.07N 98.18E
Tavy *r.* England **31** 50.27N 4.10W
Taw *r.* England **31** 51.05N 4.05W
Tawau Malaysia **60** 4.16N 117.54E
Tawe *r.* Wales **31** 51.38N 3.56W
Tay *r.* Scotland **35** 56.21N 3.18W
Tay, Loch Scotland **34** 56.32N 4.08W
Taylor, Mt. U.S.A. **90** 35.14N 107.36W
Taymyr, L. U.S.S.R. **49** 74.20N 101.00E
Taymyr Pen. U.S.S.R. **49** 75.30N 99.00E
Taynuilt Scotland **34** 56.26N 5.14W
Tayport Scotland **35** 56.27N 2.53W
Tayshet U.S.S.R. **49** 55.56N 98.01E
Tayside *d.* Scotland **35** 56.35N 3.28W
Taytay Phil. **60** 10.47N 119.32E
Taz *r.* U.S.S.R. **48** 67.30N 78.50E
Tbilisi U.S.S.R. **57** 41.43N 44.48E
Tchibanga Gabon **72** 2.52S 11.07E
Te Anau, L. New Zealand **82** 45.10S 167.15E
Te Araroa New Zealand **82** 37.38S 178.25E
Te Awamutu New Zealand **82** 38.00S 175.20E
Tebessa Algeria **42** 35.22N 8.08E
Tebuk Saudi Arabia **56** 28.25N 36.35E
Tecuci Romania **43** 45.49N 27.27E
Teddington England **27** 51.25N 0.20W
Tees *r.* England **33** 54.35N 1.11W
Tees B. England **33** 54.40N 1.07W
Teesdale *f.* England **32** 54.38N 2.08W
Tegucigalpa Honduras **96** 14.05N 87.14W
Tehran Iran **57** 35.40N 51.26E
Tehtsin China **59** 28.45N 98.58E
Tehuacán Mexico **96** 18.30N 97.26W
Tehuantepec Mexico **96** 16.21N 95.13W
Tehuantepec, G. of Mexico **96** 16.00N 95.00W
Tehuantepec, Isthmus of Mexico **96** 17.00N 94.00W
Teifi *r.* Wales **30** 52.05N 4.41W
Teign *r.* England **31** 50.32N 3.46W
Teignmouth England **31** 50.33N 3.30W
Teisenberg *mtn.* W. Germany **44** 47.48N 12.46E
Teith *r.* Scotland **35** 56.09N 4.00W
Teixeira de Sousa Angola **72** 10.41S 22.09E
Tekapo, L. New Zealand **82** 43.35S 170.30E
Tekirdağ Turkey **43** 40.59N 27.30E
Te Kuiti New Zealand **82** 38.20S 175.10E
Tela Honduras **96** 15.56N 87.25W
Telanaipura Indonesia **60** 1.36S 103.39E
Telavi U.S.S.R. **57** 41.56N 45.30E
Tel Aviv-Jaffa Israel **56** 32.05N 34.46E
Tele *r.* Zaïre **72** 2.48N 24.00E
Telford England **28** 52.42N 2.30W
Telgte W. Germany **45** 51.59N 7.46E
Telimélé Guinea **70** 10.54N 13.02W
Tel Kotchek Syria **56** 36.48N 42.04E
Tell Atlas *mts.* Algeria **68** 36.10N 4.00E
Telok Anson Malaysia **60** 4.00N 101.00E
Teluk Berau *b.* Asia **61** 2.20S 133.00E
Teluk Irian *b.* Asia **61** 2.30S 135.20E
Tema Ghana **70** 5.41N 0.01W
Tembo Aluma Angola **72** 7.42S 17.15E
Teme *r.* England **28** 52.10N 2.13W
Temora Australia **80** 34.27S 147.35E
Témpio Italy **42** 40.54N 9.06E
Temple U.S.A. **91** 31.06N 97.22W
Temple Ewell England **29** 51.09N 1.16E
Templemore Rep. of Ire. **39** 52.48N 7.51W
Tenasserim Burma **60** 12.05N 99.00E
Tenasserim *d.* Burma **59** 13.00N 99.00E
Tenbury Wells England **28** 52.18N 2.35W
Tenby Wales **31** 51.40N 4.42W
Ten Degree Channel Indian Oc. **60** 10.00N 92.30E
Tenerife *i.* Africa **68** 28.10N 16.30W
Tengchung China **59** 25.02N 98.28E
Tenghsien China **63** 35.10N 117.14E
Tengiz, L. U.S.S.R. **48** 50.30N 69.00E
Tenke Zaïre **72** 10.34S 26.07E
Tennant Creek *town* Australia **79** 19.31S 134.15E
Tennessee *d.* U.S.A. **91** 36.00N 86.00W
Tennessee *r.* U.S.A. **91** 37.10N 88.25W
Tenterden England **29** 51.04N 0.42E
Tenterfield Australia **80** 29.01S 152.04E
Teplice Czech. **44** 50.40N 13.50E
Ter *r.* England **27** 51.45N 0.36E
Ter *r.* Spain **41** 42.02N 3.10E
Tera *r.* Portugal **41** 38.55N 8.01W
Téramo Italy **42** 42.40N 13.43E
Teresina Brazil **102** 5.09S 42.46W
Termez U.S.S.R. **48** 37.15N 67.15E
Termini Italy **42** 37.59N 13.42E
Terminos Lagoon Mexico **96** 18.30N 91.30W
Termoli Italy **42** 41.58N 14.59E
Ternate Indonesia **61** 0.48N 127.23E
Terneuzen Neth. **45** 51.20N 3.50E
Terni Italy **42** 42.34N 12.44E
Ternopol U.S.S.R. **47** 49.35N 25.39E
Terre Haute U.S.A. **94** 39.27N 87.24W
Terschelling *i.* Neth. **45** 53.25N 5.25E
Teruel Spain **41** 40.21N 1.06W
Teslin *r.* Canada **92** 62.00N 135.00W
Tessaoua Niger **71** 13.46N 7.55E
Test *r.* England **28** 50.55N 1.29W
Tet *r.* France **40** 42.43N 3.00E
Tetbury England **28** 51.37N 2.09W
Tete Moçambique **73** 16.10S 33.30E
Tete *d.* Moçambique **73** 15.30S 33.00E
Teterev *r.* U.S.S.R. **47** 51.03N 30.30E
Tetney England **33** 53.30N 0.01W
Tetuan Morocco **41** 35.34N 5.22W
Teuco *r.* Argentina **103** 25.37S 60.10W
Teviot *r.* Scotland **35** 55.36N 2.27W
Teviotdale *f.* Scotland **35** 55.26N 2.46W
Teviothead Scotland **35** 55.20N 2.56W
Tewkesbury England **28** 51.59N 2.09W
Texarkana U.S.A. **91** 33.28N 94.02W
Texas *d.* U.S.A. **90** 32.00N 100.00W
Texel *i.* Neth. **45** 53.05N 4.47E
Texoma, L. U.S.A. **91** 34.00N 96.40W
Tezpur India **59** 26.38N 92.49E
Thabana Ntlenyana *mtn.* Lesotho **74** 29.30S 29.10E
Thabazimbi R.S.A. **74** 24.41S 27.21E
Thailand Asia **59** 16.00N 102.00E
Thakhek Laos **59** 17.25N 104.45E
Thala Tunisia **42** 35.35N 8.38E
Thale Luang *l.* Thailand **60** 7.30N 100.20E
Thallon Australia **80** 28.39S 148.49E
Thame England **28** 51.44N 0.58W
Thame *r.* England **28** 51.38N 1.10W
Thames *r.* Canada **94** 42.20N 82.25W
Thames *r.* England **27** 51.30N 0.05E
Thames New Zealand **82** 37.08S 175.35E
Thames Haven England **27** 51.31N 0.31E
Thana India **58** 19.14N 73.02E
Thanh Hoa Vietnam **60** 19.50N 105.48E
Thar Desert India **58** 28.00N 72.00E
Thargomindah Australia **80** 27.59S 143.45E
Tharrawaddy Burma **62** 17.37N 95.48E
Tharthar, Wadi *r.* Iraq **56** 34.18N 43.07E
Tharthar Basin *f.* Iraq **56** 33.56N 43.16E
Thásos *i.* Greece **43** 40.40N 24.39E
Thaton Burma **59** 17.00N 97.39E
Thaungdut Burma **59** 24.26N 94.45E
Thaxted England **29** 51.57N 0.21E
Thayetmyo Burma **59** 19.20N 95.18E
The Aird *f.* Scotland **37** 57.26N 4.23W
Thebes *ruins* Egypt **56** 25.41N 32.40E
The Buck *mtn.* Scotland **37** 57.18N 2.59W
The Cherokees, L. O' U.S.A. **91** 36.45N 94.50W
The Cheviot *mtn.* England **35** 55.29N 2.10W
The Cheviot Hills England/Scotland **35** 55.22N 2.24W
The Coorong Australia **80** 36.00S 139.30E
The Everglades *f.* U.S.A. **91** 26.00N 80.30W
The Fens *f.* England **29** 52.32N 0.13E
The Glenkens *f.* Scotland **34** 55.10N 4.13W
The Grenadines *is.* St. Vincent **97** 13.00N 61.20W
The Hague Neth. **45** 52.05N 4.16E
The Hebrides, Sea of Scotland **36** 57.05N 7.05W
The Little Minch *str.* Scotland **36** 57.40N 6.45W
Thelon *r.* Canada **93** 64.23N 96.15W
The Long Mynd *hill* England **28** 52.33N 2.50W
The Machers *f.* Scotland **34** 54.45N 4.28W
The Marsh *f.* England **33** 52.50N 0.10E
The Minch *str.* Scotland **36** 58.10N 5.50W
The Mumbles Wales **31** 51.34N 4.00W
The Naze *c.* England **29** 51.53N 1.17E
The Needles *c.* England **28** 50.39N 1.35W
The North Sd. Scotland **37** 59.18N 2.45W
Theodore Roosevelt L. U.S.A. **90** 33.30N 111.10W
The Ox Mts. Rep. of Ire. **38** 54.06N 8.52W
The Paps *mts.* Rep. of Ire. **39** 52.01N 9.14W
The Pas Canada **93** 53.50N 101.15W
The Pennines *hills* England **32** 55.40N 2.20W
The Potteries *f.* England **32** 53.00N 2.10W
The Rhinns *f.* Scotland **34** 54.50N 5.02W
The Six Towns *town* N. Ireland **34** 54.45N 6.53W
The Skerries *is.* Wales **30** 53.27N 4.35W
The Solent *str.* England **28** 50.45N 1.20W
Thessaloniki Greece **43** 40.38N 22.56E
Thessaloniki, G. of Med. Sea **43** 40.10N 23.00E
The Storr *mtn.* Scotland **36** 57.30N 6.11W
The Swale *str.* England **29** 51.22N 0.58E
Thetford England **29** 52.25N 0.44E
Thetford Mines *town* Canada **95** 46.06N 71.18W
The Trossachs *f.* Scotland **34** 56.15N 4.25W
The Twelve Pins *mts.* Rep. of Ire. **38** 53.30N 9.49W
The Wash *b.* England **33** 52.55N 0.15E
The Weald *f.* England **29** 51.05N 0.20E
The Woods, L. of N. America **91** 49.46N 94.30W
The Wrekin *hill* England **28** 52.40N 2.33W
Theydon Bois England **27** 51.40N 0.05E
Thiers France **40** 45.51N 3.33E
Thiés Senegal **70** 14.50N 16.55W
Thimphu Bhutan **58** 27.29N 89.40E
Thionville France **44** 49.22N 6.11E
Thíra *i.* Greece **43** 36.24N 25.27E
Thirsk England **33** 54.15N 1.20W
Thisted Denmark **46** 56.58N 8.42E
Thitu Is. Asia **60** 10.50N 114.20E
Thjórsá *r.* Iceland **46** 63.53N 20.38W
Thok-Jalung China **59** 32.26N 81.37E
Tholen *i.* Neth. **45** 51.34N 4.07E
Thomastown Rep. of Ire. **39** 52.32N 7.08W
Thomasville U.S.A. **91** 30.50N 83.59W
Thornaby-on-Tees England **33** 54.34N 1.18W
Thornbury England **28** 51.36N 2.31W
Thorne England **33** 53.36N 0.56W
Thorney England **29** 52.37N 0.08W
Thornhill Scotland **35** 55.15N 3.46W
Thornton England **32** 53.53N 3.00W
Thornwood Common *town* England **27** 51.43N 0.08E
Thorpe England **27** 51.25N 0.31W
Thorpe-le-Soken England **29** 51.50N 1.11E
Thorshavn Faroe Is. **46** 62.02N 6.47W
Thouars France **40** 46.59N 0.13W
Thrapston England **29** 52.24N 0.32W
Thrushel *r.* England **31** 50.38N 4.19W
Thuin Belgium **45** 50.21N 4.20E
Thule Greenland **93** 77.40N 69.00W
Thun Switz. **44** 46.46N 7.38E
Thunder Bay *town* Canada **94** 48.25N 89.14W
Thuringian Forest *f.* E. Germany **44** 50.40N 10.50E
Thurles Rep. of Ire. **39** 52.41N 7.50W
Thurnscoe England **33** 53.31N 1.19W
Thursby England **35** 54.40N 3.03W
Thursday I. Australia **61** 10.45S 142.00E
Thurso Scotland **37** 58.35N 3.32W
Thurso *r.* Scotland **37** 58.35N 3.32W
Tiaret Algeria **41** 35.20N 1.20E

Tibati Cameroon **71** 6.25N 12.33E
Tiber *r.* Italy **42** 41.45N 12.16E
Tiberias, L. Israel **56** 32.49N 35.36E
Tibesti Mts. Chad **71** 21.00N 17.30E
Tibet *d.* China **59** 32.20N 86.00E
Tibetan Plateau *f.* China **59** 34.00N 84.30E
Tibooburra Australia **80** 29.28S 142.04E
Tiburon I. Mexico **90** 29.00N 112.25W
Ticehurst England **29** 51.02N 0.23E
Ticino *r.* Italy **40** 45.09N 9.12E
Tickhill England **33** 53.25N 1.08W
Tidjikja Mauritania **70** 18.29N 11.31W
Tiel Neth. **45** 51.53N 5.26E
Tielt Belgium **45** 51.00N 3.20E
Tien Shan *mts.* Asia **62** 42.00N 80.30E
Tienshui China **62** 34.25N 105.58E
Tientsin China **63** 39.08N 117.12E
Tierra Blanca Mexico **96** 18.28N 96.12W
Tierra del Fuego *i.* S. America **102** 54.00S 68.30W
Tiétar *r.* Spain **41** 39.50N 6.00W
Tietê *r.* Brazil **103** 20.43S 51.30W
Tighnabruaich Scotland **34** 55.56N 5.14W
Tigris *r.* Asia **57** 31.00N 47.27E
Tihama *f.* Saudi Arabia **69** 20.30N 40.30E
Tijuana Mexico **90** 32.29N 117.10W
Tikhoretsk U.S.S.R. **47** 45.52N 40.07E
Tikhvin U.S.S.R. **47** 59.35N 33.29E
Tiko Cameroon **72** 4.09N 9.19E
Tiksi U.S.S.R. **49** 71.40N 128.45E
Tilburg Neth. **45** 51.34N 5.05E
Tilbury England **27** 51.28N 0.23E
Till *r.* England **35** 55.41N 2.12W
Tillabéri Niger **71** 14.28N 1.27E
Tillicoultry Scotland **35** 56.09N 3.45W
Tilt *r.* Scotland **37** 56.46N 3.50W
Timagami L. Canada **94** 46.55N 80.03W
Timaru New Zealand **82** 44.23S 171.41E
Timbuktu Mali **70** 16.49N 2.59W
Timişoara Romania **43** 45.47N 21.15E
Timişul *r.* Yugo. **43** 44.49N 20.28E
Timmins Canada **94** 48.30N 81.20W
Timok *r.* Yugo. **43** 44.13N 22.40E
Timoleague Rep. of Ire. **39** 51.38N 8.46W
Timor *i.* Austa. **61** 9.30S 125.00E
Timor Sea Austa. **79** 13.00S 122.00E
Tinahely Rep. of Ire. **39** 52.48N 6.19W
Tinglev Denmark **44** 54.57N 9.15E
Tingsryd Sweden **46** 56.31N 15.00E
Tinian *i.* Asia **61** 14.58N 145.38E
Tinkisso *r.* Guinea **70** 11.25N 9.05W
Tinne *r.* Norway **46** 59.05N 9.43E
Tínos *i.* Greece **43** 37.36N 25.08E
Tintagel Head England **31** 50.40N 4.45W
Tinto Hills Scotland **35** 55.36N 3.40W
Tioman *i.* Malaysia **60** 2.45N 104.10E
Tipperary Rep. of Ire. **39** 52.29N 8.10W
Tipperary *d.* Rep. of Ire. **39** 52.37N 7.55W
Tip Top Mtn. Canada **94** 48.16N 86.02W
Tiptree England **29** 51.48N 0.46E
Tiranë Albania **43** 41.20N 19.48E
Tirano Italy **42** 46.12N 10.10E
Tiraspol U.S.S.R. **47** 46.50N 29.38E
Tirebolu Turkey **56** 41.02N 38.49E
Tiree *i.* Scotland **34** 56.30N 6.50W
Tirga Mor *mtn.* Scotland **36** 58.00N 6.59W
Tîrgu-Jiu Romania **43** 45.03N 23.17E
Tîrgu Mures Romania **47** 46.33N 24.34E
Tirlemont Belgium **45** 50.49N 4.56E
Tirso *r.* Italy **42** 39.52N 8.33E
Tiruchirapalli India **59** 10.50N 78.43E
Tiruppur India **58** 11.05N 77.20E
Tisza *r.* Yugo. **43** 45.09N 20.16E
Titicaca, L. S. America **102** 16.00S 69.00W
Titograd Yugo. **43** 42.30N 19.16E
Titovo Užice Yugo. **43** 43.52N 19.51E
Titov Veles Yugo. **43** 41.43N 21.49E
Tiumpan Head Scotland **36** 58.15N 6.10W
Tiverton England **31** 50.54N 3.30W
Tizimín Mexico **96** 21.10N 88.09W
Tizi Ouzou Algeria **41** 36.44N 4.05E
Tlaxcala *d.* Mexico **96** 19.45N 98.20W
Tlemcen Algeria **41** 34.53N 1.21W
Tletat ed Douair Algeria **41** 36.15N 3.40E
Toba, L. Indonesia **60** 2.45N 98.50E
Tobago S. America **97** 11.15N 60.40W
Tobelo Indonesia **61** 1.45N 127.59E
Tobermory Scotland **34** 56.37N 6.04W
Tobi *i.* Asia **61** 3.01N 131.10E
Toboali Indonesia **60** 3.00S 106.30E
Tobol *r.* U.S.S.R. **48** 58.15N 68.12E
Tobolsk U.S.S.R. **48** 58.15N 68.12E
Tobruk Libya **69** 32.06N 23.58E
Tocantins *r.* Brazil **102** 2.40S 49.20W
Tocumwal Australia **80** 35.51S 145.34E
Todmorden England **32** 53.43N 2.07W
Toe Head Rep. of Ire. **39** 51.29N 9.15W
Toe Head Scotland **36** 57.50N 7.07W
Togian Is. Indonesia **61** 0.20S 122.00E
Togo Africa **70** 8.00N 1.00E
Tokat Turkey **56** 40.20N 36.35E
Tokoroa New Zealand **82** 38.13S 175.53E
Tokuno *i.* Japan **63** 27.40N 129.00E
Tokyo Japan **63** 35.40N 139.45E
Tolbukhin Bulgaria **43** 43.34N 27.52E
Toledo Spain **41** 39.52N 4.02W
Toledo U.S.A. **94** 41.40N 83.35W
Toledo, Montes de *mts.* Spain **41** 39.35N 4.30W
Tollense *r.* E. Germany **44** 53.54N 13.02E
Tolo, G. of Indonesia **61** 2.00S 122.30E
Tolob Scotland **36** 59.53N 1.16W
Tolosa Spain **41** 43.09N 2.04W
Tolsta Head Scotland **36** 58.20N 6.10W
Toluca Mexico **96** 19.20N 99.40W
Toluca *mtn.* Mexico **96** 19.10N 99.40W
Tomatin Scotland **37** 57.20N 3.59W
Tombigbee *r.* U.S.A. **91** 31.05N 87.55W
Tomelloso Spain **41** 39.09N 3.01W
Tomini Indonesia **61** 0.31N 120.30E
Tomini G. Indonesia **61** 0.30S 120.45E
Tomintoul Scotland **37** 57.15N 3.24W
Tomsk U.S.S.R. **48** 56.30N 85.05E
Tona, G. of U.S.S.R. **49** 72.00N 136.10E
Tonalá Mexico **96** 16.08N 93.41W
Tonbridge England **27** 51.12N 0.16E
Tönder Denmark **44** 54.57N 8.53E
Tone *r.* England **31** 50.59N 3.15W
Tonga Is. Pacific Oc. **107** 21.00S 175.00W
Tonga Trench Pacific Oc. **107** 20.00S 172.00W
Tongking, G. of Asia **60** 20.00N 107.50E
Tongland Scotland **35** 54.52N 4.02W
Tongres Belgium **45** 50.47N 5.28E
Tongue Scotland **37** 58.28N 4.25W
Tonk India **58** 26.10N 75.50E
Tonle Sap *l.* Khmer Rep. **60** 12.50N 104.00E
Tonnerre France **40** 47.51N 3.59E
Tönsberg Norway **46** 59.16N 10.25E
Toowoomba Australia **80** 27.35S 151.54E
Top, L. U.S.S.R. **46** 65.45N 32.00E
Topeka U.S.A. **91** 39.03N 95.41W
Topko, Mt. U.S.S.R. **49** 57.20N 138.10E
Topsham England **31** 50.40N 3.27W
Tor Egypt **56** 28.14N 33.37E
Tor B. England **31** 50.25N 3.30W
Torbat-i-Shaikh Jam Iran **57** 35.15N 60.37E
Torbay *town* England **31** 50.27N 3.31W
Tordesillas Spain **41** 41.30N 5.00W
Töre Sweden **46** 65.55N 22.40E
Torhout Belgium **45** 51.04N 3.06E
Torit Sudan **73** 4.27N 32.31E
Torksey England **33** 53.18N 0.45W
Tormes *r.* Spain **41** 41.18N 6.29W
Torne *r.* Sweden **46** 67.13N 23.30E
Torne Träsk *l.* Sweden **46** 68.15N 19.20E
Tornio Finland **46** 65.52N 24.10E
Tornio *r.* Finland **46** 65.53N 24.07E
Toro Spain **41** 41.31N 5.24W
Toronaíos, G. of Med. Sea **43** 40.05N 23.38E
Toronto Australia **80** 33.01S 151.33E
Toronto Canada **95** 43.42N 79.25W
Tororo Uganda **73** 0.42N 34.13E
Torpoint England **31** 50.23N 4.12W
Torquato Severo Brazil **103** 31.04S 54.10W
Torran Rocks *is.* Scotland **34** 56.15N 6.20W
Tôrre de Moncorvo Portugal **41** 41.10N 7.03W
Torrelavega Spain **41** 43.21N 4.00W
Torrens, L. Australia **79** 31.00S 137.50E
Torreón Mexico **96** 25.34N 103.25W
Torres Str. Pacific Oc. **61** 10.30S 142.20E
Tôrres Vedras Portugal **41** 39.05N 9.15W
Torrevieja Spain **41** 37.59N 0.40W
Torridge *r.* England **31** 51.01N 4.12W
Torridon Scotland **36** 57.23N 5.31W
Torridon, Loch Scotland **36** 57.35N 5.45W
Torrington U.S.A. **95** 41.49N 73.05W
Tortola *i.* Virgin Is. **97** 18.28N 64.40W
Tortosa Spain **41** 40.49N 0.31E
Tortue *i.* Haiti **97** 20.05N 72.57W
Tortuga *i.* Venezuela **97** 11.00N 65.20W
Toruń Poland **47** 53.01N 18.35E
Tory I. Rep. of Ire. **38** 55.16N 8.13W
Tory Sd. Rep. of Ire. **38** 55.14N 8.15W
Torzhok U.S.S.R. **47** 57.02N 34.51E
Tosno U.S.S.R. **47** 59.38N 30.46E
Tosson Hill England **35** 55.16N 2.00W
Tostado Argentina **103** 29.15S 61.45W
Totana Spain **41** 37.46N 1.30W
Totland England **28** 50.40N 1.32W
Totley England **33** 53.19N 1.32W
Totma U.S.S.R. **47** 59.59N 42.44E
Totnes England **31** 50.26N 3.41W
Totora Bolivia **103** 17.40S 65.10W
Tottenham Australia **80** 32.14S 147.24E
Tottenham England **27** 51.35N 0.05W
Totton England **28** 50.55N 1.29W
Touba Ivory Coast **70** 8.22N 7.42W
Toubkal *mtn.* Morocco **68** 31.03N 7.57W
Touggourt Algeria **68** 33.08N 6.04E
Toul France **44** 48.41N 5.54E
Toulon France **40** 43.07N 5.53E
Toulouse France **40** 43.33N 1.24E
Toungoo Burma **59** 19.00N 96.30E
Tourcoing France **45** 50.44N 3.09E
Tournai Belgium **45** 50.36N 3.23E
Tournus France **40** 46.33N 4.55E
Tours France **40** 47.23N 0.42E
Tovada *r.* U.S.S.R. **48** 57.40N 67.00E
Tovil England **27** 51.18N 0.31E
Towcester England **28** 52.07N 0.56W
Tower Hamlets *d.* England **27** 51.32N 0.03W
Tow Law *town* England **35** 54.45N 1.49W
Townsend, Mt. Australia **80** 36.24S 148.15E
Townsville Australia **79** 19.13S 146.48E
Towyn Wales **30** 52.37N 4.08W
Toyama Japan **63** 36.42N 137.14E
Trabzon Turkey **56** 41.00N 39.43E
Trafalgar, C. Spain **41** 36.10N 6.02W
Trail Canada **90** 49.04N 117.29W
Trajan's Gate *f.* Bulgaria **43** 42.13N 23.58E
Tralee Rep. of Ire. **39** 52.16N 9.42W
Tralee B. Rep. of Ire. **39** 52.18N 9.55W
Tramore Rep. of Ire. **39** 52.10N 7.10W
Tramore B. Rep. of Ire. **39** 52.09N 7.07W
Tranås Sweden **46** 58.03N 15.00E
Tranent Scotland **35** 55.57N 2.57W
Trang Thailand **60** 7.35N 99.35E
Trangan *i.* Asia **61** 6.30S 134.15E
Trangie Australia **80** 32.03S 148.01E
Transkei *f.* R.S.A. **74** 32.00S 28.00E
Transvaal *d.* R.S.A. **74** 24.30S 29.00E
Transylvanian Alps *mts.* Romania **43** 45.35N 24.40E
Trápani Italy **42** 38.02N 12.30E
Traralgon Australia **80** 38.12S 146.32E
Trasimeno, Lago *l.* Italy **42** 43.09N 12.07E
Traun Austria **44** 48.14N 14.00E
Travers, Mt. New Zealand **82** 42.05S 172.45E
Traverse City U.S.A. **94** 44.46N 85.38W
Travnik Yugo. **43** 44.14N 17.40E
Trébic Czech. **44** 49.13N 15.55E
Třeboň Czech. **44** 49.01N 14.50E
Tredegar Wales **28** 51.47N 3.16W
Tregaron Wales **30** 52.14N 3.56W
Tregony England **31** 50.16N 4.55W
Treig, Loch Scotland **37** 56.48N 4.49W
Treinta-y-Tres Uruguay **103** 33.16S 54.17W
Trelew Argentina **102** 43.13S 65.15W
Trelleborg Sweden **46** 55.10N 13.15E
Tremadog B. Wales **30** 52.52N 4.14W
Tremblant, Mont Canada **95** 46.15N 74.35W
Trenque Lauquén Argentina **103** 35.56S 62.43W
Trent *r.* England **33** 53.41N 0.41W
Trentham England **32** 52.59N 2.12W
Trento Italy **44** 46.04N 11.08E
Trenton U.S.A. **95** 40.15N 74.43W
Tres Arroyos Argentina **103** 38.26S 60.17W
Tres Forcas, Cap Morocco **41** 35.26N 2.57W
Treshnish Is. Scotland **34** 56.29N 6.26W
Treshnish Pt. Scotland **34** 56.32N 6.21W
Três Lagoas Brazil **103** 20.46S 51.43W
Treuchtlingen W. Germany **44** 48.57N 10.55E
Treviso Italy **42** 45.40N 12.14E
Trevose Head *c.* England **31** 50.33N 5.05W
Trier W. Germany **45** 49.45N 6.39E
Trieste Italy **42** 45.40N 13.47E
Triglav *mtn.* Yugo. **42** 46.21N 13.50E
Tríkkala Greece **43** 39.34N 21.46E
Trim Rep. of Ire. **38** 53.33N 6.50W
Trincomalee Sri Lanka **59** 8.34N 81.13E
Tring England **27** 51.48N 0.40W
Trinidad Cuba **97** 21.48N 80.00W
Trinidad S. America **97** 10.30N 61.20W
Trinidad U.S.A. **90** 37.11N 104.31W
Trinity *r.* U.S.A. **91** 29.55N 94.45W
Tripoli Lebanon **56** 34.27N 35.50E
Tripoli Libya **68** 32.58N 13.12E
Tripolitania *f.* Libya **68** 29.45N 14.30E
Tripura *d.* India **59** 23.45N 91.45E
Tristan da Cunha *i.* Atlantic Oc. **112** 38.00S 12.00W
Trivandrum India **58** 8.41N 76.57E
Troisdorf W. Germany **45** 50.50N 7.07E
Trois-Rivières *town* Canada **95** 46.21N 72.34W
Troitsko Pechorsk U.S.S.R. **48** 62.40N 56.08E
Trollhättan Sweden **46** 58.17N 12.20E
Tromsö Norway **46** 69.42N 19.00E
Trondheim Norway **46** 63.36N 10.23E
Trondheim Fjord *est.* Norway **46** 63.40N 10.30E
Troon Scotland **34** 55.33N 4.40W
Trostan *mtn.* N. Ireland **34** 55.03N 6.10W
Trotternish *f.* Scotland **36** 57.33N 6.15W

Troup Head Scotland **37** 57.41N 2.18W
Trout L. Canada **91** 51.10N 93.20W
Trowbridge England **28** 51.18N 2.12W
Troy U.S.A. **95** 42.43N 73.43W
Troyes France **40** 48.18N 4.05E
Trujillo Peru **102** 8.06S 79.00W
Trujillo Spain **41** 39.28N 5.53W
Trujillo Venezuela **97** 9.20N 70.38W
Truro Canada **91** 45.54N 64.00W
Truro England **31** 50.17N 5.02W
Trutnov Czech. **44** 50.34N 15.55E
Trysil *r.* Norway **46** 61.03N 12.30E
Tsangpo *r. see* Brahmaputra China **59**
Tsavo Nat. Park Kenya **73** 2.45S 38.45E
Tselinograd U.S.S.R. **48** 51.10N 71.28E
Tsetang China **59** 29.05N 91.50E
Tshane Botswana **74** 24.05S 21.54E
Tshela Zaïre **72** 4.57S 12.57E
Tshikapa Zaïre **72** 6.28S 20.48E
Tshofa Zaïre **72** 5.13S 25.20E
Tshopo *r.* Zaïre **72** 0.30N 25.07E
Tshuapa *r.* Zaïre **72** 0.14S 20.45E
Tsinan China **63** 36.50N 117.00E
Tsinghai *d.* China **62** 36.15N 96.00E
Tsingtao China **63** 36.04N 120.22E
Tsining Shantung China **63** 35.25N 116.40E
Tsitsihar China **63** 47.23N 124.00E
Tskhinvali U.S.S.R. **47** 42.14N 43.58E
Tsna *r.* U.S.S.R. **47** 54.45N 41.54E
Tsumeb S.W. Africa **74** 19.13S 17.42E
Tsushima *i.* Japan **63** 34.30N 129.20E
Tsuyung China **59** 25.03N 101.33E
Tuam Rep. of Ire. **38** 53.32N 8.52W
Tuamgrenay Rep. of Ire. **39** 52.54N 8.32W
Tuamotu Archipelago *is.* Pacific Oc. **106** 16.00S 145.00W
Tuapse U.S.S.R. **47** 44.06N 39.05E
Tuatapere New Zealand **82** 46.09S 167.42E
Tuath, Loch Scotland **34** 56.30N 6.13W
Tubbercurry Rep. of Ire. **38** 54.03N 8.45W
Tübingen W. Germany **44** 48.32N 9.04E
Tubja, Wadi *r.* Saudi Arabia **56** 25.35N 38.22E
Tucacas Venezuela **97** 10.46N 68.20W
Tucson U.S.A. **90** 32.15N 110.57W
Tucumán Argentina **103** 26.55S 65.15W
Tucumcari U.S.A. **90** 35.11N 103.44W
Tudela Spain **41** 42.04N 1.37W
Tudweiliog Wales **30** 52.54N 4.37W
Tuguegarao Phil. **61** 17.36N 121.44E
Tukangbesi Is. Indonesia **61** 5.30S 124.00E
Tukums U.S.S.R. **46** 56.58N 23.10E
Tukuyu Tanzania **73** 9.20S 33.37E
Tula *r.* Mongolia **62** 48.53N 104.35E
Tula U.S.S.R. **47** 54.11N 37.38E
Tulcea Romania **43** 45.10N 28.50E
Tuléar Malagasy Rep. **67** 23.20S 43.41E
Tuli Indonesia **61** 1.25S 122.23E
Tuli Rhodesia **74** 21.50S 29.15E
Tuli *r.* Rhodesia **74** 21.49S 29.00E
Tulkarm Jordan **56** 32.19N 35.02E
Tulla Rep. of Ire. **39** 52.52N 8.48W
Tullamore Australia **80** 32.39S 147.39E
Tullamore Rep. of Ire. **39** 53.17N 7.31W
Tulle France **40** 45.16N 1.46E
Tullins France **40** 45.18N 5.29E
Tullow Rep. of Ire. **39** 52.49N 6.45W
Tuloma *r.* U.S.S.R. **46** 68.56N 33.00E
Tulsa U.S.A. **91** 36.07N 95.58W
Tulun U.S.S.R. **49** 54.32N 100.35E
Tumba, L. Zaïre **72** 0.45S 18.00E
Tummel *r.* Scotland **37** 56.39N 3.40W
Tummel, Loch Scotland **37** 56.43N 3.55W
Tummo Libya **68** 22.45N 14.08E
Tump Pakistan **58** 26.06N 62.24E
Tumpat Malaysia **59** 6.11N 102.10E
Tunceli Turkey **56** 39.07N 39.34E
Tunchwang China **62** 40.00N 94.40E
Tunduma Tanzania **73** 9.19S 32.47E
Tunduru Tanzania **73** 11.08S 37.21E
Tundzha *r.* Bulgaria **43** 41.40N 26.34E
Tungabhadra *r.* India **58** 16.00N 78.15E
Tungkwan China **63** 34.36N 110.21E
Tung Ting Hu *l.* China **63** 29.40N 113.00E
Tunis Tunisia **42** 36.47N 10.10E
Tunis, G. of Med. Sea **42** 37.00N 10.30E
Tunisia Africa **68** 34.00N 9.00E
Tupelo U.S.A. **91** 34.15N 88.43W
Tupiza Bolivia **103** 21.27S 65.45W
Tura Tanzania **73** 5.30S 33.50E
Tura U.S.S.R. **49** 64.05N 100.00E
Turbo Colombia **97** 8.06N 76.44W
Turfan China **62** 42.55N 89.06E
Turfan Depression *f.* China **62** 43.40N 89.00E
Turgutlu Turkey **43** 38.30N 27.43E
Turi U.S.S.R. **46** 58.48N 25.28E
Turia *r.* Spain **41** 39.27N 0.19W
Turin Italy **40** 45.04N 7.40E
Turkana, L. Kenya **73** 4.00N 36.00E
Turkestan *f.* Asia **57** 40.00N 79.30E
Turkestan U.S.S.R. **48** 43.17N 68.16E
Turkey Asia **56** 39.00N 35.00E
Turkey *r.* U.S.A. **94** 42.58N 91.03W
Turkmenistan Soviet Socialist Republic *d.* U.S.S.R. **48** 40.00N 60.00E
Turks I. C. America **97** 21.30N 71.10W
Turku Finland **46** 60.27N 22.15E
Turneffe I. Belize **96** 17.30N 87.45W
Turnhout Belgium **45** 51.19N 4.57E
Tŭrnovo Bulgaria **43** 43.04N 25.39E
Turnu Măgurele Romania **43** 43.43N 24.53E
Turnu Severin Romania **43** 44.37N 22.39E
Turquino *mtn.* Cuba **97** 20.05N 76.50W
Turriff Scotland **37** 57.32N 2.28W
Turtkul U.S.S.R. **57** 41.30N 61.00E
Tuscaloosa U.S.A. **91** 33.12N 87.33W
Tuscola U.S.A. **94** 39.49N 88.18W
Tuskar Rock *i.* Rep. of Ire. **39** 52.12N 6.13W
Tuticorin India **59** 8.48N 78.10E
Tuttlingen W. Germany **44** 47.59N 8.49E
Tutubu Tanzania **73** 5.28S 32.43E
Tuxpan Mexico **96** 21.00N 97.23W
Tuxtla Gutiérrez Mexico **96** 16.45N 93.09W
Tuz, L. Turkey **56** 38.45N 33.24E
Tuzla Yugo. **43** 44.33N 18.41E
Tweed *r.* Scotland **35** 55.46N 2.00W
Twickenham England **27** 51.27N 0.20W
Twin Falls *town* U.S.A. **90** 42.34N 114.30W
Two Harbors *town* U.S.A. **94** 47.02N 91.40W
Twyford Berks. England **28** 51.29N 0.51W
Twyford Hants. England **28** 51.01N 1.19W
Tyler U.S.A. **91** 32.22N 95.18W
Tyndrum Scotland **34** 56.27N 4.43W
Tyne *r.* England **35** 55.00N 1.25W
Tyne *r.* Scotland **35** 56.00N 2.36W
Tyne and Wear *d.* England **35** 54.57N 1.35W
Tynemouth England **35** 55.01N 1.24W
Tyre Lebanon **56** 33.16N 35.12E
Tyrone *d.* N. Ireland **38** 54.35N 7.15W
Tyrrell, L. Australia **80** 35.22S 142.50E
Tyrrellspass *town* Rep. of Ire. **38** 53.23N 7.24W
Tyrrhenian Sea Med. Sea **42** 40.00N 12.00E
Tyumen U.S.S.R. **48** 57.11N 65.29E
Tywi *r.* Wales **31** 51.46N 4.22W
Tywyn Wales **30** 53.14N 3.49W
Tzaneen R.S.A. **74** 23.50S 30.09E
Tzekung China **62** 29.20N 104.42E
Tzepo China **63** 36.32N 117.47E

U

Ubaiyidh, Wadi *r.* Iraq **56** 32.04N 42.17E
Ubangi *r.* Congo/Zaïre **72** 0.25S 17.40E
Ubeda Spain **41** 38.01N 3.22W
Uberaba Brazil **103** 19.47S 47.57W
Uberlândia Brazil **103** 18.57S 48.17W
Ubombo R.S.A. **74** 27.35S 32.05E
Ubon Ratchathani Thailand **59** 15.15N 104.50E
Ubsa Nur *l.* Mongolia **62** 50.30N 92.30E
Ubundu Zaïre **72** 0.24S 25.28E
Uckfield England **29** 50.58N 0.06E
Udaipur India **58** 24.36N 73.47E
Uddevalla Sweden **46** 58.20N 11.56E
Uddjaur *l.* Sweden **46** 65.55N 17.50E
Udine Italy **42** 46.03N 13.15E
Udon Thani Thailand **59** 17.29N 102.46E
Uele *r.* Zaïre **72** 4.08N 22.25E
Uelen U.S.S.R. **92** 66.13N 169.48W
Uelzen W. Germany **44** 52.58N 10.34E
Uere *r.* Zaïre **72** 3.30N 25.15E
Ufa U.S.S.R. **48** 54.45N 55.58E
Uffculme England **28** 50.45N 3.19W
Ugab *r.* S.W. Africa **74** 21.10S 13.40E
Ugalla *r.* Tanzania **73** 5.15S 29.45E
Uganda Africa **73** 2.00N 33.00E
Ughelli Nigeria **71** 5.33N 6.00E
Ugie *r.* Scotland **37** 57.31N 1.48W
Uglegorsk U.S.S.R. **49** 49.01N 142.04E
Ugra *r.* U.S.S.R. **47** 54.30N 36.10E
Uig Scotland **36** 57.35N 6.22W
Uige Angola **72** 7.40S 15.09E
Uige *d.* Angola **72** 7.00S 15.30E
Uinta Mts. U.S.A. **90** 40.45N 110.30W
Uitenhage R.S.A. **74** 33.46S 25.25E
Uithuizen Neth. **45** 53.24N 6.41E
Ujiji Tanzania **73** 4.55S 29.39E
Ujjain India **58** 23.11N 75.50E
Ujpest Hungary **47** 47.33N 19.05E
Ujung Pandang Indonesia **60** 5.09S 119.28E
Uka U.S.S.R. **49** 57.50N 162.02E
Ukerewe I. Tanzania **73** 2.00S 33.00E
Ukiah U.S.A. **90** 39.09N 123.12W
Ukraine Soviet Socialist Republic *d.* U.S.S.R. **47** 49.30N 32.04E
Ulan Bator Mongolia **62** 47.54N 106.52E
Ulan Göm Mongolia **62** 49.59N 92.00E
Ulan-Ude U.S.S.R. **62** 51.55N 107.40E
Uliastaj Mongolia **62** 47.42N 96.52E
Ulindi *r.* Zaïre **72** 1.38S 25.55E
Ulla *r.* Spain **41** 42.38N 8.45W
Ulladulla Australia **80** 35.21S 150.25E
Ullapool Scotland **36** 57.54N 5.10W
Ullswater *l.* England **32** 54.34N 2.52W
Ulm W. Germany **44** 48.24N 10.00E
Ulsberg Norway **46** 62.45N 10.00E
Ulsta Scotland **36** 60.30N 1.08W
Ulster *d.* N. Ireland/Rep. of Ire. **38** 54.40N 6.45W
Ulua *r.* Honduras **96** 15.50N 87.38W
Uluguru Mts. Tanzania **73** 7.05S 37.40E
Ulva *i.* Scotland **34** 56.29N 6.12W
Ulverston England **32** 54.13N 3.07W
Ul'yanovsk U.S.S.R. **47** 54.19N 48.22E
Uman U.S.S.R. **47** 48.45N 30.10E
Ume *r.* Rhodesia **74** 16.59S 28.28E
Ume *r.* Sweden **46** 63.43N 20.20E
Umfuli *r.* Rhodesia **74** 17.32S 29.14E
Umiat U.S.A. **92** 69.25N 152.20W
Umm-al-Gawein U.A.E. **57** 25.32N 55.34E
Umm-al-Hamir Saudi Arabia **57** 29.07N 46.35E
Umm Lajj Saudi Arabia **56** 25.03N 37.17E
Umm Sa'id Qatar **57** 24.47N 51.36E
Umniati *r.* Rhodesia **74** 17.28S 29.20E
Umtali Rhodesia **74** 18.58S 32.38E
Umtata R.S.A. **74** 31.35S 28.47E
Umuahia Nigeria **71** 5.31N 7.26E
Umvukwe Range *mts.* Rhodesia **74** 16.30S 30.50E
Umvuma Rhodesia **74** 19.16S 30.30E
Umzimkulu R.S.A. **74** 30.15S 29.56E
Una *r.* Yugo. **42** 45.03N 16.22E
Unapool Scotland **36** 58.14N 5.01W
Uncompahgre Peak U.S.A. **90** 38.04N 107.28W
Underberg R.S.A. **74** 29.47S 29.30E
Undur Khan Mongolia **49** 47.20N 110.40E
Ungarie Australia **80** 33.38S 147.00E
Ungava B. Canada **93** 59.00N 67.30W
Uniondale R.S.A. **74** 33.40S 23.07E
Union of Arab Emirates Asia **57** 24.00N 54.00E
Union of Soviet Socialist Republics Europe/Asia **48** 60.00N 80.00E
United Kingdom Europe **18** 54.00N 2.00W
United States of America N. America **90** 39.00N 100.00W
Unna W. Germany **45** 51.32N 7.41E
Unnao India **58** 26.32N 80.30E
Unshin *r.* Rep. of Ire. **38** 54.13N 8.31W
Unst *i.* Scotland **36** 60.45N 0.55W
Unye Turkey **56** 41.09N 37.15E
Upavon England **28** 51.17N 1.49W
Upemba, L. Zaïre **73** 8.35S 26.28E
Upemba Nat. Park Zaïre **73** 9.00S 26.30E
Upernavik Greenland **93** 72.50N 56.00W
Upington R.S.A. **74** 28.28S 21.14E
Upminster England **27** 51.34N 0.15E
Upper *d.* Ghana **70** 10.30N 1.40W
Upper Egypt *f.* Egypt **56** 26.00N 32.00E
Upper Lough Erne N. Ireland **38** 54.13N 7.32W
Upper Taymyr *r.* U.S.S.R. **49** 74.10N 99.50E
Upper Tean England **32** 52.57N 1.59W
Upper Tooting England **27** 51.26N 0.10W
Upper Volta Africa **70** 12.30N 2.00W
Uppingham England **28** 52.36N 0.43W
Uppsala Sweden **46** 59.55N 17.38E
Upton upon Severn England **28** 52.04N 2.12W
Ur *ruins* Iraq **57** 30.55N 46.07E
Uraba, G. of Colombia **97** 8.30N 77.00W
Ural *r.* U.S.S.R. **48** 47.00N 52.00E
Uralla Australia **80** 30.40S 151.31E
Ural Mts. U.S.S.R. **48** 55.00N 59.00E
Ural'sk U.S.S.R. **48** 51.09N 51.20E
Urana Australia **80** 35.21S 146.19E
Uranium City Canada **92** 59.32N 108.43W
Urbana U.S.A. **94** 40.07N 88.12W
Urbino Italy **42** 43.43N 12.38E
Ure *r.* England **33** 54.05N 1.20W
Uren U.S.S.R. **47** 57.30N 45.50E
Urfa Turkey **56** 37.08N 38.45E
Ürgüp Turkey **56** 38.39N 34.55E
Urlingford Rep. of Ire. **39** 52.44N 7.35W
Urmia, L. Iran **57** 37.40N 45.28E
Urmston England **32** 53.28N 2.22W
Urr Water *r.* Scotland **35** 54.54N 3.50W
Uruapan Mexico **96** 19.26N 102.04W
Uruguaiana Brazil **103** 29.45S 57.05W
Uruguay S. America **103** 33.15S 56.00W
Uruguay *r.* Argentina/Uruguay **103** 34.00S 58.30W
Urumchi China **62** 43.43N 87.38E
Urunga Australia **80** 30.30S 152.28E
Uşak Turkey **56** 38.42N 29.25E

Usambara Mts. Tanzania **73** 4.45S 38.25E
Ushant *i. see* Ouessant, Île d' France **40**
Ushnuiyeh Iran **57** 37.03N 45.05E
Usk Wales **31** 51.42N 2.53W
Usk *r.* Wales **31** 51.34N 2.59W
Usküdar Turkey **43** 41.00N 29.03E
Ussuriysk U.S.S.R. **63** 43.48N 131.59E
Ustica *i.* Italy **42** 38.42N 13.11E
Usti nad Labem Czech. **44** 50.41N 14.00E
Ust'kamchatsk U.S.S.R. **49** 56.14N 162.28E
Ust Kut U.S.S.R. **49** 56.40N 105.50E
Ust'Maya U.S.S.R. **49** 60.25N 134.28E
Ust Olenek U.S.S.R. **49** 72.59N 120.00E
Ust'Tsilma U.S.S.R. **48** 65.28N 53.09E
Ust Urt Plateau *f.* U.S.S.R. **48** 43.30N 55.20E
Usumacinta *r.* Mexico **96** 18.48N 92.40W
Utah *d.* U.S.A. **90** 39.00N 112.00W
Utembo *r.* Angola **72** 17.03S 22.00E
Utete Tanzania **73** 8.00S 38.49E
Utica U.S.A. **95** 43.06N 75.15W
Utiel Spain **41** 39.33N 1.13W
Utrecht Neth. **45** 52.04N 5.07E
Utrecht *d.* Neth. **45** 52.04N 5.10E
Utrecht R.S.A. **74** 27.40S 30.20E
Utrera Spain **41** 37.10N 5.47W
Utsunomiya Japan **63** 36.33N 139.52E
Uttaradit Thailand **59** 17.38N 100.05E
Uttar Pradesh *d.* India **58** 27.50N 80.00E
Uttoxeter England **32** 52.53N 1.50W
Uusikaupunki Finland **46** 60.48N 21.30E
Uvinza Tanzania **73** 5.08S 30.23E
Uvira Zaïre **73** 3.22S 29.06E
'Uwaina Saudi Arabia **57** 26.46N 48.13E
Uxbridge England **27** 51.33N 0.30W
Uyo Nigeria **71** 5.01N 7.56E
'Uyun Saudi Arabia **57** 26.32N 43.41E
Uzbekistan Soviet Socialist Republic *d.* U.S.S.R. **48** 42.00N 63.00E
Uzhgorod U.S.S.R. **47** 48.38N 22.15E

V

Vaago *i.* Faroe Is. **46** 62.03N 7.14W
Vaal *r.* R.S.A. **74** 29.03S 23.42E
Vaal Dam R.S.A. **74** 27.00S 28.15E
Vaasa Finland **46** 63.06N 21.36E
Vaduz Liech. **44** 47.08N 9.32E
Vaggeryd Sweden **46** 57.30N 14.10E
Váh *r.* Czech. **47** 47.40N 17.50E
Vaila *i.* Scotland **36** 60.12N 1.34W
Valdai Hills U.S.S.R. **47** 57.10N 33.00E
Valday U.S.S.R. **47** 57.59N 33.10E
Valdemarsvik Sweden **46** 58.13N 16.35E
Valdepeñas Spain **41** 38.46N 3.24W
Valdez U.S.A. **92** 61.07N 146.17W
Val-d'Or *town* Canada **95** 48.07N 77.47W
Valença Portugal **41** 42.02N 8.38W
Valence France **40** 44.56N 4.54E
Valencia Spain **41** 39.29N 0.24W
Valencia Venezuela **97** 10.14N 67.59W
Valencia, G. of Spain **41** 39.38N 0.20W
Valencia, L. Venezuela **97** 10.09N 67.30W
Valencia de Alcántara Spain **41** 39.25N 7.14
Valenciennes France **45** 50.22N 3.32E
Valentia I. Rep. of Ire. **39** 51.54N 10.21W
Vale of Berkeley *f.* England **28** 51.42N 2.25W
Vale of Evesham *f.* England **28** 52.05N 1.55W
Vale of Gloucester *f.* England **28** 51.54N 2.15W
Vale of Kent *f.* England **29** 51.08N 0.38E
Vale of Pewsey *f.* England **28** 51.21N 1.45W
Vale of Pickering *f.* England **33** 54.11N 0.45W
Vale of White Horse *f.* England **28** 51.38N 1.32W
Vale of York *f.* England **33** 54.12N 1.25W
Valga U.S.S.R. **46** 57.44N 26.00E
Valinco, G. of Med. Sea **40** 41.40N 8.50E
Valjevo Yugo. **43** 44.16N 19.56E
Valkeakoski Finland **46** 61.17N 24.05E
Valkenswaard Neth. **45** 51.21N 5.27E
Valladolid Spain **41** 41.39N 4.45W
Valle Venezuela **97** 9.15N 66.00W
Valletta Malta **42** 35.53N 14.31E
Valley City U.S.A. **90** 46.57N 97.58W
Valleyfield Canada **95** 45.15N 74.08W
Valmiera U.S.S.R. **46** 57.32N 25.29E
Valnera *mtn.* Spain **41** 43.10N 3.40W
Valognes France **40** 49.31N 1.28W
Valparaíso Chile **102** 33.35S 71.20W
Vals, C. Indonesia **61** 8.30S 137.30E
Valverde Dom. Rep. **97** 19.37N 71.04W
Valverde del Camino Spain **41** 37.35N 6.45W
Van Turkey **56** 38.28N 43.20E
Van, L. Turkey **56** 38.35N 42.52E
Vancouver Canada **90** 49.13N 123.06W
Vancouver I. Canada **92** 50.00N 126.00W
Vänern *l.* Sweden **46** 59.00N 13.15E
Vänersborg Sweden **46** 58.23N 12.19E
Vanga Kenya **73** 4.37S 39.13E
Vanka Järvi *l.* Finland **46** 61.30N 23.50E
Vännäs Sweden **46** 63.56N 19.50E
Vannes France **40** 47.40N 2.44W
Vanrhynsdorp R.S.A. **74** 31.36S 18.45E
Var *r.* France **40** 43.39N 7.11E
Varanasi India **58** 25.20N 83.00E
Varangerenfjord *est.* Norway **46** 70.00N 29.30E
Varazdin Yugo. **44** 46.18N 16.20E
Varberg Sweden **46** 57.06N 12.15E
Vardar *r.* Greece **43** 40.31N 22.43E
Varel W. Germany **45** 53.24N 8.08E
Varennes France **40** 46.19N 3.24E
Varginha Brazil **103** 21.33S 45.25W
Varkaus Finland **46** 62.15N 27.45E
Varna Bulgaria **43** 43.13N 27.57E
Värnamo Sweden **46** 57.11N 14.03E
Vasilkov U.S.S.R. **47** 50.12N 30.15E
Västerås Sweden **46** 59.36N 16.32E
Västerdal *r.* Sweden **46** 60.32N 15.02E
Västervik Sweden **46** 57.45N 16.40E
Vaternish Pt. Scotland **36** 57.37N 6.39W
Vatersay *i.* Scotland **36** 56.56N 7.32W
Vatnajökull *mts.* Iceland **46** 64.20N 17.00W
Vättern *l.* Sweden **46** 58.30N 14.30E
Vaughn U.S.A. **90** 34.35N 105.14W
Vavuniya Sri Lanka **59** 8.45N 80.30E
Växjö Sweden **46** 56.52N 14.50E
Vaygach *i.* U.S.S.R. **48** 70.00N 59.00E
Vecht *r.* Neth. **45** 52.39N 6.01E
Vega *i.* Norway **46** 65.40N 11.55E
Vejle Denmark **46** 55.43N 9.33E
Vélez Málaga Spain **41** 36.48N 4.05W
Velikaya *r.* U.S.S.R. **46** 57.54N 28.06E
Velikiye-Luki U.S.S.R. **47** 56.19N 30.31E
Velletri Italy **42** 41.41N 12.47E
Vellore India **59** 12.56N 79.09E
Velsen Neth. **45** 52.28N 4.39E
Veluwe *f.* Neth. **45** 52.17N 5.45E
Venachar, Loch Scotland **34** 56.13N 4.19W
Venado Tuerto Argentina **103** 33.45S 61.56W
Vendas Novas Portugal **41** 38.41N 8.27W
Vendôme France **40** 47.48N 1.04E
Venezuela S. America **102** 7.00N 65.00W
Venezuela, G. of Venezuela **97** 11.30N 71.00W
Veniaminof Mtn. U.S.A. **92** 56.05N 159.20W
Venice Italy **42** 45.26N 12.20E
Venice, G. of Med. Sea **42** 45.20N 13.00E
Venlo Neth. **45** 51.22N 6.10E
Venraij Neth. **45** 51.32N 5.58E
Venta *r.* U.S.S.R. **46** 57.22N 21.31E
Ventnor England **28** 50.35N 1.12W
Ventspils U.S.S.R. **46** 57.22N 21.31E
Ver *r.* England **27** 51.42N 0.20W
Vera Spain **41** 37.15N 1.51W
Veracruz Mexico **96** 19.11N 96.10W
Veracruz *d.* Mexico **96** 18.00N 95.00W
Veraval India **58** 20.53N 70.28E
Vercelli Italy **40** 45.19N 8.26E
Verde *r.* Paraguay **103** 23.10S 57.45W
Verde, C. Senegal **70** 14.45N 17.25W
Verdon *r.* France **40** 43.42N 5.39E
Verdun Canada **95** 45.28N 73.35W
Verdun France **40** 49.10N 5.24E
Vereeniging R.S.A. **74** 26.41S 27.56E
Verin Spain **41** 41.55N 7.26W
Verkhoyansk U.S.S.R. **49** 67.25N 133.25E
Verkhoyansk Range *mts.* U.S.S.R. **49** 66.00N 130.00E
Vermont *d.* U.S.A. **95** 43.50N 72.50W
Verona Italy **42** 45.27N 10.59E
Versailles France **40** 48.48N 2.08E
Verviers Belgium **45** 50.36N 5.52E
Vervins France **45** 49.50N 3.55E
Verwood England **28** 50.53N 1.53W
Vesoul France **44** 47.38N 6.09E
Vesterålen *is.* Norway **46** 68.55N 15.00E
Vest Fjorden *est.* Norway **46** 68.10N 15.00E
Vestmanna Is. Iceland **46** 63.30N 20.20W
Vesuvius *mtn.* Italy **42** 40.48N 14.25E
Vetlanda Sweden **46** 57.26N 15.05E
Vetluga *r.* U.S.S.R. **47** 56.18N 46.19E
Vettore, Monte *mtn.* Italy **42** 42.50N 13.18E
Vézere *r.* France **40** 44.53N 0.55E
Viana do Castelo Portugal **41** 41.41N 8.50W
Viborg Denmark **46** 56.28N 9.25E
Vicenza Italy **42** 45.33N 11.32E
Vich Spain **41** 41.56N 2.16E
Vichuga U.S.S.R. **47** 57.12N 41.50E
Vichy France **40** 46.07N 3.25E
Victor Harbor Australia **80** 35.36S 138.35E
Victoria *d.* Australia **80** 37.20S 144.10E
Victoria Cameroon **71** 4.01N 9.12E
Victoria Canada **90** 48.26N 123.20W
Victoria Hong Kong **60** 22.16N 114.15E
Victoria U.S.A. **96** 28.49N 97.01W
Victoria, L. Africa **73** 1.00S 33.00E
Victoria, Mt. P.N.G. **79** 8.10S 147.20E
Victoria de las Tunas Cuba **97** 20.58N 76.59W
Victoria Falls *f.* Rhodesia/Zambia **74** 17.58S 25.45E
Victoria I. Canada **92** 71.00N 110.00W
Victoria Nile *r.* Uganda **73** 2.14N 31.20E
Victoria West R.S.A. **74** 31.25S 23.08E
Vidin Bulgaria **43** 43.58N 22.51E
Viedma Argentina **103** 40.45S 63.00W
Vienna Austria **44** 48.13N 16.22E
Vienne France **40** 45.32N 4.54E
Vienne *r.* France **40** 47.13N 0.05W
Vientiane Laos **60** 18.01N 102.48E
Vieques *i.* Puerto Rico **97** 18.08N 65.30W
Vierwaldstätter See *l.* Switz. **40** 47.00N 8.35E
Vierzon France **40** 47.14N 2.03E
Vietnam Asia **60** 15.00N 108.00E
Vignemale, Pic de *mtn.* France **40** 42.46N 0.08W
Vigo Spain **41** 42.15N 8.44W
Vijayawada India **59** 16.34N 80.40E
Vijose *r.* Albania **43** 40.39N 19.20E
Vikna *i.* Norway **46** 64.59N 11.00E
Vila Coutinho Moçambique **73** 14.34S 34.21E
Vila da Maganja Moçambique **73** 17.25S 37.32E
Vila da Ponte Angola **72** 14.28S 16.25E
Vila de João Belo Moçambique **74** 25.05S 33.38E
Vila de Manica Moçambique **74** 19.00S 33.00E
Vila de Sena Moçambique **73** 17.36S 35.00E
Vila Franca Portugal **41** 38.57N 8.59W
Vila General Machado Angola **72** 12.01S 17.22E
Vilaine *r.* France **40** 47.30N 2.25W
Vila Luso Angola **72** 11.46S 19.55E
Vila Mariano Machado Angola **72** 12.58S 14.39E
Vilanculos Moçambique **74** 22.01S 35.19E
Vila Nova do Seles Angola **72** 11.24S 14.15E
Vila Pereira de Eça Angola **72** 17.05S 15.44E
Vila Pery Moçambique **74** 19.04S 33.29E
Vila Real Portugal **41** 41.17N 7.45W
Vila Real de Santo Antonio Portugal **41** 37.12N 7.25W
Vila Salazar Angola **72** 9.12S 14.54E
Vila Silva Porto Angola **72** 12.25S 16.58E
Vila Teixeira da Silva Angola **72** 12.13S 15.46E
Vila Vasco da Gama Moçambique **73** 14.55S 32.12E
Vila Verissimo Sarmento Angola **72** 8.08S 20.38E
Vilhelmina Sweden **46** 64.38N 16.40E
Viljandi U.S.S.R. **46** 58.22N 25.30E
Villa Angela Argentina **103** 27.34S 60.45W
Villablino Spain **41** 42.57N 6.19W
Villacañas Spain **41** 39.38N 3.20W
Villach Austria **44** 46.37N 13.51E
Villa Cisneros W. Sahara **68** 23.43N 15.57W
Villa Constitución Argentina **103** 33.15S 60.20W
Villagarcia Spain **41** 42.35N 8.45W
Villaguay Argentina **103** 31.55S 59.01W
Villahermosa Mexico **96** 18.00N 92.53W
Villa Huidobro Argentina **103** 34.50S 64.34W
Villajoyosa Spain **41** 38.31N 0.14W
Villa Maríla Argentina **103** 32.25S 63.15W
Villa Montes Bolivia **103** 21.15S 63.30W
Villanueva de la Serena Spain **41** 38.58N 5.48W
Villanueva-y-Geitru Spain **41** 41.13N 1.43E
Villaputzu Italy **42** 39.28N 9.35E
Villarrica Paraguay **103** 25.45S 56.28W
Villarrobledo Spain **41** 39.16N 2.36W
Villa Sanjurjo Morocco **41** 35.14N 3.56W
Villefranche France **40** 46.00N 4.43E
Villena Spain **41** 38.39N 0.52W
Villeneuve France **40** 44.25N 0.43E
Villeneuve d'Ascq France **40** 50.37N 3.10E
Villeurbanne France **40** 45.46N 4.54E
Villingen W. Germany **44** 48.03N 8.28E
Vilnius U.S.S.R. **46** 54.40N 25.19E
Vilvoorde Belgium **45** 50.56N 4.25E
Vilyuy *r.* U.S.S.R. **49** 64.20N 126.55E
Vilyuysk U.S.S.R. **49** 63.46N 121.35E
Vimmerby Sweden **46** 57.40N 15.50E
Vina *r.* Cameroon **71** 7.43N 15.30E
Vincennes U.S.A. **94** 38.42N 87.30W
Vindel *r.* Sweden **46** 63.56N 19.54E
Vindhya Range *mts.* India **58** 22.55N 76.00E
Vineland U.S.A. **95** 39.29N 75.02W
Vinh Vietnam **59** 18.42N 105.41E
Vinnitsa U.S.S.R. **47** 49.11N 28.30E
Vire France **40** 48.50N 0.53W
Vire *r.* France **40** 49.20N 0.53W
Virgin Gorda *i.* Virgin Is. **97** 18.30N 64.26W
Virginia Rep. of Ire. **38** 53.50N 7.06W
Virginia U.S.A. **94** 47.30N 92.28W
Virginia *d.* U.S.A. **91** 37.30N 79.00W
Virginia Water *town* England **27** 51.24N 0.36W
Virgin Is. C. America **97** 18.30N 65.00W
Virovitica Yugo. **43** 45.51N 17.23E
Virton Belgium **45** 49.35N 5.32E
Virunga Nat. Park Zaïre **73** 0.30S 29.15E
Vis *i.* Yugo. **42** 43.03N 16.10E

Visby Sweden **46** 57.37N 18.20E
Viscount Melville Sd. Canada **92** 74.30N 104.00W
Visé Belgium **45** 50.44N 5.42E
Višegrad Yugo. **43** 43.47N 19.20E
Viseu Portugal **41** 40.40N 7.55W
Vishakhapatnam India **59** 17.42N 83.24E
Viso, Monte *mtn.* Italy **40** 44.38N 7.05E
Vistula *r.* Poland **47** 54.23N 18.52E
Vitebsk U.S.S.R. **47** 55.10N 30.14E
Viterbo Italy **42** 42.26N 12.07E
Vitim *r.* U.S.S.R. **49** 59.30N 112.36E
Vitória Espírito Santo Brazil **102** 20.19S 40.21W
Vitoria Spain **41** 42.51N 2.40W
Vittória Italy **42** 36.57N 14.21E
Vizianagaram India **59** 18.07N 83.30E
Vlaardingen Neth. **45** 51.55N 4.20E
Vladimir U.S.S.R. **47** 56.08N 40.25E
Vladivostok U.S.S.R. **63** 43.09N 131.53E
Vlieland *i.* Neth. **45** 53.15N 5.00E
Vlorë Albania **43** 40.28N 19.27E
Vltava *r.* Czech. **44** 50.22N 14.28E
Voe Scotland **36** 60.21N 1.15W
Vogelkop *f.* Asia **61** 1.10S 132.30E
Vogelsberg *mtn.* W. Germany **44** 50.30N 9.15E
Voghera Italy **42** 44.59N 9.01E
Voi Kenya **73** 3.23S 38.35E
Voil, Loch Scotland **34** 56.21N 4.26W
Voiron France **40** 45.22N 5.35E
Volga *r.* U.S.S.R. **48** 45.45N 47.50E
Volga Uplands *hills* U.S.S.R. **47** 53.15N 45.45E
Volgograd U.S.S.R. **47** 48.45N 44.30E
Volkhov *r.* U.S.S.R. **47** 60.15N 32.15E
Vologda U.S.S.R. **47** 59.10N 39.55E
Vólos Greece **43** 39.22N 22.57E
Volsk U.S.S.R. **47** 52.04N 47.22E
Volta *d.* Ghana **70** 7.30N 0.25E
Volta *r.* Ghana **70** 5.50N 0.41E
Volta, L. Ghana **70** 7.00N 0.00
Volterra Italy **42** 43.24N 10.51E
Volturno *r.* Italy **42** 41.02N 13.56E
Volzhskiy U.S.S.R. **47** 48.48N 44.45E
Voorburg Neth. **45** 52.05N 4.22E
Vopna Fjördhur *est.* Iceland **46** 65.50N 14.30W
Vordingborg Denmark **44** 55.01N 11.55E
Vorkuta U.S.S.R. **48** 67.27N 64.00E
Voronezh U.S.S.R. **47** 51.40N 39.13E
Voroshilovgrad U.S.S.R. **47** 48.35N 39.20E
Vosges *mts.* France **44** 48.10N 7.00E
Voss Norway **46** 60.38N 6.25E
Votuporanga Brazil **103** 20.26S 49.53W
Vouga *r.* Portugal **41** 40.41N 8.38W
Voves France **40** 48.16N 1.37E
Voznesensk U.S.S.R. **47** 47.34N 31.21E
Vranje Yugo. **43** 42.34N 21.52E
Vratsa Bulgaria **43** 43.12N 23.33E
Vrbas *r.* Yugo. **43** 45.06N 17.29E
Vrede R.S.A. **74** 27.24S 29.11E
Vršac Yugo. **43** 45.08N 21.18E
Vryburg R.S.A. **74** 26.57S 24.44E
Vyatka *r.* U.S.S.R. **47** 55.45N 51.30E
Vyatskiye Polyany U.S.S.R. **47** 56.14N 51.08E
Vyazma U.S.S.R. **47** 55.12N 34.17E
Vyazniki U.S.S.R. **47** 56.14N 42.08E
Vyborg U.S.S.R. **46** 60.45N 28.41E
Vyrnwy *r.* Wales **30** 52.45N 3.01W
Vyrnwy, L. Wales **30** 52.46N 3.30W
Vyshka U.S.S.R. **57** 39.19N 49.12E
Vyshniy-Volochek U.S.S.R. **47** 57.34N 34.23E

W

Wa Ghana **70** 10.07N 2.28W
Waal *r.* Neth. **45** 51.45N 4.40E
Waalwijk Neth. **45** 51.42N 5.04E
Wabash *r.* U.S.A. **94** 38.25N 87.45W
Wabush City Canada **93** 53.00N 66.50W
Waco U.S.A. **91** 31.33N 97.10W
Wad Pakistan **58** 27.21N 66.30E
Wadden Sea Neth. **45** 53.15N 5.05E
Waddesdon England **28** 51.50N 0.54W
Waddington, Mt. Canada **92** 51.30N 125.00W
Wadebridge England **31** 50.31N 4.51W
Wadesmill England **27** 51.51N 0.03W
Wadhurst England **29** 51.03N 0.21E
Wadi Halfa Sudan **69** 21.55N 31.20E
Wad Medani Sudan **69** 14.24N 33.30E
Wafra Kuwait **57** 28.39N 47.56E
Wageningen Neth. **45** 51.58N 5.39E
Wager Bay *town* Canada **93** 65.55N 90.40W
Wagga Wagga Australia **80** 35.07S 147.24E
Wahpeton U.S.A. **91** 46.16N 96.36W
Waiau New Zealand **82** 42.39S 173.02E
Waiau *r.* New Zealand **82** 42.47S 173.23E
Waigeo *i.* Indonesia **61** 0.05S 130.30E
Waihou *r.* New Zealand **82** 37.12S 175.33E
Waikato *r.* New Zealand **82** 37.19S 174.50E
Waikerie Australia **80** 34.11S 139.59E
Waimakariri *r.* New Zealand **82** 43.23S 172.40E
Waimarie New Zealand **82** 41.33S 171.58E
Wainfleet All Saints England **33** 53.07N 0.16E
Waingapu Indonesia **61** 9.30S 120.10E
Wainwright U.S.A. **92** 70.39N 160.00W
Waipara New Zealand **82** 43.03S 172.47E
Waipukurau New Zealand **82** 40.00S 176.33E
Wairau *r.* New Zealand **82** 41.32S 174.08E
Wairoa New Zealand **82** 39.03S 177.25E
Wairoa *r.* New Zealand **82** 36.07S 173.59E
Waitaki *r.* New Zealand **82** 44.56S 171.10E
Waitara New Zealand **82** 38.59S 174.13E
Wajir Kenya **73** 1.46N 40.05E
Wakatipu, L. New Zealand **82** 45.10S 168.30E
Wakayama Japan **63** 34.12N 135.10E
Wakefield England **33** 53.41N 1.31W
Wakeham Canada **93** 61.30N 72.00W
Wakkanai Japan **63** 45.26N 141.43E
Walachian Plain *f.* Romania **47** 44.30N 26.30E
Walbrzych Poland **44** 50.48N 16.19E
Walbury Hill England **28** 51.21N 1.30W
Walcha Australia **80** 31.00S 151.36E
Walcheren *f.* Neth. **45** 51.32N 3.35E
Walderslade England **27** 51.21N 0.33E
Wales U.K. **30** 52.30N 3.45W
Walgett Australia **80** 30.03S 148.10E
Wallasey England **32** 53.26N 3.02W
Wallingford England **28** 51.36N 1.07W
Wallington England **27** 51.22N 0.09W
Walls Scotland **36** 60.14N 1.34W
Wallsend England **35** 55.00N 1.31W
Walmer England **29** 51.12N 1.23E
Walney, Isle of England **32** 54.05N 3.12W
Walsall England **28** 52.36N 1.59W
Waltham Abbey England **27** 51.42N 0.01E
Waltham Forest *d.* England **27** 51.36N 0.02W
Waltham on the Wolds England **33** 52.49N 0.49W
Walthamstow England **27** 51.34N 0.01W
Walton-on-Thames England **27** 51.23N 0.23W
Walton on the Hill England **27** 51.17N 0.02W
Walton on the Naze England **29** 51.52N 1.17E
Walvis B. R.S.A. **74** 22.48S 14.29E
Walvis Bay *d.* R.S.A. **74** 22.55S 14.35E
Walvis Bay *town* R.S.A. **74** 22.50S 14.31E
Wamba Kenya **73** 0.58N 37.19E
Wamba Nigeria **71** 8.57N 8.42E
Wamba Zaïre **73** 2.10N 27.59E
Wamba *r.* Zaïre **72** 4.35S 17.15E
Wami *r.* Tanzania **73** 6.10S 38.50E
Wanaaring Australia **80** 29.42S 144.14E
Wanaka, L. New Zealand **82** 44.30S 169.10E
Wandsworth *d.* England **27** 51.27N 0.11W
Wanganella Australia **80** 35.13S 144.53E
Wanganui New Zealand **82** 39.56S 175.00E
Wangaratta Australia **80** 36.22S 146.20E
Wangeroog *i.* W. Germany **45** 53.50N 7.50E
Wangford Fen *f.* England **29** 52.25N 0.31E
Wanhsien China **63** 30.54N 108.20E
Wankie Rhodesia **74** 18.18S 26.30E
Wankie Nat. Park Rhodesia **74** 19.00S 26.30E
Wansbeck *r.* England **35** 55.10N 1.33W
Wanstead England **27** 51.34N 0.02E
Wantage England **28** 51.35N 1.25W
Warangal India **59** 18.00N 79.35E
Waratah B. Australia **80** 38.55S 146.07E
Ward Rep. of Ire. **38** 53.26N 6.20W
Warden R.S.A. **74** 27.50S 28.58E
Wardha India **59** 20.41N 78.40E
Ward Hill Orkney Is. Scotland **37** 58.54N 3.20W
Ward Hill Orkney Is. Scotland **37** 58.58N 3.09W
Ward's Stone *mtn.* England **32** 54.03N 2.36W
Ware England **27** 51.49N 0.02W
Wareham England **28** 50.41N 2.08W
Warendorf W. Germany **45** 51.57N 8.00E
Warialda Australia **80** 29.33S 150.36E
Wark Forest *hills* England **35** 55.06N 2.24W
Warley England **28** 52.29N 2.02W
Warlingham England **27** 51.19N 0.04W
Warmbad S.W. Africa **74** 28.29S 18.41E
Warminster England **28** 51.12N 2.11W
Warracknabeal Australia **80** 36.15S 142.28E
Warragul Australia **80** 38.11S 145.55E
Warrego *r.* Australia **80** 30.25S 145.18E
Warren Mich. U.S.A. **94** 42.30N 83.02W
Warren Ohio U.S.A. **94** 41.15N 80.49W
Warri Nigeria **71** 5.36N 5.46E
Warrington England **32** 53.25N 2.38W
Warrnambool Australia **80** 38.23S 142.03E
Warsaw Poland **47** 52.15N 21.00E
Warsop England **33** 53.13N 1.08W
Warta *r.* Poland **47** 52.45N 15.09E
Warwick Australia **80** 28.12S 152.00E
Warwick England **28** 52.17N 1.36W
Warwick U.S.A. **95** 41.42N 71.23W
Warwickshire *d.* England **28** 52.13N 1.30W
Washington England **35** 54.55N 1.30W
Washington U.S.A. **95** 38.55N 77.00W
Washington *d.* U.S.A. **90** 47.00N 120.00W
Washington, Mt. U.S.A. **95** 44.17N 71.19W
Wasior Asia **61** 2.38S 134.27E
Wassy France **40** 48.30N 4.59E
Wast Water *l.* England **32** 54.25N 3.18W
Waswanipi L. Canada **95** 49.30N 76.20W
Watampone Indonesia **61** 4.33S 120.20E
Watchet England **31** 51.10N 3.20W
Waterbury U.S.A. **95** 41.33N 73.03W
Waterford Rep. of Ire. **39** 52.16N 7.08W
Waterford *d.* Rep. of Ire. **39** 52.10N 7.40W
Waterford Harbour *est.* Rep. of Ire. **39** 52.12N 6.56W
Watergate B. England **31** 50.28N 5.06W
Waterloo Belgium **45** 50.44N 4.24E
Waterloo Canada **94** 43.28N 80.32W
Waterloo U.S.A. **94** 42.30N 92.20W
Waterlooville England **28** 50.53N 1.02W
Watertown N.Y. U.S.A. **95** 43.57N 75.56W
Watertown S.Dak. U.S.A. **91** 44.54N 97.08W
Watertown Wisc. U.S.A. **94** 43.12N 88.46W
Waterville Rep. of Ire. **39** 51.50N 10.11W
Waterville U.S.A. **95** 44.34N 69.41W
Watervliet U.S.A. **95** 42.43N 73.42W
Watford England **27** 51.40N 0.25W
Watlington England **28** 51.38N 1.00W
Watson Lake *town* Canada **92** 60.07N 128.49W
Watten, Loch Scotland **37** 58.29N 3.20W
Watton England **29** 52.35N 0.50E
Wau P.N.G. **61** 7.22S 146.40E
Wau Sudan **69** 7.40N 28.04E
Wauchope Australia **80** 31.27S 152.43E
Waukegan U.S.A. **94** 42.21N 87.52W
Waukesha U.S.A. **94** 43.01N 88.14W
Wausau U.S.A. **94** 44.58N 89.40W
Wauwatosa U.S.A. **94** 43.04N 88.02W
Waveney *r.* England **29** 52.29N 1.46E
Wavre Belgium **45** 50.43N 4.37E
Waxham England **29** 52.47N 1.38E
Waycross U.S.A. **91** 31.08N 82.22W
Wealdstone England **27** 51.36N 0.20W
Wear *r.* England **35** 54.55N 1.21W
Weardale *f.* England **35** 54.45N 2.05W
Weaver *r.* England **32** 53.19N 2.44W
Weda Indonesia **61** 0.30N 127.52E
Weddell Sea Antarctica **106** 73.00S 42.00W
Wedmore England **28** 51.14N 2.50W
Weert Neth. **45** 51.14N 5.40E
Wee Waa Australia **80** 30.34S 149.27E
Weiden in der Oberpfalz W. Germany **44** 49.40N 12.10E
Weifang China **63** 36.44N 119.10E
Weihai China **63** 37.30N 122.04E
Weimar E. Germany **44** 50.59N 11.20E
Weirton U.S.A. **94** 40.24N 80.37W
Weissenfels E. Germany **44** 51.12N 11.58E
Welhamgreen England **27** 51.44N 0.11W
Welkom R.S.A. **74** 27.59S 26.44E
Welland Canada **95** 45.59N 79.14W
Welland *r.* England **33** 52.53N 0.00
Welling England **27** 51.28N 0.08E
Wellingborough England **28** 52.18N 0.41W
Wellington Australia **80** 32.33S 148.59E
Wellington Salop England **30** 52.42N 2.31W
Wellington Somerset England **31** 50.58N 3.13W
Wellington New Zealand **82** 41.17S 174.47E
Wellingtonbridge Rep. of Ire. **39** 52.16N 6.45W
Wells England **28** 51.12N 2.39W
Wellsford New Zealand **82** 36.16S 174.32E
Wells-next-the-Sea England **33** 52.57N 0.51E
Welshpool Wales **30** 52.40N 3.09W
Welwyn England **27** 51.50N 0.13W
Welwyn Garden City England **27** 51.48N 0.13W
Wem England **32** 52.52N 2.45W
Wembere *r.* Tanzania **73** 4.07S 34.15E
Wembley England **27** 51.34N 0.18W
Wemyss Bay *town* Scotland **34** 55.52N 4.52W
Wenatchee U.S.A. **90** 47.26N 120.20W
Wenchow China **63** 28.02N 120.40E
Wendover England **27** 51.46N 0.46W
Wenlock Edge *hill* England **28** 52.33N 2.40W
Wenshan China **59** 23.25N 104.15E
Wensleydale *f.* England **32** 54.19N 2.04W
Wensum *r.* England **29** 52.37N 1.20E
Wentworth Australia **80** 34.06S 141.56E
Wepener R.S.A. **74** 29.44S 27.03E
Werne W. Germany **45** 51.39N 7.36E
Werris Creek *town* Australia **80** 31.20S 150.41E
Wesel W. Germany **45** 51.39N 6.37E
Weser *r.* W. Germany **44** 53.15N 8.30E
Wessel, C. Australia **79** 11.00S 136.58E
West Allis U.S.A. **94** 43.01N 88.00W
West Bridgford England **33** 52.56N 1.08W
West Bromwich England **28** 52.32N 2.01W

West Burra *i.* Scotland **36** 60.05N 1.21W
Westbury England **28** 51.16N 2.11W
West Calder Scotland **35** 55.51N 3.34W
West Clandon England **27** 51.16N 0.30W
Westcott England **27** 51.13N 0.20W
Westerham England **27** 51.16N 0.05E
Western *d.* Ghana **70** 6.00N 2.40W
Western *d.* Kenya **73** 0.30N 34.30E
Western Australia *d.* Australia **79** 25.00S 123.00E
Western Cleddau *r.* Wales **31** 51.47N 4.56W
Western Cordillera *mts.* N. America **106** 46.00N 120.00W
Western Ghats *mts.* India **58** 15.30N 74.30E
Western Hajar *mts.* Oman **57** 24.00N 56.30E
Western Isles *d.* Scotland **36** 57.40N 7.10W
Western Sahara Africa **68** 25.00N 13.30W
Western Sayan *mts.* U.S.S.R. **49** 53.00N 92.00E
Wester Ross *f.* Scotland **36** 57.37N 5.20W
Westerstede W. Germany **45** 53.15N 7.56E
Westerwald *f.* W. Germany **45** 50.40N 8.00E
West Felton England **30** 52.49N 2.58W
Westfield U.S.A. **95** 42.07N 72.45W
West Frisian Is. Neth. **45** 53.20N 5.00E
West Germany Europe **44** 51.00N 8.00E
West Glamorgan *d.* Wales **31** 51.42N 3.47W
West Haddon England **28** 52.21N 1.05W
West Ham England **27** 51.32N 0.01E
West Hanningfield England **27** 51.41N 0.31E
West Hartford U.S.A. **95** 41.46N 72.45W
West Horsley England **27** 51.17N 0.27W
West Indies C. America **97** 21.00N 74.00W
West Kilbride Scotland **34** 55.42N 4.51W
West Kingsdown England **27** 51.21N 0.14E
West Kirby England **32** 53.22N 3.11W
West Lake *d.* Tanzania **73** 2.00S 31.20E
Westland Bight *b.* New Zealand **82** 43.30S 169.30E
West Linton Scotland **35** 55.45N 3.21W
West Loch Roag Scotland **36** 58.14N 6.53W
West Loch Tarbert Scotland **36** 57.55N 6.53W
West Malaysia *d.* Malaysia **60** 4.00N 102.00E
Westmeath *d.* Rep. of Ire. **38** 53.30N 7.30W
West Mersea England **29** 51.46N 0.55E
West Midlands *d.* England **28** 52.28N 1.50W
West Nicholson Rhodesia **74** 21.06S 29.25E
Weston Malaysia **60** 5.14N 115.35E
Weston-super-Mare England **28** 51.20N 2.59W
West Palm Beach *town* U.S.A. **91** 26.42N 80.05W
Westport New Zealand **82** 41.46S 171.38E
Westport Rep. of Ire. **38** 53.48N 9.32W
Westray *i.* Scotland **37** 59.18N 2.58W
Westray Firth *est.* Scotland **37** 59.13N 3.00W
West Schelde *est.* Neth. **45** 51.25N 3.40E
West Siberian Plain *f.* U.S.S.R. **48** 60.00N 75.00E
West Sussex *d.* England **29** 50.58N 0.30W
West Terschelling Neth. **45** 53.22N 5.13E
West Thurrock England **27** 51.29N 0.17E
West Virginia *d.* U.S.A. **91** 39.00N 80.30W
West Water *r.* Scotland **37** 56.47N 2.35W
West Wickham England **27** 51.22N 0.02W
West Wittering England **28** 50.42N 0.54W
West Wyalong Australia **80** 33.54S 147.12E
West Yorkshire *d.* England **32** 53.45N 1.40W
Wetar *i.* Indonesia **61** 7.45S 126.00E
Wetheral England **35** 54.53N 2.50W
Wetherby England **33** 53.56N 1.23W
Wetzlar W. Germany **44** 50.33N 8.30E
Wewak P.N.G. **61** 3.35S 143.35E
Wexford Rep. of Ire. **39** 52.20N 6.28W
Wexford *d.* Rep. of Ire. **39** 52.20N 6.25W
Wexford B. Rep. of Ire. **39** 52.27N 6.18W
Wey *r.* England **27** 51.23N 0.28W
Weybridge England **27** 51.23N 0.28W
Weyburn Canada **90** 49.39N 103.51W
Weymouth England **28** 50.36N 2.28W
Weymouth U.S.A. **95** 42.14N 70.58W
Whakatane New Zealand **82** 37.56S 177.00E
Whale *r.* Canada **93** 58.00N 57.50W
Whaley Bridge *town* England **32** 53.20N 2.00W
Whalley England **32** 53.49N 2.25W
Whalsay *i.* Scotland **36** 60.22N 0.59W
Whangarei New Zealand **82** 35.43S 174.20E
Wharfe *r.* England **32** 53.50N 1.07W
Wharfedale *f.* England **32** 54.00N 1.55W
Wheathampstead England **27** 51.49N 0.17W
Wheeler Peak *mtn.* Nev. U.S.A. **90** 38.59N 114.29W
Wheeler Peak *mtn.* N. Mex. U.S.A. **90** 36.34N 105.25W
Wheeling U.S.A. **94** 40.05N 80.43W
Whernside *mtn.* England **32** 54.14N 2.25W
Whickham England **35** 54.57N 1.40W
Whipsnade England **27** 51.52N 0.33W
Whitburn Scotland **35** 55.52N 3.41W
Whitby England **33** 54.29N 0.37W
Whitchurch Bucks. England **28** 51.53N 0.51W
Whitchurch Hants. England **28** 51.14N 1.20W
Whitchurch Salop England **32** 52.58N 2.42W
White *r.* Ark. U.S.A. **91** 35.30N 91.20W
White *r.* Ind. U.S.A. **94** 38.25N 87.45W
White *r.* S. Dak. U.S.A. **90** 43.40N 99.30W
Whiteabbey N. Ireland **34** 54.42N 5.53W
Whiteadder Water *r.* Scotland **35** 55.46N 2.00W
White Cap Mtn. U.S.A. **95** 45.35N 69.13W
White Coomb *mtn.* Scotland **35** 55.26N 3.20W
Whitefish Pt. U.S.A. **94** 46.46N 84.58W
Whitehaven England **32** 54.33N 3.35W
Whitehead N. Ireland **34** 54.45N 5.43W
Whitehorse Canada **92** 60.41N 135.08W
Whitehorse Hill England **28** 51.35N 1.35W
White Mountain Peak U.S.A. **90** 37.40N 118.15W
White Mts. U.S.A. **95** 44.15N 71.10W
Whiten Head Scotland **37** 58.34N 4.32W
White Nile *r.* Sudan **69** 15.45N 32.25E
White Parish England **28** 51.01N 1.39W
White Russia Soviet Socialist Republic *d.* U.S.S.R. **47** 53.30N 28.00E
Whitesand B. England **31** 50.20N 4.20W
White Sea U.S.S.R. **48** 65.30N 38.00E
White Volta *r.* Ghana **70** 9.13N 1.15W
Whithorn Scotland **34** 54.44N 4.25W
Whitland Wales **30** 51.49N 4.38W
Whitley Bay *town* England **35** 55.03N 1.25W
Whitney Canada **95** 45.29N 78.15W
Whitney, Mt. U.S.A. **90** 36.35N 118.17W
Whitstable England **29** 51.21N 1.02E
Whittington England **30** 52.53N 3.00W
Whittlesey England **29** 52.34N 0.08W
Whitton England **33** 53.42N 0.39W
Whitwell England **27** 51.53N 0.18W
Whyalla Australia **79** 33.04S 137.34E
Wiay *i.* Scotland **36** 57.24N 7.13W
Wichita U.S.A. **91** 37.43N 97.20W
Wichita Falls *town* U.S.A. **90** 33.55N 98.30W
Wick Scotland **37** 58.26N 3.06W
Wick *r.* Scotland **37** 58.26N 3.06W
Wickford England **27** 51.38N 0.31E
Wickham England **28** 50.54N 1.11W
Wickham Market England **29** 52.09N 1.21E
Wicklow Rep. of Ire. **39** 52.59N 6.03W
Wicklow *d.* Rep. of Ire. **39** 52.59N 6.25W
Wicklow Head Rep. of Ire. **39** 52.58N 6.00W
Wicklow Mts. Rep. of Ire. **39** 53.06N 6.20W
Wick of Gruting *b.* Scotland **36** 60.37N 0.49W
Widford England **27** 51.50N 0.04E
Widnes England **32** 53.22N 2.44W
Wien *see* Vienna Austria **44**
Wiener Neustadt Austria **44** 47.49N 16.15E
Wiesbaden W. Germany **44** 50.05N 8.15E
Wigan England **32** 53.33N 2.38W
Wight, Isle of England **28** 50.40N 1.17W
Wigmore England **27** 51.21N 0.36E
Wigston Magna England **28** 52.35N 1.06W
Wigton England **35** 54.50N 3.09W
Wigtown Scotland **34** 54.47N 4.26W
Wigtown B. Scotland **34** 54.47N 4.15W
Wilberfoss England **33** 53.57N 0.53W
Wilcannia Australia **80** 31.33S 143.24E
Wildhorn *mtn.* Switz. **44** 46.22N 7.22E
Wildspitze *mtn.* Austria **44** 46.55N 10.55E
Wildwood U.S.A. **95** 38.59N 74.49W
Wilhelm, Mt. P.N.G. **61** 6.00S 144.55E
Wilhelmshaven W. Germany **45** 53.32N 8.07E
Wilkes-Barre U.S.A. **95** 41.15N 75.50W
Willemstad Neth. Antilles **97** 12.12N 68.56W
Willersley England **30** 52.07N 3.00W
Willesden England **27** 51.33N 0.14W
Williamsport U.S.A. **95** 41.16N 77.03W
Willington England **35** 54.43N 1.41W
Williston R.S.A. **74** 31.20S 20.52E
Williston U.S.A. **90** 48.09N 103.39W
Williton England **31** 51.09N 3.20W
Willmar U.S.A. **91** 45.06N 95.00W
Willowmore R.S.A. **74** 33.18S 23.30E
Willunga Australia **80** 35.18S 138.33E
Wilmington Del. U.S.A. **95** 39.46N 75.31W
Wilmington N.C. U.S.A. **91** 34.14N 77.55W
Wilmslow England **32** 53.19N 2.14W
Wilrijk Belgium **45** 51.11N 4.25E
Wilson *r.* Australia **80** 27.36S 141.27E
Wilson, Mt. U.S.A. **90** 37.51N 107.51W
Wilson's Promontary *c.* Australia **80** 39.06S 146.23E
Wilstone Resr. England **27** 51.48N 0.40W
Wilton England **28** 51.05N 1.52W
Wiltshire *d.* England **28** 51.20N 2.00W
Wimbledon England **27** 51.26N 0.12W
Wimbledon Park England **27** 51.26N 0.17W
Wimborne Minster England **28** 50.48N 2.00W
Winam *b.* Kenya **73** 0.15S 34.30E
Winburg R.S.A. **74** 28.31S 27.01E
Wincanton England **28** 51.03N 2.24W
Winchester England **28** 51.04N 1.19W
Windermere England **32** 54.24N 2.56W
Windermere *l.* England **32** 54.20N 2.56W
Windhoek S.W. Africa **74** 22.34S 17.06E
Windlesham England **27** 51.22N 0.39W
Windrush *r.* England **28** 51.42N 1.25W
Windsor Canada **94** 42.18N 83.00W
Windsor England **27** 51.29N 0.38W
Windsor Great Park *f.* England **27** 51.27N 0.37W
Windward Is. C. America **97** 13.00N 60.00W
Windward Passage *str.* Carib. Sea **97** 20.00N 74.00W
Wingate England **35** 54.44N 1.23W
Wingrave England **27** 51.52N 0.44W
Winisk *r.* Canada **93** 55.20N 85.20W
Winkleigh England **31** 50.49N 3.57W
Winneba Ghana **70** 5.22N 0.38W
Winnebago, L. U.S.A. **94** 44.00N 88.25W
Winnipeg Canada **91** 49.59N 97.10W
Winnipeg, L. Canada **93** 52.45N 98.00W
Winnipegosis, L. Canada **90** 52.00N 100.00W
Winnipesaukee, L. U.S.A. **95** 43.40N 71.20W
Winona U.S.A. **94** 44.02N 91.37W
Winschoten Neth. **45** 53.07N 7.02E
Winscombe England **28** 51.19N 2.50W
Winsford England **32** 53.12N 2.31W
Winslow England **28** 51.57N 0.54W
Winston-Salem U.S.A. **91** 36.05N 80.05W
Winsum Neth. **45** 53.20N 6.31E
Winterswijk Neth. **45** 51.58N 6.44E
Winterthur Switz. **44** 47.30N 8.45E
Winterton England **33** 53.39N 0.37W
Winterton-on-Sea England **29** 52.43N 1.43E
Winton Australia **79** 22.22S 143.00E
Winton New Zealand **82** 46.10S 168.20E
Wirksworth England **33** 53.05N 1.34W
Wirral *f.* England **32** 53.18N 3.02W
Wisbech England **29** 52.39N 0.10E
Wisconsin *d.* U.S.A. **94** 44.45N 90.00W
Wisconsin *r.* U.S.A. **94** 42.57N 91.07W
Wisconsin Rapids *town* U.S.A. **94** 44.24N 89.50W
Wishaw Scotland **35** 55.47N 3.55W
Wismar E. Germany **44** 53.54N 11.28E
Wissembourg France **44** 49.02N 7.57E
Wissey *r.* England **29** 52.33N 0.21E
Witham England **27** 51.48N 0.38E
Witham *r.* England **33** 52.56N 0.04E
Witheridge England **31** 50.55N 3.42W
Withernsea England **33** 53.43N 0.02E
Witney England **28** 51.47N 1.29W
Witten W. Germany **45** 51.26N 7.19E
Wittenberg E. Germany **44** 51.53N 12.39E
Wittenberge E. Germany **44** 52.59N 11.45E
Wittlich W. Germany **45** 49.59N 6.54E
Witu Kenya **73** 2.22S 40.20E
Wiveliscombe England **31** 51.02N 3.20W
Wivenhoe England **29** 51.51N 0.59E
Włocławek Poland **47** 52.39N 19.01E
Wodonga Australia **80** 36.08S 146.09E
Wokam *i.* Asia **61** 5.45S 134.30E
Woking England **27** 51.20N 0.34W
Wokingham England **28** 51.25N 0.50W
Woldingham England **27** 51.17N 0.02E
Wolf *r.* U.S.A. **94** 44.00N 88.30W
Wolfenbüttel W. Germany **44** 52.10N 10.33E
Wolf Rock *i.* England **31** 49.56N 5.48W
Wolfsburg W. Germany **44** 52.27N 10.49E
Wolin Poland **44** 53.51N 14.38E
Wollaston England **28** 52.16N 0.41W
Wollaston L. Canada **92** 58.15N 103.30W
Wollongong Australia **80** 34.25S 150.52E
Wolmaransstad R.S.A. **74** 27.11S 26.00E
Wolseley Australia **80** 36.21S 140.55E
Wolsingham England **35** 54.44N 1.52W
Wolvega Neth. **45** 52.53N 6.00E
Wolverhampton England **28** 52.35N 2.06W
Wolverton England **28** 52.03N 0.48W
Wombwell England **33** 53.31N 1.23W
Wonersh England **27** 51.12N 0.33W
Wonsan N. Korea **63** 39.07N 127.26E
Wonthaggi Australia **80** 33.33S 145.37E
Woodbridge England **29** 52.06N 1.19E
Woodford Rep. of Ire. **39** 53.03N 8.24W
Woodford Halse England **28** 52.10N 1.12W
Wood Green England **27** 51.38N 0.06W
Woodhall Spa England **33** 53.10N 0.12W
Woodmansterne England **27** 51.19N 0.10W
Woodside Australia **80** 38.31S 146.21E
Woodstock England **28** 51.51N 1.20W
Woodville New Zealand **82** 40.20S 175.54E
Wooler England **35** 55.33N 2.01W
Woolwich England **27** 51.29N 0.05E
Woomera Australia **79** 31.11S 136.54E
Woonsocket U.S.A. **95** 42.00N 71.30W
Wooroorooka Australia **80** 28.59S 145.40E
Wooster U.S.A. **94** 40.46N 81.57W
Wootton Bassett England **28** 51.32N 1.55W
Worcester England **28** 52.12N 2.12W
Worcester R.S.A. **74** 33.39S 19.26E
Worcester U.S.A. **95** 42.17N 71.48W
Workington England **32** 54.39N 3.34W
Worksop England **33** 53.19N 1.09W

Worland U.S.A. **90** 44.01N 107.58W
Wormit Scotland **35** 56.25N 2.28W
Worms W. Germany **44** 49.38N 8.23E
Worms Head Wales **31** 51.34N 4.18W
Worsbrough England **33** 53.33N 1.29W
Worthing England **29** 50.49N 0.21W
Worthington U.S.A. **91** 43.37N 95.36W
Wotton-under-Edge England **28** 51.37N 2.20W
Wowoni *i.* Indonesia **61** 4.10S 123.10E
Wragby England **33** 53.17N 0.18W
Wrangel I. U.S.S.R. **49** 71.00N 180.00
Wrangell U.S.A. **92** 56.28N 132.23W
Wrangle England **33** 53.03N 0.09E
Wrath, C. Scotland **36** 58.37N 5.01W
Wrexham Wales **30** 53.05N 3.00W
Wrigley Canada **92** 63.16N 123.39W
Wrocław Poland **44** 51.05N 17.00E
Wrotham England **27** 51.19N 0.19E
Wuchow China **63** 23.30N 111.21E
Wuhan China **63** 30.35N 114.19E
Wuhu China **63** 31.23N 118.25E
Wu Kiang *r.* China **62** 30.10N 107.26E
Wuliang Shan *mts.* China **62** 24.27N 100.43E
Wuppertal W. Germany **45** 51.15N 7.10E
Würzburg W. Germany **44** 49.48N 9.57E
Wusih China **63** 31.35N 120.19E
Wuwei China **62** 38.00N 102.54E
Wuyun China **63** 49.15N 129.39E
Wyandotte U.S.A. **94** 42.11N 83.10W
Wyangala Dam Australia **80** 33.56S 148.57E
Wye England **29** 51.11N 0.56E
Wye *r.* U.K. **28** 51.37N 2.40W
Wylye England **28** 51.08N 2.01W
Wylye *r.* England **28** 51.04N 1.48W
Wymondham England **29** 52.34N 1.07E
Wyndham Australia **79** 15.29S 128.05E
Wyoming U.S.A. **94** 42.54N 85.42W
Wyoming *d.* U.S.A. **90** 43.00N 108.00W
Wyre *r.* England **32** 53.51N 2.55W
Wyre *i.* Scotland **37** 59.07N 2.58W
Wyre Forest *f.* England **28** 52.25N 2.25W

X

Xánthi Greece **43** 41.07N 24.55E
Xau, L. Botswana **74** 21.15S 24.50E
Xauen Morocco **41** 35.10N 5.16W
Xieng Khouang Laos **60** 19.11N 103.23E
Xingu *r.* Brazil **102** 2.00S 52.00W

Y

Yaan China **59** 30.00N 102.59E
Yablonovy Range *mts.* U.S.S.R. **49** 53.20N 115.00E
Yacuiba Bolivia **103** 22.00S 63.43W
Yahuma Zaïre **72** 1.06N 23.10E
Yakima U.S.A. **90** 46.37N 120.30W
Yakutsk U.S.S.R. **49** 62.10N 129.20E
Yallourn Australia **80** 38.09S 146.22E
Yalta U.S.S.R. **47** 44.30N 34.09E
Yalung Kiang *r.* China **59** 26.35N 101.44E
Yamagata Japan **63** 38.16N 140.19E
Yamal Pen. U.S.S.R. **48** 70.20N 70.00E
Yaman Tau *mtn.* U.S.S.R. **48** 54.20N 58.10E
Yambering Guinea **70** 11.49N 12.18W
Yambol Bulgaria **43** 42.28N 26.30E
Yamethin Burma **59** 20.24N 96.08E
Yamuna *r.* India **58** 25.20N 81.49E
Yana *r.* U.S.S.R. **49** 71.30N 135.00E
Yanbu Saudi Arabia **56** 24.07N 38.04E
Yangtze Kiang *r.* China **63** 32.15N 119.50E
Yantabulla Australia **80** 29.13S 145.01E
Yao Chad **71** 12.52N 17.34E
Yaoundé Cameroon **71** 3.51N 11.31E
Yap *i.* Asia **61** 9.30N 138.09E
Yapehe Zaïre **72** 0.10S 24.20E
Yaqui *r.* Mexico **90** 27.40N 110.30W
Yare *r.* England **29** 52.34N 1.45E
Yarkand China **62** 38.27N 77.16E
Yarkand *r.* China **62** 40.30N 80.55E
Yarmouth Canada **91** 43.50N 66.08W
Yarmouth England **28** 50.42N 1.29W
Yarmouth Roads *f.* England **29** 52.39N 1.48E
Yaroslavl U.S.S.R. **47** 57.34N 39.52E
Yarrow Scotland **35** 55.31N 3.03W
Yarrow *r.* Scotland **35** 55.32N 2.51W
Yartsevo U.S.S.R. **49** 60.17N 90.02E
Yarty *r.* England **31** 50.46N 3.01W
Yasanyama Zaïre **72** 4.18N 21.11E
Yass Australia **80** 34.51S 148.55E
Yatakala Niger **70** 14.52N 0.22E
Yazd Iran **57** 31.54N 54.22E
Ye Burma **59** 15.15N 97.50E
Yealmpton England **31** 50.21N 4.00W
Yegorlyk *r.* U.S.S.R. **47** 46.30N 41.52E
Yegoryevsk U.S.S.R. **47** 55.21N 39.01E
Yei Sudan **73** 4.09N 30.40E
Yelets U.S.S.R. **47** 52.36N 38.30E
Yell *i.* Scotland **36** 60.35N 1.05W
Yellowknife Canada **92** 62.30N 114.29W
Yellow Sea Asia **63** 35.00N 123.00E
Yellowstone *r.* U.S.A. **90** 47.55N 103.45W
Yellowstone L. U.S.A. **90** 44.30N 110.20W
Yellowstone Nat. Park U.S.A. **90** 44.35N 110.30W
Yell Sd. Scotland **36** 60.30N 1.11W
Yelsk U.S.S.R. **47** 51.50N 29.10E
Yelwa Nigeria **71** 10.48N 4.42E
Yemen Asia **69** 15.15N 44.30E
Yenagoa Nigeria **71** 4.59N 6.15E
Yen Bai Vietnam **59** 21.43N 104.54E
Yenchwan China **63** 36.55N 110.04E
Yenisei *r.* U.S.S.R. **49** 69.00N 86.00E
Yenisei G. U.S.S.R. **48** 73.00N 79.00E
Yeniseysk U.S.S.R. **49** 58.27N 92.13E
Yentai China **63** 37.30N 121.22E
Yeo *r.* Avon England **28** 51.24N 2.55W
Yeo *r.* Somerset England **28** 51.02N 2.49W
Yeovil England **28** 50.57N 2.38W
Yerbent U.S.S.R. **57** 39.23N 58.35E
Yerevan U.S.S.R. **57** 40.10N 44.31E
Yershov U.S.S.R. **47** 51.22N 48.16E
Yeşil *r.* Turkey **56** 41.22N 36.37E
Yeu Burma **59** 22.49N 95.26E
Yeu, Île d' France **40** 46.43N 2.20W
Yevpatoriya U.S.S.R. **47** 45.12N 33.20E
Yevstratovskiy U.S.S.R. **47** 50.07N 39.45E
Yeysk U.S.S.R. **47** 46.43N 38.17E
Yiewsley England **27** 51.31N 0.27W
Yinchwan China **62** 38.30N 106.19E
Yingkow China **63** 40.40N 122.17E
Yingtak China **63** 24.20N 113.20E
Yinkanie Australia **80** 34.21S 140.20E
Ylikitka *l.* Finland **46** 66.10N 28.30E
Y Llethr *mtn.* Wales **32** 52.50N 4.00W
Yokadouma Cameroon **71** 3.26N 15.06E
Yoko Cameroon **71** 5.29N 12.19E
Yokohama Japan **63** 35.28N 139.28E
Yola Nigeria **71** 9.14N 12.32E
Yonkers U.S.A. **95** 40.56N 73.54W
Yonne *r.* France **40** 48.22N 2.57E
York England **33** 53.58N 1.07W
York U.S.A. **95** 39.57N 76.44W
York, C. Australia **79** 10.58S 142.40E
York Factory *town* Canada **93** 57.08N 92.25W
Yorkshire Wolds *hills* England **33** 54.00N 0.39W
Yorkton Canada **90** 51.12N 102.29W
Yoshkar Ola U.S.S.R. **47** 56.38N 47.52E
Youghal Rep. of Ire. **39** 51.58N 7.51W
Young Australia **80** 34.19S 148.20E
Youngstown U.S.A. **94** 41.05N 80.40W
Yoxford England **29** 52.16N 1.30E
Yozgat Turkey **56** 39.50N 34.48E
Ypres Belgium **45** 50.51N 2.53E
Ystad Sweden **46** 55.25N 13.50E
Ystradgynlais Wales **31** 51.47N 3.45W
Ythan *r.* Scotland **37** 57.21N 2.01W
Yuan Kiang *r. see* Red r. **59**
Yuan Kiang *r.* China **63** 29.00N 112.12E
Yucatan *d.* Mexico **96** 19.30N 89.00W
Yucatan Channel Carib. Sea **96** 21.30N 86.00W
Yucatan Pen. Mexico **96** 19.00N 90.00W
Yugoslavia Europe **43** 44.00N 20.00E
Yukon *r.* U.S.A. **92** 62.35N 164.20W
Yukon Territory *d.* Canada **92** 65.00N 135.00W
Yulin Kwangtung China **60** 18.20N 109.31E
Yuma U.S.A. **90** 32.40N 114.39W
Yumen China **62** 40.19N 97.12E
Yungera Australia **80** 34.48S 143.10E
Yun Ling Shan *mts.* China **59** 28.30N 99.00E
Yunnan *d.* China **59** 24.15N 101.30E
Yunnan Plateau Asia **107** 24.00N 107.00E
Yushu China **59** 33.06N 96.48E
Yuzhno Sakhalinsk U.S.S.R. **63** 46.58N 142.45E
Yvetot France **40** 49.37N 0.45E

Z

Zaandam Neth. **45** 52.27N 4.49E
Zabol Iran **57** 31.00N 61.32E
Zabrze Poland **47** 50.18N 18.47E
Zacapa Guatemala **96** 15.00N 89.30W
Zacatecas Mexico **96** 22.48N 102.33W
Zacatecas *d.* Mexico **96** 24.00N 103.00W
Zadar Yugo. **42** 44.08N 15.14E
Zafra Spain **41** 38.25N 6.25W
Zagazig Egypt **56** 30.36N 31.30E
Zagreb Yugo. **42** 45.49N 15.58E
Zagros Mts. Iran **57** 32.00N 51.00E
Zahedan Iran **57** 29.32N 60.54E
Zahle Lebanon **56** 33.50N 35.55E
Zaindeh *r.* Iran **57** 32.40N 52.50E
Zaïre Africa **72** 2.00S 22.00E
Zaire *d.* Angola **72** 6.30S 13.30E
Zaïre *r.* Zaïre **72** 6.00S 12.30E
Zaječar Yugo. **43** 43.55N 22.15E
Zakataly U.S.S.R. **57** 41.39N 46.40E
Zákinthos *i.* Greece **43** 37.46N 20.46E
Zambezi *r.* Moçambique/Zambia **73** 18.15S 35.55E
Zambezi Zambia **72** 13.30S 23.12E
Zambezia *d.* Moçambique **73** 16.30S 37.30E
Zambia Africa **73** 14.00S 28.00E
Zamboanga Phil. **61** 6.55N 122.05E
Zambue Moçambique **73** 15.07S 30.40E
Zamfara *r.* Nigeria **71** 12.04N 4.00E
Zamora Mexico **96** 20.00N 102.18W
Zamora Spain **41** 41.30N 5.45W
Zamość Poland **47** 50.43N 23.15E
Záncara *r.* Spain **41** 38.55N 4.07W
Zanesville U.S.A. **94** 39.55N 82.02W
Zanjan Iran **57** 36.40N 48.30E
Zanzibar Tanzania **73** 6.10S 39.16E
Zanzibar I. Tanzania **73** 6.00S 39.20E
Zaporozhye U.S.S.R. **47** 47.50N 35.10E
Zara Turkey **56** 39.55N 37.44E
Zaragoza Spain **41** 41.39N 0.54W
Zarand Iran **57** 30.50N 56.35E
Zárate Argentina **103** 34.07S 59.00W
Zardeh Kuh *mtn.* Iran **57** 32.21N 50.04E
Zaria Nigeria **71** 11.01N 7.44E
Zarqa Jordan **56** 32.04N 36.05E
Zary Poland **44** 51.40N 15.10E
Zawi Rhodesia **74** 17.00S 30.10E
Zaysan U.S.S.R. **62** 47.30N 84.57E
Zaysan, L. U.S.S.R. **62** 48.00N 83.30E
Zealand *i.* Denmark **46** 55.30N 12.00E
Zebediela R.S.A. **74** 24.25S 29.07E
Zeebrugge Belgium **45** 51.20N 3.13E
Zeehan Australia **80** 41.55S 145.21E
Zeeland *d.* Neth. **45** 51.30N 3.45E
Zeerust R.S.A. **74** 25.33S 26.06E
Zeila Somali Rep. **69** 11.21N 43.30E
Zeist Neth. **45** 52.03N 5.16E
Zeitz E. Germany **44** 51.03N 12.08E
Zelenodolsk U.S.S.R. **47** 55.50N 48.30E
Zelenogorsk U.S.S.R. **46** 60.15N 29.31E
Zemio C.A.R. **72** 5.00N 25.09E
Zenne *r.* Belgium **45** 51.04N 4.25E
Zevenbergen Neth. **45** 51.41N 4.42E
Zeya *r.* U.S.S.R. **49** 50.20N 127.30E
Zèzere *r.* Portugal **41** 40.05N 7.40W
Zhdanov U.S.S.R. **47** 47.05N 37.34E
Zhitomir U.S.S.R. **47** 50.18N 28.40E
Zhlobin U.S.S.R. **47** 52.50N 30.00E
Zhob *r.* Pakistan **58** 31.40N 70.54E
Zielana Góra Poland **44** 51.57N 15.30E
Ziguinchor Senegal **70** 12.35N 16.20W
Zile Turkey **56** 40.18N 35.52E
Zilfi Saudi Arabia **57** 26.15N 44.50E
Ziling Tso *l.* China **59** 31.40N 88.30E
Zimatlán Mexico **96** 16.52N 96.45W
Zimbabwe Ruins Rhodesia **74** 20.30S 30.30E
Zimnicea Romania **43** 43.38N 25.22E
Zinder Niger **71** 13.46N 8.58E
Zittau E. Germany **44** 50.55N 14.50E
Zlatoust U.S.S.R. **48** 55.10N 59.38E
Znamenka U.S.S.R. **47** 48.41N 32.36E
Znojmo Czech. **44** 48.52N 16.05E
Zomba Malaŵi **73** 15.22S 35.22E
Zongo Zaïre **72** 4.20N 18.38E
Zonguldak Turkey **56** 41.26N 31.47E
Zouerate Mauritania **70** 22.35N 12.20W
Zoutkamp Neth. **45** 53.21N 6.18E
Zrenjanin Yugo. **47** 45.22N 20.23E
Zug Switz. **44** 47.10N 8.31E
Zuhreh *r.* Iran **57** 30.04N 49.32E
Zûjar *r.* Spain **41** 38.58N 5.40W
Zûjar Dam Spain **41** 38.57N 5.30W
Zumbo Moçambique **73** 15.30S 30.30E
Zungeru Nigeria **71** 9.48N 6.03E
Zürich Switz. **44** 47.23N 8.33E
Zürich, L. Switz. **44** 47.10N 8.50E
Zutphen Neth. **45** 52.08N 6.12E
Zwickau E. Germany **44** 50.43N 12.30E
Zwolle Neth. **45** 52.31N 6.06E
Zyryanovsk U.S.S.R. **48** 49.45N 84.16E